Revise AS

AQA Psychology

Cara Flanagan

Contents

Specification lists

AQA A psychology

MODULE	SPECIFICATION TOPIC	CHAPTER REFERENCE	STUDIED IN CLASS	REVISED	PRACTICE QUESTIONS
Unit 1	*Cognitive psychology: Memory*				
	Models of memory	2.1			
	Memory in everyday life	2.2			
	Developmental psychology: Early Social Development				
	Attachment	3.1			
	Attachment in everyday life	3.2			
	Research methods				
	Methods and techniques	4.1			
	Investigation design	4.2			
	Data analysis and presentation	4.3			
Unit 2	*Biological psychology: Stress*				
	Stress	5.1			
	Stress in everyday life	5.2			
	Social psychology: Social influence				
	Social influence	6.1			
	Social influence in everyday life	6.2			
	Individual differences: Psychopathology (Abnormality)				
	Defining and explaining psychological abnormality	7.1			
	Treating abnormality	7.2			

Examination analysis

The AQA A specification comprises six compulsory modules (two examination units):

Unit 1 The Unit 1 exam is divided into two sections: *1½ hours 50% of AS (25% of A Level)*
    • Cognitive psychology and research methods • Developmental psychology and research methods
All questions are compulsory and structured. Questions include short answer, stimulus material and **one** 12-mark question requiring extended writing, in which QWC (quality of written communication) will be assessed.

The total mark for this paper is 72, which is divided evenly between the two sections.

Unit 2 The Unit 2 exam is divided into three sections: *1½ hours 50% of AS (25% of A Level)*
    • Biological psychology • Social psychology • Individual differences
All questions are compulsory and structured. Questions include short answer, stimulus material and **one or more** 12-mark questions requiring extended writing, in which QWC will be assessed.

The total mark for this paper is 72, which is divided evenly between the three sections.

AQA B psychology

MODULE	SPECIFICATION TOPIC	CHAPTER REFERENCE	STUDIED IN CLASS	REVISED	PRACTICE QUESTIONS
	Approaches				
	Key approaches in psychology	1.1			
	Biopsychology	5.3			
	Gender development				
	Concepts	3.3			
Unit 1	Explaining gender development	3.3			
	Research methods				
	Methods of research	4.1, 4.2			
	Preparing data and descriptive statistics	4.3			
	Ethics	4.2			
	Social psychology				
	Social influence	6.1			
	Social cognition	6.3			
	Cognitive Psychology				
Unit 2	Remembering and forgetting	2.1, 2.3			
	Perceptual processes	2.4			
	Individual differences				
	Anxiety disorders	7.3			
	Autism	7.3			

Examination analysis

The AQA B specification comprises six compulsory modules (two examination units):

Unit 1 The Unit 1 exam is divided into three sections: *1½ hours 50% of AS (25% of A Level)*
* Biopsychology and other key approaches • Gender development • Research methods

Unit 2 The Unit 2 exam is divided into three sections: *1½ hours 50% of AS (25% of A Level)*
* Social psychology (one question on social influence; one on social cognition)
* Cognitive psychology (one question on remembering/forgetting; one on perceptual processes)
* Individual differences (one question on anxiety disorders; one on autism)

*On each unit exam, candidates answer **three** questions – one from each section. Questions in each section will include short answer, stimulus material, and 10-mark questions requiring extended writing, in which QWC (quality of written communication) will be assessed. The total mark for each paper is 60, which is evenly divided between sections.*

Psychology A level: AS and A2

AS and A2

All Psychology A Level courses are in two parts. Most students will begin by studying the AS (advanced subsidiary) course in the first year and will then go on to study the second part of the A Level course (A2) in the second year. To gain the full A Level, you need to complete both the AS and A2 courses. Some students just do the AS course. Usually the full A Level takes two years: one year for AS and one year for A2. But you can take more or less time to complete it.

AS Assessment

The Psychology A Level is assessed in four unit exams: two are AS and two are A2. These are available in January and June every year so that you can take one AS unit halfway through the course and the other at the end of the first year (and one A2 unit half way through the second year and one at the end of the year). Or, you can take them both at the end of the first year – or even take them all at the end of the second year. You can re-sit any unit as often as you wish.

Even though you can re-sit unit exams as often as you like, this information may be passed on, for example, to universities.

Assessment objectives

Following an examination course means that much of your learning is guided by how it will ultimately be assessed. Examination boards set out their 'assessment objectives', which are their criteria for assessing performance. In the A Level examinations there are three assessment objectives which, in brief, are: describe (AO1); evaluate (AO2); and design, conduct and report research (AO3). There is also an assessment of the quality of written communication (QWC).

Psychology is a science subject and, therefore, shares assessment objectives with all science subjects.

Assessment objective 1 (AO1) – Knowledge and understanding of science and of how science works. Candidates should be able to:

(a) recognise, recall and show understanding of scientific knowledge

(b) select, organise and communicate relevant information.

Assessment objective 2 (AO2) – Application of knowledge and understanding of science and of how science works. Candidates should be able to:

(a) analyse and evaluate scientific knowledge and processes

(b) apply scientific knowledge and processes to unfamiliar situations, including those related to issues

(c) assess the validity, reliability and credibility of scientific information.

Assessment objective 3 (AO3) – How science works in Psychology. Candidates should be able to:

(a) describe ethical, safe and skilful practical techniques and processes, selecting appropriate qualitative and quantitative methods

(b) know how to make, record and communicate reliable and valid observations and measurements with appropriate precision and accuracy, using primary and secondary sources

(c) analyse, interpret, explain and evaluate the methodology, results and impact of their own and others' experimental and investigative activities in a variety of ways.

Quality of written communication (QWC) – Candidates are assessed on their ability to produce accurate spelling, punctuation and grammar, and on organising information.

Types of examination questions used at AS

A variety of question types are used in AS examination questions. They may draw on a combination of styles, for example, a structured question may contain some short-answer parts and a final part requiring extended writing. It might begin with stimulus material.

1. Simple questions

You may be asked to fill in boxes using a list of concepts. For example, you may be shown a diagram of the multi-store model and asked to fill in words from a list.

Example:

1 *Fill in the missing labels to complete the diagram* *(3 mark)*

MULTI-STORE MODEL

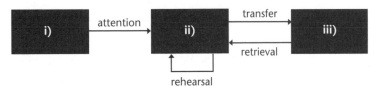

2. Short-answer questions

These questions may assess knowledge (AO1) or evaluation (AO2), and require a short answer (e.g. one sentence, or a few sentences of free writing).

Such questions may be worth 1 mark but usually they are worth 2 or 3 marks, in which case you should state your answer and then provide some further detail or elaboration to explain your point.

You should relate the length of your answer to the number of marks that are available.

Examples:

1 *Identify* **one** *method of obtaining a sample.* *(1 mark)*

2 *Outline how the multi-store model suggests that information is transferred from short-term memory to long-term memory.* *(2 marks)*

3 *Describe* **one** *explanation of why people conform.* *(3 marks)*

3. Stimulus material questions

Some questions begin with a sentence, or several sentences, to 'set the scene'. The question then follows from this stimulus material (sometimes called 'source material').

It is very important in such questions to relate your answer to the stimulus material.

Examples:

1 *Milgram's study of obedience is often criticised for being unethical, although Milgram himself made a robust defence of it.*

   Give **two** *examples of how the ethics of this study can be defended.* *(4 marks)*

2 *Nadine developed an intense fear of going to the dentist. She has toothache and her mother has told her she must go to have it checked.*

   Based on your knowledge of psychology, describe how her fear of going to the dentist might be overcome. *(3 marks)*

7

Types of examination questions used at AS

4. Structured questions

Structured questions are those that are divided into several parts. The parts usually have a common context and they often become progressively more demanding as you work your way through them. They may start with simple recall, then require more elaborate description of a study or a theory. The most difficult part of a structured question is usually at the end, where the candidate is asked to analyse the evidence relating to a specific issue. When answering structured questions, do not feel that you have to complete one question before starting the next. If you run out of ideas, go on to the next part.

Example:

1 *(a) Explain what is meant by the terms 'obedience' and 'conformity'.*

(3 marks + 3 marks)

*(b) Outline **two** explanations of why people conform to majority influence.*

(3 marks + 3 marks)

(c) 'Milgram's study provoked public outcry partly because of the actual findings but also because of the ethical issues raised.'

Discuss the ethical issues raised by Milgram's studies of obedience. *(8 marks)*

5. Extended writing questions

In AS Level psychology, questions requiring extended answers will usually form part of a structured question, or will be found on their own towards the end of the examination paper. These questions are used to assess your ability to communicate ideas and put together a logical argument involving both description (AO1) and evaluation (AO2). They are usually also the questions that are used to assess QWC.

Examples:

Outline and evaluate research into conformity. *(10 marks)*

*'Abnormality can be treated using biological or psychological methods. Discuss **two** methods used to treat abnormality.'* *(8 marks)*

Discuss the validity of studies on social influence. *(12 marks)*

The 'correct' answers to extended questions are less well-defined than those for short-answer questions. Examiners may have a list of points for which credit is awarded up to the maximum for the question. Or they may judge the 'quality' of your response as good, average or poor before allocating it a mark within a range that corresponds to that 'quality'.

Examiners may use marking guidelines similar to the ones on page 9 to assess the AO1 and AO2 (and QWC) components of extended writing questions.

Outline marking allocation for extended essay questions

Good	AO1
	Accurate, reasonably detailed, well-organised and coherent, appropriate selection of material to answer the question.
	AO2
	Broad range of issues/evidence considered with some elaboration OR narrower range of issues/evidence but with greater elaboration.
	QWC
	Clear expression of ideas, few errors in grammar, spelling and punctuation.
Average	AO1
	Generally accurate and organised but less detailed. Some evidence of selection of material.
	AO2
	Reasonable evaluation, may be some lack of focus and material not always used effectively.
	A range of issues/evidence considered in depth OR only a few considered, but in greater depth.
	QWC
	Reasonable expression of ideas, some errors in spelling and punctuation.
Poor	AO1
	Basic description demonstrating some knowledge and understanding but lacking detail, may be muddled and poorly focused.
	AO2
	Basic evaluation, restricted range of issues/evidence.
	QWC
	Expression of ideas is poor, few specialist terms used, and frequent errors in spelling and punctuation obscure meaning.

Command words

Whatever type of question you are answering, it is important to respond in the correct way to the command words at the beginning of the question. The most common command words are given below, together with a brief description of what each word is asking for.

Identify/ State/ Outline	Briefly describe without too much detail, identifying the main points.
Describe/ Explain	Provide a more detailed answer.
Distinguish between	Identify and describe differences.
Evaluate	Present criticisms, which may include positive (i.e. strengths or advantages) as well as negative (i.e. limitations or disadvantages) points, and applications or implications.
Discuss	To include both description and evaluation.

Exam advice

Do read all the questions first.

- If you have to choose between questions, make sure you choose the right question for you. Don't end up discovering that you could do parts (a) and (b) but you haven't a clue about part (c).

Do answer the question.

- This sounds obvious but, under exam conditions, students can feel very anxious and write about anything they can think of. They sometimes don't even read the whole question – they just notice certain key words and start writing.
- Don't regurgitate a prepared answer because you got a good mark for it in class. If it doesn't answer the question, it will not get any marks.

Do use psychological terms and write coherently and legibly.

- This shows the examiner you really have studied psychology, and also boosts your QWC mark. Identify the names of psychologists and use dates if you can (you don't have to be exact – 'the 1950s' is as good as '1953').

Do use the mark allocation to guide you in how much you should write.

- A total of 2 marks for a question is likely to mean that two valid points are required, or one point plus elaboration/explanation. If you write lots for a question that is worth very few marks, you won't get extra credit and you will have less time to answer the other questions.

Do elaborate on your answers.

- In many questions you are awarded 1 mark for identifying a point, and a second mark for providing some extra information – such as an explanation, an example or some research evidence. Elaboration is what makes the difference between a Grade A and a Grade C.

Don't ignore features of a question.

- If the question says 'describe how psychologists have dealt with ethical issues', don't write about ethical issues – marks would only be awarded, in this case, for writing about how psychologists *deal with* ethical issues.
- If you are unsure what a question means, explain any ambiguities to the examiner in your answer.

Don't leave out obvious material.

- It is very easy to think 'the examiner knows that' and presume that you don't have to write down the obvious things. However, the examiner cannot be sure that you know it unless you demonstrate it.

Don't waste time.

- An examination has a finite length. Don't spend time 'waffling' hoping the examiner might find something relevant in what you say. Examiners award marks only for material that is directly relevant to the question. Spend time thinking and select what you write very carefully. Selectivity is one of the criteria that examiners use when deciding how many marks to award for an answer.

Exam technique

Links from GCSE

AS Level psychology is a step up from GCSE. You can take a GCSE in Psychology but this would mean covering very much the same information. If you have studied GCSE psychology, the new AS work will be quite easy because it is familiar, and you can focus on tackling slightly more difficult assignments and focus on those areas that are new.

Most students doing AS Level psychology will be new to the subject but there are still links to your earlier GCSEs. For example, physiological psychology is concerned with the same subject matter as biology, and some of the things you have studied in mathematics will also come in useful here (e.g. drawing graphs and considering correlations).

The most important thing to realise is that the level of this AS exam is designed to be just the right sort of step up for you after studying GCSE. You will be required to learn about more complex ideas and, in the examination, to answer more extended questions than during your GCSE studies. And after AS level, the next step up is A2.

What are examiners looking for?

In psychology, examiners are looking for evidence of your knowledge, but often there are no 'right' answers. There is a range of correct answers, and any of these will receive credit – the examiner is looking for evidence of your knowledge *as appropriate to the question* set. The examiners will mark your answers *positively*. They do not subtract marks when material is missing. Instead, they aim to award marks for any material that is relevant.

A* grades

To achieve an A* grade, you need to achieve a…
- grade A overall (80% or more on uniform mark scale) for the whole A level qualification
- grade A* (90% or more on the uniform mark scale) acrosss your A2 units.

A* grades are awarded for the A level qualification only and not for the AS qualification or individual units.

Four steps to successful revision

Step 1: Understand

- Study the topic to be learned slowly. Make sure you understand the logic or important concepts.
- Mark up the text if necessary – underline, highlight and make notes.
- Re-read each paragraph slowly.

GO TO STEP 2

Step 2: Summarise

- Now make your own revision note summary:
  What is the main idea, theme or concept to be learned?
  What are the main points? How does the logic develop?
  Ask questions: Why? How? What next?
- Use bullet points, mind maps, patterned notes.
- Link ideas with mnemonics, mind maps, crazy stories.
- Note the title and date of the revision notes
  (e.g. Psychology: Attitudes and prejudice, 3rd March).
- Organise your notes carefully and keep them in a file.

This information is now in your short-term memory. You will forget 80% of it if you do not go to Step 3. GO TO STEP 3, but first take a 10-minute break.

Step 3: Memorise

- Take 25-minute learning 'bites' with 5-minute breaks.
- After each 5-minute break test yourself:
  - Cover the original revision note summary
  - Write down the main points
  - Speak out loud (record on tape)
  - Tell someone else
  - Repeat many times.

**The material is well on its way to long-term memory.
You will forget 40% of it if you do not do step 4. GO TO STEP 4**

Step 4: Track/Review

- Create a revision diary (one A4 page per day).
- Make a revision plan for the topic, e.g. 1 day later, 1 week later, 1 month later.
- Record your revision in your revision diary, e.g.
  Psychology: Attitudes and prejudice, 3rd March 25 minutes
  Psychology: Attitudes and prejudice, 5th March 15 minutes
  Psychology: Attitudes and prejudice, 3rd April 15 minutes
  ... and then at monthly intervals.

Approaches

1.1 Key approaches in psychology

After studying this section you should be able to:

- *describe the distinguishing features of the major approaches in psychology: biological, behavioural, social learning theory, cognitive, psychodynamic and humanistic approaches*
- *give strengths and limitations of each approach*
- *describe the research methods used to investigate each approach*
- *give strengths and limitations of these research methods.*

LEARNING SUMMARY

The biological (physiological) approach

AQA B — U1
AQA B — A2 (U4)

Physiological explanations are those based on parts of the body.

Distinguishing features of the biological approach

1. Physiological explanations

- **The nervous system** – The key components of the nervous system are described on page 111: central, autonomic and somatic nervous systems (CNS, ANS and SNS), the sympathetic and parasympathetic branches of the ANS, and the brain and neurons.
- **Communication in the nervous system** – Synaptic transmission is described on page 112: axons, dendrites, axon terminals and neurotransmitters are involved.
- **Hormones** – Biochemical substances such as adrenaline and testosterone. They are produced in one part of the body (endocrine glands such as the pituitary and adrenal glands) and circulate in the blood, having an effect on target organs. They are produced in large quantities but disappear very quickly. Their effects are slow in comparison to the nervous system but very powerful. Some hormones are also neurotransmitters (i.e. they are produced by neurons to transmit electrical messages from one neuron to another).

The biological approach draws on explanations used by biologists. These include both physiological and genetic explanations.

2. Genetic explanations

- **Genes** – The units of inheritance. Some characteristics (e.g. eye colour) are determined by one gene whereas for most characteristics (e.g. intelligence) many genes are involved. (Genotype and phenotype are discussed on page 116.)
- **Theory of evolution** – Genetically determined traits evolve through **natural selection**, a behaviour that promotes survival. Reproduction will be 'selected' and the genes for that trait survive. As the environment changes (or an individual moves to a new environment) new traits are needed to ensure survival. New genetic combinations produce **adaptations** and the individual who best 'fits' the environmental niche will be better able to compete, survive and reproduce (**survival of the fittest**).

Strengths and limitations of the biological approach

The strengths and limitations are discussed on pages 115 and 117–118.

Research methods used by the biological approach

The research methods are discussed on pages 113–114 and 116–117.

The behaviourist approach

AQA B   U1

AQA B   A2 (U4)

The behaviourist approach is also referred to as 'learning theory' because it is based on the idea that all behaviour is learned.

The approach was called 'behaviourism' because of its exclusive focus on external observable *behaviours*. Before behaviourism, psychologists studied what people thought by asking them to describe their thoughts. Behaviourists felt that this approach lacked scientific rigour.

Behaviourism dominated psychology in the first half of the 20th Century.

Distinguishing features of the behaviourist approach

- Humans and non-human animals are only **quantitatively** different, i.e. they differ in terms of having more or less of something, rather than differing qualitatively.
- There is no need to look at what goes on inside the 'black box' (the mind); it is sufficient to be concerned with external and **observable behaviour** only.
- All behaviour can be explained in terms of **conditioning theory** (see below): stimulus and response (S–R) links, which build up to produce more complex behaviours.
- All behaviour is determined by **environmental influences**, i.e. learning. Each individual is born as a blank slate (**tabula rasa**).

1. Classical conditioning – Learning to **associate** a stimulus with a response.

food   response   salivation

Unconditioned stimulus   **Unconditioned response**

bell   response   no salivation

Neutral stimulus   **No conditioned response**

Pavlov was the first to demonstrate classical conditioning, producing a salivation response in dogs to the sound of a bell.

Cats invariably run to you when they hear the cupboard door opening. This is an everyday example of classical conditioning.

bell + food   response   salivation

Unconditioned response

bell   response   salivation

Conditioned stimulus   **Conditioned response**

2. Operant conditioning – Learning a behaviour because of its **consequences**.

Skinner (1938) placed a pigeon in a 'Skinner box'. If it pecked at a lever, a door would open and food (a **reinforcer**) was delivered. The pigeon first pecked randomly around the box as part of its natural exploratory behaviour. Accidentally, it pecked the lever (stimulus – S) and received food (response – R).

Each time the pigeon pecked the lever and received food, the S–R link was strengthened or 'stamped in'. Reinforcement occurs when a reward is received (when the lever is pecked), which 'stamps in' the rewarded behaviour. Any unrewarded behaviour is 'stamped out' (i.e. when pecking elsewhere, no food appears). So, behaviour has been brought under stimulus control. If the pigeon also learns to get food by pecking at a button whenever it is lit up, it is learning to discriminate between different states of illumination (a discriminative stimulus).

Skinner described operant conditioning in terms of 'ABC':

Antecedents – The situation beforehand.

Behaviour – What the pigeon does.

Consequences – The probability of a behaviour being repeated depends on strengthening or weakening S–R links.

All reinforcement (positive or negative) *increases* the likelihood of a response.

1. **Positive reinforcement** increases the probability of a response recurring because the response is pleasurable. For example, receiving a smile when you give someone a kiss.
2. **Negative reinforcement** (i.e. escape from an unpleasant stimulus) is also pleasurable and increases the probability of the same response in the future. For example, finding that a smile stops your mother shouting at you.
3. **Positive punishment** (punishment by application), receiving something unpleasant, decreases the probability of a future behaviour. For example, being told off for smiling at an inappropriate moment.
4. **Negative punishment** (punishment by removal), removing something desirable, also decreases the probability of future behaviour. For example, not being allowed your dessert because you didn't finish your main course.

Skinner's approach concentrated on the effects of emitted behaviour rather than Pavlov's focus on the elicited behaviours themselves.

3. Features of conditioning

- **Generalisation** – animals respond in the same way to stimuli that are similar.
- **Extinction** – the new response disappears because it is no longer paired or reinforced.
- **Shaping** – animals gradually learn a target behaviour by being reinforced for behaviours that are closer and closer to the target.
- **Reinforcement schedules** – partial reinforcement schedules are more effective and more resistant to extinction. This may be because, under continuous reinforcement, the organism 'expects' it on every trial and, therefore, 'notices' its absence more quickly.
  Partial reinforcement includes fixed or variable ratios, and fixed or variable intervals. An example of a fixed ratio would be a reward once in every ten trials; an example of a fixed interval would be a reward every 10 minutes.

Strengths and limitations of the behaviourist approach

Strengths

- Classic learning theory has had a major influence on all branches of psychology – **methodological behaviourism** is the view that all approaches use some behaviourist concepts to explain behaviour. (See pages 52 and 154.)
- Behaviourism has given rise to many **practical applications**, such as dog training and therapies for mental disorders. (See page 159.)
- It is an empirical perspective which lends itself to **scientific research**. Broadbent (1961) argued that it is the best method for rational advance in psychology.

An empirical study is a study (such as an experiment or an interview) where data has been collected through direct observation or experience.

Limitations

- Behaviourism is a **mechanistic** (machine-like) perspective that ignores consciousness, subjective experience and emotions.
- It excludes the role of **cognitive, emotional** and **innate** factors.
- It is a very **determinist explanation** of behaviour – behaviour is determined by the environment and cannot be controlled by free will. The use of behaviourist principles to determine the behaviour of others (as in some prisons and psychiatric institutions) could be considered **unethical**. Both Watson and Skinner (in 'Walden Two') had a desire to use their principles to produce a better society.
- It is a **reductionist approach** – reducing complex behaviour to stimulus–response (S–R) links.
- Behaviourism is largely based on work with **non-human animals**. Behaviourists argue that the theory of evolution shows that human and non-human animals are quantitatively different, not qualitatively different, and, therefore, such research is meaningful.

Research methods used by the behaviourist approach

- **Laboratory experiments**, as described on page 75.
- **Non-human animal learning experiments**, such as the studies by Pavlov and Skinner.

Evaluation of research methods

- It may not be appropriate to make generalisations to human behaviour from the study of **non-human animals** because a lot of human behaviour is influenced by higher level thinking.
- Evaluation of **experiments** in general is given on page 75.

Progress check

1. Identify **two** distinguishing features of the biological approach.
2. Is the behaviourist approach an example of nature or nurture?
3. Which form of conditioning is an example of learning by association?
4. What is the effect of negative reinforcement?

4 It increases the likelihood of a behaviour being repeated.
3 Classical conditioning.
2 Nurture.
1 E.g. Physiological explanations such as nervous transmission; Genetic explanations such as the theory of evolution; Genotype and phenotype.

Social learning theory (SLT)

AQA B ▷ U1
AQA B ▷ A2 (U4)

Social learning theory is a neo-Behaviourist approach. ('Neo' means 'new'.) Social learning theory added a new dimension to traditional learning theory. It added cognitive factors.

In SLT, the term 'model' is used to describe a person who is imitated, and modelling is the process of imitation.

Child kicking a Bobo doll in the study by Bandura *et al.* (1961)

You can look at specific social learning explanations and studies on pages 70 and 162.

Distinguishing features of the SLT approach

- **Observational learning** – A significant source of learning comes from observing the behaviour of others and storing a representation of this behaviour (i.e. storing a mental representation).
- **Indirect (vicarious) reinforcement** – If the behaviour you observe has been reinforced (vicarious reinforcement) then this increases the likelihood that you will imitate the behaviour. The person stores an **expectation of future outcomes** (i.e. expectation of rewards/punishments that they will receive). Bandura was the first to describe the concept of indirect learning. He recognised that people could not acquire everything through direct reinforcement.
- **Modelling** – When an appropriate situation presents itself, a person will imitate a behaviour previously observed. They will then receive direct reinforcement, which further increases or decreases the likelihood of future behaviours.
- **Identification** – Individuals are more likely to imitate a behaviour if they **identify** with the model (e.g. people of the same gender, TV idols, parents).

Bandura *et al.* (1961) produced the classic demonstration of SLT in their 'Bobo doll study'.

Young children watched a model playing with various toys including a Bobo doll (a 3-foot inflatable toy). Some of the children saw the model behave aggressively towards the doll.

Later, the children were given an opportunity to play with the same toys. Those who had observed aggressive behaviour behaved more aggressively, including imitation of specific acts directed at the Bobo doll, such as saying 'Pow' when hitting the doll.

Strengths and limitations of social learning theory

Strengths
- SLT goes beyond traditional learning theory with the inclusion of **unobservable** and **cognitive** and **social** factors.
- SLT can explain **individual differences** – people behave differently because of different indirect and direct reinforcement experiences. It can also explain **cultural differences** – different cultures reinforce different behaviours and also model different behaviours.

Limitations
- SLT doesn't include the effects of **emotional factors or biological factors**, although Bandura acknowledged that biological factors are part of any account. For example, the urge to be aggressive is biological; what is learned (indirectly and directly) is how and when to express the aggression.

Research methods used by social learning theory

The main method used is the **laboratory experiment**, which is described and evaluated on page 75.

The cognitive approach

Chapter 2 deals with cognitive psychology, providing examples of the cognitive approach in psychology such as memory, forgetting and perception. Cognitive psychologists are also interested in other cognitive activities, such as attention, decision-making and language.

The cognitive approach is not just used in cognitive psychology, it is used throughout psychology to explain behaviour such as prejudice and abnormality.

The word 'cognitive' comes from the Latin word *cognitio* meaning 'to apprehend', understand or know. These are all internal processes which involve the mind (brain processes).

The development of techniques to scan the brain, and, therefore, find out much more about brain processes, has led to the increasing popularity of *cognitive neuroscience*, the scientific study of biological mechanisms underlying cognition.

Distinguishing features of the cognitive approach

- **Mental states** – The cognitive approach seeks to explain behaviour in terms of how the mind operates. For example, the cognitive approach to understanding prejudice looks at how our attitudes (a mental state) influence our behaviour. But prejudice could be explained in other ways, such as using psychodynamic theory.
- **An information-processing approach** – Cognitive psychology was heavily influenced by the computer revolution of the 1950s. This led to the use of information-processing terms and concepts as metaphors for what was happening in the mind. For example, models of memory focus on the input and output of information and, in between, how that information is processed.

Strengths and limitations of the cognitive approach

Strengths

- The approach lends itself to **scientific** research – the explanations produce hypotheses that can be easily tested (to confirm or refute the explanations) for example, the models of memory presented in chapter 2.
- The approach has **numerous useful applications**, from advice about the validity of eyewitness testimony (see pages 35–37), to suggestions on how to improve your memory (useful for examination candidates, see page 38), and how to improve performance in situations requiring close attention (e.g. air traffic control).

Limitations

- The **cognitive** approach has been criticised for being overly **mechanistic**, and lacking social, motivational and emotional factors. It is mechanistic because the approach is based on the behaviour of machines.
- Research studies **lack ecological validity** because they are artificial (e.g. memory experiments that use word lists) or because they are based on small samples (e.g. case studies).

Research methods used by the cognitive approach

- **Laboratory experiments** – Described and evaluated on page 75. Field and natural experiments are used as well (see page 76).
- **Case-studies of brain-damaged patients** – If a person incurs damage to part of their brain, we may be able to associate this with changes in behaviour. This allows us to determine which parts of the brain might be related to particular behaviours, as in the case study of H.M. (see page 27, and page 79 for evaluation).
- **Brain scans** – Thought processes can be observed in the living brain using modern scanning techniques to study memory. (See page 27 for examples and and page 114 for evaluation.)

The psychodynamic approach

AQA B ▸ U1

AQA B ▸ A2 (U4)

Psychodynamic refers to any approach that emphasises the processes of change and development, i.e. dynamics. Freud's psychoanalytic theory is the best known psychodynamic theory.

Psychoanalysis is a theory of personality and the therapy derived from it.

Freud (1920) gave an example of the Freudian slip: a British MP was speaking of his colleague from Hull but said 'the honourable member from Hell', thus revealing his private thoughts about the MP.

The three strands of Freud's theory of development are: the driving force (e.g. pleasure principle); personality structure (e.g. the id); and the organ-focus (e.g. oral).

Freud did not mean the term 'sexual' in the way many people interpret it. 'Sexual' roughly means 'physical' or 'sensual'.

The phallic stage is described in more detail on pages 71–72.

Distinguishing features of the psychodynamic approach

Sigmund Freud's theory of psychoanalysis emphasised the following:

- **Early experience** – Infants are born with innate biological drives, e.g. for oral satisfaction. These interact with early experience and have a fundamental influence on the developing personality. Either frustration or overindulgence at any **psychosexual stage** (see below) will result in a fixation on that stage, when the person's **libido** (life force) becomes locked into the stage.
- **Ego defences** – If innate drives are thwarted or not satisfied, anxiety is produced. The ego defends itself against anxiety using ego defence mechanisms (e.g. repression, denial, projection). Ego defences can explain abnormal and/or unconscious behaviour.
- **The unconscious** – Many aspects of personality dynamics are unconscious, and expression is indirect, for example, through dreams and in 'Freudian slips'.

The key concepts in Freud's theory are as follows:

1. The structure of the personality

- The **id** (or 'it') – The primitive, instinctive part that demands immediate satisfaction. It is motivated by the **pleasure principle** ('it' gets what 'it' wants).
- The **ego** (or 'I') – This develops in the first two years as a result of experience. Motivated by the **reality principle**, the ego makes the child adjust to the demands of the environment and modifies the demands of the id.
- The **superego** (or 'above-I') – This develops at about the age of five (during the phallic stage as an outcome of the Oedipus conflict). It is the equivalent to the conscience.

2. **Psychosexual stages**: the child seeks gratification through different body organs during development.

- **Oral stage** (0–18 months) – An oral fixation from too much or too little gratification of id, which may result in actions such as thumb-sucking.
- **Anal stage** (18–36 months) – Anal fixation could be due to strict toilet training, or pleasure playing with faeces. It may result in an anal-retentive personality.
- **Phallic stage** (3–6 years) – A fixation on genitals leads to the **Oedipus complex** – desire for mother; jealousy and guilt towards father, which is resolved by identification with father. Girls realise they have no penis and blame their mother. 'Penis envy' is resolved by a desire to have babies. This conflict resolution is weaker for girls and so, according to Freud, girls don't develop as strong a sense of moral justice as boys. Jung proposed an '**Electra complex**' – a young girl feels desire for her father and rejects her mother.
- **Latency stage** – The in-between years, when little development takes place. Boys and girls do not interact much at this stage.
- **Genital stage** (puberty) – The development of independence is now possible if earlier conflicts have been resolved.

Strengths and limitations of the psychodynamic approach

Strengths

- Freud's important **contribution** was to recognise childhood as a critical period of development, and to identify sexual (physical) and unconscious influences.

You have to ask yourself, 'Why are Freudian concepts still used so much?'. Concepts such as Freudian slips and psychoanalysis are part of everyday language. The answer must be that they contain some truths about humanity.

- The theory has been enormously **influential** within psychology, and beyond. Hall and Lindzey (1970) suggested that this is due to a fine literary style, a conception of man which is broad and deep, and which combines the world of reality with make-believe.
- It is an **idiographic** approach, meaning that it focuses more on the individual rather than general laws of behaviour (which is the **nomothetic** approach taken by, for example, cognitive psychology). Psychoanalytic theory provides a rich picture of individual personality dynamics.

Limitations

- The theory lacks rigorous **research support**, especially regarding normal development. The 'evidence' comes largely from case studies of middle-class, European females, many of whom were neurotic and adult – yet the theory is of **normal** child development. The data was retrospectively collected and given subjective interpretation, therefore, it had **potential investigator bias**.
- It reduces human activity to a basic set of structures, which are **reifications** (abstract concepts that are presented as if they are real things) and which cannot be directly studied.
- It is **deterministic** (i.e. it implies that people have little, if any, choice or free will): it suggests that infant behaviour is determined by innate forces and adult behaviour is determined by childhood experiences.
- The original theory lays too much emphasis on **innate biological forces**.

Other theorists, such as Erikson and Jung, produced psychodynamic theories that placed less emphasis on biological forces and more on the influences of social and cultural factors. Erikson's work with adolescents and Sioux Indians led him to believe that many aspects of behaviour were culturally, rather than biologically, based.

Research methods used by the psychodynamic approach

- **Case studies** such as Little Hans (see page 163). See page 79 for a description and evaluation of case studies.
- **Clinical interviews** – The interview method is described and evaluated on pages 78–79. Clinical interviews are an example of semi-structured interviews.

Progress check

1 What is vicarious reinforcement?
2 Identify **two** research methods commonly used by the cognitive approach.
3 What stage in development is associated with the Oedipus complex?
4 What are ego defences?

4 Methods by which the ego avoids feelings of anxiety, e.g. repression or projection.
3 Phallic.
2 E.g. Experiments; Case studies; Brain scans.
1 Experiencing reinforcement by seeing someone else being reinforced.

The humanistic approach

AQA B ▶ U1

AQA B ▶ A2 (U4)

In the 1950s, a number of psychologists developed humanistic psychology as a reaction against the then dominant approaches in psychology – behaviourism and psychoanalysis. They felt that these traditional approaches overlooked the role of free will and self-determination in human behaviour.

Humanistic psychology was based on the wider principles of humanism, a non-religious belief system that emphasises the personal worth of each individual and humanity as a whole.

Distinguishing features of the humanistic approach

- Each individual is **unique** – What matters is each person's subjective view rather than some objective reality. Reality is defined by the individual's perspective.
- **Personal responsibility** – Individuals are capable of **self-determination** (free will, rather than taking a deterministic view).
- Human nature is positive and inherently good. Each person strives for growth and **self-actualisation**.
- **Self-concepts** – The humanistic approach uses self-concepts to explain behaviour. For example, self-acceptance is seen to be important in healthy psychological development.

Strengths and limitations of the humanistic approach

Strengths

- This **subjective approach** has encouraged psychologists to accept the view that there is more to behaviour than objectively discoverable facts.
- The humanistic approach has had **widespread application**, for example, in counselling and client-centred therapy (Rogers, 1951).

Limitations

- It is largely a vague, unscientific and *untestable* approach.
- Some concepts are *culturally-relative*, for example, the emphasis on self-determination is a Western ideal and not as applicable to some societies (known as collectivist societies), where the group is more important than the individual.

Research methods used by the humanistic approach

- **Qualitative methods** – Humanistic psychologists believe that psychological theories should be humanly, rather than statistically, significant. They claim that objective data can tell us little about subjective experience. Qualitative methods are used that include discourse analysis (analysing human communications such as books or films) and naturalistic observations. See page 94 for an evaluation of the use of qualitative data.

Progress check

1 Name **one** assumption of the humanistic approach in psychology.
2 What is **one** advantage of the humanistic approach in psychology?

2 E.g. It is subjective; It is more humanly meaningful.
1 E.g. Uniqueness; Free will; Importance of self-concepts.

Sample question and student answers – AQA B questions

1

(a) Identify and describe **one** assumption of the behaviourist approach in psychology. *(3 marks)*

One assumption of the behaviourist approach is that all that matters is observable behaviour. Another assumption is that all behaviour can be explained in terms of learning.

1(a) The candidate has identified two assumptions where only one was required, and has not given a description of either. Only one assumption can be credited. **1 out of 3 marks.**

(b) The term modelling is used by social learning theorists. Explain what the term means, using an example from everyday life. *(2 marks)*

They are talking about imitation. One example would be watching someone on TV who goes to an exercise class and loses weight (is rewarded). Then, if the person watching saw this they might want to go to an exercise class too.

(b) All that is required for this question is a brief explanation for 1 mark and an example for 1 mark. This answer satisfies both criteria. **2 out of 2 marks.**

(c) Sharon spent a lot of time in hospitals when she was young because of a heart problem that has now been treated. The treatments she had to undergo were very painful. Recently, she had to visit a hospital again because her best friend had a baby. As soon as she walked in she felt sick.

Use the behaviourist approach in psychology to explain why Sharon felt sick when she went to visit her friend in hospital. *(4 marks)*

It is probably because she associates being in hospital with her earlier experiences in hospital, which were not very nice. This could be explained in terms of classical conditioning. The UCS (unconditioned stimulus) is the treatment that produces a UCR (unconditioned response), which is feeling sick. The hospital becomes associated with the treatment and, therefore, becomes the CS (conditioned stimulus) and produces the CR (conditioned response), which is feeling sick. So when Sharon goes to visit her friend, just being in a hospital makes her feel sick.

(c) This is an excellent answer because the explanation of classical conditioning is totally put in context. A weak answer would just provide a basic explanation of classical conditioning with no reference to the stimulus material. **4 out of 4 marks.**

(d) Discuss the cognitive approach in psychology. Refer to **at least one other** approach in your answer. *(10 marks)*

The cognitive approach emphasises the role of thinking in behaviour. This is quite different from the behaviourist approach because the behaviourist approach ignores any mental concepts and focuses only on the behaviour you can observe.

The cognitive approach is related to information processing. It started at the time of the computer revolution and used ideas like input, output and processing. This led to certain models of memory like the multi-store model. Cognitive psychologists are interested in topics related to thinking, such as memory, language, attention, perception and so on.

The cognitive approach is also used in other areas of psychology, such as explaining psychological disorders like phobias or autism. In the case of OCD it has been suggested that this develops because of maladaptive thinking patterns. Some people find it hard to dismiss intrusive thoughts, such as 'that doorknob is covered in germs'.

One of the strengths of the cognitive approach is that it is easy to conduct well-controlled lab experiments. This helps to prove or disprove any theory and, therefore, helps us advance knowledge. Another strength is that it has had many useful applications such as therapies to treat mental illnesses (e.g. cognitive behavioural therapies).

On the negative side, there are also weaknesses. It has been accused of being overly mechanistic and ignoring people's emotions. Using lab experiments is also a weakness because they are often quite artificial and contrived and may not apply to everyday life. For example, some

(d) This answer is reasonably organised though, at times, the discussion seems to change direction unexpectedly. There is a brief mention of one other approach, as required in the question and there is a good balance between description and evaluation. The material is accurate and thus is classified as a 'good answer', but not the best. **8 out of 10 marks.**

studies of memory use nonsense words which are not very memorable and, therefore, may not tell us much about 'real' memory. To be fair, other studies have tried to test memory more realistically. Recent research into memory has started to use brain scans that provide evidence about the brain in action.

Practice examination questions – AQA B questions

1

(a) Outline **two** criticisms of the psychodynamic approach. *(4 marks)*

(b) Tom is four years old and living with his mother and father. According to the psychodynamic approach, describe the psychosexual stage that Tom is going through. *(4 marks)*

(c) Describe **one** key assumption of the humanistic approach. *(3 marks)*

(d) Describe and evaluate **two** methods used by psychologists to investigate the biological approach. *(10 marks)*

2

(a) Psychologists explain some behaviours in terms of evolutionary processes.

(i) What is meant by the term evolution? *(2 marks)*

(ii) Give an example of **one** behaviour and suggest how this behaviour can be explained using the theory of evolution. *(3 marks)*

(b) Two other approaches that are used to explain behaviour are the behaviourist approach and the cognitive approach. Describe **two** differences between these two approaches. *(4 marks)*

(c) Discuss the biological approach in psychology. Refer to evidence in your answer. *(10 marks)*

Cognitive psychology

2.1 Models of memory

After studying this section you should be able to:

- describe the multi-store model of memory, including the concepts of encoding, capacity and duration
- give strengths and weaknesses of the multi-store model
- describe the working memory model and give strengths and weaknesses of this memory model
- describe the levels of processing approach and give strengths and weaknesses of this approach model.

LEARNING SUMMARY

The multi-store model (MSM)

AQA A ▷ U1
AQA B ▷ U2

Memory is the process by which we encode, store and retrieve information. It includes sensory memory, short-term memory and long-term memory.

The multi-store model of memory aims to describe the structure of memory and explain how information is transferred from STM to LTM.

Atkinson and Shriffrin (1968) proposed the multi-store model of memory. The model identifies three stores (see diagram below) and explains how information is transferred between these stores. Information enters sensory memory (SM). If attention is paid to the information, it is transferred to short-term memory (STM) where it is stored briefly. Verbal rehearsal maintains information in STM. Continued rehearsal creates long-term memories (LTM). Material may be retrieved from LTM via STM for recall or further processing.

MULTI-STORE MODEL

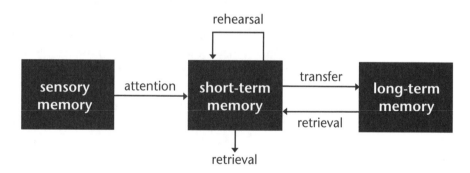

A familiar example of sensory memory is when you still 'hear' information 1 or 2 seconds after it was first heard. The information is very briefly held in sensory memory. This explains why sometimes, when you say 'Pardon?', you are simultaneously aware of what was said.

People have poor recall of events from childhood (called infantile amnesia) but particularly good recall for events from adolescence and early adulthood (reminiscence bump) and also for events from the last few years (recency effect).

The structure of memory

1. **Sensory memory (SM)** – The sensory form of a stimulus remains unaltered in the mind for a brief time. This could be an auditory or visual trace. It is rapidly lost through spontaneous decay (i.e. the physical trace disappears).

2. **Short-term memory (STM)** – Information receives minimal processing. It is relatively limited in capacity (it holds about seven items) and rapidly decays unless it is maintained through rehearsal. It may be held in a visual or auditory form (code), though it is mainly the latter.

3. **Long-term memory (LTM)** – Relatively permanent storage that has unlimited capacity. Different kinds of long-term memory have been identified:
   - **Procedural memory** – knowing how. Our knowledge of how to do things, and skills such as riding a bicycle.
   - **Declarative memory** – knowing that. Memory for specific information or facts, which is subdivided into semantic or episodic memory.

- **Semantic memory** – storage for language, other cognitive concepts and general knowledge. It is well organised, usually is not forgotten, and does not disappear in cases of amnesia. It is this kind of memory that is tested in experimental work.
- **Episodic memory** (also called **autobiographical memory**) – memory for personal events and people, i.e. the episodes of your life. Episodic memory is reconstructed as an evolving process of a person's history. A person's episodic memory may not be reliable because of memory distortions.

Recently, Schachter *et al.* (2000) added another LTM store – the **perceptual representation system (PRS)**, which is related to perceptual priming, i.e. the increased likelihood of recognising something when you have recently seen something similar.

Research evidence related to the MSM

The evidence for separate memory stores comes from empirical studies of duration, capacity and encoding. Evidence also comes from the serial position effect, case studies of brain damage, brain scans and understanding of forgetting.

1. Duration

Duration refers to how long a memory lasts in storage. Short-term memories last a short time – between 15 and 30 seconds, if not rehearsed. Long-term memories may last forever.

- **Sensory memory (SM)** – Sperling (1960) presented a display (like the one on the left) to trained participants for 50 milliseconds. After the display was presented, participants were told to report the whole array or just one row. In the whole array condition, they typically recalled 4 out of 12 items (about 33% recall). In the one row condition participants could recall 3 out of 4 items (75% recall), suggesting information decays quickly after presentation.
- **Short-term memory (STM)** – Peterson and Peterson (1959) studied the recall of trigrams (i.e. consonant triplets of letters that had no meaning). If participants had to wait three seconds before recalling the trigram they could remember 80%. But if they had to wait 18 seconds, recall was reduced to 10%. (Participants did an interference task – counting backwards – between presentation and recall to prevent rehearsal).
- **Long-term memory (LTM)** – Bahrick *et al.* (1975) demonstrated the existence of very-long-term-memories (VLTM). Nearly 400 adults of various ages were shown photographs from their high school yearbooks, and were asked to identify individuals. Even after 34 years, ex-students were still able to name 90% of their classmates. This shows that people have accurate VLTMs.

2. Capacity

Capacity refers to how much can be held in a memory store. STM has a very small capacity, whereas LTM is potentially unlimited.

- **STM** – Miller (1956) suggested that the span of STM is limited, not by the bits of information, but by the **chunks**; people can remember the same number of 10-letter words as 5-letter ones. The number of chunks that can be remembered is 7±2 (i.e. between 5 and 9). However, Simon (1974) found that there is a limit beyond which, chunk size does have an effect: participants had a shorter memory span for larger chunks (e.g. 8-word phrases) than for smaller chunks.

Chunking relies on LTM in order to determine meaningfulness. Bower and Springston (1970) showed that participants recalled meaningful chunks (e.g. FBI PHD TWA) better than they recalled meaningless chunks (e.g. FB IPH DWT A).

Recent research (Cowan *et al.*, 2001) suggests that STM may actually be limited to 4, rather than 7, chunks.

Sidebar notes:

An empirical study is a study (such as an experiment or an interview) where data has been collected through direct observation or experience.

An example of a stimulus used in Sperling's study:

7 I V F
X L 5 3
B 4 W 7

In these studies of memory, what kind of LTM memory is being tested – semantic, procedural or episodic? How does this affect the ecological validity of the findings?

Miller suggested that the magic number 7±2 might explain why things so often come in sevens – like seven days in the week or seven wonders of the world.

Think of your postcode. How many bits of information are there in it? How many chunks of information are there? Phone numbers are also presented in chunks, for example, 0181 654 3462.

- **LTM** – Merkle (1988) estimated (using the number of synapses) that LTM may have a capacity of between one thousand and one million gigabytes.

3. Encoding

Encoding describes the form or code used to store data in memory. This may be based on the sound of the information (an **acoustic** code), the way the information appears (a **visual** code) or may be in terms of meaning (a **semantic** code).

STM tends to be stored acoustically, whereas LTM is more semantic.

- Conrad (1964) found that participants made mistakes when recalling words that sounded similar (acoustic similarity), when recall was immediate (i.e. when testing STM).
- Baddeley (1966) investigated both STM and LTM by giving participants lists of words that were acoustically similar or dissimilar, or semantically similar or dissimilar.

In an experiment testing STM, he found that participants who were given words that were acoustically similar recalled about 55% of the words, compared to 75% recall in the other three conditions. In the experiment testing LTM, it was found that participants given words that were semantically similar again recalled about 55% of the words compared to 75% recall in the other three conditions.

These findings suggest that in STM, information tends to be acoustically coded (and that is why acoustically similar words were muddled up) and in LTM, information tends to be semantically coded (and that is why words with similar meanings tended to be muddled up).

Other research has found that STM does not always use an acoustic code. This depends on whether verbal rehearsal is prevented and/or whether recall is tested in an acoustic manner. For example, Brandimonte *et al.* (1992) found that participants used visual encoding in STM if they were given pictures to remember (a visual task). Verbal rehearsal was prevented (they had to say 'la la la') and they were asked to recall the items by drawing them (a visual recall task).

4. Serial position effect

Are the first words that are heard recalled best (**primacy effect**)? Or are the words that are heard most recently recalled best (**recency effect**)?

Glanzer and Cunitz (1966) asked participants to recall word lists. If this was done immediately, there was both a primacy effect and a recency effect (early and later words were better recalled) due to STM and LTM effects. If there was a delay of 10 seconds or more, there was only a primacy effect – LTM alone was affected.

Primacy is due to the fact that the first items are more likely to have entered LTM. Recency occurs because the last items on the list are still in STM.

5. Brain damage

Brain injury to specific areas can affect STM. Shallice and Warrington (1970) studied K.F., who experienced memory losses after a motorbike accident. He performed poorly on STM tasks (e.g. digit span) but his LTM was intact.

Brain injury may also affect LTM. In **anterograde amnesia**, permanent memories remain intact but sufferers cannot remember any new information for more than the normal STM span. This is probably because transfer from STM to LTM is lost.

Some examples of the word lists used by Baddeley:

Acoustically similar: cap, cab, can, mad

Acoustically dissimilar: pit, few, cod

Semantically similar: great, large, broad

Semantically dissimilar: good, huge, hot

The serial position effect refers to whether the position of words in a list affects the likelihood of recall.

3 6 2 9 8 5 1 4 7 3
Above is a string of digits. Cover up all the digits except the first four and say the digits, then shut your eyes and recall them. Were you right? Now try it with five digits. Keep going until you don't get them right. This is called the 'digit span technique' and is a way to assess the capacity of a person's short-term memory.

What are some of the weaknesses with using evidence from brain-damaged individuals?

It is not reasonable to generalise from a sample of one person. But, other studies have also supported the importance of the hippocampus. For example, Baddeley (1990) described the same symptoms in a man, Clive Wearing, whose hippocampus was damaged by infection.

Examples include Korsakoff's syndrome, which is due to severe alcohol poisoning, and the case study of H.M. (Milner, 1959). H.M. had an operation to remove both hippocampi from his brain to alleviate his severe epilepsy. H.M.'s personality and intellect remained intact, but his memory was affected. He suffered extensive anterograde amnesia, so he had no memory for events after the operation. His memory for events prior to the operation was reasonable, but not as good as it had been. He could still talk and recall all the skills he knew previously (semantic memory) but his memory did not incorporate new experiences. For many years he reported that his age was 27 and that the year was 1953. After a while he realised this was absurd and tried guessing. In other words, he tried to 'reconstruct' memories. He watched the news every night yet he had no recall for major events. He happily re-read magazines with no loss of interest. He couldn't memorise lists of words or recall faces of people he met.

This case study suggests that the hippocampus may function as a memory 'gateway' through which new memories pass before being permanently stored in LTM.

6. Brain scans

A more recent method of studying brain activity is the use of brain scans (see page 114). CAT (computerised axial tomography), MRI (magnetic resonance imaging) and PET (positron emission tomography) scans all produce images of the brain in action.

Maguire *et al.* (2000) used MRI scans to show that taxi drivers in London, who use their memory in their work, have larger hippocampi than non-taxi drivers.

Beardsley *et al.* (1997) showed that the pre-frontal cortex of the brain was active when participants were involved in an STM task.

The hippocampus is a small structure found deep inside the brain. There is one in each hemisphere of the forebrain.

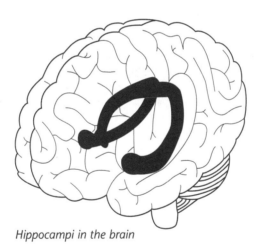

Hippocampi in the brain

7. Forgetting

Explanations for forgetting are different for STM and LTM. See pages 39–42.

Evaluation of the MSM

The scientific method revolves around theory-testing. Scientists produce theories to explain events in the world. In order to test the validity of such theories, research is conducted. A 'good' theory should be easy to test, i.e. experiments can be designed to test the specific predictions of the theory.

Strengths

- The distinction between STM and LTM is **well-supported by research evidence** (see pages 25-27).
- The MSM has **encouraged psychologists to conduct empirical research** to test the model, which has increased our understanding of memory.
- The MSM has encouraged other psychologists to **provide alternative explanations** of memory.

The MSM is no longer regarded as an adequate representation of memory processes. However, historically, it is an important theory.

Weaknesses

- The model is **over-simplified** – Research has since shown that there are more than three memory stores and more than two processes involved (see evidence on page 30).
- **More memory stores** – As we have already seen, LTM is divided into several different stores (procedural, declarative, episodic and semantic). The working memory model (see page 29) identifies subdivisions within STM.
- **Processes** – The levels of processing approach (see page 32) suggests that lasting memories are created through elaborative processing, rather than simply verbal or maintenance rehearsal, as suggested by the MSM.
- **STM and LTM are not as separate** as the MSM suggests. For example, chunking requires that LTM is accessed in order to establish the meaning of the chunks.
- The MSM presents a **passive view of memory** and cannot account for active processes such as reconstruction, that is, when memories are altered because of expectations (see accuracy of eyewitness testimony on page 35).
- **Validity** – The research studies have tended to concern only semantic memory and, therefore, the results and the MSM may be relevant only to this kind of memory rather than explaining, for example, memory for riding a bicycle or memory for events in the past.

Progress check

1 Identify **six** distinguishing features of the MSM.
2 STM and LTM differ in terms of duration. Name **one** study that illustrates this.
3 List the **six** ways that STM can be distinguished from LTM.
4 Outline **two** weaknesses with the research evidence for the MSM.

1 E.g. SM; Attention; STM; Rehearsal; LTM; Based on stores and processes.
2 E.g. Peterson and Peterson; Sperling; Bahrick *et al.*
3 Capacity; Encoding; Serial position effect; Brain damage; Brain scans; Forgetting.
4 E.g. Only one kind of memory is usually tested (semantic); Experiments may use artificial stimuli; In studies of brain damage we cannot be sure of the cause of observed behaviours; Case studies cannot be generalised.

The working memory (WM) model

AQA A U1
AQA B U2

Baddeley and Hitch (1974) suggested that short-term memory should be sub-divided. They used the phrase 'working memory' instead of short-term memory to reflect their view that this is the area of memory that is active when you are *working on* information. Working memory consists of the following parts:

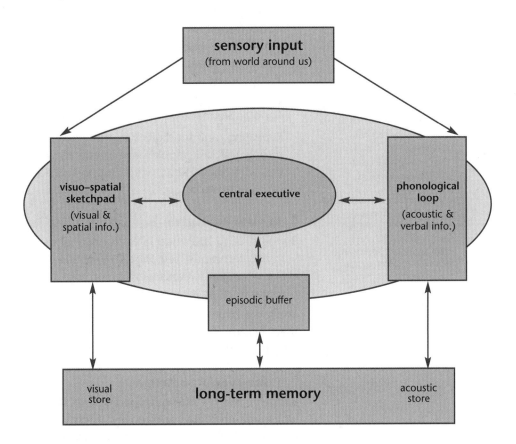

The working memory model

The structure of working memory

1. **Central executive** – This component of working memory is modality-free (i.e. not visual or auditory). It is roughly the same as attention (the concentration of mental effort on sensory or mental events). The central executive allocates resources to other components.

2. **Visuo-spatial sketchpad** (or scratchpad) – This part is used to hold visual memories, such as people's faces.

3. **Phonological loop** – This deals with verbal material and preserves the order of information. Information passes round and round in a loop as it is rehearsed. The phonological loop consists of…
   - a **phonological store**, which allows an individual to rehearse information acoustically – a kind of inner ear
   - an **articulatory process**, which is used for words that are heard or seen – a kind of inner voice.

The phonological store allows an individual to rehearse information acoustically.

4. **Episodic buffer** – This has recently been added by Baddeley (2000) because there was nowhere for information that is both visual and acoustic to be stored. The episodic buffer integrates information from the central executive, the visuo-spatial sketchpad and the phonological loop. It has a limited capacity.

Baddeley and Hitch first formulated the WM model to explain the results from various studies that showed:

(a) if you perform two tasks occupying *the same* modality (e.g. both visual tasks) they are performed less well then if either is done alone,

(b) if you perform two tasks and each involves a *different* modality (e.g. visual and auditory) then each is performed as well as when done alone.

For example McLeod (1977) showed that performance was impaired when participants played the piano and sang at the same time (both tasks are auditory). This must be due to competition within one component.

Research evidence related to the WM model

1. Dual-task processing

Baddeley and Hitch (1976) gave participants two tasks:

- **Verbal reasoning task** – Participants were given a sentence (e.g. 'B is followed by A') and then shown a pair of letters (BA). They then had to say 'true' or 'false'. This task should involve the central executive.
- **Concurrent task** – Participants had to do the verbal reasoning task at the same time as one of four set tasks:
  1. say 'the' repeatedly
  2. say 'one two three four five six' repeatedly
  3. repeat random strings of digits
  4. no additional task.

Repeating random digits was the only task that involved the central executive so only this task should have interfered with the verbal reasoning task. This was what they found, which supports the idea of separate stores in working memory.

2. Central executive

Bunge *et al.* (2000) used fMRI (functional magnetic resonance imaging – a brain scanning technique, see page 114) to see which parts of the brain were most active when participants were doing two tasks: reading a sentence, and recalling the final word in each sentence.

The same brain areas were active in either dual- or single-task conditions, but there was more activation in the dual-task condition. This showed that increased attentional demands led to greater brain activity, a central executive function.

3. Visuo-spatial sketchpad

Baddeley *et al.* (1975) gave participants the task of visualising a matrix of digits, which was presented auditorially. If this was combined with tracking a moving light, the ability to visualise was impaired.

4. Phonological loop: phonological store

Baddeley and Lewis (1981) found that articulatory suppression did *not* affect decisions involving acoustic (phonological) differences, demonstrating that there must be a separate store for this.

The articulatory process is the process of speaking.

Articulatory suppression refers to a task that stops you articulating (i.e. speaking).

5. Phonological loop: articulatory process

Baddeley (1975) gave participants a sequence of words to recall. Normally they could perform the task better with short, rather than long, words (called a **word length effect**) but when an articulatory suppression task (counting backwards) was included there was no difference, demonstrating that the word length effect depends on having access to an articulatory process.

The word length effect describes the fact that people remember short words better than long words.

6. Episodic loop

Baddeley *et al.* (1987) found that when participants were shown words and then asked for immediate recall, their performance was much better for sentences (related words) than for unrelated words.

This supports the idea of an immediate memory store for items that are neither visual nor phonological and that draws on long-term memory (to link the related words).

Evaluation of the WM model

Strengths

- The WM model is supported by **research evidence** (see page 30). This evidence is important because it cannot be explained by the multi-store model, whereas it can be explained by the working memory model. This makes the WM model the better model.
- The WM model describes **rehearsal (the articulatory process) as only one component**, which seems more appropriate than the central importance it is given in the multi-store model.
- The division of STM into further components more accurately reflects **evidence from brain-damaged patients**. For example, Shallice and Warrington's (1970) study of K.F. (see page 26) also revealed that his short-term forgetting of auditory stimuli was much greater than his short-term forgetting of visual stimuli. He could remember meaningful sounds but not words. Shallice and Warrington concluded that K.F.'s problems centred on what they called the 'auditory-verbal short-term store'.

According to Sternberg (2006), the working memory model is probably now the most widely accepted model of memory.

The working memory model does not distinguish between STM and LTM. Working memory is simply the most recently activated portion of enduring memory, rather than being a way station to and from LTM.

Weaknesses

- The description of the **central executive is considered unsatisfactory**. It is not clear whether it really explains anything and some psychologists think it may not be unitary. For example, Eslinger and Damasio (1985) studied a patient called E.V.R. who had a cerebral tumour removed. He was able to do some tasks linked to the central executive (e.g. tests requiring reasoning) but no other tasks that required involvement of the central executive (e.g. he had poor decision-making skills).
- Like the MSM, the **empirical evidence** for the WM model comes from ordinary **laboratory experiments using simplistic stimuli** (which concern only semantic memory), and from studies of brain-damaged individuals. This means that the findings lack ecological validity and cannot be generalised to all memory processes.

Progress check

1 Identify **six** distinguishing features of the WM model.
2 What happens when a person has to perform two tasks simultaneously involving the same modality?
3 Which patient had problems with his auditory-verbal short-term memory store?
4 Which part of the WM model has been criticised?

4 The central executive.

3 K.F.

2 Performance is slowed down.

1 E.g. Central executive; Visuo-spatial sketchpad; Phonological loop; Phonological store; Articulatory process; Episodic buffer.

The levels of processing approach (LOP)

AQA B ▸ U2

The key point in the LOP approach is that enduring memories are a by-product of the processing that takes place. The more meaning information has, the more memorable it should be.

Psychologists make a distinction between *implicit* and *explicit* memory. Implicit memory is when you remember things without deliberately making an effort to do so, for example, when you remember what you did last night. Explicit memory is when you focus on trying to remember something, such as revising for exams. The LOP approach can explain implicit memory.

Craik and Lockhart (1972) argued that the concept of **maintenance rehearsal** alone is not sufficient to account for long-term memory. Rehearsal is a kind of processing but it is not very deep. Craik and Lockhart believed that it is the *depth* of processing that determines whether information is stored over a long, rather than a short, period.

The main problem with this theory is defining what constitutes 'depth'. Craik and Lockhart defined it in terms of a continuum from shallow to deep processing: an example of shallow processing would be to say whether a word was written in capital letters, whereas an example of deep processing would be to say whether the word would fit in a given sentence (which involves semantic processing or a consideration of meaning).

The key study by Craik and Tulving (1975) illustrates how memory is an automatic by-product of cognitive operations. Participants were shown a word and asked a question which required a 'yes' or 'no' answer. The questions belonged to one of three levels of analysis:

1. **Shallow or structural**, for example, 'Is the word in capital letters?'
2. **Phonemic**, for example, 'Does the word rhyme with able?'
3. **Semantic or sentence**, for example, 'Would the word fit in the sentence, 'They met a ---- in the street.'?

In one experiment, participants were given an unexpected recognition test (**implicit** memory). In another experiment, they were told beforehand that they would be asked to recall the words (**explicit** memory). Participants who had been given semantic-type questions remembered most words. The phonemic coding was next best. Where participants were warned about recall (explicit memory), their performance was better. However, the differences between the three levels of analysis remained.

This shows that semantic processing creates an automatic memory, supporting the levels of processing theory. It is superior to conscious (explicit) storage, as it is used when a person is instructed to remember the information.

The graphs below show the results from the study by Craik and Tulving.

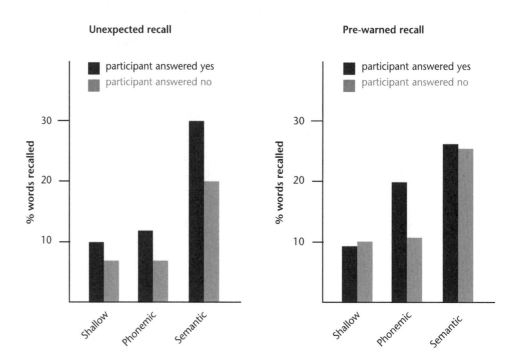

Research evidence related to the LOP approach

There are a number of ways that complex (deep) processing can take place:

1. Semantic processing

This is illustrated in the study by Craik and Tulving described on page 32.

Another classic study was conducted by Hyde and Jenkins (1973). They gave participants five different tasks: to rate a list of words for pleasantness; to estimate the words' frequency of usage; to count the occurrences of the letters 'e' and 'g' in the words; to decide what part of speech the word was; or to decide if the word fitted into certain sentences.

When tested for incidental learning (recall without warning), recall was best in the first two conditions, which involved semantic processing.

2. Elaboration

Craik and Tulving (1975) also tested the effects of elaboration. Participants were shown a word, and a sentence containing a blank. They were asked whether or not the word fitted into the incomplete sentence. Elaboration was manipulated by varying the complexity of the sentence between the simple (e.g. 'She cooked the -----') and the complex (e.g. 'The great bird swooped down and carried off the struggling ----').

Participants recalled twice as many words for the complex sentences. The improved performance was not due to increased time spent on the task because Craik and Tulving's other research showed that phonemic processing took as long as semantic processing.

The findings from this study show that elaboration (complexity) is a form of deep processing.

3. Organisation

Mandler (1967) asked participants to repeatedly sort a pack of cards into between two and seven categories, according to any system they wished. They were asked to repeat the task until they had sorted the cards identically two times in a row.

At the end, they were given an unexpected free recall test. Mandler found that recall was poorest for those who had used only two categories, and best for those who had used seven categories. Presumably, those participants who used several categories in sorting were imposing more organisation on the list and, therefore, remembered more.

4. Distinctiveness

Eysenck and Eysenck (1980) manipulated distinctiveness by using nouns containing silent letters or irregular pronunciation, such as 'comb'. Some participants were asked to say these words as they were spelled (e.g. pronouncing the 'b' in 'comb'). This was the shallow (non-semantic), distinctive condition. There was also a non-semantic, non-distinctive condition where the nouns were pronounced normally, as well as a semantic, non-distinctive condition and a semantic, distinctive condition, where the nouns were processed in terms of their meaning.

On an unexpected test of recognition memory, words in the non-semantic, distinctive condition were much better remembered than those in the non-semantic, non-distinctive condition, and almost as well as the two semantic conditions. This demonstrated that distinctiveness was as important as depth.

Whenever you read the description of a study, ask yourself, 'What does this show?' It is vital to understand *what was demonstrated* in order to communicate this in an exam.

You can use this evidence to enhance your revision – the more you organise your notes, the better you will remember it! Other ideas are to elaborate it and make it *distinctive!*

Craik (2002) commented, 'Perhaps the most enduring legacy of the Craik and Lockhart (1972) paper is the greater emphasis on memory as processing in current theories'.

Lockhart and Craik (1990) produced an updated version of their theory to deal with some of the criticisms, but essentially the levels of processing approach no longer merits much attention from cognitive psychologists.

Evaluation of the LOP approach

Strengths

- There is **considerable empirical evidence** to support the role of depth of processing, as outlined on page 33.
- The LOP approach **played an important role** in forcing psychologists to reconsider the MSM because the LOP approach showed that there is more to processing than maintenance rehearsal, i.e. elaborative processing is more important.
- The LOP approach also increased our understanding of behaviour, which is a positive feature for any theory.

Weaknesses

- It is possible that the better recall of semantic coding is due to **the way the participants' memories were tested**, as Morris *et al.* (1977) demonstrated. They found that if participants were given a rhyming recognition test they remembered the words that had received shallow processing better than the more deeply processed ones. This suggests that effective processing is related to the mode of recall, called **transfer-appropriate processing**.
- Levels of processing is an **over-simplified account**, focusing too much on depth of processing. Depth is not the only factor that affects memorability: relevance can also be important.
- The LOP approach **cannot explain** much of the evidence generated by the other models of memory.
- This model **describes rather than explains**. The concept of 'depth' is hard to define and it is circular (something which requires deeper processing is better remembered, and something that is better remembered was more deeply processed). This criticism may not be entirely fair as subsequent research has, in fact, extended what is meant by depth to include elaboration, organisation and distinctiveness. 'Depth' can be seen to be increasingly complex interaction with information to be remembered.
- Craik (2002) acknowledged that processing may be **necessary but not sufficient** to create enduring memories that need consolidation (e.g. rehearsal) as well as processing.

Progress check

1. In the LOP theory, what is said to determine how data enters permanent memory?
2. In the study by Craik and Tulving, identify the **three** types of questions asked.
3. Name **three** examples of complex processing.

3 E.g. Elaboration; Organisation; Distinctiveness.
2 Shallow, phonemic and semantic
1 Complexity or depth of processing.

2.2 Memory in everyday life

After studying this section you should be able to:

- *describe factors affecting the accuracy of eyewitness testimony, including misleading information, anxiety and age of witness*
- *describe and evaluate the use of the cognitive interview*
- *describe and evaluate strategies for memory improvement.*

The accuracy of eyewitness testimony (EWT)

AQA A   U1
AQA B   U3

Eyewitness testimony (EWT) refers to the descriptions given in a criminal trial by individuals who were present during the crime. This includes identification of perpetrators, important details of the crime scene, such as how fast a car was travelling before an accident, and/or peripheral information, such as the weather on that particular day.

Graph of results for the second experiment by Loftus and Palmer

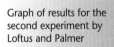
Response to 'Did you see any broken glass?'

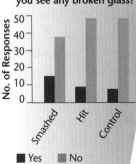
■ Yes   ■ No

The verbs used in Loftus and Palmer's experiment are a good example of **demand characteristics**. Participants look for cues about what is expected of them. This means they are receptive to certain features of the experiment, such as leading questions. These features almost demand a particular response from participants.

1. The effect of misleading information on accuracy of EWT

'Misleading information' is also called **leading questions** – questions that influence or prompt the respondent to give a particular answer.

Loftus and Palmer (1974) investigated the effect of leading questions by asking participants to estimate the speed of a car. Participants were shown film clips of automobile accidents and asked a set of questions, one of which was a *critical* question: 'About how fast were the cars going when they [hit] each other?'.

Participants were in one of five conditions, determined by the verb used in the critical question: hit, smashed, collided, bumped or contacted.

Participants in the 'smashed' group reported the highest speeds, followed by 'collided', then 'bumped', 'hit' and 'contacted' (see graph on the left). This shows that EWT was affected by misleading information – the different verbs implied faster or slower speeds.

Loftus and Palmer suggested that this effect might be either because the critical verb biases a person's response or because it actually alters their memory of the event. To test these explanations, they conducted a second experiment.

Participants were shown a film that contained a 4-second multiple-car accident. This time only 'hit' and 'smashed' were used in asking the question about speed. A week later the participants were asked to return to the psychology lab and were asked some further questions including the critical question, 'Did you see any broken glass?' The group with the word 'smashed' were twice as likely to answer 'yes' to seeing broken glass (even though there was none) than other participants (see graph on the left). This shows that misleading information (in this case **post-event information**, i.e. supplied after an event) did affect later recall.

Evaluation

- Witnessing video clips in a lab is **not very much like real-life**. For example, the task lacks the emotional impact of a real life accident (see the effects of anxiety on page 36). Yuille and Cutshall (1986) interviewed 13 people four months after they witnessed an armed robbery in Canada. They included two misleading questions in the interview. The witnesses provided accurate recall that matched their initial reports. This suggests that misleading/post-event information may *not* affect memory in real-life and that EWT can be very reliable.
- The task (estimating the speed of a car) is **not a 'concrete' task** – in fact it was specially selected because people would not be confident about estimating the speed of a car and would, therefore, be more likely to be affected by cues. When Elizabeth Loftus (1979) investigated a more concrete task, she found participants had good recall.

'Do you get headaches frequently? 'Loftus showed that this is a (mis)leading question: people reported an average of 2.2 headaches per week whereas those who were asked 'Do you get headaches occasionally, and if so, how often?' reported an average of 0.7 headaches!

The way the question was asked had a significant effect on the answer that was given.

Participants were shown a series of pictures of a man stealing a red wallet from a woman's bag and, later, 98% identified the colour correctly. Even when the wallet was later incorrectly described as brown, they recalled it as red. This shows that we may have good recall for important and concrete information, and that recall of such information may not be distorted even by misleading information.

- However, in these studies, the misleading information was supplied some time after the memories were stored. Does misleading information affect the way memories are stored or **does it just affect their later retrieval?**

Bekerian and Bowers (1983) conducted a study where participants were shown a series of slides of events leading up to a car accident – a red car approached a junction where there was either a STOP or a YIELD sign. Later, participants were asked questions including one that mentioned either a STOP or a YIELD sign. Finally, they were asked to look at pairs of slides and to identify which one was in the original set.

Participants who were shown slides and asked questions that were consistent (e.g. STOP picture and STOP mentioned in the question) were more likely to choose the correct slide, whereas those given misleading information (e.g. STOP picture and YIELD question) were less accurate. However, this effect only occurred if the recognition slides were given in a random order. When the order matched the original order of events, the misleading information had no effect. This shows that misleading information appears to affect retrieval, rather than initial storage.

2. The effect of anxiety on the accuracy of EWT

Emotional arousal enhances the accuracy of memory

Christianson and Hubinette (1993) interviewed 110 witnesses to bank robberies, and found that those who had been threatened in some way were more accurate in their recall and remembered more details than those who had been onlookers and less emotionally aroused. This continued to be true even 15 months later.

Emotional arousal reduces the accuracy of memory

Deffenbacher *et al.* (2004) conducted a review of 18 studies that looked at the effects of anxiety on the accuracy of EWT recall. They found that many of them indicated it had a negative impact.

The Yerkes–Dodson effect

The apparent contradiction may be explained in terms of the **Yerkes-Dodson effect** – arousal has a positive impact up to a certain point but too much arousal has a negative effect (see graph on the left).

3. The effect of age on the accuracy of EWT

Young children are not good eyewitnesses

Brassard (2002) found that 4 year olds were more prone to suggestibility than 8 year olds, i.e. when interviewed, their answers were influenced by cues from the interviewer.

Goodman and Reed (1986) also looked at suggestibility and found no difference between 6 year olds and adults. However, 3 year olds recalled little and were highly suggestible.

Martin *et al.* (1979) tested children and young adults and found that the amount of information recalled (they watched a film about a distressed man) increased with age.

Younger adults have better recall than older adults

Karpel *et al.* (2001) found that young adults (aged 17–25) were more accurate than older adults (aged 65–85) in their recall of information from a video about a robbery. They were also less vulnerable to leading questions.

Memon *et al.* (2003) found that younger participants (aged 16–33) had more accurate recall of a video and better recognition in a line-up than older participants (aged 60–82). However, this effect only became apparent if they were tested one week after initial viewing. If participants were tested immediately, there was no difference of recall due to age.

No difference

Yarmey (1993) found no difference in recall due to age between young participants (aged 18–29) and old participants (aged 45–65) when they were asked to identify a woman who they had spoken to 15 minutes earlier.

Own-age bias

Anastasi and Rhodes (2006) have shown that age-related differences in accuracy of recall may be related to *what* it is the participants have to recall. Younger adults were better than older people at recalling photographs of younger people, whereas older people were better than younger people at recalling photographs of older people.

> There may be a **cohort effect** when comparing young and older adults. The older adults belong to a group (cohort) who grew up at a time when diet and education were not as good as that of young adults today. A more valid approach would be to compare the same individuals over time to see if their memories decline. This is called a cross-sectional design.

4. The cognitive interview (CI)

Fisher and Geiselman (1995) developed an interviewing technique that aims to improve the quantity and quality of eyewitness recall, based on psychological research. The cognitive interview involves:

1 **Reporting every detail**, no matter how irrelevant. It may be that some irrelevant details act as important cues to recall other things.
2 **Mental recreation of original scene** – By actually visualising the original event the eyewitness may 'see' certain things that were previously overlooked.
3 **Changing the order** – If events are recalled, for example, in reverse order, this may create new cues that lead to the recovery of new information.
4 **Changing the perspective** – The interviewee is asked to recall the incident from multiple perspectives, e.g. imagining how it would have appeared to other witnesses who were present at the time.

> The reason why the CI has yet to be widely adopted is probably because it takes longer than the standard police interview and requires extensive training. An alternative would be to use brief training programmes, but these have not produced improved accuracy in eyewitness recall (Memon *et al.*, 1994).

Research evidence

Köhnken *et al.* (1999) reviewed 53 studies using the CI and found an average increase of 34% in recall when the cognitive interview was used, compared to a standard police interview.

Milne and Bull (2002) examined the relative effectiveness of each of the four components of the CI and found that no individual element led to increased recall. However, recall was enhanced when (1) and (2) were used together.

Stein and Memon (2006) tested the CI in a real life setting (in Brazil – most studies are lab-based). They found that the CI increased the amount of correct information obtained from witnesses, and was far superior in producing forensically rich information (i.e. details that would be useful in a court of law).

Strategies for memory improvement

AQA A U1

A **mnemonic** is any structured technique that is used to help people remember and (most importantly) recall later on. For example, acronyms and acrostics.

An example of an acronym: 'HOMES' – a word which stands for the names of the Great lakes in North America: Huron, Ontario, Michigan, Erie and Superior.

An example of an acrostic: 'Never Eat Shredded Wheat' – for the four points of the compass.

Memory-improvement techniques aim to structure material and thus make it more memorable and/or meaningful. They also aim to make abstract information more concrete and to provide meaningful links between meaningless items.

1. Verbal techniques

- **Acronyms and acrostics** – Make meaningless (random) material meaningful, which makes it more memorable. If we remembered everything, our memories would be overflowing with useless information. Therefore, our memories have evolved so that we remember only meaningful information.
- **Organising notes into subheadings and topics** – This makes it easier to retrieve information from your brain. Bower *et al.* (1969) showed that people remember more words when they are organised into categories than when they are presented randomly.
- **Chunking** is a strategy that is used to reduce what has to be remembered (see Miller, page 25) and create meaningful units. For example, people frequently chunk telephone numbers.
- **Cues**, such as creating a list of key words that will act as cues to recall. The most common explanation for forgetting is an inability to access what is stored in memory. It is available but not accessible, which is demonstrated when someone gives you the right cue (see retrieval failure on page 40).

2. Visual techniques

- **Mind maps or spider diagrams** (in fact, all diagrams) – Such methods organise information and establish links that help recall. Memory essentially involves making associations in the brain. This is a process that normally takes place without any effort from you, but when learning abstract or apparently random material, you need to artificially make the links.
- **Method of loci** – Placing items in positions on a route that you are familiar with, such as your route to school or around your house. Recall items by doing the walk 'in your head'.
- **Colouring items** in your notes makes them more distinctive – This is related to **elaborative processing** (see LOP theory on page 32). The *amount* of rehearsal is important (maintenance rehearsal) but the *nature* of rehearsal (elaboration) is more important.

Visual techniques may help recall because such items are double-encoded in memory (Paivio, 1971). They are first coded as verbal symbols and again as image-based symbols. This double coding increases the likelihood that they will be remembered.

Progress check

1 In Loftus and Palmer's study, which verb led to the highest speed estimates?
2 How does anxiety affect recall?
3 What is the 'own-age bias'?
4 Name **three** mnemonic techniques used to improve memory.

4 E.g. Acronyms; Cues; Diagrams.
3 Participants recognise people of their own age better than people who are older or younger.
2 Moderate anxiety enhances recall, but too much leads to poor recall (Yerkes–Dodson effect).
1 Smashed.

2.3 Forgetting

After studying this section you should be able to:

- *describe explanations of forgetting: decay, displacement, lack of consolidation, interference, retrieval failure (absence of context and cues), and motivated forgetting including repression*
- *evaluate such explanations.*

LEARNING SUMMARY

Explanations of forgetting in STM

AQA B   U2

'Forgetting' assumes that something was once stored in memory, and has now disappeared (not available), or can't be 'brought to mind' (not accessible).

A **memory trace** is the physical representation of the information in the brain.

1. Decay

The physical memory trace simply disappears because it is not rehearsed or processed sufficiently. Peterson and Peterson (see page 25) provided evidence that data in STM disappears if it is not rehearsed.

Evaluation

The disappearance of a memory trace may be due to displacement rather than spontaneous decay, i.e. if nothing else entered STM, the memory would not disappear.

2. Displacement

Information stored in STM will be displaced by new information entering STM because STM has a limited capacity. This might explain Peterson and Peterson's findings (see page 25) where the second set of information (participants had to count backwards in threes) displaced the initial material and caused information to disappear, i.e. be forgotten.

An example of a list used in the serial probe technique:

2 1 8 5 3 4 9 2 6 9 7 3
The last digit is the probe, so the answer is 4.

The serial probe technique (see explanation on the left) has been used to investigate displacement. Waugh and Norman (1965) asked participants to listen to a sequence of digits. The participants were then given a probe (one of the numbers in the list) and asked to recall the number that came next in the list. If the probe was near the end of the list, recall was good, but if the probe was early in the list, recall was poor. This demonstrates that early numbers are displaced by later ones.

Since STM has limited capacity and duration, the explanations for forgetting in STM are likely to be due to lack of availability rather than accessibility.

Evaluation

Waugh and Norman (1965) repeated the experiment, this time reading digits out at a rate of one per second (slower) or four per second (faster). The rate of presentation should not make a difference if displacement is the explanation; if decay is the explanation then recall should be poorer when the rate is slow. The findings were that the effect of the rate of presentation was relatively small compared to the effect of position. This shows that (1) most of forgetting in STM can be explained by displacement (2) some forgetting in STM is due to decay.

3. Lack of consolidation

Memory loss that arises from an accident or ECT (electro-convulsive therapy) creates amnesia (see page 157). The trauma prevents the consolidation of immediate memories and, therefore, they are lost.

Evaluation

Lack of consolidation explains a limited range of behaviour.

Explanations of forgetting in LTM

Paired associate task – to test retroactive and proactive interference, participants are asked to learn two similar lists, like those shown below:

List 1

A	B
BEM	lawn
TAQ	barge
MUZ	host
PEZ	tube
LUF	weed
ROH	mate

List 2

A	C
BEM	aisle
TAQ	cave
MUZ	bass
PEZ	vine
LUF	dame
ROH	file

You might try the following research activity to test RI and PI yourself. Compare performance when the stimulus terms are the same, or when both lists contain different words. Which causes more forgetting: RI or PI?

An example of one of the word lists used in Tulving and Psotka's study: hut, cottage, tent, hotel, cliff, river, hill, volcano, captain, corporal, sergeant, colonel, ant, wasp, beetle, mosquito, zinc, copper, aluminium, bronze, drill, saw, chisel, nail.

Can you identify the six categories?

You might try another research activity: ask people to learn the list of words above. When they have to recall the list, tell some people the names of the categories but let others produce free recall. Which group does better?

In the case of both kinds of retrieval failures (context and cues) and motivated forgetting (covered on the next page) memories are available, but not currently accessible.

1. Interference

One set of information competes with another, causing it to be 'overwritten' or physically lost. There are two forms of interference:

- **Retroactive interference** (RI) – new information 'pushes out' earlier material.
- **Proactive interference** (PI) – previous learning interferes with current learning.

Interference can be demonstrated by a **paired-associate task** (see example on the left). Participants are asked to learn two similar lists. In each list, the same nonsense syllable is paired with different words, A–B (e.g. BEM and lawn) and A–C (e.g. BEM and aisle). If participants learn list 1 (A–B), then list 2 (A–C), and are asked to recall list 1, their performance will be affected by RI. If they learn list 2 followed by list 1, and are tested on list 1 again, their performance will be affected by PI.

Findings include:

- **Similarity causes greater interference** – McGeoch and McDonald (1931) found that if the interference task was a list of synonyms to the original list, recall was poor (12%), nonsense syllables had less effect (26% recall), and numbers had least effect (37% recall). Only interference can explain such findings.
- Little proactive or retroactive interference is found when **different stimulus terms** are used in the two lists (Underwood and Postman, 1960).
- RI is stronger than PI.

Evaluation

Interference has **limited application** as an explanation of memory. It is only relevant to occasions when two sets of data are very similar. This is rare in everyday life but it does occur, for example, when you turn on the windscreen wipers instead of the indicators when driving someone else's car.

There is evidence that apparent interference effects are **experimental artefacts**. Ceraso (1967) found that, if memory was tested again after 24 hours, recognition (accessibility) showed considerable spontaneous recovery, whereas recall (availability) remained the same. This suggests that interference occurs because memories are not accessible, rather than because they have actually been lost (unavailable).

This is **further supported** in a study by Tulving and Psotka (1971). Participants were given five lists of 24 words each, and each list was organised into six categories. An example is shown on the left. The categories were not explicit but it was presumed that they would be obvious to participants.

Recall was about 70% for the first word list, but this fell as participants were given each additional list to learn. However, at the end they were given a cued recall test, i.e. told the names of the categories as a clue. Recall rose again to about 70%. This shows that the words were there (i.e. available) but interference had made them inaccessible.

2. Retrieval failure (absence of context and cues)

Tulving (1962) presented participants with a list of words followed by three successive recall trials. The specific words recalled each time differed, although the response rate remained at a fairly steady 50%. This suggests that information is there but is not always retrieved. Presumably, on each recall trial, the participants were using different retrieval cues. Tulving and Pearlstone (1966) found that performance was three times better when participants were given appropriate retrieval cues.

People always perform better on a recognition task than free recall. This can be explained by retrieval failure (cue-dependent forgetting). A recognition task provides cues for better recall.

- **Encoding specificity principle** – The closer the retrieval cue is to the information stored in memory, the greater the likelihood that the cue will be successful in retrieving the memory. Thomson and Tulving (1970) demonstrated this by showing that cues which are strongly associated (e.g. 'white' as a cue for 'black') lead to better recall than weak associations (e.g. 'train' as a cue for 'black').
- **Time of learning** – Tulving also claimed that cues should only be useful if they are encoded at the time of learning. However, Jones (1982) gave participants unrelated word pairs to learn (e.g. regal and beer). When their recall was tested, one group (the 'informed' group) were told that the cue, if reversed, gave a clue to its partner (e.g. regal–lager). The informed participants performed twice as well as uninformed participants, despite the fact that initially the cue (regal) was ineffective. Yet it was, nonetheless, there to be used if it later proved effective.

Cues do not have to be a significant word. They may also be the context or state in which something was learned.

Police reconstructions of crimes are based on context-dependence. When a person re-visits the scene of a crime their memory is jogged. A more common example is the smell of something, like the sea, which may jog your memory for a particular incident at the seaside.

- **Context-dependent recall** – Abernethy (1940) found that recall was better for a group of participants who sat in the same room and the same seat when tested, and with the same lecturer, than those who were tested in different surroundings. They may have looked around the room and certain things acted as cues that jogged their memory. Godden and Baddeley (1975) gave divers lists of words to learn on land or underwater. Recall was better when the context was constant. Godden and Baddeley (1980) found that recognition is not affected by extrinsic context, whereas recall is. This can be explained in terms of cues: recognition doesn't require cues, whereas recall does.

State-dependent recall may explain why, every time you get depressed, certain memories come flooding back.

- **State-dependent recall** – Goodwin *et al.* (1969) reported evidence of drinkers who hid money when drunk and couldn't remember where it was when they were sober. However, they could recall when drunk again.

Evaluation

Retrieval failure is the **main reason** for forgetting in LTM (Eysenck, 1988).

However, many of the studies used to support cue-dependent forgetting are **lab-based** and not much like everyday memory. Therefore, cue-dependent recall may not apply to all aspects of everyday memory. For example, procedural knowledge (e.g. remembering how to play ping-pong) may not be related to cue-dependent recall. Such memories are rather resistant to forgetting, but not totally immune. If you haven't played ping-pong in years, there is some re-learning to do, but even so, cues don't really explain this kind of forgetting/recall.

3. Motivated forgetting

Motivated forgetting is when a person wants to forget something. There are two kinds of motivated forgetting: suppression and repression.

Suppression

Suppression refers to when you consciously try to forget a memory. For example, you might 'forget' to do your homework because you didn't want to do it so you simply pushed it out of your mind.

The word 'repressed' means to be kept out of conscious awareness.

Hypnosis is one means of retrieving inaccessible memories. However, it may rely on reconstructions or 'suggestion' (putting ideas into a person's head), and, therefore, recall is inaccurate.

Freud initially used hypnosis with his patients, in order to access repressed memories, but ultimately concluded that it was too unreliable.

Decay has also been put forward as an explanation for forgetting in LTM, but it is unlikely – lack of availability is a more likely explanation. However, there are cases of actual loss of neural tissue (brain damage) through ageing, illness or injury. This would clearly affect memory.

Repression

Repression refers to when you unconsciously forget a memory. The idea of repression was proposed by Sigmund Freud over a century ago. Freud argued that painful or disturbing memories are put beyond conscious recall as a means of protecting one's ego from anxiety (Freud's theory is described on page 19).

The kinds of memory that are 'forgotten' or repressed range from the serious, such as childhood incidents of sexual abuse or extreme unhappiness, to more commonplace situations like 'forgetting' to clean your room or go to the dentist.

Research evidence

- Levinger and Clark (1993) gave participants word lists, including some emotionally-charged words, such as 'fear'. Subsequent recall was poorer for the emotional words. However, when Parkin *et al.* (1982) repeated this experiment with delayed recall, they found improvement, which suggests that arousal had only created initial repression.
- Myers and Brewin (1994) found that individuals who were classed as 'repressors' took longer to recall unhappy childhood memories and fewer were recalled as compared with other personality types. In addition, the repressors were more likely to report difficult relationships with their fathers. This means that they had more anxiety-provoking memories and appeared to repress these, though this may be 'inhibited recall' rather than true repression.
- Case histories of event-specific amnesia may be examples of repression. For example, Sirhan Sirhan, the man who assassinated Robert Kennedy, claimed he could recall nothing of the crime (Bower, 1981).

Evaluation

Repression is **hard to prove or disprove**. Someone may simply say they can't recall something (though it is there), or their eventual recall may be inaccurate.

Progress check

1 Name **two** explanations for forgetting in STM.
2 Distinguish between RI and PI.
3 How did Tulving and Psotka demonstrate that interference doesn't affect what is actually stored in memory?

3 When they used a cued-recall task, participants were able to recall much more.
2 RI: current learning interferes with material already learned. PI: current learning is affected by previously learned material.
1 E.g. Trace decay; Displacement; Lack of consolidation.

2.4 Perceptual processes

After studying this section you should be able to:

- describe perceptual set and the effects of motivation, expectation, emotion and culture on perception
- describe principles of perceptual organisation and Gestalt principles
- describe and evaluate Gibson's and Gregory's theories of visual perception
- describe distortion illusions, including the Müller-Lyer illusion and the Ponzo illusion
- describe ambiguous figures, including the Necker cube and Rubin's vase
- consider what distortion illusions and ambiguous figures tell us about perception
- describe depth cues (monocular and binocular)
- describe types of perceptual constancy, including size and shape constancy.

LEARNING SUMMARY

Perceptual set

AQA B   U2

> Perceptual set may be seen as a good thing – it speeds up the perceptual process. But it is also a bad thing, because it may lead to perceptual errors.

'Set' is the predisposition or bias to perceive a scene one way instead of any of the other ways. The following are some of the factors that may influence set:

1. **Motivation** – If you deprive a person of food, they are then motivated to satisfy their need, which appears to increase their sensitivity towards need-related objects. This would then speed the process of satisfying their need. Gilchrist and Nesburg (1952) showed slides of food to student volunteers before and after they went without food for 20 hours. As the volunteers got hungrier, the pictures of the food were perceived as being brighter. Sanford (1936) also found that the number of responses related to food (on a questionnaire) increased, the longer the participants were deprived of food.

2. **Expectation** – Bruner and Postman (1949) showed participants five different playing cards. Some of these were incongruous ('trick') cards, for example, a black three of hearts or a red six of clubs. It took participants longer to correctly identify the trick cards, and they often resolved the conflict by reporting a compromise. For example, the red six of clubs was seen as purple, and the black hearts illuminated by a reddish light.

> **Sensations** are the raw data of the perceptual system, the unaltered record of the physical stimulus.
>
> **Perceptions** are based on sensations, but they are altered through interpretation and elaboration so that what is 'seen' has meaning.

3. **Emotion** – Things that are threatening or unpleasant are ignored, or less likely to be attended to (called **perceptual defence**). McGinnies (1949) found that participants required significantly longer exposure times to correctly report emotionally threatening words such as 'penis' and 'whore'. However, this may be due to embarrassment in saying the words. Bitterman and Kniffen (1953) found that there was no effect when participants were able to write down their responses.

   Solley and Haigh (1958) found that children drew larger and larger pictures of Santa Claus the nearer it got to Christmas. This shows how positive emotions increase sensitivity and affect perceptual organisation.

4. **Culture** – Pettigrew *et al.* (1958) used binocular rivalry (i.e. when each eye is presented with a different visual stimulus). Participants from five major racial groups in South Africa (European English, Afrikaners, Coloured, Indian and African) were shown 40 pairs of photographs of members of other ethnic groups stereoscopically (one picture to one eye) for two seconds. Immediately afterwards they were asked to name the race they thought they had seen. Afrikaners tended to see either white or black, rather than in-between. This shows that culture influences their perceptions.

Perceptual organisation and Gestalt principles

AQA B U2

The term 'Gestalt' means 'unified whole' in German.

Figure and ground – Rubin's vase

Do you see two faces or a vase in the picture above?

Closure

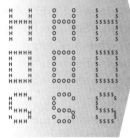

You automatically close the gaps and 'see' the letter E.

Perceptual organisation is the process of turning visual data into meaningful units. Gestalt psychologists argued that humans tend to organise sensory data in certain typical ways in order to build up perceptual units:

1. **Figure and ground organisation** – When looking at a picture, we see figures (i.e. the forms or shapes of things) set against a background. In certain ambiguous drawings, what is figure and what is ground may change. Nevertheless, at any time, only one part is figure. It is not truly possible to see both as 'figure' at the same time (see illustration on the left).

2. **Similarity** – When viewing a group of objects, we tend to group together those that are similar. For example: OOOOOXXXXXOOOOOXXXXX

3. **Proximity** – This effect occurs when elements are placed close together. They are then perceived as a group. The squares on the immediate right are not seen as a group, whereas the ones on the far right are. Proximity can be achieved in space and time.

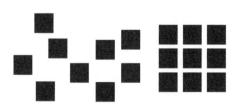

Example of proximity effect

4. **Closure** – We tend to complete images that have sections missing. When people are shown pictures, such as the one on the left, and later asked to draw them, they fill in the missing gaps.

5. **Continuity** – A series of dots that make a recognisable shape, such as the arrow on the right, are seen as an arrow rather than as than their constituent parts.

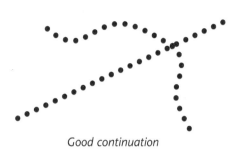

Good continuation

6. **Global precedence** – Initial perceptions are based on the overall representation, rather than the overall picture being built up from its individual elements (top-down rather than bottom-up processing, explained on pages 45–46).

Research example – Navon (1977) displayed stimulus pictures similar to those on the left for 500 milliseconds each. The large letter is termed the 'whole' or 'global' letter, and the smaller letters are the 'constituent' or 'local' parts. On some trials, the stimuli were consistent (i.e. the global and local letters were the same). On other trials, they were conflicting. Participants were asked beforehand to identify either the global or local letter. In all, they were shown 288 stimuli. Global letters were identified more quickly. When local and global letters were in conflict, participants were slowed in their identification of the local letters, but not the global ones. This supports the idea of global precedence. This would be useful in speeding up the perceptual process so that important objects in the visual scene can be identified with minimal delay.

However, it is not always true. In a later study, Kinchla and Wolfe (1979) found that when the global letter takes up a greater part of the visual field, or if the local features were larger or more prominent, then the local features were easier to respond to. Nevertheless, it certainly explains some aspects of early perceptual processing.

Stimuli similar to those used by Navon

Theories of visual perception

AQA A ▶ A2 (U3)

AQA B ▶ U2

Direct perception involves **bottom-up** or **data-driven** processing. This is when perception is primarily determined by the physical stimulus.

The retina contains the cells that are sensitive to light. It records the physical stimulus received by the eye.

Texture gradients, such as the stones in the picture below, indicate distance.

Gibson was asked to prepare training films for World War II pilots and observed that the 'flow' of data past a viewer (the pilot) provided unambiguous perceptual information.

Gibson's theory is sometimes called the 'ecological theory' because perception is explained solely in terms of the environment.

Direct perception theory does explain some aspects of perception. Changes in the optic array do provide rich data and perception can be very accurate.

1. Direct theory (Gibson, 1979)

Gibson believed that the amount of data contained in the **retinal** image (the **optic array**) contains a great deal of information about objects in the visual world, and about the movement of those objects (and the observer) within it. Such data is sufficient to explain perception.

- **Optic flow patterns** are produced as we move around the environment; thus movement produces perceptual data. Gibson felt that movement (action) was a key part of perception.
- **Invariants** – Some aspects of the optic array remain the same when you move, such as a pole (i.e. a point towards which someone is moving), **horizon–ratio relation** (the horizon is used to judge object size because it intersects the image of an object at eye height, see illustration on page 47), and **texture gradients** (which provide information of depth from sensory data alone). We collect this invariant data in an automatic way – called **resonance** – in the same way that a radio collects radio waves; perceptual data 'resonates' in the environment and this is perceived by the viewer.
- **Affordance** explains how the meaning of an object is perceived directly because its use is obvious. One look at a postbox and you can 'see' its meaning (as a place to put letters). The concept of affordance conforms to the notion that there is a close relationship between perception and action.

Research evidence

Gibson *et al.* (1955) found that all the information that a pilot required was in the optic array: a horizon line, a runway outline, ground texture, apparent movement and so on, and this gave sufficient information for landing a plane.

Lee and Lishman (1975) built a swaying room so that they could manipulate optic flow patterns. Children typically fell over but adults were able to adjust, showing that sensory and motor processes are linked and that we learn to adjust them.

Time-to-contact is the idea that animals can judge distance and speed of actions with respect to time using visual (direct) information only. Lee *et al.* (1982) demonstrated this by videotaping long jumpers. As they approached takeoff, their stride length varied so that their final take-off footfall position was correct.

Evaluation

- Direct theory explains **animal perception** and some aspects of human perception, particularly where data is **unambiguous** (e.g. when in a brightly lit situation).
- It can explain 'seeing' but not '**seeing as**', i.e. attaching meaning to what you see (Fodor and Pylyshyn, 1981).
- It cannot explain **perceptual set**, or all visual constancies and illusions (it can only explain some of them). However, **illusions are artificial** and do not represent perceptual behaviour in the real world.
- It cannot explain **concept-driven processing** or internal representations. For example, Menzel (1978) showed monkeys 20 hidden food items, which they could later locate. They must have relied on cognitive maps and not solely on sensory data.

Constructivist theory is **top-down** or **data-driven** processing. Perception is primarily determined by 'best guesses' based on past experience.

The Ames Room

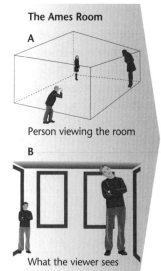

A

Person viewing the room

B

What the viewer sees

Constructivist theory can be applied to understanding certain accidents, such as when an aeroplane pilot makes on error because what he 'sees' is affected by preconceived ideas.

The two approaches (bottom-up and top-down processing – as suggested by Gibson and Gregory respectively) can be seen as complementary:

- Bottom-up may represent innate sensory mechanisms, whereas top-down depends on learned experience.
- Their relative importance varies with particular circumstances – direct perception is used in good lighting conditions whereas expectations are relied on in situations of ambiguity, such as poor lighting.

2. Constructivist theory (Gregory, 1966)

Gregory described the process of perception as 'hypothesis testing' – a perceived object is a hypothesis, which is first suggested and then tested by sensory data. The stimulus provided to our senses is often incomplete or ambiguous, therefore, Gregory believed that perception must rely on cognitive expectations to help resolve ambiguities.

Research evidence

The effect of expectation can be seen in:

- **The effects of perceptual set** (see page 43).
- **Perceptual constancy** (see page 48) – We manage to perceive such things as size and shape as constant, despite a changing retinal image, e.g. a book always looks rectangular. Size constancy is demonstrated in the **Ames Room** (on the left) where one person appears larger because constancy cues are confused. One corner of the room is actually further away but the ceiling is adjusted to maintain the appearance of a rectangular room (see drawing A). The result is that a person viewing the room 'sees' one person's head touching the ceiling and appearing much larger (see drawing B). If the person in the far corner is very familiar, the size effect disappears and the room is seen as distorted.
- **Studies of context**, for example, Palmer (1975), showed participants a contextual scene such as a kitchen and asked them to identify objects. They correctly identified an object looking like a loaf of bread 80% of the time. However, they were much less accurate with a drum or a mailbox (40% identification), presumably because their perceptions were affected by expectation about what was likely to be found in a kitchen.
- **Visual illusions** are used to illustrate the perception of ambiguous information (see examples on page 47). Gregory explained them in terms of mistaken hypotheses. For example, **misapplied size-constancy theory** (Gregory, 1970) states that size-constancy rules for 3D objects are sometimes applied inappropriately to the perception of 2D objects. This can only explain some illusions, e.g. the Ponzo illusion (see page 47). It does not fully explain the Müller-Lyer illusion (see page 47) because when the fins are replaced with circles, the effect persists. On the other hand, cross-cultural research has found that people who do not live in 'carpentered environments' (i.e. they do not experience square edges) do not 'see' the Müller-Lyer illusion – their lack of experience with corners means they have not developed the expectations that lead to the illusion (Segal *et al.*, 1963).

Evaluation

- Constructivist theory explains **perceptual set** (e.g. the effect of emotion on perception), and **perceptual constancy** (e.g. size and depth perception).
- It explains some **visual illusions**, however, these are artificial and, therefore, the theory may only explain some aspects of real-world perception.
- It cannot explain why vision is generally so **accurate** even in novel situations.
- It cannot explain why the perceptual system is sometimes **slow to adjust** (as in inverted images) and sometimes faster (as in seeing ambiguous images).
- It can't explain how the system **reacts so fast** when having to search through a store of cognitive schemas.

Visual illusions

AQA B   U2

The Ponzo illusion – which line is longer?

The Müller-Lyer illusion – which line is longer?

The Necker cube – which face of the cube is closer?

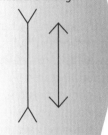

There are also auditory illusions, for example Warren and Warren (1970) showed that, if a sentence is tampered with so that a bleep occurs instead of a particular phoneme, the listener still 'hears' the phoneme even when they know it's missing (phonemic restoration).

Illustration of the horizon–ratio effect

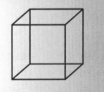

Illusions are distinct from hallucinations because they are based on real sensory data. Illusions are usually associated with an element of surprise. However, many commonplace visual techniques, such as using shadow to imply 3D in pictures, are also illusions.

Visual illusions can be classified as distortion illusions or ambiguous figures:

1. Distortion illusions

- **The Ponzo illusion** – The horizontal lines are the same length yet we perceive them as different. The oblique (slanting) lines seem to show perspective and, therefore, our perceptual processes 'adjust' for size. A distant object of the same retinal size is seen as longer because we 'see' it as further away. This illustrates size constancy.

- **The Müller-Lyer illusion** – Gregory (1970) claims that the Müller-Lyer illusion occurs because the longer fin represents the corner of a building moving away from you whereas the smaller fin is an internal angle. However, the Müller-Lyer effect persists when the fins are replaced with circles.

  Further evidence against Gregory's explanation comes from DeLucia and Hochberg (1991) who used 3D models (so real depth cues were available, rather than 2D) and the effect did not persist.

  Wraga *et al.* (2000) found no Müller-Lyer effect when participants indicated the length of a 3D model of the lines by walking blindfolded around real models. This fits Gibson's view that movement is an important part of visual perception.

2. Ambiguous figures

- **The Necker cube** is the classic example of hypothesis testing. There is no clue about which face of the cube is closer and so the faces move in and out as the perceptual system settles on one hypothesis and then the other.

- **Rubin's vase** (see picture on page 44) – When two fields have a common border, one is seen as figure and the other as ground. It is not possible to see figure and ground at the same time.

What do visual illusions tell us about perception?

Visual illusions are the unconscious 'mistakes' of perception. In fact, they are not really mistakes, but are normal, relatively consistent phenomena that are subject to regular rules of perception. Therefore, they give insight into perceptual processes.

We assume that our visual images are photographs of the real world. But visual illusions illustrate that the light patterns recorded by the eye are organised before they make sense.

Many visual illusions can be explained in terms of top-down processes (Gregory's theory). Others can be explained in terms of Gestalt principles, and some can be explained by Gibson's bottom-up theory – the Ames room can be explained by **horizon–ratio**. When two people have the same ratio to the horizon they appear to be the same size but when they have a different ratio to the horizon, they appear to be different sizes (see illustration on left).

Depth cues and perceptual constancy

AQA B ▶ U2

These are monocular cues because you only need one eye to see them. They are all examples of direct perception.

Monocular cues are sometimes known as *pictorial cues*, because they are used by artists to create the impression of 3D scenes.

Depth

Depth is perceived using a variety of monocular or binocular cues:

1. **Monocular cues** include:
   * **relative size** – more distant objects are smaller
   * **linear perspective** – parallel lines converge
   * **texture gradients** – distant things appear denser because the constituent parts are closer together
   * **shading**
   * **brightness** – a brighter object appears closer
   * **relative clarity** – things in the distance are less in focus and bluer, **interposition** – one object overlaps another
   * **motion parallax** – things that are closer move faster with respect to those further away.

2. **Binocular cues** – Binocular disparity (**stereopsis**) is the slight difference between two retinal images produced when viewing an object. Julesz (1964) produced computer-generated random dot patterns with some of the dots in one picture shifted horizontally in relation to corresponding dots in the other picture so that, when viewed stereoscopically, an illusion of depth is created and an 'image' emerges. Binocular cells in the visual cortex compare corresponding points from both retinas and compute depth from the disparity.

Perceptual constancy is a similar process to perceptual set – our perceptions are influenced by expectations and cues.

Perceptual constancy

Perceptual constancy enables us to see things as the same, despite a changing retinal image.

1. **Shape constancy** – A book 'looks' rectangular from any angle, despite the fact that the retinal image is usually not rectangular. We use our existing knowledge of shape to influence our perceptions (constructivist theory).
2. **Size constancy** – Size is determined by apparent distance (as in the Ponzo illusion, page 47). In the Ames Room, one person appears larger because constancy cues are confused (see page 46). However, horizon–ratio (direct theory) can also be used to explain this illusion (see page 47).
3. **Brightness and colour constancy** – A white shirt 'looks' white in any light, and a blue shirt still 'looks' blue in red light. This occurs because the relative frequencies of each colour remain the same. However, there are some circumstances where colour constancy does not apply, for example, under fluorescent light all colours are washed out. In this case, the relative frequencies have changed.

Progress check

1 Identify **two** effects of emotion on perception.
2 Name **three** Gestalt principles of perceptual organisation.
3 Give **one** example of a 'bottom-up' theory of visual perception.
4 Name **one** visual illusion that is an ambiguous figure.

4 E.g. Necker cube; Rubin's vase.
3 Gibson's theory.
2 E.g. Figure-ground; Similarity; Proximity; Closure; Continuity; Global preference.
1 It may lead to repressed or enhanced recall.

Sample questions and student answers – AQA A and AQA B questions

1

(a) Identify one theory or model of memory. *(1 mark)*

One model of memory is the multi-store model.

1(a) A simple answer is all that is required. **1 out of 1 mark.**

(b) Describe the theory or model of memory you identified in part (a).

(4 marks)

The multi-store model has many different memory stores, as the name suggests. There is sensory memory, short-term memory and long-term memory. The way information is passed from one store to another is as a result of verbal rehearsal. If material is not rehearsed then it disappears and is not remembered.

(b) The key features of the model have been identified but a few more details are needed to get full marks, such as explaining the nature of the stores, or how material is transferred between stores. **3 out of 4 marks.**

(c) Explain **one** strength and **one** weakness of the theory or model of memory you identified in part (a). *(6 marks)*

The main strength is that there is a lot of empirical evidence to support the theory. Peterson and Peterson (1959) showed that duration in STM is limited to less than 30 seconds, by asking participants to recall trigrams. Whereas Bahrick et al. (1975) found that adults had excellent recall of individuals' faces from their high school years.

One weakness is that the model is over-simplified. There is evidence that LTM can be further divided into lots of other kinds of memory, such as procedural and episodic.

(c) There is a lot of detail in the first paragraph, though it is not clear how the evidence described actually relates to the model. One extra sentence saying 'This shows that …' is crucial. The weakness is briefer but clearer, though again some explanation is required. **4 out of 6 marks.**

2

(a) Write down the missing answers in the table.

Memory store	Duration	Capacity	Encoding
Short-term memory	(i)	(ii)	Mainly acoustic
Long-term memory	Unlimited	Unlimited	(iii)

(3 marks)

(i) Short
(ii) 7±2 chunks
(iii) Semantic

2(a) All three answers are correct but the first one is too vague for a mark to be awarded – 'detail' is a key criterion for awarding marks, so answers need to be as exact as possible. For example, some idea of 'how short' must be given, e.g. saying STM is measured in seconds rather than hours or minutes. **2 out of 3 marks.**

(b) Tom wants to do very well in his AS exams, but he finds it difficult to revise successfully. He always seems to forget the material he learned by the time he gets into the exam.

Using your psychological knowledge, explain **two** strategies he could use in his revision to improve his memory. (4 marks)

Two strategies he could use would be mind maps and organised lists. Mind maps are good because they help you remember things because they are put into groups and are organised. The same is true of writing lists. They help you to organise the material and may give you cues to help your memory.

(b) The trick in such questions is ensuring that your answer is sufficiently psychological – it must show that you have been studying psychology! There is some psychology in this answer but not enough and it is repetitive. **3 out of 4 marks.**

Sample question and student answers – AQA A question

1

(a) Outline **two** factors that might affect eyewitness testimony. *(4 marks)*

One factor is age and another is anxiety.

(b) Briefly explain the cognitive interview. *(4 marks)*

Fisher and Geiselman (1995) developed this technique to enable police to interview eyewitnesses more effectively and get more information. The interview consists of 4 steps:

1) Report every detail. Eyewitnesses may not realise that certain details are important and might leave them out.

2) Mentally recreate the original scene as if you were there, to help remember more details.

3) Go through the events in a different order, such as backwards, as this may trigger some different memories.

4) Recall the facts from someone else's perspective.

(c) 'Many psychologists claim that eyewitness testimony tends to be inaccurate.'

Use psychological evidence to discuss whether eyewitness testimony is accurate. *(12 marks)*

The study by Loftus and Palmer showed that eyewitness testimony (EWT) can be inaccurate because it is affected by leading questions. In their study they showed people slides of a car accident and then asked them differently phrased questions about how fast the car was travelling. The participants who were asked the question using the word 'hit' gave higher speed estimates than other participants and were also more likely to say that one of the headlights was smashed. This shows that the way questions are asked can affect what people recall.

However, this was a lab experiment so it may not represent real life very well because people may behave differently when they have witnessed a real accident. For example, they may feel more anxious and this could increase or decrease how much they recall. Some studies have looked at real life eyewitnesses and found that their recall was actually better than Loftus and Palmer found. It wasn't affected so much by leading questions. This does suggest that doing the lab experiment might not tell us much about real life.

Another study conducted by Loftus also showed that EWT may actually be quite accurate if people have to recall more concrete or important information. In this study, participants saw a man stealing a wallet from a woman's bag. Almost all of them later identified the colour of the wallet correctly. Even when they were given some misleading information about the wallet being brown, they still recalled it correctly as red.

This evidence shows that EWT can be inaccurate, but isn't always inaccurate.

Practice examination question – AQA A question

1

(a) Explain what psychologists mean by 'encoding'. *(2 marks)*

(b) Distinguish between short-term and long-term memory in terms of encoding *(2 marks)*

(c) Describe and evaluate **two** strategies for memory improvement. *(8 marks)*

Sample question and student answer – AQA B question

1(a) One cue has been named and there is sufficient explanation for 2 marks. But the second half of the question (about a monocular cue) has not been answered. **2 out of 4 marks.**

(b) This is a thorough answer that satisfies the criteria of the question – an explanation and examples are provided. **3 out of 3 marks.**

(c) A very brief response but packed with information. However, the question gives clear guidance about what to provide so it is surprising that the question has not been fully answered – there is no information about why the study was conducted. There is some information about the procedure and findings but nothing about the conclusion drawn. **2 out of 4 marks.**

(d) This is a rather short answer. It is accurate and well-organised but lacks detail in both the description and evaluation. The description of the theory is brief and could be usefully extended by giving some examples. The theory is evaluated with reference to research studies but the details of these studies are rather vague. Naming the study (Palmer, 1975) would add more detail. **7 out of 10 marks.**

1

(a) Describe **one** binocular and **one** monocular depth cue. *(4 marks)*

Binocular disparity is one binocular cue which happens because you get two different images from each eye and these are slightly different.

(b) Explain what is meant by an ambiguous figure, using examples in your answer. *(3 marks)*

An ambiguous figure is a type of visual illusion where the object can be viewed in different ways. For example the vase and faces used by Gestalt psychologists (Rubin's vase) can be seen as a vase or two faces, or Necker Cube where the two faces of the cube move in and out because there is no way to judge which is the front.

(c) Describe **one** study in which the effect of culture on visual perception was investigated. Indicate why the study was conducted, the procedure used, the results obtained and the conclusion drawn. *(4 marks)*

One study by Pettigrew showed that people of different races actually see things differently. In this study the participants were shown photographs of various racial groups and then had to name the race they had seen.

(d) Describe and evaluate Gregory's theory of visual perception. *(10 marks)*

Richard Gregory proposed that perception is the process of interpreting the physical information that is perceived by the eyes. This information is usually incomplete and ambiguous and, therefore, the perceiver has to fill in the gaps. This is done by drawing on expectations based on past experience. Various studies have shown that this is true. For example, a study where people were shown various objects in the context of a kitchen or another room. What they reported they saw depended on the context.

Gregory himself used visual illusions to illustrate his theory. He said they showed how the perceptual process works. For example, the Müller–Lyer illusion is seen because we are using our knowledge of depth cues to misinterpret the images.

Critics of Gregory's approach say that this theory cannot explain everything. Often perception is very accurate and Gibson said that there is sufficient information in the visual array to explain perception. It is probably likely that both processes are operating. That is, in conditions such as poor lighting we do rely on expectations and in conditions of good lighting we use direct perception.

Practice examination question – AQA B question

1

(a) Explain displacement as an explanation of forgetting in short-term memory. *(3 marks)*

(b) At this time of year, thousands of students are taking exams and many of them will find they have forgotten key pieces of information that they spent weeks trying to learn.
Describe and evaluate **two** likely explanations for their forgetting. *(10 marks)*

Developmental psychology

3.1 Attachment

After studying this section you should be able to:

- describe and evaluate explanations of attachment, including learning theory and the evolutionary perspective (Bowlby)
- describe and evaluate types of attachment, including secure and insecure attachment
- describe and evaluate studies by Ainsworth
- describe and evaluate cultural variations in attachment
- describe and evaluate the effects of disruption of attachment, failure to form attachment (privation) and institutionalisation.

LEARNING SUMMARY

Explanations of attachment

AQA A ▶ U1
AQA B ▶ A2 (U3)

Attachment is a mutual and intense emotional relationship between two individuals. It is especially used to describe the relationship between an infant and his/her caregiver(s).

An explanation of attachment seeks to identify what factors determine the formation of attachments, and why infants become attached to one person rather than another.

In a nutshell, behaviourists believe that infants become attached to the person who feeds them – it has been nicknamed the 'cupboard love' theory.

1. Learning theory

Learning theory (behaviourism) is described in chapter 1 (see page 14). Learning theorists (behaviourists) believe all behaviour is acquired through conditioning:

1. Classical conditioning – Food (unconditioned stimulus) produces a sense of pleasure (unconditioned response). The food becomes associated with the person doing the feeding, who then becomes a conditioned stimulus, also producing a sense of pleasure.

2. Operant conditioning – Dollard and Miller (1950) adapted the principles of operant conditioning to incorporate the concept of mental states. The hungry infant feels uncomfortable, which creates a drive to lessen the discomfort. Being fed reduces the discomfort and the drive. Drive reduction is rewarding and the infant learns that food is a reward or **primary reinforcer**. The person who supplies the food is associated with the food and becomes a **secondary (or conditioned) reinforcer**, and a source of reward in his/her own right.

3. Social learning theory – Social learning theory proposes that learning can take place indirectly through vicarious reinforcement and modelling. Hay and Vespo (1988) suggested that attachment occurs because children learn to imitate the affectionate behaviour shown by their parents. Parents/caregivers also teach children in an explicit way to show affection.

Evaluation

- The explanation is **at least partially correct**. We do form attachments through conditioning. However, food may not be the main factor; it may be that responsiveness from a caregiver is an important reward that creates the bond.
- Learning theory accounts suggest that infants should become most attached to the person who feeds them but **the evidence does not support this**. Schaffer and Emerson (1964) found that fewer than half of the infants they studied developed a primary attachment to the person who usually fed them. Harlow's research (1959) with rhesus monkeys also showed that feeding was less important than contact comfort. The infant monkeys became attached to a cloth-covered wire 'mother' rather than the one with the feeding bottle.

To what extent do you think it is appropriate to generalise from the behaviour of monkeys to human attachment behaviour?

2. The evolutionary approach – Bowlby's theory

The main strands of John Bowlby's theory are:

Bowlby developed the most influential theory of attachment.

1. Attachment is adaptive

Attachment behaviour promotes survival because it ensures safety and food for offspring. It is an adaptive behaviour because individuals who are attached are more likely to survive and go on to reproduce.

2. Critical period

Bowlby claimed that if attachment does not take place before the age of 2½, then it is much more difficult thereafter.

3. Social releasers

Infants are born with innate social releasers, such as crying and smiling, and they have cute faces, which elicit care-giving. Attachment is a two-way process: it depends on the involvement of both parent/caregiver and infant, and on social releasers.

In Harlow's study, the infant monkeys grew up to be emotionally maladjusted. This supports the view that attachment must be reciprocal (a two-way process). Those monkeys had contact comfort but it was passive (i.e. it lacked responsiveness).

4. Quality rather than quantity of care

Ainsworth *et al.* (1974) proposed the **care-giving sensitivity hypothesis**. Secure attachments are the result of mothers being responsive to children's needs.

Isabella *et al.* (1989) found that mothers and infants who were more responsive to each other at one month were more likely to have a secure relationship at twelve months. Those that had a more one-sided pattern of interaction tended to have insecure relationships.

Schaffer and Emerson (1964) also found that responsiveness was important in their detailed observational study of 60 infants and mothers.

The word monotropy means focused on one individual.

According to Bowlby, primary and secondary attachments are formed with those individuals who are most responsive to the infant's social releasers.

5. Monotropy

Bowlby claimed that infants need one special attachment relationship that is qualitatively different from all others. This **primary attachment** forms with the individual who has offered sensitive responsiveness.

Infants also have **secondary attachments**, which are important for emotional development.

The primary attachment forms the basis of the internal working model and underlies the ability to experience deep feelings.

6. The internal working model

Infants have many mental models (internal working models) of their environment. One of these 'internal working models' represents the infant's knowledge about his/her relationship with the primary attachment figure. The model generates expectations about other relationships so that, whatever the child's primary relationship was like, it will lead the child to have similar expectations about other relationships, and will serve as a template for all future relationships.

This idea of a 'continuity' between infant relationships and later adult relationships is called the continuity hypothesis.

Hazan and Shaver (1987) showed that there is a link between early attachment experiences and later romantic relationships. Good early attachment is associated with happy and trusting adult relationships, whereas poor early relationships are linked to behaviours such as lack of trust, falling in and out of love, and extreme sexual attraction and jealousy.

Attachment is important for cognitive, as well as emotional, development because secure attachment promotes independence, which permits a child to explore and engage with their environment. Some people see attachment as a dependent relationship, whereas Bowlby saw it as encouraging independence. For example, Hazen and Durrett (1982) found that securely attached young children were more independent explorers of their environment and were also more innovative in their approach to problem solving.

Belsky and Rovine (1987) concluded that both caregiver responsiveness and temperament are jointly responsible for the development of attachment.

All psychologists (including Bowlby) agree that an infant has multiple attachments. The issue is about whether there is only one primary attachment that serves a special purpose in emotional development and that this attachment is qualitatively different from all others.

Evaluation

- **Influential** – This theory has had an enormous effect on people's lives, in particular the care of children who lack attachment.
- **Evolutionary argument** – The notion that attachment is adaptive is unfalsifiable (cannot be proven wrong) though it is highly plausible insofar as being close to a caregiver provides protection, and helps the infant be fed, which must enhance survival.
- **Critical period** – The concept of a critical period may be too strong. Ethologists now prefer the idea of a 'sensitive period', which suggests that children might well be able to form attachments at any time, if the opportunity presents itself.
- **Internal working model** – This would lead us to expect children to form similar sorts of relationships with all people because they are always working from the same template. However, there are actually few correlations among a child's various relationships (Howes *et al.*, 1994). Even if there are positive correlations (as suggested in the study by Hazan and Shaver), there is an alternative explanation to that of the internal working model – namely, that some infants may simply be better than others at forming relationships, and they do this as infants, and again later in life. This is called the **temperament hypothesis** (Kagan, 1984), the view that infants have an innate temperament such as being 'easy-going' or 'socially difficult', and this influences both early attachments and later relationships.
- **Sensitive responsiveness** – Research supports the view that quality, rather than quantity, is important. For example, Fox (1977) studied infants raised on Israeli kibbutzim (a commune), and found that they remained most attached to their mothers, despite the fact that they spent more time with their metapelet (carer). The fact that there is quite a high turnover rate of metapelets might explain the low attachment there, but there was still maternal attachment despite long and early separations.
- **Monotropy** – Research has shown that infants appear to form one primary attachment. This is not a behaviour specific to our culture and our method of child-rearing. For example, Tronick *et al.* (1992) studied an African tribe, the Efe, from Zaire, who live in extended family groups. The infants were looked after, and even breastfed, by different women but they usually slept with their own mother at night. Tronick *et al.* found that, by the age of 6 months, the infants still showed only one primary attachment.
- However, some psychologists believe that an infant's many attachments are **qualitatively** equivalent, as opposed to Bowlby's view of monotropy. Thomas (1998) suggested that a network of close attachments provides an infant with a variety of social and emotional interactions that meet their various needs.

Progress check

1 How does the caregiver become a conditioned reinforcer?
2 In what way does Harlow's research provide evidence against the learning theory explanation of attachment?
3 Explain the concept of monotropy.
4 Identify **two** other key features of Bowlby's theory.

4 E.g. Adaptiveness; Critical period; Social releasers; Sensitive responsiveness; Internal working model; Continuity hypothesis.
3 An infant has a special, primary emotional attachment to one person, but also has other attachments.
2 Harlow showed that feeding is not the key factor in attachment.
1 By being associated with drive reduction (e.g. reducing the drive (desire) to eat) and providing a reward.

Types of attachment

AQA A ▷ U1

AQA B ▷ A2 (U3)

Types of attachment are *patterns* of behaviour, i.e. each type consists of a cluster of various behaviours that tend to appear together.

Mary Ainsworth was the first to identify attachment types in her 'strange situation' research. She identified types A, B and C. Type D was added later by Main and Solomon (1986).

The **strange situation procedure** consists of seven 3-minute episodes designed to be used with children aged 12–18 months:

1. Parent/caregiver and infant enter a room; infant plays.
2. Stranger enters and talks with caregiver; gradually approaches infant.
3. Caregiver leaves. Stranger leaves child playing (unless appears distressed and then offers comfort).
4. Caregiver returns, stranger leaves.
5. Caregiver leaves, after infant has again begun to play.
6. Stranger returns and behaves as described in 3.
7. Caregiver returns and stranger leaves.

Psychologists have identified the following types of attachment:

- **Secure attachment** (Type B) – According to Ainsworth and Bell, 71% of infants in the **strange situation** show mild protest on their caregiver's departure. On the caregiver's return, the infants seek the caregiver and are relatively easily comforted. This is the optimal type of attachment and is associated with healthy socio-emotional development.
- **Insecure-avoidant attachment** (Type A) – 12% of infants in the strange situation show indifference when their caregiver leaves, and do not display stranger anxiety. When reunited, they actively avoid contact with their caregiver, and the caregiver generally ignores the infant during play.
- **Insecure-resistant attachment** (Type C) – 17% of infants in the strange situation are very distressed when their caregiver leaves and are not easily consoled on their return. The infant seeks comfort, yet rejects it at the same time. The caregiver is also inconsistent: either rejecting and angry towards the infant, or overly responsive and sensitive.
- **Insecure-disorganised attachment** (Type D) – The infant shows no set pattern of behaviour at separation or reunion (i.e. 'disorganised'). This type of attachment may develop when a caregiver is chronically depressed.
- **Disinhibited attachment** – A type of **disorganised** attachment where infants do not discriminate between the people they choose as attachment figures. Such children will treat strangers with inappropriate familiarity, and may be attention-seeking.

Measuring types of attachment: The strange situation

Ainsworth and Bell (1970) developed a method of controlled observation to assess the security of an infant's attachment to a caregiver. The intention was to place an infant in a mildly stressful and also novel situation in order to elicit certain attachment behaviours:

- **Separation anxiety** – This is the unease that the child shows when he/she is left by his/her caregiver.
- **Infants' willingness to explore** – A more securely attached child will explore more widely.
- **Stranger anxiety** – Security of attachment is related to greater stranger anxiety.
- **Reunion behaviour** – Insecurely attached children often greet their caregiver's return by ignoring them or behaving ambivalently.

The concept of **validity** refers to the extent to which a measurement is actually assessing something that is real (see page 87).

Evaluation

Strengths

- **Valid form of measurement** – Smith and Noble (1987) showed that the classification of attachment from the strange situation is related to children's reactions when they are separated in more natural circumstances, such as when a child is left with a baby-sitter. This suggests that it tests a real characteristic of a child.

  Sroufe (1983) found that infants rated as secure in their second year have been found later to be more popular and have more initiative. They have higher self-esteem, are less aggressive and more likely to be social leaders. This also suggests that the strange situation is measuring a psychologically real characteristic that continues through childhood.

- **Reliable form of measurement** – Main and Cassidy (1988) found similar types of attachment at age 1 and age 6. When differences occur, these are often associated with changes in the form of care, such as changes in family structure (Melhuish, 1993).

Reliability concerns the extent to which a measure is consistent – the test should give the same result every time it is used.

Limitations

- **Lacks validity** – The strange situation may test the child's relationships, rather than a characteristic of a child, i.e. it isn't assessing attachment type, but just attachment type within a particular relationship. This is supported by research that shows children have different attachment classifications with different caregivers. For example, Lamb (1977) found that some children were securely attached to their mothers but avoidantly attached to their fathers. This makes the strange situation classification meaningless (lacking in validity).

If a child has different attachments with different caregivers, how do you think this will affect their development?

- **Lacks reliability** – Some children may simply be better at forming relationships (the **temperament hypothesis** described on page 54). This means they do well with their caregivers and they do well later in life, giving rise to a spurious positive correlation between early attachments and later relationships.

Other studies by Mary Ainsworth

Uganda

Ainsworth (1967) observed 26 mothers and infants in Uganda. She noted that sensitive mothers (e.g. those who were able to provide more details about their infants) tended to have 'securely attached' infants who cried little and seemed content to explore in the presence of their mother, i.e. secure attachment led to increasing competence and independence (the 'secure base').

Ainsworth realised that learning theory could not explain the importance of sensitivity in attachment, but Bowlby's evolutionary theory could.

Baltimore, USA

Ainsworth *et al.* (1971) observed 26 mothers, and infants from birth, in Baltimore.

She found that the mothers of the infants subsequently classified as 'secure' had behaved most sensitively with them at home during the first three months of life.

Learning theorists found this difficult to understand. They were convinced that responsiveness to, for example, crying, should act as a reinforcer and increase the crying, rather than Ainsworth's prediction that crying would decrease with caregiver responsiveness.

Cultural variations in attachment

AQA A ▶ U1

AQA B ▶ A2 (U3)

If attachment is an innate process, then we should find similar patterns of attachment types all over the world (which would support Bowlby's view of attachment as an adaptive and innately-driven process). If attachment is relative to different child-rearing methods, then we would expect to find cultural variations in the distribution of types of attachment.

The term **culture** refers to the rules, customs, morals and ways of interacting that bind together members of a society or collection of people. We learn all these customs, etc. through the process of *socialisation*. Different social classes have different attitudes to, among other things, child-rearing and, therefore, might be regarded as different 'sub-cultures'.

A **collectivist society** is one where individuals share tasks, belongings, etc. and value interdependence.
Individualist societies emphasise individuality, individual needs and independence.

Cross-cultural similarities

The studies by Tronick *et al.*, Fox, and Ainsworth (see pages 54 and 56 respectively) all showed that attachment processes in different cultures were similar.

Van IJzendoorn and Kroonenberg (1988) examined over 2,000 strange situation classifications from 32 studies conducted in eight different countries. They found that the differences between countries were small. Secure attachment was the most common classification in every country. Insecure-avoidant attachment was the next most common in every country except Israel and Japan. There were bigger differences *within* countries – this was *1.5 times* greater than the variation between cultures.

Sagi (1990) found that securely attached Israeli infants were later rated as having better social skills. This further supports the view that secure attachment is important in all cultures for healthy psychological development.

Grossmann and Grossmann (1991) studied attachment in German families and found that more of the infants were insecurely attached. However, maternal sensitivity was positively related to secure attachment, as found in Ainsworth's studies. Children who were securely attached to their mothers as infants enjoyed close friendships later in childhood, whereas those who were avoidant or anxious reported having either no friends or few friends, supporting the **continuity hypothesis**. Overall, this supports the innate view of attachment.

Bee (1995) concluded that there is considerable consistency across cultures and that it is likely that the same caregiver–infant interactions contribute to secure and insecure attachments in all cultures.

Cross-cultural differences

Van IJzendoorn and Kroonenberg, and Grossmann and Grossmann found that secure attachment was not the main attachment type in some other cultures.

Rothbaum *et al.* (2000) have argued that attachment theory is only relevant to Western culture. In other cultures, such as Japan, attachment processes are fundamentally different. For example, in Japan, the aim of the attachment relationship is to create dependence rather than the Western aim of fostering independence, so maternal sensitivity is associated with insecure, rather than secure, attachment.

Dependence is common in **collectivist** cultures where children are taught not to express their individual emotions (as in an **individualist** society) but, instead, to be group-oriented.

Evaluation

- Almost all of the research has used the strange situation classification. The question is **to what extent the strange situation is meaningful in other cultures**. In Japan, for example, infants very rarely leave their mother (Miyake *et al.*, 1985). Therefore, the strange situation is a particularly stressful event for them. This is in contrast with American children, who are more familiar with being cared for by people other than their primary attachment figure. This might explain why infants in Japan *appear* to be more insecurely attached – because they react anxiously in the strange situation, due to the unusualness of the situation rather than lack of primary attachment.

The strange situation is an **imposed etic**. A 'tool' developed in one culture and applied to another culture is likely to have a different meaning in that other culture and, therefore, the results are meaningless.

- Studies frequently **equate country with culture**, whereas there are usually many distinct cultures (i.e. 'sub-cultures') within a country. For example, in the US, working class and middle class 'sub-cultures' have quite different attitudes towards child-rearing.
- **Cross-cultural research has many problems**, such as the issue of **imposed etics** (views of cultures). Another problem is that researchers from another culture (such as Ainsworth) may not understand local customs and communications. It is also likely that Western researchers are influenced by their own expectations and this may bias their observations.

Progress check

1 Name **three** types of insecure attachment.
2 Identify **two** studies by Ainsworth.
3 Identify **one** key finding from Van IJzendoorn and Kroonenberg's cross-cultural analysis.
4 In what way is the strange situation an imposed etic?

4 It is a procedure designed in one culture (e.g. USA) but then used in other cultures.
3 E.g. There was a lot of similarity across cultures; There was a lot of variation within cultures.
2 E.g. Strange situation; Uganda; Baltimore.
1 E.g. Avoidant; Resistant; Disorganised; Disinhibited.

The effects of disruption of attachment

AQA A	U1
AQA B	A2 (U3)

Bowlby (1953) said that depriving a young child of maternal care for a long time may have serious effects on his/her character in the same way as depriving a child of vitamins many have serious effects on his/her development.

Note that the use of the term 'maternal' was to describe mothering – this does not necessarily have to be done by a woman.

Michael Rutter (1981) made some other criticisms of Bowlby's maternal deprivation hypothesis in his book *Maternal deprivation reassessed*. Most importantly he suggested that Bowlby confused deprivation and *privation*. Some children experience temporary bond disruptions (**deprivation**) whereas others have failed to form any attachment bond (**privation**). On pages 61–63 we will consider the more serious consequences of privation.

In general though, Rutter agreed with Bowlby that early experiences do have special importance and may have lasting effects.

Attachments may be disrupted when an infant is physically separated from his/her primary attachment figure. If a child is given adequate substitute emotional care then research suggests that there are no negative consequences. However, this is not the case when emotional care is lacking.

Bowlby's maternal deprivation hypothesis

Bowlby (1951) formulated the **maternal deprivation hypothesis** – the view that early deprivation has long-term consequences for emotional development. He believed that a child needs a warm, intimate and continuous relationship with a mother (or permanent mother-substitute) for normal emotional development. If this is disrupted before the age of 2½ years there will be long-term consequences, and children are still sensitive to such separations up to the age of 5.

Bowlby's '44 thieves study'

Bowlby (1946) worked in a Child Guidance Clinic in London and observed that there seemed to be a link between early separation and later emotional maladjustment. To confirm this, he selected some of the children who attended the clinic and asked their parents about the children's early experiences of separation.

The children were divided into two groups: 44 'juvenile thieves' (who had been involved in stealing and therefore, presumably, lacked a social conscience), and 44 'controls' (disturbed but emotionally functional). Their ages ranged from 5 to 16 years.

Bowlby found that some of the thieves displayed an 'affectionless' character, e.g. a lack of normal affection, shame or sense of responsibility (**affectionless psychopaths**). 86% of these affectionless children had, before the age of two, repeatedly been in foster homes or hospitals, often not visited by their families.

Bowlby concluded that affectionless psychopathy was caused by attachment bonds being disturbed in early life.

However, the evidence is flawed in several respects:

- The key data were collected **retrospectively**, (i.e. the information about a child's early history was based on what parents recalled) and, therefore, may be unreliable.
- Some children had in fact been separated from their mothers for **very short periods**, so why would separation have had such a major impact?
- The evidence is **correlational**: we cannot be certain that the cause of affectionless psychopathy was maternal separation, or if some other factor caused both separation and emotional disruption. Rutter suggested that early separation and maladjustment may both be caused by family discord. The 'Isle of Wight study' by Rutter *et al.* (1976) involved interviews with over 2,000 boys, aged between 9 and 12, and their families. They found that boys were four times more likely to become delinquent (i.e. emotionally damaged) if separation was related to family discord, rather than through illness or death of their mother. This was the same conclusion reached by Clarke and Clarke (1976), who analysed data from a study of children born in Great Britain during one week in 1946. The children were tested every two years over the next 26 years.

- Douglas (1975) originally concluded that a hospital admission of more than a week, or repeated admission in a child under 4 years old, was associated with an increased risk of behaviour disturbance and poor reading in adolescence.

  However, Clarke and Clarke found that many of the children were in hospital because of problems associated with disadvantaged homes, and this might explain their subsequent problems, rather than early separations (deprivation). Social, rather than maternal, deprivation was more likely to be the main cause of subsequent delinquency.

The consequences of bond disruption

Robertson and Robertson (1968) made films of young children in brief separation. Laura, aged 2, was in hospital for 8 days and was visited occasionally. The films show her distress. John, aged 17 months, was in a residential nursery for 9 days and received only occasional visits from his father. The nursing staff attended to his physical needs but he became progressively more distressed.

In contrast, they observed four other children (Jane, Lucy, Thomas and Kate, all aged under 3 years) in brief separation while their mothers were in hospital. They received plentiful emotional care from their foster mother, Joyce Robertson, who also ensured lots of contact with home. These children greeted their parents happily whereas Laura and John had become withdrawn and rejected their parents' return.

> The important distinction here is between deprivation (separation with harmful consequences) and avoiding bond disruption (separation with no consequences, probably because emotional care is sustained).

The difference was **bond disruption**. The distressed children were physically well cared for in a residential nursery/hospital but no mother-substitute was provided. The children who coped well stayed with the Robertsons, bringing their toys with them and maintaining contact with their family.

Individual differences

Bowlby *et al.* (1956) studied 60 children under the age of 4 years who were hospitalised because they had TB, and spent up to two years in a sanatorium outside London. The nurses in the sanatorium did not provide substitute maternal care and the children were only visited once a week. Therefore, the children *probably* experienced a lack of emotional care. When they were assessed later by their teachers and a psychologist, there were very few differences between them and their school peers in terms of intellectual development and emotional adjustment. Some members of the TB group were more maladjusted (63%) but there was no serious maladjustment. Bowlby *et al.* concluded that those children who coped better may have been more securely attached and, therefore, more resilient.

Progress check

1 What is the 'maternal deprivation hypothesis'?
2 What did the Isle of Wight study by Rutter *et al.* show?
3 What is the distinction made between deprivation and privation?
4 How can bond disruption be prevented when children are physically separated from their primary attachment figure?

4 By providing adequate substitute emotional care.
3 Deprivation is disruption (loss of attachment) whereas privation is absence of attachment (no attachments have formed).
2 Emotional maladjustment and frequent separations are both caused by family discord.
1 The theory that early disruption of attachment leads to permanent emotional damage.

The effects of failure to form attachment (privation)

AQA A ▶ U1
AQA B ▶ A2 (U3)

Evidence comes from several sources, as described below.

Case studies

Privation is the failure to form any attachments during early development.

1. Genie (Curtiss, 1989)

Genie spent most of her childhood locked in a room at her home in Los Angeles. At age 13½, when she was 'rescued', she looked like a child half her age, could not stand erect, and could not speak. She never fully recovered mentally or socially.

Rymer (1993) reports that Genie showed a *disinterest* in other people. She didn't reject them, but simply treated them in the same way she treated inanimate objects, i.e. she was emotionally maladjusted.

All case studies suffer from one major flaw. They concern individuals who may be atypical and, therefore, it is not reasonable to make generalisations about all human behaviour on the basis of these single cases. On the other hand, case histories provide rich data.

This seems to show that emotional privation has serious long-term effects. However, these effects may have been due to physical rather than psychological deprivation, or they may be because she was retarded (that was the reason given by her father for locking her away), or because her care after 'discovery' was very unsettled. In addition, her mother claimed that she did in fact give Genie emotional care.

2. Czechoslovakian twins: P.M. and J.M. (Koluchová, 1976)

Koluchová studied Czechoslovakian twins P.M. and J.M. who spent the first seven years of their lives locked up. When discovered, they couldn't talk. They were then looked after by two loving sisters and by age 14 had near normal intellectual and social functioning.

By the age of 20, they were of above average intelligence and had excellent relationships with the members of their foster family (Koluchová, 1991).

3. Other case studies

Isabelle (Mason, 1942), Anna (Davis, 1947), sisters Mary and Louise (Skuse, 1984), and a Japanese brother and sister (Fujinaga *et al.*, 1992), when discovered (after being locked up for years), were physically underdeveloped and showed cognitive, social and emotional delays. Those who were young (i.e. prior to puberty) when discovered were able to recover reasonably well, though never completely.

Children who experience emotional deprivation appear to be physically smaller, a condition called **deprivation dwarfism**.

Widdowson (1951) documented this in orphanage children who failed to thrive despite good physical conditions. When a new supervisor arrived, who gave them better emotional care, their weight improved.

This suggests that the stress of having no attachment affects physical development (stress hormones affect physical health, as we will see in Chapter 5).

Conclusions

- **Age matters** – Those children who were discovered early enough appeared to have a better chance of recovering. Genie may have been too old.
- **Experiences during privation** – Some of the children were able to form attachments with peers or siblings, which may have protected them from total privation.
- **Subsequent care** – Some children were very well looked after following their discovery, which then assisted their recovery. Without it they might not have recovered.

Attachment disorder

This is a recognised mental disorder. The symptoms are: being unable to form relationships, showing little emotion, having poor social skills, and engaging in very aggressive and controlling behaviour, as well as a lack of attachments.

There are two kinds of attachment disorder:

- **reactive / inhibited attachment**: shy and withdrawn, unable to cope with most social situations
- **disinhibited** attachment: overfriendly and attention-seeking.

Children with attachment disorder have often been adopted after the age of 6 months, subsequently experiencing multiple foster homes or institutional care, which is why no attachments have formed. When they are offered the chance to develop a relationship, it comes too late.

Attachment disorder children have a poor prognosis, as predicted by Bowlby's maternal deprivation hypothesis. They seem to have no conscience, which may be caused by their lack of trust. They become so dependent on themselves that they ignore the needs of others to the point that they steal, damage or destroy anything they feel hinders their control.

The effects of institutionalisation on attachment

1. Anaclitic depression

Institutionalisation is one effect of institutional care. An 'institution' is a place dedicated to a particular task, such as looking after children awaiting adoption. Institutional care involves full-time caring over a significant period of time (i.e. not 9–5, or for just a few days).

Spitz (1945) used the term **anaclitic depression** to describe the severe and progressive depression found in institutionalised infants as a result of prolonged separation from their mothers. The term 'anaclitic' means 'arising from emotional dependency on another'.

Spitz and Wolf (1946) studied 100 apparently 'normal' children who were hospitalised. They became apathetic and sad, but recovered quickly when reunited with their mothers if the separation lasted less than three months.

However, longer separations were rarely associated with complete recovery. It is possible that other factors associated with being in hospital were also distressing.

2. Delayed cognitive development

As a consequence of Bowlby's research, institutional care (e.g. in hospitals) in the UK has changed. It now strives to provide adequate substitute emotional care. However, in some countries, limited resources mean that it is still not possible to offer very much emotional care in institutions.

Attachment is important for both emotional and cognitive development. Skeels and Dye (1939) observed how two apparently retarded children developed near normal IQs when transferred from their orphanage to a women's ward in an institution for the mentally retarded, possibly due to the increased attention (attachments).

Skodak and Skeels (1949) tested this by transferring 13 mentally retarded children aged under 2 years from their orphanage to an institution for the mentally retarded. After 19 months in the new institution, the transferred children's mean IQ had increased from 64 to 92, whereas another group who had stayed in the orphanage showed a decrease in IQ from 87 to 61 over the same period. Skeels (1966) assessed the children 20 years later and found that the differences between the groups remained.

One criticism should be considered: the children may have been responding to the researcher's expectations and it was this, rather than the increased stimulation, that led to their intellectual improvements.

3. Poor peer relations

Hodges and Tizard (1989) studied 65 children placed in an institution under the age of 4 months. There was an explicit policy in the institution against the 'caretakers' forming attachments with the children. Some of the children remained in the institution, some were adopted and some returned to their natural homes.

Bowlby had claimed that bad homes were better than good institutions but this study suggests that he was wrong.

Follow-ups at ages 4 and 8 years found that the adopted children were doing best in virtually every way when compared with those who returned home ('restored' children). However, they were having more social and cognitive difficulties than a control group of children who had never been in care. This shows that some recovery is possible after the age of 4 and that a child's natural home may not necessarily be the best place for the child.

In the institution it is likely that the most 'attractive' children were chosen to be adopted, which means the two groups might not be equivalent.

Five of the original children had remained in the institution but were not included in the final analysis because their behaviour could tell us little about recovery from the effects of institutionalisation.

At age 16, twenty-three adopted children and eleven 'restored' children were again assessed, and compared with a matched control group of 'normal' children:

- Those who were adopted were able to form close bonds with their adoptive parents, whereas the 'restored' group where much less likely to be closely attached. Restored children were also reportedly less cuddly, harder to give affection to, and were less involved with their families.
- Both groups of ex-institution children (adopted and restored) had problems with relationships in school, both with adults and peers. They were less likely to have a special friend, to be part of a crowd, or to be liked by other children. They were also more quarrelsome and more likely to be bullies.

This suggests that early privation had permanent effects on emotional and social development, despite excellent subsequent home relationships. However, it may be that all ex-institution children lag beyond their peers in emotional development, and that is why they couldn't cope.

4. Poor parenting

Quinton *et al.* (1984) compared a group of 50 women who had been brought up in institutions (childrens' homes) with a control group of 50 'normal' women. When the women were in their 20s, it was found that the ex-institution women were experiencing extreme difficulties acting as parents. For example, more of the ex-institution women had children who spent time in care, and were rated as lacking in warmth when interacting with their children.

5. Recovery from institutional care

Rutter *et al.* (2007) studied a group of about 100 Romanian orphans over a number of years, assessing them at ages 4, 6 and 11 years old. The orphans spent their early lives in extreme physical and emotional privation in Romanian institutions and were then adopted by British families. Those adopted before the age of 6 months have shown 'normal' emotional development when compared with UK children adopted at the same age. However, many of those Romanian orphans adopted *after* 6 months of age showed **disinhibited attachments** (similar to children with attachment disorder) and had problems with peers.

This research suggests that long-term consequences may be less severe than was once thought *if* children have the opportunity to form attachments. However, when children do not form attachments (i.e. continuing failure of attachment) then the consequences are likely to be severe. This is supported by Triseliøtis (1984) who recorded the lives of 44 adults who had been adopted late and whose prognosis had been poor. The adults showed good adjustment, which was attributed to the fact that they had escaped from severe privation to a good, caring environment.

Progress check

1. Name **one** case study where a child/children appeared to recover from early privation.
2. What group of children appear to be unable to recover from early privation?
3. Name **two** possible negative effects of early privation.
4. What period of time did the study by Hodges and Tizard cover?

4 About 16 years.

3 E.g. Attachment disorder; Poor peer relations; Poor parenting.

2 Children with attachment disorder.

1 E.g. The Czechoslovakian twins.

3.2 Attachment in everyday life

After studying this section you should be able to:

- describe and evaluate the impact of different forms of day care on children's social development, including the effects on aggression and peer relations
- describe the implications of research into attachment and day care for child care practices.

LEARNING SUMMARY

The impact of day care on social development

AQA A | U1

The term **day care** refers to situations where children are looked after by temporary caregivers and thus separated from their main attachment figure(s). The maternal deprivation hypothesis would predict that such separations could have permanent consequences for social development.

The data show that day care and aggressiveness are linked in some way but that does not mean that day care *causes* aggressiveness. There may be an intervening variable, such as poor home background which increases the likelihood of attending day care and also increases aggressiveness.

It may also be that day care only increases aggression in some circumstances, e.g. when it is of poor quality.

1. Negative effects on aggression

In 1991 the NICHD (National Institute of Child Health and Human Development) started an ongoing study of American children. Over 1,000 children from diverse families and locations are continuing to be involved.

At age 5, the study found that the more time a child spent in day care of any kind or quality, the more they were rated as disobedient and aggressive (NICHD, 2003).

Children in full-time day care were found to be almost three times more likely to show behavioural problems than those cared for at home. The behavioural problems included frequent arguing, temper tantrums, lying, hitting and unpredictable conduct.

Belsky *et al.* (2007) analysed data from this study as the children neared the end of their primary education and still found a link between day care experience and increased aggressiveness.

A UK study (Melhuish, 2004) also found evidence that high levels of day care, particularly nursery care in the first two years, may elevate the risk of developing anti-social behaviour.

Evaluation

- **Not all research has found a negative correlation.** For example, Prodromidis *et al.* (1995) studied Swedish children and concluded that child care arrangements were not associated with aggression or non-compliance. The ALSPAC (Avon Longitudinal Study of Parents and Children) study followed 14,000 children born in the UK between 1991 and 1992 and found no evidence of negative effects from day care (Gregg *et al.*, 2005).
- In addition, the NICHD results have been reported in a way that **magnifies the effects on aggression**. There may be a slight negative correlation, but in fact 83% of children who spent between 10 and 30 hours per week in day care did not show higher levels of aggression. NICHD data also showed that a mother's sensitivity to her child was a better indicator of reported problem behaviours than was time in day care.
- All studies assess attachment using the strange situation (see page 55). However, this method has been criticised, for example, children who are used to separations because of day care may react differently in this controlled observation to children who spend most of their time with one caregiver.

2. Positive effects on peer relations

Shea (1981) videotaped playtimes at nursery school and found that the children became progressively more sociable from when they started day care. The children stood closer together and engaged in more rough-and-tumble play and peer interactions. They were less aggressive and had less need to cling to the teacher.

Clarke-Stewart *et al.* (1994) studied 150 children attending school for the first time and found that those who had attended day care could cope better in social situations and interact better with peers.

The EPPE (Effective Provision of Pre-School Education) project in the UK has studied over 3,000 children between the ages of 3 and 7 years and found that day care was associated with increased independence and peer sociability at 5 years (but also increased anti-social behaviour) (Melhuish *et al.*, 2002).

Interestingly, an early start at pre-school (between 2 and 3 years) was also linked with being more sociable with other children (often, early day care is associated with negative outcomes).

Evaluation

* Again, we cannot assume that day care has caused **any differences** in social behaviour. It could be, for example, that children who are shy are less likely to stay in day care.
* Belsky and Rovine (1988) found that there was an **increased risk of an infant developing insecure attachments** if they were in day care for at least four months and if this had begun before their first birthday. Such insecure attachment might damage their ability to form relationships and be popular in school.
* However, Clarke-Stewart *et al.* (1994) found **no effects on attachment security** from day care. They compared attachment security in 15-month-old children who spent a lot of time in day care (i.e. 30 hours or more a week from the age of 3 months) with children who spent less than 10 hours a week there.

3. Individual differences

The term **individual differences** is used by psychologists to describe the fact that people differ from each other. This may sound obvious but it is often overlooked in psychological research where it is assumed that the same 'laws' apply to everyone.

* Some children are insecurely attached before attending day care but may actually benefit more from day care. Egeland and Hiester (1995) studied about 70 children either at home or in day care. Day care appeared to have a negative effect on secure children, but a positive effect on insecure children.
* Different temperamental types may cope less well with day care. Pennebaker *et al.* (1981) found that the nursery experience was threatening for those children who were shy and unsociable.
* Some day care provision is poor – the children lack stimulation, and/or bond disruption is not avoided by the provision of close emotional contact with substitute caregivers. This means that different children have different experiences.

The implications for child care practices

AQA A   U1

Implications of attachment research

- **Providing substitute emotional care (avoiding bond disruption)**, for example, when children have to spend time in hospitals. This prevents the child becoming distressed due to a disruption to attachment.
- **Avoiding late adoptions**, which are associated with attachment disorder. If children do not have the opportunity to form attachments early in life they may never be able to form them (see Rutter *et al.* (2007), page 63). Today, most babies are adopted within the first week of birth. Research shows that adopted children are just as securely attached as non-adopted children (Singer *et al.*, 1985).
- **Parenting programmes** help parents who are having difficulty coping with young children. For example, the 'Circle of Security' project teaches parents to respond more sensitively to their young children and thus, promote secure attachments.

Implications of day care research

- **Quality of care is important** – Quality care is linked to reduced anti-social behaviour and high sociability in children in day care. Quality can be achieved by having low child : staff ratios (e.g. 3 : 1), with each child assigned to one member of staff who has special responsibility for that child, and training in sensitive responsiveness. This increases the extent to which day care offers adequate substitute emotional care.
- **Individual differences matter** – If some children are more negatively (or positively) affected by day care experiences, this should be taken into account when parents (or the state) decide how day care provision should be given. The American **Head Start programme**, which began in the 1960s to provide extra intellectual stimulation through day care for disadvantaged children, was an example of using day care to suit individual needs.

Progress check

1 Name the large scale longitudinal study conducted in America.
2 Identify **one** important individual difference in the effects of day care.
3 What would count as a low child : staff ratio in day care?

3 3 : 1.
2 E.g. Security of attachment; Temperament; Quality of care.
1 NICHD

3.3 Gender development

After studying this section you should be able to:

- *define gender concepts, such as sex, gender and androgyny, sex-role stereotypes, cultural variations in gender-related behaviour, nature and nurture*
- *describe and evaluate biological explanations of gender development, including typical and atypical sex chromosome patterns (Klinefelter's syndrome and Turner's syndrome) and the influence of androgens (testosterone and oestrogen)*
- *describe and evaluate social learning theory explanations of gender development, including reinforcement, modelling, imitation and identification*
- *describe and evaluate the cognitive approach to explaining gender development, including gender schema theory, Kohlberg's cognitive-developmental theory (gender identity, gender stability and gender constancy)*
- *describe and evaluate the psychodynamic approach to explaining gender development, including Freud's psychoanalytic theory (Oedipus complex, Electra complex and identification).*

LEARNING SUMMARY

Gender concepts

AQA B   U2

Many people use the terms 'sex' and 'gender' as if they refer to the same thing, but this is not true.

1. Sex and gender

- Sex is a biological fact – whether someone is male or female.
- Gender refers to what it is to be male or female.

2. Androgyny

Bem (1974) proposed that it was not necessary to regard 'male' and 'female' as mutually exclusive categories. A person can be both male and female, i.e. androgynous. For example, a person might be independent (a masculine trait) and at times show vulnerability (a feminine trait).

Bem also proposed that an androgynous person will be psychologically healthier than an individual who is tied to behaving as only a male or a female. Bem suggested that individuals who are less sex-stereotyped are freer to do things appropriate to the situation, rather than being tied to behaving in a manner appropriate to their gender.

A schema can be described as an organised packet of information or a cluster of related concepts.

3. Sex-role stereotype

A stereotype is a set of related concepts (a **schema**) that tell us what behaviours are appropriate for our sex/gender, i.e. how males and females should behave. They are learned through direct and indirect reinforcement, and exposure to role models. (See the social learning explanation of gender development on page 70.)

Can you think of an example of a behaviour that would be reinforced in boys but not in girls?

4. Cultural variations in gender-related behaviour

Williams and Best (1982) explored gender stereotypes in 30 different national cultures, finding many similarities across cultures. Men were more dominant, aggressive and autonomous, whereas women were more nurturant, deferent and interested in affiliation.

A **collectivist society** is one where individuals share tasks and belongings, and value interdependence.

Individualist societies emphasise individuality, individual needs and independence.

Williams and Best (1992) found that such consensus was strongest in **collectivist** societies and weaker in **individualist** societies where gender equality is more influential.

Mead's classic studies (1949) found that, for example, in some cultures, both men and women behaved in a way Westerners would regard as feminine. This must be due to social influences. At the same time, in all cultures men were more aggressive, indicating the effects of nature.

5. Nature and nurture

Some aspects of gender role are biologically determined (nature), whereas other aspects are learned (nurture).

- **Nature** – Hormones (e.g. testosterone in males and oestrogen in females) control many sex-related behaviours (such as puberty and menstruation). The presence of male hormones during pre-natal development may affect brain growth, which influences behaviour. (See biological explanations of gender development, page 69.)
- **Nurture** – Weinberg *et al.* (1979) found that some sex differences disappeared if girls were given raised expectations and boys were given lowered ones. This suggests that socialisation is responsible for apparent sex differences. Evidence from studies of cultural diversity also supports this.

Maccoby and Jacklin (1974) conducted a review of over 1,500 studies of gender differences in children under the age of 12. They found that:

- girls are marginally superior on tests of verbal ability
- boys are marginally better on tests of visual/spatial ability, for example, identifying the same figure from different angles
- boys are marginally better on tests of arithmetic reasoning, especially in adolescence
- boys are physically and verbally more aggressive than girls, from the age of two
- considering overall intelligence, 10 studies favoured girls, one favoured boys and 18 found no difference.

Maccoby and Jacklin concluded that the sex differences observed were minimal and suggested that most popular sex-role stereotypes are 'cultural myths' that have no basis in fact. Such myths are perpetuated by expectations arising from gender stereotypes, rather than real factors, thus supporting the nurture view.

Maccoby and Jacklin's review may underestimate sex differences because it pools results from studies that used different tests, methods, sample sizes, etc.

On the other hand, studies of sex differences tend to overestimate sex differences, because studies that fail to find any differences tend not to get published!

Progress check

1 What does the term 'gender' mean?
2 What is meant by 'sex-role stereotype'?
3 Do studies of cultural variations in gender-related behaviour support nature or nurture?

1 Your masculinity or femininity, not whether you are a male or female.
2 The schemas you have about what is appropriate behaviour for males or females.
3 Nurture.

Explanations of gender development

The four approaches to explaining gender development considered here (biological, social learning, cognitive and psychodynamic) are outlined in chapter 1.

In both of the first two case studies, described on the right, biological sex had a greater effect on gender identity than sex of rearing (i.e. the sex they are told they are). In both cases male hormones would also have affected the brain during development, which may have affected their gender identity. However, the third case study shows that biological sex need not match gender identity.

Klinefelter's syndrome occurs in 1 in every 1,000 births. Turner's syndrome occurs in about 1 in every 2,500 female births.

Androgens such as testosterone are male hormones. They are present in small amounts in women. Oestrogen is a female hormone.

Research shows that genetic sex and gender need not correspond. Therefore, biological explanations are not sufficient on their own, but biological factors clearly contribute to gender development. Biosocial explanations combine biological and social explanations.

1. Biological explanations

1. Typical sex chromosome patterns

Typical sex chromosome patterns are XX for a female and XY for a male, so-called because of their shapes. The Y chromosome carries very little genetic material.

There is usually a direct link between chromosomal sex and gonads (i.e. XX genes and vagina and womb or XY genes and penis and testicles). However, there are exceptions:

- **The Batista family** – Four children were born with normal female genitalia and grew up as girls. At puberty, testicles descended and penises appeared. They were genetically XY but had not developed male genitalia because of an insensitivity to the male hormone **testosterone**. During puberty, massive amounts of testosterone are produced and this caused the male genitalia to appear. The girls seemed to accept their change of sex without difficulty.
- **Twin study** – Diamond and Sigmundson (1997) reported that 'David', the twin studied by Money, whose penis was accidentally removed while being circumcised and who was raised as a girl, eventually elected to go back to being a man, despite prolonged attempts to socialise him into being a girl. He said he had never felt that he was a girl.
- Goldwyn (1979) described the case of **Daphne Went**, an XY individual with Testicular Feminising Syndrome (TFS), an insensitivity to testosterone which results in female external genitalia. Mrs. Went was content with her female role and adopted two children.

2. Atypical sex chromosome patterns

- **Klinefelter's syndrome** (XXY) results in a male with small gonads and reduced fertility. Individuals may have a range of other physical and behavioural problems, such as lack of body hair and small breasts. Replacement hormone therapy may increase male characteristics. Severity varies and many boys and men with the condition have few detectable symptoms.
- **Turner's syndrome** (XO – one sex chromosome missing) results in females who are likely to be infertile, and fail to develop secondary sexual characteristics during teenage years (unless treated). They may have learning difficulties, heart problems, short stature and other physical abnormalities.

3. Hormones

- Chromosomes determine a person's sex, but most sexual development and activity is governed by hormones.
- All embryos start developing the same genital structures, then male hormones cause the female parts to be absorbed and the male parts to develop.
- Testosterone also has a significant masculinising effect on the developing brain in the foetus. Dörner (1974) injected rats with male hormones during pre-natal development and they showed male behaviours. It is also argued that testosterone promotes development of the areas of the brain that are often associated with spatial and mathematical skills. Oestrogen is thought to do the same in the areas of the brain that are often associated with verbal ability (Brosnan, 2004).

2. Social learning theory

Gender role behaviour is learned through indirect and direct reinforcement:

Indirect reinforcement

Children identify with certain people (e.g. parents, peers, pop stars) and model their gender behaviours on them, most particularly if the behaviour is seen to be rewarded (**vicarious reinforcement**).

Direct reinforcement

When children reproduce behaviours that they have observed, they will be reinforced (or not) directly and this will determine future behaviour.

The principles of social learning theory are outlined in Chapter 1, on page 17. The key concepts are indirect (vicarious) reinforcement and direct reinforcement, modelling, imitation and identification.

Research evidence for social learning theory

- **Parental reinforcement** – Smith and Lloyd (1978) gave mothers a set of feminine-, masculine- and neutral-type toys. When a 6-month-old baby was dressed and named as a boy, the mothers encouraged more physical activity and gave masculine-type toys to the baby.
- **Peer reinforcement** – Lamb and Roopnarine (1979) observed preschool children at play. Children generally reinforced peers with sex-appropriate play and were quick to criticise sex-inappropriate play. Children responded more readily to reinforcement by the same sex rather than opposite sex peers. This suggests that children already know what is sex-appropriate; their peers are just reinforcing that knowledge.
- **Television reinforcement** – Williams (1985) studied the effects of the arrival of television on a town called 'Notel', which had had no television previously. He found that the children's sex-role attitudes became more traditional and sex-stereotyped after two years of exposure to television.

Research evidence against social learning theory

- **Real gender differences** – Jacklin and Maccoby (1978) introduced unfamiliar 2½ year olds to each other and dressed them in neutral clothing. The researchers found that interactions were most lively and positive with same-sex pairs. This may well reflect an early incompatibility between girls and boys, partly based on biological differences such as boisterousness, and partly due to learned preferences for toys and activities.
- **Variable reinforcement** – Fagot (1985) found evidence that teachers tend to reinforce 'feminine' behaviours in both boys and girls, such as quiet, sedentary activities. However, only girls acquire them. This suggests that reinforcement alone does not explain the acquisition of gender-appropriate behaviours.

Evaluation

- Reinforcements are **not sufficiently consistent** to explain all observed differences, but gender-appropriate behaviours are clearly reinforced.
- Social learning theory **overlooks** the role of **biological** (innate) factors.
- Social learning theory explains **cultural differences** and accounts for the influence of **stereotypes**.

3. The cognitive approach

1. Kohlberg's cognitive-developmental theory

Kohlberg (1966) argued that gender identity is a combination of social learning mediated by maturational and cognitive factors:

- Different stages of gender identity develop only when a child has aged (matured) to the right point.
- Gender identity is the result of a child's active structuring of his/her own experience (a cognitive process), not just the passive product of social learning. Kohlberg proposed three stages:

(1) **Basic gender identity** (2–3½ years) – gender known but still believe it is possible to change sex

(2) **Gender stability** (3½–4½ years) – awareness that gender is fixed

(3) **Gender constancy** (4½–7 years upwards) – recognition that superficial changes do not alter gender.

Research evidence

Slaby and Frey (1975) showed preschool children a film that had men on one side and women on the other side of the screen. Those children who had previously been rated as having gender consistency watched more same-sex models. This shows how they actively seek information that will help them to develop gender-appropriate behaviour.

Evaluation

- The cognitive approach **combines social learning** with some aspects of **biological** development.
- This view assumes that **development proceeds in stages**, and that gender identity is mediated by cognitive factors. This may not be universally true.

2. Gender schema theory

Martin and Halverson (1981) suggested that once a child has a basic gender identity, they are motivated to learn more about the sexes and incorporate this information into a gender schema. Like all schemas, this serves to organise relevant information and attitudes, and will influence behaviour.

Research evidence

Martin and Little (1990) found that preschool children had very little gender understanding, yet they had strong gender stereotypes about what boys and girls were permitted to do. Masters *et al.* (1979) showed that children aged 4–5 were more influenced in their choice of toy by the gender label (e.g. 'It's a girl's toy') than by the gender of the model seen playing with the toy.

Evaluation

- The gender schema theory offers a **middle ground** between social learning and cognitive-developmental explanations.
- The gender schema theory explains how **gender stereotypes persist**, because people are more likely to remember information that is consistent with their schemas.
- The gender schema theory explains how gender behaviours occur **before gender identity**.
- The gender schema theory lacks mention of **biological factors** and assumes that all gender behaviour is mediated by cognitive factors.

The essence of the cognitive approach is that it is what you *think* that has the greatest influence on your behaviour.

You can read more about it in Chapter 1 – see page 18.

According to the cognitive approach, children attend to same-sex models because they have already developed a consistent gender identity, not vice versa (as suggested by the social learning theory).

Remember that a **schema** can be described as an organised packet of information or a cluster of related concepts. It is a bit like a stereotype.

In Kohlberg's theory, a child must recognise the permanence of their gender before they can begin to acquire gender schema. In gender schema theory, gender schema begin to be formed as soon as the child recognises that there is a difference between men and women.

Social learning theory portrays gender development as a passive process, whereas cognitive theories suggest that the child is an active seeker of information.

Freud's theory is an example of the psychodynamic approach. The key concepts of his theory are outlined in Chapter 1, see page 19.

Freud suggested that there are five stages in personality development:
Oral stage (0–1½ years)
Anal stage (1½–3 years)
Phallic stage (3–6 years)
Latency stage (6 years–puberty)
Genital stage (puberty)

Identification also results in the formation of the conscience and ego-ideal, which embody the moral values of the same-sex parent.

Shaffer (2002) has suggested a synthesis of all accounts:
- Biology determines initial identity and behaviours.
- Differential reinforcement emphasises existing tendencies and socialises the child.
- Socialisation results in acquisition of gender schema (gender-typing, and in group and out group schema).
- Gender schema lead to collecting gender-consistent information.

4. The psychodynamic approach

Sigmund Freud proposed that gender development was related to the **phallic** stage of development (which takes place between 3 and 6 years of age).

Around the age of 3 years, a child's sexual interest focuses on their genitalia and they feel desire for their opposite-sex parent. This makes them see their same-sex parent as a rival. The child feels unconscious hostility, resulting in guilt. The child also feels anxiety and fear of punishment should his/her true desires be discovered.

Resolution occurs through **identification** with the same-sex parent. Identification is the process of 'taking on' the attitudes and ideas of another person. Unsatisfactory resolution can result in amorality, homosexuality or rebelliousness.

Freud described this process in boys as the **Oedipus complex**. Oedipus was a figure in Greek mythology, who physically desired his mother and killed his father. Freud described the phallic stage for boys as a time when they want their mother and, therefore, feel jealous of their father, wanting to remove him. The fear that the father will discover these feelings is expressed as a fear of castration, but is eventually resolved through identification with the father.

In girls, the same process was termed the **Electra complex** by Jung. In Greek mythology, Electra urged her brother to kill her mother. According to Freud, the young girl had 'penis envy' and resented her mother for not providing her with one. 'Penis envy' is resolved by a desire to have babies. This conflict resolution is weaker for girls and, therefore, according to Freud, gender identity and moral development are not complete in girls.

Evaluation

- Freud's important **contribution** was to recognise childhood as a critical period of development, and to identify sexual (physical) and unconscious influences.
- The theory lacks rigorous **research support**, especially regarding normal development. The 'evidence' for gender development comes from the case study of Little Hans (Freud, 1909, see page 163) who loved his mother and was jealous of his father. This conflict was resolved through identification with his father.
- The account of development is **gender-biased** – female gender development was not well-described (which may reflect women's role in Victorian society).

Progress check

1. How are sex and gender different?
2. Which **two** explanations draw on the concept of identification?
3. Explain the fundamental difference between Kohlberg's theory and Martin and Halverson's theory.
4. According to Freud, during what stage does gender development take place?

4 Phallic.
3 Whether permanence of gender comes before or after identity.
2 Social learning and psychodynamic theory.
1 Sex is a biological fact, gender refers to your sense of maleness/femaleness.

Sample questions and student answers – AQA A questions

1

1(a) Two characteristics have been identified. **2 out of 2 marks.**

(a) Identify **two** characteristics of a securely attached child. *(2 marks)*

A securely attached child is not too upset when his mother (or caregiver) leaves him, and the child is easily comforted upon her return.

(b) Bowlby's theory, rather than learning theory, was a wise choice because there is so much that can be written. The description of the theory is both accurate and well-detailed, and covers various features of the theory. It clearly deserves full marks. **6 out of 6 marks.**

(b) Outline **one** explanation of attachment. *(6 marks)*

Bowlby proposed a theory of attachment which explained how attachment is an adaptive behaviour because it helps survival (and ultimately reproduction) and also acts as a basis for emotional development. The child's first main attachment relationship provides a template for later relationships in the form of an internal working model. Bowlby proposed that this template is based on the primary attachment relationship (monotropy), which is determined by the sensitive responsiveness of one caregiver. Bowlby also claimed that attachments have to form before the child is 2½ years old, otherwise it will be too late and the child will be forever emotionally scarred. A further part of his theory was that attachment acts as a secure base for exploration.

(c) It would have been helpful to state an example of the 'evidence' that is referred to, such as Tizard's research. **2 out of 3 marks.**

(c) Give **one** criticism of this theory *(3 marks)*

The idea of a critical period for the development of attachments is probably wrong. There is lots of evidence that, given the right circumstances, children can recover and develop normally even when they have had no opportunity to form early attachments.

2

2(a) When a question does not specify how many points to make, you can assume that maximum marks will be available for one answer that is well explained, providing detail, or for giving several answers in less detail. The answer here has provided one answer with some detail. However, no psychological research has been specifically identified in the answer. **2 out of 4 marks.**

(a) Sarah is five years old and has to go to hospital to have her appendix removed. Naturally, she is feeling very anxious about this operation and also about staying away from home for a week.

Explain what the nurses might do to help Sarah feel less anxious, referring to psychological research on attachment in your answer. *(4 marks)*

One thing the nurses might do is make sure Sarah is emotionally well-cared for, providing substitute emotional care so that Sarah's attachment bonds with her mother are not disrupted. Such disruption would create further anxiety.

(b) An excellent, detailed answer. Names and dates are not required but they do add detail to the answer. **6 out of 6 marks.**

(b) Outline research into the effects of day care on peer relations. *(6 marks)*

Shea (1981) observed children in nursery school and found that they became more sociable over time, suggesting that day care led to increased sociability (although they might just have become more relaxed). In another study, Clarke-Stewart et al. (1994) compared children who went to day care with those who didn't. The day care children coped better socially and could interact better with peers. The EPPE project (3,000 UK preschool children) also found that day care was associated with increased independence and peer sociability.

Practice examination question – AQA A question

1

(a) Describe **two** implications of research into attachment for child care practices. *(4 marks)*

(b) Discuss the effects of institutionalisation. *(12 marks)*

Sample question and student answers – AQA B question

1

(a) Identify **one** way that Turner's syndrome might affect an individual. *(1 mark)*

1(a) An appropriate answer. **1 out of 1 mark.**

The girl is likely to be infertile.

(b) Explain how the study of people with abnormal chromosome patterns can help our understanding of normal gender development. *(4 marks)*

(b) For full marks the answer should be well-detailed and well-organised, which this answer is. It is a thoughtful response and the example is essential because the command word was 'explain'. **4 out of 4 marks.**

Abnormal chromosome patterns highlight the importance of genes in determining normal gender development. So, you can compare someone with an abnormal pattern, such as XO, and if this is associated with infertility, that suggests that the presence of a second X gene (normal female is XX) is involved in fertility. Of course it might well be that a host of other factors are involved.

(c) Describe and evaluate the social learning explanation of gender development. Refer to **one other** explanation of gender development in your answer. *(10 marks)*

(c) This is a very good answer, though there are a few flaws, which prevent the awarding of top marks. The answer starts with a good description of SLT, however, it is slightly too general. Even though there are attempts to link it to gender development, it reads more like a description of SLT than an account of gender development. The same is true for the evidence from Bandura – a little bit general and a little superficial.

As required by the question, the student answer refers to other theories of gender development. This is done well because the other explanations are not described but are used as a valuable contrast to the SLT explanation. **8 out of 10 marks.**

According to social learning theory, we acquire gender (and all behaviour) through direct and indirect reinforcement. You observe people behaving in certain ways and store memories of this. If you see someone being rewarded for behaving in a particular way (such as playing with girls' toys) then this increases the likelihood that you will repeat the same behaviour. When you do repeat it, you may be punished for such behaviour and this is direct reinforcement, so it becomes less likely that you will repeat the behaviour.

Bandura showed evidence for social learning theory in a study of aggression with the Bobo doll. However, even though it was about aggression we can apply the same principles to gender.

Social learning theory explains the effects of stereotypes. We are exposed to stereotypes that are then imitated because we see people being rewarded for behaving according to stereotype. This has similarities with the cognitive explanations of gender development because they suggest that children acquire gender concepts through modelling, but only once they have understood that there is a difference between men and women.

Smith and Lloyd (1978) conducted a study that showed how mothers reinforce gender-stereotyped behaviours. The mothers were given toys to play with, with a baby dressed in girl's or boys' clothing. They tended to give masculine-type toys to the boys, thus reinforcing stereotypes.

However, SLT cannot account for all gender behaviours. There is evidence that biological factors are fundamentally important. For example, in Money's study of the twin boys, the one boy who was raised as a girl nevertheless always felt he was a boy and ultimately chose that sex.

Practice examination question – AQA B question

1

(a) Distinguish between the terms **sex** and **gender**. *(3 marks)*

(b) Outline **two** criticisms of the psychoanalytic explanation of gender development. *(4 marks)*

Research methods

4.1 Research methods and techniques

After studying this section you should be able to:

LEARNING SUMMARY

- *describe experimental methods of research: laboratory, field and natural (quasi) experiments, including their advantages and weaknesses*
- *describe and evaluate non-experimental methods of research, including investigations using correlational analysis, and observational techniques/ studies*
- *self-report techniques (questionnaires and interviews), and case studies.*

Experimental methods

AQA A   U1
AQA B   U1

A research method or technique is a systematic method of *empirical* data collection.

'Empirical' research is based on observed facts, i.e. data that is collected through direct observation (as opposed to data collected by rational thought).

In an experiment, the relationship between two things is investigated by deliberately producing a change in the **independent variable** (IV) and recording what effect this has on the **dependent variable** (DV). The main features are:

- **Causal relationships** between the independent and dependent variables can be demonstrated – changes in the DV are assumed to be caused by the IV.
- **Greater control** – Features of the experimental environment can be controlled by the experimenter.
- **Replication** – The study can be repeated because all variables have been identified and operationalised and, as far as possible, controlled.

1. Laboratory experiments

Laboratory experiments are conducted in a specially designed environment where variables can be well controlled. Therefore, it is a highly contrived and controlled situation, often described as 'artificial'.

Advantages
- This is the **ideal form** of the experiment because there is the possibility of good control of all variables, especially extraneous ones (high internal validity).
- **Replication** is relatively easy.

Weaknesses
- In reality, **total control is never possible**. The results may be affected by, for example, experimenter bias and demand characteristics (see page 83).
- The laboratory experiment is a **contrived situation**, therefore, the results may not generalise to everyday life (lack ecological/external validity).

2. Field experiments

Field experiments are conducted in more natural surroundings. The independent variable (IV) is still manipulated by the experimenter.

One key difference between a laboratory and field experiment is that, in a field experiment, participants are often not aware that they are being studied and, therefore, may behave more naturally.

Advantages
- They tend to have greater **ecological validity** because the setting is more natural and, therefore, behaviour may be more natural.
- The technique generally **avoids experimenter effects** because the participants are usually unaware of the experiment.

Field studies do not necessarily have greater ecological validity. For example, Hofling *et al.'s* study (see page 126) only tells us about the obedience of nurses and does not necessarily apply to all situations of authority. It was also a highly contrived study – when conditions were made more natural, obedience dropped to 11% (Rank and Jacobsen, 1975).

Natural experiments are sometimes called 'quasi-experiments' because they are not genuine experiments, which is what 'quasi' means (not quite the real thing).

Strictly speaking, studies that look at gender or age differences are not natural experiments because the IV has not been altered. It is a 'state of being'. Such studies can be described as **difference studies**.

When comparing laboratory and field experiments, you can see that each has advantages. Field experiments tend to have higher external validity whereas laboratory experiments have higher internal validity because the greater control means fewer extraneous variables.

Weaknesses

- Extraneous variables are **harder to control**.
- **Some design problems** remain, such as sample bias and some demand characteristics.
- It may be **more time-consuming** and expensive than laboratory experiments because it is conducted in 'the field'.

3. Natural experiments (quasi-experiments)

If conditions vary naturally, the effects of an independent variable (IV) can be observed without any intervention by the experimenter. The research is still an experiment in the sense that there is an IV and a DV, but it is not a 'true' experiment because:

- **The IV is not directly manipulated** – Lack of direct manipulation of the IV means that you cannot be certain that the IV is the *cause* of any observed effect.
- **Participants are not randomly allocated** to conditions, therefore, participants in different conditions may not be comparable.

Advantages

- A natural experiment is the **only way** to study cause and effect in certain situations, for example, where there are practical and/or ethical objections to manipulating the variables, such as looking at the effects of deprivation.
- Natural experiments tend to have greater **ecological validity** because they are conducted in a natural setting.

Weaknesses

- You cannot establish **cause and effect** because the IV is not deliberately changed and participants are not randomly allocated to conditions.
- It is not easy to **replicate** such studies, and may not be possible at all.
- They can **only be used when conditions vary naturally**. Such conditions are not always possible to find.
- The unusualness of the circumstances may reduce **external validity**.

Progress check

1 Name the **three** kinds of experiment.
2 Name **one** difference between a laboratory and field experiment.
3 Name **one** difference between a laboratory and a natural experiment.

3 E.g. In natural experiments the IV is not directly manipulated.

2 E.g. Lab experiments have more control than field experiments; Field experiments are more natural and participants are not aware of being studied.

1 Laboratory, field and natural/quasi.

Non-experimental methods

AQA A ▶ U1
AQA B ▶ U1

Correlation is a method of analysis rather than a research method. Thus, we talk about 'investigations using a correlational analysis', rather than a 'correlation study'.

Note that +1.00 and -1.00 are equally strong correlations – the minus sign just means that one variable increases as the other decreases. There is more discussion of this on page 93.

It is only in an experiment that you have an IV and DV. In a correlation you have **co-variables**. Both experimental and non-experimental methods may have a hypothesis, or a number of hypotheses.

1. Investigations using correlational analysis

Correlation concerns the extent to which two variables (**co-variables**) are related. For example, you might compare the IQ scores of twins, or a person's verbal and non-verbal IQ score.

A numerical value is calculated to represent the degree to which two sets of data are correlated, called a **correlation coefficient**. The reason for the relationship can only be supposed because a strong correlation does not demonstrate cause and effect.

Perfect positive correlation is +1.00; perfect negative correlation is –1.00.

Advantages

- Correlational analysis can be used **where experimental manipulation would be unethical** or impossible.
- It indicates **possible relationships** between co-variables, and might suggest future research ideas, which would look at possible causal relationships.
- It can **rule out causal relationships** – if two variables are not correlated, then one cannot cause the other.

Weaknesses

- Correlational analysis does not establish **cause and effect**.
- The relationship may be due to other **extraneous variables**. For example, height and IQ might be linked because diet influences both.

2. Observational studies

In a **naturalistic observation**, behaviour is observed in the natural environment. All variables are free to alter, and interference is kept to a minimum. No IV is manipulated but nevertheless a hypothesis may be tested.

Observations may be unstructured or structured. 'Structured' means the use of behavioural categories and sampling methods, which are discussed on page 84.

Advantages

- Observational studies are useful when studying behaviour for the first time. Naturalistic observation is needed to **establish possible relationships**.
- It offers a way to study behaviour where there are **ethical objections** to manipulating variables.
- It gives a more **realistic picture** of spontaneous behaviour because participants are in their own environment and may not be aware that they are being observed. It tends to have higher ecological validity.

Most non-experimental methods actually produce **quantitative data** (i.e. data that can be counted), rather than qualitative data.

Inter-observer reliability is discussed again on page 88.

Weaknesses

- It is not possible to infer **cause and effect**.
- It is **difficult to replicate** and, therefore, you cannot be certain that the result was not a 'one off'.
- It is difficult to **control** extraneous variables, which reduces internal validity.
- **Observer bias**: the observer sees what he 'wants' to see.
- **Observer reliability**: there may be differences between different observers (low inter-observer reliability) or the same observer on different occasions, which means that the data collected is unreliable.

Note that a controlled observation differs from a naturalistic one in terms of control over environmental factors but not in terms of the control over recording methods. In both controlled and naturalistic observations, the data may be recorded using structured or unstructured techniques.

Other kinds of observation

- **Controlled observation** – Not all observations are naturalistic. Some are highly controlled and conducted in a laboratory environment. An example of a controlled observation is detailed on page 55 – Ainsworth's strange situation study.
- **Participant and non-participant observation** – Other participants may regard the observer as 'one of them' (participant), or the observer may watch (non-participant). Participant observation is likely to be biased, but may produce richer data.
- **Covert or overt observation** – Participants may not be aware they are being observed, e.g. through a one-way mirror (covert) or participants may be aware of being watched (overt). Covert observation raises ethical objections whereas overt observations mean participants may not behave naturally.
- **Content analysis** – A form of indirect observation of behaviour using, for example, books, diaries or TV programmes, and counting the frequency of particular behaviours, such as gender-related words.

3. Self-report techniques

Self-report techniques may:

- Be used as a way to measure a DV in an experiment, for example, to determine how participants felt after seeing an aggressive or non-aggressive film.
- Form the basis of a whole research study. For example, a study to find out about obedience might ask people whether they would obey in certain situations.

Self-report techniques may be written (questionnaires) or conducted face-to-face (interviews).

All self-report techniques allow researchers to access what people think and feel. The alternative is to observe what people do.

1. Questionnaires and structured interviews

All questions in questionnaires and structured interviews are determined beforehand.

Advantages

- Questionnaires and structured interviews can collect information about people's **feelings and attitudes** that cannot be obtained through observation.
- Questionnaires are an efficient form of data collection because once they are designed they can be given out to thousands of people.

Students often say that an advantage of questionnaires is that they are cheap and easy to use and collect lots of data. They are not. Designing questionnaires takes time and skill. They do not collect more data than any other method. The key advantage is that they can be given out to lots of people at relatively little cost, both financially and in terms of time.

Weaknesses

- People often **don't know what they think** and so their answers may be 'guesses', or influenced by the way a question is phrased.
- They may result in a reduction of truthfulness in answers, due to **social desirability bias** (i.e. providing answers that make the respondent 'look good').
- In comparison with unstructured interviews, the data collected will be **restricted** by a pre-determined set of questions.
- They are only **suitable for certain kinds of participants** – those who are literate and willing to spend time filling in a questionnaire. This leads to a biased sample.

Unstructured interviews are also called **clinical interviews** because it is the technique used by doctors to collect information.

2. Unstructured interviews

The interviewer may have some general aims and start with a few prepared questions, but mainly lets the interviewee's answers guide subsequent questions.

Many of the advantages and weaknesses given for questionnaires/structured interviews also apply to unstructured interviews.

One weakness of interviews is that the interviewer's *expectations may influence* the interviewee's performance. This is called an **interviewer** or **investigator** bias.

Another weakness of interviews is that they may not be comparable because different interviewers ask different questions (**low inter-interviewer reliability**). Reliability may also be affected by the same interviewer behaving differently on different occasions.

Advantages

- **Rich data** (i.e. 'rich' in detail, usually qualitative) can be obtained, more than in a structured interview/questionnaire.

Weaknesses

- Unstructured interviews require **well-trained interviewers**, which makes it more expensive to produce reliable interviews.

4. Case studies

A case study is a detailed account of a single individual, a small group, an institution or an event. It might contain data about personal history, background, test results, and the text of interviews.

Advantages

- It may be the only option when a behaviour is **rare**.
- It provides rich data and insights from an **unusual perspective**.
- It relates to real-life (i.e. it has **high ecological validity**).

Various examples of case studies are included in this book. See Genie (page 61) and H.M. (page 27).

Note that case studies are both high and low in ecological validity!

Weaknesses

- The close relationship between experimenter and participant introduces **bias**.
- It does not use rigorous methodology – it is often unstructured and **unreplicable** and difficult to establish **cause and effect**. It usually involves recall of earlier history and may, therefore, be **unreliable**.
- It produces a limited sample, and lacks generalisability (**low in ecological validity**).

Progress check

1. What research method(s) enable causal relationships to be demonstrated?
2. What kind of observational study takes place in a lab?
3. Name **two** advantages of investigations using correlational analysis.
4. Name **two** research methods that collect rich data.

1 Any kind of experiment.
2 Controlled observation.
3 E.g. Used where experimental manipulation would be unethical; Indicates relationships between co-variables; Can rule out causal relationships.
4 E.g. Interviews; Case studies.

4.2 Investigation design

After studying this section you should be able to:

Psychology and psychologists use the scientific method to produce explanations about human (and animal) behaviour. The scientific method consists of four important steps:

1. Observations of behaviour.
2. Explanations produced for these observations, which lead to the production of one or more hypotheses.
3. A research study designed to test each hypothesis.
4. If the hypothesis is not supported, the explanation/theory needs to be adjusted.

- *identify and write your own research aims and hypotheses, including directional and non-directional hypotheses, and the operationalisation of variables (such as independent and dependent variables)*
- *describe and evaluate experimental designs (independent groups, repeated measures and matched pairs), and the use of counterbalancing*
- *describe issues relating to control (including extraneous and confounding variables)*
- *explain how to conduct pilot studies and why they are used*
- *describe and evaluate sampling techniques, including random, opportunity and volunteer sampling*
- *describe and evaluate techniques used in observational studies, including the development and use of behavioural categories*
- *describe and evaluate the design of questionnaires and interviews*
- *describe issues relating to validity and reliability*
- *describe and evaluate ethical issues and how psychologists deal with them, including an awareness of the BPS Code of Ethics.*

Formulating research questions

AQA A ▶ U1
AQA B ▶ U1

A hypothesis should be written in the present tense. It is not a prediction of what is expected to happen. It is a statement of what is believed to be true.

A hypothesis is sometimes called the **alternative hypothesis** – because it is alternative to the **null hypothesis**.

An example of a (alternative) hypothesis in an experiment is 'Participants recall more words from list A than list B'. This is a directional hypothesis. An example of an alternative hypothesis in a study using a correlational design is 'There is a relationship between a participant's score on test A and test B'. This is non-directional.

Note that AQA A students are not required to know about the null hypothesis.

Research aims are the stated intentions of the questions that are going to be answered in an investigation.

A **hypothesis** is a formal, unambiguous statement of what a researcher believes.

- In an experiment, the hypothesis provides a statement about the effect of the **independent variable** (IV) on the **dependent variable** (DV).
- The **independent variable** (IV) is the one that is specifically manipulated so that we can observe its effect on the **dependent variable** (DV). The DV is usually the one we are measuring or assessing.
- The hypothesis should include all **levels** of the IV, e.g. 'Participants recall more words from list A' is not sufficient. You must also add '…than list B'. In this case, there are two levels or conditions of the IV: list A and list B. List A might be nouns and list B might be verbs.
- **Operationalisation** is necessary in order to make a variable measurable and unambiguous. It is a definition of the variable based on a set of operations or objective components. For example, hunger might be defined in terms of the number of hours since a participant last ate, or a rating scale of how hungry they feel.
- A **directional** or **one-tailed hypothesis** predicts the direction of the effect.
- A **non-directional** or **two-tailed hypothesis** anticipates a difference or correlation but not the direction of that difference/correlation.

In a study using a correlational analysis the hypothesis states the relationship predicted between the co-variables.

The **null hypothesis** (H_0) is a statement of 'no difference' or 'no relationship' between the populations being studied.

The **alternative hypothesis** (H_1) is the statement of what the researcher believes to be true.

Designing experiments

Experimental design

1. Independent groups design

Comparison is made between two unrelated groups of participants. The participants are in groups. One group receives the experimental treatment. The other receives a different experimental treatment or no treatment (this is the **control group**). Performance on the DV is compared between the two groups.

An **order effect** occurs when the order in which tasks are done affects performance. For example, if participants do the same test twice they may do better on the second test because of practice. Or they may do worse because they have got bored.

Advantages

- Independent groups design is used **where repeated measures are not possible**, e.g. in a study where taking part in both conditions means participants would realise the purpose of the experiment.
- **There are no order effects** or other problems of repeated measures.

Weaknesses

- It lacks control of **participant variables** (see page 82).
- It needs **more participants** than a repeated measures design.

2. Repeated measures design

The same participant is tested before and after the experimental treatment. Therefore, all participants are tested twice, for example, doing a memory test with and without noise. Performance on the DV is compared to see if there was a difference before and after.

Advantages

- It gives good control for **participant variables**.
- It needs **fewer participants** than an independent groups design.

Order effects can be dealt with by using **counterbalancing**, described on page 82.

Weaknesses

- **The order effects** (e.g. practice or boredom effects) can affect final performance.
- The participants may **guess the purpose** of the experiment after the first test.

When matching participants, it is not always appropriate to use gender or age or any other obvious variable *unless* there is evidence to suggest that it could be a significant variable. For example, when testing short-term memory you don't need to match participants on gender unless you have reason to suspect that girls might have better memories than boys.

3. Matched pairs design

Participant variables are controlled by matching pairs of participants on key attributes. One partner is exposed to the IV, and both are compared in terms of their performance on the DV.

Advantages

- **There are no order effects** or other problems of repeated measures design.
- **Participant variables** are partly controlled.

Weaknesses

- Matching is **difficult**, time-consuming and may 'waste' participants, because some participants do not match and, therefore, cannot be used. For example, if you are matching on gender, you may have too many girls and cannot, therefore, use all of them.
- Matching is **inevitably inexact**.

The following two terms are used interchangeably: **extraneous variable** and **confounding variable** ('confounding' because it may confound or confuse the results).

Strictly speaking, an **extraneous variable** is any variable that can affect the outcome of a study, whereas a **confounding variable** is an extraneous variable that has a systematic effect and is, therefore, likely to confound the results.

In the example on the right, the extraneous variable (room temperature) would be a confounding one as it varies systematically with the IV.

When considering situational variables, remember that noise and other distractions do not always matter. Hovey (1928) gave two groups of students an IQ test and both performed equally well, despite the fact that one group were in a hall with bells and buzzers, a circular saw, four acrobats and a photographer taking pictures!

Experimenter effects are not exclusive to experiments. When they occur in other methods of research, they are referred to as **researcher** or **investigator effects**.

Note that **experimenter effects** are different from **experimental effects**, which are the effects of the experimental treatment.

A **demand characteristic** is a feature of an experiment that invites a certain response from participants and thus, leads all participants to behave in the expected way.

The experiment is a social situation. Participants prefer to behave in a socially-acceptable manner. This is true even when performing anonymously or when answering questions on paper.

Control (part 1)

In an experiment, the IV is controlled by the experimenter. Any changes in the DV are due to the deliberate changes in the IV *unless* there are *extraneous variables*, i.e. variables other than the IV that have affected the DV and are, therefore, acting as an alternative IV. This would mean that the experimental result is meaningless.

1. Participant variables

Participant variables are features of the participants, such as their gender, age, social class or education. Such characteristics are important when using an independent groups design, and also when assessing the extent to which a sample is representative. They may also be relevant when matching participants in a matched pairs design.

Participant variables can be controlled using **random allocation** to conditions. Any bias in placing participants in experimental or control groups can be overcome by randomly determining the group they are placed in.

2. Situational variables

Situational variables are features of the situation that act as extraneous variables.

For example, if the effect of time of day is tested by giving Group 1 a test in the morning, and Group 2 the same test in the afternoon, but when Group 1 do the test the room is colder than when Group 2 do it, then room temperature is an extraneous variable (i.e. it acts as an alternative IV).

- **Systematic effects** (constant error), e.g. when testing the effects of noise on memory, all of those tested in the noise condition are tested in the morning whereas those tested in the no-noise condition are tested in the afternoon. Time of day is a systematic effect (or constant error). Better performance may be due to time of day, rather than lack of noise.
- **Random errors** are features of the experiment that occur with no pattern. They occur equally in both conditions and are assumed to cancel each other out. In this case, noise would be an extraneous variable but not a confounding one.

Situational variables include **order effects** that can be controlled using **counterbalancing**, such as giving half the participants condition A first, while the other half get condition B first. This prevents improvement due to, for example, practice, or poorer performance due to, for example, boredom.

Standardised procedures are used to ensure that conditions are equivalent for all participants. This includes the use of **standardised instructions**.

3. Experimenter effects

The behaviour of the experimenter may act as an extraneous variable.

- **Experimenter bias** – An experimenter has expectations about the outcome of an experiment and may indirectly and unconsciously communicate them to the participant. This affects the participants' behaviour.
- **Demand characteristics** – Cues that communicate the experimental hypothesis. Participants search for clues about what is expected of them and, therefore, respond to demand characteristics. This leads them to unconsciously behave along the lines expected by the experimenter. Orne (1962) tested this by telling participants they were in an experiment investigating sensory deprivation. In fact, they were not deprived at all, yet they displayed the classic symptoms – they did what they were expected to do.
- **Hawthorne effect** – A person's performance may improve, not because of the experimental treatment, but because they are receiving unaccustomed attention (a confounding variable). Such attention increases self-esteem and

leads to improved performance. (The effect is named after the Hawthorne electrical factory where it was first observed.)

- **The Greenspoon effect** – Participants may be subtly reinforced by the experimenter's comments. Greenspoon (1955) was able to alter participants' responses by saying 'mm-hmm' whenever the participant said a plural word, or 'uh-huh' after other responses. This led respectively to increased or decreased production of plural words in random word generation.

Experimenter/investigator effects may be controlled using the **double blind technique** where neither the participant, nor the experimenter, is aware of the 'crucial' aspects of the experiment.

Standardised instructions help to prevent experimenter bias by controlling what the experimenter says to the participants.

Control (part 2)

In an experiment, the term 'control' is also used in a second way – when referring to **control groups** or **control conditions**.

- In an independent measures design, the group that receives the experimental condition is the **experimental group**. In order to determine whether the experimental treatment has had an effect a comparison group is needed, called the **control group**.
- In a repeated measures design, there is an **experimental condition** and a **control condition**.

Sometimes, there is no control condition; instead, there are two experimental conditions. Or there may be a **placebo condition**. Placebos are a control for the effects of expectations – participants think they are receiving the experimental treatment when they are not. They receive a 'treatment' which appears to be the same as the real thing but does not have its critical effects.

> Note that the experimenter is the person actually carrying out the research, whereas the investigator designs and directs the research and may also be the person conducting the study. Demand characteristics are investigator effects, rather than experimenter effects.

> If we study the effects of noise on memory performance, then one group is exposed to noise during learning (this is the experimental group) and their recall is compared to that of another group which is not exposed to noise during learning (this is the control group).
>
> If this was designed as repeated measures then each participant would take part in both the noise condition (i.e. the experimental condition) and the no-noise condition (i.e. the control condition).

Progress check

1 Which variable is controlled by the experimenter?
2 Which experimental design is affected by order effects?
3 When is counterbalancing used?
4 What is a demand characteristic?

4 A cue that communicates the aims/hypothesis of an experiment and invites a certain predictable response from participants.
3 When order effects may affect performance.
2 Repeated measures.
1 IV.

Pilot studies

AQA A ▸ U1
AQA B ▸ U1

A pilot study is a smaller-scale, preliminary study (using a small group of participants), which makes it possible to check out standardised procedures and the general design of an investigation before investing time and money in the major study. Any problems can be adjusted.

Sampling techniques

AQA A ▸ U1
AQA B ▸ U1

If a sample is not representative of the target population then we cannot make generalisations.

A difficulty for all sampling techniques is that some participants may refuse to take part. Therefore, in a sense, the *final* sample is a volunteer sample of sorts.

Most research involves opportunity sampling. It is the easiest method in terms of both time and money. A close second is volunteer sampling, which is often used in universities where notices are put up asking for willing participants.

All sampling techniques, except for random sampling, suffer from **sampling bias**. Some people have a greater or lesser chance of being selected than they should be given how frequently they are found in the population.

Sample – Part of a population selected such that it is considered to be representative of the population as a whole.

Population – The group of people from whom the sample is drawn. The population may also be unrepresentative of the target population (the group about which we aim to make generalisations), for example, selecting a sample from one school.

Sampling techniques (methods of drawing a sample):

- **Random sample** – Every member of the population has an equal chance of being selected, therefore, it is an unbiased sample. This can be achieved using random number tables or numbers drawn from a hat. However, the population that the sample is drawn from may be biased, e.g. if you take names from the phonebook, you only include people with telephones.
- **Systematic or quasi-random sample** – For example, every 10th case, or the name at the top of each page in the phonebook. There is no bias in selection. However, every person does not stand an equal chance of being selected (therefore, quasi-random).
- **Opportunity sample** – Selecting participants because they are available, for example, asking people in the street. This is sometimes mistakenly regarded as random, whereas it is invariably biased because the sample is selected from a restricted group, for example, people in a shopping centre.
- **Volunteer or self-selected sample** – Participants who become part of an experiment because they volunteer when asked. The results are likely to suffer from a volunteer bias because such participants are usually more highly motivated and perform better than randomly selected participants.
- **Stratified sample** – The population is divided into sections (strata) in relation to factors considered relevant, for example social class or age. The researcher then randomly selects a set number of individuals from each strata.
- **Quota sample** – This also uses stratified methods, but the sample is not randomly determined. The researcher seeks any five individuals satisfying each criterion.

Progress check

When an exam question asks you 'how', make sure you describe how you would do something rather than explaining what it is or why you would do it.

1 How would you do a pilot study?
2 What is meant by the term 'population'?
3 What method of sampling is most commonly used?

3 Opportunity or volunteer.
2 The group from whom a sample is drawn.
1 E.g. Give a test to a group of typical participants.

Designing observational studies

AQA A — U1
AQA B — U1

Observational techniques may be used in an observational study or, for example, to assess the DV in an experiment.

Observational studies require techniques for categorising behaviour to ensure consistency and enable observers to identify important behaviours. They also require techniques for sampling behaviour.

1. Methods of categorising behaviour

Behavioural categories/checklist – Categories are identified when making preliminary observations to cover all behaviours observed. An observer then uses this to record the behaviours of a target individual or group. It is important that these categories:

- Refer to **explicit** behaviours that can be identified by observers
- Cover all possible **component** behaviours
- Avoid having a '**waste basket**' category where observers have to score too many behaviours in this category because they don't belong anywhere else
- Are **mutually exclusive**, so observers are not confused by knowing where to score a behaviour.

Coding system – A system of symbols or abbreviations is developed as a shorthand for each behavioural category.

2. Sampling techniques

In many situations, there is too much going on to record everything that is happening during an observation. Therefore, a sampling system is needed:

- **Event sampling** – A list of behaviours is drawn up and a record is made every time they occur. This method is useful when the target behaviours occur sporadically, and might be missed using time sampling.
- **Time sampling** – Observations are made at regular intervals, such as once every minute. This method is suitable when behaviours-to-be-recorded are frequent and, therefore, a time sample will be representative.
- **Point sampling** – Observations are made of one individual for a fixed period of time, such as five minutes, and then the next individual is observed.

> When we observe a person's behaviour, it is a seamless stream of activity. The difficulty for observational research is breaking this stream into chunks that can be recorded. To do this, observers need ways to categorise behaviour and need sampling techniques.

> An example of the behavioural categories that might be used when observing children in a dining hall:
> - Eats silently
> - Talks to neighbour
> - Talks to supervisor
> - Shouts to someone
> - Walks to/from table
> - Other.

Progress check

1 List some behavioural categories that might be used for an observational study at a bus stop.
2 In an observational study, an observer notes what is going on every 10 seconds. What method of sampling is this?

2 Time sampling.

1 E.g. Person on own; Person with one friend chatting; Person in a group.

Designing questionnaires and interviews

AQA A ▸ U1
AQA B ▸ U1

Leading questions are questions that influence or prompt the respondent to give a particular answer.

Open questions produce **qualitative data** and closed questions produce **quantitative data** (i.e. data that can be counted).

1. Good questions

- Avoid complex, ambiguous, negative, emotive, and/or **leading questions** (see page 35, where leading questions are discussed in relation to eyewitness testimony and the study by Loftus and Palmer.)
- **Open questions** can have an infinite variety of answers (e.g. 'How do you reduce stress?') and are best for maximum information.
- **Closed questions** have a limited range of answers, e.g. providing a list of stress reduction techniques from which participants have to choose their answer. This makes it easy to analyse the responses, but limits the answers that respondents can give. This means participants may not be able to fully express themselves.
- **Forced choice** questions (e.g. 'Do you smoke to reduce stress?' Yes/No) may bias the results because participants can't give their real answer.
- 'Don't know' categories may get overused.

2. Structured interviews/questionnaires

- Develop **sub-topics** to investigate. A 'top down' approach should be used in generating questions: start with broad questions and break each one down into a number of different specific behaviours.
- It may help to include some irrelevant questions – **filler questions** – to mislead the respondents from the main purpose of the survey.
- When thinking about the **question sequence**, it is best to start with easy questions, saving difficult questions, or ones that raise emotional defences, until the respondent has relaxed. Also, respondents may resist answering 'yes' or 'no' too many times in a row.
- Write **standardised instructions**, and debriefing notes.
- The questionnaire should now be given a **pilot run**. Test it on a small sample (their feedback will be useful). Redraft the questionnaire, removing or rewriting questions that were confusing to respondents or tended to elicit unhelpful responses (e.g. where all respondents said 'other').
- Decide on a **sampling technique** (see page 84).

Progress check

1. What is meant by a 'closed question'?
2. Which type of question produces qualitative data?
3. Name **one** sampling technique that might be used when collecting data with a questionnaire, and explain why it would be suitable.

1 A question that has a limited range of possible answers.
2 Open questions.
3 E.g. Volunteer sampling because you'd get respondents who would be willing to spend time filling in the questionnaire; A stratified sample because then you would get people from a range of different strata to increase the representativeness of the sample.

Validity and reliability

Internal validity concerns what goes on *inside* a study. External validity is about drawing conclusions from the study and making generalisations about everyday life, i.e. *outside* the study.

Some students think that validity means that a researcher finds out what they expected to find – this is not validity.

Lab experiments have high internal validity because maximum control is possible.

A study that is low in internal validity produces meaningless results and this affects external validity because the results cannot be generalised.

Validity

Validity is the extent to which something is legitimate, real and/or true. Validity can be internal or external:

1. Internal validity

Internal validity describes the extent to which a test or research study measures what it intended to measure.

Research studies – Internal validity is the extent to which all extraneous variables have been controlled and the extent that we can be certain that any changes in the DV were due to manipulation of the IV (rather than any extraneous variable). The more controlled an experiment is, the higher the internal validity.

Other factors that affect internal validity include:

- **Experimental realism** – This refers to when a participant does not believe in the experimental setup and they may simply play-act, so the results are meaningless. The higher the experimental realism, the more a participant is involved with the task as if it was a real event.
- **Mundane realism** – This refers to things that are similar to everyday activities. For example, memorising a list of nonsense words lacks mundane realism, whereas a list of French verbs to be learned is higher in mundane realism.

Psychological tests – Is the test 'true'? For example, we might question whether a test of anxiety actually measures anxiety. It might measure phobias rather than anxiety.

Internal validity can be assessed using:

- **Face validity** – The items look like they measure what the test says it measures. For example, on a creativity test, do the items look like they are measuring creativity?
- **Criterion validity** – Do people who do well on the test do well on other things that you would expect to be associated? For example, does someone who performs well on an intelligence test also do well at school?
- **Predictive validity** – Do people who perform well on a test go on to be good at the things you would predict them to be good at? For example, performing well on an intelligence test in primary school should predict the students who go on to get a good degree at university.

Ecological validity is sometimes used to refer to both internal and external validity. Strictly speaking it is a form of external validity. However, you can't have external validity without internal validity. So, they are all part of the same thing.

The more you control an experiment (high internal validity), the less external/ecological validity it may have, because greater control reduces realism.

2. External (ecological) validity

External validity describes the extent to which the findings from a study can be generalised to everyday life ('real life') and situations other than the context of the study.

- **Ecological validity** – Describes the extent to which the findings of a study can be generalised from the setting (ecology) in which it was conducted, to other settings.
- **Population validity** – A study may use a restricted group of participants, such as university students. This limits how much the findings can be generalised because university students are likely to have unique characteristics (e.g. high intelligence).

Reliability

Reliability is the extent to which something is consistent or stable.

A reliable measurement produces the same findings under the same circumstances.

1. Internal reliability

Internal reliability describes the extent to which a measure is consistent within itself. It can be demonstrated or checked using:

A test that lacks reliability will also lack validity because, without consistency, the results are meaningless.

- **Split-half method** – The test is randomly divided into two so that each half is equivalent. Internal reliability is demonstrated if participants' scores are similar on both halves (i.e. high positive correlation between scores from both halves).
- **Item analysis** – Performance on each item is compared with the overall score. A good positive correlation suggests high internal reliability.

2. External reliability

External reliability describes the extent to which a measure varies from one use to another. It can be demonstrated or checked using:

- **Test–re-test** – The same person is tested twice over a period of time. Similar scores demonstrate high external reliability.
- **Inter-observer reliability** – The ratings from more than one person are correlated to check for agreement. If correlation is low, it may be due to poorly designed behavioural categories (i.e. observers don't know which categories to use), or poorly trained observers.
- **Inter-interviewer reliability** – Different interviewers should produce the same result when interviewing the same person, or the same interviewer should produce the same result when interviewing the same person on two different occasions. If the results are not the same, it suggests that the interviewers are behaving differently and may need more careful training.
- **Replication** – Any research study should produce similar findings if repeated.

Progress check

1. What is the difference between internal and external validity?
2. Name **two** methods of assessing validity.
3. Name **two** methods of assessing reliability.
4. How could you improve low inter-observer reliability?

1. Internal validity concerns what is happening inside the experiment (e.g. control, realism). External validity concerns generalisation.
2. E.g. Face; Criterion; Predictive.
3. E.g. Split-half technique; Item analysis; Test–re-test; Inter-observer reliability; Inter-interviewer reliability; Replication.
4. E.g. Refine the behavioural categories; Train observers more carefully.

Ethical issues and dealing with them

Any group of professionals must have a set of rules they can use to 'police' themselves. The BPS has a set of ethical principles for human and non-human animal research, as well as for clinical practice. The same is true in other countries (e.g. the American Psychological Association – APA). There are also Home Office regulations for the use of non-human animals in research.

An **ethical issue** is a conflict between the rights of participants and the needs of researchers in designing valid research.

An **ethical guideline** is one of the methods used to resolve ethical issues. Some ethical issues are the same as ethical guidelines.

Consider this: Milgram's participants (see page 125) were deceived about the true purpose of the study but they were not deceived about what they would be required to do, i.e. deliver shocks to a 'learner'. So, they were able to provide a reasonable degree of informed consent.

There is no conflict about whether or not participants should be debriefed, therefore, debriefing is usually not considered to be an ethical issue. It is a means of dealing with ethical issues.

The British Psychological Society (BPS) principles for conducting research with human participants list key ethical issues and also provide guidelines for how these issues should be dealt with. Some of the key points are described below.

1. Introduction

Good psychological research is possible only if there is mutual respect and confidence between investigators and participants.

2. General

All investigations should be considered from the standpoint of all participants. The best judges of whether an investigation will cause offence may be members of the population from which the participants in the research are drawn.

3. Informed consent

Whenever possible, participants should be informed of the objectives of the investigation and about all other aspects of the research which might reasonably be expected to influence their willingness to participate.

Therefore, informed consent can be obtained even when the true aims of a study are not revealed. Participants should also be informed of other rights, e.g. to confidentiality, to leave the study, and to withhold their data.

Informed consent may not be possible when:

- **Deception is involved.**
- **Participants are unable to fully understand,** such as children or participants who have impairments that limit understanding. (An alternative is to seek the informed consent of, for example, a parent or relative.)
- **Field experiments or observational studies** are used, when participants are not even aware that they are taking part in psychological research. For example, the research by Hofling *et al.* (see page 126).

4. Deception

Intentional deception of the participants over the purpose and general nature of the investigation should be avoided wherever possible. Deception is unacceptable if participants are likely to object or show unease once debriefed.

Participants should never be deliberately misled without extremely strong scientific or medical justification.

Remember:

- **Deception is sometimes relatively harmless,** as in some memory experiments. For example, Mandler (see page 33) did not inform participants that their memories would be tested. Christiansen (1988) reported that participants do not object to deception as long as it is not extreme.
- **Deception is sometimes necessary.** For example, in Asch's study (page 122) knowledge about the purpose of the research would have made the study pointless.

5. Debriefing

The investigator should provide the participants with any necessary information to complete their understanding of the nature of the research.

The investigator should also discuss the participants' experience in order to monitor any unforeseen negative effects or misconceptions.

Part of obtaining informed consent is to advise participants of their right to withdraw.

In some studies it may be possible to identify participants even when their names have been withheld, for example, in a case study or a study of a unique group of individuals.

In many studies it has been claimed that participants experienced distress. For example, Baumrind (1964) criticised Milgram for the stress and emotional conflict experienced by participants. Milgram believed that the distress was not sufficient to stop the experiment.

Watson and Raynor (see page 162) argued that the anxiety experienced by Little Albert was no more than in real life and, thus, was acceptable. Genie's mother (see page 61) objected to the extensive testing her daughter was subjected to, saying that it caused her undue distress. This was upheld by a court and she was awarded damages.

Ethical guidelines suggest that there are some universal 'truths' yet the guidelines vary in different countries and with respect to changing social attitudes. For example, the French code concentrates on fundamental rights rather than guidelines on conducting research. The American code includes examples of how individual psychologists have resolved ethical dilemmas. Concrete examples may make it easier for psychologists to resolve their own ethical dilemmas.

6. Withdrawal from the investigation

Participants should be made aware from the outset, that they have the right to withdraw from the research at any time, irrespective of whether or not payment or other inducement has been offered.

Participants also have the right to withdraw any consent retrospectively, and to demand that their own data be destroyed.

7. Confidentiality

Participants should be aware of the requirements of legislation: information obtained about a participant during an investigation is confidential unless otherwise agreed in advance. If confidentiality cannot be guaranteed, participants must be advised of this.

8. Protection of participants

Investigators have a primary responsibility to protect participants from physical and mental harm. Normally, the risk must be no greater than encountered in their normal lifestyles.

Mental (psychological) harm includes anxiety and distress. Participants should leave a study in a similar state to when they began the study.

9. Observational research

Studies based upon observation must respect the privacy and psychological well-being of the individuals studied. Unless those being observed give their consent to being observed, observational research is only acceptable in situations where those observed would expect to be observed by strangers.

10. Giving advice

During research, an investigator may obtain evidence of psychological or physical problems. The participant should be informed and an appropriate source of professional help advised.

11. Colleagues

A psychologist who believes that another psychologist may be infringing ethical guidelines should encourage the investigator to re-evaluate the research.

Dealing with ethical issues

1. Ethical guidelines

The BPS principles for conducting research outline ethical issues and also give guidelines for conducting research.

For example, they identify consent as an issue (participants should be informed of the key details of an investigation). This should be dealt with by providing information that might reasonably be expected to influence participants' willingness to participate.

How effective and useful are such guidelines? If a researcher does not follow the guidelines, the severest penalty is disbarment from the professional organisation, which is not the same as imprisonment, but is serious nonetheless.

2. Debriefing

One of the guidelines concerns debriefing as an important aspect of ethical behaviour.

One of the difficulties with debriefing is that it doesn't turn the clock back. For example, in Milgram's study, the participants were debriefed but they may have still felt distressed by what they did.

Baumrind (1975) pointed out that cost-benefit analyses inevitably lead to moral dilemmas, yet the function of ethical guidelines is precisely to avoid such dilemmas.

3. Cost-benefit analysis

Inevitably, ethical decisions involve weighing costs (e.g. harm to participants, infringement of rights, financial considerations) against benefits (e.g. what the research can tell us about behaviour). Diener and Crandall (1978) have identified the following problems with this:

- It is **difficult to predict** costs and benefits prior to conducting a study. In Milgram's study there was no expectation that participants would continue and, therefore, the potential stress (costs) was not anticipated. Also, the ultimate findings (benefits) were not anticipated.
- **It is hard to quantify** costs and benefits, even after a study, because such judgements inevitably require subjective judgements (what one person regards as harm differs from another's view), and the participant and researcher will have different viewpoints.
- Cost-benefit analyses tend to **ignore the rights of individuals** in favour of practical considerations because one is focusing on issues of, for example, benefits to human kind.

4. Ethical committees

When a researcher wishes to conduct a study, he/she must first present a proposal for the study to an ethical committee for approval. The committee may consist of both psychologists and non-psychologists.

The committee considers ethical issues and existing guidelines, and weighs up the costs and benefits of the research before deciding whether to approve any particular study.

5. Alternative methods

- **Presumptive consent** – Seeking approval from the general public prior to an experiment, as Milgram did (see page 125). If others approve, then it is presumed that the actual participants would have also agreed.
- **Role play or questionnaires** – Participants are asked to behave as if they were in a certain situation (role play) or to state how they would behave in certain situations (questionnaires). However, this is likely to be unreliable. Consider the findings from Milgram's prior survey (people said they wouldn't obey), and the evidence that attitudes and behaviour (see page 142) are not the same. Consider also Zimbardo's study (page 123) which used role play and yet participants experienced severe stress.

Progress check

1 What do the letters BPS stand for?
2 When is deception acceptable?
3 Suggest **one** drawback to using the cost-benefit analysis.
4 What is presumptive consent?

4 Seeking approval from the general public prior to an experiment.

3 E.g. Impossible to predict, or to quantify.

2 If participants are not likely to object or show unease once they are debriefed.

1 British Psychological Society.

4.3 Data analysis and presentation

After studying this section you should be able to:

Sometimes people talk about 'qualitative research' or 'quantitative research'. The terms quantitative and qualitative actually refer to the data, not the research method.

- *distinguish between quantitative and qualitative data, and describe the strengths and limitations of each*
- *describe, interpret and present quantitative data, including graphs (bar charts, histograms, scattergrams/scattergraphs) and tables, measures of central tendency (mean, median and mode) and measures of dispersion (range and standard deviation)*
- *describe, interpret and present correlational data, including positive, negative and zero correlations and correlation coefficients*
- *presentation of qualitative data*
- *describe processes involved in content analysis.*

Quantitative data

AQA A ▶ U1
AQA B ▶ U1

Quantitative data is concerned with 'how much', whereas qualitative data provides non-numerical information ('what something is like').

Both interviews and observational studies can produce either kind of data. Even an experimental study (such as Milgram's) can generate qualitative data from post-experimental interviews.

In the exam you may be asked to interpret data in a table or graph, or to sketch your own table/graph.

Variables can be measured at different levels of detail (called 'levels of measurement'). Each level expresses more information about what we are measuring:
Nominal – Data is in categories.
Ordinal – Data is ordered in some way.
Interval – Data is measured using units of equal intervals.
Ratio – There is a true zero point.

Quantitative data concerns quantities of things – data that can be counted.

- **Strengths** – easy to analyse and, therefore, easier to produce simple conclusions.
- **Limitations** – may oversimplify human behaviour by reducing complex feelings, thoughts, etc. to numbers; may actually distort reality by forcing people to make choices, e.g. in a questionnaire.

Quantitative data can be displayed using **descriptive statistics** – methods of **describing** the data so that the meaning of the data becomes more apparent. For example, by looking at a bar chart or the median of a set of numbers you can see at a glance the meaning of the data.

Graphs and tables

- **Table** – Numerical data is arranged in columns and rows.
- **Bar chart** – Visual display of *frequency*, the highest bar is the mode. The data on the x-axis can be categories (nominal), i.e. not continuous, as well as ordinal, interval and ratio (i.e. continuous). The y-axis represents frequency.
- **Pie chart** – Frequency is translated into degrees of a circle.
- **Histogram** – Differs from a bar chart in that the area of the bars must be proportional to the frequencies represented, and the x-axis must contain continuous data. Not suitable for nominal data.
- **Curved lines** – A sketch of an approximate line may be the best way to represent the data, rather than using a jagged line graph.
- **Scattergram (or scattergraph)** – Used to plot correlational data (see page 93). Each pair of values is plotted against each other so you get a scatter of dots (each dot represents one pair of values). The dots show if a consistent trend is present. The correlation may be positive (trend from bottom left to top right), negative (trend from top left to bottom right) or none (evenly spread).

Measures of central tendency

'Central tendency' refers to ways of giving the most typical or central value.

- **Mean** – Add up all the values and divide by N. Its advantage is that it is a sensitive measure because it takes all the values of the numbers into account. However, it can be misleading with extreme values, requires calculation, and cannot be used with nominal data.

- **Median** – The middle or central value in an ordered list. All the numbers need to be arranged in order so you can identify the middle number. The median is not affected by extreme scores. However, it is not very sensitive because not all the scores are used in the calculation, and it cannot be used with nominal data.
- **Mode** – The modal group is the most common group of scores, identified by arranging all the numbers in order. **Bimodal** means having two modes. This is the only measure appropriate for nominal data. However, it is not useful in data with more than one mode.

Measures of dispersion

'Dispersion' refers to the spread of the data.

- **Range** – The difference between the lowest and highest values. The range is quick to calculate. However, it is affected by extreme values.
- **Standard deviation** – An indication of the spread of the data around the mean. It is calculated by working out the difference between each value and the mean, and then the mean of these differences is worked out. This is the most accurate measure because it takes the distance between all the values into account. However, it requires calculation.

Age and height are positively correlated, whereas age and number of brain cells are negatively correlated. You can also have a curvilinear relationship such as the Yerkes–Dodson effect (see page 36). This is still a correlation but the data would not produce a significant correlation coefficient.

Correlational data

The scattergrams below show various kinds of correlation.

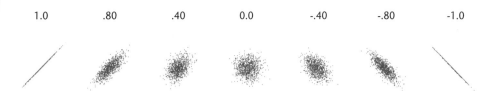

The numbers above each scattergram are called the **correlation coefficient** – the numerical value that represents the closeness of correlation.

- +1.0 is a perfect **positive correlation** – both values increase together.
- -1.0 is a perfect **negative correlation** – as one value increases the other decreases.
- +.80 and -.80 are strong positive and strong negative correlations respectively.
- +.40 and -.40 are weak positive and weak negative correlations respectively.

In an exam you may be asked to comment on the strength of correlation shown by data in a scattergram. Use the correlation coefficient to guide your answer but don't forget to mention whether it is a positive or negative correlation.

Progress check

1 Which measure of central tendency would be suitable for nominal data?
2 Which measure of central tendency uses all the data?
3 Which measure of dispersion is easiest to calculate?
4 What kind of correlation would have a correlation coefficient of +.75?

4 Strong positive correlation.
3 The range.
2 Mean, median and mode use all the data – but only the mean uses all the values.
1 The mode.

Qualitative data

AQA A ▶ U1
AQA B ▶ U1

People often say that the difference between qualitative and quantitative data is that qualitative data concerns what people think and feel. But, quantitative data can do this too. It is the depth of understanding and the openness that is crucial.

A common criticism of qualitative analysis is that it tends to be subjective. However, when the same data is analysed qualitatively by various people it becomes more objective.

Qualitative data expresses the experiences of participants and the meanings they attach to their data. It is concerned with how things are expressed, what a behaviour feels like and what it means, i.e. the quality.

- **Strengths** – It represents the true complexities of human behaviour, and gains access to what people think and feel in a way that is not possible with quantitative methods. It gives people free range to express themselves and, therefore, may uncover new information.
- **Limitations** – It is more difficult to detect patterns and draw conclusions, and subjective analysis may lead to biased data.

Foster and Parker (1995) suggested the following possibilities for presenting qualitative data:

- **'Giving voice'** – Represent and/or summarise what the interviewee has said using selective quotations to represent an entire interview.
- **Grounded theory** – Use the data to develop theoretical accounts. The theoretical account is 'grounded' in the data. It is 'theoretical' in the sense that it is an attempt to produce a coherent account of the facts. The researcher might identify certain themes that recur, or categorise types of behaviour.
- **Thematic analysis** – Organise the interview material in relation to certain research questions or themes that were identified before the research started. This differs from 'grounded theory' in that the themes arise prior to the research. Grounded theory comes out of the interview text.
- **Discourse analysis** – This aims to reveal how the text is organised by a number of competing themes or discourses.

Content analysis

Content analysis is a form of indirect observation – data that already exists is analysed, e.g. from a newspaper, magazine, book, photograph, interview transcript, etc.

Quantitative or qualitative data may be analysed by producing categories and then counting occurrences within a category (quantitative) or giving examples within each category (qualitative). For example:

- **Quantitative** – Television advertisements could be analysed to investigate gender stereotypes. Categories would be identified (e.g. product types used by male or female characters) and then instances would be counted.
- **Qualitative** – Interviews could be analysed to investigate issues of central concern to adolescents. Categories would be identified (e.g. parental disagreements, peer relationships), and appropriate quotes would be provided for each category from the interviews.

Progress check

1 Identify **one** difference between quantitative and qualitative data.
2 Whose voice is used in 'giving voice'?

2 Participant's voice.
1 E.g. Ease of analysis; Richness of data.

Sample question and student answers – AQA A and AQA B question

1 A group of psychology students decided to conduct a study to see whether there were gender differences in memory.

They decided to look at short-term memory and test it by giving participants 20 words to remember. They also decided that it would be better to match the participants on certain key variables.

	Mean score	*Standard deviation*
Boys	13.5	3.7
Girls	12.8	6.2

(a) Write a suitable directional hypothesis for this study. *(2 marks)*

Boys have better memories than girls.

1. (a) Hypothesis is not fully operationalised but it is directional. **1 out of 2 marks.**

(b) What would you conclude from the findings in the table above? *(3 marks)*

It looks like boys do have better memories than girls. However, the difference is rather small, therefore, I think you would conclude that their memories are pretty much the same. The standard deviations are quite different, which suggests a greater variability in the girls.

(b) A very thorough answer, which has presented conclusions instead of just describing the results (boys remembered more than girls). Results are facts; conclusions are generalisations. **3 out of 3 marks.**

(c) Describe what words might be suitable to use as the stimulus material. *(2 marks)*

You could use nouns such as table and chair.

(c) Although the answer is a bit brief, it would still get 2 marks. **2 out of 2 marks.**

(d) The boy–girl pairs were matched in this study. Name **two** variables that might be used to match the participants. *(2 marks)*

Match on IQ (from an IQ test) and also on age.

(d) Appropriate criteria for matching. **2 out of 2 marks.**

(e) Give **one** advantage of using a matched pairs design in this study. *(2 marks)*

It helps to exclude participant variables, such as age or IQ.

(e) A correct answer but not really enough context (question says 'in this study'). **1 out of 2 marks.**

(f) Identify an appropriate sampling method that could be used in this study and give **one** advantage of using this method. *(3 marks)*

You could use opportunity sampling. An advantage of this would be that it is easy.

(f) One mark for identifying an appropriate sampling method but no marks for saying it is easy. Why is it easy? **1 out of 3 marks.**

(g) (i) Explain what is meant by the term 'validity'. *(2 marks)*

Validity means you are testing what you intended to test.

(ii) Explain **one** possible threat to the validity of this study. *(2 marks)*

One threat to the validity of this study would be that there might be an extraneous variable such as some people being more intelligent – the boys might have been more intelligent.

(g) Perfect definition for (i) and good answer for (ii) which has been clearly explained. **4 out of 4 marks.**

Sample question and student answers – AQA A and AQA B question

2 After conducting the experiment, the students thought it might be interesting to do a further study on memory and age because it seemed that the young people they tested had better memories than the older people. Their results are shown in the graph below. The correlation coefficient was -.70

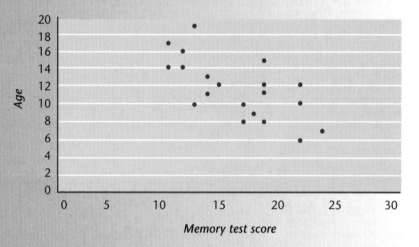

Memory test score

(a) Either scattergram or scattergraph is correct. **1 out of 1 mark.**

(a) What kind of graph is shown above? *(1 mark)*

It is a scattergraph.

(b) Credit for 'strong' and 'negative' but for full marks the student should have described the relationship between age and memory, i.e. as age increases memory score decreases. **2 out of 3 marks.**

(b) Describe what the students found out about the relationship between age and memory. *(3 marks)*

They found a strong negative correlation.

(c) An appropriate ethical issue has been identified and the 'how' fully explained – many students cannot think of what to write when asked how they would do it. **3 out of 3 marks.**

(c) Name **one** ethical issue that the students should have dealt with and describe how they would have dealt with it.

They should have obtained informed consent from the participants. They could have done this by explaining the purpose of the study and including any information that would affect the participants' decision to take part, and then asking them to agree.

(d) Appropriate and detailed answer for (i) but not enough for 3 marks (always let the number of marks guide the length of your answer). The answer for (ii) is also not sufficiently detailed. **3 out of 5 marks.**

(d) (i) The data in this study are quantitative. Give an example of some qualitative data that the students might collect related to age and memory. *(3 marks)*

They might interview some of the participants afterwards and ask them to comment on their memories. They might interview some older and some younger people.

(ii) Explain **one** advantage of collecting quantitative data. *(2 marks)*

An advantage of using quantitative data is that it is easy to analyse.

(e) The student has described the test–re-test method though there is no need to name it; the method is well described. **2 out of 2 marks.**

(e) The students wondered how reliable their memory test was. Describe **one** method they could use to check the reliability of the test. *(2 marks)*

They could do this by giving the test to a group of people and then giving them the same test a few weeks later. If the test is reliable they should get fairly similar scores.

Practice examination questions – AQA A and AQA B questions

1   A psychologist intends to conduct a naturalistic observation of people's behaviour in a fast food restaurant, focusing on what people do when they are sitting down at a table and eating their meals.

The psychologist wishes to focus on the interactions between people and intends to look only at the behaviour of dyads – groups where there are only two people. She intends to record her observations using behavioural categories that will produce quantitative data.

(a)   Describe the aims of this study.   *(2 marks)*

(b)   Explain the difference between a naturalistic observation and a field experiment.   *(2 marks)*

(c)   Describe **two** behavioural categories that might have been used to record the data.   *(2 marks)*

(d)   Sketch a graph, with appropriate labels, for displaying the findings from this study.   *(3 marks)*

(e)   Explain **two** factors that might have affected the validity of this study.
                                                     (2 marks + 2 marks)

2   Previous research has found that teenagers are more conformist that older people.

A study is conducted to investigate this relationship between age and conformity using a questionnaire. For each participant, a score will be calculated expressing his or her conformity rating. This will be established by asking them questions about situations where they might or might not conform. The mean score will be calculated for people under 20 and people over 20.

(a)   Explain why it might have been a good idea to use a pilot study.   *(2 marks)*

(b)   Identify a suitable sampling method that might have been used and give **one** advantage of using this method in the study.   *(3 marks)*

(c)   Give an example of **one** closed question that could have been used in the questionnaire and explain why it is a closed question.   *(2 marks)*

(d)   Explain why it might be better to interview the participants instead of using a questionnaire.   *(2 marks)*

(e)   The mean is a measure of central tendency. Name **two** other measures of central tendency.   *(2 marks)*

(f)   Name **one** measure that the psychologist could use to find out about the spread of scores in each group and give **one** weakness of using this method.   *(3 marks)*

Biological psychology

5.1 Stress

After studying this section you should be able to:

- describe the body's response to stress, including the pituitary-adrenal system and the sympathomedullary pathway in outline
- describe and evaluate stress-related illness and the immune system.

The body's response to stress

AQA A   U2
AQA B   A2 (U3)

Stress is a state of psychological tension and physiological arousal produced by a stressor, which makes the individual ready to respond. It is an *adaptive response* – important for survival when dealing with emergency situations.

A **stressor** is a physical or psychological stimulus that threatens an individual's psychological and/or physiological well-being.

There are two major responses to stress: one for dealing with immediate or **acute stress**, and the other for long-term or .**chronic stress**.

Acute stress: The sympathomedullary pathway

1 **Sympathetic nervous system** – Perception of a stressor leads to activation of the sympathetic branch of the autonomic nervous system (ANS, see page 111). This is called the **fight or flight response** – the body is ready to fight or flee.

2 The **adrenal medulla** is activated by the sympathetic nervous system (SNS) and releases **adrenaline** and **noradrenaline**. The adrenal medulla lies in the adrenal gland just above the kidneys.

3 **Adrenaline** and **noradrenaline** have the effect of increasing heart rate and blood pressure, and mobilising fat and body sugars, all to prepare the animal for sudden activity. Americans use the terms **epinephrine** and **norepinephrine** for adrenaline and noradrenaline respectively.

Chronic stress: The pituitary-adrenal system

This is also called the **hypothalamic-pituitary-adrenal axis (HPA axis)**. This system responds to prolonged stressors.

1 **The hypothalamus** in the midbrain produces hormones in response to stress, e.g. **corticotrophin-releasing factor (CRF)**, which stimulates the anterior pituitary gland to secrete its hormones.

2 **The pituitary gland** releases **adrenocorticotrophic hormone (ACTH)**, which stimulates the adrenal cortex in the adrenal gland.

3 **The adrenal cortex** secretes at least 20 different hormones, including **cortisol**, which has a variety of effects. Some of these effects are positive (e.g. increased energy and lowered sensitivity to pain), and some are negative (e.g. reduced immune responses).

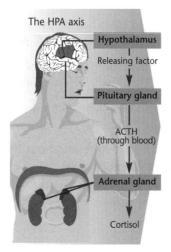

The HPA axis

Hypothalamus
|
Releasing factor
↓
Pituitary gland
↓
ACTH
(through blood)
↓
Adrenal gland
↓
Cortisol

Evaluation

- **People without adrenal glands** (i.e. people who are adrenalectomised) have to be given additional quantities of glucocorticoids in order to live (Tyrell and Baxter, 1981). This shows that the ANS stress response is vital for survival.
- Most of the evidence is based on **research with male participants**. The 'fight or flight' response may be more typical of males than females, who produce a 'tend and befriend' response to stress (Taylor *et al.*, 2000). This gender difference may be adaptive because survival would be enhanced if males fought off an attack whilst females protected their young.

Stress and the immune response

AQA A ▶ U2
AQA B ▶ A2 (U3)

The immune system protects us from disease.

The main components are **antibodies** and **white blood cells (leucocytes)**. There are different kinds of leucocytes including T-cells, B-cells and natural killer cells. They fight viruses and tumours. The presence of adrenaline and cortisol (produced when stressed) reduces the production of these components.

Research evidence

AIDS has an immunosuppressive effect because the HIV virus attacks T-cells. AIDS does not kill in itself, but it prevents the body from protecting itself against other viruses and tumours.

- **Lymphocyte activity and tumours** – Riley (1981) created stress in mice by placing them on a turntable rotating at 45rpm. After five hours, their lymphocyte count was reduced.
  In another study, cancer cells were implanted in mice. The mice that were given 10 minutes of rotation per hour for three days (high stress condition) developed large tumours, whereas the mice that were not exposed to stress did not develop any tumour growth.
- **T-cell activity** – Kiecolt-Glaser *et al.* (1984) conducted a natural experiment with medical students. The researchers took a blood sample from each student one month before the students' final examinations, and again during their exams. The samples were tested for T-cell activity. The students were also given questionnaires on psychiatric symptoms, loneliness and life events. T-cell activity was significantly lower on the second occasion, when the students were presumably most stressed. It was particularly low for students who reported feeling most lonely, and those experiencing other stressful life events and psychiatric symptoms, such as depression or anxiety. This shows that stress lowers immune system activity, especially where social support is lacking.

Remember that 'acute' is immediate stress, whereas 'chronic' is long-term.

- **Chronic stress** – Kiecolt-Glaser *et al.* (1987) analysed blood samples from married, separated and divorced women. Happily married women had better immune functioning than those who were dissatisfied. Separated and divorced women, who found their separation/divorce hard to bear, also had weaker immune functions.
  However, these findings may be unsound because of so many potentially confounding factors, such as money, diet, etc.
- Stress may sometimes **enhance immune system activity** – Evans *et al.* (1994) measured immune responses in students who either had to give a public speech (acute stress) or were taking exams (chronic stress). They measured the activity of the SIgA antibody, which is found in saliva and is an important protection against infection. They found that SIgA levels increased with acute stress, and decreased with chronic stress.

Evaluation

- The functioning of the immune system in most stressed individuals is **actually within the normal range**, therefore, it is not clear why stress might have such big effects.
- The straightforward physiological account does not explain how the stress response **varies depending on the type of stressor and individual differences**. Mason (1975) found that levels of adrenaline and noradrenaline secretion varied in different individuals when exposed to situations of fear, anger or uncertainty.

Stress-related illness

AQA A ▶ U2

Stress has been linked with a range of physical and psychological illnesses.

- **The common cold** – Cohen *et al.* (1991) exposed participants to the cold virus. Those who had highest stress levels (as measured in life-change units, see page 101) and felt most 'out of control' were twice as likely to become ill as those with lower levels of stress.
- **Hypertension** (high blood pressure) is diagnosed when a person has experienced raised blood pressure for at least several weeks. It is a major risk factor for coronary heart disease. Cobb and Rose (1973) found that hypertension rates were several times higher in air traffic controllers, and especially in those controllers working in busy airports, than other people working at the airport.
- **Coronary heart disease (CHD)** – Friedman and Rosenman (1959) demonstrated a link between stress and CHD (see page 104).
- **Cancer** – Morris *et al.* (1981) found evidence that cancer is associated with Type C individuals (i.e. people who are industrious, conventional and sociable, but tend to be repressed and react to stress or threat with a sense of helplessness). In this study, women who developed malignant, rather than non-malignant (benign), breast cancer reported that they both experienced and expressed far less anger. Emotional suppression is linked with increased stress, lowered effectiveness of the immune system and illness.
- **Post-traumatic stress disorder (PTSD)** – This psychiatric disorder is linked to the experience of stress, and is observed in a range of situations, from war veterans to rape victims and people living in extreme poverty.

How does stress cause illness?

- **Directly** – by reducing the immune activity and the body's ability to fight disease.
- **Indirectly** – by leading the stressed individual to adopt an unhealthy lifestyle (e.g. increased smoking, drinking, 'comfort'-eating). Cohen and Williamson (1991) found that people who were stressed tended to smoke more, drink more alcohol, take less exercise, and sleep less than people who were not stressed. However, others (e.g. Ogden *et al.*, 1996) suggest that alcohol may reduce stress.

There are various factors that appear to moderate the effects of stress. One of these is social support (see study by Kiecolt-Glaser *et al.*, 1984, on the previous page). Another is having a sense of control (see Cohen *et al.*, 1991, on this page).

All of this research is correlational. There is no evidence that stress has *caused* illness, though this may be true.

Progress check

1 Where is adrenaline produced?
2 What hormone stimulates the stress response in the pituitary gland?
3 What are leucocytes and what do they do?
4 Name **one** factor that moderates the stress response.

4 E.g. Social support; Control.
3 White blood cells that attack invading viruses and tumours.
2 Corticotrophin-release factor (CRF).
1 In the adrenal medulla.

5.2 Stress in everyday life

After studying this section you should be able to:

- *describe and evaluate life changes*
- *describe and evaluate daily hassles*
- *describe and evaluate workplace stress*
- *describe and evaluate personality factors, including Type A behaviour*
- *outline the distinction between emotion-focused and problem-focused approaches to coping with stress*
- *describe and evaluate psychological methods of stress management, including Cognitive Behavioural Therapy*
- *describe and evaluate physiological methods of stress management, including drugs.*

LEARNING SUMMARY

Sources of stress

AQA A ▶ U2

1. Life changes

Two medical doctors, Thomas Holmes and Richard Rahe (1967) observed that patients who were in poor health had often experienced, in the recent past, a variety of **life events** – events that all involved change from a steady state, even when the change was for the better. They suggested that changes absorb 'psychic energy', leaving less energy available for other things, such as physical defence against illness.

Holmes and Rahe developed the Social Readjustment Rating Scale (SRRS) as a means of measuring life change units (LCUs). They constructed the scale by analysing 5,000 patient records and identifying 43 life events that seemed to precede illness. Then they asked people to rate the events in terms of stress. Some examples are shown on the left.

Some example items for the SRRS are shown below.

LCUs are shown in brackets.

Death of spouse (100)
Divorce (73)
Jail term (63)
Personal illness (53)
Marriage (50)
Retirement (45)
Pregnancy (40)
Death of close friend (37)
Child leaves home (29)
Trouble with boss (23)
Holiday (13)
Christmas (12)

Research evidence

- Rahe *et al.* (1970) assessed stress and illness in 2,500 naval personnel. Just before a tour of duty, participants were asked to fill in a questionnaire relating to significant changes in their lives over the past six months, providing an LCU for each of them. During the next six months on board ship, a health record was kept for each participant by the ship's physician. Rahe *et al.* found a significant positive correlation of +.118 between LCUs and illness.
- Rahe and Arthur (1977) found an increase of various psychological illnesses, athletic injuries, physical illnesses and even traffic accidents, when LCUs were raised.
- Jacobs and Charles (1980) investigated a possible link between life events and cancer in children. They asked parents to complete the SRE (an adaptation of the SRRS) in order to assess family stress. Children who developed cancer had families with a higher life-change rating than a control group of children being treated for non-cancerous illnesses.
- DeLongis *et al.* (1988) studied stress in 75 married couples and found no relationship between life events and health. However, they did find a significant positive correlation of +.59 between hassles and next-day health problems such as flu, sore throats, headaches and backaches.

To use the scale, you should circle events that have happened to you in the last 12 months. Your LCU total is an estimate of the amount of life stress you have experienced.

Evaluation of life changes as a source of stress

- The SRRS muddles different kinds of life events, most particularly those that you have some control over and those that you do not. It is these latter events that may be most stressful.

Remember that the results of studies looking at life change units and illness are correlational. It does not mean that stress *causes* illness. It may be that there is an intervening variable or the relationship is spurious. For example, Brown (1974) suggested that people with high levels of anxiety are more likely to report negative life events and are also more prone to illness.

Examples of items on the daily hassles and uplifts scale:

- Time spent with family
- What you look like
- The weather
- Workload
- Drinking
- Smoking
- Pets
- Housework
- Amount of free time
- Social commitments

- The SRRS scale does not allow for the fact that **different people interpret the same event differently** and, therefore, it is not realistic to assign a single number to the experience of stress.
- Studies using the scale have found only a **small correlation** between life events and illness, and some studies have found no correlation.
- The importance of the SRRS scale is not in its **usefulness**, but in its status as a breakthrough. It triggered off a wealth of research and encouraged efforts to develop a more effective tool. For example, Sarason *et al.* (1978) sought to improve on the SRRS by asking participants to indicate to what extent a particular life event was personally desirable or undesirable, and also to indicate the personal impact of the events. This 57-item scale is called the Life Experiences Survey (LES).

2. Daily hassles

DeLongis *et al.* (1982) noted that most people do not often experience major life events, therefore, the strains of everyday life (**daily hassles**) might be a better measure of stress and a better predictor of physical illness. In fact, the same events can be both a hassle and an uplift simultaneously.

So, DeLongis *et al.* developed a 'Hassles and Uplifts Scale' with 53 items (some examples are shown on the left).

Research evidence

- DeLongis *et al.* (1982) studied 100 individuals for a period of one year, monitoring their health, life events, and daily hassles and uplifts. They found a significant negative correlation between hassles and health status (i.e. the more hassles experienced, the lower the health status). There was also a significant negative correlation between hassle intensity and health status, but no significant correlation with uplifts.
- In the 1988 study (see previous page) DeLongis *et al.* found no correlation between uplifts and illness but did find a significant positive correlation of +.59 between hassles and next-day health problems. They also found individual differences in stress responses: people high in self-esteem and social support were not as affected by stress.

Evaluation of daily hassles as a source of stress

- Research suggests that daily **hassles have a more significant effect** on health than life events. For example, Ruffin (1993) found a stronger correlation between illness and daily hassles than negative life events.
- **There isn't a simple causal relationship** between hassles and illness. Since they are usually repeated events, it is a circular model: hassles affect health and health affects the subjective experience of hassles.
- The **chronic sources of stress** should also be considered. These are more general, ongoing life difficulties, such as poor housing, low income, strains of family life, unsatisfying work, etc. Moos and Swindle (1990) produced the LISRES (Life Stressors and Social Resources Inventory). They identified eight areas of ongoing life stressors: health, home, finance, work, partner, child, extended family and friends. The LISRES also includes an assessment of social resources available to the individual, as these moderate the effect of stressors.
- **Individual differences** affect the degree of stress experienced. This explains why correlations between life events, hassles and physical illness are not as high as might be expected.
- **Situational differences** mean that the same hassle can be experienced in different ways on different occasions. For example, a traffic jam may sometimes give you time to relax, whereas at other times it seems highly stressful.

The Work Foundation (2005) claims that:
- about half a million people in the UK experience work-related stress at a level they believe is making them ill
- up to 5 million people feel 'very' or 'extremely' stressed by their work
- work-related stress costs society about £3.7bn every year (at 1995–6 prices).

Remember that a stressor is any physical or psychological stimulus that threatens an individual's psychological and/or physiological well-being.

Whenever you read the description of a study, ask yourself 'What does this show?' It is vital to understand *what was demonstrated* and to communicate this in an exam.

The **galvanic skin response (GSR)** is used to measure stress levels. When the ANS is aroused, the electrical conductivity of the skin is altered. This is measured by attaching electrodes to the skin.

One comment that is made about many psychological experiments is that they only involved American male undergraduates – a population sample that is by no means typical of everyone. On the other hand, Glass's research involved *female* students – different, but still potentially biased. It is possible that women are more sensitive to noise than men.

3. Workplace stress

The pressures of work and the work environment are a major cause of stress. Work problems feature both as major life events and as hassles and uplifts.

Similar stress is experienced by paid workers, volunteers, students and housewives.

Causes of workplace stress include job uncertainty, organisational change, interpersonal conflicts, sexual harassment, punitive management, work overload, under-utilisation of skills, difficult tasks, decision-making, lack of support, and dangerous, unpleasant or uncomfortable work environments.

Effects of workplace stress include absenteeism, high staff turnover, alcohol and drug abuse, and poor performance in terms of quantity and quality.

The costs of work stress are high, both for the employee and the employer.

Research evidence

- **Role conflict** – The demands of the organisation conflict with the needs of the worker, e.g. number of hours worked. Shirom (1989) found that there was a significant correlation between perceived role conflict and cases of coronary heart disease (CHD).
- **Shift work** – Having to adjust your body clock to different sleep patterns results in considerable stress and has been associated with major industrial accidents. Czeisler *et al.* (1982) found that shift work amongst manual workers in an industrial setting in Utah, USA, correlated with raised accident rates, absenteeism and chronic feelings of ill health.
- **Relationships** – Matteson and Ivancevich (1982) found that the most common source of work stress was the inability to get on with other workers.
- **Noise** – Many work environments are very noisy. Glass *et al.* (1969) arranged for participants to complete various cognitive tasks, such as number work and letter searches, whilst listening to noisy tapes. Later, the participants had to complete four puzzles. Two of the puzzles could not be solved. Frustration was measured in terms of the time that participants persisted at these tasks, and stress was measured throughout using galvanic skin response (GSR – see explanation on the left).
Participants did adapt to the noise, as shown by the fact that their GSR levels and number of errors were considerably reduced by the end of the first set of tasks. However, if the noise was intermittent, participants made more errors and later showed less task persistence. This suggests that unpredictable noise has a 'psychic' cost because it requires attention, whereas constant noise can be 'tuned out'.
- **Lack of control** – Glass *et al.* (1969) tried a further variation where some participants were given a button to ostensibly control the noise. These participants showed greater task persistence than those who thought they had no control. Perceived control avoids a sense of helplessness and anxiety, which would increase stress and frustration. Similar results were found by Marmot *et al.* (1997) who followed a sample of over 7,000 UK civil servants over a five-year period. Cardiovascular problems were highest among the lower grade workers, who expressed a weaker sense of job control. This again suggests that low control increases stress.
- **Responsibility** – In contrast with 'lack of control' studies, other research has found that increased responsibility (presumably greater control) is linked to higher stress levels. For example, Margolis and Kroes (1974) found that foremen (who had a lot of responsibility) were seven times more likely to develop gastric ulcers than shop-floor workers (who had little responsibility).

Evaluation of workplace stressors as a source of stress

- There are **individual differences**. Schaubroeck *et al.* (2001) found that some workers are less stressed when they have no control or responsibility. In this study, Schaubroeck *et al.* found that some people had higher immune responses in low-control situations. Some people view negative work outcomes as being their fault. For these employees, control can actually exacerbate the unhealthy effects of stress.

- Such individual differences might explain the **conflicting findings**. For example, in Marmot's study, the higher grade individuals (who had more responsibility) experienced less stress, whereas Johansson *et al.* (1978), in a study of sawyers in a Swedish sawmill, found that stress was highest in those with most responsibility.

- The **research methods used to collect data** may produce biased data. Keenan and Newton (1989) produced some quite different results using interviews instead of questionnaires to collect information. For example, they found that time-wasting job demands were significant job stressors.

- The **consequences** of workplace stress are enormous in terms of costs to the organisation (i.e. days off work). Therefore, workplace stressors are an important area of research.

4. Personality factors

Individual differences are important in understanding the effects of stress. Personality type is a kind of individual difference.

- **Type A and B** – Friedman and Rosenman (1959) looked at people who experienced higher levels of stress, calling them personality Type A (typically impatient, competitive, time-pressured and hostile). Individuals who lack these characteristics and are generally more relaxed were called Type B.
  Friedman and Rosenman assessed 3,154 healthy men aged between 39 and 59, living around San Francisco in 1960.
  Eight and a half years later, (Friedman and Rosenman, 1974) they found that 257 of the total sample had developed CHD. 178 of these men had been assessed as type A (69%), whereas only half as many were Type B.
  Twenty-two years later (Friedman, 1996), 214 men had died from CHD: 119 were Type A and 95 were Type B, a rather less marked difference. One explanation for the less impressive results twenty-two years later is that the men had followed health advice and, therefore, even Type A individuals were experiencing less stress.

- **Type C** – Type C individuals cope with stress by suppressing their emotions, which leads to chronic stress that affects the functioning of the immune system. Type C is associated with increased rates of cancer (see page 100).

- **Type D** (D = distressed) – Type D individuals are generally gloomy, socially inept and worry a lot. Denollet *et al.* (1996) interviewed 300 adults (men and women) who had suffered heart attacks. Ten years later, those who had a tendency to suppress emotions (Type C) and experience negative emotions (Type D) were four times more likely to have had a further heart attack.

The findings about Type A and CHD have been applied to improving health. For example, Friedman *et al.* (1986, the Recurrent Coronary Prevention Project) found that, after five years, those CHD patients who had been taught how to modify their stress response had fewer second heart attacks than those who received counselling or no treatment.

The notion of a hardy personality type has been extended to a form of treatment for stress – hardiness training which is discussed on page 108.

- The **hardy personality type** – Kobasa *et al.* (1982) found that managers of large companies who were psychologically 'hardy' suffered less illness. The characteristics of hardiness are: greater sense of commitment to work and personal relationships; seeing stressful situations as a challenge and an opportunity; and a stronger sense of personal control.

Evaluation

- Some recent research has found that **hostility** may be the key component in the Type A vulnerability to stress (Myrtek, 2001).
- It is not clear whether personality types are a **cause or an effect**, whether they are actually directly related to stress responses (e.g. whether they cause the immune system to underfunction) or whether they are actually indirectly related (e.g. they lead to increased smoking).

Progress check

1 What is an LCU and what does it measure?
2 What scale did DeLongis *et al.* construct?
3 Name **three** workplace stressors.
4 Give **two** characteristics of the Type A personality.

4 E.g. Impatient; Competitive; Time-pressured; Hostile.
3 E.g. Role conflict; Shift work; Relationships; Noise; Control; Responsibility.
2 Hassles and uplifts scale.
1 Life change unit. It measures the amount of stress in terms of change.

Coping with stress

Lazarus and Folkman (1984) used their **Ways of Coping Scale** to identify the two different styles of coping – emotion-focused and problem-focused.

The idea of *coping* with stress is similar to *managing it* (see stress management techniques on pages 107–110). They both mean the same thing – aiming to deal with a situation effectively. However, there is an implication that *methods of stress management* are more formal approaches, whereas *coping with stress* suggests an *ad hoc* strategy developed by the individual.

Men tend to prefer problem-focused coping, whereas women prefer emotion-focused coping (Brody and Hall, 1993), possibly because they are socialised to use such approaches.

Emotion-focused and problem-focused approaches

1. Emotion focus

Some methods of coping with stress focus on reducing the emotion associated with stress.

These methods tend to be **physiological** methods, such as relaxation, drugs or biofeedback (see page 109), but also include more casual activities, such as watching television (relaxing and distracting), drinking and socialising.

Emotion focus:
- Is useful when the situation itself cannot be changed.
- Often requires less effort, for example, taking a drug to reduce anxiety.
- Can be re-applied in different settings, for example, relaxation techniques may help in future stress situations.
- Does not usually provide long-term solutions for a particular problem because only the symptoms are dealt with, rather than the problem itself.
- May have a negative effect because it delays an individual actually dealing with a problem, such as being stressed because of work difficulties.

2. Problem focus

Other methods focus on coping with the *problem* itself, rather than just dealing with the symptoms of the stress.

A person can try to find some way of changing it or avoiding it in the future, or he/she may learn **psychological** stress management techniques (see pages 107–108). Less formal techniques include taking control and thinking through different options.

Problem focus:
- Provides long-term solutions because the problem changes.
- Means that psychological stress management techniques can be re-applied in new situations.
- May not be appropriate in some situations, for example, when the problem cannot be changed or when it is a short-term problem that will alter in time.
- May not work for everyone: people with low self-esteem tend to avoid problem-focused coping (Mullis and Chapman, 2000).

Evaluation
- Different techniques are **appropriate for particular problems**, for example, emotion focus is appropriate for a situation that cannot be changed.
- Different techniques **suit different people**. Some people prefer problem-focus.
- It is **difficult to assess coping styles** because answers to questionnaires on coping style are related to the kind of problem presented.
- Endler and Parker (1990) developed a different scale for measuring coping styles – the **Multidimensional Coping Inventory**. They found a third coping style – **avoidance-oriented**. This involves denying or minimising the seriousness of the situation, similar to Freud's ego-defence mechanisms (see page 19), but at a more conscious level.

Psychological techniques focus on thoughts and feelings, whereas physiological techniques involve the body.

The term 'cognitive' refers to mental activity, so cognitive therapies are those techniques concerned with thinking. (These are discussed further on pages 154 and 159.)

Psychological methods of stress management

The psychological approach to stress reduction involves the use of techniques that help the person to cope with the situation itself, rather than dealing with the symptoms of their stress. (Physiological methods of stress management deal with symptoms).

1. Stress inoculation therapy (SIT)

Meichenbaum (1985) proposed a form of therapy to protect an individual ('inoculate' them) before dealing with stress, rather than coping with it afterwards.

This is a form of cognitive therapy because it aims to change the way the individual *thinks* about their problem (and thus change the experience of stress), rather than changing the problem itself.

There are three main phases of the therapy:

1 **Conceptualisation phase** – The therapist and client discuss potential problem areas in order for the client to reconceptualise their problem.

2 **Skills acquisition phase (and rehearsal)** – Stress-reduction techniques are taught based on a variety of skills, for example, relaxation, positive thinking, social skills and using self-coping statements (e.g. 'Stop worrying because it's pointless' and 'One step at a time').

3 **Application and follow-through** – The client practises stress-reduction techniques in role-play, and then uses them in real-life situations.

Research evidence

Meichenbaum (1977) compared stress inoculation with systematic de-sensitisation (a form of learning therapy where patients learn to relax with their feared object – see page 159).

Patients had both snake and rat phobias, one of which was treated with either stress inoculation or systematic de-sensitisation.

Meichenbaum found that both were effective for the target phobia, but stress inoculation also greatly reduced the non-treated phobia, showing that the patient had learned general strategies for coping with anxiety.

Sheehy and Horan (2004) used SIT with first year undergraduates. After four weekly sessions of 90 minutes, the students had lower anxiety levels than a control group and they also performed better academically.

Evaluation

- SIT provides a **long-lasting method** of coping with problems that create stress, and clients learn skills that are generally useful.
- It is **good for coping with moderate stress**, but is not as effective for severe stress.
- It is **time consuming** and requires clients to be highly **motivated**.
- **Individual differences** mean that not all individuals are able to use this method effectively.

2. Increasing hardiness (hardiness training)

Kobasa (1986) suggested that people who are psychologically more hardy (see page 105) find it easier to cope with stress. She therefore suggested that it might be possible to train people to be more hardy, so that they could cope better with stress.

Hardiness training consists of three techniques:

1 **Focusing** – People are often unaware that they are stressed, so, in order to deal with stress, they should become more aware of the signs, such as tight muscles and increased heart rate, and then identify the sources of this stress.

2 **Reconstructing stress situations** – The client thinks of a stressful situation and writes down how it could have turned out better and how it could have turned out worse. This allows them to understand their current coping strategies, and to focus on the positive. It also lets them see that it could have been worse.

3 **Compensating through self-improvement** – Insights can then be built upon and new techniques can be mastered. This can be applied to reassure the client that he/she can cope.

Research evidence

Wiebe (1991) assessed male and female undergraduates for hardiness and then gave them a task to do under stressful conditions. The hardy individuals displayed greater tolerance and reported that they found the task less threatening. The men also showed less increase in heart rate during the task.

Salvatore Maddi worked with Suzanne Kobasa and now runs the Hardiness Training Institute in the US claiming many successful outcomes.

Maddi (1987) conducted a course for managers who, after an initial training programme, reported more job satisfaction and spoke of tremendous improvements in their work and personal relationships. Their levels of anxiety, depression and obsessiveness dropped quite noticeably, as did some physical symptoms of mental strain such as headaches and loss of sleep. Their blood pressure dropped as well.

None of these changes occurred in a comparison group of managers who did not take the course.

Evaluation

- Some people find that **this sort of strategy does not work**. In Maddi's research the technique did not work for everyone – a few of the trainees showed no improvement, possibly because they were reluctant participants. But this would mean the strategy was not right for them.
- The technique requires considerable **effort and determination** – the characteristics of a hardy personality. This suggests that it works with people who are already fairly hardy.
- It provides a **long-lasting method of coping** with any problems that create stress, and clients learn skills that are generally useful.

Physiological methods of stress management

Physiological strategies focus on alleviating the **physiological** symptoms associated with a stressful situation, even if the situation itself cannot be changed.

They may achieve this in a number of ways, including the use of relaxation to control some aspects of the body's stress response.

1. Drugs

Anxiolytic drugs are drugs that reduce anxiety, for example:

All anxiolytic drugs are related to the bodily processes involved in the stress response, i.e. they intervene in the activity of the ANS.

GABA stands for Gamma–aminobutyric acid

A **neurotransmitter** is a chemical substance that enables communication from one nerve cell to another. See diagram on page 112.

- **Barbiturates** depress activity in the central nervous system, and reduce anxiety. For a long time these were used in stress management but they have undesirable side-effects (such as slurred speech) and can be addictive. •
Benzodiazepines (BZs, e.g. Valium and Librium) are currently the most commonly used anxiolytic drugs. They enhance the effect of the neurotransmitter **GABA**, the body's natural form of anxiety relief. GABA reduces activity in the nervous system by slowing down transmission between nerve cells and thus making a person feel calmer. BZs also reduce the activity of serotonin, a neurotransmitter that is related to arousal and aggression. The common side-effects of BZs are sleepiness and dependence.
- **Betablockers** (BBs) reduce the activity of the sympathetic nervous system, which, as we saw on page 98, is critical in arousing the body to deal with a stressor. Therefore, the physical symptoms of stress (sweatiness, faster heart rate, etc.) are reduced. BBs do this by binding to the receptors of cells in the heart and around the body that usually react to adrenaline (which is both a neurotransmitter and a hormone).

Evaluation

There is a more general section on the use of drugs for psychological disorders on page 156.

- Drugs can be **effective** in reducing stress in the short term.
- They are **easy to use and are popular**. BBs are often used by sportsmen and musicians for short-term stressful situations where only the symptoms need to be dealt with.
- Drugs **do not tackle the problem**; they only treat the symptoms of stress and may, therefore, prevent a person actually dealing with the real problem.
- In the long term, drugs often have **unpleasant side-effects** and problems of dependence. Barbiturates caused major problems with addiction, but it is now recognised that even low doses of BZs create withdrawal problems. It is, therefore, recommended that they are only taken for four weeks at a time (Ashton, 1997).

2. Biofeedback

Biofeedback is a technique used to learn voluntary control of involuntary muscles, or voluntary muscles that are not normally controlled.

This leads to the control of various autonomic functions, such as blood pressure and heart rate.

Biofeedback involves four processes:

1 **Feedback** – The patient is attached to a machine, which gives information (feedback) about ANS activity. For example, the patient can hear his/her heart beat or is given a signal (light or tone) to show higher or lower blood pressure.

2 **Relaxation** – The patient is taught techniques of relaxation.

Remember that operant conditioning involves a behaviour being 'stamped in' as a result of rewards or reinforcement. Operant conditioning is described on page 14.

3 **Operant conditioning** – Relaxation leads to a target behaviour, for example, heart rate is decreased or muscle tension is relaxed. This is rewarding, which increases the likelihood of the same behaviour being repeated. Such learning (conditioning) takes place without any conscious thought. The reward leads to an unconscious 'stamping in' of the behaviour.

4 **Transfer** – The patient then transfers the skills learned to the real world.

Research support

The operant conditioning of involuntary responses was demonstrated by Miller and DiCara (1967) by paralysing rats with curare (they had respirators to keep them breathing). This was to ensure that the rats could not use any form of voluntary control.

Half of the rats were rewarded whenever their heart rates slowed down; the reward was delivered by electrically stimulating the pleasure-centre in the brain. The other half were rewarded when their heart rates speeded up. In both groups there were significant changes in heart beats after repeated reinforcement.

Evaluation

* Biofeedback has been shown to be **effective** with many conditions associated with stress, such as asthma, hypertension, migraine and bed-wetting (Underhill, 1999).
* Biofeedback certainly works with **voluntary** responses. However, apparent changes in **involuntary** control may be due to relaxation and control of unused voluntary muscles. Attempts to replicate the work of DiCara and Miller have never been as successful (Dworkin and Miller, 1986).
* It is **time-consuming** and requires **effort and commitment**.
* On the other hand, it is **non-invasive**, has virtually **no side effects**, and can be effective over the long-term.

Progress check

1 Identify **two** examples of emotion-focused coping.
2 What does SIT stand for?
3 Give **one** drawback of using drugs to manage stress.
4 Give **one** advantage of using biofeedback to manage stress.

4 E.g. Can be long-lasting; Non-invasive; No side effects.
3 E.g. Side effects; Drugs may mask the problem.
2 Stress inoculation therapy.
1 E.g. Watching TV; Taking drugs to control stress.

5.3 Physiological and genetic explanations of behaviour

After studying this section you should be able to:

- *outline the structure and function of the divisions of the nervous system, including neurons and synaptic transmission*
- *describe localisation of function in the brain (cortical specialisation), including motor, somatosensory, visual, auditory and 'language' centres*
- *describe and evaluate methods used to identify areas of cortical specialisation, including neurosurgery, post-mortem examinations, EEGs, electrical stimulation and scanning techniques (e.g. PET)*
- *explain the difference between genotype and phenotype*
- *describe types of twins: monozygotic (MZ) and dizygotic (DZ)*
- *describe and evaluate the use of twin studies, and family and adoption studies to investigate selective breeding and the genetic basis of behaviour.*

LEARNING SUMMARY

Physiological psychology

AQA B   U1

The nervous system

1. Central nervous system (CNS)

The CNS comprises the brain and spinal cord, containing about 12 billion nerve cells (neurons), and about ten times as many glia cells – packing cells that provide nutrition and waste removal. The brain is divided into the following parts:

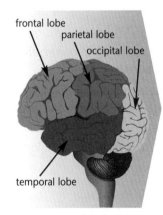

frontal lobe
parietal lobe
occipital lobe

temporal lobe

- **Forebrain** – The **cerebral cortex**, the outer, much-folded grey matter, which is responsible for higher cognitive functions, accounts for 50% of the human nervous system. It is divided into two **hemispheres** joined by fibres including the **corpus callosum**. Each hemisphere has four lobes: **frontal** (for fine motor movement and thinking); **parietal** (for bodily senses, e.g. pain); **occipital** (for vision); and **temporal** (for hearing, memory, emotion and language). The forebrain also contains various subcortical (i.e. outside the cortex) structures, such as the **hypothalamus**, which integrates the autonomic nervous system (important in stress and emotion).
- **Midbrain** – Contains, for example, the **reticular activating system (RAS)**, which controls sleep, arousal, consciousness and attention.
- **Hindbrain** – Contains, for example, the **cerebellum** (for controlling voluntary movement) and the **medulla** (for controlling heart beat and respiration).

2. Somatic nervous system

In the somatic (soma = body) nervous system, messages are sent from the brain to control voluntary movement, and messages are sent back regarding sensations.

3. Autonomic nervous system (ANS)

The **ANS** controls involuntary muscles, such as the stomach and the heart, and the **endocrine system** which produces and distributes **hormones**. The ANS is largely self-regulating (automatic or autonomous).

There are two branches of the ANS that work in a correlated but antagonistic fashion to maintain internal equilibrium (homeostasis):

- The **sympathetic branch** activates internal organs for vigorous activities and emergencies: 'fight or flight'.
- The **parasympathetic branch** conserves and stores resources, monitors the relaxed state, and promotes digestion and metabolism.

Neurons and synaptic transmission

Neurons are electrically excitable cells that form the basis of the nervous system.

Each neuron consists of:

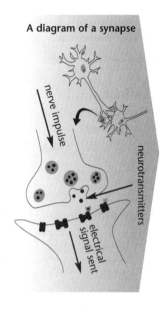

A diagram of a synapse

nerve impulse

neurotransmitters

electrical signal sent

- The **soma**, which contains the nucleus of the cell where protein synthesis takes place.
- The **axon**, which can be many centimetres long and carries nerve signals away from the soma, as well as bringing some types of information back to the soma. The axon is insulated by a **myelin sheath**.
- **Dendrites**, which are at the end of the axon and have many branches enabling communication with many target cells. This is where information is received by the neuron. Information outflow (i.e. from dendrites to other neurons) can also take place.
- The axon terminal, which is at the end of each dendritic branch. It contains **synapses**, which is where chemical messengers (**neurotransmitters**) are released in order to communicate with target neurons.

Electrical transmission occurs along the **axon** due to changes in potassium and sodium ions.

Chemical transmission occurs at the **synapses**. The electrical signal stimulates **presynaptic vesicles**, which release **neurotransmitters**.

The neurotransmitters travel across the **synaptic cleft** or **gap** (which is about 20 nanometres wide) and act upon the adjacent neuron. The effect may be to excite or inhibit the other neuron.

Some common neurotransmitters are dopamine, serotonin (sleep and arousal), adrenaline, GABA (decreases anxiety), and endorphins (pain blockers).

Localisation of function in the brain

Localisation refers to the fact that particular areas of the cerebral cortex are associated with specific physical or behavioural functions.

Localisation of function allows more specialised development, for example, if an area of the brain is pre-set to interpret visual information it reduces the amount of learning that is necessary.

On the other hand, localisation means that damage to a specialised region may result in permanent loss of function.

1. Laterality (sidedness)

- **Bilateral** – Functions are equally represented in the same areas in both hemispheres.
- **Contralateral** – One hemisphere controls the opposite side of the body, e.g. your right hand is controlled by the left hemisphere.
- **Ipsilateral** – Connections are between the same side of the brain and body. Hearing is both contralateral and ipsilateral – most of the information from one ear travels to the auditory cortex on the opposite side of the brain, but some also goes to the same side. This allows comparisons to be made so that the direction of the sound can be calculated.
- **Laterality (hemispheric asymmetry)** – One hemisphere is preferred over the other even though both sides are capable, as illustrated by the fact that most people prefer to write with one hand rather than the other.

2. Localisation

Many functions are restricted to one area of the brain (**cortical specialisation**), and may or may not have laterality.

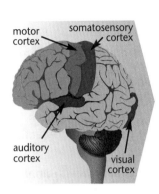

motor cortex

somatosensory cortex

auditory cortex

visual cortex

- **Language** is localised and lateralised. It is directed by areas of the frontal and temporal cortex that are usually found on the left side of the brain. **Broca's area** is in the anterior frontal lobe and is involved with language production. **Wernicke's area** is in the posterior temporal lobe and is mainly concerned with language comprehension. In some people, the language centres are in the right hemisphere or are present in both hemispheres, which may lead to stuttering.
- **Hearing** is controlled by the auditory cortex located in the temporal lobe and is both contralateral and ipsilateral. Cells in the primary auditory cortex are sensitive to specific frequencies of sound. Cells in the secondary auditory cortex respond to combinations of sounds such as human speech.
- **Vision** is controlled by the visual cortex in the occipital lobe. Each hemisphere receives the input of one side of the visual field of the eye (contralateral and ipsilateral). This means that, if one eye is damaged, both hemispheres continue to get visual input. This arrangement also means comparisons can be made between both visual fields, which is important for depth perception.
- **The motor centre** is located in the frontal lobe. Electrical stimulation of parts of the motor cortex results in movements of groups of muscles. The motor cortex is in charge of general movement plans, rather than individual muscle contractions. It is related to voluntary and complex actions, rather than more involuntary movements such as sneezing or laughing.
- **The somatosensory cortex** responds to touch and other body information. It is located in the parietal lobe. The somatosensory cortex receives largely contralateral information, though some information is passed across the hemispheres to compare sensations from the right and left sides.

Methods used to investigate the brain

1. Neurosurgery

Neurosurgery refers to operations on the brain. Individuals may require surgery for removal of tumours, which results in damage to specific areas, and indicates the function of that area.

Non-human animals are often used in physiological research because of the ethical problems involved with human participants. The methods listed here are the 'more' ethical approaches used with humans.

For example, the case of H.M., whose right and left hippocampi were removed to reduce his epilepsy (see page 27). This resulted in serious memory loss, indicating the importance of the hippocampus for memory.

The split brain operation is also used to treat severe epilepsy: the structures that connect the two hemispheres (e.g. the corpus callosum) are severed.

Sperry (1968) studied patients who had had this operation and was then able to demonstrate the separate functions of the right and left hemispheres. For example, if a patient touched an object that was out of sight with his left hand (right hemisphere), the patient could not say what it was (left hemisphere function).

Evaluation

Patients may have suffered brain damage as a result of their condition and, therefore, their brains are atypical.

2. Post-mortem

Brains are examined after a person's death to check, for example, for abnormal structures.

Albert Einstein, a very intelligent person, was shown after his death to have had a brain of normal size. However, when his brain was examined more closely, there were some differences in how densely the neurons were packed together (they were more densely packed than normal). This shows that it may not just be the size of a person's brain that is important for IQ, but the way that the brain is organised.

Post-mortem examinations of the brains of people who had suffered schizophrenia have been found to have enlarged ventricles (cavities) (Torrey, 2002).

Research on intelligence and brain size has used autopsy data to show that men's brains on average are heavier than women's brains. However, women's brains may be better organised (Johnson *et al.*, 1996).

Evaluation

Brain-scanning techniques can now collect the kind of data that used to be available only after a post-mortem. Brain-scanning techniques have the advantage of allowing researchers to link structure and behaviour better.

3. EEG (electro-encephalogram)

Microelectrodes are attached to the patient's scalp to detect electrical activity in specific parts of the brain.

EEGs show that the awake brain has two characteristic brain waves – alpha and beta. The asleep brain has theta and delta waves and REM (rapid eye movement) activity.

Dement and Kleitman (1957) studied dreams and REM sleep using EEGs to indicate brain state. The participant would be awoken during REM sleep or NREM (non rapid eye movement) sleep and asked to report any dreams.

Evaluation

EEGs are useful in understanding states of awareness, but they cannot tell us much about precise regions of the brain.

When considering the precision of any method, you can think of *spatial* precision (some techniques provide information about the functioning of particular neurons) or *temporal* precision (some techniques provide information about brain activity on a millisecond-by-millisecond basis).

4. Electrical stimulation

A weak current is applied to a small part of the brain in a conscious patient to see what experience they report.

For example, Penfield (1955) produced recollections of specific memories and sounds by stimulating specific areas of the brain.

Evaluation

Very weak current may not truly emulate a real nervous impulse.

One common problem with methods of investigating the brain is that you cannot be certain that a primary cause has been located. For example, if you sever a person's vocal chords they cannot speak, but that does not mean the chords are central to speech.

5. Brain-scanning techniques

- **Positron emission tomography (PET scan)** – A radioactive form of glucose is injected into the body. This is taken up by active parts of the brain because they need glucose for energy. The scanner measures the positrons emitted from the radioactive glucose. Only tiny amounts of radioactivity are involved. PET scans show us the brain in action, but areas are not identified with precision. PET scans are taken over 60 seconds or more so they sum up activity over a prolonged time (lacks temporal precision).
- **Magnetic resonance imaging (MRI scans)** – Radio waves excite atoms, producing magnetic changes that are detected by a large magnet surrounding the patient.
- **Functional MRI (fMRI)** provides both anatomical and functional information by taking repeated scans of the brain in action. MRI scans produce precise 3D images and are used to detect very small brain tumours.

Evaluation

These methods cause no permanent damage, and allow the brain to be observed in action. But they take a long time and can be uncomfortable for patients.

Evaluation of the physiological approach

The term **'reductionist'** means that something is being reduced to its most basic components.

The term **'determinist'** means that behaviour is established by factors other than one's own will.

Strengths

- Physiological explanations offer an **objective, reductionist, determinist** and **mechanistic** (machine-like) explanation of behaviour, which **facilitates experimental research**.
- Physiological explanations are also very **determinist**, suggesting that all behaviour is entirely predictable. We may not yet be able to explain everything in physiological terms, but this approach suggests that such explanations are theoretically possible and then *everything* can be described in terms of biology.
- Physiological explanations can be used to **treat psychological problems**, such as treating depression by altering levels of neurotransmitters through drug therapies (see page 156).

Weaknesses

- Physiological explanations are **oversimplified**. There are positive aspects of this oversimplification (see above) but they may not fully explain human behaviour because other important influences are omitted, such as emotions and self-determination.
- The determinist aspect suggests that **free will is not possible**, and certain behaviours are inevitable, for example, people with abnormal brains are predestined to develop certain disorders.
- It overlooks the **experiential** aspect of behaviour.
- Physiological explanations are **more appropriate for some kinds of behaviour** (such as vision) than other kinds, where higher order thinking is more involved (e.g. emotion). Although all human behaviour, even vision, involves some higher order mental activity. Therefore, physiological explanations on their own are usually inadequate.

Progress check

1 What is the difference between the CNS and the ANS?
2 What is the function of the cerebral cortex?
3 What is a synapse?
4 Where is language localised in the brain?

4 The left hemisphere, frontal and temporal cortex.
3 The junction between neurons.
2 Higher cognitive functions.
1 The CNS (brain and spinal cord) controls voluntary activity; the ANS controls involuntary muscles and the endocrine system.

Genetic basis of behaviour

Genotype and phenotype

In the 19th Century, Gregor Mendel conducted experiments with plants and demonstrated that particles (**genes**) explained heredity. Each characteristic (such as flower colour) is determined by a pair of **alleles** (2 alleles = a gene). One allele is inherited from each parent.

The total set of genes is an individual's **genotype**. Some genes are dominant and some are recessive. Each human gene occurs in a pair, and only the dominant one is expressed. Recessive genes are not expressed unless they occur as a pair. (Humans have a total of 23 pairs of genes.)

An individual's **phenotype** is the observable characteristics of the individual, which results from interaction between the genes he/she possesses (i.e. his/her **genotype**) and the environment.

According to the principles of **natural selection**, characteristics and behaviours that are adaptive (i.e. increase an individual's chances of survival and reproduction) will be perpetuated. Such selection takes place at the level of genes.

The principle of **kin selection** is that any characteristic or behaviour that promotes an individual's gene pool will be selected.

Methods used to investigate nature and nurture

1. Twin studies

Monozygotic (MZ) twins, or identical twins, come from a single egg and have identical genes.

Dizygotic (DZ) twins come from two separate eggs and are as genetically similar as any brothers or sisters . However, they do share many experiences, such as developing in the same womb and growing up in a more similar environment than most siblings (e.g. if the family moved house this would be experienced by the twins at the same age, whereas one sibling might be 2 and the other 10 years old, which would make the experience quite different).

The nature–nurture debate and intelligence was studied by Bouchard and McGue (1981). They reviewed a number of studies and found an MZ correlation of +.85 and a DZ correlation of +.58. If MZ twins are reared apart they should nevertheless have very similar IQs. They are identical genetically but have had different environments.

Through an appeal on the BBC, Shields (1962) gained access to a sample of 44 twins, some of whom were reared apart and some of whom were together. The concordance for MZ twins reared apart was +.77 and reared together was +.76. This suggests little environmental influence.

Bouchard *et al.* (1990) used data from over 100 twins in the Minnesota Study of Twins Reared Apart. They found that about 70% of the variation in IQ scores is due to genetic factors.

Evaluation

The problem with twin studies is that the twins often share the same environment, so the effects of nature and nurture are muddled.

This is overcome by studying twins who have been reared apart. But such samples are small and the twins often spent their early life together and/or were raised in similar environments.

Side notes:

It is genotype that is naturally selected. However, selective pressure works on phenotype.

Most behaviours are determined by more than one gene (polygenetic inheritance).

Gottesman (1963) described the concept of a **reaction range**, e.g. our potential height is inherited, but actual height is determined by environmental factors such as diet. Your potential is your *genotype* and your realised potential is your *phenotype*.

Nature refers to behaviour that is determined by inherited factors. **Nurture** is the influence of environmental factors, including learning.

The debate about which has the greater influence on development is called the **nature–nurture debate**, or the **heredity versus environment debate**.

If intelligence was entirely inherited, the MZ correlations should be +1.00. The fact that scores are lower shows a significant environmental component.

A correlation is not evidence that one factor caused another. A third (or more) factor may have been involved.

2. Familial studies

Genetic comparisons can be made between family members. The closer individuals are genetically, the more similar they should be. Siblings share 50% of their genes, as do parents and children. Cousins are 25% similar.

Bouchard and McGue (1981) surveyed over 100 studies that looked at familial correlations of IQ. They found that the closer the genetic link, the higher the correlation in IQ. For example, siblings reared together had a correlation of +.45 and cousins had a correlation of +.145.

Evaluation

This would seem to support the genetic position, but genetically related people usually live in the same environment, making it difficult to separate the influences of nature from the influences of nurture.

> **Heritability** is the proportion of phenotypic variation in a population that is attributable to genetic variation among individuals.

3. Adoption studies

Heritability of certain traits can also be examined using data from children who were adopted. The comparisons can be made between an adopted child and his/her natural parent, adopted parent or adopted sibling.

Horn (1983) reported on the Texas Adoption Study, which looked at about 300 families with adopted children. The biological mothers had all given the children up within one week of birth. The children at age 8 had a correlation of +.25 with their biological mother (genetic link) and +.15 with their adopted mother (environmental link).

Plomin (1988) reported on the same children at age 10. They had a correlation of +.02 with their adoptive siblings.

Evaluation

Adoptions are often made to similar environments, which means that it is difficult to separate nature and nurture. Research has shown that genetic contributions increase with age, so data should be used cautiously when children are tested.

4. Selective breeding

Humans artificially select animals for breeding to increase certain characteristics in a population, such as producing cows with higher milk yields or dogs with friendlier temperaments. The success of such breeding programmes shows the influence of genes on certain traits. In the 19th Century, Francis Galton proposed that we could breed a superior race of humans through selective breeding programmes, using the term **eugenics** to describe this idea.

Evaluation

The idea may work with animals but it raises serious ethical problems with humans and may, in any case, be unsuccessful as human behaviour is caused by a complex interaction of factors.

Evaluation of the genetic approach

Many of the same criticisms (strengths and weaknesses) that apply to the physiological approach apply to the genetic approach as well.

> **Phenylketonuria (PKU)** is given as the classic example of interaction. It is an inherited metabolic disorder where phenylketones build up and cause brain damage unless the child is given a diet (nurture) low in phenylalanine.

Strengths

- Psychologists generally take an **interactionist approach** (i.e. behaviours are explained in terms of an interaction between nature and nurture). This offers a sound explanation of behaviour. One example is the **diathesis-stress model** of mental disorder: individuals are born with an innate vulnerability for certain mental disorders, but these will only develop if the individual is exposed to environmental stressors, such as a difficult childhood or a stressful job (see page 152).

A **concordance rate** is the extent to which two things are related, in this case, how frequently both twins have the same characteristic.

Weaknesses

- Genetic explanations are **determinist**, but the relationship between genes and behaviour is not a simple one. Even identical twins who are 100% identical genetically never show 100% concordance rates for any physical or psychological characteristic.
- Attempts to map particular genes onto particular traits have led people to believe that behaviour (such as intelligence or sexual preferences) can be controlled. Such **genetic engineering** works with plants and, in some cases, with animals, but it is unlikely to work with humans because all behaviours are caused by an array of genes, none of which are necessary.

Progress check

1 Are genes a component of nature or nurture?
2 How can researchers conduct twin studies and rule out the influence of the environment?
3 Explain the concept of concordance rate.

3 The extent to which two things are related, for example, how frequently both twins have the same disorder.

2 By using twins who have been reared apart.

1 Nature.

Sample question and student answers – AQA A question

1

(a) Identify the main components of the pituitary-adrenal system. *(2 marks)*

> The hypothalamus, pituitary and adrenal glands.

1(a) The three basic components have been identified but 'adrenal glands' is not sufficiently detailed for full marks; should have been adrenal cortex. **1 out of 2 marks.**

(b) A small company employs a psychologist to give advice on workplace stress. Levels of absenteeism have risen recently at the company and the director wishes to try to reduce this with expert help.
Imagine that you are the psychologist.

Explain **two** strategies that you would suggest to reduce the stress currently experienced by the office staff, basing your answer on psychological evidence. *(6 marks)*

> One strategy would be to give them an increased sense of control. Marmot et al. found that greater control was associated with less illness in Civil Servants.
>
> A second strategy would be to reduce noise. Cohen et al. found that participants were less stressed and worked best (greater task persistence) when the environment was less noisy.

(b) A short but well-informed, well-organised and clear answer. **6 out of 6 marks.**

(c) Describe the role of personality factors in stress. *(6 marks)*

> One study that investigated how individuals vary in terms of how stress affects them is Friedman and Rosenman's study of over 3,000 middle-aged men.
>
> At the start of the study the men were given questionnaires and interviewed to assess their personality type. The way they responded to the questions was a way to assess their personality type.
>
> Type As are people who are impatient, competitive, time-pressured, and hostile. Type B individuals lack these characteristics and are generally more relaxed.
>
> After 8½ years they had a look to see how many of the men had suffered heart attacks, as a measure of how stressed they had been. About 250 of the men had developed CHD; of these 69% had been assessed as Type A and about 35% had been Type B. This suggests that being a Type A personality may make you more susceptible to CHD.

(c) This is a very detailed description of the Friedman and Rosenman study. However, it is not a complete answer to the question. The same material could have been used to support an answer but the question has not been directly answered. **4 out of 6 marks.**

Practice examination question – AQA A question

1

(a) (i) Explain the difference between 'life changes' and 'daily hassles'.
(2 marks)

(ii) Outline research findings on the effect of life changes on stress.
(4 marks)

(b) Explain how the body responds to stressors. *(6 marks)*

(c) Psychologists have conducted research into a variety of methods for managing stress, ranging from the physical to the psychological.

Discuss **one or more** stress management techniques, considering how successful they are at coping with stress. *(12 marks)*

Sample question and student answers – AQA B question

1

(a) Identify **one** method used to study cortical specialisation, and give **one** strength of this method. *(3 marks)*

> One method is using brain scans and the strength is that they show the brain when it is alive and active.

(a) There is one mark for naming a method and two marks for the strength, but only one mark would be awarded for the strength here as it lacks detail and really is appropriate to a range of different methods (such as EEG). **2 out of 3 marks**.

(b) Give **one** example of a function that is localised in the brain and use this to explain localisation of function (cortical specialisation). *(4 marks)*

> One function that is localised is language, which is localised in the left hemisphere of the brain and in a particular region. The concept of localisation of function is that certain areas of the brain are dedicated to particular functions so if that area is damaged then that particular function is affected. Other areas of the brain are unlikely to be able to take over. This is a good thing because it means that the brain is ready to take on certain functions so it doesn't all have to be learned.

(b) A full and detailed answer, probably more than required for the 4 marks available. However, the answer doesn't quite fulfil the question's requirements – the example has not been used to explain localisation of function. Instead there is material explaining why localisation takes place and the effects of localisation – all unfortunately not worthy of credit. **3 out of 4 marks**.

(c) Explain how the autonomic nervous system functions. *(4 marks)*

> The ANS is divided into two branches. The sympathetic branch is aroused when an animal is stressed and produces adrenaline to prepare for fight or flight. The result is that heart rate increases, sweat is produced, digestion is stopped and so on. Once the threat is passed, the parasympathetic branch steps in and returns the body to a state of relaxation.

(c) A clear and well-organised account of the ANS, in sufficient detail for full marks. **4 out of 4 marks**.

Practice examination question – AQA B question

1

(a) Explain the difference between genotype and phenotype. *(3 marks)*

(b) Below is a diagram of the brain with four labels A, B, C and D. Write which letter, **A**, **B**, **C** or **D**, matches each of the structures listed below:

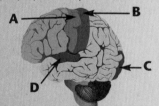

    (i) Somatosensory cortex

    (ii) Auditory cortex

    (iii) Motor cortex

    (iv) Visual cortex   *(4 marks)*

(c) Bill is taking his driving test. When the examiner gets in the car, Bill starts to feel tense, his heart is pounding and he is feeling sweaty. He manages to get through the test and passes. When it is all over he heaves a sigh of relief and his heart stops pounding. He suddenly feels quite hungry.

    (i) Identify **two** actions of the parasympathetic division of the autonomic nervous system.

    (ii) Identify **two** actions of the sympathetic division of the autonomic nervous system.   *(4 marks)*

Social psychology

6.1 Social influence

After studying this section you should be able to:

The word 'influence' comes from ancient astrologers who believed that human behaviour could be explained in terms of an airy fluid flowing down from the heavenly bodies. This fluid exerted a force called **influentia**, which was invisible yet powerful.

- *describe and evaluate types of conformity, including internalisation and compliance*
- *describe and evaluate explanations of why people conform, including informational social influence and normative social influence*
- *describe and evaluate research into obedience, including Milgram's work*
- *describe and evaluate explanations of why people obey*
- *describe and evaluate social facilitation, including dominant responses, causes of arousal, evaluation apprehension and distraction, and effects of arousal.*

LEARNING SUMMARY

Conformity

AQA A U2
AQA B U2

Conformity is a change in behaviour or attitudes as a result of real or imagined group pressure or norms. Kelman (1958) suggested that there are three kinds of conformity:

- **Compliance** – Conforming to the majority, in spite of not really agreeing with them. It is likely to involve a public, but not private, change of opinions.
- **Identification** – Conforming to the demands of a given role because of identification with that role, as in the behaviour of a traffic warden. This kind of conformity generally extends over several aspects of behaviour. There still may be no change to personal opinion.

Norms are the rules established by a group to regulate the behaviour of its members.

- **Internalisation** – Personal opinion does change because the new norms are internalised.

The opposite of conformity is **independent behaviour**, i.e. resisting social influences. **True independence** means following your conscience, rather than being disobedient or non-conformist. For example, Galileo's resistance to ideas of his time was based on principled thinking, whereas driving round a roundabout in an anticlockwise direction is not principled and, therefore, is not true independent behaviour.

Apparent non-conformity occurs when an individual is apparently not conforming to group norms, but is in fact conforming to a different set of group norms.

Explanations of why people conform

There are likely to be **individual differences** in whether people conform or not. There are often claims, for example, that women are more easily influenced than men. Eagly (1978) suggests that women may be more oriented towards interpersonal goals and thus *appear* more conformist. Individual differences are considered more on page 134.

- **Informational social influence** – People like to be right and assume that if most people share a particular view, it must be right. The majority are assumed to supply correct information. Informational social influence operates especially in situations of ambiguity and may lead to internalisation.
- **Normative social influence** – People want to be accepted by social groups and they fear rejection. This creates social pressure and, therefore, people seek to conform to the norms for that group. Normative social influence may have greatest effect with groups of strangers and is likely to lead to compliance rather than internalisation.
- Other factors include **uncertainty** (people are most likely to conform when they are uncertain), **group membership** (people conform most to groups they identify with) and **deindividuation** (anonymity often increases conformity).

121

Research studies

1. Informational social influence in *ambiguous* situations

In many situations, especially social ones, there is no 'right' answer (i.e. it is ambiguous) and, therefore, we look to others for *information*. This may change an individual's private opinion because he/she now regards the majority opinion as the correct one.

Sherif (1936) used the autokinetic effect (a point of light moves erratically when viewed in total darkness) to demonstrate group influence. He showed the light to individuals and asked them to estimate how far, and in which direction, it moved.

After about 100 trials the individuals had reached a consistent level of judgements. Sherif then asked groups of participants to work together. They were not asked to arrive at a group estimate but, nevertheless, after a few exposures, the judgements of the group tended to converge and persisted when the individuals were tested later. The group performance had created a socially-determined standard or norm. This convergence towards a norm is useful in ambiguous situations. It helps us know how to behave (i.e. informational social influence).

2. Normative social influence

People also conform because they want to be liked by the other members of the group, and do not want to be rejected. Normative influence may have played a part in Sherif's study. Normative influence is not likely to change private opinion.

Solomon Asch (1952) wished to see if conformity would still occur when the situation was totally unambiguous. He showed a set of three lines to participants, and asked them to identify which line was the same as a fourth 'standard line'. The confederates all gave the same wrong answer on 12 'critical trials' (out of 18). The 'true' participants answered after the confederates. About 75% of the true participants conformed at least once on critical trials, 5% conformed all of the time, and the average rate of conformity was 37%. In a control study, Asch found that people make mistakes about 1% of the time.

Evaluation of Asch's study

The consequences of complying in this study were not harmful and the pressure to comply was great. In some real life situations this would not be true. Therefore, the study lacks mundane realism and ecological validity.

Other research on normative social influence

Asch conducted several variations on his 1952 study with sets of lines:

1. the presence of a dissenter (i.e. a deliberate non-conformist) cut conformity rates by 25%, even when the dissenter disagreed with the participant as well as the group

2. conformity decreased if the participants were not face-to-face

3. a group of three was sufficient to increase conformity (larger numbers did not increase conformity).

In a group of strangers, the need to establish social contact is greater than the need to be correct. The same might not be true for established groups, though there may be other pressures to conform. Williams and Sogon (1984) found that conformity was even higher when they tested participants who all belonged to the same sports club.

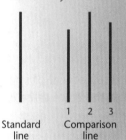

Example of lines used in Asch's study.

Standard line

Comparison line

1 2 3

A **confederate** is an ally of the researcher who is thought to be a true participant but is in fact acting on instructions from the researcher.

The participants in Asch's study were all males. How might this affect the validity of the findings from this study?

Participants in Asch's study were deceived about the true purpose of the study. Would knowledge of the true aims have affected their decision to participate? (see BPS ethical guidelines on page 90).

Asch interviewed participants after his study and asked them to explain why they conformed. They gave one of three answers:

1. *Distortion of perception* – Majority opinion had actually altered what they thought they saw (i.e. internalisation).
2. *Distortion of judgement* – Participants thought they simply must be seeing things and altered their response (i.e. identification).
3. *Distortion of action* – Participants yielded to the majority because they did not want to be ridiculed (i.e. compliance).

Zimbardo's study is sometimes used when discussing obedience. The guards and prisoners were *conforming* to norms but the prisoners were also *obeying* the guards.

Moscovici pointed out that if majority influence was the only process, then opinions would never change because we all would continue to follow the majority. Yet history is littered with examples of changing attitudes, such as those towards females and homosexuals. Such changes are due to minority influence. Moscovici (1980) proposed the two-process model of attitude change:

- *Majority influence* is likely to result in a public change of behaviour but no private change.
- *Minority influence* produces conversion, i.e. a change of private opinion.

Venkatesan (1966) found that in some situations, **reactance** is displayed, i.e. a reaction against a group norm. In his study, groups of students were asked to select one of three identical suits labelled A, B and C (they were told that the suits were from different manufacturers). The true participant (last to register an opinion) conformed to majority opinion except when most of the confederates made statements strongly favouring one suit. When individuals feel forced to conform they may react by asserting their independence.

Philip Zimbardo (Haney *et al.*, 1973) conducted a classic study of conformity to social roles. He sought to find out whether prisoners and prison guards behave aggressively because of their personalities (a dispositional explanation) or because they are conforming to social expectations attached to their roles (a situational explanation).

Student volunteers were randomly assigned to the role of guard or prisoner and were placed in a mock prison. The guards were told that they could set their own rules and were given reflective sunglasses and uniforms, and were allowed to go home between shifts – all to increase their sense of power and anonymity.

The prisoners had to wear stocking caps, chains around their ankles and loose-fitting smocks – all aimed at emasculating them. The guards grew increasingly tyrannical, waking prisoners in the night and getting them to clean the toilet with their bare hands.

Five prisoners had to be released early because of extreme depression (crying, rage and acute anxiety). In fact, the whole study was ended after six days, despite the intention to continue for two weeks. This was a remarkable demonstration of the strength of social norms and people's reluctance to ignore them. The participants' behaviour was the result of normative social influence and identification, rather than internalisation, since they probably did not change their personal beliefs.

Evaluation of Zimbardo's study

It is possible that the participants took on very specific role behaviours because that is what they were asked to do (**demand characteristic**).

In real life a person may adapt a role to suit their personal beliefs and the requirements of the situation.

3. Minority influence

In some situations, social influence occurs as a result of minority, rather than majority, influence. The processes are different with minority influence – the views of a consistent and persuasive minority cause people to question their existing views and gradually change their opinions. The result is usually internalisation rather than compliance.

In Asch's study, one additional dissenter had the effect of reducing conformity to majority opinion. A minority of one dissenter was able to change the group behaviour.

Moscovici *et al.* (1969) demonstrated minority influence in a study where groups were shown an unambiguous stimulus – 36 blue-coloured slides of different intensities. Two people in a group of six were confederates and named the colour of some slides as green. Overall, there was 8.42% conformity to the wrong answers; 32% of participants gave the same answer as the minority at least once. The conformity dropped to 1.25% when the confederates were not consistent (answering green only 24 times out of 36).

Evaluation of research into conformity

1. Experimental artefacts, i.e. features of the experiment that are artificial:

- **Demand characteristics** – Participants behave in certain ways because features of the experiment 'demand' a typical response.
- **Anxiety** fosters conformity.
- **Paid volunteer** participants may feel they have entered into a social contract and, therefore, should obey norms about behaviour in experiments.
- **Experiments are social situations** – In Asch's study (1955) the participants expressed how much like outsiders they felt by dissenting (not conforming). Belonging to the group is more important than correctness.

2. Ecological validity – To what extent do the results generalise to other situations and to real life?

- **In real life** people sometimes have the option to simply do nothing, which may not be possible in an experiment.
- Many of the experimental situations were **oversimplified**.
- All of the experiments involved **strangers**. We may behave differently with individuals or groups who know us (and who are known by us).
- **Cultural differences** – The research is mainly from Western society, where people may actually be less conformist. (**Collectivist societies** are more oriented towards group norms and, therefore, might be more conformist, see page 134).

3. Child of the times – Social norms are always changing.

- Perrin and Spencer (1980) replicated Asch's study using British students. However, they did not obtain evidence of conformity, concluding that people may have now learned to be more self-reliant. However, they repeated the study with youths on probation as participants and the probation officers as the confederates. This time conformity levels were as high as in Asch's study.
- Doms and Avermaet (1981) did reproduce the same results as Asch, and suggested that Perrin and Spencer's use of science and engineering students could have biased their results because they would be more confident about judging the length of lines. It is also possible that Asch's findings have influenced subsequent behaviour.

A **collectivist society** is one where individuals share tasks and belongings, and value interdependence, unlike **individualist societies**, which emphasise individuality, individual needs and independence.

Progress check

1. Define conformity.
2. What kind of conformity results in a change of personal opinion?
3. What psychological term describes the following: 'You gave the same answer as all the other people in a group, even though you knew it was wrong'.
4. What does the phrase 'a child of its times' mean?

4 Refers to research that is relevant to the historical period when it was conducted and, therefore, may not be relevant today.

3 Normative social influence.

2 Identification

1 A change in behaviour or attitudes as a result of real or imagined group pressure or norms.

Obedience

AQA A U2
AQA B U2

Conformity and obedience both involve changing behaviour in response to social influence. Conformity is a response to group pressure (be it a majority or minority). Obedience is to a single individual or law.

Obedience means behaving as instructed, but not necessarily changing your opinions (i.e. compliance rather than internalisation). Obedience happens when you are explicitly directed to do something, whereas conformity is affected by example and group (normative) pressure. Most obedience is reasonable, but when it is to unjust authority, the consequences may be disastrous.

Milgram's research

Milgram (1963), the baseline study

Stanley Milgram recruited 40 male participants using newspaper advertisements and flyers through the post. The participants were aged between 20 and 50, and their jobs ranged from unskilled to professional. When they arrived for the supposed memory experiment they were paid $4.50 at the onset and drew lots for their roles, though the confederate always ended up as the 'learner' while the true participant was the 'teacher'. There was also an 'experimenter' dressed in a lab coat, played by an actor. Participants were told they could leave the study at any time.

History provides evidence to suggest that people obey unjust authority, most infamously the behaviour of many Germans in response to their Nazi leaders. Is such obedience due to dispositional or situational factors?

The 'learner' was strapped in a chair in another room and wired with electrodes. The teacher was required to give the learner an increasingly severe electric shock each time the learner made a mistake on a learning task (learning word pairs).

The shock level started at 15 volts (labelled 'slight shock' on the shock machine) and rose through 30 levels to 450 volts (danger – severe shock). When the teacher got to 300 volts (intense shock) the learner pounded on the wall and then gave no response to the next question. When the 'teacher' turned to the experimenter for guidance, he was given a standard instruction, 'An absence of response should be treated as a wrong answer'. After the 315 volt shock the learner pounded on the wall again but after that there was no further response from the learner. If the teacher felt unsure about continuing, the experimenter used a

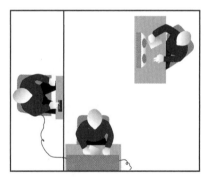

Diagram showing experimenter, 'teacher' and 'learner'.

sequence of four standard 'prods', which were repeated if necessary, e.g. 'The experiment requires that you continue' and 'You have no other choice, you must go on'.

The participants were not actually giving real shocks, but they thought they were.

Results

It is questionable as to whether this study is an experiment. Can you identify an independent and dependent variable? Some people argue that the increasing shock levels are the IV.

- No participants stopped below 300 volts. 12.5% (five participants) stopped at 300 volts (intense shock), and 65% continued to the highest level of 450 volts.
- Prior to the experiment, Milgram asked 14 psychology students to predict the naïve participants' behaviour. The students estimated that no more than 3% of the participants would continue to 450 volts.
- The participants showed signs of extreme tension. Many of them were seen to do things like sweat, tremble and bite their lips. Three even had full-blown seizures.

Would you have obeyed? The survey prior to the experiment suggests that people think they would not obey yet, in reality, people do.

- All participants were debriefed, and assured that their behaviour was entirely normal. They were also sent a follow-up questionnaire. 84% reported that they felt glad to have participated, and 74% felt they had learned something of personal importance.

Participants showed obedience to unjust authority beyond what anyone expected. The sheer strength of obedience and the tension created by the social pressure to obey were surprising. This is the result that is often overlooked: the surprise is that we are surprised by human behaviour. This is the value of psychological research compared with reasoned argument – we may uncover counter-intuitive results.

If we want to decide on whether Milgram's research had high or low validity, one question we can ask is 'Did he measure what he intended to measure'? In other words, was he testing obedience to unjust authority? If the answer is yes, then this study has high **internal validity** (see page 87).

The conclusion from all of these studies is that obedience is due to *situational*, rather than *dispositional*, factors.

Students often think that the study by Hofling *et al.* had high ecological validity because it was conducted in a natural setting. However, it was very *contrived*. Also, the findings may be restricted to nurses/doctors rather than obedience in everyday life, and therefore, is rather low in generalisability (**ecological validity**).

N.B. A field study is conducted in a more natural setting and, therefore, participants will behave more naturally. But this does not necessarily make the study higher in **ecological validity** – there may be unique features of the situation (such as a hospital setting), which means that it is not reasonable to generalise the results to everyday life.

In a field study, participants can still be affected by **experimenter bias** but they are less likely to be affected because they are not aware of being participants and, therefore, are not actively looking for clues about how to respond.

Variations conducted by Milgram and others

- **Proximity of 'learner'** – If the 'teacher' was placed in the same room as the 'learner' and had to press the learner's hand on the shock plate, obedience fell to 30%.
- **Proximity of experimenter** – When instructions were given over the phone, the 'teachers' often said they were giving the shocks when they were not. Overall, 21% of 'teachers' continued to obey.
- **Perceived authority** – When the experiment was conducted in a run-down building rather than a prestigious university setting, obedience fell to 47.5%.
- **Individual differences** – The experiment was repeated with over 1,000 participants from all walks of life. It was found that educated participants were less obedient, and military participants were more obedient. This may be related to their group norms (i.e. conformity) or greater confidence.
- **Social support** – If the 'teacher' was paired with two other 'teachers' (confederates) who dissented, then only 10% of the real participants continued to 450 volts.
- **Deindividuation** – Zimbardo (1969) arranged for the learner to be introduced to the participant and wear a name tag, or to wear a lab coat and hood. The latter condition led to more electric shocks.
- **Cultural differences** – Cultural differences can be understood in terms of conformity to group norms. Milgram (1961) repeated his research with French and Norwegian participants and found differences. Smith and Bond (1993) report a number of cross-cultural replications with different rates of obedience, for example, 85% in Germany and 40% for male Australians. However, it is likely that such studies did not exactly replicate Milgram's study and, therefore, the studies are not comparable.
- **Gender differences** – Milgram found that female participants were equally obedient, but Kilham and Mann (1974) found much lower conformity rates in Australian women (12% compared to males at 40%).

Other research studies

1. Field studies

Hofling *et al.* (1966) conducted a study in a more natural environment, where nurses were told to administer a drug to a patient. The instruction given was contrary to their rules: nurses were not permitted to accept instructions over the telephone, nor from an unknown doctor, nor for a dose in excess of the safe amount. Nevertheless, 21 out of 22 nurses obeyed the order (95%). Nurses defended themselves by saying it often happens and a doctor would be annoyed if they refused. However, their behaviour might be interpreted as conforming to expected role behaviour, rather than being obedient.

Rank and Jacobsen (1977) conducted a similar but less contrived study. This time nurses were asked to give doses of a known drug (Valium) and were allowed to consult other nurses. The result was that only 11% obeyed.

Bickman (1974) arranged for experimenters dressed either in a milkman's uniform, a guard's uniform, or in casual dress, to issue orders to New York pedestrians (e.g. 'Pick up this bag for me', 'This fellow is overparked at the meter but doesn't have any change. Give him a dime'). Participants were most likely to obey the experimenter when he was dressed as a guard. This supports the finding that obedience can be related to the amount of perceived authority.

Most of the time people are on auto-pilot: Langer (1978) approached people who were using a photocopier and said 'Can I make a copy?', 93% of the users made no objection even when no excuse was offered. If the request increased to making 20 copies, only 24% obeyed. This suggests a social norm to obey 'reasonable' requests. This kind of routine behaviour does allow us to think about more important things.

2. The obedience alibi

Mandel (1998) described an event in the Second World War where people did not behave as Milgram's results would predict. Major Trapp had orders to kill all the Jews in a small Polish town – but Trapp told his men that if they did not wish to obey orders he would assign them to other duties. Nevertheless, most of the men did obey – despite the fact that the task involved many of the factors Milgram had found led to reduced obedience (e.g. face-to-face contact, some disobedient peers, absence of pressure from an authority figure).

> **Internal validity** concerns what goes on inside the experiment – are the findings meaningful?

Mandel suggests that Milgram has provided an 'obedience alibi' – allowing people to deny responsibility because of situational factors, whereas there is more to behaviour than that. A large number of Milgram's participants did not obey (35% in the baseline study). This is considered further on page 128.

Evaluation of obedience research

Milgram's research has been criticised for three main reasons, some of which apply to the other obedience studies:

1. Internal validity

Did the participants actually believe in what they were being asked to do, or did they just go along with giving the shocks to please the experimenter? How 'real' did they think the study was?

- **Orne and Holland** (1968) claimed Milgram's participants must have been aware that something did not add up, for example, why wasn't the experimenter giving the shocks himself? However, in a replication of Milgram's experiment by Rosenhan (1969), nearly 70% of participants reported that they believed the whole arrangement, i.e. that it was a genuine learning experiment.
- The participants were seen to sweat, tremble and bite their lips. This suggests that **they did believe** in the task.

> A **demand characteristic** is a feature of an experiment that invites participants to behave in certain, predictable ways. Participants are susceptible to such cues because they want to know how they are expected to behave.

- Milgram suggested various reasons why obedience was so high, such as the prestigious environment (Yale University), and that the participant believed the experimenter is earnest in pursuit of knowledge and, therefore, obedience is important. In short, features of the experimental set-up actually enhanced the tendency to obey (**demand characteristics**).

2. Ecological (external) validity

> **Ecological (or external) validity** concerns what goes on outside the study – can we generalise the findings to other settings?

- **Laboratory experiments** are contrived and so they are low in ecological validity. However, in Milgram's experiment, the contrived setting was appropriate – it was an authority-subordinate task used to measure what Milgram wanted to measure, i.e. obedience to authority.

> Adolf Eichmann, one of the Nazi leaders in World War II, claimed at his trial that he was only following orders. Milgram's research supports this explanation for obedience. But was Milgram just providing an alibi? His conclusions suggest that most of us will behave brutally if directed by unjust authority.

- **Replications** generally support Milgram's findings – those he conducted himself and those conducted by other people (including one by Slater *et al.*, 2006, conducted in virtual reality). This suggests that the study has ecological validity (i.e. it can be generalised to other settings). However, Mandel's evidence does question Milgram's situational explanation, which leads people to overlook more plausible explanations. For example, Goldhagen (1996) argues that German behaviour in the Second World War can be better explained in terms of anti-Semitism (prejudice). Milgram's findings may only apply to short-term situations, such as those encountered in the studies described previously.
- **Cross-cultural support** also suggests that Milgram's findings apply to human nature, not just certain situations or certain groups of people.

Aronson (1988) argued that there might have been no ethical objections to Milgram's research if the findings had been less distasteful. In other words, it is the findings rather than the methods that are distasteful.

It is important to remember that ethical issues have no bearing on the results of the study, but they do affect decisions to replicate it.

One point that is often made is that there were no ethical guidelines at the time of Milgram's research, but this is not correct. It is also stated that he was suspended from the American Psychological Association because of the ethical issues surrounding this work. This is true, but he was later reinstated and was even made President of the APA.

Obedience to authority does depend on what you are being asked to do. It is obedience to *unjust* authority that especially needs to be explained. In many situations, obedience and conformity are healthy and appropriate responses.

Obedience to authority does depend on what you are being asked to do. It is obedience to *unjust* authority that especially needs to be explained. In many situations, obedience and conformity are healthy and appropriate responses.

3. Ethical considerations

Baumrind (1964) claimed that Milgram's experiment caused psychological damage to participants that cannot be justified. Milgram defended himself by raising the following points:

- Participants **did agree to take part** in an experiment which involved shocking a fellow participant so, in a sense, they did give informed consent. Milgram also gained a form of **presumptive consent** by asking people to predict how participants would behave – he could, therefore, argue that he had no reason to expect such high levels of obedience.
- Milgram did **thoroughly debrief** participants and most of them said they were glad they took part. However, participants would still have experienced psychological effects and even if change was for the good, it was still change.
- It is not clear whether participants did have the **right to withdraw**. They were told they could leave at any time and some participants did, however, the 'prods' throughout the experiment made this very difficult.

Explanations of why people obey

1. Situational explanations

- **Socialisation** – We are taught that it is the norm to obey authority. Individuals have past experience of being rewarded for obedience, so we obey because that is what we have learned to do. There are situations where both conformity and obedience are adaptive features of behaviour, such as doing what your parents tell you. There are roles that require obedience, such as being a nurse or being an experimental participant.
- **Graduated commitment** – A person may be unaware of the level of their obedience before they have gone further than they intended. In Milgram's study the shocks increased by only 15 volts each time – what does one more step matter? Having obeyed initially, to a small request, **binding factors** ensure continued obedience.
- **The agentic state** – Milgram (1974) proposed that the participant becomes an 'agent' of the person in authority. This is a feature of certain situations, such as when you are at work or in a large crowd – you are likely to obey the commands of those in authority. When an individual is in an agentic state, he/she ceases to act according to his/her own conscience and lacks a sense of responsibility for his/her actions. The opposite is true of an **autonomous state**.
- **The role of buffers** – People are more prepared to obey when they are 'buffered' from the consequences of their actions, e.g. giving shocks to someone in another room. This explains why soldiers are more obedient when they do not have to face their enemy.
- **Uncertainty** – In some situations, such as the psychology experiment or many occasions in real life, people are not sure how to behave and, therefore, they respond to social cues (demand characteristics).

2. Dispositional explanations

- **Socialisation** – Some people have experiences that enable them to resist the pressures to obey unjust authority. One of Milgram's later participants, Gretchen Brandt, had been in Germany during the Second World War and said she had seen too much pain. She refused to go further because, she said, 'We are here of our own free will'.
- **The authoritarian personality** – Adorno *et al.* (1950) proposed that some individuals are more likely to be obedient (and conformist) because of the way they were brought up. (See page 144 for more detail.)

The desire to understand obedience and tyranny has important real world applications – to help us understand and better control tyrannies that exist today. Haslam and Reicher (2008) suggest that such tyrannies depend on leaders who convince us that our group is in crisis and is threatened by an 'outgroup'. Salvation lies in destroying the outgroup.

- **Self-esteem and the need for social approval** – Stang (1972) found that individuals with high self-esteem are less likely to obey. Crowne and Marlowe (1964) used the Marlowe–Crowne Social Desirability Scale and found that those who were low in need for social approval were less likely to conform in an Asch-type experiment.
- **Mindlessness** – Much of the time, people are on auto-pilot, which predisposes them to being put in an agentic state.
- **Social identity theory** (explained on page 143) – Haslam and Reicher (2008) suggest that people obey unjust authority because they identify with the group. They argue that Milgram's participants did not mindlessly obey, but wrestled with their conscience about what they were doing and found some justification, such as doing it for the sake of science.

Progress check

1. What percentage of Milgram's participants stopped at 300 volts?
2. What levels of obedience were found in Milgram's face-to-face situation?
3. Name **one** researcher who has investigated obedience, besides Milgram.
4. What is the 'agentic shift'?

4 The shift from personal responsibility to being an agent of another person.
3 E.g. Hofling et al.; Rank and Jacobsen; Bickman.
2 Obedience fell to 30%.
1 12.5%.

Social facilitation

Social facilitation refers to the enhancement of an individual's performance when working in the presence of other people (an audience). It is also called the **audience effect**. Audience effects enhance performance on dominant (familiar) tasks and may occur even if members of the audience are blindfolded and wearing headphones.

The term **social inhibition** refers to the opposite effect – when individual performance decreases in the presence of others. This is true for non-dominant (unfamiliar) responses, or when considering quantity rather than quality.

1. Co-action

> Triplett's experiment was the first true social psychology experiment.

The presence of an audience may lead to improved performance just because others are there. Norman Triplett (1987) first observed this. He was intrigued by the fact that cyclists performed better when in a race or with a pacemaker, than when they practised on their own.

He considered various theories put forward, such as the 'shelter theory', which suggested that they sheltered each other from the wind. His own explanation was that the presence of others might be psychologically stimulating because of the sense of competition. This stimulation would release energy not previously available.

> **Co-action** is when two or more people perform side-by-side but without interacting, i.e. they work independently.

Triplett designed an experiment to test his hypothesis. The participant had to turn a reel as fast as possible so that a flag sewn to a thread made four circuits of a four-metre course. Participants did this on their own or alongside someone else (i.e. co-acting). Each participant performed six trials, alternating between the two conditions. In all, he tested 225 people of all ages.

> This result has an application in examination practices. Do people revise better on their own, or when in a library? Do students perform better in an exam when in groups or alone?

The participants who were co-acting performed faster than those working alone. This supports the hypothesis. Triplett acknowledged that other factors are important, but to a lesser extent. For example, seeing another person apparently working faster probably increases your self-expectations.

The result was replicated in a number of experiments using different tasks and even with animals. For example:

> Caution should always be exercised in making inferences about human behaviour from animal studies because animal behaviour is less influenced by thinking about a task. However, in this case, the lack of thinking is a plus – the animal research shows that even without thinking, the audience effect occurs.

- Allport (1920) compared the performance of participants doing a variety of tasks, such as multiplication problems, word associations and debating. The participants worked faster when they were co-acting than when they were alone.
- Zajonc *et al.* (1969) placed a bright light at the start of a maze for cockroaches. If the cockroaches were in pairs they ran away faster. Performance was also increased when an audience of four cockroaches watched!

2. Quality versus quantity

Speed may be increased by the presence of others, but errors may also increase.

- **Quantity** improves when people are co-acting.
- **Quality** improves when people are working alone.

Research evidence

Dashiell (1930) found that participants may be faster at multiplication when co-acting, but they also made more errors.

Pessin (1933) arranged for participants to learn a set of nonsense syllables, a novel task. Those who worked in front of an audience, rather than alone, took longer and made more errors.

Dominant responses are shown on well-learned, instinctive, often simple, motor tasks.

Non-dominant responses are shown on conceptual, novel, complicated or untried tasks.

The results from the study by Schmitt *et al.* are given below, showing mean response times in seconds for participants to complete simple and difficult tasks in the three conditions.

	Simple	Difficult
1	15	52
2	10	73
3	7	63

Evaluation apprehension occurs because a person feels anxious about being evaluated or assessed by someone else.

3. Dominant and non-dominant responses

Zajonc suggested that there are different kinds of task: tasks requiring dominant responses and tasks requiring non-dominant responses.

- Dominant tasks are improved by the presence of others.
- Non-dominant tasks result in depressed performance when conducted in the presence of an audience.

Research evidence

Schmitt *et al.* (1986) asked participants to perform two tasks: a simple, well-learned task (typing their name into a computer) and a difficult, novel task (typing their name backwards with ascending numbers placed between each letter). This task was performed in one of three conditions:

1. alone (no audience)
2. mere presence (experimenter wore a blindfold and earphones)
3. evaluation apprehension (the experimenter assessed the participant's performance).

Participants performed the simple task faster under both audience conditions than when alone. Participants performed the difficult task slower under both audience conditions than when alone. When the audience created 'evaluation apprehension', the participants were faster still on the simple task, but performance was poor on the difficult task.

Markus (1978) asked participants, prior to the supposed experiment, to take off their shoes (dominant response) and put on a lab coat, some large socks and shoes (non-dominant response) so that they were dressed identically. This was done either alone, while an observer watched, or while the observer was present but had their back turned. They recorded the time taken to do this. The results showed the same order as above.

Zajonc (1969) found task effects in cockroaches. If the maze task was made more complex, by adding a right turn, the lone cockroaches did better.

Bartis *et al.* (1988) gave participants the basic task of thinking of different uses for a knife. However, half were asked to think of creative uses of a knife (complex) and half to merely list all uses of a knife (simple). These two groups were further divided between those who were told they would be individually identified (evaluation apprehension) and those whose results would be pooled with everybody else's.

In the evaluation apprehension condition, the simple task gave more results, but the complex task gave fewer uses for a knife. This shows the importance of evaluation apprehension and the different effects this has on dominant and non-dominant tasks.

The Yerkes-Dodson law expresses the curvilinear relationship between arousal and performance, as illustrated in the graph below.

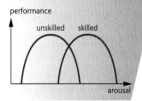

In the study by Cottrell *et al.* the task involved learning supposedly Turkish words. Some were repeated more often than others so that recognition of some was a dominant response (better learned words). It is possible that in this study there wasn't a sufficient difference between the dominant and non-dominant task and this is why the audience effect disappeared when observers were blindfolded.

4. Explanations of social facilitation

1. Drive theory (Zajonc, 1965)

The presence of other people creates arousal (a higher state of alertness). Greater arousal leads to faster performance, though too much arousal will lead to reduced performance, resulting in an inverted U relationship (see graph on the left). When the task is not complicated (i.e. a dominant task or a skilled performance) the inverted U is 'higher' on the x-axis (arousal has less effect) than when performing a complicated, non-dominant task where a person is unskilled (see graph). This explains why you need to be well-practised at a skill in order to perform it in public.

2. Evaluation apprehension (Cottrell, 1972)

Cottrell suggested that arousal is created by the presence of others, because they are evaluating you and this makes you feel nervous (apprehensive) and so you are aroused.

Cottrell *et al.* (1968) tested participants on a task where the audience was blindfolded, so they could not judge performance. In this situation, the audience effect disappeared, supporting the idea that evaluation apprehension is important in social facilitation.

On the other hand, Schmitt *et al.* (1986) found that the effect did not disappear with a blindfolded observer (see previous page) which undermines the evaluation apprehension explanation. This suggests that there is possibly a more complex relationship between evaluation apprehension and performance because it does not always have an effect.

3. Distraction-conflict (Saunders *et al.*, 1983)

It is possible that the mere presence of others causes a distraction. This interferes with attention available for a task, which creates conflict over whether to attend to the task or to the people. The conflict produces arousal.

Saunders *et al.* (1978) gave participants the same or a different task to others who were co-acting – there should be less distraction from those who were doing a different task.

Participants in the high distraction condition (i.e. performing the same task with a co-actor) performed better on the simple task, but worse on the complex one, supporting distraction-conflict.

This explanation could account for the fact that social facilitation has been demonstrated in animals (for example, ants and cockroaches) because these animals can hardly be affected by evaluation apprehension.

Progress check

1 What is a co-action effect?
2 What term is used to describe tasks that are simple and well-rehearsed?
3 Name **one** study that demonstrates the effects of evaluation apprehension.
4 Why are people aroused when co-acting?

4 Possibly evaluation apprehension but more likely to be distraction.
3 E.g. Schmitt *et al.*; Bartis *et al.*; Cottrell.
2 Dominant responses.
1 When two or more people are performing a task side-by-side but are not interacting.

6.2 Social influence in everyday life

After studying this section you should be able to:

- describe and evaluate explanations of independent behaviour, including how people resist pressures to conform and pressures to obey authority
- describe and evaluate the influence of individual differences on independent behaviour, including locus of control
- describe and evaluate implications for social change of research into social influence.

Independent behaviour

AQA A   U2

How people resist pressures to conform

1. Presence of other dissenters

Asch (see pages 122 and 123) found, in a variation of his baseline study, that the presence of a dissenter cut conformity rates by 25%, even when the dissenter disagreed with the participant as well as the group. The effect of an ally may be due to informational social influence. The social support given by a fellow dissenter provides the individual with an independent assessment of reality that makes them feel more confident in their own decision, and more confident in rejecting the majority position.

2. Moral conviction

One of the criticisms of Asch's research is that the task was an insignificant one. In situations where people have strong convictions, there may be less willingness to conform. Hornsey *et al.* (2003) found remarkably little movement toward the majority on attitudes that had moral significance for the individual (e.g. cheating), even when this involved public (rather than just private) behaviours.

> In an exam answer, if necessary, 'evaluation' can be achieved by using research evidence to support your point. Or research evidence can be used as part of your description. It is all determined by the way you use the material.

3. Personality

Asch found that students were less conformist (28%) than other participants (37%) in his studies. This may be because they are more self-confident in their opinions or simply more intelligent. When Perrin and Spencer replicated Asch's study (see page 124), conformity levels dropped. This may be because they used science and engineering students who were more confident in opinions on line length. Locus of control is also an important aspect of personality (see 'the influence of individual differences' on page 134).

4. Experience

Adorno *et al.* (1950) described the **authoritarian personality** – people who are more likely to be conformist because of the way they were brought up (see page 144). The fact that there are cultural differences in conformity (see page 124 and page 134) shows that people **learn** to be more or less conformist.

How people resist pressures to obey authority

1. Presence of other dissenters

Milgram found that levels of obedience dropped to 10% if the 'teacher' was paired with two other 'teachers' (confederates). However, Mandel reported that the presence of dissenters did not reduce obedience in a real life situation (see page 127).

Lawrence Kohlberg's main work was a theory of the development of moral understanding, which included a description of the stages of moral development.

2. Moral conviction

Milgram (1974) interviewed many of the participants in his studies and found that the individuals who resisted unjust authority often explained their behaviour in terms of moral convictions. For example, Gretchen Brandt (see page 129) was confident that it was wrong because of her past experiences, and a participant who was a minister said that his ultimate authority was God and this experiment trivialised human behaviour.

Kohlberg (1969) interviewed some of Milgram's participants and found that those who resisted the pressure to obey presented arguments typical of people who were at a higher stage of moral development.

3. Personality

Adorno's concept of the authoritarian personality applies to obedience as well as conformity. It is a concept that can be linked to both personality and experience (because it develops as a result of upbringing).

The authoritarian person is more obedient, conformist and also finds it difficult to cope with ambiguity.

4. Experience

Interviews by Milgram with his participants showed the importance of experience. For example, Gretchen Brandt's convictions stemmed from her own experiences in Nazi Germany.

Milgram also found that military people were more obedient, whereas educated people were less obedient.

Zimbardo (2007) argues that there is nothing special about resisting obedience: most heroes describe themselves as just ordinary people. Zimbardo believes that the key lies in having a 'heroic imagination', an orientation to behave heroically when the situation demands it. Zimbardo argues that people can be prepared to behave heroically by having the opportunity to think about it beforehand.

5. Deindividuation

Zimbardo (1969) showed that people were more willing to obey when the 'learner' was deindividuated (i.e. anonymous). Milgram found that obedience dropped in face-to-face situations. So lack of anonymity ('humanisation') reduces obedience.

The influence of individual differences

Personality is an individual difference – we have already seen how it interacts with increased or decreased conformity and obedience. Experience also creates individual differences, and is an important factor. Other key individual differences are gender, culture and locus of control:

1. Gender

Eagly and Carli (1981) found that women are more easily influenced than men. However, Eagly (1978) analysed numerous studies and concluded that this gender difference only occurs in studies where the task involves group pressure, rather than persuasion. Eagly suggests that women may sometimes appear to be more conformist because they are more oriented towards interpersonal goals, and so they conform on group pressure tasks.

Milgram found that female participants were equally obedient, but Kilham and Mann (1974) found much lower conformity rates in Australian women (12% compared to males at 40%). This may be because the confederate was female, and women were less willing than men to give shocks to a woman.

When psychologists investigate the effect of culture, they are actually looking at countries rather than cultures.

People in a **collectivist** society would be expected to be more conformist than people in an **individualist** society because they are more oriented towards group goals.

2. Culture

Bond and Smith (1996) analysed conformity studies carried out between 1952 and 1994 that had used the same (or similar) procedures as Asch's original study. They found that collectivist countries tended to show higher levels of conformity than individualist countries.

Moreover, the impact of the cultural variables on conformity levels was greater than any other variable (such as majority size or gender). Bond and Smith also found that levels of conformity in the US had declined steadily since Asch's studies in the 1950s, with the date of study negatively correlated with the level of conformity found in the study.

Eagly (1981) found a significant difference in conformity between studies conducted before and after 1970. In later studies, women were rarely found to be more conformist, which suggests that social expectations (where women had higher status) is linked to levels of conformity.

Smith and Bond (1993) surveyed studies that replicated Milgram's baseline study and found differences. For example, Australians were less obedient (40% obedience for males), and in Spain there was higher obedience (90% for a sample of students). The difficulty is that there are small but significant differences in replications, for example in the Australian study, shocks were given to a long-haired student rather than a businessman, which may help to explain lowered shocks (because participants may feel more positively-disposed towards a student and therefore, less inclined to give shocks).

3. Locus of control

Locus of control (Rotter, 1966) refers to where you place the responsibility (or blame) for things that happen to you.

- **Internals** have an internal locus of control. They believe that they are responsible for the things that happen to them. Therefore, internals are less likely to move to the agentic state, preferring to take responsibility for their actions. They are less likely to rely on the opinions of others, are more likely to be leaders and are more able to resist coercion from others.
- **Externals** have an external locus of control. This can make them feel comfortable because when things go wrong, they blame someone or something else ('a bad workman blames his tools'). On the other hand, this makes an individual feel that things 'happen to them'. Life is simply a matter of luck or fate.

The following are some sample items from Rotter's Locus of Control Scale.

Respondents are asked to select a or b – whichever statement they agree with.

2. a. Many of the things in people's lives are partly due to bad luck.
b. People's misfortunes result from the mistakes they make.

4. a. In the long run people get the respect they deserve in this world.
b. Unfortunately, an individual's worth often passes unrecognised no matter how hard he tries.

28. a. What happens to me is my own doing.
b. Sometimes I feel that I don't have enough control over the direction my life is taking.

Research evidence

Anderson and Schneier (1978) found that internals were more likely to emerge as group leaders. Burger and Cooper (1979) found that people high in a desire for personal control were less likely to conform to a confederate who was expressing his opinion about the funniness of cartoons.

Strickland (1970) found that internals and externals were both equally influenced in a conditioning experiment (the experimenter reinforced certain responses, thus increasing the likelihood that the participant made similar responses). However, when interviewed afterwards, internals were more likely than externals to deny having been influenced, i.e. they saw themselves as more independent. But this was not true for all internals: those internals who realised that the experimenter was reinforcing the choice of certain verbs were less influenced, i.e. when conscious of being controlled by others, internals exert their independence. This suggests a complex relationship between locus of control and social influence.

Historical differences are an example of the effects of culture because they can be related to changes in the norms within a society.

If levels of obedience vary in different cultures, this can be explained in terms of conformity to group norms.

2a 4b and 28b are examples of an external locus of control; 2b, 4a and 28a are examples of an internal locus of control.

Implications for social change

Social change refers to a shift in the status quo of a group or society. Research into social influence has largely been concerned with the factors that maintain the status quo, e.g. conformity to the views/behaviour of the majority, or obedience to those in a position of authority. However, the findings can be turned around to suggest how social change may be achieved.

1. Minority influence

Minority views that are consistent and persistent lead individuals to question their own thinking and change their views. Such change may initially be private, for fear of being ridiculed by the majority, but gradually the minority position becomes the majority opinion (the **snowball effect**). This suggests that attitudes can be changed by a few who feel strongly about their views and are prepared to speak out repeatedly. An example of this would be advocates of gay rights.

2. Disobedient role models

One of the variations conducted by Milgram involved two further 'teachers' (confederates) who defied the experimenter and refused to punish the 'learner'. In this case, obedience fell to 10%.

This suggests the importance of disobedient role models, such as Rosa Parks' refusal to obey segregation laws in the southern US in the 1950s, an act which sparked off the American civil rights movement.

3. Importance of moral principles and internal locus of control

Social influence research shows that people with strong moral convictions and those who have an internal locus of control are less likely to be influenced by others. This suggests that children should be encouraged to act on moral principles (rather than blindly obeying or disobeying) and to develop a sense of responsibility for their own behaviour in order to resist unjust influence.

In 1955 Rosa Parks, a black American, boarded a bus, tired after a day's work. She sat down and when a white man demanded to take her seat, she refused and was arrested because the law stated that black people had to give up their seats for white people.

Progress check

1 Identify **three** factors that may affect the willingness of people to conform.
2 Are 'authoritarian personalities' more or less likely to obey?
3 Milgram's study has been carried out in many different cultures. Why is it problematic to compare these studies with each other?
4 What are 'internals'?

4 People who believe they are in control and are responsible for their own actions.

3 E.g. Because they may each use slightly different methods.

2 More likely to obey.

1 E.g. Presence of dissenters; Moral conviction; Personality; Experience.

6.3 Social cognition

After studying this section you should be able to:

- *describe and evaluate factors affecting impression formation, including social schemas, primacy and recency effects, central traits and stereotyping*
- *describe and evaluate the concept of attribution: dispositional and situational attributions; attributional biases, including the fundamental attribution bias; the actor–observer bias and the self-serving bias*
- *describe and evaluate the structure and function of attitudes: cognitive, affective and behavioural components; adaptive, knowledge and ego-expressive functions*
- *describe and evaluate explanations of prejudice, including competition for resources, social identity theory and the Authoritarian Personality.*

LEARNING SUMMARY

Impression formation

AQA B   U2

Impression formation concerns how we form an impression of another individual's personality. It consists of taking a limited amount of information and producing a global perception of that individual.

Biases in impression formation

Interestingly, in Asch's experiments, no one said, 'How am I to know?'. Participants do their best in experiments, but this may well result in **demand characteristics** (features of an experiment that help participants work out what is expected of them, and lead them to behave in certain predictable ways).

1. Central traits

When considering the description of an individual, adjectives such as 'warm', 'cold' or 'intelligent' have greater *weight* than other words, such as 'polite' and 'blunt'.

Asch (1946) gave participants descriptions of an individual (e.g. 'energetic', 'assured', 'talkative', 'cold', 'ironical', 'inquisitive', 'persuasive'), and asked them to rate that individual on a number of personality characteristics. If key words were changed (e.g. 'warm' instead of 'cold') participants gave different descriptions of the target individual.

Kelley (1950) arranged real-life encounters where students were given a description of a substitute lecturer. After the lecture, they were asked to assess the lecturer. The central words 'warm' and 'cold' again affected impressions.

Primacy refers to something that comes first, **recency** refers to what has been heard most recently (i.e. last).

2. Primacy/recency

First impressions do count (**primary effect**), though when there is a time interval, the **recency effect** may come into play.

Asch (1946) conducted a different experiment, with the words 'intelligent', 'industrious', 'impulsive', 'critical', 'stubborn' and 'envious'. Participants who were given the word list with positive qualities first, rated the person more positively than those who had the word list in the reverse order (negative qualities first).

The studies used to understand impression-formation are rather low in **mundane realism** (see page 87). They often do not reflect the complexity of real life encounters with people.

Luchins (1957) asked participants to read two paragraphs about 'Jim'. Paragraph A described him as extroverted; paragraph B described him as introverted. When participants were asked to indicate which traits were typical of Jim, they showed a primacy effect, i.e. those who had read paragraph A first used words such as 'sociable', 'happy', and 'athletic', whereas those who read paragraph B first said 'shy', 'unfriendly', 'unpopular', 'weak'. However, this effect was reversed when the two 'Jim' paragraphs were presented with a gap of one minute in between while participants did some arithmetic tasks. There was now a recency effect. A recency effect was also shown when participants were warned at the beginning not to make a snap judgement.

A **schema** is a cognitive structure that contains knowledge about a thing, including its attributes and the relations among its attributes (Fiske and Taylor, 1991).

A **stereotype** is more fixed and culturally-determined.

A nice illustration of the self-fulfilling prophecy was given by Guthrie (1938). A group of students played a trick on an unattractive female classmate, pretending that she was the most desirable girl in the college and taking turns asking her out. By the sixth date, the general opinion was that she had actually become more attractive. Presumably, she came to believe that she was attractive and this led her to behave differently.

It is important to investigate when people act as 'motivated tacticians' because then we can avoid the influence of stereotypes.

Explanations – social schemas and stereotyping

Both schemas and stereotypes provide a means of organising information and generating future expectations that simplify our social perceptions. Schemas and stereotypes influence our views for a number of reasons:

1. Cognitive misers

Stereotypes/schemas allow us to conserve cognitive energy because they summarise large amounts of information and provide a fairly accurate picture from meagre data. Such simplified cognitive processing depends on **heuristics** (methods or rules used to solve a problem) and **categorisation** (i.e. identifying groups of individuals).

2. Halo effect

A person who possesses one desirable characteristic, such as being physically attractive, will be assumed to possess other desirable traits.

3. 'Grain of truth' hypothesis

At least some stereotypes are derived from experience and contain some truth. Once formed, they are resistant to change because they tend to be **self-fulfilling**.

There are important biases in stereotyping:

- **False consensus effect** – Individuals overestimate the degree to which others think the same. For example, Sherman *et al.* (1984) found that smokers gave higher estimates of smokers (51%) than non-smokers did (38%).
- **Confirmatory bias** – We seek out information that confirms, rather than challenges, our beliefs. Cohen (1981) found that people tended to remember data that is consistent rather than non-consistent with stereotypes.

Evaluation

- Stereotypes **aid cognitive processing** but they are at least **partly inaccurate**.
- The **motivated tactician** – People don't always use heuristics; they can also act as a 'fully engaged thinker', but perhaps only in certain situations. Kruglanski and Freund (1983) asked participants to assess the quality of dissertations attributed to individuals of different ethnic origins. When time was limited and there was no expectation of evaluation, participants were more affected by the ethnic origin of the writer.
- **Complex situations** – Most people are aware of the effects of stereotypes and try to control them, but this may break down in complex situations. Darley and Gross (1983) showed videos of 'Hannah' playing in a high-class or run-down neighbourhood, and asked participants to estimate her academic ability. If the information was minimal they resisted the influence of stereotypes but when shown further videos, their judgements were more affected by stereotypes.

Progress check

1 Give an example of a central trait.
2 Which has a greater effect – primacy or recency?

2 The primacy effect is stronger except when there is a time gap, or participants are warned against making snap judgements.

1 E.g. Warm; Cold; Intelligent.

Attribution

Attribution is the process of explaining causes of behaviour. We do not observe traits; we observe behaviours and infer personal attributes.

Does your mother ever say 'I think that jumper wants to be safely in your cupboard'? This is an example of **anthropomorphism** – attributing human feelings to an inanimate object. Notice also that such anthropomorphic attributions tend to be dispositional.

'**Personalism**' is when a behaviour is seen as directly intending to benefit or harm the perceiver. '**Hedonic relevance**' refers to behaviour having specific effects for the perceiver.

An example of a correspondent inference is when we assume that film stars have similar personalities to the roles they play.

Things that co-vary are things that tend to happen at the same time, such as grey clouds and rain, or drinking and hangovers. Their co-variance leads us to expect that one causes the other.

Heider (1958) proposed that people have a strong tendency to attribute causes of behaviour to behaviour that can be seen in our descriptions of inanimate objects.

Heider and Simmel (1944) found that participants described objects (e.g. triangles) in a film in anthropomorphic terms (e.g. saying that one triangle liked the other one). This indicates our tendency to infer 'personalities', even when no causation could possibly be involved.

Heider suggested that our explanations of behaviour are related to two sources:

- The **person** – internal or dispositional factors, such as a person's beliefs.
- The **situation** – external or situational factors, such as social norms or luck.

People prefer to make dispositional attributions. This is called the **fundamental attribution error** (FAE). Ross *et al.* (1977) demonstrated the FAE. Observers watched participants giving answers to a quiz. The observers knew that some participants had written the original questions so it was no wonder they did better, yet they were rated as superior to the others, a dispositional attribution even when situational factors were clearly involved.

1. Correspondent inference theory (Jones and Davis, 1965)

We assume (infer) that an individual possesses a corresponding disposition when a behaviour is intentional, unusual, low in social desirability, and/or has personalism and/or hedonic relevance.

Research evidence

Jones and Harris (1967) showed that participants judged an essay writer's opinion to be the same as expressed in their essay (pro- or anti- Castro), even if the raters knew the essay was written under no-choice conditions, i.e. they gave a dispositional attribution.

Evaluation

- Attribution may be **more complex** in real life. Jones and Nisbett (1971) gave extra information about essayists' political views, which affected judgements.
- Some behaviours are **not intentional** (e.g. clumsiness) but this still leads to dispositional attributions.
- Some behaviours **confirm expectations** (e.g. stereotypes) and, thus, are not unusual, but they nevertheless lead to correspondent inferences.

2. Co-variation model (Kelley, 1967)

Kelley proposed that attributions are based on co-variations, determined by three factors or axes:

- **Consistency**, e.g. John always laughs at this comedian (high consistency).
- **Distinctiveness**, e.g. John laughs at just this comedian (high distinctiveness).
- **Consensus**, e.g. everyone laughs at this comedian (high consensus).

External attributions are made when there is sufficient evidence of all three. Internal attributions occur when distinctiveness and consensus are low and consistency is high.

Research evidence

McArthur (1972) gave participants 12 event-depicting sentences, which contained information (high or low) about all three axes. Participants attributed external or internal causes, as the model predicted.

Evaluation

- The evidence is based on **artificially-created situations**. Real-life is different.
- It is possible to **explain the results differently**, e.g. people may simply be attending to the most salient (noticeable) feature.
- In order to make a judgement, you need to have observed the behaviour on a number of occasions, whereas **the information is often rather incomplete**.

3. Causal schemata (Kelley, 1972)

Kelley suggested that observers use causal schemata (heuristics) to provide rapid interpretation of often ambiguous social data, for example:

- **Multiple necessary causes** – a group of behaviours are jointly necessary.
- **Multiple sufficient causes** – attributions are made on the basis of only one instance of behaviour using, e.g. the **discounting principle** (select most obvious potential cause) or the **augmenting principle** (a behaviour 'against the odds' is given greater weight).

Evaluation

- Causal schemata can explain how attributions are made when information is **incomplete**.
- However, the model lacks **empirical support**.

Errors and biases in the attribution process

1. Fundamental attribution error (FAE)

FAE refers to the over-emphasis on dispositional, rather than situational, factors.

Research evidence

- Ross *et al.* (1977) and Jones and Harris (1967), described on page 139.
- **Cultural bias** – Western cultures emphasise individualism and dispositional explanations. Miller (1984) found that Indian Hindus preferred situational to dispositional explanations.
- The **English language facilitates** dispositional explanations (e.g. we refer to an honest person but not an honest situation), though this may reflect innate tendencies.

2. Actor–observer bias

We prefer to explain our own (the actor's) behaviour in terms of situation, and the behaviour of others (those who we are observing) in terms of disposition. This may be because the actor knows about his/her own disposition but has to make inferences about another person.

Research evidence

Nisbett *et al.* (1973) asked students to provide an explanation for selecting a particular course of study, relating to both themselves and to a friend. They made situational attributions about themselves (e.g. what the course has to offer) but dispositional ones about the friend (e.g. being clever).

3. Self-serving bias

We take credit for our successes and disassociate from our failures, blaming external factors. This protects self-esteem, and gives us a sense of control.

Research evidence

Jones *et al.* (1968) arranged for participants to teach two pupils. The 'teachers' attributed improved performance to themselves, but blamed the pupils for failure.

A heuristic is a general guideline for solving a problem. It does not guarantee a solution, but tends to work well most of the time.

All attribution theories assume that people make judgements in a *logical and rational* manner, which may not always be true.

A **bias** is a prejudice, a systematic factor that produces mistakes. People behave in a predictably biased manner when making attributions.

In his obedience studies, Milgram found that participants' behaviour was quite different from what people had predicted beforehand (see page 125). This can be explained by the FAE. People 'prefer' a *dispositional* explanation (someone would only give strong electric shocks if they were inhuman) rather than a *situational* one (in a laboratory people may feel they have to obey).

- **Ingroup bias** (i.e. the tendency to show a preference towards members of your own group) is an example of a self-serving bias because it enhances personal self-esteem. Duncan (1976) showed white participants a video of a white or black person violently pushing another during a heated conversation. Participants made internal attributions (e.g. 'violent personality') when the pusher was black and external ones for the white aggressor (e.g. 'he was provoked').
- Self-serving bias explains why 'actors' sometimes explain their behaviour in situational terms (when it enhances self-esteem), which is the **reverse of the actor–observer bias**.
- **Depressed** individuals may behave in the opposite way. Abrahamson *et al.* (1978) suggested that depressives tend to attribute failure to themselves (internal) rather than to external factors, and such individuals see these attributions as unchanging (stable) and as global, rather than specific.
- **Cultural bias** – The self-serving bias is stronger in individualist cultures. Kashima and Triandis (1986) found that Americans were more likely to explain successes in terms of high ability, and failures in terms of low ability, whereas the opposite was true of Japanese participants (a collectivist society).

An **individualist** society emphasises the rights and interests of the individual, in contrast with a **collectivist** society, where individuals share tasks, belongings and income. In an **individualistic** society, the emphasis is on 'I' rather than 'we'.

Progress check

1 Explain the FAE.
2 Name the three axes of Kelley's co-variation model.
3 Which bias predicts that people tend to give situational explanations for their own behaviour and dispositional explanations for the behaviour of others?
4 Name **one** cultural difference in attribution.

4 E.g. Indian Hindus preferred situational to dispositional explanations; Self-serving bias is stronger in individualist cultures.
3 Actor–observer bias.
2 Consistency, distinctiveness, consensus.
1 People prefer dispositional rather than situational explanations.

Attitudes and prejudice

Prejudice is an unjustified, usually negative, attitude towards an individual, based solely on their membership of a particular category or group.

Structure and function of attitudes

> If we put the three components on the right together, we have a definition for attitudes: 'A liking or disliking of an object based on cognitions about the object that leads to a readiness to behave in a certain way'.

1. The structural approach

Attitudes have three components:
- **Cognitive** – Beliefs (*cognitions*) about something.
- **Affective** – The extent to which you like or dislike something.
- **Behavioural** – The readiness to *behave* in a certain way.

2. The functional approach

Attitudes are essential to the well-being of an individual, and serve three functions:

- **Adaptive** – Attitudes help us to avoid unpleasant things and seek out favourable ones. They are also important when identifying with people/groups. For example, feeling wary of dangerous sports might enhance your survival.
- **Knowledge** – Attitudes are part of our knowledge about the social world, and are an integral part of stereotypes that help us simplify our social perceptions. Most of the things we 'know' also have a positive or negative connotation (i.e. personal meaning). For example, you know about city life but you also have an attitude about this as distinct to your views about rural life.

> The concept of **ego** was introduced by Freud to represent the rational or realistic self as distinct from the **id** (primitive self) and **super-ego** (ideal self). Freudian concepts are discussed on page 19.

- **Ego-expressive** – Attitudes are a means of expressing our emotions. We use them to show like or dislike. Attitudes protect our ego by:
  - Promoting a positive self-image through positive self-attitudes. For example, a woman can make herself feel better by feeling good about women generally.
  - Projecting feelings of threat or conflict onto others, as in the case of prejudice. For example, people make themselves feel good by attributing their undesirable characteristics to others, such as by saying that everyone is late to important meetings.

3. Attitudes and behaviour

There is evidence to suggest that people do not always behave in a manner that is consistent with their attitudes.

> Gordon Allport (1935) made the point that if an individual does not have guiding attitudes, he/she is 'confused and baffled'. However, there is evidence that behaviour cannot be so simply predicted from attitudes, which questions the usefulness of the concept of attitudes.

- DeFleur and Westie (1958) asked white students to be photographed with black students. 30% of the students behaved differently from their previously expressed views: either they said they were prejudiced but agreed to be photographed, or they said they were unprejudiced, but refused to be photographed i.e. they said one thing but did another (attitudes and behaviour were not the same).
- On the other hand, Bagozzi (1981) questioned people about their attitudes, intentions and behaviour with respect to donating blood. He later checked to see which of his participants did actually give blood and found that, as expected, attitudes did equate to intentions and ultimately to behaviour (i.e. those who expressed pro-donation attitudes did actually give blood).

Prejudice

The three main explanations for prejudice are: competition for resources; social identity theory; and the authoritarian personality.

1. Competition for resources (Realistic conflict theory)

Prejudice stems from direct competition between social groups over scarce and valued resources, such as unequal distribution of wealth, unemployment or disputes over territory. Ingroup and outgroup attitudes are turned into hostility because the outgroup becomes the scapegoat for economic problems.

- **Robbers Cave Experiment** (Sherif *et al.*, 1961) is the classic study of how prejudice forms through the effects of ingroup and outgroup behaviour. They selected 22 well-adjusted, white 11-year-old boys to go on a summer camp for three weeks. In stage 1, the ingroup was developed. The boys were divided into two groups, and were given lots of co-operative activities and a sense of group identity (a name, hats and t-shirts). In stage 2, the groups became aware of each other and a tournament was organised. There was aggression and fights after every match. In stage 3, the researchers resolved the conflict through co-operative activity, involving super-ordinate goals, such as repairing a failed water supply. By the time they went home, all traces of ingroup and outgroup prejudice had disappeared. Three factors led to the prejudiced behaviour: ethnocentrism (ingroups and outgroups), competition and stereotypes.
- However, a similar study by Tyerman and Spencer (1983) observing an annual scout camp with conditions similar to Sherif's study, concluded that the presence of competition did not lead to intergroup conflict and hostility.
- Hovland and Sears (1940) found a negative correlation between the number of lynchings (mainly black people) in the southern US between 1882 and 1930, and the economic indices of the time. High aggression (measured by lynchings) towards black people may be one consequence of prejudice. The economic index is an indication of frustration (when the price of cotton was low there were fewer jobs and, therefore, greater hardship).
- Langford and Ponting (1992) interviewed non-Aboriginal Canadians and concluded that continuing prejudices towards Aboriginals (individuals who originated in that country) was positively related to perceived conflict over things like jobs. The researchers suggest that Aboriginal rights movements should deal directly with feelings of perceived competition, in order to reduce prejudice.

Evaluation

- Prejudice is likely to **exist prior to conflict**, but conflict is the trigger to hostile behaviour.
- The theory can be **applied** to reducing prejudice by creating **super-ordinate goals**. Aronson *et al.* (1978) developed the jigsaw method to foster mutual interdependence. Schoolchildren worked in groups where each member had a piece of work to prepare and teach to other group members for an end-of-project test. This led to moderate attitude change.

2. Social identity theory (SIT) (Tajfel and Turner, 1979)

A person's self-image has two components: personal identity and social identity. Social identity is determined by the various social groups you belong to, such as your gender or football club. There are three causal processes:

- **Categorisation** – We group people into social categories. This leads to the formation of ingroups and outgroups. This categorisation process simplifies interpersonal perception.
- **Social comparison** – Comparisons are made between groups in order to increase **self esteem**, and we all have a need to increase our self-esteem. **Ingroup favouritism** and **outgroup negative bias** enhance social and personal esteem, and lead to biased perceptions of ingroup and outgroup members. Tajfel (1982) demonstrated this in his study of the minimal group (the ingroup). Arbitrary group membership was sufficient to create ingroup and outgroup behaviour.
- **Social beliefs** – Our beliefs/attitudes generate different social behaviours.

Research support

SIT generates various predictions that can be tested:

- **Illusion of outgroup homogeneity** – Members of an outgroup are perceived as less diverse than members of the ingroup, thus confirming existing stereotypes. Linville *et al.* (1989) asked elderly people and college students to rate their own group and the other group in terms of traits, such as friendliness. Both tended to perceive the ingroup as more differentiated (e.g. there were both friendly and unfriendly group members) and the outgroup as more homogenous (i.e. all group members were much the same).
- **Intergroup comparisons** – SIT would predict that people will naturally make ingroup and outgroup judgements. Haeger (1993) asked participants from six European countries to write down whatever came to mind when they thought of their own country. Analysis of their responses showed that 20% had spontaneously drawn comparisons between their country and other countries, in a way that favoured their country (e.g. 'People are free to speak their mind here, unlike in some other countries.').

A 'good' theory should be easy to test, i.e. an experiment should be designed to test the specific predictions of the theory. It should also generate lots of ways of being tested.

Evaluation

- SIT generates a number of **testable propositions**, which in turn provide support for the theory.
- SIT can account for prejudice in situations of **minimal information**.
- SIT does not fully explain the **violence** associated with some prejudices.
- SIT offers a **good explanation** of why members of an ingroup favour themselves over an outgroup, and that this might lead to prejudice. However, while research has supported ingroup favouritism it has shown relatively little support to outgroup discrimination (which would create prejudice). In fact, Mummendey *et al.* (1992) found that when participants were asked to award unpleasant tones to other participants they did so equally to ingroup and outgroup members.

3. The Authoritarian Personality

Adorno *et al.* (1950) proposed that some individuals may have more prejudiced, conformist and obedient personalities, and that such behaviour might be explained in terms of having an authoritarian upbringing that leads to a particular cognitive style.

In order to test this explanation, Adorno *et al.* developed a set of scales for testing authoritarianism, such as the potentiality for Fascism scale (F scale). They tested about 2,000 white, middle-class Americans, finding that people with an authoritarian personality had the following characteristics:

- **Cognitive style** – They tend to be rigid, find ambiguity harder to cope with and have a simplistic way of thinking about the world, for example, they hold rather fixed stereotypes. They deny negative feelings in order to maintain consistency and deal with ensuing repressed feelings by projecting these onto scapegoats (realistic conflict).
- **Values** – They favour law and order, and are more concerned with status, success and traditional customs.
- **Personal style** – They avoid psychological interpretations and repressed feelings.
- **Child rearing** – Their parents tended to give conditional love, strict discipline, expected unquestioning loyalty and were insensitive to the child's needs. Such experiences would create an insecure adult who respects authority and power, conforms more readily to group norms, and who may increase their self-esteem through in-group favouritism (social identity), leading to prejudice.

Evaluation

- The Authoritarian Personality explanation **accounts for both the existence of prejudices and the hostility element**.
- McFarland and Adelson (1996) found that almost all prejudice can be accounted for by **right-wing authoritarianism and social dominance orientation** – key characteristics of the authoritarian personality.
- There were a number of **criticisms of the data collected**, for example, the data was subjectively analysed. There were also **criticisms of the questionnaires**, for example, a response set on the F-scale (agreement leads to authoritarian-type answers), and that left-wing authoritarianism was overlooked.
- The study was **correlational** so we cannot say that authoritarian parenting style **caused** the prejudiced personality.

An authoritarian parenting style is one that relies on having a clear social hierarchy and expects obedience to those in authority.

This is a *dispositional* explanation of prejudice, whereas realistic conflict theory is a *situational* explanation – the reason that people are prejudiced is either explained in terms of personality or in terms of factors that trigger prejudiced behaviour.

The Authoritarian Personality explanation grew out of a desire to understand the anti-Semitism of the 1930s.

Altmeyer (1998) concluded, from available research, that the many different kinds of prejudice are mainly matters of personality.

Progress check

1 Name the three components of an attitude.
2 What is 'ingroup favouritism'?
3 Which explanation(s) can account for the hostility associated with prejudice?
4 Name **two** causal processes in social identity.

4 E.g. Categorisation; Social comparison; Social beliefs.
3 Realistic conflict theory and the Authoritarian Personality.
2 The perception that your own social group has more positive characteristics.
1 Affect, behaviour, cognition.

Sample question and student answers – AQA A and B question

1

(a) Distinguish between the terms 'conformity' and 'obedience'. *(4 marks)*

Conformity means being influenced by norms, whereas obedience is being influenced by a person.

(b) Outline **two** explanations for why people conform. *(6 marks)*

One reason why people conform is because of informational social influence. There is no clear way to behave and, therefore, they look to others to establish the 'correct' way. This may not necessarily involve a change in their attitudes, but it might. A second reason why people conform is because of normative social influence. People conform in order to be liked by others and to avoid being rejected or ridiculed. This may involve just going along with a group and not necessarily changing personal attitudes.

(c) Many people focus on the ethical objections raised by research into obedience but there are arguments on both sides.

Discuss psychological research into obedience, in terms of the ethical issues it raises. *(12 marks)*

Milgram found that 65% of his original participants were willing to administer the highest level of shocks to the 'learner'. For all the participants knew, they could have killed the person they were giving shocks to. In Milgram's film, one of them clearly said he thought he'd killed him. The ethical objections to this research include the issues of deception, harm, and the right to withdraw.

The participants were deceived because they were not told the true purpose of the research. However, there would be no point conducting the study if they did know the true purpose. The ethical guidelines say that deception is acceptable if there is no alternative. Other studies of obedience have also had to use deception, such as those by Hofling et al. and Bickman. Therefore, it would seem inevitable that deception is used in this kind of study. One way to compensate for deception is to debrief participants afterwards so they do know the true aims of the experiment and they have an opportunity to withhold their data if they want to. Milgram did all of this after his experiment. However, in a field study such as Bickman's, this was not possible. One difficulty with this debriefing is that participants may feel even worse when they discover they have been cheated, and upset that they fell for the deception.

In terms of psychological harm, all obedience research involved high levels of anxiety and stress for participants. Just having to decide whether to obey, even though someone else is suffering, imposes great stress on a participant. Simply debriefing someone afterwards doesn't remove the stress that they felt. They might say that they feel OK but they may be denying their true feelings. They may feel quite depressed about the way that they behaved. It is true that most of Milgram's participants said that they were glad to have participated and had learned something valuable.

The final ethical issue is the right to withdraw. Milgram told participants that they were free to go, yet the standardised prods made it very difficult for them to leave.

1(a) This is a fairly basic answer but at least a contrast has been made (as required by the command words 'distinguish between') rather than just explaining each term separately. A fuller answer might explain how 'norms' are established and might note that obedience is 'usually' in response to authority but not always. **2 out of 4 marks.**

(b) A well-detailed answer. **6 out of 6 marks.**

(c) The student's response concentrates on Milgram's study though the question referred to 'obedience research' generally – though there is some reference to other research. The response does focus on ethical issues rather than the common mistake of too much time spent actually describing the studies. There is also a reasonable amount of evaluation (commentary) on the points made about ethical issues but not enough to constitute a broad range of issues (see marking criteria on page 9). There are probably more than enough AO1 (descriptive) points and not enough evaluative (AO2) points, therefore **10 out of 12 marks.**

Sample question and student answers – AQA A question

1

(a) What is meant by 'locus of control'? *(3 marks)*

1(a) Not a particularly well-worded answer but it is accurate and detailed and shows understanding of the concept. There is enough for full marks. **3 out of 3 marks.**

A locus of control is what kind of control a person has over themselves. It can be internal or external. Internal means you take responsibility for your own actions, whereas external means you think that factors outside yourself are in control, such as luck or other people.

(b) Many psychology students learn about Milgram's research as part of their AS studies. What can this research tell us about independent behaviour? *(4 marks)*

(b) The question leaves it up to you whether you provide lots of different answers with little explanation, or only one or two answers each with some explanation (as here). Two implications have been identified and explained for full marks. Notice the focus on what the research can tell us. **4 out of 4 marks.**

One thing that was shown was that those people who obeyed tended to move into an agentic state where they just followed orders. Therefore, it is important that, instead of just following orders, people think about whether what they are doing is right or wrong. Some of Milgram's participants stood up for themselves because they had a more highly developed moral sense. This suggests that it is probably important to study morals at school.

(c) Milgram's research has been criticised for being low in validity. Outline **two** reasons why this study might be low in validity. *(4 marks)*

(c) As required by the question, this answer provides two reasons and in each case there is some further elaboration to explain the reason, so **4 out of 4 marks.** Often students just write 'the study was an experiment so it was artificial' and do not explain how this would reduce validity.

One reason is that it was conducted in an artificial and contrived situation and, therefore, the participants might not have behaved as they would behave in everyday life. The second reason is that the participants may not have actually believed that the shocks were real so they just went along with it to please the experimenter.

(d) Describe **one** implication for social change of research into social influence. Refer to psychological research in your answer. *(4 marks)*

(d) A clear and detailed answer, based on psychological research as required in the question. For full marks some further details of the actual research is required. **3 out of 4 marks.**

One implication is that social change can be achieved by having disobedient role models. Both Milgram and Asch showed that the presence of disobedient models or allies led people to resist the pressures to conform or obey. Therefore, if you want to bring about social change you should stand up and speak out and others may follow.

Practice examination question – AQA A question

1

(a) Psychologists have investigated conformity and resistance to conformity. Describe **one** problem they have encountered in doing such research. *(4 marks)*

(b) Brian and his sister Diana are very different to each other. Brian tends to be quite independent and not go along with the crowd, being a bit of a loner. But Diana always wants to be with her group of friends; she likes the same things they like – music, clothes and so on.

Use the examples of Brian and Diana to explain individual differences in independent behaviour. *(3 marks)*

(c) Describe and evaluate research related to how people resist pressures to conform. *(12 marks)*

Sample question and student answers – AQA B question

1(a) There is just about enough detail here for full marks. **2 out of 2 marks**.

(b) An appropriate weakness has been identified but the explanation is rather limited – some further explanation of why the questionnaire was flawed or why the data was not valid would have increased the marks. A generous **2 out of 3 marks**.

(c) A clear explanation of social identity theory but the link to prejudice is a little vague. **3 out of 4 marks**.

(d) A good example of prejudice in everyday life has been identified and then social identity theory has been used to explain this in sufficient detail. **3 out of 3 marks**.

1

(a) Explain what is mean by the Authoritarian Personality. (2 marks)

The Authoritarian Personality consists of certain characteristics, such as rigid thinking style and a tendency to be conformist and also more prejudiced.

(b) Explain **one** weakness with the Authoritarian Personality as an explanation for prejudice. (3 marks)

The questionnaire used to collect data in the original study was flawed, which means the data may not have been valid.

(c) Outline **one** other explanation for prejudice. (4 marks)

Social identity theory proposes that prejudice develops because part of one's identity comes from membership of social groups, and also self-esteem. If your ingroup is high in esteem this makes you feel better, (like when your football team wins). To make your ingroup feel better people discriminate against the outgroup and this leads to prejudice.

(d) Use the explanation you have outlined in (c) to explain an everyday example of prejudice. (3 marks)

An everyday example would be when people who support one football team are very rude about people who support a different team and this is because of outgroup discrimination. It makes the people feel better about their team by putting the other team supporters down and thus, better about themselves.

Practice examination questions – AQA B questions

1

(a) Explain the difference between situational and dispositional attributions, giving examples of each kind of attribution. (6 marks)

(b) Identify **one** factor that affects impression formation and give an example of it in everyday life. (3 marks)

(c) Describe and evaluate **at least two** functions of attitudes. Illustrate your answer with examples. (10 marks)

2

(a) Explain how the concept of the Authoritarian Personality has been used to explain conformity. (3 marks)

(b) Describe and evaluate research on social facilitation. (10 marks)

Individual differences

7.1 Defining and explaining psychological psychopathology (abnormality)

After studying this section you should be able to:

'Abnormal' means to deviate from what is usual or from some sort of standard. The problem lies in establishing a standard.

Psychopathology refers to the study of the causes (pathology) of psychological disorders.

- *describe definitions of abnormality, including deviation from social norms, failure to function adequately and deviation from ideal mental health*
- *describe limitations associated with these definitions of psychological abnormality*
- *describe and evaluate key features of the biological approach to psychopathology*
- *describe and evaluate key features of psychological approaches to psychopathology, including the psychodynamic, behavioural and cognitive approaches.*

LEARNING SUMMARY

Definitions of abnormality

AQA A ▶ U2

The term 'clinical' is used to distinguish an abnormality that has been diagnosed by a trained professional (e.g. a clinical psychologist) from the everyday use of the term 'abnormality'.

Cultural relativism is an issue for all definitions of abnormality, i.e. the fact that any definition is relative to what is considered acceptable (or not) for any particular cultural group. The term 'culture' refers to the rules, customs and ways of interacting that are shared by a collection of people.

1. Deviation from social norms

Abnormality can be defined in terms of standards of social behaviour. For example, it is acceptable to wear very little clothing on a beach, but not when walking down the high street. Such standards are socially agreed and culturally-based, though there are many cross-cultural similarities.

Many people who are labelled as clinically abnormal do behave in a socially deviant way, for example, schizophrenics behave anti-socially and erratically.

Advantages of this approach

- This has the benefit of including some consideration of the **effect of deviant behaviour** on others.

Limitations of this approach

- Social deviations vary according to **prevailing moral perspectives** and this approach allows serious abuse of individual rights. Examples of deviation through history have been witchcraft, homosexuality, unmarried motherhood, delinquency and political dissent.
- Social deviation is related to **social and cultural context**. What is deviant behaviour in Britain may not be deviant elsewhere, and vice versa.
- Social deviation **can be a good thing**, as in the case of people who resisted German occupation in the Second World War, so it may be dangerous to regard deviancy as automatically abnormal.

2. Failure to function adequately

Certain behaviours are distressing and dysfunctional for the individual. For example, being depressed disrupts a person's ability to work, to look after him/herself and/or to conduct satisfying relations with other people.

149

Rosenhan and Seligman's list does include some universal indicators of undesirable behaviour, such as distress to oneself or others, i.e. it is not all culturally relative.

Rosenhan and Seligman (1989) suggested that certain elements jointly determine abnormality. Singly, they may cause no problem, but when several co-occur, they are symptomatic of abnormality and are related to a failure to function adequately. These elements are suffering, maladaptiveness (personally and socially), irrationality and incomprehensibility, unpredictability and loss of control, vividness and unconventionality, observer discomfort, and violation of moral standards.

Advantages of this approach

- Using the concepts of dysfunction and distress acknowledges the subjective experience of the individual.

Limitations to this approach

- In some situations, apparently dysfunctional behaviour **may be functional**, for example, depression can be an adaptive response to stress.
- Personal distress **may not be a good indicator of an undesirable state**. Although many people do seek psychiatric help because they feel distressed, not all mental disorders are accompanied by a state of distress (e.g. anti-social personality disorder). However, in other situations, distress is a 'healthy' response up to a point (e.g. the death of a close friend). This means having to make subjective decisions about how much distress is tolerable. It might be helpful to include the distress of others as a criterion of adaptive behaviour.
- Diagnoses of dysfunction and distress require judgements to be made by others, which are inevitably **influenced by social and cultural values**.

Anti-social personality disorder is similar to Bowlby's concept of affectionless psychopathy. People with anti-social personality disorder have a disregard for the feelings of others. However, this causes no distress to the person with the disorder.

3. Deviation from mental health

Doctors use the concept of physical health as a yardstick to measure ill-health, for example, a body temperature outside the normal range indicates illness.

Jahoda (1958) suggested that we could similarly define psychological well-being in terms of signs of psychological health in order to recognise mental illness. The key features would be self-acceptance, potential for growth and development, autonomy, accurate perception of reality, environmental competence, and positive interpersonal relations.

There is some overlap between Jahoda's list and the one from Rosenhan and Seligman.

Advantages of this approach

- It is preferable to have **some absolutes** (signs of healthiness) rather than relying on subjective criteria that are prone to cultural relativism.

Limitations of this approach

- Such approaches are nevertheless **influenced by cultural attitudes**, for example, autonomy is not a universal ideal.
- The list is **idealistic** – few people actually manage to achieve most of the behaviours identified.
- It is possible to measure physical illness objectively (e.g. blood pressure), but the **concepts for mental health are too vague** for the purpose of diagnosis.

Carl Rogers (1959) was the 'father' of the counselling movement. Like Jahoda, Rogers defined abnormality in terms of the characteristics of a mentally healthy person. He emphasised the importance of having a sense of self and being self-accepting as pre-requisites for mental health.

Progress check

1 Give an example of a socially acceptable definition of behaviour.
2 Name **two** behaviours from Jahoda's list.

2 E.g. Self-acceptance; Autonomy; Accurate perception of reality; Positive interpersonal relations.
1 E.g. Wearing a bikini / swimming shorts on the beach but being covered up when walking down the street.

Explanations of abnormality

The biological approach generally is discussed on page 13.

The biological approach is also called the **medical model** because it is based on the idea of diagnosing physical symptoms and providing appropriate treatments, as is done with physical illness.

A 'concordance rate' is the extent to which two things are related, in this case how frequently both twins have the same disorder.

The medical approach involves the diagnosis of *syndromes* (or diseases) by identifying *symptoms* and then deciding on appropriate treatment. The medical model involves the use of classification systems, such as DSM (**Diagnostic and Statistical Manual of Mental Disorders**) in which each mental disorder is given a list of typical symptoms to help diagnose mental illness. DSM is used in America, whereas ICD (**International Classification of Diseases**) is used in the UK and Europe.

The medical model is the dominant model for explaining and treating mental illness. It tends to be favoured by psychiatrists, whereas clinical psychologists favour psychological models.

1. The biological approach / medical model

The biological approach is based on the view that psychological disorders can be explained in the same way as physical disorders, i.e. they are manifestations of an underlying biochemical or physiological dysfunction, which may or may not have a known cause.

- **Genetic transmission** – Mental illness is the result of an inherited gene or group of genes. Evidence comes from twin or family studies. For example, Gottesman and Shields (1972) found that **concordance rates** for schizophrenia in non-identical twins is about 9%, whereas it rises to 42% in identical twins, indicating some environmental influence, but a larger genetic component for the disorder. Other studies have used **gene-mapping** to demonstrate the location of the actual gene(s) that cause the disorder. For example, Meyer *et al.* (2001) found that a mutation in the gene WKL1 showed up in seven family members with a particular form of schizophrenia, but not in six others who had no symptoms of the disorder.
- **Biochemical abnormalities** – Many studies have found abnormal levels of certain neurotransmitters and/or hormones (see page 112). For example, depression has been linked to low levels of noradrenaline and serotonin, and schizophrenia has been linked to high levels of dopamine. Some forms of depression are related to disordered hormone levels, such as post-partum depression and pre-menstrual syndrome. Abnormal brain chemistry may be the result of faulty genes – Meyer *et al.* propose that the unusual form of WKL1 found in some schizophrenics may cause abnormal protein production. Or, abnormal brain chemistry could be the effect of mental illness. Either way, the use of drugs to return neurotransmitters or hormones to normal levels has been shown to be effective (see page 156).
- **Neuroanatomy** – The structure of the brain has sometimes been found to be different in people with certain mental disorders. For example, Chua and McKenna (1995) reported that the brains of schizophrenic patients were smaller and had larger ventricles than the brains of normal individuals.
- **Infection** – Mental disorders may be caused by a virus or bacteria. For example, general paresis was regarded since the 16th Century as a mental illness, but has since been found to be caused by the syphilis bacterium. Crow (1984) proposed that schizophrenia is caused by a retrovirus, which becomes incorporated into DNA.

Strengths

- The medical treatment of insanity was a move in the direction of **humaneness**. The illness, rather than the patient, was blamed. On the other hand, control is taken away from the patient, who relies on expert guidance.
- At least some disorders have a **biological basis**. However, an exclusive emphasis on biological bases may mean that other factors are overlooked.

Weaknesses

- In many cases, it is not clear whether the physical factor is actually an **effect rather than a cause**.
- The medical model may be appropriate for **physical illness**, but not for mental illness where symptoms are less objective. It overlooks the fact that mental disturbance is often defined in terms of social difficulties. In fact, Clare (1980) pointed out that many physical illnesses also have a social-psychological component and, therefore, the medical model may be insufficient on its own even for physical illnesses.

- The medical approach may **prevent us understanding the true causes** of mental disorders. Szasz (1960) argued in his book *The Myth of Mental Illness* that the medical model is 'worthless and misleading' and 'scientifically crippling'. He claimed that it is a modern day version of demonology and serves the same political purposes, namely social control, by those invested with undisputed authority – the medical profession.
- The medical approach purports to be **value-free** and scientific, but is just as subject to prevailing attitudes as other models.

A combined approach: The diathesis–stress model

It may be more realistic to combine the biological and psychological models. Mental illness arises when both factors combine:

- **Diathesis**: a genetic vulnerability or predisposition.
- **Stress**: some environmental event that triggers the predisposition.

The **diathesis–stress model** explains why, when one identical twin develops a disorder, their twin does not always develop the disorder – because they do not both experience the same environmental triggers. It also explains why people who share certain traumatic experiences do not all develop, for example, depression – because some people are more vulnerable to develop depression.

Progress check

1 Identify **one** key feature of the biological approach.
2 Would you expect identical or non-identical twins to have a higher concordance rate for schizophrenia?
3 Identify **one** similarity between mental and physical illnesses.
4 What is the diathesis–stress model?

4 An explanation that combines diathesis (genetic vulnerability) with stress (environmental trigger).
3 E.g. They both have psycho-social components.
2 Identical twins.
1 E.g. Mental illnesses have a physical cause; Symptoms can be identified and diagnosed.

2. The psychological approach: the psychodynamic model

The psychodynamic approach generally is discussed on page 19.

This model is largely based on Sigmund Freud's psychoanalytic theory. Psychoanalysis is the name used for the theory and the therapy.

- **Psychological causes** – Mental illness is the result of psychological, rather than physical, causes. Freud's first patient, Anna O. (Freud, 1910) suffered from paralysis. He demonstrated that these physical symptoms were psychological because, as soon as she was able to express her unconscious conflicts related to her father's death, her paralysis recovered. (Anna O. later threw some doubt on Freud's explanations).
- **Early experience** – Mental illness can be understood in terms of early experiences. In childhood, the ego is not sufficiently developed to cope well with traumatic experiences and, therefore, these may be repressed. Freud suggested that depression occurs when a child experiences early loss (e.g. the death of a parent) and represses the associated feelings. If, later in life, the individual has further experiences of loss, this awakens the earlier repressed feelings and leads to depression.
- **Unconscious conflicts** – Conflict creates anxiety in the ego. Ego defences form to protect the ego, e.g. projection or repression, and the conflicts become unconscious. Recovery depends on making the unconscious conscious and dealing with repressed anxieties. The associated method of treatment, psychoanalysis, is described on page 158.

Students often confuse *definitions* and *explanations* of abnormality. Consider a person who is severely depressed. Why do we regard this as abnormal? Perhaps because their depression prevents them functioning adequately. However, we might also ask why that person has become depressed. Perhaps it is because of some abnormal neurotransmitters? First, we have *defined* what is abnormal about their depression, then we *explained* why they might have become depressed in the first place.

Strengths
- Freud's explanation of mental illness was the **first attempt** to explain mental illness in psychological terms.
- It is supported by **extensive theory** and therapeutic practice.

Weaknesses
- It is **not a scientifically rigorous** approach. The model is based on concepts that are difficult to prove or disprove (i.e. they lack **falsifiability**) and Freud based his ideas about the development of the normal personality on studies of abnormal adults (only one child was studied – Little Hans).
- It is a **reductionist** model, suggesting that the patient is controlled by instinctual forces and help must come from an expert.
- It is also a **determinist** model based on biological mechanisms (e.g. id and ego, psychosexual stages) and their interactions with life experiences.
- Freud was overconcerned with **sexual factors**, though this may reflect the culture in which he lived. Subsequent psychoanalytic theories (e.g. Erikson) have replaced sexual with social influences.

3. The psychological approach: The behavioural model

The behavioural approach generally is discussed on page 14.

- **Learning theory** – Behaviourists base explanations of all behaviour on learning theory. Abnormal behaviours, like any other behaviours, are learned through the processes of classical and operant conditioning. For example, a phobia may develop because a dog bites you (**classical conditioning**), or because avoidance of something fearful is rewarding (**operant conditioning**) or because you model your behaviour on someone else (**social learning theory**).
- **The focus is on behaviour only** – Only behaviours that are currently observable are important. The patient's history does not matter, nor does any understanding of feelings or thoughts. There is no conscious activity involved in learning. It occurs through conditioning (i.e. association, reinforcement or punishment).

According to the behaviourist view, there are no *mental* disorders because the mind is irrelevant. Psychological disorders are maladaptive behaviour patterns that have arisen through traumatic or inappropriate learning.

- **Treatment** – What can be learned can be unlearned using classical and operant conditioning techniques and focusing only on behaviours (symptoms rather than causes).

Strengths

- The firm scientific basis and operationalised procedures make the theory and therapies **easy to research**.
- The approach has produced **successful therapies** for a range of disorders, e.g. systematic de-sensitisation for phobias (see page 158), exposure and prevention therapy for obsessive-compulsive disorder (see page 164) and aversion therapy for developmental disorders (see page 168). In fact, for some disorders, it is the only viable option, e.g. when the brain is injured. On the other hand, if there are causes of a particular disorder, then just treating the symptoms is only a short-term solution, and the success of behavioural therapies may be quite **unrelated to learning theory**. For example, it may be a matter of giving increased attention.

Weaknesses

The cognitive-behavioural approach draws on both cognitive and behavioural explanations. You can read about examples of cognitive-behavioural therapies on page 159.

- Behaviourist explanations on their own **do not provide adequate explanations** of many disorders, such as depression and schizophrenia. Cognitive-behavioural explanations are a subsequent development and have been more successful as therapies than behaviourist therapies on their own.
- Behaviourist explanations **do not fully explain behaviour**. For example, not everyone who is bitten by a dog becomes a phobic, and equally, some people who have phobias have not necessarily had a fearful experience (e.g. spider phobias).
- Behaviourist explanations are **oversimplified** and based more on animal behaviour than human behaviour, which is more greatly influenced by thoughts and feelings.

4. The psychological approach: the cognitive model

The cognitive model emphasises the role of thoughts, expectations and attitudes (i.e. cognitions) in mental illness, either as causes or as mediating factors.

The cognitive approach generally is discussed on page 18.

- **The role of thinking** – All behaviour is directed by thinking. The cognitive (or cognitive-behavioural) model **grew out of the behavioural model** because the latter was seen as inadequate in its focus on external behaviour only.
- **Faulty thinking** – It is the way you *think* about a situation that is maladaptive, which is different to having maladaptive *behaviour* (as suggested by the behavioural model). 'Cure' can be achieved by restructuring a patient's thinking and enabling them to change their self-beliefs and motivations.

The client is the only one who knows their own cognitions.

- **Client-centred approach** – The cognitive model, unlike the other models, sees the client as being in control of their own behaviour. In all the other models, mental disorder is explained as the consequence of some external force controlling a person's behaviour (biological factors or life experiences). The cognitive model describes mental disorder as the product of a person's own faulty control and, therefore, the only one who can change their behaviour is that person, with the guidance of a therapist.

Strengths

- The cognitive model has led to cognitive/cognitive-behavioural therapies that have been **successful** for disorders such as depression, and are becoming **increasingly popular**.
- It is an **objective approach** that lends itself to research.

Weaknesses

- Like the behavioural model, this approach **does not investigate causes** but just treats behaviours. However, this appeals to some patients, who prefer not to search for deep meanings.
- **Irrational beliefs may be realistic**, for example, a depressed person may have a realistic view of their situation, and trying to change this view may be unrealistic and unhelpful.
- Irrational beliefs may be an **effect rather than a cause** of mental disorder and, therefore, the explanation of faulty thinking may be erroneous (flawed).

Progress check

1 Identify **one** explanation for abnormality, offered by the psychoanalytic model.
2 Suggest **one** key difference between the psychodynamic and behavioural approaches.
3 Which model suggests that the patient is in control?
4 What is meant by 'faulty thinking'?

4 Thinking that is maladaptive.
3 The cognitive model.
2 E.g. The behavioural model focuses on external behaviour only.
1 E.g. Unresolved conflicts create anxiety; Ego defences against anxiety lead to neurotic behaviour.

7.2 Treating abnormality

After studying this section you should be able to:

- describe and evaluate biological therapies, including drugs and ECT
- describe and evaluate psychological therapies, including psychoanalysis, systematic de-sensitisation and Cognitive Behavioural Therapy.

Biological therapies

AQA A   U2

The biological approach to abnormality suggests that there are physical causes for mental disorders. If one believes that mental disorders have a physical basis then it follows that they should be treated using physical or somatic methods (soma = body).

1. Drugs

The main classes of drugs are described below.

- **Anxiolytic drugs** (anti-anxiety) such as benzodiazepines and beta-blockers are used to treat stress and anxiety (see pages 108–109).
- **Anti-psychotic drugs** are used to treat psychotic illnesses such as schizophrenia.
  - **Typical** anti-psychotics, for example, chlorpromazine, are used to treat the positive symptoms of schizophrenia, such as hallucinations. They bind to *dopamine* receptors at the ends of neurons and block the action of dopamine, reducing the positive symptoms (see page 112 for a diagram of a neuron synapse).
  - **Atypical** anti-psychotics, such as clozapine, treat negative symptoms, such as reduced emotional expression, as well as positive symptoms of schizophrenia. They act on the *serotonin* system as well as the dopamine system by temporarily occupying receptor sites and then allowing normal transmission. This may explain why side effects are less severe than when typical anti-psychotics are used.
- **Anti-depressant drugs** (stimulants), such as Prozac, promote activity of *noradrenaline* and *serotonin*, which leads to increased arousal but can be affected by rebound (depression after initial euphoria).
  - **Tricyclics** increase activity of these neurotransmitters by blocking their re-uptake. When a neuron fires, the neurotransmitters are released into the synapse affecting the adjoining neuron; they are then re-absorbed by the neuron, preventing further action. By blocking re-uptake the neurotransmitter levels are increased.
  - **SSRIs (selective serotonin re-uptake inhibitors)** block mainly serotonin.
  - **Selective noradrenaline re-uptake inhibitors** are also now available.

Evaluation of drug therapy

Relapse is a key issue when evaluating treatments for mental disorders. A patient may be relieved of their symptoms for a while but then 'relapse', i.e. go back to having the same symptoms. Therefore, there may initially appear to be a cure (and this is cited as a success for the therapy) but this 'cure' is only temporary.

- Drug treatment is **easy**, **requiring little effort** from the patient.
- Drugs can be particularly **effective** when used in conjunction with **psychotherapy**. They can relieve some of the disabling symptoms and allow the contributing psychological factors to be dealt with.
- The use of drug therapies has offered **significant relief** to many sufferers. For example, WHO (2001) reported that schizophrenics were less likely to relapse when taking anti-psychotics.

The advent of drug therapies in the 1950s led to a large decrease in the number of people in mental institutions.

- However, some of this success may be due to the **psychological effects** of drugs. Kirsch *et al.* (2002) reviewed 38 studies of anti-depressants and found that treatments using **placebos** were almost as effective as using drugs.
- There are problems of **addiction** and **dangerous side-effects**. For example, anti-psychotics cause tardive dyskinesia (involuntary movements of the mouth and tongue). Other symptoms range from high blood pressure to constipation. Such effects explain why many patients stop taking drugs, which is a key reason why they do not work.
- Drugs are **not cures**. They are short-term remedies that very often become long-term. They may mask the underlying problem, preventing a real cure.

2. Electroconvulsive therapy (ECT)

ECT today involves little discomfort, as the patient is given an anaesthetic and a muscle relaxant. An electric shock is applied to the brain to create a seizure.

- **Unilateral ECT** – An electrode is placed above the temple on the non-dominant side of the brain, and another electrode is placed in the middle of the forehead.
- **Bilateral ECT** – An electrode is placed above each temple.
- A very small electric current (about 0.6 amps) is passed through the brain for about half a second and the seizure lasts about a minute. The individual awakes soon after and remembers nothing of the treatment, which is desirable. However, they may also suffer some long-term memory loss.
- The treatment is usually given three times a week over a period of one to five weeks.

Evaluation of ECT

- ECT appears to be **successful for cases of severe depression**. Janicak *et al.* (1985) found that 80% of all severely depressed patients respond well to ECT, compared with 64% recovery when given drug therapy. However, Sackheim *et al.* (2001) found that 84% of patients relapsed within 6 months.
- The method is **potentially dangerous** (death from using anaesthetic) and there are **side effects** such as memory loss, fear and anxiety.
- Some critics believe it should not be used because we don't know the **basis for its success** – it's like hitting a TV to make it work again. However, there are proposed explanations, such as suggesting that the seizure may re-structure disordered thinking or it may alter the biochemical balance of the brain and thus lead to recovery.

Progress check

1 Identify the neurotransmitter that SSRIs enhance.
2 What is a placebo?
3 What kind of ECT affects only one side of the brain?

3 Unilateral ECT.
2 A substance that has no pharmacological effects.
1 Serotonin.

Psychological therapies

Psychological therapies (or psychotherapies) are all derived from psychology approaches to explaining abnormality, i.e. they propose that psychological, rather than physical, factors underlie mental disorder and, therefore, treatments should target the way people think, feel and behave.

Freud did not subscribe to the idea of dream dictionaries. He believed that some items symbolised particular things (for example, a lighthouse might symbolise a penis). But such symbolism was not universal because it depends on experience – a lighthouse would have a different meaning for a lighthouse keeper (it might symbolise the power of a person's employer).

When two researchers find completely different results using the same data, it is worrying! It suggests that possibly the researcher's expectations affected the analysis performed on the data. Researchers sometimes appear to find what they want to find.

1. Psychoanalysis

Psychoanalysis is derived from Freud's theory of personality, which is also sometimes called his theory of psychoanalysis. Thus, psychoanalysis is both the theory and the method for dealing with mental disorders. Freud believed that mental disorder arises from early experiences that create anxiety and so the associated feelings are repressed into the unconscious mind.

However, unconscious thoughts and feelings affect behaviour and create mental disorder. Cure relies on the therapist's ability to make the unconscious conscious and guide the patient in resolving their conflicts. The therapist uses the following techniques to achieve this:

1. **Free association** – The therapist introduces a topic and the patient talks freely about anything that comes into his/her mind. This enables unconscious thoughts and feelings to be uncovered.
2. **Rich interpretation** – The therapist explains the patient's thoughts and feelings using Freud's dynamics of personality development. If a patient resists the interpretation offered, this can be taken as evidence that the therapist is correct because he/she has uncovered issues that create anxiety and are repressed.
3. **Analysis of dreams** – Dreams express the innermost workings of the mind. By talking through a patient's dreams the therapist accesses the 'royal road to the unconscious'. In Freudian therapy, dreams are repressed 'wishes'.
4. **Transference** – The patient transfers their feelings about others onto the therapist, therefore, recreating some of the original anxieties. For example, the therapist may become the hated parent. The therapist then has to deal with these transferred feelings and, therefore, deals with the original repressed anxieties.

Evaluation of psychoanalysis

* Eysenck (1952) examined 10,000 patient histories and found a 44% improvement in patients receiving psychoanalysis, but higher rates for mixed therapies. However, when Bergin (1971) reanalysed the same data using different outcome criteria the psychoanalysis success rose to 83% and the mixed group fell to 65%.
* The emphasis on early conflicts means that **present conflicts** may be overlooked.
* Psychoanalysis has **limited applicability**. It is suitable for intelligent and verbally-able patients, and for wealthy clients with time on their hands, as appointments are usually several times a week over a period of years (sometimes called YAVIS – young, attractive, verbal, intelligent, successful).
* It is only suitable for those mental illnesses where some **insight is retained**, i.e. it is not helpful with schizophrenics.
* Therapy may create **false memories**. This has led to some serious court cases in the USA.

Systematic de-sensitisation is derived from the behavioural approach and is based on the principles of **classical conditioning** (see page 14). At the start of therapy, the S–R link is: feared object (stimulus) → anxiety (learned response). Through SD the patient learns to associate the stimulus with a new response – relaxation.

2. Systematic de-sensitisation (SD)

Systematic de-sensitisation (SD) is mainly used to treat phobias, such as fear of flying or snake phobias. It was a method devised by Wolpe (1958) in which a patient learns to pair the feared thing with relaxation, rather than anxiety.

1. **Relaxation** – The patient is taught deep muscle relaxation. Relaxation will later become associated with the feared object, replacing the existing link between feared object and anxiety. Relaxation also works through **reciprocal inhibition** – the fact that it is impossible to maintain two incompatible emotional responses simultaneously (anxiety and relaxation).
2. **De-sensitisation hierarchy** – The patient constructs a hierarchy of increasingly threatening situations. Typically, there might be 15 items in the hierarchy, such as looking at a picture of the feared object, watching someone else holding it, touching it and so on.
3. **Visualisation** – The patient is asked to imagine each scene whilst deeply relaxed. At any time, if the patient feels anxious, the image is stopped and relaxation is regained. This may take several attempts.
4. **Progression** – When a particular scene can be imagined without creating anxiety, then the patient can move on to the next step in the hierarchy, finally mastering the feared situation.

The whole process typically takes three or four weeks with two sessions per week, but it can be completed more quickly.

Evaluation of SD

- SD has been demonstrated to be **successful** for a certain range of disorders, such as phobias. For example, McGrath *et al.* (1990) found that 75% of patients with phobias recover after a course of SD. However, people may recover spontaneously from phobias so the recovery rate would be almost as good without treatment.
- SD does not require a therapist. It can be **self-administered** by reading about what to do and following the instructions. This makes it a highly accessible method.

An alternative way to explain why SD works is that cognitive restructuring takes place.

- The success of SD **may have nothing to do with relaxation**. Other therapies (e.g. flooding) just expose a person to the feared thing with no hierarchy and no relaxation. Marks (1973) suggests that SD works because of exposure to the feared stimulus, which can be achieved by flooding. Flooding may be rather traumatic, but quicker.
- There is some evidence that SD only works with 'acquired' phobias, rather than those with an innate component, such as fear of open spaces, rather than fear of being bitten by a dog (see page 161 for an explanation of biological preparedness). This would explain why it works for some people (who have learned their phobias) and not others (whose phobias are based on innate fears).

The cognitive approach suggests that mental disorders are due to faulty thinking. Therefore, the therapy aims to change the way the person thinks. This is a particularly useful approach when you cannot change the problem itself – but you can always change the way you think about something.

3. Cognitive Behavioural Therapy (CBT)

Stress inoculation therapy is described and evaluated on page 107. This is an example of a Cognitive Behaviour Therapy – a method of treatment that targets the way a person thinks, as well as the way he/she behaves.

Perhaps one of the best known forms of CBT is **rational-emotional behaviour therapy** (REBT). Ellis (1957) suggested that patients develop a set of irrational beliefs that lead them to react to situations with undesirable emotions. He used the ABC model to describe what happens:

Activating event → **B**eliefs about the activating event → **C**onsequences

For example:
  A. a boy fails on an important school test
  B. he believes that he must be competent in everything he does in order to be a worthwhile person, so
  C. he is plunged into despair.

CBT combines the cognitive and behavioural approaches. The therapies aim to change the way a person thinks *and* behaves.

The therapist is directive and aggressive and challenges beliefs (called 'disputing'), e.g. by asking, 'Who says you must be perfect?'. This leads the patient to ask the same questions and ultimately exchange irrational beliefs for rational ones. There are various types of disputing, such as logical disputing (questioning whether a belief follows logically from available information), and pragmatic disputing (questioning whether a belief is useful).

Evaluation of CBT

- CBT and REBT are **successful** methods. Ellis (1957) claimed a 90% success rate for REBT, and Smith and Glass (1975) reported that REBT was second only to systematic de-sensitisation as a successful therapy (they reviewed 475 studies).
- CBTs are **popular** because they are relatively quick and do not require any search for deep meanings. However, they do require effort from the patient to be successful and, therefore, they do not appeal to everyone.
- The same methods can be applied by the person to **many different situations** once the principles (such as 'disputing') are understood. Therefore, the therapy has a wide application.
- REBT is a fairly aggressive therapy and is also judgemental because the therapist's values may not be shared by the client. This raises **ethical issues**.

Progress check

1 What is the primary aim of psychoanalysis?
2 What is transference?
3 Which method of psychotherapy is Wolpe associated with?
4 What does ABC stand for in REBT?

4 activating event, belief and consequences.
3 Systematic de-sensitisation.
2 Moving the emotions associated with one person onto another person.
1 To make the unconscious conscious and, therefore, deal with repressed emotions.

7.3 Psychological disorders

After studying this section you should be able to:

- describe the symptoms of anxiety disorders: phobias (agoraphobia, social phobias and specific phobias) and obsessive-compulsive disorder (distinguishing between obsession and compulsion)
- describe and evaluate explanations of phobias and obsessive-compulsive disorder, including biological, behavioural, cognitive and psychodynamic
- describe the symptoms of autism, including lack of joint attention and the triad of impairments (autism as a syndrome)
- describe and evaluate explanations of autism, including cold-parenting, biological (genetic and neurological correlates) and cognitive (theory of mind, central coherence deficit and failure of executive functioning)
- describe methods of studying autism, including the Sally–Anne experiment, the 'Smartie tube' test, and comic strip stories
- describe and evaluate therapeutic programmes for autism, including behaviour modification, aversion therapy for self-injuring behaviour, language training (including the Lovaas technique) and parental involvement.

LEARNING SUMMARY

Anxiety disorders: phobias

AQA B   U2

The DSM is explained on page 151.

A phobic disorder involves extreme, persistent and irrational fear together with a lack of control, which is strongly out of proportion to the danger.

Three categories are distinguished by DSM-IV:

- **Agoraphobia** – Fear of open spaces or public places. In most cases, the panic disorder starts first, then the fear of having another attack makes the individual feel insecure about being in public. About 50% of all clinically-diagnosed phobics are suffering from agoraphobia with panic disorder.
- **Social phobias**, such as talking or eating in public, extreme concern about the individual's own behaviour and the reactions of others towards that behaviour.
- **Specific phobias** such as zoophobias (animals), fear of water, fear of heights, etc. Specific phobias generally have little impact on overall quality of life.

The biological approach to abnormality is described on page 151.

1. Biological explanations of phobias

Genetic – Individuals may inherit a genetically-determined predisposition to develop phobias. This is supported by **twin studies**, such as Torgersen (1983), who found 31% concordance for panic disorder with agoraphobia in MZ twins versus zero concordance in DZ twins, though none of them shared the same phobias.

A 'concordance rate' is the extent to which two things are related, in this case, how frequently both twins have the same disorder.

It is also supported by **family studies**. Solyom et al. (1974) found that 45% of phobic patients studied had a family history of the disorder, compared with 17% of 'normal' controls.

Evolutionary – Fear and anxiety are adaptive responses. A fear becomes a phobia when it interferes with normal functioning. The concept of **biological preparedness** (Seligman, 1971) proposes that there would be an adaptive advantage to develop certain ('ancient') fears more readily than others, for example, fear of heights or of strangers, because such fears would increase the survival (and ultimate reproduction) of an individual.

This explains why people acquire certain fears more readily than others, such as a fear of snakes rather than a fear of fast cars.

The diathesis–stress model suggests that illness occurs when a person has a genetic vulnerability or predisposition to develop a particular disorder (**diathesis**) but the disorder only develops if it is triggered by some environmental event or experience (a **stressor**).

Evaluation

- Kendler *et al.* (1992) concluded that **specific phobias have only a small genetic component**, whereas agoraphobia appears to be more related to genetic vulnerability.
- Genetic explanations are only part of the explanation. The **diathesis–stress model** is a fuller explanation. Kleiner and Marshall (1987) reported that 84% of agoraphobics had experienced family problems in the months before they had their first panic attack. This supports the diathesis–stress model.
- Bennett-Levy and Marteau (1984) found that fear was highly correlated with certain aspects of an animal's appearance – the more the animal's appearance was different to human form, the more the animal was feared. This suggests some innate predisposition – a tendency to fear strangeness.
- The concept of biological preparedness cannot explain fears of **harmless situations** or things.

2. Behavioural explanations of phobias

Classical and operant conditioning are explained on page 14, and social learning theory is explained on page 17.

Classical conditioning – Watson and Rayner (1920) conditioned 'Little Albert' to fear white furry objects by pairing a loud noise with a furry object.

It is likely that most phobias are learned through the association of trauma with some neutral stimulus. In addition, the fact that phobics avoid their feared situation means the response is never extinguished.

Operant conditioning – Mowrer (1947) proposed a **two-process theory**: the first stage of developing a phobia involves classical conditioning (as outlined above). The second stage is operant conditioning because the avoidance of the phobia stimulus reduces fear and is, therefore, reinforcing.

Social learning theory – Fears may be learned through imitation. Mineka *et al.* (1984) found that monkeys could develop snake phobias simply by watching another monkey experience fear in the presence of a snake.

Evaluation

- Some fears **may be innate** (see above).
- **Not everyone who is exposed to conditioning** develops phobias. For example, DiNardo *et al.* (1988) found that as many people without dog phobias as those with dog phobias reported negative experiences with dogs.

3. Cognitive explanations of phobias

Phobias may be the result of irrational thoughts. For example, the sensation of crowding in a lift may develop into a cognition that lifts are associated with suffocation.

Cognitive explanations centre on irrational thinking and faulty cognition. See page 18 for a general explanation of the cognitive approach and page 154 for the cognitive approach to abnormality.

Eysenck (1997) reports research on biological challenges (e.g. breathing a mixture of carbon dioxide and oxygen). This often provokes a panic attack in patients suffering from panic disorder with agoraphobia, but rarely in normal controls. Panic attack patients may differ in the way they *interpret* their bodily symptoms.

Evaluation

- The **success of behavioural and cognitive-behavioural therapies** in treating phobias supports their value as explanations.

4. Psychodynamic explanations of phobias

The basics of Freudian theory are described on page 19, and on page 153 it is applied to abnormality.

Freud (1909) suggested that phobias arise when anxieties are displaced onto the phobic object that symbolises the initial conflict. If the conflict is resolved the phobia will disappear.

Freud used the classic case study of Little Hans to illustrate the process. Hans developed a fear of horses because the horse represented the boy's unconscious fear of his father. He was also afraid of being bitten by a horse, whereas he was actually scared that his mother would leave him.

Evaluation

Falsifiability refers to the ability to prove a theory wrong. It is possible to present a Freudian explanation to fit any facts.

- Freudian explanations lack **falsifiability**. There are other, possibly more plausible explanations, for example, Hans might have developed his fear through **classical conditioning**.
- Data collection in such studies relies on **retrospective recall**, which may be unreliable.
- Such data is **correlational** and does not demonstrate a causal link.

Anxiety disorders: *Obsessive-compulsive disorder (OCD)*

AQA B   U2

The AQA B specification requires that you know about treatments of phobias and OCD – you can read about these on pages 156–160. In particular, the AQA B specification mentions drug therapy, psychodynamic therapy (psychoanalysis), systematic de-sensitisation and flooding, and cognitive therapy.

OCD involves two components:

- **Obsessions** – Recurrent, intrusive thoughts that are classed as inappropriate or forbidden. The individual feels unable to control them, which creates intense anxiety.
- **Compulsions** – They develop as a means of controlling the obsessive thoughts. These compulsions are repetitive behaviours or thoughts, such as repeated hand-washing. Most OCD patients recognise that their compulsions are unreasonable, but they cannot control them. This creates further anxiety.

1. Biological explanations of OCD

Genetic – Individuals may inherit a genetically-determined predisposition to develop OCD. This is supported by family studies, such as Nestadt *et al.* (2000) who found that people who had a relative with OCD were five times more likely to develop OCD than members of the general population.

Remember that evolutionary explanations for mental disorders are based on the assumption that such disorders are inherited, or a predisposition for the disorder is inherited.

Evolutionary – It may be that some aspects of OCD behaviour are adaptive and, therefore, humans are predisposed to develop the disorder. For example, ritualistic behaviours often concern hygiene (e.g. repeated hand-washing) and may be adaptive insofar as extra vigilance over cleanliness might promote survival.

Brain biochemistry – OCD has been linked to low levels of the neurotransmitter serotonin, and high levels of dopamine.

Evaluation

- **Concordance rates in twin studies are quite high** for OCD. For example, Rasmussen and Tsuang (1986) found as much as 87% concordance for identical twins. This supports a genetic explanation. However, relatives do not have the same obsessive rituals so this suggests that what is inherited is a tendency to be obsessive.
- One problem with biochemical explanations is that it is not clear whether abnormalities are **the cause or the effect**.

Drug therapies do not provide a permanent solution as patients relapse when they stop taking the drugs.

- The success of drug therapies indicates the involvement of biochemical factors. For example, the use of SSRIs to increase serotonin levels has been shown to be effective. Piggott *et al.* (1996) found improvement in 42% of patients over a period of two years.

2. Behavioural explanations of OCD

Mowrer's two-process theory for phobias can be applied to OCD.

Classical conditioning – Some thoughts become associated with an event that creates anxiety, and then take on the associated properties of the event. For example, a mother looks at her baby and thinks 'I could smother this child'. Such thoughts create intense anxiety and in the future, just looking at the child creates intense anxiety.

Operant conditioning – Distress and compulsive behaviours are maintained because the person learns to avoid the anxiety by escaping (e.g. going to wash their hands).

Evaluation

- OCD patients are **not always able to identify a traumatic event** that may have triggered the disorder. Several obsessions can be present within one individual and the obsessions can change without the occurrence of new traumas. This suggests a predisposition to develop the disorder as a response to everyday events.
- The behavioural explanation has led to a successful therapy for OCD patients called **exposure and prevention therapy (ERP)**. Patients are exposed to situations that trigger their obsessions but are prevented from engaging in their usual compulsive response. This enables the person to experience a lack of anxiety following the trigger behaviour. ERP therapy provides opportunities for re-learning. Albucher *et al.* (1998) reported that 60–90% of OCD patients improve considerably using ERP.

ERP is a form of Cognitive Behavioural Therapy because it deals with thoughts and behaviour.

3. Cognitive explanations of OCD

OCD patients suffer from impaired information-processing (faulty thinking). People often have unwanted or intrusive thoughts (such as being infected by germs or harming someone) but these are usually easily dismissed. However, for some people they cannot be ignored. Such individuals think in terms of rigidly defined categories, or believe they should have total control, both of which are examples of maladaptive or faulty thinking. The thoughts create self-blame, depression and anxiety. Neutralising thoughts or acts reduce the obsessive thoughts and these become compulsive, because each time they are performed they reduce the unwanted thoughts and this makes them harder and harder to resist.

Cognitive explanations are similar to behavioural ones but there is greater emphasis on thought processes (faulty thinking).

Faulty thinking may be a product of genetic factors.

Evaluation

- There is some evidence that OCD patients do have **more intrusive thoughts** than normal people (Clark, 1992).
- There is no evidence to show that faulty thinking is the **cause, rather than a consequence** of OCD symptoms.

4. Psychodynamic explanations of OCD

OCD develops when the id produces unacceptable impulses that create anxiety for the ego and thus are dealt with by ego defences. The three most common ego defences for OCD are:

- **Isolation** – The ego isolates itself from the unacceptable impulses, but occasionally they intrude as obsessive thoughts.
- **Undoing** – This takes over when obsessive thoughts intrude, and deals with the anxiety by producing compulsive acts that symbolically undo the unacceptable impulses from the id, for example compulsive hand-washing is a symbolical undoing.
- **Reaction formation** – Behaviours are performed that are the opposite to the unacceptable impulses, as a means of reducing anxiety. For example, being exceptionally kind when experiencing very aggressive impulses.

The **id** is the primitive 'I want' part of the self, motivated by the pleasure principle. The **ego** is the realistic part of the self that tries to avoid feelings of anxiety.

Evaluation

See pages 20 and 153 for general criticisms of Freud's psychoanalytic theory.

- Psychoanalysis (the therapy related to Freud's psychodynamic theory) may actually have a **negative effect** on OCD recovery, which does not support the Freudian explanation.
- Adler (1931) produced a **different psychodynamic explanation** for OCD, which suggests that OCD develops because of feelings of inferiority. Therefore, the treatment derived from this approach focuses on building confidence.

Progress check

1 Seligman proposed that certain fears are adaptive and innate. What did he call his explanation?
2 What is Mowrer's two-process theory?
3 What neurotransmitters are linked to OCD?
4 What is the key concept in cognitive explanations?

4 Irrational, faulty or maladaptive thinking/cognitions/information-processing.
3 Serotonin (low levels) and dopamine (high levels).
2 A behavioural explanation for the development of anxiety disorders, involving classical and operant conditioning.
1 Biological preparedness.

Autism

Autism is a condition that becomes apparent very early in life. People with autism usually have three areas of difficulty: (1) social interaction (indifference to other people); (2) social communication (e.g. difficulty understanding social gestures); (3) imagination (e.g. lack of imaginative play).

People with autism also have a range of other difficulties, such as learning difficulties, obsessive interests, resistance to changes in their routine, odd mannerisms and repetitive behaviour patterns.

Asperger's syndrome is a similar condition to autism except that individuals tend to have normal or high IQs. In fact, the range of different symptoms has led to the term 'autistic spectrum disorders'.

Autism is a complex disorder and is likely to be caused by an array of genes rather than one single gene.

Cognitive explanations centre on irrational thinking and faulty cognition. (See page 18 for a general explanation of the cognitive approach and page 154 for the cognitive approach to abnormality.)

Explanations of autism

1. Cold-parenting

Leo Kanner (1943) first identified the common features of autism and claimed that the condition was due to a genuine lack of maternal warmth towards a child, and a lack of attachment to the child (the 'refrigerator mother').

Bettelheim (1967) popularised these ideas, comparing the autistic child to a prisoner in a concentration camp and parents to SS guards. He suggested that autistic children withdrew as a response to the cruel and unloving situation at home. Bettelheim based this on his own observations of the parents of autistic children.

Evaluation

- Kanner may have confused **cause and effect**. Cold-parenting might be an effect of a child lacking important social skills.
- This explanation is now regarded as **over-simplistic and erroneous** – blame is no longer placed on parents. Bettelheim claimed an 85% success rate for his work, but this was discredited after his death.

2. Biological explanations

Genetic – Various studies have identified certain genes as being common to individuals with autism. For example, Geschwind *et al.* (2005) found a gene on chromosome 17 linked to autism in boys. The effect of this gene on boys rather than girls may explain the increased incidence of autism in boys.

Neurological correlates – Some studies have found evidence of a link between autism and low levels of serotonin. Sutcliffe *et al.* (2005) found that serotonin abnormalities in autistic individuals were also linked to chromosome 17.

Evaluation

- The research on the biological basis of autism reflects the **complexity of the disorder**. There are no clear genetic or biochemical causes, probably because autism is in fact a range of disorders where a range of autism-related genes are sufficient, but none are necessary.
- The fact that 100% concordance has not been found between the presence of a gene and autism suggests that **biology cannot be the sole explanation**.

3. Cognitive explanations

Theory of mind (ToM) is the ability to understand what is going on in another person's mind, to 'guess' what they are thinking or feeling. Lack of ToM is a kind of 'mind-blindness'. The lack of ToM in autistic people would explain the social difficulties that are common in autistic people, as well as their lack of pretend play.

Baron-Cohen *et al.* (1985) tested this using the Sally–Anne test (see page 167) and showed that almost all autistic children could not cope, whereas children with a low mental age (Down's syndrome) could cope, ruling out the influence of intelligence.

Central coherence deficit (Weak central coherence, WCC) – People favour different cognitive styles. Frith (1989) suggested that some people focus more on the individual components of any experience or event, rather than seeing the 'bigger picture'. Such a 'weak' central coherence means more difficulty in switching attention flexibly and more difficulty with social relations. There is evidence that autistic people are *better* on tasks where a figure has to be divided into constituent parts (e.g. the Embedded Figures Task where hidden shapes in drawings have to be found, Happé, 1994).

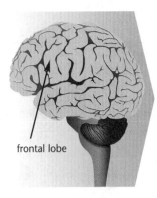

frontal lobe

Failure of executive functioning – The term 'executive functioning' refers to higher cognitive functions, such as planning, working memory, impulse control and mental flexibility, which are all located in the frontal lobe of the brain (see diagram on left). Autism may be, in part, caused by deficits in these functions, which fits with some of the characteristic behaviours, such as stereotyped behaviours.

Evaluation

- Cognitive explanations fit with **biological explanations** because deficits probably have a physical basis.
- The 'difference' view, put forward by WCC, is a more **positive approach** because it suggests that autism is not a deficit but instead it is a different kind of information processing.
- There is **good research evidence** for all these explanations, though also **some lack of support**. For example, Mottron *et al.* (1999) report that some studies have found evidence of intact central coherence among people with autism, and also some studies have found that executive function deficits are not found in young autistic children.

The term 'autistics' is commonly used as a short hand – however, it is preferable to use the phrase 'people with autism' to indicate that autism does not affect the whole personality; there is a danger that a person with autism (or any mental disorder) becomes perceived as nothing but their condition.

Methods of studying autism

1. Sally–Anne test

- Sally puts her ball in her basket and leaves the room.
- Anne moves the ball to her box.
- Sally returns. Where will she look for her ball?

People who have a theory of mind will say that Sally will look in her basket, whereas people lacking a theory of mind (e.g. autistic children) will say that Sally will look in Anne's box (because they cannot perceive that another person will think differently to them and they know that the ball is in Anne's box).

1.

This is Sally   This is Anne

2.

Sally puts her ball in the basket

3.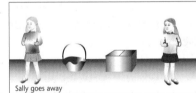

Sally goes away

4.

Annes moves the ball to her box

5.

Where will Sally look for her ball?

2. The 'Smartie tube' test

A child is shown a tube of Smarties and asked what is inside. The answer is inevitably 'Smarties'.

The child is then shown that a pencil is inside and then again asked what is inside and answers 'pencil'. Finally, the child is told that another child (Susan) is going to play the game and is asked what Susan will answer to the question, 'What is inside?'. A child with a theory of mind will say 'Smarties', but autistic children (lacking theory of mind) tend to answer 'pencil'.

3. Comic strip stories

Mechanical story

Behavioural story

Belief story

Theory of mind can be tested by asking children to arrange pictures into simple stories. In order to do this, a child has to imagine what the story character is thinking.

Baron-Cohen *et al.* (1986) tested the three groups of children (autistic, Down's Syndrome and 'normal') on the three types of stories. Autistic children found most difficulty with the belief story (requiring a theory of mind), but did better than 'normal' children on the mechanical story (no theory of mind).

Therapeutic programmes for autism

The therapies described here are based on behaviourist principles and are particularly suitable for individuals with limited intellectual abilities, which is a characteristic of many autistic people.

1. Aversion therapy for self-injuring behaviour

An individual is given an unpleasant shock or some aversive stimulus each time they do something that is self-harmful. This results in an association between self-injury and the unpleasant experience, reducing the likelihood of repeating the self-damaging behaviour.

Aversion therapy is based on **classical conditioning** (see page 14 for a fuller explanation).

Aversion means avoidance.

- **Before** conditioning: UCS (shock) creates UCR (fear and aversive or avoidance behaviour).
- **During** conditioning: Shock and harmful behaviour are paired.
- **After** conditioning: Harmful behaviour becomes CS, producing CR (fear and aversive behaviour).

Evaluation

- This is an **unpleasant treatment** and may result in psychological problems such as resentment. However, it **may be the only way** to prevent severe self-injury in children with limited mental ability, so the benefits may outweigh the costs.
- The method has been used with **some success** when treating alcoholics, smokers and sexual deviants.

2. Behaviour modification

There are a number of behaviour modification techniques, such as:

Behaviour modification is based on **operant conditioning** (see page 14).

Shaping – Behaviour can be changed or modified through a system of progressive rewards. Initially, almost any behaviour is rewarded but gradually rewards are given for behaviours that are closer and closer to the target behaviour.

Token economy – Autistic people are given tokens for achieving target behaviours. The tokens can be exchanged for rewards such as sweets or special activities.

Evaluation

- Behavioural techniques **may not provide cures**; once rewards are withdrawn, behaviours may relapse.
- Behavioural techniques are **most effective** when started in early childhood and when they are very structured. One danger is that rewards are given for peripheral behaviours (e.g. the child gets attention for being naughty, which acts as a kind of reinforcement) and this spoils the effectiveness of the target rewards.

3. Language training

The Lovaas technique (also called **Applied Behaviour Analysis, ABA**) was established by Lovaas (1987). It is a form of behaviour modification therapy and is appropriate for children.

The programme identifies a range of target behaviours that are causing difficulties, such as language problems, self-care skills and self-damaging behaviour. Lovaas originally used punishments (e.g. shocks) as well as rewards to modify behaviour. Punishments are used less today, although some claim that this lessens the effectiveness of the method (Dawson, 2004).

Evaluation

- There is considerable **evidence of the success** of the technique. For example, Anderson *et al.* (1987) found that even an average of 20 hours a week of one-to-one support over a period of a year brought about significant improvement in cognitive functioning in half the sample of children treated.
- The method relies on **intensive interaction** (Lovaas recommended 40 hours a week) which means high costs, and it may not be successful with all children.
- The research evidence has been criticised because of selective sampling (some autistic children were rejected as unsuitable) and also because the studies tend to be conducted by supporters of the technique and, therefore, lack objectivity.

4. Parental involvement

Division TEACCH started in 1966 as part of the Department of Psychiatry at the University off Carolina, USA.

Special home programmes have been devised, such as the TEACCH (Treatment and Education of Autistic and Related Communication Handicapped Children) model, where parents were advised about their children's particular cognitive strengths and needs.

Evaluation

- Lovaas *et al.* (1973) found that children with autism tended to relapse at the end of treatment if they returned to an institutional setting rather than to their homes. No relapse was observed among those children who returned home to parents who had learned to implement behavioural techniques.

Progress check

1. What explanation of autism was suggested by Kanner?
2. Name **one** cognitive explanation for autism, other than ToM.
3. Name **one** method used to study ToM.
4. Which therapy for autism is based on classical conditioning?

4 Aversion therapy.
3 E.g. Sally–Anne test; Smartie tube test.
2 Central coherence deficit or failure of executive functioning.
1 Cold parenting.

Sample question and student answers – AQA A question

1

1(a) The first two answers are correct but ECT is not a behavioural therapy – systematic desensitisation would have been acceptable. **2 out of 3 marks.**

(a) For each approach listed in the table below, identify a method of treatment based on the approach. *(3 marks)*

Biological approach	(i)
Psychodynamic approach	(ii)
Behavioural approach	(iii)

(i) Drugs, (ii) Psychoanalysis, (iii) ECT

(b) Outline **two** attempts to define abnormality. *(6 marks)*

(b) The question requires an outline of two definitions and the candidate has fulfilled this requirement. Both definitions are clearly explained and accurate. **6 out of 6 marks.**

One way to define abnormality is in terms of social norms. The standard for what is normal is set in terms of what most people in any society think is an appropriate way to behave. Any behaviour that is inappropriate is then regarded as abnormal. A second way to define abnormality is in terms of mental health. This means that we say what kind of psychological behaviours are signs of good mental health, such as autonomy and accurate perception of reality. If these are lacking in an individual then they are psychologically abnormal.

(c) Describe **one** limitation of one of the definitions you described in part (b). *(3 marks)*

(c) An appropriate limitation, but it is a little unclear (in what way is it 'abuse') and also there is not sufficient detail for the 3 marks available, so some more examples might have been provided. A generous **2 out of 3 marks.**

One limitation of the social norms definition is that it allows abuse to take place because societies may define some behaviours as unacceptable, such as homosexuality.

(d) Tom was involved in a major car accident and since then has refused to get into a car. In fact, he becomes sweaty and anxious when he even hears a car. Explain how Tom's fear might have developed, using **one** explanation of abnormality that you have studied. *(4 marks)*

(d) In questions that require you to apply your knowledge, there is always a danger that you become too focused on the psychology and forget to engage with the stimulus – as here. The student has not answered the question and, despite having presented lots of good psychology, would get only **1 out of 4 marks.**

One way to explain Tom's fear is using the behavioural approach. This suggests that people develop mental disorders through either classical or operant conditioning, or both. In classical conditioning a person learns to associate a previously neutral stimulus to a response, forming a new S–R link. In operant conditioning a behaviour is rewarded, which increases the likelihood that it will be repeated.

(e) Describe **one** method that psychologists have used to study explanations of abnormality. *(4 marks)*

(e) A well-detailed and accurate answer. **4 out of 4 marks.**

One method is twin studies, which are used to demonstrate whether a certain mental disorder has a genetic basis. For example, a researcher looks at identical and non-identical twins to see if concordance rates are higher in the identical twins. If this is true then this suggests that the disorder has a genetic basis. A concordance rate is the extent to which two things are the same.

Practice examination question – AQA A question

1

Describe and evaluate the cognitive approach to explaining abnormality.

(12 marks)

Sample question and student answers – AQA B question

1

(a) Use your knowledge of psychology to explain why a young girl may develop a fear of spiders because her mother is very afraid of them.

(2 marks)

1(a) The other obvious answer would be a genetic link, but this student answer is fine. **2 out of 2 marks.**

The young girl may imitate her mother, which is a social learning explanation. She is modelling her mother's behaviour.

(b) Autism is a disorder that affects a person's social abilities. Describe **one** method used to investigate autism.

(3 marks)

(b) This is a clear description of the Sally–Anne method – as far as it goes, but the end isn't quite right. The point is that a child without a theory of mind will behave differently when questioned, and this has not been included. **2 out of 3 marks.**

The Sally–Anne test is used to test autism. What happens is that a child is told that Sally puts a ball in her basket and then leaves a room. While she's gone, Anne moves the ball into her box. When Sally comes back, the question is where does she think the ball is.

(c) Discuss explanations of autism.

(10 marks)

(c) This is a good student answer, demonstrating sound knowledge and understanding. The answer is well-organised and gives a brief outline of each explanation followed by an evaluation of the explanation – the command word 'discuss' requires both description and evaluation in equal measure. A good range of explanations has been examined in reasonable detail. Alternatively, the student might have described only two or three explanations but in greater detail – there is a requirement to cover at least two explanations. **10 out of 10 marks.**

One explanation of autism is that it is biological. Certain people inherit a gene, or genes, that lead to autism. This is supported by studies that have looked at genes and linked autism to a particular gene. Geschwind found evidence linking autism in boys to a gene on chromosome 17. However, the genetic explanation is not likely to be the whole story because 100% concordance is not found in identical twins. It may act as a predisposition to develop the disorder, as suggested by the diathesis–stress model.

Another kind of explanation is cognitive explanations. For example, Theory of Mind. This explains why people with autism have difficulty with social relationships – because they lack the ability to understand what another person is thinking (this is theory of mind). It could be that the lack of ToM is genetic. Evidence from Baron-Cohen shows that many autistic children do lack ToM (using the Sally–Anne test) but it is not true of all autistic people.

Another cognitive explanation is central coherence deficit. This is a good explanation because it suggests that autistic people are not necessarily deficient but just different. They tend to focus more on the individual components rather than the whole. It has been supported by research as well, such as using the Embedded Figures Task (Happe).

One of the first explanations of autism was put forward by Kanner and later Bettleheim, who both suggested it was due to cold parenting, i.e. parents who were unresponsive and did not become attached to their children. However, today this explanation is not given much credit. Cold parenting could be the effect, rather than the cause, of autism.

Practice examination questions – AQA B question

1

(a) Identify **two** types of phobia.

(2 marks)

(b) Explain how systematic de-sensitisation can be used to treat phobias.

(3 marks)

(c) Describe and evaluate a biological explanation for obsessive compulsive disorder.

(10 marks)

Revise
A2

Psychology
AQA

Cara Flanagan

Contents

Part 3 : AQA B Unit 3

Part 4 : AQA B Unit 4

Specification lists

MODULE		SPECIFICATION TOPIC	CHAPTER REFERENCE	STUDIED IN CLASS	REVISED	PRACTICE QUESTIONS
Unit 3		Biological rhythms and sleep	1.1, 1.2, 1.3			
		Perception	2.1 (AS Unit 2.4), 2.2, 2.3			
		Relationships	3.1, 3.2, 3.3			
		Aggression	4.1, 4.2, 4.3			
		Eating behaviour	5.1, 5.2, 5.3			
		Gender	6.1, 6.2, 6.3			
		Intelligence and learning	7.1, 7.2, 7.3			
		Cognition and development	8.1, 8.2, 8.3			
Unit 4	Section A	Schizophrenia	9.1, 9.2, 9.3			
		Depression	10.1, 10.2, 10.3			
		Anxiety disorder – phobias	11.1, 11.2, 11.3			
		Anxiety disorder – OCD	12.1, 12.2, 12.3			
	Section B	Media psychology	13.1, 13.2, 13.3			
		The psychology of addictive behaviour	14.1, 14.2, 14.3			
		Anomalistic psychology	15.1, 15.2, 15.3			
	Section C	Psychological research and scientific method	16.1, 16.2 (AS Units 4.1, 4.2 and 7.3), 16.3 (AS Unit 4.3)			

Examination analysis

The A2 AQA A specification comprises two examination units: Unit 3 and Unit 4.

Unit 3 Topics in Psychology   *1½ hours 50% of A2 (25% of A level)*

The unit exam is divided into eight sections, each containing one essay-style question. There is one section for each of the topics listed in the table above. Each question is worth 25 marks. Candidates must answer three out of the eight questions. QWC (quality of written communication) will be assessed in each question.

The total mark for this paper is 75.
Available in January and June.

Unit 4 Psychopathology, Psychology in Action and Research Methods   *2 hours 50% of A2 (25% of A level)*

The unit exam is divided into three sections:
- **Section A** Psychopathology: one essay-style question to be answered from a choice of three (on schizophrenia, depression and anxiety disorder). QWC will be assessed in this essay.
- **Section B** Psychology in Action: one question to be answered from a choice of three (one from each topic).
- **Section C** Research methods: one compulsory structured question.

The total mark for this paper is 85 (Sections A and B are worth 25 marks; Section C is worth 35 marks.)
Available in January and June.

AQA B Psychology

MODULE		SPECIFICATION TOPIC	CHAPTER REFERENCE	STUDIED IN CLASS	REVISED	PRACTICE QUESTIONS
Unit 3	Section A	**Child Development**				
		Social development	17.1 (AS Unit 3.1)			
		Cognitive development	8.1, 17.2			
		Moral development	8.2, 17.3			
	Section B	**Applied Options**				
		Cognition and law	18.1 (AS Unit 2.2)			
		Schizophrenia and mood disorders	9.1, 9.2, 9.3, 10.1, 10.2, 10.3, 18.2			
		Stress and stress management	18.3 (AS Unit 5.1 and 5.2)			
		Substance abuse	18.4			
		Forensic psychology	18.5			
Unit 4		Approaches in psychology	19.1 (AS Unit 1.1)			
		Debates in psychology	16.1, 19.2			
		Methods in psychology (AS Unit 4.1, 4.2,	16.2, 16.3, 19.3, 4.3 and 7.3)			

Examination analysis

The A2 specification comprises two examination units: Unit 3 and Unit 4.

Unit 3   Child Development and Applied Options   2 hours 50% of A2 (25% of A level)
The unit exam is divided into two sections:

- **Section A** *Child Development: one structured question to be answered from a choice of three (one from each topic). QWC (quality of written communication) will be assessed in this essay.*
- **Section B** *Applied Options: two structured questions to be answered from a choice of five (one from each topic). QWC will be assessed in these essays.*

The total mark for this paper is 60, divided equally between the three questions.
Available in January and June.

Unit 4   Approaches, Debates and Methods in Psychology   2 hours 50% of A2 (25% of A level)
The unit exam is divided into three sections:

- **Section A** *Approaches in Psychology: one structured question to be answered from a choice of two. QWC will be assessed in this essay.*
- **Section B** *Debates in Psychology: one compulsory structured question. QWC will be assessed in this essay.*
- **Section C** *Methods in Psychology: one compulsory structured question.*

The total mark for this paper is 60, divided equally between the three questions.
Available in June only.

Psychology A level: AS and A2

AS and A2

All Psychology A level courses are in two parts. Most students will start by studying the AS (Advanced Subsidiary) course in the first year and then go on to study the second part of the A level course (A2) in the second year. To gain the full A level you need to complete both the AS and A2 courses. Some students just do the AS course. Usually the full A level takes two years, allowing one year for AS and one year for A2. But you can take more or less time to complete it.

The Psychology A level is assessed in four unit exams: two are AS and two are A2. These are generally available in January and June every year.

> Even though you can resit unit exams as often as you like, this information may be passed on by the exam board.

Assessment objectives

> Psychology is a science subject and, therefore, it shares assessment objectives with all science subjects.

Following an examination course means that much of your learning is guided by how it will ultimately be assessed. Examination boards set out their 'assessment objectives', which are their criteria for assessing performance. In the A level examinations there are three skill clusters or *assessment objectives*, which, in brief, are **describe** (AO1), **evaluate** (AO2) and **conduct** (AO3). There is also an assessment of the **quality of written communication** (QWC).

Assessment objective 1 (AO1)

Knowledge and understanding of science and of *How Science Works*. Candidates should be able to:
(a) recognise, recall and show understanding of scientific knowledge
(b) select, organise and communicate relevant information.

Assessment objective 2 (AO2)

Application of knowledge and understanding of science and of How Science Works. Candidates should be able to:
(a) analyse and evaluate scientific knowledge and processes
(b) apply scientific knowledge and processes to unfamiliar situations, including those related to issues
(c) assess the validity, reliability and credibility of scientific information.

Assessment objective 3 (AO3)

How Science Works in Psychology. Candidates should be able to:
(a) describe ethical, safe and skilful practical techniques and processes, selecting appropriate qualitative and quantitative methods
(b) know how to make, record and communicate reliable and valid observations and measurements with appropriate precision and accuracy, through the use of primary and secondary sources
(c) analyse, interpret, explain and evaluate the methodology, results and impact of their own and others' experimental and investigative activities in a variety of ways.

Quality of Written Communication (QWC)

Quality of written communication refers to the use of accurate spelling, punctuation and grammar, and the ability to organise information.

Types of examination questions used at A2

A2 questions come in three varieties, as shown below.

Essay-style questions

Essay-style questions are used in AQA A questions only. In such cases the question is not parted. There is a requirement to include description (AO1), evaluation (AO2) and commentary on methodology (AO3). Question examples:
- *Describe and evaluate Piaget's theory of cognitive development. (25 marks)*
- *Discuss **two** biological explanations of schizophrenia. (25 marks)*

Structured questions

Most A2 questions are structured questions where the question is divided into two or more parts. The parts usually have a common context and often become progressively more demanding as you work your way through the question.
Each part may be wholly description (AO1), for example:
- *Describe psychological research into circadian rhythms. (9 marks)*
- *Describe what Piaget meant by class inclusion. (3 marks)*

Or, each part may be wholly evaluation (AO2), for example:
- *Evaluate research related to circadian rhythms. (10 marks)*

Or, each part may be a mixture of AO1 and AO2, for example:
- *Outline and evaluate biological explanations of addiction. (10 marks)*
- *Discuss the humanistic approach to psychology. (15 marks)*

Some parts may focus specifically on methodology (AO3), for example:
- *Suggest **three** behavioural categories that could be used by researchers in an observational study of friendship in children aged four years. (3 marks)*

In the AQA A exam AO3 marks are combined with AO2 marks. This is because it is difficult to separate AO2 and AO3 in practice, as any evaluation is likely to include reference to methodology (see mark schemes on pages 10–11).

Stimulus material questions

Some questions begin with a sentence or several sentences to 'set the scene'. The question then follows from this quotation or stimulus material (sometimes also called 'source material'). It is important in such questions to relate your answer to the quotation or stimulus material. This style is used in research methods questions where the details of a research study are outlined, followed by a series of questions.

Command words

To some extent you can work out what skills are required by the command word at the start of the question. However, there is some flexibility in the way these are used. For example, 'explain' may be all AO1 or may be a combination of AO1 and AO2 marks. The best advice is to just answer the question, but at the same time you should be aware of the meaning *usually* attached to the common command words (shown on the next page).
You can also study the meaning of the command words by looking at the mark schemes published on the AQA website.

Examples of A2 command words (injunctions)

Outline, suggest	To briefly describe without too much detail, identifying the main points.
Describe	To provide a detailed description.
Explain	Present an explanation of an issue; this involves more than just describing something; you should also try to make the concept clear or intelligible so that a person can undestand it.
Distinguish between	Identify and describe differences.
Briefly evaluate	To evaluate without too much elaboration.
Evaluate (or critically evaluate)	Present criticisms, which may include positive (i.e. strengths or advantages) and negative (i.e. limitations or disadvantages) points, as well as other means of evaluation, such as applications or implications, and especially methodology.
Discuss	To include both description and evaluation, including considerations related to research methodology.

What are examiners looking for?

In Psychology examiners are looking for evidence of your knowledge, but often there are no 'right' answers. There are a range of correct answers and any of these will receive credit – the examiner is looking for any evidence of your knowledge *as appropriate to the question set*.

The examiners mark your answers *positively*. They do not subtract marks when material is missing. Instead they aim to award marks for any material that is relevant.

A* grades

To achieve an A* grade, you need to achieve a...

- grade A overall (80% or more on uniform mark scale) for the <u>whole</u> A level qualification
- grade A* (90% or more on the uniform mark scale) acrosss your A2 units.

A* grades are awarded for the A level qualification only and not for the AS qualification or individual units.

Important information

This book is based on the latest specifications, however, these do change and candidates should always consult the exam board website for the latest versions, and to look at recent mark schemes.

Mark schemes used at A2

AQA A A2 marking criteria

AQA A AO1 mark bands (questions worth 9 marks)

Examiners use marking guidelines similar to the ones on this page and the following pages to assess the AO1, AO2 and AO3 components of extended writing questions.

9–8 marks	**Sound** Knowledge and understanding are accurate and well-detailed. A good range of relevant material has been selected. There is substantial evidence of breadth/depth. Organisation and structure of the answer are coherent.
7–5 marks	**Reasonable** Knowledge and understanding are generally accurate and reasonably detailed. A range of relevant material has been selected. There is evidence of breadth and/or depth. Organisation and structure of the answer are reasonably coherent.
4–3 marks	**Basic** Knowledge and understanding are basic/relatively superficial. A restricted range of material has been presented. Organisation and structure of the answer are basic.
2–1 marks	**Rudimentary** Knowledge and understanding are rudimentary and may be muddled and/or inaccurate. The material presented may be very brief or largely irrelevant. Lacks organisation and structure.
0 marks	No creditworthy material.

In the AQA A A2 exam, all questions are marked out of a total of 25 marks, divided between 9 AO1 marks and 16 AO2/AO3 marks (except for the research methods question).

A summary table of AO1 mark bands (for questions worth 9 marks)

An examiner decides on which mark to award by first identifying the band that best describes the essay answer. They then decide on the actual mark within the band by considering whether they were more drawn to the band above or the band below, or neither. It is likely that an answer contains elements of several band descriptors but the examiner selects the best fit.

Marks	Knowledge and understanding	Range of relevant material	Breadth and depth	Organisation and structure
9–8	Accurate and well-detailed	Selected	Substantial	Coherent
7–5	Generally accurate and well-detailed	Selected	Evidence	Reasonably coherent
4–3	Basic/relatively superficial	Restricted		Basic
2–1	Rudimentary, muddled and/or inaccurate	Brief or largely irrelevant		Lacking
0	No creditworthy material			

AO1 marks bands (for questions worth 5 marks)

5–4	Outline is reasonably thorough, accurate and coherent.
3–2	Outline is limited, generally accurate and reasonably coherent.
1	Outline is weak and muddled.
0	No creditworthy material

AQA A AO2/AO3 mark bands

If a question is marked out of 10 or out of 6 the same mark bands apply as for questions marked out of 16. The marks are shown in brackets in the column on the left.

QWC refers to quality of written communication.

16–13 [10–9] [6]	**Effective** Commentary and evaluation demonstrate sound analysis and understanding. The answer is well focused and shows coherent elaboration and/or clear line of argument. Issues/debates/approaches are used effectively. There is substantial evidence of synopticity. QWC: Ideas are well-structured and expressed clearly and fluently. Consistently effective use of psychological terminology. Appropriate use of grammar, punctuation and spelling.
12–9 [6–8] [5–4]	**Reasonable** Commentary and evaluation demonstrate reasonable analysis and understanding. The answer is generally focused and shows reasonable elaboration and/or line of argument is evident. Issues/debates/approaches are used reasonably effectively. There is evidence of synopticity. QWC: Most ideas are appropriately structured and expressed clearly. Appropriate use of psychological terminology. Minor errors of grammar, punctuation and spelling only occasionally compromise meaning.
8–5 [5–3] [3–2]	**Basic** Commentary and evaluation demonstrate basic, superficial understanding. The answer is sometimes focused and shows some evidence of elaboration. Superficial reference may be made to issues/debates/approaches. There is some evidence of synopticity. QWC: Expression of ideas lacks clarity. Limited use of psychological terminology. Errors of grammar, punctuation and spelling are intrusive.
4–1 [2–1] [1]	**Rudimentary** Commentary and evaluation are rudimentary, demonstrating very limited understanding. The answer is weak, muddled and incomplete. Material is not used effectively and may be mainly irrelevant. If reference is made to issues/debates/approaches, it is muddled and inaccurate. There is little or no evidence of synopticity. QWC: Deficiency in expression of ideas results in confusion and ambiguity. The answer lacks structure and is often a series of unconnected assertions. Errors of grammar, punctuation and spelling are frequent and intrusive.
0	No creditworthy material is presented

A summary table of AQA A AO2/AO3 mark bands (for questions worth 16 marks)

Marks	Analysis and understanding	Focus	Elaboration	Line of argument	Issues/ debates/ approaches	Synopticity
16–13	Sound	Well focused	Coherent	Clear	Used effectively	Substantial evidence
12–9	Reasonable	Generally focused	Reasonable	Evident	Reasonably effective	Evidence
8–5	Basic, superficial	Sometimes focused	Some evidence		Superficial reference	Some evidence
4–1	Rudimentary, little understanding	Weak, muddled and incomplete	Not effective	May be mainly irrelevant	Absent or muddled/ inaccurate	Little or none

Quality of written communication (QWC) marks

Marks	Structure of ideas and expression	Use of psychological terminology	Spelling, punctuation, grammar
16–13	Well structured, clear, fluent	Effectively used	Appropriate
12–9	Most appropriately structured, clear	Appropriate use	Minor errors that occasionally compromise meaning
8–5	Lacks clarity	Limited use	Errors are intrusive
4–1	Lacks structure, often unconnected assertions, confused and ambiguous		Errors frequent and intrusive

AQA B A2 marking criteria

In the AQA B A2 exam all questions are marked out of a total of 20. This is divided up across the different parts of the question. The final part of each question is usually worth 12 marks. This part is marked using the scheme on the right.

The mark scheme below is for those question parts marked out of 12. In such questions there are four AO1 (description) marks and eight AO2 (evaluation) marks. However, the overall mark is determined by a combination of these, as shown in the bands below.

12–10 marks **Excellent answers**	
AO1	Thorough description, showing sound and accurate knowledge and understanding.
AO2	Evaluation is full and well-balanced with appropriate analysis. Any references to research are accurate. Evaluative comment is not simply stated but is presented in the context of the discussion as a whole. The answer is well-focused, organised and mostly relevant with little, if any, misunderstanding.
QWC	The candidate expresses most ideas clearly and fluently, with consistently effective use of psychological terminology. Arguments are well structured, with appropriate use of sentences and paragraphs. There are few, if any, minor errors of grammar, punctuation and spelling. The overall quality of language is such that meaning is rarely, if ever, obscured.

9–7 marks **Good to average answers**	
AO1	Answer shows knowledge and understanding.
AO2	There is an attempt to present a balanced evaluation. Some analysis is evident and the answer is mostly focused on the question, although there may be some irrelevance and/or misunderstanding. Any references to research are relevant but are perhaps not linked so clearly to the discussion as for the top band.
QWC	The candidate expresses most ideas clearly and makes some appropriate use of psychological terminology. The answer is organised, using sentences and paragraphs. Errors of grammar, punctuation and spelling may be present but are mostly minor, such that they obscure meaning only occasionally.

6–4 marks **Average to poor answers**	
AO1	Answer shows some knowledge and understanding of the area. Answers in this band are likely to be mostly descriptive and there is likely to be irrelevance and/or inaccuracy. Answers constituting reasonable description with minimal focus on the question are likely to be in this band.
AO2	There must be some evaluation in order to gain 5/6 marks.
QWC	The candidate expresses basic ideas clearly but there may be some ambiguity. The candidate uses key psychological terminology inappropriately on some occasions. The answer may lack structure, although there is some evidence of use of sentences and paragraphs. There are occasional intrusive errors of grammar, punctuation and spelling, which obscure meaning.

QWC refers to quality of written communication.

An examiner decides on which mark to award by first identifying the band that best describes the essay answer. They then decide on the actual mark within the band by considering whether they were more drawn to the band above or the band below, or neither. It is likely that an answer contains elements of several band descriptors but the examiner selects the best fit.

Exam advice

Some dos and don'ts

Do answer the question.

- This sounds obvious but, under exam conditions, students can feel very anxious and write about anything they can think of. They don't even read the whole question; they just notice certain key words and start writing.

- Don't regurgitate a prepared answer because you got a good mark for it in class. If it doesn't answer the question, it will not receive any credit.

Do use psychological terms and write coherently and legibly.

- This shows the examiner you really have studied psychology, and also boosts your QWC mark. Identify the names of psychologists and use dates if you can (you don't have to be exact – 'the 1950s' is as good as '1953').

Do use the mark allocation to guide you in how much you should write.

- A total of 5 marks for a question, for one part of a question, indicates what proportion of time you should spend on that part. If you write a lot for a question with very few marks, you won't get extra credit and you will have less time to answer the other questions.

Do take note of the injunctions.

- The injunctions tell you whether you should be describing, evaluating or both. These injunctions are described on page 8.

Do elaborate on your answers.

- In many questions you are awarded 1 mark for identifying a point, and a second mark for providing some extra information, such as an explanation, an example, or some research evidence. Elaboration is what makes the difference between a grade A and a grade C.

Don't ignore features of a question.

- If the question says 'describe how psychologists have dealt with ethical issues', don't write about ethical issues. Marks would only be awarded, in this case, for writing about *how psychologists deal with* ethical issues.

- If you are unsure what a question means, explain any ambiguities to the examiner in your answer.

Don't leave out obvious material.

- It is very easy to think 'the examiner knows that' and think that you don't have to write down the obvious things. However, the examiner cannot be sure that you know it unless you demonstrate it.

Don't waste time.

- An examination has a finite length. Don't spend time 'waffling', hoping the examiner might find something relevant in what you say. Examiners award marks only for material that is directly relevant to the question. Spend time thinking and select what you say very carefully. Selectivity is one of the criteria that examiners use when deciding how many marks to award for an answer.

Four steps to successful revision

Step 1: Understand

- Study the topic to be learned slowly. Make sure you understand the logic or important concepts.
- Mark up the text if necessary – underline, highlight and make notes.
- Re-read each paragraph slowly.

GO TO STEP 2

Step 2: Summarise

- Now make your own revision note summary:
  What is the main idea, theme or concept to be learned?
  What are the main points? How does the logic develop?
  Ask questions: Why? How? What next?
- Use bullet points, mind maps, patterned notes.
- Link ideas with mnemonics, mind maps, crazy stories.
- Note the title and date of the revision notes
  (e.g. Psychology: Attitudes and prejudice, 3rd March).
- Organise your notes carefully and keep them in a file.

This information is now in your short-term memory. You will forget 80% of it if you do not go to Step 3. GO TO STEP 3, but first take a 10-minute break.

Step 3: Memorise

- Take 25-minute learning 'bites' with 5-minute breaks.
- After each 5-minute break test yourself:
  - Cover the original revision note summary
  - Write down the main points
  - Speak out loud (record on tape)
  - Tell someone else
  - Repeat many times.

**The material is well on its way to long-term memory.
You will forget 40% of it if you do not do step 4. GO TO STEP 4**

Step 4: Track/Review

- Create a revision diary (one A4 page per day).
- Make a revision plan for the topic, e.g. 1 day later, 1 week later, 1 month later.
- Record your revision in your revision diary, e.g.
  Psychology: Attitudes and prejudice, 3rd March 25 minutes
  Psychology: Attitudes and prejudice, 5th March 15 minutes
  Psychology: Attitudes and prejudice, 3rd April 15 minutes
  ... and then at monthly intervals.

Chapter 1

Biological rhythms and sleep

1.1 Biological rhythms

After studying this topic you should be able to describe and evaluate:

- circadian, infradian, and ultradian rhythms, including the role of endogenous pacemakers and exogenous zeitgebers
- the consequences of disrupting biological rhythms, for example, shift work and jet lag.

LEARNING SUMMARY

Types of biological rhythm

AQA A ▶ U3

Biological rhythms are not the same as *biorhythms* (a pseudoscientific technique that uses biological rhythms to predict a person's behaviour on a given day).

The term 'zeitgeber' is German for 'time-giver'.

A **circadian rhythm** is one that recurs about once every day (every 24 hours). The word *circadian* comes from two words: 'circa' (about) and 'dies' (day).

The term 'free-running' refers to how the rhythm would function if it is unaffected by any external zeitgebers, such as daylight changes or clocks.

When doctors collect samples of blood or urine for medical testing they record the time of day the sample was taken because some substances fluctuate naturally over the course of the day. This is a further application of research into biological rhythms.

A biological rhythm is a biologically-driven behaviour that is periodically repeated. Biological rhythms may be controlled by **endogenous pacemakers**, i.e. by internal biological mechanisms, or they may be controlled by **exogenous zeitgebers**, i.e. by external factors in the environment, such as daylight.

Circadian rhythms

1. Sleep/waking cycle

During a 24-hour period we sleep/wake once. Normally our sleep/wake pattern is entrained by external events, such as clocks, meal times and daylight changes.

We also have a free-running daily cycle governed by our endogenous body clock. For example, Michel Siffre (1972) spent six months in an underground cave. His sleep/waking cycle settled down to 25–30 hours.

The endogenous rhythm can only be controlled to a limited amount. Folkard *et al.* (1985) used artificial light to reduce the circadian cycle. Participants coped at a 23-hour cycle, but when it was reduced to 22 hours their bodies reverted to a natural cycle.

2. Temperature

Core body temperature rises and falls during the course of a day (along with heart rate, urine secretion, or any measure that indicates metabolic rate). It reaches a trough around 4am and returns to normal level by about 8pm.

Colquhuon (1970) concluded, from a review of research, that cognitive performance is positively correlated with temperature. Long-term recall is best when body temperature is highest. In contrast, research has found that alertness is best when body temperature is lowest, in the early morning and early evening (Monk and Embrey, 1981).

Evaluation

- **Individual differences** – Aschoff and Wever (1976) observed that some people, when isolated from daylight, maintain 24–25 hour cycles, whereas others develop idiosyncrasies such as 29 hours awake and 21 hours asleep. Marks and Folkard (1985) suggested that 'morning' types may peak in their daily rhythms a few hours earlier than 'evening' types.
- **Application** – The field of **chronotherapeutics** aims to match medical treatments to circadian cycles in order to maximise benefits of certain treatments and minimise adverse effects. For example, asthma symptoms worsen during the night, possibly due to increased levels of cortisol. Therefore, some doctors prescribe unequal doses of medication.

'Infra' means 'below; **infradian rhythms** occur less than once every 24 hours, i.e. they are cycles that take longer than one day to be completed.

Pheromones are biochemical substances that act like hormones, except they are secreted into the air and are then transmitted to other animals of the same species and absorbed into their bloodstream.

Infradian rhythms

1. Menstrual cycle

The menstrual cycle occurs once a month. It is controlled endogenously by hormones produced by the pituitary gland. Reinberg (1967) documented the menstrual cycle of a woman who spent three months in a cave, with only dim lighting. Her sleep–wake cycle lengthened slightly and her menstrual cycle became shorter. However, the menstrual cycle can apparently be synchronised by external factors. Russell *et al.* (1980) collected daily samples of women's underarm sweat, mixed it with alcohol and applied this to the upper lip of their female participants. The participants' menstrual cycles began to synchronise, probably due to **pheromones** that acted as exogenous zeitgebers.

Evaluation

- The **purpose of a menstrual cycle** (rather than having constant fertility) is to conserve energy; it is better to restrict periods of fertility and, therefore, there is a need to have endogenous control of the rhythm.
- There are '**side effects**' of the menstrual cycle – pre-menstrual tension has been associated with increased aggressive behaviour in women and has even been used as a defence in criminal trials (Lewis, 1990).

2. Circa-annual rhythms

There are various circa-annual rhythms (i.e. occur once a year), for example:

Migration – Gwinner (1986) kept wild birds in cages for three years, exposing them to 12 hours of light and 12 hours of darkness. Despite a lack of external stimuli they still showed signs of migratory restlessness, suggesting endogenous control. Migration may also be triggered by the availability of food (exogenous cue).

Hibernation – Pengelly and Fisher (1957) artificially controlled squirrels' exposure to light (12 hours on/off) and temperature ($0°C$). Nevertheless, the squirrels hibernated from October to April.

Evaluation

- What happens when biorhythms go wrong? **Seasonal affective disorder** (SAD) affects some people during winter. They become depressed, possibly because darkness leads to increased production of melatonin, which affects mood.
- Such understanding has led to **phototherapy** as a treatment for SAD, i.e. exposure to bright lights for several hours a day to reduce the effect of too much darkness/melatonin.

'Ultra' means 'more than'. **Ultradian rhythms** occur more often than once a day, such as heart beats.

Ultradian rhythms

1. Sleep stages

During a night's sleep you pass through different sleep cycles. (These are described on page 19). Each cycle takes about 90 minutes.

2. Basic rest activity cycle (BRAC)

During the daytime biorhythms follow this same 90-minute cycle. For example, Klein and Armitage (1979) tested participants' performance on verbal and spatial tasks through the day and found a 96-minute cycle, the same duration as the sleep cycle. Gerkema and Dann (1985) found that smaller animals tend to have more rapid cycles.

Evaluation

- This 90-minute cycle appears to be controlled by a **different biological clock** to the one governing the circadian rhythm. If the circadian clock is destroyed the 90-minute cycle continues.

Control of biological rhythms

AQA A U3

The **suprachiasmatic nucleus** (SCN) takes its name because it is located directly above the *optic chiasma* – the place where the optic nerves cross over.

The diagram shows the location of the SCN, the main biological clock.

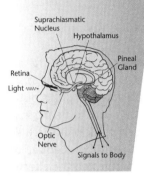

In animals, such as birds and reptiles, light falls directly on the pineal gland through the skull and affects the production of melatonin.

The concept of 'adaptiveness' comes from evolutionary theory and refers to the idea that behaviours that persist are likely to be those that promote an individual's survival and reproduction and, thus, the potential survival of their genetic line.

The role of endogenous (internal) pacemakers

In mammals, the main endogenous pacemaker is the **suprachiasmatic nucleus** (SCN), a small group of cells in the **hypothalamus** located behind the eyes in the brain. Evidence comes from studies of animals, for example, Morgan (1995) removed the SCN from hamsters and found that their circadian rhythm disappeared. The rhythm could be re-established using transplanted SCN cells. The SCN generates a circadian rhythm but is reset by light from the eyes, even when they are shut. The mechanism underlying this rhythm is an interaction between four proteins: the first two (CLOCK + CYCLE) cause the levels of two other proteins (PERIOD + TIM) to increase, whereas PER + TIM cause CLK + CYC to decrease, so as PER + TIM levels increase, CLK + CYC levels decrease, and as CLK + CYC decreases then so do PER + TIM and then CLK + CYC increases! This produces a rhythm and is the basis of the biological clock (Darlington *et al.*, 1998). Biological rhythms are also endogenously regulated by **hormones**, as in the female menstrual cycle.

There are other regions of the body that produce oscillating rhythms, such as cells in the liver and heart. It has been found that eating times, rather than light, reset some of these other clocks. In fact, research has shown that each cell in the body has an internal ticking clock, affected by a series of clock proteins. There is also evidence that there are separate internal clocks controlling the sleep/waking cycle and temperature. Hawkins and Armstrong-Esther (1978) studied nurses on shift work and found that their circadian rhythms changed, but not their temperature cycles.

Endogenous rhythms are also related to the **pineal gland**. In humans, the pineal gland is regulated by the SCN and leads to changes in levels of **melatonin**. Increases in melatonin are associated with decreases in arousal and sleepiness.

The role of exogenous (external) zeitgebers

External stimuli may themselves be rhythmic. Day length is the dominant **zeitgeber**. Also important are the seasons, weather, temperature, phases of the moon, tides (in aquatic animals), availability of food, and social stimuli.

Miles *et al.* (1977) studied a blind man who had a 24.9 hour circadian rhythm despite being exposed to a variety of zeitgebers that should have set his 'clock' to 24 hours (such as the radio). He had to use stimulants and sedatives to coordinate his sleep/wake cycle with the rest of the world. This demonstrates that light really is the dominant time-giver. However, light cues can be overcome. Luce and Segal (1966) pointed out that people who live within the Arctic Circle still sleep for about 7 hours, despite the fact that during the summer months the Sun never sets. In this case, social cues are dominant.

Evaluation

- It is **adaptive** to have biological rhythms to **govern the biochemical processes** (like the conductor of an orchestra).
- It is also adaptive for these endogenous rhythms to be **reset by external cues** so that animals are in tune with seasonal variations, and daytime/night-time.
- It might be **life threatening** to be solely at the mercy of environmental cues, therefore, endogenous cues are important too.

Consequences of disrupting biological rhythms

AQA A ▶ U3

Staying up later than normal is an example of phase delay, whereas making yourself go to sleep earlier is phase advance. Most people do find it easier to go to bed late and feel fine the next day, than to get up earlier than normal and feel OK.

It is likely that shift work is a major cause of industrial accidents because these often occur at night. Moore-Ede (1993) estimated the cost of shift worker fatigue in the US to be $77 billion annually. Therefore, this research has important applications.

When external cues (e.g. daylight) change suddenly, we have to re-adjust our internal clock and our ability to cope may be harmed. Generally, **phase delay** (delaying your internal clock) is easier to adapt to than **phase advance** (skipping ahead).

Shift work

On average it takes about three days to adjust to a 12-hour shift in time (which applies to jet lag as well). Artificial lighting is moderately effective in re-setting the circadian rhythm, but it takes time. Performance is affected because some body clocks are slower to reset and, therefore, the body's rhythms are desynchronised.

Evaluation

- **Individual differences** – Those people whose circadian rhythms change least may cope best overall (Reinberg *et al.*, 1984).
- **Harmful effects of shift work** – May be caused by other problems, for example, shift workers suffer from sleep deprivation because it is more difficult to sleep during the day (it tends to be noisier than night-time and daylight is disturbing). Shift work also disrupts family and social life, which can lead to depression.
- **Applications** – Dawson and Campbell (1991) exposed participants to a 4-hour pulse of bright light on their first night. This helped their subsequent adjustment as measured by body temperature. Czeisler *et al.* (1982) tested the effects of rotating shifts with the clock (phase delay), rather than against it, so people were doing early shifts and then later shifts. The result was that workers felt better and the management also reported increased productivity and fewer errors.

Jet lag

Klein *et al.* (1972) found that adjustment was faster for westbound flights (phase delay). Schwartz *et al.* (1995) found that East coast US Baseball teams did better when travelling west than West coast teams travelling east, again showing that phase delay has less effect. On the other hand, on short trips, returning home may be easier than the outward journey because other body clocks haven't changed, meaning that on the return home it may take less time to readjust.

Evaluation

- **Coping with jet lag.** Redfern (1989) suggested the use of **benzodiazepines** (BZs) to increase melatonin levels and resynchronise the body clock. Webb and Agnew (1971) interviewed regular travellers and found that they used various non-pharmacological approaches, such as a rigid schedule of meals, exposure to light and outdoor activity.
- One of the reasons for jet lag may be that the **temperature clock** is not reset so easily and, therefore, the body is experiencing desynchronised rhythms such as what happens in shift work (see Hawkins and Armstrong-Esther on page 17.)

Key points from AS

- BZs are also used to decrease anxiety as discussed in *Revise AS Unit 5.2, page 109.*

Practice essays 1.1

(a) Outline the research studies that have investigated circadian rhythms.

(9 marks)

(b) Assess the consequences of disrupting circadian rhythms.   *(16 marks)*

1.2 Sleep states

After studying this topic you should be able to describe and evaluate:

- *the nature of sleep*
- *the functions of sleep, including evolutionary explanations and restoration theory*
- *lifespan changes in sleep.*

The nature of sleep

AQA A ▶ U3

Key points from AS

- The electrical activity of the brain during sleep is recorded using an electroencephalograph (EEG) – see *Revise AS Unit 5.3, page 114* for details.

The phrase 'descending the sleep staircase' is used to describe moving through these sleep stages into decreased consciousness.

Paralysis during REM sleep may serve the useful function of preventing us from acting out our dreams.

Note that dreams also occur in NREM sleep (i.e. stages 1–4).

REM sleep is not found in more primitive animals like reptiles.

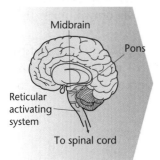

Sleep is not unconsciousness, it is an altered state of consciousness such that there is a decreased responsiveness to the external environment. It occurs daily (**circadian**) and has distinct stages (**ultradian**).

Sleep stages

Stage 1 – Relaxed state, brain waves change from the beta waves characteristic of being awake to **alpha waves**, which are slower (8–12 hertz, i.e. 8–12 waves per second), more regular and have a greater amplitude (i.e. the height of the wave). Alpha waves are seen during meditation. The transition from stage 1 is often accompanied by a **hypnagogic state**, which may include hallucinatory images.

Stage 2 – Slower, larger brain waves (theta, 4–8 Hz), short bursts of high-frequency **sleep spindles** and **K-complexes** (responses to external stimuli). This is light sleep and the sleeper is easily woken.

Stage 3 – More slowing down of brain waves and bodily activity (e.g. heart rate). Long, slow delta waves (1–5 Hz) with some sleep spindles.

Stage 4 – **Slow-wave sleep (SWS)** with more delta waves than stage 3. It's hard to be woken except by personally significant noises (such as your baby crying). Some physiological activities take place, such as the production of growth hormones. Also, sleep walking and night terrors are experienced in this stage.

Stage 5 or REM sleep – Stage 4 sleep is followed by Stage 3, Stage 2 and then Stage 5: **rapid eye movement (REM) sleep**, and active (beta 13–20 Hz) brain waves. Jouvet called this **paradoxical sleep** because of the contradictions: eye movement, heart rate, breathing, etc. are increased, but the body is in a state of near paralysis and it is difficult to wake a person up.

Sleep stages alternate through the night, starting with a rapid descent into deep sleep. Most sleepers complete about five ultradian cycles during a normal night's sleep, with progressively less SWS and more REM activity as morning approaches.

The physiology of sleep

The brain stem is the area of the brain that controls arousal, alertness and sleep. The brain stem is (in an evolutionary sense) the oldest part of the brain, which controls vital functions. Three neurotransmitters are involved in sleep:

- **Serotonin**: The SCN (see page 17) responds to changes in light and controls production of **melatonin** in the pineal gland which, in turn, leads to production of **serotonin** in the **raphe nuclei** (part of the reticular activating system, **RAS**). Increased levels of serotonin reduce RAS activity and assist the onset of sleep.
- **Noradrenaline** from the **locus coeruleus** (part of the pons) triggers REM sleep.
- **Acetylcholine** is associated with brain activation during wakefulness and REM sleep. It is produced in the **pons** and controls PGO waves that trigger REM.

The function of sleep

Beware of evolutionary arguments that sound as if the animal has made some deliberate choice about behaviour. The 'choice' is made through **natural selection**, a process which has taken place over thousands of years. Behaviours persist only if they are adaptive in some way for the individual. Other behaviours are not selected.

Infant sleep could be explained as an adaptive behaviour to help exhausted parents cope with finding food and other things.

The **EEA** is the environment to which a species is adapted. The selective pressures at that time explain the behaviours that we observe today. In humans it is suggested that our EEA was the period from 1.8 million to 11,000 years ago, when humans lived on the plains in Africa.

There are a few important observations about sleep: (1) All animals sleep, which suggests that sleep serves some important function; (2) Different species have quite different sleep habits, which suggests that sleep patterns are an evolutionary adaptation to environmental conditions; (3) Sleep deprivation studies show that there are some physical effects of both NREM and REM deprivation, but these may be related to motivation as much as some kind of reduced capacity.

Evolutionary explanations

The evolutionary approach proposes that sleep patterns have evolved because they are adapted to the needs of individual species. Each species has developed different sleep habits and patterns to deal with environmental pressures of predation, energy conservation and foraging requirements.

1. Protection from predation (Meddis, 1975)

Meddis suggests that sleep has evolved because it helps keep animals safe from predation. Animals have to gather food (and are then exposed to predators) but at other times they should stay out of harm's way. Siegel (2008) claims that being awake is riskier than being asleep because of the likelihood of injury. Sleep may ensure that animals stay still when they have nothing better to do with their time.

2. Energy conservation or Hibernation theory (Webb, 1982)

Sleep is adaptive because it is a means of conserving energy, in the same way that hibernation enhances survival by reducing physiological demands. An animal that is constantly active requires more food, and this is likely to decrease survival. Sleep ensures quietness and energy conservation.

3. Foraging requirements

Sleep is also related to the amount of time an animal has to spend finding food. Cows (herbivores) spend a lot of time grazing and, therefore, cannot afford to spend as much time sleeping as, for example, cats (carnivores).

Evaluation

- It is **difficult to falsify** evolutionary theory.
- There are problems with applying this theory to **human sleep**. In the **environment of evolutionary adaptedness (EEA)**, sleep may have enhanced survival, but this isn't true now.
- Empson (1989) calls ecological theories **'waste of time'** theories because they propose that sleep happens in order to waste time. However, deprivation studies do suggest that lack of sleep has distinct consequences so it can't just be a waste of time. For example, animal studies have shown that sleep deprivation eventually results in death (e.g. Jouvet, 1964). Deprivation of REM sleep results in REM rebound, i.e. an increase in REM sleep on subsequent nights, suggesting that REM sleep may serve a particular function.
- In fact, in Meddis' view, sleep is not just a 'waste of time', but he argues that if an animal has to sleep then it is best to do it **out of harm's way**.
- Support for the evolutionary approach to explaining the function of sleep comes from the fact that it is **present in all animals**, which suggests that it serves some adaptive function.
- Support for the evolutionary approach also comes from the fact that the sleep **patterns of individual species are all different** and can be related to environmental pressures. For example, some dolphins sleep one hemisphere at a time, which may be related to the fact that they will drown unless they surface regularly to breathe.
- Siegel (2008) claims that existing research points to just **one consistent factor** that explains sleep patterns in those species studied – **ecology rather than biology**. He argues that the best strategy for passing on your genes is to be asleep for as long as you can get away with.

Restoration theory (Oswald, 1980, and Horne, 1988)

Sleep allows various physiological and psychological states to be recovered. For example, infancy is a time of needing high sleep, possibly because of the enormous brain and body growth, and the learning that is taking place.

1. Physiological restoration

During slow wave sleep the body makes repairs, waste products are removed, and there is increased production of growth hormone. Stern and Morgane (1974) argue that the normal function of REM sleep is to restore levels of neurotransmitters after a day's activities. Anti-depressants seem to reduce REM activity, possibly because they increase neurotransmitter levels. Cirelli *et al.* (2004) found that genes for proteins, which are involved in adjusting synaptic connections, are switched on during NREM sleep.

2. Psychological restoration

Naitoh (1975) reviewed research and found that sleep-deprived individuals described themselves as less friendly, less relaxed, less good-natured, and less cheerful. Berry and Webb (1983) found that when people slept well during the night, their level of anxiety the next day was lower than when they had slept poorly. Also, during REM sleep, memories may be consolidated (according to neurobiological theories of dreams) and emotional experiences may be relived (according to psychological theories of dreams, such as Freud).

Evaluation

- **Deprivation research** partly supports the restoration view; people do less well when deprived of sleep. In general, memory improves by about 15% after a night's sleep. However, the effects of sleep deprivation may be as much about motivation, i.e. lack of sleep makes people feel less motivated and that's why they don't perform so well.
- However, some studies of sleep deprivation actually suggest there is **little effect from deprivation**. In one famous case study in 1965 Randy Gardner stayed awake for 11 days and simply slept a bit longer when he did go to sleep. However, people deprived of sleep have brief episodes of **microsleep** when some sleep functions may take place. Relaxed wakefulness may also permit some physiological/psychological restoration.
- The idea of **physiological/psychological restoration whilst apparently awake** is supported by recent research with pigeons (Benca *et al.*, 2007). SWS deprivation led to increased slow wave brain activity (as measured by EEG) when awake. Migratory birds can cope for long periods without sleep so they may have evolved a way for parts of the brain to sleep during wakefulness.
- According to restoration theory we would expect to find **increased sleep in relation to increased activity**. Shapiro *et al.* (1981) found that marathon runners did require extra sleep, whereas Horne and Minard (1985) tried to exhaust their participants and found that they went to sleep faster, but not for longer.
- On the other hand, Empson (1989) claims that it is **impossible to go without sleep** and remain fine, and Horne (1988) points out that sleep-deprived participants do show a **rebound effect**, i.e. they sleep longer after deprivation.

Conclusion

Neither theory accounts for why animals have reduced consciousness when sleeping. It is not necessary for restoration, and from a safety (adaptive) point of view it makes little sense. The fact that all animals sleep means it must perform some restorative function. The fact that each species evolves a particular style suggests an adaptive element as well.

Self-report studies tend to be biased by self-expectations.

It is important to remember, when considering the function of REM sleep, that REM sleep is not the same as dreaming.

Horne (1988) proposed that a distinction should be made between **core sleep** (SWS and REM) and **optional sleep**. During core sleep, brain recovery takes place, whereas bodily processes are recovered during optional sleep and this can also occur during relaxed wakefulness. Therefore, sleep deprivation only requires the recovery of core sleep.

Horne also made the important point that sleep probably serves different purposes in different species. Thus, no single theory of the functions of sleep is likely to be adequate.

The restoration approach provides some views on *why* sleep is important, whereas the adaptive approach also focuses on *when* different species sleep.

Lifespan changes in sleep

Newborn babies – Newborn babies tend to sleep for about 2/3 of the day (16 hours in every 24 hours). They display two kinds of sleep: quiet and active sleep, which are immature versions of REM and SWS respectively. At birth there is more active sleep than quiet sleep, but this gradually decreases.

- It has been suggested that babies' sleep is an adaptive mechanism to make their parents' lives easier.
- The greater amount of active/REM sleep may be explained in terms of the considerable learning and brain development that is taking place.

EEG (electro-encephalograph) is used to measure electrical activity in the brain (see sleep stages on page 19).

One year – Over the first year of life there is a gradual maturation of sleep EEG patterns so they begin to look more like the adult form. There is a decrease in active/REM sleep to about 50%, and consolidation of sleep periods: rather than sleeping in short bursts throughout the day, young children sleep through the night and may have one or two naps totalling 10–12 hours of sleep.

Five years – Full EEG patterns of sleep are shown by the age of 5, but the frequency is different to adult sleep patterns; there is more REM sleep (about 33% of total sleep time) and less Stage 1 sleep. Most children of this age sleep for about 10 hours, boys sleeping slightly more than girls. There are more instances of **parasomnias** (sleep disorders, such as sleep walking or night terrors – see page 24).

Adolescence – At this age, individuals sleep for an average of 9–10 hours per night. The amount of REM sleep is less than in childhood. One distinguishing feature of adolescent REM sleep is that it is sometimes accompanied by orgasm and ejaculation, which is significantly less likely at other ages.

Middle age – At this age, parasomnias are very rare but there is an increasing frequency of sleep disorders (such as insomnia and snoring).

Old age – Total sleep time remains the same, but the type of sleep differs. REM sleep decreases to about 20% of total sleep time with a corresponding increase of stage 2 sleep (about 60%). The amount of slow wave sleep is also considerably reduced to as little as 5% and may be non-existent for some older people. Older people have more difficulty going to sleep and wake up more frequently (up to six times a night).

Decreases in slow wave sleep are accompanied by decreased production of growth hormones, supporting the view that SWS is important for the production of growth hormone.

Research studies

Floyd *et al.* (2007) looked at the results of nearly 400 sleep studies and concluded that the percentage of REM decreases with age (decreasing about 0.6% per decade) until the age of about 70, when it starts increasing. This is probably because the total sleep time decreases.

Van Cauter *et al.* (2000) studied data from sleep studies of about 150 men. They found that sleep deteriorates at two points in a person's life – between the ages of 16 and 25 and again between the ages of 35 and 50. Men over 45 have virtually no SWS, which affects hormone production.

Practice essay 1.2

Describe and evaluate **two** theories of the function of sleep.   *(25 marks)*

1.3 Disorders of sleep

After studying this topic you should be able to describe and evaluate:

- *explanations for insomnia, including primary and secondary insomnia and factors influencing insomnia, for example, apnoea and personality*
- *explanations for other sleep disorders, including sleep walking and narcolepsy.*

Insomnia

AQA A U3

Insomnia is characterised by having prolonged difficulties falling asleep and/or remaining asleep, despite the opportunity to do so.

Some estimates suggest that as many as 50% of all older adults report insomnia problems.

The term 'secondary' is used because the insomnia is a side effect (i.e. secondary) to some other problem. Primary insomnia is its own disorder.

'Sleep hygiene' is often mentioned as a cause of insomnia, referring to behaviours that affect your sleep for good or bad, e.g. smoking, drinking, napping and exercise. The implication is that people need to improve the hygiene or healthiness of their sleep habits.

A distinction is made between **primary** and **secondary insomnia**; the former has no known medical, psychiatric or environmental cause, whereas the latter has. Insomnia is diagnosed when:

- a person has been experiencing sleep difficulties for more than one month
- the resulting daytime fatigue causes severe distress or impairs work, social or personal functioning.

1. Causes of primary insomnia

In cases where insomnia has been a lifelong problem, the cause may be due to a brain abnormality involving the sleep circuits (a physical, but not medical condition).

In other cases the cause may be stress. The insomnia should disappear when the source of the stress is dealt with – though sometimes anxiety resulting from insomnia becomes a cause of further insomnia. The person who has difficulty sleeping starts to worry that they can't sleep and this worry in itself becomes the cause of persistent insomnia.

2. Causes of secondary insomnia

Causes of secondary insomnia include certain illnesses, such as some heart diseases; mental disorders, such as depression or general anxiety disorder; substances, such as medicine, caffeine, tobacco or psychoactive drugs; and medical conditions, such as hyperthyroidism and Wilson's syndrome. Specific sleep disorders may also be the cause of the problem:

- **Circadian rhythm disorders** are caused when circadian rhythms are disrupted, for example, because of shift work or jet lag.
- **Apnoea** is a disorder characterised by pauses in breathing, which may last a few seconds or minutes and may occur 5–30 times an hour. Normal breathing may restart with a loud snort. The most common cause of apnoea is blockage of the airways (airway collapses), which may occur in people who are overweight. This is called **obstructive sleep apnoea**. **Central sleep apnoea** is less common and occurs because of faulty signals from the brain to the breathing centres.

Personality may be a factor in insomnia, for example:

- Kales *et al.* (1976) gave 124 insomniacs a personality test and found that 85% showed signs of abnormal personality. Kales *et al.* suggest that the emotional arousal associated with 'abnormal personality' is a factor in insomnia.
- Bardwell *et al.* (1999) found that insomniacs scored more highly on anger measures than non-insomniacs.
- Grano *et al.* (2006) found a link between impulsivity and insomnia in men. In women impulsivity was just associated with difficulties getting to sleep.

Other sleep disorders

AQA A ▷ U3

Sleep disorders are medical disorders that interfere with normal physical, mental and emotional functioning.

Sleep disorders include snoring and restless legs syndrome (an irresistible urge to move your legs because they tingle or burn).

1. Sleep walking (SW) or somnambulism

'Sleep walking' refers to a range of activities that are normally associated with wakefulness (e.g. eating, getting dressed or walking about) and which take place during sleep without the conscious knowledge of the subject. It is most common in childhood, affecting about 20% of children and only about 1–3% of adults (Hublin *et al.*, 1997). Adolescents and adults with SW tend to have an increased prevalence of anxiety and personality disorders.

SW occurs during NREM sleep. The individual usually has their eyes open and may act as if awake, but any speech is nonsensical. In the morning they have no memory of the episode. In severe cases (one or more episodes a night) it may have a considerable effect on a person's life and there may be a risk of injury.

Some psychologists suggest that NREM parasomnias such as SW, sleep terrors and confusional awakenings are on a continuum and share a genetic cause.

Research has found that SW has a significant genetic component. Evidence comes from familial studies. For example, Broughton (1968) found that the prevalence of SW in first-degree relatives of an affected subject is at least 10 times greater than that in the general population. Twin studies have also been used; Lecendreux *et al.* (2003) report about 50% concordance in identical (MZ) twins compared to 10–15% in non-identical (DZ) twins. They have also identified a gene that may be critical in SW as well as night terrors – the **DQB1*05 gene**.

2. Night terrors

Night terrors are a childhood problem. Like SW they occur during NREM sleep and are not related to dreams. The child appears very frightened but, unlike in a nightmare, the child can't be woken and has no memory of the event in the morning.

3. Narcolepsy

Narcolepsy means 'seized with sleepiness'.

Narcolepsy is a disorder of the system that regulates the sleep/wake cycle. It results in sudden and uncontrollable attacks of sleep at irregular and unexpected times, which may last minutes or hours. The most obvious symptom is excessive daytime sleepiness (EDS). The person may appear drunk whereas they are actually just very sleepy, and, after a microsleep, the person may wake without realising they had been asleep.

The prevalence of narcolepsy is not accurately known. It is significantly under-reported because its severity varies from the barely noticeable to the profoundly disrupting. However, the reported prevalence of narcolepsy in the population ranges from 5 in 10,000 (0.05%) in Europe and North America, to 16 in 10,000 in Japan (www.narcolepsy.org.uk).

The most obvious symptom of narcolepsy is a sudden loss of muscular control (**cataplexy**) triggered by amusement, anger or excitement. Other symptoms that occur when falling asleep or awakening are sleep paralysis (on falling asleep or awakening) and hallucinations (**hypnagogic** when falling asleep and **hypnopompic** when waking up). There may also be moments of trance-like behaviour and interruption of night-time sleep by frequent waking periods.

Narcolepsy usually begins in adolescence and may have a biological basis. It may be the result of a genetic abnormality (related to the HLA complex on chromosome 6), the result of an auto-immune disease or caused by a shortage of the neurotransmitter **hypocretin**.

Practice essay 1.3

Discuss explanations for **two or more** sleep disorders, including sleep walking and narcolepsy.

(25 marks)

Chapter 2

Perception

2.1 Theories of perceptual organisation

After studying this topic you should be able to describe and evaluate:

AS

- This unit is covered in *Revise AS Unit 2.4, pages 45–46.*

- *Gregory's top-down/indirect theory of perception*
- *Gibson's bottom-up/direct theory of perception.*

2.2 Development of perception

After studying this topic you should be able to describe and evaluate:

- *the development of perceptual abilities, for example, depth/distance and visual constancies*
- *infant and cross-cultural studies of the development of perceptual abilities*
- *the nature–nurture debate in relation to explanations of perceptual development.*

The development of perceptual abilities

AQA A   U3

Depth (distance) perception refers to our ability to perceive that some objects are further away than others.

The visual cliff

The development of depth/distance perception

1. Evidence that depth/distance perception is innate

Gibson and Walk (1960) used the **visual cliff** (see drawing on left) to test depth perception in infants aged 6–14 months. Most of the infants (92%) refused to crawl over the 'cliff' even if they had a patch across one eye, which showed that (a) they perceived depth, and (b) they were using monocular cues only to perceive depth (since they could see depth with a patch over one eye. Binocular cues depend on the use of both eyes.). However, this may be due to learned rather than innate factors as the infants tested had plenty of sensorimotor experience. However, even younger infants were tested by Campos *et al.* (1978) (and their heart rates were slower then when on the shallow side).

Bower *et al.* (1970) observed even younger infants (6–20 days old) and tested their response to an approaching object. If the infant had no depth perception their response to a large disc stopping further away should be the same as their response to a smaller, closer one because they both create the same retinal image. In fact the infants were so upset by the smaller, closer one that the experiment was abandoned early, without testing all the infants.

2. Evidence that depth/distance perception is learned

Yonas *et al.* (1986) showed that infants' ability to respond to depth cues in pictures emerges rather late. The ability to respond to **overlap** emerged at about 6 months and responsiveness to **texture gradient** and **linear perspective** was only apparent by about 7 months.

Bremner (1994) concluded that the ability to interpret dynamic cues (e.g. as in the study by Bower *et al.*) appears earlier than the ability to use static pictorial depth cues.

Key points from AS

- **Overlap**, **texture gradient** and **linear perspective** are all cues used in 2D pictures to represent 3D. These cues are discussed in *Revise AS Unit 2.4, page 48.*

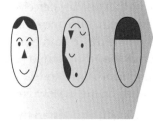

There are important ethical considerations when using infants as participants, as infants are especially affected by experience and perhaps should not be exposed to any experimental manipulation. Equally, their parents should never be deceived, though briefing parents might bias the research.

The development of visual constancies

1. Shape constancy

Bower (1966) conditioned 6–8 week-old infants to turn their heads towards a certain sized or shaped cube by rewarding them with a game of 'peek-a-boo' every time a correct response was made. When he changed the distance or angle (retinal image changes), the infants continued to produce the conditioned response, therefore demonstrating size and shape constancy. If the infant had a patch over one eye, their performance remained the same, but not if they were shown slides. This indicates that they were using **motion parallax** to determine depth.

2. Size constancy

Granrud (2006) tested whether 4-month-old infants respond primarily to the physical size of an object or its retinal image size. This was tested by first of all habituating the infants to either a 6cm-diameter disk at a distance of 18cm or a 10cm disk at 50cm. ('Habituation' means they got used to it so it was no longer a novel stimulus and, therefore, would not attract their interest – infants are drawn to look first at something novel). The infants were then tested with 6cm and 10cm disks, presented side by side at a distance of 30cm. For each infant, one test object had a novel physical size but a familiar retinal image size, and the other had a familiar physical size but a novel retinal image size. The infants showed a preference for the object that had a novel physical size, suggesting that they had not developed shape constancy.

Evaluation

- Testing somewhat **immobile and unresponsive participants** is difficult and prone to subjective interpretation and experimenter bias. For example, many of the studies assess infant perception in terms of which image the infant attends to most – assuming that this means the image is more novel to them.
- Research tends to be **laboratory based** and behaviour is possibly atypical.
- Sensorimotor **learning takes place even before birth**, in the womb, so we can't be sure that abilities present at birth are innate or learned.

Infant studies of the development of perceptual abilities

The studies described above suggest that perception is due to both nature and nurture. Another area of study has concerned infant face perception. In a classic study Fantz (1961) found that neonates (up to 6-months old) could discriminate certain visual forms (see example 'faces' on the left). The infants preferred more complex patterns to just black and white, and preferred a real face rather than a scrambled set of the same features. This 'facial preference' finding has been replicated in a number of studies, such as Goren *et al.* (1975) who used slightly different heads.

An interest in complexity may be important in stimulating the visual development of the brain. However, the preference for a face cannot be solely due to pattern complexity because the scrambled face was less preferred. It may be due to a liking for things that are symmetrical or it may have adaptive importance: a neonate who can recognise and respond to its own species will better elicit attachment and caring.

Evaluation

- **Separating maturation from learning** is difficult. Facial preference may develop very early because infants are positively reinforced when they respond to faces.
- **Studies of face perception in adults** provide mixed support for innate perception of faces (see page 29).

Cross-cultural studies of the development of perceptual abilities

A **cross-cultural study** is one that makes comparisons across two or more cultures. However, in much of the research this comparison is implicit, i.e. no actual comparison is made between the cultural groups studied and Western norms. In an exam question it may be helpful to make the comparative nature of this work explicit.

An example of a **split style** drawing.

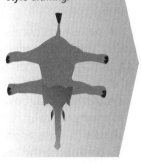

The **Müller–Lyer illusion**.

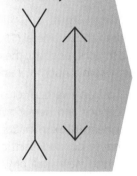

The **horizon-ratio effect** is when two people have the same ratio to the horizon, they appear the same size, but when they have a different ratio to the horizon they appear to be different sizes. This is illustrated in the size constancy drawing on the previous page.

Depth/distance perception

Turnbull (1961) described how a pygmy guide thought that buffalo grazing in the distance were insects. Having lived in a forest all his life, the guide had acquired no knowledge of depth cues, nor of size constancy.

Hudson (1960) tested over 500 children and adults, black and white, from southern Africa. He showed them pictures of a hunting scene or a flying bird and found that the 'school-going' participants interpreted the depth cues correctly whereas the 'non-school-going' participants did not, suggesting that the ability to decode depth cues is learned. Inability to interpret depth cues may be because the pictures are presented on paper. Deregowski *et al.* (1972) found that the Me'en people in Ethiopia did not respond to drawings of animals on paper, but they did if they were on cloth.

Interpretation of pictures

Drawing is not a direct representation of the real world. We learn cultural forms of representation. Aborigines (natives of Australia) use a semi-circle to represent people; a family group is a group of semi-circles around a circle (people sitting round a campfire) (Cox, 1992). The **split-style** drawing technique is used by some Africans (Deregowski, 1972) where objects are represented from above in a flattened form.

Visual illusions

Segall *et al.* (1963) found that the **Müller–Lyer illusion** would only be perceived by those with experience of a **carpentered environment** (an environment where there are straight lines and rectangles, unlike the round shapes of African dwellings). Rural Zulus did not experience the Müller–Lyer illusion. On the other hand, Allport and Pettigrew (1957) found that Rural Zulus showed the **horizon-ratio effect** to a greater extent than Europeans, presumably because of greater familiarity with large open spaces.

However, Gregor and McPherson (1965) found no differences between Australian Aborigines living in carpentered or open-air environments in terms of Müller–Lyer or the horizon-ratio effect. Cross-cultural differences in perceiving visual illusions may be related more to training and education than environment.

Evaluation

- Cross-cultural studies are fraught with **difficulties**, such as biased interpretations by observers and limited samples.
- This research has focused on **limited aspects of perception** (e.g. visual illusions) and may tell us little about cultural differences in everyday perception.
- There is a tendency, in psychology, to **confuse 'culture' with 'country'**. A cultural group shares a set of beliefs, values and practices. Within any one country there are many cultural groups. Many so-called cross-cultural studies in psychology actually involve comparisons between different national groups.
- Studies of human neonates (reviewed on the previous pages) suggest that many perceptual abilities are innate. If this view is correct, and abilities such as depth perception are inborn, then we **should find that all people develop these abilities** regardless of their different personal experiences.

The nature–nurture debate in relation to perceptual development

AQA A ▶ U3

Is perception an innate process (nature) or do we have to learn how to interpret sensory data (nurture)?

'**Nature**' refers to behaviours that are inherited or innate, but this is not the same as behaviours that are present at birth – some biologically-determined behaviours appear later in life, such as changes during adolescence. Additionally, at birth, a young animal has already been alive for some time and environmental factors may have altered behaviour.
'**Nurture**' refers to behaviours that are the result of experience or environmental influence.

Sensory deprivation has major emotional effects, which could explain the physical effects of such deprivation.

There are some applications of this debate. For example, Banks *et al.* (1975) found that if children with squints are operated on before the age of three, they subsequently develop normal vision. But, if the operation is left any later, the deprivation appears to result in some degree of abnormal binocular vision.

The nature–nurture debate is discussed further on page 183.

Gibson's direct theory proposes that perception is largely innate. James Gibson and his wife Eleanor (Gibson and Gibson, 1955) outlined **differentiation theory** – the view that perceptual development involves learning to differentiate between the distinctive features of different classes of objects. Gregory's indirect theory suggests that perceptual abilities are influenced by learned expectations.

Evidence for nature

Studies of infant perception show that some abilities are innate (see pages 25 and 26), such as aspects of depth perception and also face perception. Some cross-cultural studies support the idea of innate perceptual characteristics (see previous page). In another cross-cultural study, Rosch (1978) found that members of the Dani (from New Guinea) were quicker at learning the colour name for fire-engine red than other reds, which suggests that this is an innately perceived colour.

Hubel and Wiesel (1962) demonstrated the biological basis of pattern recognition, which is evidence of innate perceptual abilities. They placed microelectrodes in different parts of a cat's visual cortex and found **simple cells** that only fired when the cat was shown a line of unique orientation in a particular part of the visual field. They also found cells sensitive to other features (e.g. a stationary or moving dot, a moving line), and **complex cells**, which responded to several simple cells, and **hypercomplex cells**, which responded to simple patterns or shapes (such as angles). These cells are organised into **functional columns**, which may predispose the brain to be able to make certain comparisons, such as those used in depth perception.

Evidence for nurture affecting nature

Visual deprivation leads to a loss of innate biological abilities. For example, Wiesel (1982) sewed one eye of a kitten shut. If this is done early enough and for long enough, the eye becomes blind, suggesting that without experience the innate system is not maintained.

Blakemore and Cooper (1970) placed kittens in a drum that had only vertical, or only horizontal, lines. The kittens later had difficulties with depth perception and were virtually blind, except for the contours perpendicular to those they experienced. Examination of their visual cortex showed that there were no cells remaining that responded electrically to the orientation not experienced by the cat. This supports the view that physical degeneration results from a lack of experience during a critical period.

Gregory and Wallace (1963) studied SB, who was blind from birth due to cataracts. In later life the cataracts were removed but SB was never fully able to use his newly acquired sight even though he was not blind. Von Senden (1932) found the same in other cataract patients.

Conclusions

The conclusion from studies of deprivation is that experience modifies innate abilities. Innate systems are present from birth but require experiential input to be maintained and to adapt to changed circumstances (nature and nurture). The process of differentiation or bottom-up processing (Gibson) may explain innate systems of perception, whereas enrichment or top-down processing (Gregory) is related to those perceptual abilities that are learned. In any one situation the relative contributions of each will vary according to particular circumstances (such as lighting conditions).

Practice essay 2.2

'Is perception due to nature or nurture, or both?' Discuss the nature–nurture debate in relation to perceptual development.   *(25 marks)*

2.3 Face recognition and visual agnosias

After studying this topic you should be able to describe and evaluate:

- *Bruce and Young's theory of face recognition, including case studies and explanations of prosopagnosia.*

Bruce and Young's theory of face recognition

AQA A U3

Face recognition is the process by which the brain and mind understand and interpret the human face.

Bruce and Young (1986) developed a model for face recognition, which suggests that there are two different mechanisms for familiar and unfamiliar face recognition.

- The recognition of **familiar faces** involves structural encoding first, followed by face recognition units, person identity nodes, and name generation.
- The **recognition of unfamiliar faces** probably involves recognition of configuration (Yin, 1969). In the Bruce and Young model, recognition of unfamiliar faces involves structural encoding first and then expression analysis, facial speech analysis, and directed visual processing.

The study of face recognition has important applications, for example, in the production of machines that will recognise faces for security, and in assisting police to produce accurate eyewitness records of faces (i.e. identikit pictures).

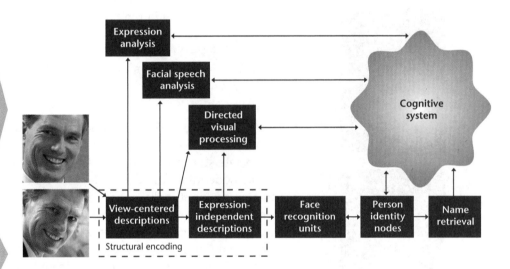

Face recognition has important survival value because we need to distinguish between friends and foes.

Research evidence

1. Prosopagnosia

Prosopagnosia is a special case of **visual agnosia**, where patients can describe objects in their visual field (including details of colour, texture and shape), but are unable to recognise the objects.

Patients with prosopagnosia cannot recognise faces, but their ability to recognise other objects may be relatively intact. Prosopagnosia is not a unitary disorder – different people show different types and levels of impairment. This supports Bruce and Young's notion that face perception has a number of stages, each of which can be separately damaged.

2. Case studies

Brunsdon *et al.* (2006) studied AL, an 8-year-old with prosopagnosia. The child could not recognise familiar or unfamiliar faces, therefore, the deficit was at the level of structural encoding. However, he could recognise individual features and this ability was used to train him to name familiar faces.

de Haan *et al.* (1991) studied a patient with amnesia, ME, who was good at matching famous faces and names but didn't know any information about them. This supports the separate units of the Bruce and Young model.

Malone *et al.* (1982) studied a patient who was able to recognise photographs of famous statesmen but coped poorly with matching unfamiliar faces, and another patient who could do the opposite.

Young *et al.* (1985) studied normal people and not one of the participants reported being able to put a name to a face without also knowing something else about the person. They could often remember a lot about the person, just not their name.

3. Experimental studies

Bauer (1984) showed familiar and unfamiliar faces to patients with prosopagnosia. Despite being unable to identify which faces were familiar, the patients showed a positive **GSR** to the familiar faces, showing an unconscious response.

Thompson (1980) demonstrated the **Thatcher effect** (see left). People find it difficult to detect local feature changes in an upside-down face, but can detect them in an upright face. When a face is upside-down, the configural processing cannot take place, and so minor differences are more difficult to detect. This supports the notion of a unique face processor.

4. Neurophysiological evidence

Various studies (e.g. Sergent et al., 1992) have used scanning techniques to identify the areas of the brain that are active when identifying faces. The **fusiform face area (FFA)** is active when processing faces and not as active when identifying other objects, especially in the right hemisphere.

5. Infant face perception

Evidence that infants have an innate preference for faces supports the view that face perception is hardwired in a special region of the brain (see pages 25–26).

Evaluation

- Burton and Bruce (1993) developed a **more precise version** of the Bruce and Young model. The new model has been used in computer simulations. It has no separate store for names, and the familiar face recognition is at the person-identity node rather than at the face recognition unit.
- Some psychologists believe that face recognition is **no different to the recognition of any other complex stimuli**. Faces are simply complex perceptual objects that we become very practised at identifying. Support for this comes from Gauthier *et al.* (2000) who have shown that the FFA is also active when participants are asked to discriminate between different types of birds and cars. This suggests that the FFA may have a general role in the recognition of similar visual objects, rather than just specialising in faces. It is clear that the FFA is important in face recognition but may not be exclusive to it.

GSR stands for galvanic skin response, a method of measuring emotional arousal by testing the electrical conductivity of the skin. When a person is emotionally aroused the ANS is activated and sweatiness increases the electrical conductivity of the skin.

The **Thatcher effect** – look at this picture upside-down and you will see that the features are actually in the wrong direction – this is only detected when the face is viewed the right way up.

Practice essay 2.3

Discuss Bruce and Young's theory of face recognition. *(25 marks)*

Chapter 3

Relationships

3.1 The formation, maintenance and breakdown of romantic relationships

After studying this topic you should be able to describe and evaluate:

- *theories of the formation, maintenance and breakdown of romantic relationships, for example, reward/need satisfaction and social exchange theory.*

LEARNING SUMMARY

Formation of romantic relationships

AQA A ⟩ U3

This is a **learning theory** account of relationship formation, as it is based on the concept of conditioning (see page 72).

The reinforcement-affect model can be used to explain why politicians like to be seen at award ceremonies. You can also use it to win the affections of your heart throb – appear at events that make them happy (e.g. a football match).

Is a simple explanation a bad thing? **Occam's razor** is the principle that one should avoid complex explanations when a simpler one exists. On the other hand, a simple explanation may oversimplify complex behaviours.

Evolutionary explanations of human reproductive behaviour (see page 34) can also be used to explain why people form romantic relationships.

1. Reinforcement-affect model (Clore and Byrne, 1974)

- 'Reinforcement' leads us to like (and, therefore, wish to form relationships with) people who reward us (**operant conditioning**). Such reinforcement (rewards) might be someone else acting positively towards us (e.g. smiling or being friendly) or a situation involving someone else rewarding us.
- 'Affect' refers to the positive feelings that are associated with a good experience. This is an example of **classical conditioning** – learning by association. If a particular event or situation (unconditioned stimulus) creates positive feelings (unconditioned response), then a person (neutral stimulus) who is associated with the event becomes a conditioned stimulus producing the conditioned response (positive feelings). Increased 'affect' towards that person leads to relationship formation.

Research evidence

Veitch and Griffitt (1976) placed participants in a waiting room where they listened to either good or bad news with a stranger present. When they were asked to rate the stranger, the degree of liking was related to the kind of news they had been listening to.

Cunningham (1988) found that men who watched a happy rather than a sad movie later interacted with a female confederate more positively.

Evaluation

- This is a relatively **simple** model (both an advantage and a disadvantage).
- The research support is rather **contrived and artificial** (Duck, 1992).
- The model does not account for **relationships** where rewards are irrelevant.

2. Reward/need satisfaction (Argyle, 1994)

People form relationships because interpersonal relationships satisfy parts of the seven basic human motives or needs: biological (e.g. eating together); dependency (e.g. being comforted); affiliation (seeking company); dominance (establishing social order); sex (reproduction); aggression (interpersonal hostility); and self-esteem (being valued by others).

Evaluation

- This explanation is more appropriate to **individualist societies** because the 'needs' are focused on the individual and not the group.

Maintenance of romantic relationships

Social exchange theory is sometimes called an **economic theory** because it explains relationships in terms of maximising rewards, minimising costs and gaining profits. Such 'economic theories' are more relevant to **individualist** societies rather than **collectivist** ones where people are more concerned with the needs of others.

Social exchange theory can also be used to explain the formation and breakdown of relationships. But, if you do this when answering an essay question, make sure you shape your description to explain formation or breakdown rather than maintenance.

Equity theory is a version of social exchange theory, which suggests that balance is achieved more through perceived fairness (equity) rather than exchange. Both over- and under-benefits are not fair.

The maintenance of relationships can be explained more simply in terms of daily routines – such routines provide comfortable predictability and people prefer not to disrupt this.

Much of the early research has been based on studies with college students as participants and, therefore, may explain a certain kind of romantic relationship – one between young people. Long-term, middle-aged relationships may be governed by other factors, such as daily routines.

1. Social exchange theory (Thibaut and Kelley, 1959)

'Social exchange' refers to the exchange of **rewards** between two people, such as being cared for, companionship and sex. Relationships also incur **costs**, such as money spent or opportunities missed. According to this theory, people wish to maximise their rewards and minimise costs so they receive a **profit** from a relationship (i.e. satisfaction).

In order to judge the rewards in a relationship people make two comparisons: (1) between actual and expected rewards (called the **comparison level, CL**), and (2) the comparison level for alternative relationships (referred to as **CLalt**).

Thibaut and Kelley suggest relationships develop through key stages:
- **Sampling** – Explore rewards and costs directly or indirectly (observing others).
- **Bargaining** – Prospective partners establish sources of profit and loss.
- **Commitment** – Routines are established.
- **Institutionalisation** – Norms and mutual expectations are established.

Research evidence

Rusbult (1983) found that 'costs' are only calculated after the honeymoon phase.

Simpson *et al.* (1990) found that participants who were dating at the time of the study rated members of the opposite sex as less attractive, demonstrating that they closed themselves off from attractive alternatives.

Evaluation

- Social exchange theory can be applied to **all sorts of relationships**, e.g. families, friends.
- **Mechanistic** approach. In reality, relationships are more complex; it is difficult to define rewards or costs and to quantify satisfaction or 'profit'. It also focuses too much on the individual perspective rather than social aspects of a relationship, such as how partners talk with each other and interpret shared events (Duck and Sants, 1983).

2. Active maintenance strategies

Relationships are maintained through strategies that couples develop. Rusbult *et al.* (1986) suggested there are four strategies which can be combined: active or passive, constructive or destructive. For example, loyalty is a passive, constructive strategy where a partner waits for the situation to improve. Dindia and Baxter (1987) found 49 different strategies in their study below.

Research evidence

Dindia and Baxter (1987) examined the strategies used by 50 married couples. The strategies ranged from the fairly trivial (e.g. talking about each other's experiences during the day) through to more meaningful strategies (e.g. reminiscing about shared experiences). There were more strategies for maintaining relationships than for repairing them.

Yum (2000) found that partners prefer constructive to destructive strategies.

Dainton (2000) found that those couples who used maintenance strategies reported greater levels of satisfaction in their relationship, supporting the role of strategies in the maintenance of relationships.

Evaluation

- This is a **more recent approach** – looking at the interaction between partners rather than the individual's perspective.
- It is a more **qualitative approach** than social exchange theory.

Breakdown of romantic relationships

AQA A ▶ U3

Social exchange theory would predict that dissolution is the result of an imbalance in rewards and costs, and/or the existence of a better alternative.

Lee (1984) proposed an alternative stage theory of relational breakdown based on a study of over 100 pre-marital romantic break-ups:

- **Dissatisfaction:** problems recognised.
- **Exposure:** problems identified and brought out into the open.
- **Negotiation:** discussion about the issues raised during the exposure stage.
- **Resolution attempts:** both partners try to find ways of solving the problems.
- **Termination:** if the resolution attempts are unsuccessful.

Felmlee's (1995) 'fatal attraction theory' suggests that the same characteristic(s) that initially caused attraction, ultimately lead to dissolution. Such characteristics might initially be exciting or different but later appear predictable or strange.

1. Stage model of relational dissolution (Duck, 1984)

Duck described breakdown in terms of five stages:

- **Breakdown** – Dissatisfaction leads to breaking point. Repair strategy: correct own behavioural faults.
- **Intra-psychic phase** – Thinking about the relationship, at first in private, then with confidants, and finally with partner. Repair strategy: re-establish liking for partner.
- **Dyadic phase** – Deciding whether to break up or repair. Repair strategy: express conflict, clear the air and reformulate rules for a future relationship.
- **Social phase** – Including others in the debate, enlisting support for your 'side'. Repair strategy: outsiders may help patch things up or encourage separation.
- **Grave dressing phase** – Post-mortem for public and private re-adjustment. Repair strategy: decide on a mutually acceptable version of events, and/or attempt to salvage friendship out of the break up.

Evaluation

- A **strength** of this model is the inclusion of repair strategies, useful for **marriage guidance** to identify the stage of dissolution reached and strategies appropriate to that stage.
- Duck focused on the processes that take place **after breakdown** and focused less on the early events. This is in contrast with **Lee's model** (see left), which is mainly concerned with events leading up to breakdown.
- Stage models do not explain why breakdown occurs; they are **descriptive**.

2. Risk factors (Duck, 1982)

Duck suggested that breakdown can be explained in terms of 'risk factors':

1. **Predisposing personal factors** (dispositional) – distasteful personal habits, change in interests, poor role models (e.g. divorced parents), dissonance (e.g. partners from different religious backgrounds) or poor social skills.

2. **Precipitating factors** (situational) – deception, boredom, relocation, conflict or a better alternative.

Research evidence

Rohlfing (1998) found that reduced proximity (a possible predisposing factor) may not lead to breakdown; 70% of students questioned had experienced at least one long-distance romantic relationship (LDRR). Holt and Stone (1988) found that there was little decrease in relationship satisfaction as long as lovers are able to reunite regularly.

Evaluation

- These factors offer an **explanation** for dissolution.
- **Many relationships are stable** despite the presence of such factors.
- Some of the factors are **intervening variables,** for example, lower educational levels may be associated with divorce, but are not the cause.

Practice essays 3.1

(a) Outline **two or more** theories of the maintenance of romantic relationships. *(9 marks)*

(b) Evaluate **one** of the theories you outlined in part (a). *(16 marks)*

3.2 Human reproductive behaviour

After studying this topic you should be able to describe and evaluate:

- the relationship between sexual selection and human reproductive behaviour
- evolutionary explanations of parental investment, for example, sex differences, parent–offspring conflict.

LEARNING SUMMARY

The relationship between sexual selection and human reproductive behaviour

Darwin proposed sexual selection as a variation of natural selection. **Sexual selection** is the selection for traits that are solely concerned with increasing mating success. For example, if a peacock's tail increases his chances of being selected as a mate then the trait becomes perpetuated – it has been sexually selected.

Because of **anisogamy** (the fact that each sex has different gametes – eggs and sperm), males (sperm) compete and females (eggs) select.

Dunbar (1995) found that the male–female patterns shown in personal ads were not shown in gay and lesbian personal ads – presumably because mate choice in these individuals is not driven by reproductive criteria.

Males must compete to be selected by females.

Any behaviour that increases an individual's reproductive success will be selected and appear in future generations. 'Reproductive success' includes the number of offspring produced, their healthiness, survival and ultimately their reproductive success. In general, each sex behaves differently because of different selective pressures arising from the differences between eggs and sperm (**anisogamy**).

- **Sperm** – males produce millions of sperm and can potentially fertilise hundreds of females at a minimal cost to future reproductive potential. Natural selection will favour strategies that maximise the number of fertilisations, leading to **intrasexual** competition and polygamy.
- **Eggs** – female investment is greater because the egg contains nutrients, which have a physiological cost. Therefore, eggs are produced in limited numbers and females need to be more careful to ensure that each reproduction is successful (e.g. seek good mate, high parental investment and monogamy). Natural selection will favour discrimination in females, which leads to **intersexual** selection strategies.

Research evidence

The consequence of this is that men should seek partners who have good reproductive potential, whereas females do best with partners who have good genetic potential and are able to provide resources to aid the survival of the young.

Various studies have provided such support. For example, Buss (1989) found that, in 37 cultures, men preferred partners who were young and physically attractive (this indicates good reproductive potential), whereas women valued males with high resource potential, i.e. good financial prospects, ambition, and industriousness. Dunbar and Waynforth (1995) analysed personal ads and found that 42% of males sought a youthful mate, compared to 25% of females. 44% of males sought a physically attractive partner, compared to 22% of women.

However a recent study using speed dating events found no gender differences in the importance placed on physical attractiveness and earning potential (Todd *et al.*, 2007).

1. Male (intrasexual) strategies

Courtship routines – The classic example from the animal world is the peacock, who parades in front of a peahen to show off his fabulous tail as an advertisement of his genetic quality. In humans, men buy chocolates and flowers. Miller (1998) suggested that stories, jokes, dance, music and art may all be forms of courtship displays to aid sexual conquests.

Male size and adornment – Males evolve weaponry (e.g. antlers) and are bigger for fighting (competition between males for females). Penis size is related to male competition: in species where competition is greatest, penis sizes are larger. In some human groups, men wear penis sheaths to advertise their quality.

Williams (1966) suggested that courtship is a contest between male salesmanship and female sales resistance.

Sperm competition – Males also compete at the level of sperm. When females mate with more than one male, a successful male strategy is to produce sperm that will be more successful. As a result, males evolve larger testicles, ejaculate more and produce faster-swimming sperm.

Sneak copulation – A non-dominant male discretely copulates when the first male is not looking. Sasse *et al.* (1994) found, in a study in Switzerland, that less than 1.4% of the children's presumed father was not their biological one. Unpartnered males gain from sneak copulation. Women may gain from having varied partners because it increases the quality of their offspring.

Rape – Thornhill and Thornhill (1983) controversially argued that men who are unable to mate are driven to select an alternative strategy. Thornhill (1980) cites the behaviour of the male *Panorpa scorpion fly* who inseminates unwilling females by securing the female's wings in an abdominal clamp, showing that rape occurs 'naturally' and, therefore, this suggests that it is an adaptive strategy.

2. Female (intersexual) strategies

Females have more to lose because their investment in reproduction is higher. Therefore, females who are 'choosier' have evolved through selective pressure, in particular basing their choice on 'good genes' in order to produce offspring that are fitter (i.e. have a greater chance of survival and reproduction). This choosiness has certain predictable outcomes, as seen, for example, in the runaway process and handicapping theory.

This explanation is also called the 'sexy sons' or 'good taste' hypothesis.

As long as the advantages outweigh the disadvantages, the 'bizarre' characteristic will be perpetuated.

Runaway process – Fisher (1930) suggested that females select males with attractive characteristics because they will then produce sons who have inherited those characteristics, increasing the sons' reproductive success (and, therefore, enhancing the continuance of the mother's genes). Initially, the characteristics would have some survival value (e.g. long tail) but, because females actively select mates with this feature, it becomes exaggerated. The classic example of such runaway or bizarre characteristics is the peacock's tail. Miller (1992) argues that the overlarge human brain is an example of the runaway process – our intellectual abilities evolved because of the demands of courtship.

Evaluation

- Support comes from, for example, Petrie *et al.* (1987) who found that peacocks with the best tails (most eyespots) were most likely to be selected and had the biggest offspring that also survived longest.

Handicapping theory is also called the 'good genes' or 'good sense' hypothesis. 'Good genes' are for survival, as opposed to Fisher's hypothesis where the 'good genes' would be for producing attractive male offspring.

Handicapping theory – Zahavi (1975) proposed that females prefer mates with handicaps (such as an over-long tail) because this is evidence of their superior genetic quality. Superior genetic quality is also demonstrated through symmetry and good quality hair/feathers. Møller (1992) suggested that symmetry is a handicap because it requires a great deal of genetic precision. Only good genes can produce a symmetrical body and this explains why symmetricality is attractive.

Evaluation

The fact that diseases continue to evolve means that this mechanism would be particularly advantageous.

- **Support** comes from, for example, Møller (1990) who studied barn swallows, a species troubled by the blood-sucking mite. He found that parents with longer tails had offspring with smaller mite loads even when they were reared in a foster nest (where the mites could be passed through contact from foster parents with greater mite loads).
- Critics point out that the **same might apply to males who have been injured**, but this 'handicap' would not be heritable and in fact individuals who get injured tend to be weaker to begin with. Females who mated with males handicapped through injury would not provide any genetic benefit for their offspring so this behaviour would not be perpetuated.

Evolutionary explanations of parental investment

Trivers (1972) defined **parental investment** (PI) as 'any investment by a parent in one of her/his offspring that increases the chance that the offspring will survive at the expense of that parent's ability to invest in any other offspring (alive or yet to be born)'.

Who ends up holding the baby? It isn't always females. For example, the male stickleback remains with the eggs he has gathered from a number of females until they hatch; the male seahorse carries fertilised eggs around in a brood pouch.

External fertilisation does not always result in male care, nor does internal fertilisation always lead to maternal care. For example, the female jacana lays a clutch of eggs for each male in her harem and then leaves them for the male to incubate and rear entirely on his own.

Sex differences in parental investment

1. Eggs and sperm

Parental investment begins with the gametes. Female investment is greater. Either sex may use one of two strategies: r or K.

- **r strategy** – The individual produces many eggs/sperm and devotes little extra care. Survival is ensured through numbers alone, or by having several mates and leaving the partner to care.
- **K strategy** – The individual produces relatively few eggs (female) or mates with one partner, and devotes more energy to ensuring survival.

2. Who provides the care?

Mode of fertilisation may be a way of explaining which sex becomes the carer:

- **Paternity certainty hypothesis** – Ridley (1978) proposed that males are more likely to care for young when fertilisation is external because the care increases the certainty that the offspring are his own. In the case of internal fertilisation the male can desert, knowing (or thinking) that the offspring are his.
- **Order of gamete release hypothesis** – Dawkins and Carlisle (1976) proposed that both sexes prefer not to be left 'holding the baby' because this decreases their future reproductive potential. Internal fertilisation allows the male to get away first; with external fertilisation the female can leave first.
- **Association hypothesis** – Williams (1975) proposed that the adult who is left in close proximity to the embryo tends to care for the young. Where external fertilisation takes place this is the male; with internal fertilisation this is the female.

However, in mammals, shared care is common because, after birth, the young are still quite dependent. The male's investment may be better protected by staying and sharing the care, and protecting the female and young so this behaviour is naturally selected.

3. Parental certainty

Female mammals can be certain that their child is their own, whereas males cannot. The same applies to grandparents – maternal grandmothers are most certain that a grandchild is their own, whereas paternal grandfathers are least certain. Research has supported this. For example, Pollett *et al.* (2007) studied the visiting patterns of grandparents living within 30km of their grandchildren. Over 30% of the maternal grandmothers had contact daily or a few times a week with their grandchildren. In the case of maternal grandfathers, there was on average 25% contact. However, paternal grandparents had much less contact – 15% of the paternal grandmothers and little more than 15% of the paternal grandfathers regularly saw their grandchildren.

Evaluation

- **Support** for this comes from Andersson *et al.* (1999), who looked at the investments made by fathers in the college education of their biological children and their stepchildren. The investments were highest when a father was still living with the biological mother of his children, but otherwise investments were the same, which doesn't fit evolutionary theory. Andersson *et al.* suggest that men are willing to invest in stepchildren because it demonstrates to their partner that they are a good provider (a criterion for sexual selection).

4. Sexual jealousy

One of the consequences of gender differences in PI is sexual jealousy. Buss (1995) suggests that sexual jealousy has evolved differently in males and females because each sex has different concerns. For a male it is important that his partner is sexually faithful in order to ensure an offspring is his own. For a female, emotional infidelity is more important because she doesn't want to lose her breadwinner and risk more difficulties raising her offspring.

This was supported by a study by Buss *et al.* (1992) who found that American male students indicated more concern about sexual infidelity, whereas female students expressed more concern about emotional infidelity. In addition, the men showed much higher **GSR** responses (indicating distress) when shown pictures of sexual infidelity than emotional infidelity. However, Harris (2003) found this difference did not apply to real-life experiences. When actual reports from men and women about their partner's infidelity were examined there were no gender differences.

Parent–offspring conflict

Parental investment is not determined solely by parents. Offspring behaviour often influences the process in order to maximise offspring **fitness**. A parent has an equal interest in each offspring, although the amount of resources allocated to each offspring decreases as the child gets older and needs less care to ensure survival. From the offspring's point of view, decreased care is undesirable and this leads to certain behaviours, as listed below.

1. Sibling rivalry

In most sexually reproducing species (including humans), individual offspring will want to receive more than their 'fair share' at the expense of other offspring, in order to maximise their own fitness. As a result, sibling rivalries may develop for the attention and available resources of parents. Mock and Parker (1998) document many examples in animals species, for example, egrets who push siblings out of the nest, and shark embryos who eat their embryonic siblings.

Lalumière *et al.* (1996) suggested that human parents cope with sibling rivalry by steering siblings along different developmental paths, maximising each individual's strengths, so that there is reduced sibling competition and also less subsequent competition for the same mates. This might explain why siblings turn out to be so different.

2. Parent–offspring conflict before birth

Parent–offspring conflict does not only develop after birth, but begins at the moment a mother's egg is fertilised by the father's sperm (Buss, 1999). High blood pressure in pregnancy (which may lead to the potentially fatal condition called **pre-eclampsia**) may be caused by the foetus secreting hormones when it 'perceives' the need for more nutrition. The higher blood pressure results in more nutrient-containing blood being delivered to the foetus. This mechanism benefits the foetus at the expense of the mother (Haig, 1998).

Research has found that mothers who do have high blood pressure during pregnancy tend to have fewer spontaneous abortions (Haig, 1993) and larger babies at birth (Xiong *et al.*, 2000), both of which suggest that high blood pressure is associated with more healthy foetuses and is, therefore, an adaptive strategy.

> **GSR** stands for galvanic skin response, a method of measuring emotional arousal by testing the electrical conductivity of the skin. When a person is emotionally aroused the ANS is activated and sweatiness increases the electrical conductivity of the skin.

> The concept of **fitness** is central to evolutionary theory. It describes the reproductive capability of an individual – the fitter you are the more likely you are to reproduce successfully. Fitness is measured by the proportion of the individual's genes in all the genes of the next generation.

Practice essay 3.2

Discuss the relationship between sexual selection and human reproductive behaviour.
(25 marks)

3.3 Effects of early experience and culture on adult relationships

After studying this topic you should be able to describe and evaluate:

- the influence of childhood and adolescent experiences on adult relationships, including parent–child relationships and interaction with peers.

LEARNING SUMMARY

Influence of childhood experiences on adult relationships

AQA A   U3

Key points from AS

- John Bowlby's attachment theory, and related research evidence, is discussed in more detail in *Revise AS Unit 3.1, page 53.*

Hazan and Shaver (1987) extended Bowlby's theory to adult relationships. They argued that the **attachment behavioural system** that develops in infancy leads to three aspects of adult behaviour: romantic relationships, caregiving and sexuality.

A lot of research looks at the consequences of being a secure or insecure adult. However, the key question is whether these temperament types are due to childhood experiences or to some other factor, such as the innate temperament of the individual. For the purposes of this section, however, we are only concerned with the link between early experience and later behaviour, rather than the question of whether early experience *caused* later behaviour.

Fraley (2004) concludes that early attachment and later romantic relationships are only moderately related at best.

John Bowlby (1969) proposed that the relationship between a primary attachment figure and his/her infant creates an **internal working model** of relationships. This internal working model creates expectations about future relationships, described as a **continuity hypothesis** – people who are securely attached as infants will continue to form similar relationships throughout life. They are more likely to be sociable and popular with peers, to form lasting romantic relationships and to offer secure attachment to their children.

Research evidence

Friendships

Simpson *et al.* (2007) followed 78 individuals from infancy to their early 20s. Those individuals who were securely attached were more socially competent in school and were more likely to have secure friendships at age 16. In early adulthood these individuals had more positive daily emotional experiences.

Romantic relationships

Hazan and Shaver (1987) found that adults who were securely attached as infants believed that love was enduring, and were more mutually trusting, and were less likely to have been divorced. In contrast, adults who had been insecurely attached felt true love was rare, fell in and out of love easily and generally found relationships less easy.

McCarthy (1999) studied women whose attachment types were recorded in infancy. Those who had been classified as avoidant had the greatest difficulty in romantic relationships and those who had been classified as resistant had the poorest friendships. Women who were securely attached as infants had the most successful romantic relationships and friendships.

However, Steele *et al.* (1998) found a correlation of only .17 between secure attachment type at age 1 and at age 20.

Caregiving and parenting

Quinton *et al.* (1984) compared a group of 50 women who had been reared in institutions (children's homes) with a control group of 50 'normal' women. When the women were in their 20s it was found that the ex-institution women were experiencing extreme difficulties acting as parents. For example, more of the ex-institution women had children who had spent time in care and more of the ex-institution women were rated as lacking in warmth when interacting with their children.

Sexuality

Avoidant romantic attachment is associated with more accepting attitudes of casual sex (Schachner and Shaver, 2002).

Influence of adolescent experiences on adult relationships

AQA A ▶ U3

Key points from AS

- You can read a description of Freud's theory and stages of development in *Revise AS Unit 1.1, page 19.*

Erikson's eight stages of life

First year – Trust vs. mistrust

Second year – Autonomy vs. shame and doubt

Third to sixth year – Initiative vs. guilt

To puberty – Industry vs. inferiority

Adolescence – Identity vs. identity confusion

Early adulthood – Intimacy vs. isolation

Middle age – Generativity vs. stagnation

Old age – Integrity vs. despair

Parent–child relationships

Freud suggested that adolescence was a period of identity formation and the development of independence (the **genital stage**). Erik Erikson (1968) developed Freud's ideas, proposing that adult intimacy could only be achieved if earlier crises in development had been successfully negotiated. Erikson suggested that there were eight crises or 'tasks' that occurred during a person's life (see left). Negative outcomes in one stage make successful resolution of the developmental crisis of the next stage more difficult. In early adulthood, intimacy is the main task but this stage cannot be resolved if earlier stages had a negative outcome. This includes attachment experiences in the first year (trust versus mistrust) and also includes, most importantly, the identity crises during puberty. Erikson suggested that a young person who cannot establish their own identity will have problems with intimacy because the individual fears loss of identity if they commit to others.

Erikson's view has been supported by research, for example, Kahn *et al.* (1985) found that students assessed as being low in identity development later had less success in relationships (e.g. men likely to not be married, women more likely to be separated). There may, however, be a gender difference in the link between intimacy and identity. Erikson believed that the relationship between identity and intimacy was different for men and women. He suggested that female identity development was different – for a woman, identity depends on finding a partner first so identity comes *after* intimacy. For males, identity comes *before* intimacy. This may be a gender bias or a real difference.

More recent research has also showed that warm and close parental relationships (attachment) during adolescence are important for the development of autonomy (which is important for adult relationships). This has been called '*inter*dependence' or '**connectedness**' (Coleman and Hendry, 1999).

Interaction with peers

Ainsworth (1989) suggested that peers were important in adolescent emotional development because they provide attachment relationships and also feedback about social behaviour.

Peers provide an emotional way-station on the way to adulthood; in order to become independent, young people transfer their dependence from parents to peers (Steinberg and Silverberg, 1986). However, there is a different view, which is that peer attachments don't replace parental attachments, they are simply different. Peer relationships are more symmetrical, i.e. each person in the relationship is equal. At the same time, parental relationships during adolescence also change and become more like the new peer relationships – more symmetrical and less critical (Hendry *et al.*, 1993).

Peers also provide opportunities for practising adult romantic relationships; too much practice or practice in poor quality adolescent relationships may negatively impact on young adult relationships. Meier *et al.* (2005) used data from the US National Longitudinal Study of Adolescent Health and found that both adolescent relationship type and the quality of those relationships contribute to the type and quality of young adult relationships.

Practice essay 3.3

Discuss the influence of adolescent experiences on adult relationships, including parent–child relationships and interaction with peers. *(25 marks)*

Chapter 4

Aggression

4.1 Social psychological approaches to explaining aggression

After studying this topic you should be able to describe and evaluate:

Aggression refers to behaviour that is intended to cause harm or pain.

- *social psychological theories of aggression, for example, social learning theory, deindividuation*
- *explanations of institutional aggression.*

LEARNING SUMMARY

Social psychological theories of aggression

AQA A   U3

Vicarious reinforcement occurs when you observe someone else being reinforced for certain behaviour (e.g. on TV). This increases your own expectation of future rewards and punishments.

See page 72 for an explanation of operant conditioning.

'Social' learning is learning that involves other people – therefore it is 'social'.

Key points from AS

- **Social learning theory** is discussed in more detail in *Revise AS Unit 1.1, page 17.*

More evidence of the effects of indirect reinforcement on aggression can be found in Chapter 13 on media psychology, see page 125.

You are more likely to imitate (or '*model*') your behaviour on someone you admire or respect (e.g. rock stars, parents, teachers, friends) because you *identify* with them. **Modelling** and **identification** are important concepts in SLT.

1. Social learning theory (SLT)

Aggression is learned:

- **Indirectly** – through **observational learning** (you observe what others are doing). Such behaviour is only repeated if **vicarious reinforcement** occurs.
- **Directly** – when a behaviour is performed, it may be directly reinforced and, therefore, more likely to be repeated. If it isn't reinforced, the probability that it will be repeated is decreased.

Both indirect and direct reinforcement are examples of **operant conditioning**.

An individual learns (a) the value of aggressive behaviour (thus increasing tendency to aggress) and (b) to imitate specific acts of aggression.

Albert Bandura first outlined SLT. He suggested that there are four steps in the **modelling** process:

- **Attention** – If a person (model) is attractive, prestigious, or similar you will pay more attention.
- **Retention** – Actions must be remembered (i.e. cognitive processes involved).
- **Reproduction** – Vicarious reinforcement is not enough, imitation can only occur if the person possesses appropriate skills.
- **Motivation** – Imitation is related to direct and indirect reinforcements and punishments.

Research evidence

Bandura *et al.* (1961, 1963) showed that, if children watched someone else behave aggressively towards a Bobo doll (punching it, shouting at it and hitting it with a hammer), they were more likely to be aggressive themselves later on, and also imitated specific actions when they were placed on their own with the doll (after being mildly frustrated). Later variations found that a filmed version was as effective as a live model, and also that imitation was even more likely if:

- The model was **rewarded**. When the model was punished children did not imitate the behaviour. This shows that observational learning only results in imitation when it is vicariously reinforced.
- The child **identified** with the model. For example, a favourite hero or heroine on TV, or same sex model.
- The participant had low **self-esteem**.

Aggressive video games provide an opportunity to observe the effects of models on behaviours (see page 26).

Aggression can also be explained in terms of **disinhibition** (see page 125) – seeing someone else behave aggressively may reduce one's own inhibitions about behaving in this way.

Key points from AS

- Social explanations of aggression can be evaluated by considering the relative strengths and limitations of biological explanations. See, for example *Revise AS Unit 1.1, page 13*.

See biological explanations of aggression on pages 43 and 44.

Deindividuation describes the loss of a sense of personal identity that can occur when, for example, in a crowd or wearing a mask. It is associated with a reduced sense of personal responsibility and increased anti-social behaviour.

In Zimbardo's view, deindividuation results in anti-social behaviour. Prentice-Dunn and Rogers propose a 'normative' view – deindividuation results in people following groups' norms rather than going against them.

Key points from AS

- Zimbardo's classic **Stanford Prison study** involved deindividuated behaviour from both prisoners and guards. It is described in *Revise AS Unit, page 123.*
- Obedience studies are described in *Revise AS Unit 6.1, page 128.*

Evaluation

- Research findings may be due to **demand characteristics** in an unfamiliar social situation (the children had to look for cues of what to do with Bobo).
- SLT can explain **media influences** on anti-social behaviour (see page 125).
- SLT can explain the influence of **coercive home environments**. Parents solve disputes aggressively and children model their behaviour on this (Patterson *et al.*, 1989).
- People are not consistently rewarded for aggression. Often they are punished, which suggests that SLT may be an **oversimplified** account.
- Research doesn't include the effects of **emotional factors or biological factors**, although Bandura acknowledged that biological factors are part of any account. For example, the urge to be aggressive is biological; what is learned (indirectly and directly) is how and when to express the aggression.
- It can explain **individual differences** (people behave differently because of different indirect and direct reinforcement experiences), and can explain **cultural differences** (different cultures reinforce different behaviours and also model different behaviours).
- It explains the fact that people imitate **specific acts** of violence.

1. Deindividuation

Anonymity – The presence of a crowd (or group) leads individual members to feel anonymous and act according to a different set of rules than they would normally. Zimbardo (1969) suggested that:

- **Individuated behaviour** is rational, consistent with personal norms.
- **Deindividuated behaviour** is unrestrained, acting on primitive impulses, and leads to anti-social acts.

Reduced self awareness – An alternative explanation (Prentice-Dunn and Rogers, 1982) for deindividuation effects is that being in a crowd leads to reduced *private* awareness rather than reduced *public* awareness (i.e. anonymity). Normally, people are aware of their personal morals but within a group they may lose sight of 'private' principles and follow the group.

Research evidence

Zimbardo (1963) repeated Milgram's (1963) obedience experiments with participants either wearing a name tag (individuated) or in a hood (deindividuated). When wearing a hood, participants gave more shocks.

Diener *et al.* (1976) observed the behaviour of over 1,000 children on Halloween. The house owner asked some of the children to give their names. Those who remained anonymous were more likely to steal some money and/or extra chocolate when briefly left alone (i.e. they were more likely to behave anti-socially).

Evaluation

- In some instances, deindividuation leads to **increased pro-social behaviour** (e.g. at a peace rally). Johnson and Downing (1979) compared the behaviour of people wearing uniforms either like the Ku Klux Klan or like nurses. The latter gave fewer shocks, i.e. deindividuation did not result in anti-social behaviour.
- As with obedience, an individual can elect whether to behave **autonomously**; deindividuation is not inevitable.
- Understanding deindividuation has led to useful **practical applications**, for example, using video cameras at football matches so that people can see themselves and, therefore, be more publically self-aware.

Explanations of institutional aggression

'**Institutional aggression**' includes:

1. The behaviour of people who belong to institutional groups, such as the military and police (and terrorist groups). In general, this kind of institutional aggression does not involve anger and is likely to be **instrumental aggression** rather than **hostile aggression** (i.e. aggression as a means to another goal).

2. The behaviour of people living in institutions, such as prisoners or people in mental hospitals. In general, this kind of institutional aggression is likely to be hostile (i.e. aggression stemming from feelings of anger).

An **institution** is a structure for a particular social group governed by a set of rules and identified with a particular purpose. It may be an actual place (such as a prison or school) or a conceptual structure (such as the armed forces, the judiciary or marriage). Institutions are social constructions, artifacts of a particular time, culture and society, produced by collective human choice.

Essentially, any explanation of aggressive behaviour could be used to answer essays on this topic as long as you link your answer to institutions.

Key points from AS

- Zimbardo's Stanford Prison experiment is described in *Revise AS Unit 6.1, page 123.*
- Social identity theory is described in *Revise AS Unit 13.7, page 144.*

1. Warfare

Warfare is sometimes seen as uniquely human because it requires a culturally-transmitted technology or political organisation. However, 'wars' are frequently observed between animal groups. One long-term study of wolves (Mech, 1970) found that 25% of all deaths were due to intra-species killing (i.e. within species).

Ardrey (1961) suggested that humans engage in warfare because they have a killing instinct, which evolved because humans are, by nature, carnivorous hunters.

Ehrenreich (1997) proposed the **defence hypothesis of warfare** – that the origins of warfare lie in group defence against predators. She argued that humans survived not just because they hunted but because they protected themselves from being hunted. For example, early Americans defended themselves from uncivilised savages by destroying the Indian nation.

Freud (1930) suggested that wars occurred because humans have a death instinct (**thanatos**), which leads the id to be driven towards self-destruction. The ego diverts this urge towards others so that thanatos becomes a desire to destroy and be aggressive towards others. Freud suggested that the only way to prevent people being aggressive is to redirect these urges into sport or other cathartic activities.

Lorenz (see page 45) suggested that animals evolve safety mechanisms to reduce actual physical harm during intra-species conflict, e.g. displays of strength prior to battle, and signals that indicate defeat. In more modern warfare, humans no longer fight face-to-face and are, therefore, capable of greater destruction.

Watson (1974) looked at the role of deindividuation, such as the use of war paint and uniforms. He examined data from 23 societies and found that of those who behaved most aggressively (killed, tortured, and maimed their enemies), 80% were societies who changed their appearance before going to war.

2. Terrorism

Terrorism can be explained in terms of minority influence (Kruglanski, 2003). This applies to women seeking the vote at the turn of the 20th Century, as well as militant groups of today. Terrorists seek to bring about social change by changing majority opinion. They do this by being consistent and persistent in their claims and activities. Initially, opinion change may not be apparent. For example, a secret poll conducted by the Ministry of Defence (2005) found that a majority of Iraqis *supported* terrorist attacks, although this was not the public impression. A psychodynamic explanation would be that our instinctive aggressive impulses are normally controlled by the superego. But, when a cause is morally justified (e.g. for the sake of religious ideals), then the superego encourages aggressive behaviour.

3. Behaviour of prisoners

Zimbardo, in his classic Stanford Prison experiment (1973), found that the aggressive behaviour of prisoners and guards was due to situational rather than dispositional factors ('a bad barrel rather than a bad apple').

In contrast, Haslam and Reicher (2006) argue that people do not simply behave according to assigned roles; the behaviour of prisoners and guards can be better explained in terms of **social identity theory**.

Practice essay 4.1

Outline and evaluate **two or more** social psychological theories of aggression.

(25 marks)

4.2 Biological explanations of aggression

After studying this topic you should be able to describe and evaluate:

- *the role of neural and hormonal mechanisms in aggression*
- *the role of genetic factors in aggressive behaviour.*

LEARNING SUMMARY

The role of neural and hormonal mechanisms in aggression

AQA A ▶ U3

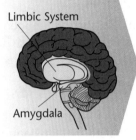

Limbic System

Amygdala

Moghaddom (1998) distinguishes between explanations of aggression which are *normative*, and those which are *causal*. **Normative explanations** explain aggression as being influenced by the norms and rules of particular cultures, i.e. social explanations. **Causal explanations** suggest that aggression is determined by particular factors, such as hormones or hot temperatures, i.e. they are biological explanations.

Key points from AS

- Stress response is discussed in *Revise AS Unit 5.1, page 98.*

Neuroanatomy

Bard (1929) found that cats that had their cortex removed displayed 'sham rage' (i.e. anger without the real emotional content). This suggested that the cortex normally inhibits the **limbic system** (a sub-cortical system including the amygdala, hippocampus and hypothalamus), thus preventing aggression. Later research implicated the **amygdala** in particular. Kluver and Bucy (1939) removed the temporal lobes from monkey's brains and found that they showed little fear or aggression (called the Kluver-Bucy syndrome). Electrical stimulation of the amygdala in animals increases aggression.

Raine *et al.* (1997) used brain scans to demonstrate that murderers were more likely to have abnormalities in their limbic system than normal individuals.

In humans there is evidence that tumours in the limbic system are associated with aggressive behaviour. For example, Charles Whitman, the Texas tower sniper, was found after death to have had a brain tumour that pressed on his amygdala.

Evaluation

- The link with aggression is **complex**. For example, different areas of the limbic system are associated with offensive, defensive and predatory aggression in rats (Adams, 1986).
- Raine *et al.* point out that brain abnormalities may create a predisposition to be violent but they alone do not **cause** violent behaviour.

Neurotransmitters

Low levels of **serotonin** are linked to aggression, as shown, for example, by the fact that drugs which increase serotonin reduce aggression (Delville *et al.*, 1997).

Hormones

Testosterone is a male hormone (present in smaller amounts in females). High levels are associated with aggressiveness in animals (e.g. Gilberto *et al.*, 1997), however, some experiments have not shown a relationship between testosterone levels and aggression in humans (Albert *et al.*, 1993).

High levels of **adrenaline** have also been linked to aggression; adrenaline is linked to the fight/flight response.

The female hormones **oestrogen** and **progesterone** increase just before menstruation (creating pre-menstrual tension – see also page 16) and have also been linked to greater hostility (Hoyenga and Hoyenga, 1993).

Evaluation

- Testosterone has been linked to particular **kinds of aggression** – physical aggression (violence). It may amplify it, but it does not cause it (Simpson, 2001).
- Hormones may be an **effect, rather than a cause**, of aggression.

The role of genetic factors in aggressive behaviour

AQA A ▶ U3

The Y chromosome is the male chromosome. All humans have 23 pairs of chromosomes. In a normal male, one pair is XY, which creates a male. Normal females are XX. (See biological explanations of gender differences, page 59.)

Various lines of research have suggested that higher aggression can be linked to certain genes.

The Y chromosome

Witkin *et al.* (1976) found an over-representation of **XYY** men in prison populations (i.e. one Y chromosome too many). This has been supported by later research.

Criminal families

Mednick *et al.* (1984) found that adopted children whose biological fathers were criminals were more likely to become criminals themselves, than adopted children whose adopted fathers were criminals. This suggests that a tendency to being criminal (and presumably more aggressive) is in your genes.

This line of argument has been used by various criminals, such as Stephen Mobley who killed a man in 1981. His defence was that it wasn't his fault because his family had a history of violence so he had inherited the gene. The court didn't accept his argument and he was sent to the electric chair.

MAOA gene

Biological data is often from studies of non-human animals, which overemphasises the importance of biological factors. In humans, innate behaviour is more modifiable.

The MAOA (monoamine oxidase A) gene is important in eliminating excess amounts of certain neurotransmitters, such as adrenaline and serotonin. Caspi *et al.* (2002) studied over 400 New Zealand men and found that those with low MAOA gene activity *and* who had been abused in childhood were four times more likely to have been convicted of a violent crime by the age of 26.

Brunner *et al.* (1993) studied a family of impulsive, aggressive males who also had a mutation in the gene coding for MAOA.

Selective breeding

The genetic basis of aggression has also been demonstrated in selective breeding programmes. More (or less) aggressive breeds of dogs, bulls or other animals are developed by selecting suitable males and females for breeding.

Evaluation

- This research often assumes that being **criminal is equal to being aggressive**. However, many people in prison are there for crimes that are not connected with aggression. It may simply be that certain genes are linked with low intelligence, and less intelligent men are more likely to end up in prison!

General evaluation of biological explanations

You can contrast biological explanations of aggression with social explanations described on pages 40 and 41.

- If hormones or genes are the cause of aggression, they can be used to **reduce aggression/violence**. However, drug therapies have not been found to be successful in the treatment of aggression (Tyrer *et al.*, 2008).
- Biological accounts explain the motivation to be aggressive but **not the methods used or the targets of aggression** (e.g. violence towards other racial groups).
- Biological accounts cannot explain **cultural differences**.

Practice essay 4.2

Outline and evaluate **one** social psychological explanation of aggression and **one** biological explanation of aggression.   *(25 marks)*

4.3 Aggression as an adaptive response

After studying this topic you should be able to describe and evaluate:

- *evolutionary explanations of human aggression, including infidelity and jealousy*
- *explanations of group display in humans, for example, sports events and lynch mobs.*

LEARNING SUMMARY

Evolutionary explanations of human aggression

AQA A ▶ U3

Aggression is a solution to a range of adaptive problems – i.e., solving these problems would have enhanced the survival and reproductive benefits of the actor; hence, this mental module (aggressive response) would have spread through the population.

Lorenz's view is that aggression is an instinct. Freud's theory (page 42) of aggression is also an 'instinct theory', i.e. he suggested aggression is an innate tendency, but he was not considering it from an evolutionary point of view.

Konrad Lorenz, in his book '*On Aggression*' (1966), proposed that aggression evolved in all animals (including humans) because it is adaptive – the most aggressive animals control access to resources such as mating, territory and food. Lorenz proposed a **hydraulic model** – certain environmental signals (such as the sight of a rival male) acts as a 'releaser' of 'action specific energy'. Over time this energy builds up (like a cistern of water filling up) and will eventually lead to an outburst of aggressive behaviour if not released earlier in some acceptable way such as engaging in sports (a process called **catharsis**).

A more recent evolutionary approach has been outlined by Buss (2005), where aggression is seen as a means of solving various adaptive problems: getting valuable resources that others possess, defending oneself against exploitation or physical attack, deterring others from aggression against you, climbing up in the dominance hierarchy of a group, inflicting costs on intrasexual rivals, deterring long-term mates from (sexual) infidelity and gaining access to mates.

Evaluation

- Evolutionary accounts are **determinist**, suggesting that human aggressive behaviour may be inevitable in certain situations.
- The evolutionary approach emphasises the **positive aspects** of aggression and recognises its survival value.
- The evolutionary approach does not account for **cultural differences**.

Evolutionary stable strategy (ESS)

Maynard-Smith (1982) proposed that uncontrolled violence is not a stable strategy. If all members of a population are violent, they will kill each other. At the other extreme, a population that is totally non-violent (called 'doves' as opposed to 'hawks') will not work – a chance mutation producing one 'hawk' will wipe out the 'doves'. Therefore, in any population, there will be a balance of hawks and doves. This was supported by Barrett *et al.* (2002) who drew on 'Njál's Saga (13th Century Viking blood feuds) to demonstrate that genetic groups are more likely to survive if they have some members who are violent. In the case of the Viking saga, those families who had family members who were **berserkers** (warriors) were more likely to survive than those families who didn't have berserkers in their family group.

A **ritual** is a stylised set of actions which has evolved socially or biologically to communicate information. An example of ritualised human aggression can be seen in Australian Aboriginal structured violence – two combatants are only allowed to cut/stab their opponent in the back (it's very hard to kill a person that way). At the end village elders examine the warrior's wounds to determine the winner.

Ritualised forms of aggression

Lorenz also argued that intra-species aggression does not naturally lead to death or injury because this would lead to the extinction of the species. He suggested that ritualised forms of aggression evolve to prevent actual harm taking place. For example, two male stags circle each other, make threatening noises and lock horns but usually one will back down before there is major injury. In humans the lack of face-to-face contact in modern warfare may explain why warfare is lethal, whereas 'naturally' it would not be.

Jealousy concerns something you have and are afraid of losing, especially losing an important relationship to a rival. Envy is the desire for something you haven't got.

Infidelity refers to being unfaithful, but it extends beyond sexual unfaithfulness.

A man whose wife cheats on him is referred to as a cuckold. But no equivalent word exists for a woman whose husband has cheated on her.

You can contrast evolutionary explanations of aggression with social explanations (e.g. social learning theory), discussed on page 40.

Jealousy

Jealousy is cited as one of the top three causes of murders. From an evolutionary perspective, there are various ways to explain why jealousy is a source of murder and aggression.

1. Infidelity

Evolutionary theory predicts a different response to infidelity in men and women because for each gender the loss of a partner has different consequences. Men are more concerned with sexual infidelity because they cannot be certain that any child is theirs unless their partner is sexually faithful and, from an evolutionary point of view, men (and their genes) do 'best' by preventing sexual infidelity. Women on the other hand, are more concerned in the resources a partner can provide and do 'best' if they do not share these with other women. Women, therefore, have evolved a greater concern with emotional infidelity. This was supported in a study by Buss *et al.* (1992, see page 37). Daly *et al.* (1982) found the same was true for relationship violence – men were more violent when their partner was sexually unfaithful.

2. Male-to-male rivalry

Males compete with other males to gain access to females. Such competition arises because females tend to be the ones who choose and males compete with each other to be chosen (see page 34). This male-to-male competition can be seen in contests between males, and is supported by research that has found that male-to-male violence is prevalent among young males in virtually all societies (Daly and Wilson, 1988). The universal nature of such behaviour supports the evolutionary perspective.

3. Female-to-female rivalry

Males prefer to mate with physically attractive females because physical attractiveness is linked to fertility (see Buss, 1989, page 34). This leads to female-to-female rivalry. As predicted by evolutionary theory, Buss and Dedden (1990) found that women were more likely than men to verbally belittle the physical appearance and promiscuity of their same sex rivals, a tactic that would reduce the attractiveness of a rival.

4. Sibling rivalry

Siblings are often jealous of each other. Parental investment theory (see page 36) suggests that sibling rivalry (and jealousy) has evolved in order for each child to try to maximise the resources allocated to that child inevitably at the expense of any other offspring. Harris (2004) suggests that this may be a better explanation of the origins of jealousy rather than infidelity.

Evaluation

- Violence is **not necessarily a natural outcome of jealousy**. If it was, then rates of uxoricide (murdering one's wife) would be constant across cultures, whereas Daly and Wilson (2006) report that the rates of uxoricide are twice as high in the US compared to the UK, but considerably lower than they were 20 years ago.
- Harris (2003) also found that the gender difference existed in imagined scenarios (as in Buss *et al.'s* research, see page 37). But, when she examined **actual reports** from over 100 men and women about a partner's infidelity the gender difference disappeared. Both men and women were more concerned with emotional infidelity.
- Harris also found **cultural differences** – European and Asian men are less likely than American men to say sexual fidelity is worse. This suggests that cultural factors are more significant than innate factors.

Explanations of group display in humans

Group display is a ritualised form of aggressive threat, akin to the ritualised aggression suggested by Lorenz (see page 45).

Group displays are related to dominance in terms of mating and territorial possession.

Evolutionary stable strategies are described on page 45.

Sports events

War dances – A number of national sports teams have adapted native war dances to use in opening ceremonies. The New Zealand rugby team starts each match by performing the *haka*, a traditional Maori war dance. The Tongans also perform the *Kailao*. War dances are performed by warriors before battle to proclaim their strength and intimidate the enemy, and also to motivate the warriors and show their obedience, skill and weapons. War dances involve fierce facial expressions and the waving of weapons. Other examples of group display include cheerleading and the Mexican wave, both of which may relate to war dances. Such group displays motivate fans and increase social identity.

'Owner wins' strategy and territorial behaviour – Group displays may be related to territorial behaviour. They are a means of staking out a group territory and thus increasing confidence in winning. Sports teams are more likely to win home games – and the same is true in the animal kingdom where 'owner wins' is an evolutionary stable strategy (Maynard-Smith and Parker, 1976). The group display is an attempt to declare ownership, which is particularly important for visiting teams.

Ritual behaviour – Marsh (1982) argued that sporting events serve as occasions for 'ritual confrontations' between fans. This involves verbally abusing rival fans, threatening them with attack, and general horseplay. His views were based on extensive observations of football fans. He concluded that these confrontations are relatively harmless and are just symbolic displays of aggressive energy. They are highly structured and predictable, and serve to control the extent to which people are aggressive. Marsh believed that if the aggressive behaviours associated with football were suppressed, the rates of violent crime and fighting behaviour in non-sport settings would increase.

Evaluation

- Some believe (e.g. Dunning *et al.*, 1988) that Marsh's account **underplays the amount of violence** that does occur at football matches.
- An alternative account is that young men are socialised to value displays of aggression and masculinity, which **emphasise their social identity** (i.e. the groups they belong to that increase their self-esteem).

Lynch mobs

A **lynch mob** is a group of people who have assembled with the intention of inflicting violence on another person, which results in the death of that person. It is an example of an aggressive mob; another example is a riot mob – a highly emotional crowd (temporary collection of people) that pursues some violent or destructive goal.

Le Bon (1903) presented an influential account of mob behaviour. He proposed that people behave in an extreme way in crowds because they lose their sense of identity (deindividuation). Anti-social behaviour spreads through a crowd like a disease – a process termed '**social contagion**'. An alternative view was presented by Turner and Killian (1957). Their **emergent norm theory** is related to social identity theory (see page 42) and suggests that distinctive behaviours emerge as a crowd interacts, creating norms for that group. In this account the behaviour of the crowd is seen as rational rather than irrational, and it also allows for the fact that not all members behave in the same way.

Practice essays 4.3

(a) Outline explanations of group display in humans. *(5 marks)*

(b) Outline and evaluate evolutionary explanations of human aggression.
(20 marks)

Chapter 5

Eating behaviour

5.1 Eating behaviour

After studying this topic you should be able to describe and evaluate:

- *factors influencing attitudes to food and eating behaviour, for example, cultural influences, mood, health concerns*
- *explanations for the success or failure of dieting.*

LEARNING SUMMARY

Factors influencing attitudes to food and eating behaviour

AQA A ▶ U3

Our eating behaviour is due to a mix of both nature and nurture, i.e. innate factors (discussed on page 50) and acquired/learned factors, which are discussed on this page.

The term **culture** refers to all the rules, customs, morals and ways of interacting that bind together members of a society or some other collection of people. We learn all these rules, customs, etc. through the process of socialisation. Different social classes have different attitudes to, among other things, attachment and also eating behaviour, and therefore, might be regarded as different '**subcultures**'.

The appearance, smell, taste and texture of food are probably the most important determinants in food preferences (Hetherington and Rolls, 1996). Other factors are also important, such as the price of food and a person's socioeconomic status, ethical concerns and hunger.

1. Cultural influences

Chrisler (1997) suggested that cultural factors moderate individual differences in eating behaviour, i.e. they modify innate preferences (see page 51).

Social learning – We model our behaviour on what we see other people doing, especially when they are rewarded (vicarious reinforcement) and when the models are people we identify with (e.g. parents, siblings). Therefore, we learn to like eating the same things that we see other people enjoying. Equally, we learn to avoid eating things that we see other people disliking.

Mere exposure – People like things which are familiar (Zajonc, 1968). Research shows that the more frequently a food is tasted, the more it is liked. Rozin (1987) claims that mere exposure is the overriding factor in acquired food likes.

Social context – Eating is often a social occasion and is likely to be affected by family food rules at a younger age as well as later learning experiences.

2. Mood

'Emotional eaters' are individuals who eat to comfort themselves. This may lead to bulimia, an eating disorder where overeating is subsequently compensated for by purging (for example, by self-induced vomiting or laxative use). Depression may cause people to overeat because low levels of the neurotransmitter **serotonin** are linked to depression.

Emotional distress may also lead to undereating because joy and anger can inhibit hunger contractions.

3. Health concerns

Many people today consider what they eat in terms of the healthiness of the food, for example, choosing low fat items or fresh vegetables. People who rate nutrition as important prefer healthy foods (McFarlane and Pliner, 1997). However, healthy food may sometimes have a negative effect. For example, a Finnish study (Kähkönen and Tuorila, 1998) found that young men had a lower expectation in terms of tastiness of low fat Bologna sausages compared with regular ones.

Evaluation

- Such accounts **don't explain why children** typically avoid certain adult foods such as mushrooms and tomatoes. A full account includes nurture and nature.
- Understanding health-based choices is **useful in designing programmes** to encourage healthy-eating lifestyles.

Explanations for the success or failure of dieting

AQA A ▶ U3

See page 72 for an explanation of operant conditioning.

On page 54 an evolutionary explanation is presented for anorexia, which suggests that some people may be genetically programmed to respond in the opposite way to food restriction.

Traditional dieting strategies tend not to work for emotional eaters because the psychological aspects of weight management aren't fully addressed by most plans.

Research into the success and failure of dieting has grown in popularity because of the recent epidemic levels of obesity and also the obsession by many men and women to become thinner.

The evidence related to diet failure can be turned around and used to discuss dieting success.

Biological explanations of eating behaviour can help understand the success and failure of dieting. These are discussed on the following pages. In addition, explanations of obesity (on pages 57 and 58) are relevant.

Success

Operant conditioning – A small degree of success will act as a reinforcer, encouraging a person to continue dieting. This may explain why diet plans often start with a rigorous first few weeks, which should result in significant losses.

Social support – The success of the organisation *Weight Watchers* is explained in terms of the support provided by other members. Such self-help groups (as distinct from individual dieting regimes) provide successful role models, vicarious reinforcement and a social identity that empowers individuals. Miller-Kovach *et al.* (2001) showed that a *Weight Watchers* programme was more successful than using an individual self-help method over a period of two years. Lowe *et al.* (2004) reported that weight losses are reasonably well maintained even after five years; an average of 71.6% of participants maintained a loss of 5% or more.

Failure

Hormones – Cummings *et al.* (2002) studied the hormone **ghrelin**, which is produced in the stomach. Low levels of ghrelin stimulate appetite. They found that it increases by an average of 24% when people are on low-calorie diets, therefore, making people even more hungry! The researchers concluded that severe food restriction results in a physiological response of increasing appetite to avoid starvation. The result is that weight loss is made more difficult. Interestingly, patients who had stomach reduction surgery experienced reduced levels of ghrelin because there is less stomach to produce the hormone, which may explain part of the success of such operations.

Cognitive factors – Williams *et al.* (2002) linked failure in dieting to cognitive factors. They measured eating behaviour (using the Dutch Eating Behaviour Questionnaire) and attention, and found that people who have difficulties with sustained attention are less successful at dieting.

Personality factors – A number of studies compare high and low 'restrainers'. High restrainers are individuals who diet by restraining the amount they eat, as opposed to 'low restrainers' who find it easy to simply restrict their food intake. Mensink *et al.* (2008) suggest that high restrainers are very sensitive to food cues and, therefore, find it more difficult to resist food. In order to diet successfully they have to make bigger efforts to resist food than low restrainers and so they are more likely to fail. For example, Stirling *et al.* (2004) looked at the effects of forbidden food on subsequent eating behaviour in restrained and unrestrained normal-weight women. Despite being told not to eat some chocolate, the high restrainers consumed a small quantity of the forbidden food.

Type of diet – Low-fat diets may be counter-productive and lead to diet failure because such diets can lead to anxiety, depression and other mental health problems (Food and Mood Project, 2008). This can create a vicious cycle because low mood then leads to overeating. For example, Nolen-Hoeksema (2002) found that 80% of women who coped with low mood by binge eating went on to develop full-blown depression within five years.

Evaluation

• Diet success and failure is likely to have **multi-causal explanations**.

Practice essays 5.1

(a) Discuss **two** factors that influence attitudes to food / eating behaviour.
(10 marks)

(b) Discuss **two** explanations for the failure of dieting. *(15 marks)*

5.2 Biological explanations of eating behaviour

After studying this topic you should be able to describe and evaluate:

- *the role of neural mechanisms involved in controlling eating and satiation*
- *evolutionary explanations of food preference.*

LEARNING SUMMARY

Neural mechanisms involved in eating and satiation

AQA A | U3

Satiation refers to feeling full.

The **hypothalamus** is part of the **limbic system** which is generally concerned with emotion and homeostasis (maintaining a steady state).

Diagram of hypothalamus and the LH and VMH.

Thalamus

Ventromedial zone | Lateral zone

See page 43 for an illustration of the limbic area.

Serotonin is a neurotransmitter that is generally associated with mood. Levels of serotonin are commonly low in depressed people and anti-depressants often work by increasing serotonin levels. The same treatment has been used with anorexics to increase their appetite.

Understanding how non-biological factors interact with, and can override, physiological satiety signals and promote overeating, is important in successful diet control.

1. Hypothalamus

The hypothalamus is the hunger centre of the brain, located in the midbrain. It regulates eating, acting like a thermostat to start/stop eating:
- The **ventromedial hypothalamus (VMH)** is associated with cessation of eating, i.e. hunger is suppressed in response to body signals of satiation.
- The **lateral hypothalamus (LH)** is stimulated by low serotonin levels and creates sensations of hunger, which leads to eating.

Animals that overeat (**hyperaphagia**) or undereat (**aphagia**) have been found in post-mortem examinations to have damaged VMH and LH respectively. Recent naturalistic studies of animals by de Araujo *et al.* (2006) confirmed the role of the LH as the most important brain region for hunger motivation. This is confirmed by human studies, for example, Reeves and Plum (1969) performed a post-mortem examination of a patient who had doubled her body weight in two years. They found a tumour in the VMH. Quaade (1971) found that electrical stimulation of the LH in obese patients led to reports of feeling hungry.

2. Other regions of the limbic system

Other parts of the limbic system have also been implicated in hunger/satiation, such as the **orbitofrontal complex** and **hippocampus**. Wang (2006) found that these two regions were activated by signals from the stomach, indicating fullness. The involvement of the limbic system indicates the complex set of information involved in hunger because this brain region is not just linked to emotional behaviour but also to learning and memory, movement, and the processing of sensory information.

3. Blood-glucose levels

Glucostatic theory suggests that the brain monitors blood-glucose levels; glucoreceptors may be located in the VMH. One source of glucose comes from the intestine, which produces **cholectystokinin (CCK)** in response to the presence of food. CCK causes the liver to produce glucose and to signal the brain.

4. Lipids (fats)

Lipostatic theory suggests that reduced fat levels may create sensations of hunger. **Leptin** is a hormone derived from fat. London and Baicy (2007) found that leptin reduces activation in regions of the brain linked to hunger, whilst enhancing activation in regions linked to inhibition and satiety.

Evaluation

- The **brain alone is not responsible** for eating behaviour. However, the stomach does not play a major role in hunger because people with no stomach still feel hungry.
- Fullness (satiation) may also be explained by **cognitive factors** ('I have eaten, therefore, I am full') and **activity in the stomach** (stretch sensors in the stomach report fullness, which is why liquids make you feel full).

Evolutionary explanations of food preference

AQA A   U3

Food preferences evolved because liking particular kinds of food is adaptive (i.e. it prompted survival and thus, reproduction). Such preferences can be observed in terms of eating behaviours that are innate; if they are innate they are likely to be adaptive.

The **EEA** (environment of evolutionary adaptiveness) is the environment to which a species is adapted. The selective pressures at that time explain the behaviours that we observe today. In humans it is suggested that our EEA was the period from 1.8 million to 11,000 years ago when humans lived on the plains in Africa.

The term '**sauce béarnaise syndrome**' was coined by Martin Seligman after he had eaten a sumptuous dinner including the rich sauce béarnaise, followed by a concert with music by the composer Wagner. Later that night he developed stomach flu resulting in nausea and a lot of vomiting. For the next 10 years he felt very queasy any time he smelled sauce béarnaise. This led him to reflect on the acquired association. He had also spent the evening listening to Wagner but did not feel queasy when he heard that music again. This led him to suggest that we have an innate predisposition to learn links between tastes and nausea.

Sweet foods

Davis (1928) looked at eating behaviour in three infants and found an innate preference for sweet foods. A liking for sweetness might be adaptive: our evolutionary ancestors in the EEA often experienced food shortages, so a preference for high-calorie (sweet) foods would be adaptive. In addition, sweet foods are generally not poisonous, making them doubly valuable to primitive humans. This explanation is supported by Araujo's (2008) research with mice, which showed a preference for the calorie content of foods, rather than sweetness.

Variety

Davis (1928) also found an innate liking for a variety of food. Research has in fact found an interest in new foods that is coupled with a fear of them. This reflects the risks and benefits of new foods. Liking for variety and newness would be important, from an adaptive viewpoint, in order to ensure a plentiful food supply. However, there is also the risk that new foods might be poisonous, so some cautiousness is important and adaptive.

Meat

Young children generally don't like eating meat; it is a taste acquired later. Dunn (1999) claims that human beings are not instinctively attracted to eating live or dead meat in nature. If a child was given an apple and a live chicken, they would instinctively play with the chicken and eat the apple. If a cat was presented with the same choice, their natural impulse would be the opposite.

Salt

Salt (sodium chloride) is vital for survival because if a person is deprived of salt, their body becomes dehydrated, resulting in death. Research shows that people innately respond to sodium deficiency by eating saltier foods (Beauchamp *et al.*, 1983), which would be important in maintaining sufficient amounts of sodium in the body. Desor *et al.* (1975) found that preferences for salt emerge in infants at about 4–6 months rather than being present at birth. This is due to maturation of the nervous system.

Bitter and sour tastes

Bitter/sour tastes are avoided because of their linkage to poisonous plants. However, Liem and Mennella (2003) demonstrated that children have a greater liking for sour tastes than adults. This might be because they have a greater interest in trying new foods than adults, which would have adaptive advantages. By adulthood, learned preferences have overtaken innate tendencies.

Distaste-nausea linkage

Seligman and Hager (1972) suggested that animals have an innate predisposition to learn associations between foods that cause nausea and avoidance. This has been called the **sauce béarnaise syndrome** (see left). This kind of one trial learning would have an adaptive advantage especially when the food is novel (i.e. tasted for the first time). The effect was demonstrated by Bernstein (1978) in children receiving chemotherapy. Those who were given ice cream flavoured with Maple syrup prior to chemotherapy avoided the ice cream subsequently.

Evaluation

- **Testing neonatal preferences is problematic.** Research is based on the infants' facial expressions when offered different foods and may not produce reliable results.

Practice essay 5.2

Discuss evolutionary explanations of food preference.   *(25 marks)*

5.3 Eating disorders

After studying this topic you should be able to describe and evaluate:

Note that the specification states you only have to study one eating disorder. This book covers all three of the listed disorders and you should select one of them.

- *psychological explanations of one eating disorder, for example, anorexia nervosa, bulimia nervosa, obesity*
- *biological explanations, including neural and evolutionary explanations, for one eating disorder, for example, anorexia nervosa, bulimia nervosa, obesity.*

LEARNING SUMMARY

Anorexia nervosa: psychological explanations

AQA A ▷ U3

1. Psychodynamic explanations

Family systems theory – Minuchin *et al.* (1978) suggested that anorexics' families are enmeshed. The members don't have a clear identity and the family finds it hard to resolve conflicts. This leads to anxiety, which may be projected onto the 'ill' child, i.e. the eating disorder arises as a means of dealing with family conflict. Humphrey *et al.* (1986) did find that families who had a child with an eating disorder have more negative and fewer positive interactions than 'normal' families.

Autonomy – Anorexics tend to be somewhat obsessive personalities, with low self-esteem and a fear of their own autonomy. Bruch (1987) suggested that certain mothers wish their daughters to remain dependent and, therefore, encourage anorexia. Equally, the daughters wish to remain children. Anorexia develops as a means of asserting autonomy by exerting control over the body. The fact that most anorexics come from middle-class families where there are high expectations supports this.

> **Anorexia nervosa** literally means a 'nervous lack of appetite'. The main characteristics are:
> - *Severely underweight* due to deliberate and prolonged restriction of calorie intake.
> - Intense *fear of gaining weight*.
> - Anorexics have a *disturbed body image* and usually continue to see themselves as overweight despite large weight loss.

Evaluation
- The role of autonomy could explain why anorexia is especially **common during adolescence**. Blos (1967), a psychodynamic theorist, proposed that adolescence is a time of reindividuation.
- Psychodynamic theories cannot explain the **recent increase** in anorexia.
- Parental conflict may be an **effect rather than a cause** of anorexia.
- The accounts are difficult to prove wrong (**falsify**).

2. Behavioural explanations

Classical conditioning – Leitenberg *et al.* (1968) suggested that anorexics have learned that eating is associated with anxiety, because eating too much makes people overweight and unattractive.

Operant conditioning – Weight loss is reinforcing because people praise it and the individual has escaped from an aversive stimulus.

Social learning theory (SLT) – Feminine stereotypes in the media and the current emphasis on dieting promote a desire to be thin, which is exaggerated by vulnerable individuals.

> **Key points from AS**
>
> - The study of individual differences at AS level included three psychological approaches to explaining abnormality: the psychodynamic, behavioural and cognitive approaches. These approaches are used here to explain anorexia. You can use the evaluations of these approaches when considering the explanations of anorexia – see *Revise AS Unit 7.1, pages 153–155*.

See page 72 for an explanation of classical and operant conditioning.

Evaluation
- Unlike biological explanations, SLT can account for **increased incidence** of anorexia. Becker (1999) found that the introduction of television in Fiji was associated with an increased incidence of eating disorders in young Fijian girls.
- SLT can also explain **cultural differences**, though Hoek *et al.* (1998) claim that rates of anorexia are fairly constant across cultures.
- Conditioning theory can explain how the disorder is **maintained**.

- **Behavioural therapies have been successful** in treating anorexia, e.g. through rewards for attaining and maintaining target weight (Sue *et al.*, 1994). This supports learning theory as an explanation.
- **Social factors alone** cannot explain anorexia because otherwise more people would suffer from it. This can be explained in terms of the diathesis-stress model (see next page).

3. Cognitive explanations

Distortion of body image – Garfinkel and Garner (1982) found that anorexics typically overestimate their body size compared with 'normal' controls. This distorted thinking may explain why they wish to lose more weight than other individuals.

Females more than males – Fallon and Rozin (1985) found that females rated their ideal body weight as significantly lower than the weight males thought most attractive, whereas males rated their ideal body weight as higher than their actual weight.

Evaluation

- The disordered thinking may be an **effect rather than a cause** of anorexia.

Anorexia nervosa: biological explanations

AQA A ▶ U3

1. Genetic explanations

Twin studies – Holland *et al.* (1984) found a 55% concordance rate for identical (MZ) twins compared with only 7% for non-identical (DZ) twins. This suggests that there is a significant genetic component in anorexia.

Obsessive-compulsive personality type – Klump *et al.* (2000) suggest that people with anorexia and their parents have an obsessive, compulsive personality disorder that produces perfectionist behaviour. This can be seen in their obsessive interest in food. What drives obsession? One possibility is that it is **serotonin**, and abnormal levels of serotonin could be genetically caused.

Evaluation

- The fact that not all MZ twins develop the disorder means that genetic transmission **cannot be the sole explanation**.
- However, the diathesis-stress model proposes that **genetic vulnerability** must be part of the explanation, though there also needs to be some trigger ('stress').
- Biological explanations can't explain the **recent increases** in cases of anorexia.

2. Neural explanations

Hypothalamus – Gorwood *et al.* (1998) suggest that genes may cause abnormal levels of abnormal development of the **hypothalamus**. The **lateral hypothalamus** (LH) may be innately damaged, resulting in undereating because no feelings of hunger are produced, and the **ventromedial hypothalamus** (VMH) continues to send signals to suppress hunger.

Serotonin – There is considerable evidence that increased serotonin activity in the brain is associated with a suppressed appetite and also with increased anxiety, obsessive behaviour, phobias and even vomiting – all characteristics of people with anorexia. It may be that restricted food intake alleviates related problems because, if no food is eaten, a substance called **tryptophan** is produced and body serotonin levels drop. Therefore, people with anorexia feel better by starving themselves.

Adrenaline and cortisol are produced at times of stress and they reduce appetite. When stress dies down, appetite should return to normal. But, it's possible that this does not happen in people with anorexia since they lack the hormone to switch the appetite back on (**AVP**) (Collier *et al.*, 1999).

Adolescence may be a prime time for anorexia because it is the time that girls (especially) are aware of making themselves attractive. They also often put on weight with puberty and this triggers slimming.

It is worth reading through the explanations of bulimia and obesity, on the following pages to gain further insights into explanations of eating disorders.

MZ twins share the same genes, whereas DZ twins are only as similar as any siblings – they share 50% of the same genes.

Key points from AS

- A general outline of biological explanations of abnormality can be found in *Revise AS Unit 7.1, pages 151–152.*

The role of the LH and VMH is hunger and satiety. (See page 50).

It is preferable to talk about individuals with anorexia rather than use the term 'anorexics' because the latter term makes it sound as if the disorder overwhelms the whole person. There is more to an anorexic person than anorexia. However, it is convenient shorthand to use when writing about the disorder.

Key points from AS

- The activity of the sympathetic nervous system suppresses hunger. See *Revise AS Unit 5.1, page 98.*

Both psychological and biological explanations are **determinist** – suggesting that a person's behaviour is determined by factors outside their own control.

This means they remain in a state of suppressed appetite. A key characteristic of anorexia is that they can resist the need to eat, and this explanation accounts for this.

The hippocampus regulates production of **cortisol**, which then has the effect of shrinking the size of the hippocampus, causing further cortisol to be produced. This could explain why people with anorexia get stuck in a vicious cycle and can't start eating again even when they want to.

Evaluation

- It isn't always possible to distinguish **cause and effect**. For example, which comes first – stress or hippocampal shrinkage?

- The cycle of non-eating caused by hippocampal shrinkage explains why it is **hard to break out of anorexic behaviour** once weight loss has started.

3. Evolutionary explanations

An important strength of all evolutionary explanations is that they are **ultimate explanations**, i.e. why people are predisposed to develop certain behaviours. All other psychological explanations are **proximate** – they explain the immediate events around the acquisition of a behaviour and ignore the underlying value of such behaviours.

Starvation strategy – Guisinger (2004) has suggested that anorexia evolved as a consequence of the problems faced by nomadic populations in the EEA (see page 51). Such populations would frequently experience scarcity of food and starvation. Normally animals respond to starvation by feeing intensely hungry and having low activity levels. In contrast, individuals who have a genetic tendency toward anorexia react to starvation by feeling no hunger and feeling full of energy. This would enable such individuals to cope better with starvation because they would move on to find food, whereas 'normal' behaviour (feeling hungry and sluggish) would actually be counter-productive to survival. This anorexic reaction is triggered when an individual loses a significant amount of weight, which explains why anorexics find recovery so difficult – once they have lost a key amount of weight this turns off their hunger.

Intrasexual competition – Abed (1998) proposed that eating disorders are related to competition between females. Thinness is an important factor in female attractiveness, especially because it distinguishes younger women (who are more fertile and, therefore, preferable to men for mating) from older women. In modern society older women are now often quite thin (called 'pseudo-nubile women'), which increases female competition for mates causing 'runaway' female intrasexual competition whereby the originally adaptive strategy spirals out of control in response to a range of environmental factors.

You can read more about sexual selection on page 34.

Evaluation

- Starvation theory is **supported by research**. For example, Kron *et al.* (1978) has noted that anorexic patients have a tendency towards hyperactivity and compulsions to move.

- The intrasexual competition explanation can account for the fact that **eating disorders affect mainly young females**, and decline with advancing age.

The importance of all explanations is that they highlight the *best route to recovery*. In the case of evolutionary explanations the suggestion is that the biological block to eating needs to be overcome.

4. Diathesis-stress model

The most significant criticism of all psychological models is that they cannot explain the biological evidence, and vice versa (biological models cannot explain psychological evidence).

You can evaluate explanations of anorexia with those for bulimia and obesity on the following pages.

The diathesis-stress model offers a good compromise position. It suggests that people are born with a genetic vulnerability (diathesis) to develop certain disorders. However, a disorder like anorexia nervosa will only surface if events in the person's life (stressors) trigger it. Such stressors include emotional difficulties at home or school (e.g. bullying) and/or exposure to thin role models. The diathesis-stress model explains why one MZ twin may develop anorexia but the other may not.

Bulimia nervosa: psychological explanations

Bulimia nervosa literally means 'hungry as an ox'. It is a more common problem than anorexia and probably more related to dieting. The main characteristics are:

- Periods of *compulsive bingeing*, which often involves eating enormous amounts of *high-calorie food*.
- Bingeing creates guilt so it is followed by forced vomiting or the use of laxatives (*purge*).
- Occurs *more than 2 times a week* for over 3 months
- *Weight obsession*, though it is usually nearer normal than anorexics.
- *Secondary problems* arise from the persistent vomiting, for example, tooth decay from the acid of the vomit.

Key points from AS

- The study of individual differences at AS level included three psychological approaches to explaining abnormality: the psychodynamic, behavioural and cognitive approaches. These approaches are used here to explain bulimia. You can use the evaluations of these approaches when considering the explanations of bulimia – see *Revise AS Unit 7.1, pages 153–155*.

It is worth reading through the explanations of anorexia and obesity, on the previous and following pages to gain further insights into explanations of eating disorders.

There is a considerable degree of overlap in the explanations offered for anorexia nervosa and bulimia nervosa, so reference should be made to pages 52–54, especially when considering evaluations.

1. Psychodynamic explanations

Family conflicts have also been identified in families with bulimics (see notes related to anorexia on page 53).

Abuse – Individuals deal with being abused by repressing such memories and then repressed feelings are expressed through the symptoms of bulimia. Bulimia is a means of punishing the body, and expressing self-disgust. Gender differences can be explained because females are more likely to turn blame inwards and are, therefore, more likely to develop bulimia. On the other hand, an abused male becomes hostile towards others and is less likely to develop bulimia. Abuse is probably more common in girls.

Conflict – Chassler (1998) suggests that bulimia represents conflicting wishes for merger and autonomy. Bingeing is an attempt to regain a momentary experience of the mother and merge with the engulfing maternal object. However, the terror of engulfment results in purging, rejecting this 'bad' object.

Evaluation

- A number of bulimics have experienced abuse (McLelland *et al.* (1991) report that about 30% have). However, not all people who are abused develop bulimia, and not all bulimics have been abused, so this **can only explain some cases**.

2. Behavioural explanations

Conditioning – Rosen and Leitenberg (1985) suggest that bingeing causes anxiety. Purging reduces that anxiety. This is a cycle that is reinforcing.

Social learning theory – Lee *et al.* (1992) related the lack of bulimia among Chinese girls to socio-cultural factors, such as cultural attitudes to being fat (fat is desirable and, therefore, overeating doesn't create anxiety) and the rarity of dieting (therefore, lack of role models). Such factors support the view that social learning determines whether or not dieting and bulimia occur.

Evaluation

- Research evidence supports the influence of cultural factors. For example, Nasser (1986) found that 12% of Egyptian women who were studying in London developed bulimia compared with no cases in Cairo.

3. Cognitive explanations

Disinhibition hypothesis – Ruderman (1986) suggested that dieters who have rigid cognitive styles respond to situations of overeating by going over the top (becoming disinhibited). Once they have overeaten, they purge in order to rectify their mistake.

Distorted body image – Cooper and Taylor (1988) reported that bulimics usually show a substantial discrepancy between their estimation of their true body size and the size they would ideally like to be. This distorted thinking would encourage the desire to lose weight.

Coping style – Vanderlinden *et al.* (1992) suggested that bulimics have a tendency to perceive events as more stressful than most people, and use binge/purge as a means of coping with the stress or gaining a sense of control.

Evaluation

- Distorted cognitions may be a **cause rather than an effect** of eating disorders.

Bulimia nervosa: biological explanations

AQA A ▶ U3

Key points from AS

• A general outline of biological explanations of abnormality can be found in *Revise AS Unit 7.1, pages 151–152.*

Binge–purge is the key characteristic of bulimia that distinguishes it from anorexia and, therefore, explanations should focus on both of these behaviours.

It is estimated that bulimia affects up to 10% of the female population, and some males.

It is preferable to talk about individuals with bulimia rather than use the term 'bulimics' because the latter term makes it sound as if the disorder overwhelms the whole person. There is more to a bulimic person than bulimia. However it is a convenient shorthand to use when writing about the disorder.

The role of the LH and VMH in hunger and satiety is discussed on page 50.

See page 54 for evolutionary evaluations of anorexia.

1. Genetic explanations

Kendler *et al.* (1991) found a concordance for bulimia of 26% for MZ twins and 16% for DZ twins. Bulik *et al.* (2000) concluded that bulimia is 83% genetically influenced, whereas anorexia nervosa is 58% genetic.

Lilenfeld *et al.* (2000) suggested that inherited factors may predispose some individuals to impulsivity and that such individuals develop bulimia.

Evaluation

• The fact that there is not 100% concordance for MZ twins supports the **diathesis-stress model** (see below).
• One of the difficulties in studying anorexia and bulimia is the **reliability in diagnosis**. All studies rely on identifying characteristics of a disorder and, inevitably, different criteria may be employed, leading to different rates of diagnosis.

2. Neural explanations

The ventromedial hypothalamus (VMH) may be damaged. The lateral hypothalamus (LH) stimulates eating and the VMH usually stops eating. But if the VMH is damaged then there is no sense of satiety and overeating occurs. In an individual who wishes to be thin, overeating is controlled as far as possible but then may result in an excessive binge, which further results in compensation through purging.

Serotonin is linked to this process because it helps to regulate the feeding centres of the hypothalamus. Low levels of serotonin stimulate the LH (Galla, 1995). Serotonin either predisposes an individual to develop bulimia, or perpetuates the disorder, or both.

Evaluation

• This makes sense because **bulimics have an enhanced rather than absent appetite**. They overeat and then feel guilty because of the desire to be thin.
• Further evidence **links serotonin and bulimia**. People with bulimia suffer specifically from carbohydrate craving (Turner *et al.*, 1991) and increased consumption of carbohydrates increases production of serotonin. This has led to the use of selective serotonin reuptake inhibitors (SSRIs) to treat bulimia.

3. Evolutionary explanations

A strategy for dealing with food shortage – In the EEA (see page 51) nomadic humans would have to cope with intermittent periods of food shortage. One physiological adaptation would be to prepare for a coming famine by increasing baseline weight and appetite. Dieting may activate this system resulting in overeating (bingeing), especially craving carbohydrates for quick weight gain and energy.

Intrasexual competition as an explanation of anorexia has also been applied to bulimia. Faer *et al.* (2005) suggest that in the case of bulimia it has been proposed that competition is for mates, whereas for anorexia it is for status. However, the research evidence collected from their questionnaire did not support this.

Evaluation

• This explanation can be **contrasted with the evolutionary explanations for anorexia and obesity**.

4. Diathesis-stress model

See page 54.

Obesity: psychological explanations

AQA A ▶ U3

Obesity is when a person is carrying too much fat for their height and sex. It is associated with many illnesses, such as cardiovascular disease and diabetes.

Obesity rates are set to increase dramatically in the coming years to become an epidemic.

Key points from AS

- Obesity is discussed in *Revise AS Unit 1.1, page 21*.

See page 72 for an explanation of classical and operant conditioning.

Key points from AS

- The study of individual differences at AS level included three psychological approaches to explaining abnormality: the psychodynamic, behavioural and cognitive approaches. These approaches are used here to explain obesity. You can use the evaluations of these approaches when considering the explanations of obesity – see *Revise AS Unit 7.1, pages 153–155*.

Obesity can be measured in terms of **BMI (body mass index)**. It is calculated by dividing your weight (kg) by your height (m). A BMI of over 30 is classed as obese.

It is worth reading through the explanations of anorexia and bulimia, on the preceding pages to gain further insights into explanations of eating disorders.

CBT stands for cognitive-behavioural therapy.

1. Psychodynamic explanations

The psychodynamic explanation is that obese individuals have experienced some serious disturbance during the oral stage of psychosexual development, i.e. when their libido was focused on their mouth and the infant sought oral gratification. It could either be a case of emotional deprivation or a case of overindulgence, which would mean that the libido remains locked into that form of gratification.

There may be other factors that lead to obesity, such as depression or low self-esteem. Psychodynamic explanations of such factors, therefore, can be used to explain obesity (see pages 90 and 108).

Evaluation

- All psychological explanations have **important implications** for treatments (weight loss programmes). It is not just a matter of reducing weight but targeting the root cause of the emotional disorder.
- Factors such as depression or low self-esteem may be the **effects of obesity** rather than the initial cause, but either way they may serve to perpetuate the problem.

2. Behavioural explanations

Operant conditioning – In our society, food is one of the key reinforcers. Children are given sweets for being good and we are often encouraged to reward ourselves by having an edible treat. Such reinforcement encourages weight gain.

Classical conditioning – Food is naturally associated with a sense of pleasure; a person can be trained to dislike food if it is associated with something unpleasant.

Social learning theory – There are some stereotypes that encourage obesity, for example, fat men are regarded as 'jolly' and mother figures are portrayed as being rotund. Such role models may encourage overeating.

Evaluation

- **Cultural differences** in obesity are likely to be related to differential reinforcement, which is derived from social norms. In the UK, about 22% of the adult population are classed as obese; slightly more women are obese than men. In some countries there is a very significant difference between men and women, for example, in Egypt 45% of women are obese compared to 22% of the men. Gender differences may be biological as well as cultural.
- **Acceptance of fatness** is also related to social norms. Data from the Framingham heart study followed over 30,000 children for 32 years and found that BMI change was linked to BMI changes in family and friends, even when they lived far apart. This suggests that the key factor in a person's weight was the attitudes shared by people around them.
- **Behavioural therapies may work in the short term** but in the long-term attention is needed to emotional and cognitive factors.

3. Cognitive explanations

Cognitive explanations focus on information-processing biases for food-relevant stimuli. Braet and Crombez (2003) studied 34 children and found that obese children showed a greater sensitivity to food words than control children. Such hypersensitivity may initiate or maintain dysfunctional eating behaviour.

Evaluation

- The **success of CBT** suggests that cognitive factors are important.

Obesity: biological explanations

AQA A ► U3

Key points from AS

• A general outline of biological explanations of abnormality can be found in *Revise AS Unit 7.1, pages 151–152.*

Compulsive overeating is a form of addictive behaviour, so explanations of addiction can be applied here (see pages 133–134).

Genetic linkage is never 100%, which means that environmental factors continue to be important. In addition, some people with, for example, two copies of the FTO gene are not obese. Therefore, genetics cannot be the whole explanation.

The role of the LH and VMH in hunger and satiety is discussed on page 50. The roles of ghrelin and leptin are also discussed on pages 49 and 50 respectively.

1. Genetic explanations

There are a number of genetic conditions (such as Prader-Willi syndrome) where obesity is a classic symptom, suggesting that there is a genetic link to obesity.

Wardle *et al.* (2008) analysed 5000 twins aged 8–11 years and compared them in terms of BMI and waist circumference (a measure of abdominal fatness or adiposity). They found a heritability figure of 77%, with a relatively small environmental factor, half of which was due to shared environmental effects (i.e. same home, same upbringing) and the other half due to non-shared effects.

Frayling *et al.* (2007) researched the FTO (fat mass and obesity) gene, finding that people who possessed two copies of this gene had a 70% increased risk of obesity; people with one copy had a 30% increased risk. Price *et al.* (2008) also found an association between the FTO gene and obesity when comparing about 600 extremely obese women with normal controls, and with non-obese sisters.

Evaluation

• Wardle *et al.* (2008) suggest that the **obesity epidemic is clearly due to environmental factors** (e.g. changing availability of food, attitudes to eating) because genes have not altered. However, Musani *et al.* (2008) argue that there is support for the view that genes may be changing. For example, moderately obese people are more fertile and this would increase the gene pool for obesity.

2. Neural explanations

The **hypothalamus** regulates hunger. Lesions in the ventromedial hypothalamus (VMH) caused massively obese rats. Two hormones, **leptin** and **ghrelin** provide important information to the hypothalamus. Leptin is produced by adipose (fat) tissue and signals the presence of fat reserves. Its effect on the hypothalamus is to release appetite-suppressing substances; lack of leptin leads to feelings of extreme hunger. Some fat people may lack leptin because of a faulty gene.

Evaluation

• Early research on leptin was with mice and the effects are **not as straightforward as in humans** (Paracchini *et al.*, 2005).
• Use of leptin in **obesity treatment** has not been found to be effective.

3. Evolutionary explanations

Thrifty gene hypothesis – Some ethnic groups may be more prone to obesity because of this gene. In the **EEA** (see page 51) there would have been periods when food was scarce. This gene enables an individual to make use of periods of abundance and store energy efficiently. People with greater adipose reserves are more likely to survive famine.

Evaluation

• This explanation can be **contrasted with the evolutionary explanations for anorexia and bulimia**.

See pages 54 and 56 for evolutionary evaluations of anorexia and bulimia respectively.

4. Diathesis-stress model

See page 54.

Practice essay 5.3

Discuss **two or more** biological explanations for **one** eating disorder. Include neural and evolutionary explanations in your answer.   *(25 marks)*

Chapter 6

Gender

6.1 Biological influences on gender

After studying this topic you should be able to describe and evaluate:

- *the role of hormones and genes in gender development*
- *evolutionary explanations of gender roles*
- *the biosocial approach to gender development.*

LEARNING SUMMARY

The role of hormones and genes in gender development

AQA A   U3

Many people use the terms 'sex' and 'gender' as if they refer to the same thing, whereas this is not true.

Sex is a biological fact, the fact of whether someone is male or female.

Gender refers to what it is to be male or female.

X and Y chromosomes.

female   male

X   X   X   Y

The term foetus refers to the stage of development before birth.

Evidence of cultural similarities supports biological (innate) explanations of gender roles (page 67).

Genes

Typical sex chromosome patterns are XX for a female and XY for a male, so-called because of their shapes (see illustration on the left). The Y chromosome carries very little genetic material. There is usually a direct link between chromosomal sex and gonads (i.e. the vagina/womb or penis/testicles). However, there are exceptions, for example, the case of the Batista family. Four children were born with normal female genitalia but at puberty male genitalia appeared. They were genetically XY but had not developed male genitalia because of insensitivity to the male hormone **testosterone**. During puberty, massive amounts of testosterone are produced and this caused the male genitalia to appear. The girls seemed to accept their change of sex without difficulty.

Hormones

Chromosomes determine a person's sex, but most sexual development and activity is governed by hormones. During prenatal development all embryos start developing the same genital structures, then male hormones such as **testosterone** cause the female parts to be absorbed and the male parts to develop. However, even though testosterone may not have affected the development of genitalia it may have a significant masculinising effect on the developing brain in the foetus. For example, testosterone promotes development of the areas of the brain associated with spatial and mathematical skills, whereas **oestrogen** is thought to do the same in the areas of the brain associated with verbal ability (Brosnan, 2004).

Research evidence

Dörner (1974) injected female rats with male hormones during pre-natal development and they showed male behaviours.

Money and Ehrhardt (1972) demonstrated the effects of testosterone on female development by using a group of 25 normal XX girls whose mothers had been prescribed drugs containing **androgen** (a male hormone) during pregnancy to reduce the risk of miscarriage. The androgenised girls were not more aggressive than a control group but preferred vigorous outdoor activity and boys' sports and had less interest in playing with dolls or playing games involving mothering-roles.

Berenbaum and Hines (1992) studied 60 girls with **congenital adrenal hyperplasia** (see page 64) and found that they were more aggressive and more interested in male-type activities than their sisters, which could be due to the effects of androgen on the brain during foetal development.

Evaluation

- The evidence clearly shows the **importance of biology** (genes and hormones).
- **Social factors** are important too.

Evolutionary explanations of gender roles

AQA A ▸ U3

The **EEA** is the environment to which a species is adapted. The selective pressures at that time explain the behaviours that we observe today. In humans it is suggested that our EEA was the period from 1.8 million to 11,000 years ago when humans lived on the plains in Africa.

The key to evolutionary explanations is that any behaviour that increases an individual's reproductive success will be selected and appear in future generations, and is, therefore, adaptive.

'Caringness' is also related to moral understanding (see page 162).

These evolutionary explanations can be evaluated by contrasting them with social explanations for gender roles.

A criticism of the evolutionary approach is that it is **determinist**. In the case of gender differences it suggests that such differences are inevitable.

In the **EEA** males and females faced different adaptive problems, which led to different gender role behaviours.

Mating strategies

The most basic difference between men and women lies in their method of reproduction. Men produce millions of sperm and can potentially fertilise hundreds of females at a minimal cost to future reproductive potential. This means their most successful strategy will be to reproduce as frequently as possible with the most fertile women. Women make a greater investment in each reproduction because each egg contains nutrients, which has a physiological cost and they carry the baby during prenatal development and nurse their infants for a considerable time after. Therefore, women do best by being choosy about mates.

Several gender differences arise from these differences:

- Men seek signs of fertility in potential mates (e.g. full lips, rosy cheeks and a thin waist all signal youth and fertility) whereas women seek mates who will provide a good home (e.g. have money and power). Analysis of personal ads by Waynforth and Dunbar (1995) has supported this prediction (see page 34).
- Males will compete with other males to be chosen, which increases the likelihood of inter-male competitivess and aggression. Females also compete to be seen as the most attractive.
- Males are more likely to be sexually indiscriminate (because this maximises the genes they pass to the next generation). Females are more likely to be choosy and also coy (coyness is a strategy to allow a female time to make her choices).

Interpersonal orientations

The stereotype of female caringness may be based on evolved differences due to different adaptive problems faced by ancestral males and females. In the EEA, work was largely segregated between the sexes with men hunting and women being responsible for child care. In situations of threat (stress) it would have been adaptive for men to respond with the **fight or flight response** and women to respond with tend and befriend in order to care for themselves and their offspring. The tend and befriend response is associated with the hormone **oxytocin**. The female hormone **oestrogen** enhances the effects of oxytocin, whereas the male hormone **testosterone** reduces its effects (McCarthy 1995). Research shows that women are, in fact, more likely to seek the company of others in times of stress, compared to men (Tamres *et al.*, 2002).

Adaptive advantage of sex roles

Kuhn and Stiner (2006) argue that humans (*homo sapiens*) had the evolutionary edge over Neanderthals (*homo neanderthalensis*) because they developed different sex roles. The Neanderthal diet was mainly animals, and men and women both hunted. There is evidence for this from the fact that male and female skeletons showed injuries that occurred during hunting, and also there is a lack of evidence of reliance on subsistence foods; Neanderthals were large and needed high-calorie foods. When hunting was unsuccessful the groups starved. In human groups a division of labour evolved – men were the hunters while women engaged in subsistence farming and skill-intensive crafts (e.g. milling grain, making clothing and shelter). This enabled human groups to avoid starvation and live at higher population densities. The result was the beginning of complementary sex roles related to a division of labour that provided a strong adaptive advantage for *homo sapiens*, and may explain why Neanderthals disappeared.

The biosocial approach to gender development

AQA A ▶ U3

The **biosocial** approach proposes that gender is determined jointly by biological and social factors, and most importantly takes the view that they cannot be separated. Biological and social factors combine to produce masculine and feminine behaviours and identities.

Dr John Money believes that social factors override biological ones in shaping gender identity, which is a **behaviourist** view. According to Money, assigned gender is more crucial than biological factors. However, the data that Money gathered to support his views is now treated with some degree of skepticism as he may have allowed his expectations to affect his observations.

Social influences on gender role are considered on page 65, including the effects of parents, peers and the media – these are all examples of social factors.

The contribution of biological factors

On page 59 we examined the contribution of biological factors to gender development. Support for the importance of biological factors comes from a classic case study begun by John Money (1972). He documented the case of twin boys, one of whom accidentally had his penis cut off when he was being circumcised (due to an infection) in infancy. Money believed that gender is entirely determined by socialisation in the early years of development, so he advised the boy's parents to deal with the absence of his penis by raising him as a girl (called Brenda). Brenda knew nothing about this gender re-assignment until her mid-teens. When she did discover, she/he elected to return to her/his biological gender and become a man (Diamond and Sigmundson, 1997).

Evaluation

- This case study suggests **that biology does have a significant role to play**. Other case studies support these findings. For example, Reiner and Gearhart (2003) studied 16 genetic males who were born with no penis and were reassigned as females at birth. All showed relatively male interests and attitudes and 10 of them elected to become males again by the time they were 16.
- However, other case studies show that **biological sex does not need to match gender identity**. See, for example, Goldwyn (1979) on page 64. Indeed, Money (1991) reported 250 cases where people were content with their gender reassignment.

The contribution of social factors

There are various explanations for the contribution of social factors:

Indirect reinforcement – Children identify with certain people (e.g. parents, peers, pop stars and the media generally) and model their gender behaviours on them, most particularly if the behaviour is seen to be rewarded (vicarious reinforcement). See evidence on page 65.

Direct reinforcement – When a child experiences vicarious reinforcement it leads them to repeat such behaviours. If their own behaviour is then rewarded (reinforced) this will increase the likelihood of future similar behaviour, whereas if it is punished the likelihood will be decreased.

Evaluation

- Social learning theory explains **cultural differences** (see page 67) and accounts for the influence of **stereotypes**.
- **Variable reinforcement** – reinforcements are **not sufficiently consistent** to explain all observed differences, but gender appropriate behaviours are clearly reinforced.
- Children **do not imitate (model) every behaviour they observe**. For example, boys observe girls' behaviour being rewarded but don't imitate it. This shows that social learning isn't just passive but is also related to cognitive factors (see cognitive-developmental theories on page 62). Perry and Bussey (1979) found that children only imitate those behaviours that fit their gender stereotypes, which means that they actively organise the effects of vicarious reinforcement.

Practice essay 6.1

Describe and evaluate evolutionary explanations of gender roles.

(25 marks)

6.2 Psychological explanations of gender development

After studying this topic you should be able to describe and evaluate:

LEARNING SUMMARY

- *cognitive developmental theory, including Kohlberg, and gender schema theory*
- *explanations for psychological androgyny and gender dysphoria, including relevant research.*

Cognitive developmental theories of gender development

AQA A   U3

The essence of the **cognitive approach** is that it is what you *think* which has the greatest influence on your behaviour. The cognitive-developmental approach is concerned with how thinking develops. In this case we are looking at the development of thinking about gender.

According to the cognitive approach, children attend to same-sex models because they have already developed a consistent gender identity, not vice versa. The social learning approach takes the opposite view (see page 65).

1. Kohlberg's theory

Kohlberg (1966) argued that we acquire our gender concepts through interactions with the environment (social learning), mediated by maturational cognitive factors.

- Different stages of gender identity develop only after a child's way of thinking has aged (matured) to the right point.
- Gender identity is the result of a child's active structuring of his/her own experience (a cognitive process), not just the passive product of social learning.

Kohlberg proposed three stages:

(1) **Basic gender identity** (2–3½ years) – Children recognise their gender but this is based on outward appearance and can easily be changed. Therefore, they have no gender identification with the gender and no need to acquire gender-appropriate behaviours.

(2) **Gender stability** (3½–4½ years) – Awareness that gender is fixed across time ('I will become a man'), but children still think that dressing like a girl makes you a girl, and dressing like a boy makes you a boy.

(3) **Gender constancy** (4½–7 years upwards) – Recognition that superficial changes do not alter gender; that gender is consistent across time and situation. This is similar to the conservation skills that Piaget described in general cognitive development (see page 82). It is only after stage (3) that a child can begin to acquire gender concepts appropriate to his/her own gender.

Research evidence

Thompson (1975) showed that gender identification was more accurate in 3 year olds (90% correct) than in 2 year olds (76%).

Slaby and Frey (1975) asked children questions about gender stability, such as, 'Will you be a mummy or a daddy when you grow up?' Children did not know the correct answer until the age of 3 or 4.

Slaby and Frey (1975) also showed pre-school children a film with men on one side and women on the other. Those children who had previously been rated as having gender consistency watched more same-sex models. This shows how they actively seek information that will help them develop gender-appropriate behaviour.

Evaluation

- This approach **combines social learning** with some aspects of **biological** development.
- This view assumes that **development proceeds in stages**, and that gender identity is mediated by cognitive factors. This may not be universally true.

2. Gender-schema theory

Martin and Halverson (1981) presented an alternative view to Kohlberg's, but which was still a cognitive view of gender development. Their theory emphasises the importance of **schema**; as soon as a basic gender identity develops, children are then motivated to learn more about their gender and will incorporate this information into a gender schema. Like all schemas, this serves to organise relevant information and attitudes and will influence behaviour.

Early gender identity leads to the formation of **ingroup schemas**, i.e. attitudes and expectations about your own gender. The child also develops outgroup schemas. Such ingroup/outgroup schemas lead to **ingroup favouritism** – being more positive about your own group as a means of boosting your own self-esteem. These schemas also mean that children spend more time with their own group (same-sex peers) and reject opposite-sex peers. This will reinforce their gender stereotypes because they spend time within their own group and are exposed only to same-sex concepts.

Research evidence

Martin and Little (1990) found that pre-school children had very little gender understanding, yet they had strong gender stereotypes about what boys and girls were permitted to do.

Masters *et al.* (1979) showed that children aged 4–5 years were more influenced in their choice of toy by the gender label (e.g. 'It's a girl's toy') than by the gender of the model seen playing with the toy.

Martin and Halverson (1983) found that when children were asked to recall pictures of people, children under 6 recalled more of the gender-consistent ones (such as a male firefighter or a female teacher) than gender-inconsistent ones (such as a male nurse or a female chemist).

Evaluation

- The theory offers a **middle ground** between social learning and cognitive-developmental explanations.
- It explains how **gender stereotypes persist**, because people are more likely to remember information that is consistent with their schemas.
- It explains how gender behaviour occurs **before gender identity**.
- It lacks mention of **biological factors** and assumes that all gender behaviour is mediated by cognitive factors.

Compromise position

Stangor and Ruble (1989) have proposed a way in which both approaches (Kohlberg and Martin and Halverson) can be combined: gender constancy and gender schema may relate to different aspects of development.

- Gender constancy is related to motivation. Once you realise you are always going to be a girl you are *motivated* to find out about this role and this will be associated with things like activity choice.
- Gender schemas are concerned with organisation of information and, therefore, should affect cognitive variables, such as memory.

Stangor and Ruble tested children aged 4–10 years and found that: (a) preference for same-sex toys increased with increased gender constancy (therefore, supporting gender constancy theory); and (b) memory for gender-consistent pictures increased with age (therefore, supporting gender schema theory).

Explanations for psychological androgyny and gender dysphoria

Androgyny refers to the mixing of masculine and feminine traits. The word androgyny literally means male-female.

Psychological androgyny

Sandra Bem (1976) suggested that traditional views of gender emphasise gender difference – you are a boy or a girl. Bem proposed that it is psychologically more healthy to have a mixture of male and female traits (**androgyny**) because it allows a person to select the best and most appropriate behaviours for them. Bem (1983) reformulated her approach in terms of gender schema theory, suggesting that androgynous people have a different cognitive style to a traditionally sex-typed person. An androgynous person, when faced with a decision as to how to behave in a particular situation, responds independently of any gender concepts (**gender aschematic**), whereas a traditionally sex-typed person determines what would be appropriate for their gender using gender schemas (**gender schematic**).

The BSRI is different to other measures of gender behaviour because it allows a person to select both male and female options. Forced choice scales (having to select male or female) may have produced false information about gender inclinations.

Research evidence

Bem designed the Bem Sex Role Inventory (BSRI) to test her ideas. Bem (1975) found that 34% of the male participants and 27% of the female participants in her study were androgynous. Bem and other researchers (e.g. Flaherty and Dusek, 1980) have found that androgynous subjects are more adaptable in different situations, have higher self-esteem and a greater sense of emotional well-being.

Evaluation

• Other research has **not been so supportive**. For example, Whitley (1988) found that masculine identity led to greater self-esteem than androgyny.

Gender dysphoria is a condition where an individual feels uncomfortable with the gender they have been assigned at birth and may wish to change gender. It is also called **gender identity disorder, gender incongruence** or **transgenderism**.

Gender dysphoria

Psychological explanations – Freud suggested that 'normal' gender development involves identification with your same-sex parent (in the phallic stage).

Biological explanations – A person's genetic sex (XX or XY) may not accord with aspects of their gender (as determined during prenatal development). Such mismatches can be caused by additional hormones in the mother's system, or by the foetus's insensitivity to the hormones, known as **androgen insensitivity syndrome (AIS)**, which results in female genitalia, despite having male genes. There are other rare conditions, such as **congenital adrenal hyperplasia (CAH)**, where abnormally high levels of male hormones are produced in a female foetus, causing enlarged female genitals, which may mean that the baby is assumed to be male when she is born.

It is estimated that 1 in 4000 people in the UK are receiving medical help for gender dysphoria. It is also estimated that 1 in 2000 people are born with anomalous genitals (external genitals do not match biological sex) and may be given an erroneous gender assignation (Colapinto, 2000).

Research evidence

Rekers (1995) examined over 70 boys with dysphoria and found no evidence of biological causes but did find a general absence of appropriate male role models. In cases of AIS, female reassignment may not lead to dysphoria. Goldwyn (1979) described the case of Daphne Went, an XY individual with AIS who was content with her female role and adopted two children. Further gender-anomalous case studies are described on pages 60 and 61.

This view of gender identity is similar to John Money's approach to understanding gender – social factors have greater importance than biology.

Evaluation

• Many transgender people do not regard their cross-gender feelings and behaviours as a disorder. They argue that **gender characteristics are socially constructed** and, therefore, naturally unrelated to biological sex.

Practice essays 6.2

(a) Discuss **one** explanation of psychological androgyny. *(10 marks)*

(b) Discuss **one** cognitive developmental theory of gender development.

(15 marks)

6.3 Social constraints on gender role

After studying this topic you should be able to describe and evaluate:

- social influences on gender role: for example, the influence of parents, peers, schools and the media
- cross-cultural studies of gender role.

LEARNING SUMMARY

Social influences on gender role

AQA A ▷ U3

The research in this section represents the **social learning** approach to understanding gender development – the influence of our social world on our gender development.

Parents, peers, teachers and the media provide indirect (vicarious) reinforcement of gender behaviours. Parents, peers and teachers directly reinforce gender behaviours.

The influence of parents

Parents have expectations (stereotypes) about gender behaviour and these will affect their patterns of reinforcement. For example, Smith and Lloyd (1978) gave mothers a set of feminine, masculine and neutral toys. When a 6-month-old baby was dressed and named as a boy, the mothers encouraged more physical activity and gave masculine toys to the baby.

Parents also provide direct reinforcement and reinforce their children's behaviour differentially. For example, Eccles *et al.* (1990) found that parents encouraged their children to play with gender-appropriate toys, i.e. girls to play with dolls and engage in housekeeping games, and boys to play with cars and do sporting activities. Fagot *et al.* (1992) found that parents who showed the clearest differential reinforcement had children who were quickest to develop strong gender preferences, indicating that differential reinforcement is effective.

There are differences between mothers and fathers. Ruble (1988) found that fathers reinforced gender stereotypes more than mothers. Idle *et al.* (1993) found that fathers reacted more negatively than mothers when their sons played with girls' toys.

Evaluation

- Maccoby (1998) argued that **peers, not parents**, are the prime socialising influence on gender development.
- However, other researchers (e.g. Santrock, 1994) suggest that **parents are the primary influence** during the important early years.

The evidence on this page demonstrates the importance of social factors in the development of gender roles. But, there is a lot of evidence to support the other side of the coin – the importance of biological factors (see pages 60 and 61) and also the way that children think about their own gender (see pages 62 and 63).

The influence of peers

Peers act as role models. Children are more likely to imitate same-sex role models. Slaby and Frey (1975) found that this was more likely in children with higher levels of gender constancy (see page 62), i.e. after they had begun to identify with their own gender.

Peers are important in reinforcing existing stereotypes. Lamb and Roopnarine (1979) found that pre-school children generally reinforced peers for sex-appropriate play and were quick to criticise sex-inappropriate play. Bussey and Bandura (1972) found that 3–4 year olds disapproved of gender-inconsistent behaviour by peers (e.g. boys playing with dolls).

Maccoby and Jacklin (1974) undertook a massive review of more than 1500 studies of gender differences and concluded that the differences observed were minimal and that most popular gender-role stereotypes are 'cultural myths', which are perpetuated by social influences.

Evaluation

- **Direct instruction may override peer influence**. Martin *et al.* (1995) found that boys would imitate girls' toy choice *if* the toys were labelled 'boys' toy' (and the same was true for girls). The label acts as a form of direct instruction.
- Peers are likely to be **important in middle childhood** but not in the first few years of life when important aspects of gender development are taking place. In early life, parents and family may be more important.

The influence of schools

In school, peers will have an effect on gender development, but teachers may moderate this influence by presenting more gender neutral reinforcement.

However, there may also be the reverse trend, where teachers are more likely to reinforce gender-stereotypical behaviour. For example, they may encourage male students to dress traditionally (no earrings, short hair), whereas peers might encourage anti-stereotypical behaviour (Johnson and Workman, 1994).

Evaluation

Children may respond selectively to reinforcement. Fagot (1985) found evidence that teachers tend to reinforce 'feminine' behaviours in both boys and girls, such as quiet, sedentary activities but only girls acquire them, which supports the cognitive approach.

The influence of the media

Media influences are discussed in chapter 13 (see page 125 onwards)

Stereotypes abound in the media. For example, Hodges *et al.* (1981) found that men on television are more likely to be shown as being in control, whereas women are more at the mercy of others. Meehan (1983) found that 'good' women are portrayed as submissive, sensitive and domesticated, whereas 'bad' women are independent and rebellious. Women are generally characterised as being younger than men (Elasmar *et al.*, 1999).

The media (especially television) is linked to sex stereotyping behaviour in children. For example, Williams (1985) found that the children's sex role attitudes became more traditional and sex-stereotyped after two years of exposure to television in a town called 'Notel', which previously had no television. McGhee and Frueh (1980) found that children who watched more television had more stereotypical gender role expectations.

Television is not the only source of media influence. Books also create and reinforce stereotypes. Crabb and Bielawski (1994) found that gender stereotypes in books had been changing in a review of children's books between 1938 and 1989.

Two theories have been used to explain media effects:

- **Social learning theory** – children model the stereotypes presented on television.
- **Cultivation theory** – the more time spent watching television, the more the individual's picture of the world will reflect what they see on television.

Evaluation

- Some research **overestimates the influence of the media** on gender development. Children under the age of 4 are probably not very affected by the media, yet that is an important time for gender development. Television probably has most influence during adolescence, but the effects may just be to reinforce existing stereotypes, rather than to create them.
- The media can be used to **change gender stereotypes**. Pingree (1978) found that gender stereotyping was reduced when children were shown advertisements with women in non-stereotypical roles. Similarly, Johnston and Ettema (1982) found that children modelled non-traditional behaviours on a television series called *Freestyle*, and such changes were noticeable nine months later.
- There has been a **reduction in gender stereotypes** on television (Signorelli, 2001) thus, reducing the effects that the media has on children's stereotypes. For example, women are portrayed in a less negative way on television. They are more often employed outside the home and their jobs are more prestigious. In the 1970s, women were more often seen in traditional female occupations (nursing, teaching, etc). However, the reverse trend has been slower (men portrayed in traditional female jobs/activities).

Cross-cultural studies of gender role

AQA A ▶ U3

The influence of social factors can be seen when making cross-cultural comparisons. The existence of cultural differences in gender roles supports the view that social factors are important, whereas the existence of cultural similarities emphasises the role of innate, biological factors.

Cultural differences

Margaret Mead (1935) conducted a classic cross-cultural study of gender differences in Papua New Guinea (an island in the south Pacific). She studied three primitive societies:

- **Arapesh** – the men and women were peaceful in temperament.
- **Mundugumor** – both the men and women were war-like in temperament.
- **Tchambuli** – the men spent their time decorating themselves while the women worked and were the practical ones, the opposite of traditional Western cultures.

Mead concluded that gender roles were culturally determined (**cultural determinism**). However, later (1949), she supported cultural relativism – the view that some behaviours are innate and universal. In all three societies, all the men were more aggressive in comparison with the women, though both sexes of the Arapesh were not aggressive and both sexes of Mundugumor were aggressive.

More recent studies support the existence of cultural differences. For example, Sugihara and Katsurada (2002) found differences between traits considered desirable in Japan and America; Japanese men do not seek to be 'macho' types like Americans but instead value being well-rounded in the arts.

Cultural similarities

Williams and Best (1990) explored gender stereotypes in 27 different national cultures, finding many similarities across cultures. Participants were given a list of 300 psychological characteristics and asked to identify which were more frequently associated with men or women. There was a broad consensus across countries about the different characteristics common in each gender. Men were seen as more dominant, aggressive and autonomous, whereas women were more nurturant, deferent and interested in affiliation. This suggests that there are universal gender stereotypes about male–female roles.

Interestingly, Williams and Best also asked children to rate the characteristics and found the same patterns as in adults, which seems to support a biological source to the perceived differences in gender stereotypes.

Williams and Best also investigated expectations about gender roles in 14 countries using the sex role ideology (SRI) scale. In 12 of the countries, men expressed more traditional views about how women should behave, whereas women were more egalitarian (e.g. they thought men and women should share household duties).

Evaluation

A **collectivist** society is one where individuals share tasks and belongings and value interdependence, unlike **individualist** societies, which emphasise individuality, individual needs and independence.

- Mead's early conclusions about **cultural relativism** seem to be supported.
- Williams and Best (1992) found that **consensus about stereotypes** was strongest in collectivist societies and weaker in individualist societies, where gender equality is more influential.
- In recent years there has been a **reduction in the differences** between male and female gender roles, which suggests that social influences may override biological predispositions. People have become more flexible in how different roles are allocated in a society.

Practice essays 6.3

(a) Describe social influences on gender role. *(9 marks)*

(b) To what extent can gender development be explained in terms of social factors? *(16 marks)*

Chapter 7

Intelligence and learning

7.1 Theories of intelligence

After studying this topic you should be able to describe and evaluate:

- *theories of intelligence, including psychometric, information processing, Gardner's theory of multiple intelligences and learning approaches.*

LEARNING SUMMARY

Theories of intelligence

AQA A   U3

Intelligence refers to mental abilities, such as the ability to reason, to solve problems, to think abstractly, to learn, etc. Intelligence is also an adaptive trait, particularly among our ancestors, because individuals who are more intelligent are more likely to survive and reproduce.

The term **psychometric** refers to techniques that measure some aspect of human behaviour, such as personality tests or intelligence tests.

Factor analysis is a statistical technique used to identify the variables that explain correlations between scores on tests of different abilities. Imagine that you give various mental tests to a large group of people. You then correlate the scores of each test with the scores of every other test in turn, producing a **correlation coefficient** for each pair of tests. If there is a strong correlation between any two tests this suggests that they share a common variable or factor.

1. The psychometric approach

One approach to explaining intelligence is to identify the factors that underlie successful performance on IQ tests, using a method called **factor analysis**.

Spearman's two-factor theory – Spearman (1904) found that children's scores on different mental tests were positively correlated and concluded that there was one general mental ability (the *g* factor) which underlies performance on lots of different mental tasks. He suggested that there are also specific factors (*s* factors). The differences between individuals is largely due to the g factor but s factors explain why a person does not do equally well on all tasks.

Thurstone's primary mental abilities (PMAs) – Thurstone (1938) also did a factor analysis of performance on IQ tests but found no single factor; he identified seven distinct primary mental abilities: spatial ability, perceptual speed, numerical reasoning, verbal meaning, word fluency, memory, and inductive reasoning (generating rules from a set of observations). Thurstone regarded g as an average of these PMAs. The PMAs are independent and are not correlated, so g will vary depending on which mental tests are used and which PMAs they tap.

Vernon's hierarchical model – Vernon (1950) proposed that g is what all tests measure. **Major group factors** are what some tests measure, **minor group factors** are what particular tests measure, and **specific factors** are what particular tests measure on specific occasions. This reconciles the Spearman and Thurstone models.

Cattell's fluid and crystallised intelligence – Cattell (1963) again used factor analysis and concluded that g could be divided into **fluid intelligence (gf)** and **crystallised intelligence (gc)**. Fluid intelligence is basically abstract reasoning and is innate (for example, selecting problem-solving strategies appropriate to the problem). **Crystallised intelligence (gc)** encompasses knowledge that comes from experience (for example, vocabulary).

Evaluation

- Factor analysis produces **objective statistical facts**.
- However, the factors that are identified are just **arbitrary categories** and different methods produce different factors (as shown above). Therefore, it is in fact a **subjective approach**.
- Many of the theories are based on **rather restricted samples**. For example, Spearman and Vernon used mainly schoolchildren. It is unlikely that crystallised intelligence would have been found in such samples.
- Recent evidence from Duncan *et al.* (2000) supports the existence of g. **PET scans** assessed the mental activity of participants while they completed three types of general intelligence test (spatial, verbal, and perceptual-motor). They showed that, despite the diverse tests, one region (the lateral prefrontal cortex) was missing when participants were engaged on high g tasks, but not the control tasks.

The **information-processing approach** is based on computer analogies – input, output, storage, programmes, routines and so on. Information-processing theories assume that one person is more intelligent than another because they can process information more efficiently.

Key points from AS

- Working memory is discussed in *Revise AS Unit 2.1, page 30*.

Sternberg's view is that there are three subtheories that explain an individual's intelligence. Traditional theories overlook the key interaction between the three subtheories or components: intelligence (analytic skills), context (practical skills) and experience (creativity).

2. The information processing approach

Case's information-processing theory – Robbie Case (1992) suggested that information-processing ability is related to the use of **mental space** (M space). M space is a concept rather similar to 'working memory'. There is a limit to the amount of information that can be held in M space at any one time, but processing efficiency increases with age because:

- **The brain matures** – Changes in the myelin sheath (a fatty protective layer around the nerves, which increases) leads to faster neural transmission rates.
- **Cognitive strategies develop** – As children get older the amount of M space needed for well-practised mental tasks is reduced, thus increasing the amount of available space.
- **Metacognitive skills** (thinking about thinking) – Important for efficient use of M space, for example, being aware of which words you don't understand when reading something, monitoring your own progress on a mental task, etc.

Sternberg's triarchic theory – Robert Sternberg (1988) incorporated information-processing into a broader theory of intelligence. He felt that intelligence consists of three aspects, rather than the traditional view that it is concerned just with analytic skills.

- **Componential** (analytical) subtheory – the individual's internal world. Intelligence comprises reasoning ability and metacognitive processes that control the strategies and tactics used in intelligent behaviour.
- **Contextual** (practical) subtheory – the individual's external world. To be intelligent you have to be able to apply your skills in everyday life and adapt to changing conditions – in work, relationships, etc. It is a kind of streetwise knowledge, such as knowing how to manipulate others for their own good, or working out the quickest way to get from A to B using public transport.
- **Experiential** (creative) subtheory – an individual's past experiences link the internal and external world. Intelligence is being able to produce new ideas from previously unrelated information based on past experience, i.e. being creative.

According to Sternberg, a complete explanation of intelligence must entail all of these three subtheories. Conventional notions of intelligence miss this important interaction between components, context and experience.

Evaluation

- A strength of the information-processing approach is that it is concerned with **how people actually solve complex problems**, whereas the psychometric approach provides a **description** of the human intellect.
- Information processing theory also goes beyond psychometric theories and identifies a **wider range of skills** that contribute to intelligence.
- Case's theory **lends itself to research investigation**, which is a strength. For example, Chi (1978) tested M space by comparing the ability of children who were chess experts with adults who had no chess experience. The task was their ability to remember chess board positions. The children could recall more, presumably because they had developed relevant strategies through experience.
- Case's theory **can be used to measure intelligence** by assessing the capacity of M space.
- Both theories can be **applied to education**, for example, by training students in metacognitive skills.
- Information processing theories link theories of intelligence (in the domain of individual differences in psychology) with the **domain of cognitive psychology** (see Piaget's theory of cognitive development, page 81).

3. Gardner's theory of multiple intelligences (MI theory or MIT)

Howard Gardner (1983, 1995) also regarded the traditional view of intelligence as too limited. He suggested that just because a person is not good at maths it doesn't mean that person has low overall intelligence. According to MIT, each person has a unique 'cognitive profile' based on eight different intelligences:

- **Linguistic** – Communicating well (e.g. poet, orator).
- **Logical-mathematical** – Handling logical arguments (e.g. scientist).
- **Spatial** – Able to sense your position in relation to other things (e.g. sailor, sculptor, surgeon).
- **Bodily-kinesthetic** – Using your body well (e.g. dancer, athlete, surgeon).
- **Musical** – Performing and composing music (e.g. musician, composer).
- **Interpersonal** – Sensing other people's feelings (e.g. sales person, teacher, politician).
- **Intrapersonal** – Self-awareness (e.g. therapist).
- **Naturalistic** – Recognising patterns in nature (e.g. biologist, naturalist).

Key points from AS

- Autism is discussed in *Revise AS Unit 7.3, page 166*.

Key points from AS

- There is a discussion of brain localisation in *Revise AS Unit 5.3, page 112*. For example, language centres are normally located in the frontal and temporal cortex on the left side of the brain, whereas the motor centre is in the frontal lobe.

An empirical approach is one where data has been collected through direct observation or experience.

Gardner drew up this list after extensive research involving case studies of unusual people, such as child prodigies or autistic savants. Steven Wilshire is an example of an autistic savant, a young man who has an exceptional artistic ability and photographic memory but has profound social and learning disabilities (autism). Evidence also comes from studies of people with brain damage who continue to function normally in some areas of mental activity, but not others. Studies of the brain also provide evidence for **localisation** of function in the brain – particular abilities (or intelligences) are associated with specific areas of the brain. Finally, Gardner based his theory on the evolutionary relevance of certain capacities and data from subtests on intelligence tests.

Gardner has considered other intelligences. **Spiritual** and **moral intelligences** were excluded because the evidence (from sources listed above) does not suggest that they are separate entities. **Existential intelligence** (the ability to think philosophically) meets most of the criteria, except it is not linked to any specific region of the brain.

Evaluation

- Many psychologists attack the theory because they say it is based on **intuition more than empirical data**. A recent review (Waterhouse, 2006) concluded that there was little hard evidence for the theory; it is a line of rational argument rather than a science.
- A second key criticism is that the term 'intelligences' is misleading. For example, Eysenck (1994) claims that Gardner is talking about nothing more than **talents and abilities**. However, Gardner's response is that if spatial or musical ability must be called a 'talent', then language and logic must be called merely a talent as well.
- The approach is actually rather similar to **Thurstone's and Vernon's** multifactor models (see page 68).
- It is a **popular approach with some educators**. Schools traditionally emphasise logical and linguistic intelligence, which means that students who have other talents/intelligences are not valued and Gardner's approach challenges this. The educational value is supported by research, for example, Kornhaber (2004) looked at 41 American schools that based their curriculum on MIT and concluded that it led to high quality work.

The **learning approach** is related to the **behaviourist approach**, which is concerned with observable behaviour rather than anything that might be going on inside a person's mind.

4. The learning approach

Intelligence can be defined as the capacity of an organism to learn to adjust successfully to novel or difficult situations, and to solve new problems drawing on past experience, i.e. it is the capacity to learn. This approach is not concerned with how we think, but instead concerned with measurable outcomes – what a person has learned.

The learning approach applies to human and non-human intelligence. Psychologists are interested in how one individual differs from another in terms of intelligence, but are also interested in how one species differs from another in terms of intelligence. For example, Warden (1951) tested animal intelligence using plates. First, the animal learns that if it steps on a plate it will be rewarded (a cage door opens and the animal can get food). Next, a second plate is introduced and the animal must now learn to step on the two plates in the correct sequence in order to get the reward, then a third plate is added and the animal must learn to step on all three in a given order, and so on. The limit reached is a kind of intelligence score – for guinea pigs it's one plate, for rats it's two plates, for cats seven plates, and for some monkeys 22 plates.

The learning approach to intelligence has similarities with the experiential aspects of Sternberg's theory (previous page), which was concerned with a person's ability to solve new problems based on past experience, i.e. to learn.

Another widely used test of animal (and human) intelligence involves **discrimination**. For example, you show the animal three objects, of which two are the same. Food is hidden under the different object and the animal is expected to be able to learn the principle of identifying the odd one out in order to get the reward. Monkeys learn this quickly but rats don't, suggesting that rats have 'low intelligence'.

It is important to distinguish between simple reflex learning (as in classical conditioning) and higher order learning, where complex links have to be acquired (as in Warden's study). The latter is related to intelligence.

However, when testing animal intelligence, it is important to test them under the right circumstances. In the case of the rats mentioned above, further research showed that they were not as dim as it seemed. Langworthy and Jennings (1972) had the bright idea to test rats using objects that smelled (two smelled the same and one was different). The rats then coped well because they have a well-developed sense of smell but a less well-developed visual ability (see also instinctive drift, page 74).

Animal learning often involves **trial and error**, whereas primates and humans display **insight learning** – a more intelligent approach. Köhler (1925) gave a classic demonstration of insight learning with a chimpanzee called Sultan. Sultan was in a cage and a banana was placed outside the cage, just out of reach. Inside the cage were a stick and some boxes. Sultan first tried to reach the fruit with his hand. He sat down and gazed around. Suddenly he grabbed the stick and got the fruit. Sultan had solved the problem without any reinforcement, though he may have been applying his experience from previous situations and, therefore, demonstrating intelligence.

Evaluation

- The learning approach **contrasts with all other theories**, in focusing on behaviour rather than mental activity. This is also a limitation because mental states are an important part of intelligent behaviour.
- On the positive side, it enables the focus to be on observable behaviour and thus provides a useful means of **measuring intelligent behaviour**.

Practice essays 7.1

(a) Describe **one or more** information processing theories of intelligence.

(9 marks)

(b) Evaluate **one** of the theories you described in part (a). *(16 marks)*

7.2 Animal learning and intelligence

After studying this topic you should be able to describe and evaluate:

- *the nature of simple learning (classical and operant conditioning) and its role in the behaviour of non-human animals*
- *evidence for intelligence in non-human animals, for example, self-recognition, social learning, Machiavellian intelligence.*

LEARNING SUMMARY

The nature of simple learning

AQA A ▷ U3

Classical and operant conditioning are the basics of learning theory or the behaviourist approach. Social learning theory was a later development (sometimes called neo-behaviourism), which added cognitive and social factors.

Pavlov was the first to demonstrate classical conditioning, producing a salivation response in dogs to the sound of a bell.

Guthrie (1935) suggested that, in fact, all learning takes place on a single trial. The reason it appears to take more trials is because a large number of simple components are being acquired.

Classical conditioning

Classical conditioning involves learning to **associate** a stimulus with a response. Before conditioning takes place an organism has an innate link between a stimulus and reflex response, such as the smell of food leading you to salivate, or a puff of air to the eye causing you to blink. Classical conditioning involves acquiring (learning) an association between a **neutral stimulus (NS)** and the **unconditioned stimulus (UCS)**, so that the neutral stimulus will produce the **unconditioned response (UCR)**. The NS is now called a **conditioned stimulus (CS)** and the UCR is now the **conditioned response (CR)**.

   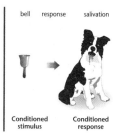

| food response salivation | bell response no salivation | bell + food response salivation | bell response salivation |

Unconditioned stimulus / Unconditioned response | Neutral stimulus / No conditioned response | Unconditioned response | Conditioned stimulus / Conditioned response

- **One-trial learning** – Usually the NS and UCR have to be paired more than once for learning to take place, but under some conditions one trial is sufficient. For example, one fearful incident in childhood may lead to a lifelong fear of dogs.
- **First-order conditioning** – Initially, conditioning acts on reflex responses.
- **Higher-order conditioning** – The CS from the original (first-order) conditioning series is used as the UCS in a new series. For example, a bell might be the first CS, which can then be associated with a time of day.

Operant conditioning

Operant conditioning is learning a behaviour because of its **consequences**.

Skinner (1938) placed a pigeon in a 'Skinner box'. If it pecked a lever, a door would open and food (a **reinforcer**) was delivered. The pigeon first pecked randomly around the box as part of its natural exploratory behaviour. Accidentally, it pecked the lever (stimulus) and received food (response). Each time it does this the S–R link is strengthened or 'stamped in' and also any unrewarded behaviour is 'stamped out' (i.e. when pecking elsewhere no food appears). So, behaviour has been brought under stimulus control.

If the pigeon learns to peck at a button whenever it is lit, in order to get food, it is learning to discriminate between different states of illumination of the button (a discriminative stimulus).

Skinner described operant conditioning in terms of ABC: **A**ntecedents (the situation beforehand); **B**ehaviour (what the pigeon does); and **C**onsequences (the probability of a behaviour being repeated depends on strengthening or weakening S–R links).

1. Positive reinforcement (receiving something pleasant) increases the probability of a response recurring because the response is pleasurable. For example, receiving a smile when you give someone a kiss.

2. Negative reinforcement (escape from an unpleasant stimulus) is pleasurable and increases the probability of the same response in the future. For example, finding that a smile stops your mother shouting at you.

3. Positive punishment (punishment by application), receiving something unpleasant, decreases the probability of a future behaviour. For example, being told off for smiling at an inappropriate moment.

4. Negative punishment (punishment by removal), removing something desirable, also decreases the probability of future behaviour. For example, not being allowed a dessert because you didn't finish your main course.

Features of conditioning

- **Generalisation** – Animals respond in the same way to stimuli that are similar.
- **Extinction** – The new response disappears because it is no longer paired or reinforced.
- **Shaping** – Animals gradually learn target behaviour by being reinforced for behaviours that are closer and closer to the target.
- **Reinforcement schedules** – Partial reinforcement schedules are more effective than continuous reinforcement, and are more resistant to extinction.

Evaluation

- It is a very **reductionist and determinist explanation** of behaviour – behaviour is determined by the environment and cannot be controlled by free will. The use of behaviourist principles to determine the behaviour of others (as in some prisons and psychiatric institutions) could be considered **unethical**. Both Watson and Skinner (see his book 'Walden Two') had a desire to use their principles to produce a better society.
- Behaviourism ignores influences on behaviour such as **emotion**. It also ignores **cognitive factors** and cannot explain behaviours such as the use of cognitive maps (mental representations of the environment used, for example, in navigation).
- Learning theory also cannot explain **innate influences**. For example, Seligman (1970) suggested that a species is biologically predisposed to acquire certain conditioned responses more easily than others (see next page for more details).
- Skinner believed in **equipotentiality** – that any response could be conditioned in any stimulus situation. However, Breland and Breland (1961) showed that learning is constrained by innate capabilities (see next page for details).

Any **reinforcer** results in a pleasurable state of affairs and *increases* the likelihood that the behaviour will be repeated. This applies to positive *and* negative reinforcement. Any **punisher** *decreases* the likelihood that the behaviour will be repeated.

Some people argue that classical and operant conditioning are actually the same thing. In the classical conditioning experiment is food a UCS or a reward? The bell is a signal that the food is coming; salivating is an anticipatory response to food. If the bell comes immediately after the food it should still result in conditioning (backward conditioning) but such conditioning is rare, which suggests that the food is a reward and this paradigm is operant conditioning.

Key points from AS

- For more evaluations of the behaviourist approach, see *Revise AS Unit 1.1, pages 15 and 16*.

The role of learning in the behaviour of non-human animals

AQA A ▶ U3

On the previous two pages we looked at how classical and operant conditioning can be used to explain the behaviour of non-human animals. On this page the focus is on applying these principles to learning in the natural environment.

Biological preparedness is considered again on page 113 and taste aversion is discussed on page 51.

Avoidance behaviour also involves operant conditioning as outlined by Mowrer (see page 114).

The BBC reported that the RSPCA has recently started playing CDs of birdsong to birds in their care before releasing them back into the wild so they can sing the right songs. Birds reared in captivity don't learn to sing the right songs.

Conditioning is in itself an innate characteristic. All animals are 'hardwired' to be conditioned by experience, i.e. to learn to respond to their environment. Being conditionable is an adaptive behaviour, i.e. being able to respond to the particulars of your environment.

Classical conditioning in the natural environment

It is likely that animals learn fears through classical conditioning, and even one-trial learning. For example, Garcia and Koelling (1966) demonstrated that rats soon learned to avoid a sweet-tasting liquid when it was accompanied by an injection of a substance that made them ill. In this case, the UCS–UCR is the injection that produces nausea, the NS is the sweet-tasting liquid that has become associated with the UCS and, thus, becomes a CS producing the CR of nausea.

Seligman's concept of **biological preparedness** suggests that some animals have an innate tendency to acquire certain conditioned responses more easily than others because they are adaptive. In this case it would be adaptive to learn to avoid anything linked to nausea. When Garcia and Koelling paired the injection with an electric shock the rats did not acquire an aversion to the sweet liquid – presumably because there is not an innate tendency to avoid things linked to electric shocks.

Operant conditioning in the natural environment

Trial and error learning is an example of operant conditioning. Errors act as punishers and decrease the likelihood of a response being repeated. Gradually, an animal learns to produce the appropriate response. For example, a predator learns which prey are easiest to catch through trial and error (reward and punishment).

Animals cannot be conditioned to acquire just any response. This was demonstrated by Breland and Breland (1961) who tried to train a pig to insert a wooden token into a piggy bank for a reward. But the pigs handled the token like any object – tossing it up and rooting with it. What animals learn tends to resemble their instinctive behaviour (**instinctive drift**).

Social learning in the natural environment

Bird species vary in the extent to which their song development is innate. Some birds have almost no facility for learning and the full adult song is present even in birds raised in isolation, for example, the Alder Flycatcher. However, most birds need to hear the adult song to develop their innate version, therefore, they are learning through imitation.

Slater (1981) showed that chaffinches produce only a very basic song repertoire if they are hand-reared, and are strongly inclined to copy the song of any bird they hear. Some birds have a highly developed ability to learn by imitation, for example, parrots and mynah birds can imitate sounds produced by other species.

Social learning involves **mentalistic processes** and is, therefore, also included as evidence of intelligence (see next page).

Evaluation

- The lower you go down on the phylogenetic scale, the less an animal's behaviour is affected by learning. There is an **important trade off** – instinctive responses mean that an animal can deal with its environment reasonably well because an adaptive behavioural repertoire has evolved to fit its environmental needs. Instinctive behaviours ensure a quick response, rather than one that has to be learned through trial and error. However, instinctive repertoires are also fixed and mean that an animal cannot respond to changing conditions. The ability to modify behaviour in the light of unpredictable environmental changes is a sign of intelligence, and gives such animals a selective advantage, but at some cost.

Evidence for intelligence in non-human animals

AQA A   U3

Mentalistic abilities are those that involve some form of mental activity or 'intelligence'. Conditioning is a non-mentalistic ability.

Lewis and Brooks-Gunn (1977) used the mirror test to demonstrate that infants of a certain age had developed a self-concept (see page 90).

In order to imitate a behaviour, the animal who is observing must understand that the particular behaviour is linked to the particular outcome. This requires some form of intelligence.

A 'tutor' probably needs to have some idea of what the learner is thinking, which involves a theory of mind. Deception also requires a theory of mind – a concept which is discussed on page 91. It is not a formal psychological theory (like Bowlby's theory or Piaget's theory), but a collection of ideas that an individual has when trying to understand what is going on in another animal's mind.

Theory of mind is likely to be favoured by natural selection, insofar as it promotes social relationships.

Self-recognition

If a person can recognise him/herself, this implies the possession of a self-concept, which is a **mentalistic state**. Gallup (1971) used the mirror test to demonstrate self-recognition. A red mark is placed on an animal's forehead (when anaesthetised). Comparison is then made between how often the animal touches this mark without and with a mirror. Gallup (1977) found that chimpanzees and orangutans are capable of self-recognition, but other primates and non-primate animals are not.

However, Epstein *et al.* (1981) found that pigeons can learn to use a mirror to help them remove bits of paper stuck to their feathers. This suggests that they have self-recognition and leads us to question whether the mirror-test really does demonstrate mentalistic abilities because pigeons are not generally regarded as being 'thinking animals'.

Social learning

Kawai (1965) observed Japanese snow monkeys on a small island. Sweet potatoes were left on the beach for the monkeys, one of whom (Imo) 'invented' the idea of washing the sand off the potatoes in the sea. Soon, other monkeys imitated her, thus evolving a new kind of behaviour, which was passed to subsequent generations. Imo also invented a way of washing wheat. However, Nagell *et al.* (1993) suggested that the behaviour in Kawai's study could be explained in terms of **stimulus enhancement** (non-mentalistic behaviour), rather than imitation. When the other monkeys observed Imo washing potatoes this simply drew their attention to both the potatoes and the water, and enhanced their ability to solve the same problem.

Imitation is a passive process where the individual animals don't deliberately perform an action so it can be imitated. **Tutoring** is an active process where the tutor modifies its behaviour to accommodate the needs of the learner. Boesch (1991) observed tutoring in chimpanzees. Mothers sometimes intervened when offspring were having difficulties cracking open nuts. The offspring were imitating what they had seen but not getting it right. The mother might leave a 'hammer' nearby (stimulus enhancement) or might place the nut in a better position (tutoring).

Machiavellian intelligence

Machiavellian intelligence refers to the ability to intentionally deceive another individual. In order to intentionally deceive another individual, you have to have an understanding of what they know, or don't know.

Whiten and Byrne (1991) compiled a record of 250 naturalistic examples of deception, such as a vervet monkey making a fake alarm call.

Experimental evidence was produced by Premack and Woodruff (1979) who arranged for a chimpanzee to see a trainer place food under one of two containers that were out of reach. A second trainer entered the room in a green coat (the chimpanzee was trained to know that he was co-operative) or a white coat (known to be competitive). On most trials, they manipulated both trainers to obtain food – they helped the cooperative trainer and deceived the competitive one. The chimpanzee knew that the competitive trainer would act on their false information, which is evidence of Machiavellian intelligence.

Practice essay 7.2

Discuss the nature of simple learning (classical and operant conditioning) and its role in the behaviour of non-human animals.   *(25 marks)*

7.3 Evolution of intelligence

LEARNING SUMMARY

After studying this topic you should be able to describe and evaluate:

- *evolutionary factors in the development of human intelligence, for example, ecological demands, social complexity, brain size*
- *the role of genetic and environmental factors associated with intelligence test performance, including the influence of culture.*

Evolutionary factors in the development of human intelligence

AQA A U3

Intelligence is the ability to deal effectively and adaptively with the environment. An animal that can respond more effectively to environmental challenges will be more likely to survive and reproduce.

Foraging is an ecological (environmental) demand.

Ecological demands

The ecological approach suggests that aspects of an animal's environment (ecology) demand intelligent behaviour. In particular, being a good forager (obtaining food) requires intelligence, therefore, intelligence would have increased survival and been naturally selected. Hunting and finding food requires memory, planning, co-ordination and tool use, which all involve considerable intelligence. A good forager is more likely to be chosen as a mate, thus enhancing reproduction of such genes.

Dunbar (1992) suggested that the evolution of human intelligence can be explained in terms of the change from a leaf-eating diet to fruit-eating. Leaf-eaters (**foliovores**) have a small home range and less difficulty managing their food source, whereas modern humans became fruit-eaters (**frugivores**) and had to remember the location of their food supply, evaluate the ripeness of fruits, develop a harvesting plan and so on. Individuals who were more successful were naturally selected.

Social complexity

Animals live in groups because there are advantages (e.g. for foraging, reproduction and predation), but group living also presents problems (e.g. conflicts, inter-relationships between group members, managing cooperation). An individual who can solve social problems is more likely to survive and reproduce.

One particular facet of sociality is the ability to understand the intentions of others (**theory of mind**) and the ability to cheat (**Machiavellian intelligence**) and detect cheats. Both are evidence of intelligence (see previous page).

Another outcome of sociality is communication between species' members in order to coordinate social activity. Humans are the only species to have developed language, which is probably the outcome of intelligence rather than cause of it. However, once language evolved, it then had a significant effect on the further development of intelligence. Vygotsky (see page 82) proposed that it is language that transforms elementary mental functions (possessed by all animals, such as attention) into higher mental functions.

The **Wason four card selection task** requires a participant to decide which of four cards needs to be turned over in order to prove a logical statement right or wrong (such as 'If a card has a vowel on one side, then it has an even number on the other side.'). The cards have the letters/numbers A, D, 4 and 7 on them.

Evaluation

- Cosmides (1989) showed that participants, when doing the **Wason four card selection task**, cope better with a concrete example that involves social relations rather than an abstract version because our intelligence is adapted to cope with such problems.
- Dunbar (1993) found no relationship between the size of the **neocortex** (part of the brain involved in higher order thinking) and environmental complexity in a range of different primates, but did find a **strong correlation between size of neocortex and group size**, as an indication of the complexity of social relationships. This supports the social complexity explanation for the evolution of human intelligence.

Brain size

Large brains have evolved:

(1) in bigger animals to coordinate bigger bodies

(2) to cope with the demands for greater intelligence (such as social complexity).

Having a large brain incurs a cost because it requires more energy and makes birth more difficult. Therefore, it is likely that there is some adaptive advantage to a proportionately bigger brain.

Comparative studies of different species support the role of brain size in intelligence. Rumbaugh *et al.* (1996) *tested primate intelligence by training them* on two tasks: if one set of learning facilitated the second task then this was taken as evidence of intelligence. They found that primates with proportionally larger brains did best. However, poorer performance may be because an animal is asked to perform a task that comes less naturally to them (consider instinctive drift, page 74), rather than because they are less intelligent.

When conducting comparative studies it is necessary to take account of body size. Jerison (1978) developed the **encephalisation quotient** (EQ), where the actual brain mass of a species is divided by its 'expected' brain size for that body size. Using this scale, humans have the highest EQ (7) of any animal. Other primates score around 2.34 and dolphins score 4.5.

Human studies indicate a small but significant correlation between brain size and intelligence. Early studies found no correlation between brain size and intelligence but that may be because they couldn't measure brain size accurately (they used skull size). Willerman *et al.* (1991) used brain scans and correlated IQ scores of college students with brain size, finding a positive correlation of 0.51 between IQ and brain : body ratio. A further study by Andreasen *et al.* (1993) used a more representative sample (advertising through a newspaper) and found a lower but significant correlation.

Sexual selection – Miller (1992) argues that the rapid change in human brain size (trebling in the last three million years) can be best explained in terms of sexual selection because it directly selects for reproductive success. Intelligence is a runaway sexy trait. The cost of a large brain is outweighed by its selective advantage. This view explains why people list intelligence as one of the most important characteristics in a prospective partner. It also explains why men have larger brains relative to body weight.

Evaluation

- Some research suggests that relative brain size **may not be related to intelligence**. The spiny anteater has a comparatively larger neocortex (taking body size into account) than a human, yet it does not have a greater intelligence.
- Research also shows that the **relationship between brain size and IQ is not a simple one**. For example, Sassaman and Zartler (1982) studied nearly 200 children with microcephaly (an abnormally small brain). About 40% were not retarded and 7% were of average IQ. Skoyles (1999) suggests that the problem may be that IQ tests measure a particular aspect of intelligent behaviour. He believes that '**expertise**' is not important in IQ tests but this would have had an adaptive advantage and may be the factor that is related to increased brain size.
- **Organisation** may be more important than size. Albert Einstein's brain, when examined at postmortem, showed no size advantage but there were some differences in terms of organisation, such as more tightly packed neurons in his prefrontal cortex. Holloway (1979) claims internal structural complexity is more important in the evolution of intelligence.

Sexual selection is explained on page 34 and runaway process is explained on page 35.

Miller (1998) points out that this theory can explain why men have historically been more creative in the arts, because this allows them to demonstrate their intelligence.

It is impossible to know whether such brain organisation is a cause or an effect of intelligence. Human brains are more highly organised than the brains of other animals.

Intelligence test performance

This section looks at intelligence test performance (i.e. IQ tests) rather than intelligence. This is because psychologists can only investigate the relationship between intelligence and other factors by operationalising intelligence, i.e. using IQ tests.

Monozygotic (MZ) twins share the same genes, whereas dizygotic (DZ) twins share 50% of the same genes. If MZ twins have more similar IQs this suggests that IQ is inherited.

A **gene** is a unit of inheritance. Studies of genetics aim to show that IQ is inherited.

It is probably best to think of genetic factors as a **'reaction range'**. They provide a potential which is very much dependent on environmental influences as to whether it is maximised or minimised. This is similar to the concept of diathesis-stress described on page 54 (genetic vulnerability related to life experiences determine an individual's behaviour).

The role of genetic factors

1. Twin studies – Research shows that MZ twins (genetically identical) have more similar IQs than DZ twins. For example, Bouchard and McGue (1981) reviewed a number of studies and found an MZ correlation of .85 and a DZ correlation of .58. Even when MZ twins are reared apart (which means IQ similarity can be due to a shared environment) they have very similar IQs. Pedersen *et al.* (1992) reported on the Swedish Adoption/Twin Study of Ageing (SATSA), that MZ twins reared apart or together had IQ correlations of about .79; DZ twins reared apart were .32 and DZ twins reared together were .22. This suggests that about 80% of IQ is inherited.

Evaluation

- If intelligence was entirely inherited, the **MZ correlations should be 100%**; the fact that scores are lower shows a significant environmental component.
- The **assumption that MZ twins are identical is wrong**. Allen *et al.* (1976) found constitutional differences based on different birth and intrauterine experiences, and found that these could be related to different parental perceptions and expectations of the twins.

2. Familial studies – Bouchard and McGue (1981) surveyed over 100 studies looking at familial correlations of IQ, and found that the closer the genetic link, the higher the correlation between IQs. For example, siblings reared together had a correlation of .45 and adopted siblings had a correlation of .31.

Evaluation

- This would seem to support the genetic position, but it could be taken equally as **evidence for environment**.
- Comparisons from one study to another (**meta-analysis**) involve grouping together many different tests which may not be comparable.

3. Adoption studies – Skodak and Skeels (1949) followed 100 adopted children and their natural mothers. At age 4 their IQs were correlated by .28. At 13 it had risen to .44, i.e. genetic effects became stronger. Plomin (1988) followed children involved in the Texas Adoption Study, and found that correlations between adoptive parents and their adopted children fell from .15 to .02 at age 10. This again suggests that genetic factors are ultimately more significant.

Evaluation

- Adoptions are often made to **similar environments**.
- Adoption studies can also be used to **support the environmental position** (see next page).

4. Gene mapping studies – Various studies have identified genes related to IQ test performance. For example, Chorney *et al.* (1998) identified a gene (IGF2R) found in 33% of 'super-bright' children but only 17% of 'average' IQs. Dick *et al.* (2007) found a link between the gene, CHRM2, and performance IQ, which involves a person's ability to organise things logically.

Evaluation

- Since intelligence is determined by many genes (polygenic), **an array of genes are involved**. No individual set of genes will create high IQ.
- Gene mapping studies have important **ethical implications**. Such research evidence might be used to classify the potential abilities of individuals, which would overlook the role of environmental factors in determining a person's actual intelligence.

5. Indirect genetic influences – The effects discussed so far are direct effects of genes on IQ. Indirect genetic effects occur in several ways. Genetically-determined characteristics create a child's **microenvironment**, which then influences development. For example, a child who has an innately pleasant temperament gets on better with people, and increased social contacts may enhance mental development. Indirect influences also include the fact that genetically more intelligent parents may well create a more stimulating home environment, which increases the IQ of their children.

The role of environmental factors

1. Adoption studies – Scarr and Weinberg (1977) found that, on average, adopted children have IQs that are 10–20 points higher than those of their natural parents.

Evaluation

- Adoptive families are generally wealthier and better educated than natural families, which would **cause environmental factors to appear stronger**.
- Early adopted children do better, favouring the idea that **environment is important under suitable circumstances**.

2. Family influence – Parent–child interactions affect the development of IQ. Yarrow (1963) found a correlation of .65 between IQ at six months and the amount of time the mother spent in social interaction with her child.

Family influence can also be seen in the fact that birth order is related to IQ, presumably because first-born children get more parental attention that children born later. Zajonc and Markus (1975) examined the IQ data of 40,000 Dutch males born in 1944, finding that IQ declines with family size and birth order. In larger families, each child has a smaller share of parental attention, less money and more physical deprivation.

3. Diet – IQ scores in Japan have increased by an average of 7.7 points over the last ten years, whereas IQ has only increased by 1.7 points in the US. This can only be explained in terms of improved environmental factors, probably diet (Lynn, 1986).

Harrell *et al.* (1955) gave low-income, expectant mothers supplementary diets. When their children were tested at age 3 they had higher IQs than those whose mothers had been given **placebos**.

4. Enrichment – **Operation Headstart** (started in 1965) resulted in initial IQ gains, but these turned out to be small and short-lived, and the costs were high. Follow up studies, such as Lazar and Darlington (1982), found that participants were less likely to become pregnant, to need welfare assistance or become delinquent. They were more likely to complete high school, to be employed after high school, and/or to continue in further education. This shows some benefit from the enrichment programme. Ramey *et al.* (1999) reviewed 10 studies that randomly allocated children to treatment and no-treatment groups (improving on the original design where children were not randomly allocated) and concluded that there was firm evidence that Headstart did boost IQ.

The Milwaukee Project – Heber *et al.* (1972) worked with newborn infants and their low-social-class black mothers who had IQs below 75. Half the group were 'controls' and received no extra treatment. The mothers in the experimental group were given help with job-related skills, parenting and housekeeping, and their children were involved in a regular day-care programme from the age of 3 months. By the time the children entered school, the experimental group had a mean IQ of 124, whereas the control group's mean IQ was 94. By the age of 10 there was still a 10 point IQ difference.

You can use research on environmental factors to evaluate genetic explanations, and vice versa.

The question of whether genetic or environmental factors contribute most to IQ is one of the best examples of the **nature–nurture debate** (see page 183). It isn't just a theoretical debate but is highly relevant to decisions about who to educate and how.

Placebos are substances that have no pharmacological effects but the person taking them thinks they are the real thing. This means you can separate the psychological from the physical effects of being given a drug treatment.

If IQ was genetically fixed then enrichment programmes would not be effective.

Any study that looks at IQ has the potential for being socially sensitive research.

The influence of culture

Culture refers to the rules, customs, morals and ways of interacting that bind together members of a society or some other collection of people. The concept of culture embraces all aspects of an individual's environment: methods of child-rearing, diet, education, etc.

1. **Culture bias in tests** – Almost all IQ tests have been designed by white, middle-class Westerners, and have been standardised on similar populations. Inevitably, people from other cultures do less well on 'our' IQ tests, although alternative explanations may be offered for their poorer performance (such as race or social class).

2. **Race and IQ** – Jensen (1969) sparked off a controversy when he suggested that black people have innately lower IQs because, on average, they scored 15 points less than white people.

   This finding may be due to test culture bias. This was demonstrated by Dove (1968) who created **Dove Counterbalance General Intelligence Test** to show that if you asked a set of questions that were based on black culture then white people perform poorly.

   Poor test performance by certain racial groups may also be due to lower stimulation, social deprivation, etc.

   Mackintosh (1986) compared white and West Indian children in England. When the groups were unmatched in terms of environmental factors, such as family education, there was a 9 point difference but when matched there was a 2.6 point difference, showing that environmental factors are important.

What is intelligence? People from different cultural backgrounds would define, and assess, it differently.

3. **Social class** – Bernstein (1961) introduced the notion of **restricted language** (code) as opposed to **elaborated code** (a richer form of language). Children from low social classes learn a limited form of language which lacks, for example, abstract concepts and limits their cognitive development and verbal intelligence. Labov (1970) rejected this idea and claimed that Bernstein was confusing social and linguistic deprivation, and had failed to recognise the subtleties of non-standard English.

   Sameroff *et al.* (1987, 1993) conducted the Rochester Longitudinal study, following over 200 children since birth. They found a clear negative (about .60) association between number of risk factors and IQ; risk factors include parental mental health, education, occupation, family support, stressful life events, and family size (all of these are related to social class). They also found that, at age 4, high-risk children were 24 times more likely to have IQs below 85 than low-risk children. When a child is not exposed to risk factors, genetic factors will be important in determining intelligence. When there are risk factors, these will be of more importance than the inherited ones.

4. **Motivation** – Lower class children may have less desire to do well. Zigler *et al.* (1973) found that such children improved their test performance by 10 IQ points if they had a play session with the tester beforehand to increase familiarity and decrease anxiety, whereas middle class children only gained 3 IQ points.

Evaluation

- It is impossible to conduct definitive research on race because we cannot **define race** nor can we exclude the **effects of deprivation**.
- The concept of 'race' is in itself problematic as it is not true that, for example, whites and blacks form separate biological groups. There is **more genetic variation within** any so-called racial group than **between** racial groups.
- Such research raises important **ethical issues** and is socially sensitive.

Practice essay 7.3

Discuss evolutionary factors in the development of human intelligence.

(25 marks)

Chapter 8

Cognition and development

8.1 Development of thinking

After studying this section you should be able to describe and evaluate:

- *theories of cognitive development, including Piaget, Vygotsky and Bruner*
- *applications of these theories to education.*

LEARNING SUMMARY

Piaget's theory of cognitive development

AQA A ▸ U3
AQA B ▸ U3

Cognitive development is the study of how mental abilities develop.

The term '**schema**' is used in many areas of psychology; it is a cluster of related concepts that represent particular aspects of the world.

'**Equilibration**' means the desire for balance or equilibrium.

An '**operation**' is an internally consistent, logical mental rule, such as the rules of arithmetic.

Piaget's theory is sometimes called an '*ages and stages theory*' because of the concept of stages. However, the structure of the intellect and the way development takes place (through disequilibrium and accommodation) is just as important.

Horizontal décalage describes the fact that not all aspects of the same stage appear at the same time, for example, the ability to conserve number and volume. Uneven cognitive performance is probably due to different learning experiences.

Jean Piaget (1896–1980) developed the most influential theory of cognitive development. It has two important assumptions:

- There are **qualitative** differences between child and adult thinking, thus, there is a sequence of distinct stages in development.
- It is a **biological** approach: biological readiness is the prerequisite for change.

The structure of the intellect

Variant cognitive structures, which develop with age: **schemas** and **operations**.

Invariant cognitive structures: **assimilation** (information taken in) and **accommodation** (schema adjusted). The process is 'driven' by **equilibration**.

Stages in cognitive development

Sensorimotor stage (0–2 years) – Early reflex activities, circular (repetitive) reactions co-ordinate sensory and motor activity.

Pre-operational stage (2–7 years) – Development of the use of symbols to represent experience (e.g. language). Thought processes lack adult logic (they are not 'operational'), e.g. egocentric thought and animism (i.e. the belief that inanimate objects have human feelings). This stage is subdivided into the pre-conceptual stage (i.e. when concepts are not fully formed) and the intuitive stage (i.e. when appearance, not reality, is important).

Concrete operational stage (7–11 years) – The child has developed adult (internally consistent) logic, but only in concrete situations. Problem solving is random rather than systematic.

Formal operational stage (11+ years) – Abstract and systematic thought.

Research evidence

Object permanence (sensorimotor stage) – The realisation that objects continue to exist even when they cannot be seen. Piaget claimed that this developed after the age of 8 months. Bower (1981) showed that infants aged 5–6 months old showed surprise when an object that had been hidden behind a screen was no longer there. Baillargeon and DeVos (1991) used the rolling car task to show that 3–4 month old infants were aware of object permanence (see page 159).

Reality-appearance distinction – Pre-operational children focus on the appearance of things and not the reality (i.e. they lack internal consistency). DeVries (1969) showed children a cat, and then hid the cat's head behind a screen while strapping on a dog's head; 3 year olds thought it was a dog even though they saw the transformation; 6 year olds were able to distinguish appearances from reality.

The three mountains task

Piaget's methods involved naturalistic observation and semi-structured interviews, using small samples – often his own children. He did spend over 50 years amassing a detailed record of individual behaviour (an **idiographic approach** – see page 185). Piaget also conducted research with Inhelder of a more experimental nature, which did involve large samples of children.

Critics tend to take Piaget's model too rigidly, and supporters suggest it should be viewed as a metaphor. The stages are not fact but a useful structure for understanding behaviour and generating research.

Class inclusion – McGarrigle *et al.* (1978) showed that the class-inclusion (centration) questions don't make sense in the pre-operational stage. However, if they asked children, 'Are there more black cows or more sleeping cows?' instead of Piaget's 'Are there more black cows or more cows?' the percentage who answered correctly moved from 25% to 48%.

Egocentrism – Piaget and Inhelder (1956) used the **three mountains task** to show that pre-operational children couldn't take the perspective of another – they tended to describe what the doll saw in terms of what they actually saw. However, when Hughes (1975) used a more realistic task with a toy policeman, pre-operational children did better.

Conservation (concrete operational stage) is the ability to understand that quantity is not changed even when a display is transformed so it looks bigger. Piaget used counters, beakers and balls of clay to demonstrate that children under 7 cannot conserve. Samuel and Bryant (1983) found that younger children coped better with one question, but there were still age differences. McGarrigle and Donaldson (1974) used 'naughty teddy' to create the transformation and young children did better, though Moore and Frye (1986) suggested that this is because naughty teddy unduly distracted the children.

Formal operational thinking – Bryant and Trabasso (1971) showed that difficulty on transitive inference tasks may be due to memory failure rather than lack of ability. Piaget and Inhelder's (1956) beaker problem showed that formal thinkers are systematic. Shayer and Wylam (1978) found that only 30% of 15–16 year olds had achieved formal operational thinking.

Evaluation

- Piaget's theory was the **first comprehensive account** of cognitive development. It changed the traditional view of the child as **passive**, and stimulated research.
- The evidence largely supports the **stage sequence**, though Piaget's tasks may have confused children and created demand characteristics.
- The influence of **language** and **social and emotional** factors were overlooked.
- If Piaget was right and cognitive development depends on maturation then **practice should not matter**. However, some studies show that practice can improve performance. For example, Hughes (1975) found that 90% of pre-operational children could cope with the three mountains task when their errors were explained to them.
- Piaget suggested that **disequilibrium** would be the driving force in cognitive development. However, conflict does not tell a child how to solve the problem.

Vygotsky's theory of cognitive development

| AQA A | U3 |
| AQA B | U3 |

Vygotsky was born in pre-Revolutionary Russia but his work was not known to the West until it was published in English in 1962.

An 'expert' is anyone with greater knowledge.

An important way to evaluate any theory is by how it might be applied to everyday life. Page 85 has information about how all three theories of cognitive development can be applied to educational practice.

Lev Semenovich Vygotsky (1896–1934) produced a theory that contrasted with the dominant Russian view (stemming from Pavlov) that learning was a product of passive conditioning. He suggested that cognitive development is the outcome of:

- The **social construction** of knowledge.
- The **social environment** (language and other cultural symbols, and experts).

The structure of the intellect

Elementary mental functions are innate capacities, such as attention and perception, possessed by all animals. These will develop to a limited extent through experience.

Cultural influences transform elementary functions into *higher mental functions*. Culture teaches children what to think and how to think.

'Sociocultural' refers to the social and cultural context in which learning takes place.

The **ZPD** is the distance between a child's current and potential abilities. The aim of instruction is to stimulate those functions that lie waiting in the ZPD.

Guided participation is related to scaffolding but emphasises the fact that at all times the learner is an active participant and is merely guided by the expert rather than being led by experts.

Vygotsky emphasised how knowledge is acquired through social interaction, whereas Piaget described it as a process of self-discovery.

Piaget and Vygotsky need not be seen as opposites. Glassman (1999) argues that in fact the two theories are remarkably similar, especially at their central core. An attempt to integrate the two approaches would be productive.

Piaget represents the Western, individualist approach shaped by the European society in which he lived, whereas Vygotsky's views are shaped by the collectivist, communist society in which he lived.

Stages in cognitive development

- **Pre-intellectual, social speech** (0–3 years).
- **Egocentric speech** (3–7 years). Language controls one's own behaviour.
- **Inner speech** (7+). Language serves for thought and social communication. Since social processes shape language, they also shape thought.

The process of sociocultural influence

Cultural influences affect cognitive development in several ways, for example:

1. **The ZPD (zone of proximal development)** – Cultural influences and **experts** guide a child through the ZPD and enable the child to cope with tasks beyond their current abilities. Effective instruction supports the learner using **guided participation** and **scaffolding** (i.e. providing instructions that give hints about what to do next. In time, the learner can 'self-scaffold' (self-regulation).
2. **Social and individual planes** – Learning starts as a social, shared activity, and shifts to an individual, self-regulated activity.
3. **Semiotics** – Knowledge is transmitted using semiotics (signs and symbols), such as language, and mathematical symbols. Conversations between expert and learner enable development/learning to take place. Language is first used for social and emotional functions (pre-intellectual language). At the same time, thought is conducted without language (pre-linguistic thought).

Research evidence

Influence of culture – Gredler (1992) noted that the counting system in Papua New Guinea (cultural influence) limits cognitive development. They use fingers, arms, etc. to count, which limits their mathematics.

Scaffolding – McNaughton and Leyland (1990) observed mothers and their children solving progressively more difficult jigsaw puzzles. Mothers' help changed as the puzzles became harder (they gave progressively more explicit help) and showed their sensitivity to the ZPD. When a puzzle was below the ZPD, the mother just kept the child on the task. When a puzzle was within the ZPD, the mother gave hints.

ZPD – McNaughton and Leyland (1990) re-tested the children a week later and identified the highest level of difficulty the children could achieve unaided. This was a measure of their *ability*, whereas the level achieved with their mother was a measure of their *capability*. The difference between the two sessions defined each child's ZPD.

Self-regulation – Wertsch *et al.* (1980) measured self-regulation by watching the time a child spent gazing at his/her mother while working on jigsaw puzzles. Less gaze represented more self-regulation. Such gazes decreased with age, suggesting increased self-regulation. In another study children were again observed as they solved puzzles; the more puzzles they did the less they gazed at their mother, showing that regulation was transferred from other to self.

Inner speech – Berk (1994) observed children while they worked at school. Most of their comments either described or served to direct the child's actions, suggesting a self-regulating function. She also found that children talked to themselves more when they were faced with a difficult task, when working by themselves, or when a teacher was not available to help.

Evaluation

- The theory has less **empirical support** than Piaget's because it is less easy to test.
- It exaggerated the importance of the **social environment**. Motivation is important too and social interaction may actually have negative effects.
- If the help of others was all that was required, the **learning of complex skills should be faster** than it is.
- It may be more relevant to **collectivist societies** because of the emphasis on social learning, whereas Piaget's theory is an individualist approach.

Bruner's theory of cognitive development

AQA A U3

Bruner stands somewhere between Piaget and Vygotsky in his views.

This is an **information processing approach**, concentrating on how strategies for organising information change with age. (See information processing approaches to the topic of intelligence on page 69.)

Development involves the mastery of the increasingly more complex modes of thinking – enactive to iconic to symbolic. This involves translating one mode into the next. For example, conducting an experiment (iconic mode) and then discussing the conclusions that can be drawn (symbolic mode).

Jerome S. Bruner (1915) based his theory on a general interest in thinking. He was foremost a cognitive psychologist and this is a major influence on his theory of cognitive development, which was also influenced by Vygotsky's views.

- Thought requires ways of representing the environment, which we do through action, image and word (enactive, iconic, and symbolic modes of thinking).
- Development is due in part to the maturation of biological systems.
- Development is also due in part to language, social frameworks and experience, which shape the development of thought.

The structure of the intellect

Categories and hierarchies – Discovering and learning takes place by organising information into categories. Commonalities across experiences are recognised so that categories are identified. Categories are further organised into **hierarchies** – frameworks with the more general (generic) information at the top.

Modes of thinking – Modes of thinking are 'recurrent themes': **enactive** skills (e.g. manipulating objects, spatial awareness), **iconic** skills (visual recognition, the ability to compare and contrast) and **symbolic** skills (abstract reasoning).

Skill acquisition – Infants learn physical skills, such as grasping, during the enactive stage. These become automatic and act as modularised units that can be combined in different ways to build up a repertoire of new skilled behaviours and to allow attention to be freed for other things. As children grow older they also develop representational skills.

Stages in cognitive development

Each mode of thinking is present throughout life, but each mode is dominant during particular developmental phases:

- Early years – The **enactive mode**, learning through one's own actions, such as learning to walk or play a musical instrument.
- Middle childhood – The **iconic mode**, learning to use diagrams and numbers.
- Adolescence – The **symbolic mode**, working with abstract concepts.

Research evidence

Iconic and symbolic mode – Bruner and Kenney (1966) arranged nine glasses on a 3x3 grid, in order of height and diameter. If the glasses were scrambled, all the children were able to simply replace them (reproduction task). If the left and right glasses in the bottom row were swapped, 5 year olds found it impossible to replace them all in the same manner (transposition task) because this requires use of the symbolic mode.

Learning strategies – Mosher (1962) looked at the strategies used by children aged 6 to 12 in the game of twenty questions, to ascertain why a car went off the road. Older children used constraint-locating questions ('was it night-time?') whereas younger children asked direct hypothesis-testing questions ('did a bird hit the window?').

The role of tutoring – Bruner followed Vygotsky in suggesting that expert instruction was important in stretching a child's capabilities (see evidence on previous page).

Evaluation

- Bruner's theory is a **more general approach**, i.e. it applies to thinking, as well as cognitive development.
- The theory emphasises both the role of **biology** and of **experience, language and social factors**. Without language, thought is limited.

Many evaluation points related to Vygotsky's theory can be applied to Bruner's theory as both theories involve the influence of social/cultural factors.

Applications of these theories to education

AQA A ▶ U3
AQA B ▶ U3

Each theory of cognitive development has had specific implications for education, as indicated below.

Piaget's theory

Readiness – Offer moderately novel stimuli when the child is ready.

Self-discovery and self-motivation lead to complete understanding.

Individualised – Children mature at different rates, therefore, learning programmes need to be individualised.

The notion of education includes not just teachers but extends to anyone who is expanding the knowledge and understanding of children, e.g. parents, playleaders and toy manufacturers.

Discovery learning – Learning should be child-centred and active. The teacher's role is not to impart knowledge but to ask questions, thus creating disequilibrium and forcing children to make accommodations and, therefore, develop.

Logic is not an innate mental process, it is the outcome of cognitive development. It needs to be taught. Logic, maths and science subjects facilitate cognitive development.

Concrete materials should be used to teach young children (because they are in the stage of concrete operations).

Piaget's key idea was that, if you tell children something they could have discovered for themselves, then you prevent them from ever completely understanding it because they cannot invent the schema for themselves.

Motivation comes from the desire for equilibration; disequilibrium is caused by cognitive conflict.

Evaluation

- Piaget never specifically applied his theory to education. Others used it to influence **nursery and primary education** in particular, but also in Nuffield secondary science, which relies on children making their own discoveries.
- Discovery activities require **experienced teachers** who can guide students.
- Discovery learning means **less time for content learning**. Modgil *et al.* (1983) suggested that it may lead to backwardness in reading and writing in children who need more direction.

Walkerdine (1984) has argued that the move to child-centred education was not because of Piaget's theory. Educationalists just used his theories to justify the changes they wished to make. In any case the ideas are not new; the Greek philosopher Plato advocated child-centred education.

- Some research suggests that, with **practice**, children can do many things before they are 'ready'. For example, Bryant and Trebasso (1971) successfully trained young children to perform certain logical tasks before they were 'ready'. However, there is also research that shows there are limits, for example, Danner and Day (1977) found that only older adolescents could actually improve with training on abstract tasks; younger adolescents not yet in the abstract stage did not benefit.

Vygotsky's theory

Expert intervention (by peers or adults) is most effective when the expert is aware of the limits of the child's ZPD.

Scaffolding – An adult advances children's thinking by providing a framework (scaffolding) on which children can climb. Wood *et al.* (1976) found that when a learner runs into difficulty, the expert provides specific instructions. When the learner is coping well only general encouragement is needed. In time, we all learn to scaffold ourselves (self-instruction).

Vygotsky's key idea was that assistance is needed to set a learner on the road to independent behaviour.

Cooperative and collaborative learning – Students work together on a common task in which each individual depends on and is accountable to each other. This social construction of knowledge then enables each individual to cope better when working on their own. Gokhale (1995) found that students who participated in collaborative learning performed significantly better on a critical-thinking test than students who studied individually.

Peer tutoring – Peers can be experts. Research shows that it is often the peer tutor who gains most from tutoring.

Motivation comes from the people around you, encouraging you through the ZPD.

Evaluation

- Vygotsky's approach **may not work as well in an individualist setting** where children are encouraged to be more competitive and self-reliant, and where groupwork may be less successful.
- The approach requires that teachers are **sensitive to their students' ZPD**, which may be unrealistic and, again, requires experience.
- Cooperative group work requires **careful organisation to work well**; some members of a group may be 'loafing' and not benefit.

> When evaluating any of the applications of theories of cognitive development to education, you can refer to general criticisms of the theoretical basis for the application.

Bruner's theory

Discovery learning – Like Piaget's approach of the same name, this emphasises the active role of the learner, but places more emphasis on the teacher's activity than Piaget did. Teachers should take a direct role in instructing children, and identify what cognitive abilities and strategies are needed for good performance on a task, avoid overloading short-term memory, identify consistent errors, and encourage 'metacognitive' knowledge about strategies. At the same time, children must organise new information for themselves by integrating it into existing hierarchies or adapting hierarchies to fit new situations. Learning is not a matter of mastering facts but inventing the structure for the facts.

> 'Metacognition' is knowing about knowing. Learning about how to acquire knowledge is important.

Scaffolding – As suggested by Vygotsky, involving peers and/or adults.

Spiral curriculum – Successful learning is related to developing and redeveloping concepts at different ages with increasing complexity, i.e. important topics are revisited using progressively more mature modes of thinking.

Choice of materials and activities – Choice should match the dominant mode of thinking for a child, although a combination of concrete, pictorial then symbolic activities, will lead to more effective learning.

Motivation – This arises from using intrinsically interesting learning materials, rather than extrinsic rewards, such as getting good grades or emphasising the value of education.

> It is difficult to provide a truly valid assessment of any of these approaches because it is impossible to decide on a common outcome measure to assess and compare the approaches. In addition, we can't be certain that a teacher is strictly using one particular approach.

Evaluation

- The **spiral curriculum model has been very influential** as well as Bruner's view that learning needs to be structured.
- **Combines Piaget and Vygotsky's approach** by including the active role of the learning as well as the importance of scaffolding from teachers.

A combined approach

The different approaches need not be mutually exclusive and can be combined usefully. For example, the CASE project (Cognitive Acceleration through Science Education) involved developing formal operations (Piaget) by giving children problems that created cognitive conflict (Piaget), but children worked together to create solutions (Vygotsky).

Practice essays 8.1

(a) Outline and evaluate Piaget's theory of cognitive development.   *(15 marks)*
(b) Outline and evaluate **one** other theory of cognitive development. *(10 marks)*

8.2 Development of moral understanding

After studying this section you should be able to describe and evaluate:

- *theories of moral understanding (Kohlberg) and/or pro-social reasoning (Eisenberg).*

Kohlberg's theory of moral understanding

AQA A   U3
AQA B   U3

Piaget (1932) produced an early account of moral development, which is described on page 161. This account focused on what choices children made when given moral dilemmas. Kohlberg's interest was in *why* people made moral choices (i.e. moral reasoning).

Lawrence Kohlberg (1966) tested moral understanding by devising a set of moral dilemmas (situations with no straightforward solution), such as Heinz, and the druggist who wouldn't sell a drug to save Heinz's dying wife. The key feature of these dilemmas was that participants were asked a series of questions such as, 'Should Heinz steal the drug?', 'Why or why not?', 'Does it make a difference whether or not he loves his wife?', 'Why or why not?'.

Kohlberg tested a group of 10–16 year old boys, and used their reasoning to construct the classification scheme below.

Level	Age	Stage
Level I Pre-conventional	6–13	1. Deference to authority, heteronomous (basing judgment on the outcome rather than intention).
		2. Doing good to serve one's own interests, egocentric.
Level II Conventional	13–16	3. Care for the other, interpersonal conformity, 'good boy/girl'.
		4. The primacy of social order, importance of conscience, unquestioning acceptance of authority.
Level III Post-conventional or principled	16–20	5. Concern with individual rights, questioning the law and authority to ensure justice.
		6. Universal, ethical principles.

Research evidence

A longitudinal study by Colby *et al.* (1983) followed Kohlberg's initial participants over 20 years, ending up with 58 men. They were re-tested every 3 years. By the age of 36, participants were mainly reasoning at stage 4 (65% of their responses), stage 3 still accounted for about 30%, and stage 5 was 5%.

Kohlberg (1975) predicted that people who reason at a higher level should behave in a more mature fashion. He provided support for this in a study looking at whether students would cheat on a test, given the opportunity. He found that only 15% of those in the post-conventional stage cheated, whereas 70% of those in the pre-conventional stage did.

Walker *et al.* (1987) used nine stages to allow for the fact that many children's reasoning falls between two stages, and found general agreement with Kohlberg. They found that stage 2 reasoning dominates at age 10 and stage 3 dominates at age 16. Colby and Kohlberg (1987) performed a more careful analysis of the original data and found that only 15% reached stage 5 and there was no evidence whatsoever of stage 6 judgments.

Fodor (1972) found that delinquents operate at a much lower level on the Kohlberg scales than non-delinquents, as we might expect, since delinquents are likely to have less-developed morals.

Evaluation

- This may be the **best available approach** and has generated much empirical interest, despite the criticisms below.
- This is a theory of **moral principles** not behaviour; moral behaviour may not be related to moral principles. For example, the classic study by Hartshorne and May (1928) found that behaviour was more governed by the probability of being caught than by any principles of morality (see page 162).
- Stages 5 and 6 may be **moral ideals**, never achieved by some people.
- Judging moral dilemmas is not the same as making **real life** *decisions*.
- **Age bias** – The dilemmas are biased towards older participants and some of the dilemmas are simply irrelevant to children. Perhaps the seemingly immature behaviour of younger children is because they don't relate to the scenarios. Eisenberg (1982) found that Kohlberg had underestimated children's moral understanding abilities.
- **Gender bias** – The classification scheme is biased towards male morality (justice) because the scenarios were **justice-oriented** and the participants were male. Kohlberg claimed that women tended to be 'less' morally developed, but it may be that they only *appeared* to be less mature because they operate a morality of care. Gilligan and Attanucci (1988) asked a group of men and women to produce accounts of their own moral dilemmas. They found that, overall, men favoured a justice orientation and women favoured a care orientation. However, Kohlberg's theory may **not be as gender biased as is claimed**; Funk (1986) used Kohlberg's dilemmas and found that women scored higher than men.
- **Culture bias** – Kohlberg claimed that the moral stages are universal. In fact, his stages reflect Western values of democracy. There are cultural differences, for example, Ma (1988) constructed a Chinese version of Kohlberg's stages, including 'Good Will' (acting in a way that complies with nature). On the other hand, there is evidence of cultural similarities. Snarey (1985) listed 27 different cross-cultural studies, which found a progression from stages 1 to 4 at about the same ages. Very few studies found any stage 5 reasoning and, where it occurred, it was likely to be in urban areas.

> Carole Gilligan developed her own stage theory of moral development (see page 162). If a man's moral perspective was assessed using Gilligan's stage theory, he might appear to be morally inferior.

> Gender differences may also be related to the 'tend and befriend' responses typical of women (see page 60).

Eisenberg's theory of pro-social reasoning

AQA A ▶ U3
AQA B ▶ U3

> **Pro-social** behaviours are those that aim to benefit others. Further research related to pro-social behaviour/moral development is discussed on pages 161–163.

Nancy Eisenberg broadened the idea of moral behaviour to include pro-social behaviour and emphasised role-taking skills (taking the perspective of another person) in moral development. Eisenberg created a stage theory of pro-social development.

Level	Age range (approx.)	Brief description
1 Hedonistic (self-centred)	Pre-school and early primary.	Pro-social behaviour is most likely when it will benefit self in some way.
2 Needs oriented	A few pre-schoolers, mainly primary.	Sometimes considers needs of others. Not much evidence of sympathy or guilt.
3 Approval oriented	Primary and some secondary.	Pro-social behaviour in return for approval and praise from others.
4 Empathetic or transitional	Older primary and secondary.	Some understanding of abstract principles. Evidence of sympathy and guilt.
5 Strongly internalised	Some secondary and a few primary.	Internalised principles that are important to self-respect.

Research evidence

Eisenberg's stage theory was based on evidence from Eisenberg *et al.* (1983, 1991). They used a different kind of moral story than Kohlberg's; for example, a moral story where a child has to decide whether to help someone when the pro-social act would be at some cost (e.g. the child sees an injured child while on their way to a birthday party – do they go to the party where they will have lots of fun, or stop and help the injured child?).

Eisenberg *et al.* (1991) found that empathy (which develops during level 4) plays an important role in producing pro-social thinking. Adolescents were more likely to help if they thought about another person's feelings of pain and anxiety.

Eisenberg suggested that pro-social development relies on a child's ability to experience **empathetic concern**; personal distress on its own does not lead to pro-social behaviour. This was supported by Caplan and Hay (1989) who found that 3–5 year olds were often very upset by another child's distress, but rarely offered to help. Hughes *et al.* (1981) found that younger children felt sad about unhappy things but only gave egocentric explanations (i.e. ones that related to the effects on themselves). Slightly older children (aged 7–9) were able to see how a situation might affect someone else, for example, if someone's dog ran away, they realised it would make the other person unhappy and that made them sad.

> According to Eisenberg, the ability to distinguish between personal distress and empathetic concern hinges on this ability to take the perspective of another person; perspective-taking is discussed on page 91.

Role-taking skills are related to pro-social behaviour generally. For example, socially maladjusted girls who received training in role-taking skills became more concerned about needs of others than age mates who received no training (Chalmers and Townsend, 1990).

Gender differences – Feshbach (1982) found significant gender differences in empathetic responses with females being more empathetic than males. Eisenberg *et al.* (1991) found that girls aged 10–12 were more empathetic and caring but suggests this may be because girls mature earlier; by adolescence boys have caught up.

Cross-cultural support – Eisenberg (1986) found similar stages in other European countries, but Kibbutz-reared Israeli children showed little needs-orientation; instead they provided reasoning based on community values (as fits with being in a collectivist society).

Evaluation

- Eisenberg broadened the conception of moral behaviour, **emphasising emotional factors** and focusing on pro-social reasoning rather than wrongdoing.
- Eisenberg's dilemmas are **more appropriate to younger children** than Kohlberg's dilemmas. Nevertheless, the stages of development are roughly similar to Kohlberg's stages, thus supporting both theories.
- This theory has **real world application** for teachers and parents. It can be used to enhance pro-social development by focusing on the development of empathy.
- Some evidence suggests that **empathy appears much earlier** than Eisenberg predicted. Zahn-Waxler *et al.* (1979) found that children aged 18–30 months showed concern when they saw other children in distress.
- Explanations of altruism in adults also dispute whether it is **selfish or selfless**. Like Eisenberg, Batson (1991) suggested that empathy was the key to pro-social behaviour (i.e. selfless), whereas Cialdini (1985) argued that pro-social behaviour is due to relieving one's own distress (i.e. selfish), thus contradicting Eisenberg.

Practice essay 8.2

Discuss Kohlberg's theory of moral understanding. *(25 marks)*

8.3 Development of social cognition

After studying this section you should be able to describe and evaluate:

- *the development of the child's sense of self*
- *the development of children's understanding of others, including Theory of Mind (Baron-Cohen) and perspective taking (Selman)*
- *biological explanations of social cognition, including the role of the mirror neuron system.*

LEARNING SUMMARY

Development of the child's sense of self

AQA A ▶ U3

The concept of **self** refers to the attitudes you have about yourself as a unique individual, separate from others.

The **mirror test** has been used to assess whether animals are capable of self-recognition (see page 75).

Self-recognition

Lewis and Brooks-Gunn (1979) tested self-recognition by colouring infants' noses with rouge and putting them in front of a mirror (called the **mirror test**). A child who responds by touching their own nose shows self-recognition. At 9–12 months, all the children smiled at the image in the mirror, but none of the children touched their noses. By 21 months, 70% touched their noses. Lewis and Brooks-Gunn also found that, by 18 months, most children can point to a photograph of themselves.

Gender concept

A key aspect of one's self-concept is gender. Gender identity develops around the age of 3 (see page 62) and is linked to Piaget's concept of conservation (see page 82).

The physical versus the psychological self

Children of 3–4 years can distinguish a thinking, psychological self from their physical self. Children of this age typically describe themselves in concrete terms. However, Eder (1990) also found that they can describe how they usually behave in particular situations, which is evidence of a psychological self-concept. Selman (1980) used dilemmas to evaluate the development of private and public self. He found that by the age of 8 most children recognise the difference between their inner states and outward appearances.

Self-esteem is the feeling an individual has about all the components of their self-concept.

Self-esteem

A key aspect of the self-concept is the value attached to it, i.e. self-esteem. Carl Rogers (1951) suggested that self development begins when a child distinguishes what is 'me' (the conscious concept of self) from the rest of the world. This happens as a result of interaction with the environment, and at the same time a child learns the values attached to the self concept. Rogers linked low self-esteem to lack of self-acceptance and unhealthy personal development. Vershueren *et al.* (2001) found that children aged 4–5 have a sense of self-esteem and that this was linked to their attachment history; children who were securely attached had more positive self-esteem.

Key points from AS

- Rogers' approach to understanding human behaviour is an example of the humanistic approach, an approach that focuses on behaviour from the point of view of the person experiencing it, see *Revise AS Unit 1.1, page 21.*

Key points from AS

- This research links with studies on attachment and Bowlby's view that healthy emotional development is related to secure attachment, see *Revise AS Unit 2.1, page 53.*

Understanding of others

A sense of self is used as a reference point for understanding others, so the two are inextricably linked – the development of a sense of self is related to being able to understand others, a topic examined on the next page.

Bischof-Kohler (1991) used the mirror test to assess self-recognition. He also assessed a child's empathy when playing with an experimenter who is sad when a teddy bear's arm falls off. There was a high correlation between self-recognition and empathy regardless of age, suggesting that both develop at about the same time – around 18–20 months.

Development of children's understanding of others

AQA A   U3

Theory of mind (ToM) is the ability to understand what is going on in another person's mind, to 'guess' what they are thinking or feeling. It is regarded as a feature of intelligent behaviour and is only found in some animals (see page 75).

Theory of Mind (ToM)

ToM is tested using a false belief task – can other people have false beliefs? Baron-Cohen *et al.* (1985) created the **Sally–Anne test** to assess ToM. Typically, children aged 4 can cope with this task, but 3 year olds can't.

Harris (1989) argues that ToM develops from pretend play. A child first becomes aware of their own emotional state and then has to be able to use this to pretend to be someone else and share their feelings (e.g. 'My teddy bear is feeling sad'). This then enables the child to comprehend that another person may feel/think differently to what they are feeling, which happens by the age of 4.

Under the age of 4 children begin to distinguish mental states. For example, by the age of 2 they use words for emotional states, and by the age of 3 they meaningfully use words like 'thinking' (Shatz *et al.*, 1983).

Sally–Anne Test
• Sally puts her ball in her basket and leaves the room
• Anne moves the ball to her box.
• Sally returns. Where will Sally look for her ball? People who have a theory of mind say that Sally will look in her basket, whereas people lacking a theory of mind say that Sally will look in Anne's box (because they cannot perceive that another person will think differently to them and they know the ball is in Anne's box).

The understanding of the reality-appearance distinction (see Piaget's theory, page 81) is also linked to ToM because it requires understanding that one representation is false. Flavell *et al.* (1986) found that 4 year olds could correctly identify a sponge that looked like a rock as a being a sponge, whereas 3 year olds called it a rock despite the fact that it felt like a sponge.

Simon Baron-Cohen has been especially interested in individuals who *lack* a theory of mind ('mindblindness'). For example, autistic children, even those with high intelligence, cannot cope with the **Sally–Anne task** (see left). This is linked to their difficulties with social communication and relationships, because ToM underlies these. Baron-Cohen has also suggested that women are better than men at empathising and that autism is an example of the 'extreme male brain'.

Key points from AS

See Sally–Anne test illustration in *Revise AS Unit 7.3, page 167*.

Deception

The ability to deceive someone else depends on a theory of mind and is seen as a sign of intelligence in animals (see Machiavellian intelligence on page 75). By the age of 3, children can deceive others by hiding their own emotion. For example, Cole (1986) found that 3 year olds didn't show disappointment when receiving the worst (rather than best) present in front of others, but did show it when filmed on their own.

On page 88 we looked at Eisenberg's theory of pro-social development. She suggested that the ability to distinguish between personal distress and empathetic concern hinges on this ability to take the perspective of another person. Perspective or role-taking marks the beginning of pro-social behaviour in children.

Perspective taking

Selman (1980) proposed that children gain a greater understanding of themselves and others through being able to discriminate between their own perspective and those of other people, i.e. perspective-taking or role-taking; he called this **role-taking theory**. In particular, a child needs to understand the thoughts, feelings, motives and intentions.

To assess this, Selman gave children a set of interpersonal dilemmas, for example: Tom's friend Mike has lost his dog but says he doesn't want another. Tom wants to buy Mike a birthday present and sees some puppies for sale – what should he do? Selman based his stage theory on the explanations that children provided.

Altogether there are 5 stages in this model. Stage 3 is mutual role-taking (10–12 years) and stage 4 is societal role taking, taking the views of society into account.

Stage 0 Egocentric, 3–6 years	Views based on self, e.g. 'I'd get him a puppy because I like dogs'.
Stage 1 Subjective, 6–8 years	Can recognise another's perspective but assume different views are because the other person has different information, e.g. 'Mike says he doesn't want the dog, therefore, he'll be angry if Tom gives him a dog'.
Stage 2 Self-reflective, 8–10 years	Can't consider both perspectives simultaneously.

Biological explanations of social cognition

AQA A   U3

> **Social cognition** is the study of how thinking (cognition) affects social behaviour.

Theory of Mind Module (ToMM)

Is ToM biologically programmed? Baron-Cohen (1995) has suggested that there are innate mental structures related to ToM, in the same way that there are innate structures in the human brain for language. The ToMM develops between 18 and 48 months and enables a child to understand mental states, such as beliefs, desires and intentions.

Shared attention mechanism (SAM)

Baron-Cohen has proposed another possible system that may be involved in mindreading. He has suggested that the SAM system develops between 9 and 18 months and allows two individuals to understand that they are attending to the same thing. The SAM system is a precursor to the development of ToM.

> A **mirror neuron** is a neuron (or nerve) in the brain that is active when an animal performs a specific task, but is also active when the animal watches another animal perform the same specific task. It means that the observer's brain experiences the behaviour of another as if it were its own behaviour.

The role of the mirror neuron system

Mirror neurons are very important in imitation, empathy and Theory of Mind.

Mirror neurons have been observed directly in primates. Rizzolatti *et al.* (1996) recorded electrical activity in single neurons in the brains of macaque monkeys. In some of the neurons of the frontal and parietal lobes they found mirror properties – the neuron would respond in the same way when the monkey saw a person pick up a piece of food as it would when the monkey picked up the food.

In humans it has not been possible to study single neurons, but brain imaging studies suggest the presence of a mirror neuron system, i.e. a network of neurons in the **frontal** and **parietal regions** of the brain that respond in the same way to the single neurons observed in monkeys (Rizzolatti and Craighero, 2004).

The importance of this neural system is that it enables the observer to share the experiences of another and, thus, to understand their actions, and more importantly, their feelings and intentions.

Evaluation

> ### Key points from AS
>
> Alternative explanations are presented in *Revise AS Unit 7.3, page 166.*

- One **application** of this knowledge is as a means of **explaining autism**. The suggestion is that autistic people have a dysfunction in the mirror neuron system and this impairs their empathising ability. However, there is no evidence to support this.
- A further application is the **development of psychological tests** related to biological abilities, such as Baron-Cohen's early screening test for autism, the Checklist for Autism in Toddlers (CHAT). This quick test is used at 18 months to determine whether the child is not showing behaviours, such as pointing and gaze following, which are examples of shared (or joint) attention; lack of such behaviours might suggest autistic difficulties.
- The fact that social intelligence is **present only in certain higher animals** (see page 75) suggests that there is a biological basis for such behaviour, otherwise all animals would be capable of such behaviour.

Practice essays 8.3

(a) Explain the concept of Theory of Mind.	(4 marks)
(b) Outline research related to the Theory of Mind.	(5 marks)
(c) Evaluate research into the Theory of Mind.	(16 marks)

See pages 9–11 for a breakdown of the marking criteria used to mark this question.

The question requests more than one evolutionary approach. This answer contains two – one from Meddis and one from Webb, plus a general evolutionary discussion. If the candidate had only presented one explanation, full marks would not be available (partial performance penalties would apply where a maximum of about 2/3 of the marks would be available).

The description is accurate and well structured and material has been selected wisely. These are the criteria for the top band of AO1. However, there is one other AO1 criteria –substantial balance of depth and breadth; both explanations could have been a little sharper/more detailed for the top band. So **8 out of 9 AO1 marks.**

The commentary (AO2) is all in the second half of the answer, starting from the fourth paragraph. The candidate has used restoration theory as a means of evaluation and managed to avoid the 'AO2 description trap' where you end up giving a load of description instead of using the material as commentary.

The AO2 has been used effectively and shows coherent elaboration and a focused line of argument. However, it is not highly effective or thorough and there is only some evidence of issues/debates or approaches. Therefore, it is closer to the top of band 2 = **12 out of 16 AO2 marks.**

The total mark is 19 out of 25 marks.

1

Describe and evaluate evolutionary explanations of the function of sleep. *(25 marks)*

The basis of the evolutionary approach is that the reason why all animals sleep (and it is a fact that all animals sleep) is because sleep serves some adaptive function. The notion of adaptiveness comes from the theory of evolution. The idea is that any behaviour that has continued in an animal's gene pool is because it must have been naturally selected because it, in some way, has helped promote the survival and reproduction of an animal possessing that characteristic.

So sleep is likely to serve some adaptive function. Meddis proposed that the function is a protective one. When an animal does not have to be out and about finding food, then it would be adaptive for them to be quiet and hidden. At the same time an animal that is likely to be preyed upon would be better off sleeping very little, whereas predators can afford to sleep a lot because they are not in much danger.

Another evolutionary explanation was suggested by Webb. This is the hibernation theory. This theory suggests that sleep is adaptive because when an animal is asleep it is not using up energy. For most animals finding food is their biggest problem so there is a vicious cycle: the more active the animal is, the more food has to be found; the more food finding, the more energy that is used. When an animal hibernates or sleeps this reduces the amount of food that is needed and would increase survival.

Evolutionary theory can be used to explain why different animals sleep in different ways. For example, one species of dolphin sleeps one hemisphere at a time possibly in order to surface regularly and breathe. Observations of the animal world support Meddis' theory. Predator species, such as cats, sleep a lot more than prey species such as gazelles. Herbivores have to spend a lot of time finding food and will sleep little. The cow is not preyed upon and sleeps only a little. The point is that the evolutionary argument can be used to explain almost any sleep pattern!

Certainly some aspects of sleeping are adaptive, however, it may not be the main function of sleep. The alternative theory is the restoration theory, which proposes that all animals sleep because certain functions take place during sleep, which help the animal restore itself physiologically and psychologically. Of course this in itself may be adaptive. Physiological and psychological restoration can take place when an animal is relaxing, so why then is it necessary to become unconscious during sleep? In terms of protection one would think it is more adaptive for animals not to lose consciousness. Perhaps the reason is that for good restoration to take place the brain has really got to go off-line. So this suggests that restoration theory may be more correct than the evolutionary approach.

One of the key criticisms made, in relation to evolutionary theories of sleep, is that many of them suggest that animals sleep in order to waste time (Empson called them 'waste of time' theories). Whereas the restoration view is that sleep is not wasting time but offers the opportunity for key functions to take place.

Another criticism that is made is that evolutionary theories may not be suitable for explaining human sleep. Sleep may have been adaptive during the environment of evolutionary adaptation (EEA) but this hasn't been true for a long time and one wonders why humans haven't evolved different patterns of sleep if evolution was all there was to patterns of sleep. We haven't got predators and don't need to waste time so we should be sleeping less.

In general, evolutionary approaches have been criticised for lacking research evidence to support the 'just so' stories, however, this may not be justified.

See pages 9–11 for a breakdown of the marking criteria used to mark this question.

2

(a) Outline **one** theory of cognitive development. *(9 marks)*

(b) Assess the research evidence that has been used to support this theory.

(16 marks)

(a) This answer contains a sound description of Piaget's theory, perhaps too much detail of the ages and stages and no mention of other key features of the theory (such as disequilibrium and schema). But, answers are marked positively so marks are not deducted for concepts that may be missing as long as a good range of material has been included, as here. **9 out of 9 AO1 marks**.

(a) Piaget's theory is the best known and most comprehensive theory of cognitive development. It has been called an 'ages and stages' theory because Piaget identified the stages that an infant and child pass through as they develop cognitively. The key point about these stages is that they represent differences in biological maturation. As the child gets older they are capable of progressively different kinds of thinking rather than just having an increase in their general knowledge (a quantitative change). A child moves from one stage to another when their mind is mature enough. The first stage is sensori-motor, when the infant is learning to co-ordinate what he sees/hears with what his body is doing. The infant repeats actions (circular reactions) in order to establish these sensori-motor links.

At the end of the first year the child starts to use language and this is the beginning of the second stage, the pre-operational stage. 'Operations' are mental rules of logic. In this second stage the child cannot cope with internally consistent logic. They have their own form of logic but it wouldn't be any use in mathematics. They are 'fooled' by the appearance of things and mistake that for reality. This explains why they find the conservation task difficult.

The third stage is the stage of concrete operations (age about 7) where the child can now cope with conservation and with logical operations – but only if they are presented in a concrete form rather than abstract. The child's problem-solving abilities also tend to be rather random. The game called 'Mastermind' is one way to demonstrate this because younger children can't deduce the solution using logical steps.

At the age of 11 children move into the formal operational stage, when they are capable of abstract and systematic (scientific) thought. It may not be a universally-achievable stage.

(b) The most obvious point is that this answer is rather thin on AO2 – there should be significantly more AO2 than AO1 given the mark division. The commentary that has been provided shows sound analysis/ coherent elaboration – the student is able to expand each critical point and present relevant evidence and explain the implications. These are criteria for the top band. Quality of written communication (QWC) is also excellent. On the down side, the answer does not provide a thorough commentary and also lacks mention of issues/debates and approaches. It therefore clearly belongs in Band 2 and would receive **11 out of 16 AO2 marks**.

(b) Piaget's methods largely involved naturalistic observation of his own children. He may have been biased in making observations. He also used semi-structured interviews. These are good for eliciting unexpected information because there are no preset directions to take. However, the way an interviewer asks a question may bias a child's response.

In the area of object permanence, Piaget claimed that infants were only aware of this after the age of 8 months. However, a study by Bower showed that younger infants were surprised when a screen was lifted and an object was not there. This suggests that Piaget underestimated the age that infants could achieve this cognitive step, thus, challenging Piaget's evidence.

Piaget's research on conservation has been especially challenged. One suggestion has been the fact that he used two questions, which may have confused younger participants who thought that if there is a second question, there perhaps is a second answer. Therefore, they changed their answer in the second condition. Older children were less confused, which is why they appear to do better on the conservation task. Research by Samuel and Bryant supports this, showing that younger children are more capable than Piaget suggested – however, there are still age differences.

Piaget's theory claimed to be a biological and, therefore, universal theory, of behaviour yet some of this research may not generalise to other cultures, though its usefulness in education suggests that it does have a place there.

The total mark is 20 out of 25 marks.

Schizophrenia

9.1 Classification and diagnosis of schizophrenia

After studying this section you should be able to describe and evaluate:

*Note that AQA A students only need to study **one** mental disorder, i.e. they only need to study chapter 9 or 10 or 11 or 12.*

- *clinical characteristics of schizophrenia*
- *issues surrounding the classification and diagnosis of schizophrenia, including reliability and validity.*

LEARNING SUMMARY

Clinical characteristics of schizophrenia

AQA A ▶ U4
AQA B ▶ U3

The term **psychotic** refers to disorders where the patient has lost touch with reality.

Schizophrenia is one of the most chronic and disabling of the major mental illnesses affecting thought processes. A sufferer is unable to separate reality from unreal experiences, such as hallucinations. Some patients may only have one **psychotic** episode, and others may have many episodes during a lifetime, but lead relatively normal lives during interim periods.

In order for a diagnosis of schizophrenia to be made, two or more of the symptoms listed below must be present for more than one month, along with reduced social functioning. The symptoms are divided into **positive** and **negative** symptoms, though not all symptoms fit this pattern. Positive symptoms are an excess or distortion of normal functions and negative symptoms are a diminution or loss of normal functions.

Schizophrenia means literally 'split-mind', but it is wrongly confused with multiple personality disorder (or dissociative identity disorder). Schizophrenia refers to a group of psychoses, which are not enduring disorders of the whole personality.

- **Thought disturbance** (positive symptoms), such as thought insertion (e.g. thoughts controlled by aliens), hallucinations (e.g. hearing voices) and delusions (e.g. of grandeur).
- **Language impairments** (positive symptoms) are also characteristic. Patients may repeat sounds (echolalia) or use invented words (neologisms).
- **Inappropriate of affect/volition** (positive symptoms), such as smiling when told bad news.
- **Blunted and flat affect/volition** (negative symptoms), such as showing little emotion, reduced motivation and interest, and difficulty planning actions.
- **Psychomotor disturbances**, such as catatonia (immobility, bizarre statues), stereotypy (e.g. rocking) and frenetic activity (e.g. strange grimaces).

Types I and II

Schizophrenia occurs in about 1% of the population, though there is a wide difference between rural and urban environments; different research has shown prevalence rates of between 0.33% and 15%.

A distinction is made between Type I schizophrenia, which is dominated by positive symptoms, and Type II schizophrenia, which features negative symptoms and has a poorer prognosis (i.e. a less favourable outcome).

Subtypes

DSM-IV identifies five main subtypes:

Paranoid type – positive symptoms; awareness and language are relatively unimpaired.

Disorganised type – disorganised speech and behaviour, vivid hallucinations, flat emotion, and inappropriate affect; the most severe form, onset in early adulthood.

Catatonic type – apathy and psychomotor disturbances.

Schizophrenia may be better characterised as a range of disorders with different causes, rather than one single disorder.

Undifferentiated type – psychotic symptoms are present, but the criteria for paranoid, disorganised, or catatonic types have not been met.

Residual type – where positive symptoms are present at a low intensity only.

Issues surrounding the classification and diagnosis of schizophrenia

Reliability

General issues

Reliability concerns consistency of measurements. In relation to classification and diagnosis, this can be established in two ways:

- **Inter-rater reliability** – Whether two or more clinicians make the same diagnosis when independently assessing a patient. Some of this error may be due to the fact that the same patient may give different information to different clinicians, but some studies provide written material to control for this.
- **Test-retest reliability** – Whether the same clinician gives the same diagnosis when presented with the same information on separate occasions.

Obviously, a diagnosis is meaningless if it is not consistent. Current versions of DSM and ICD are regarded as being considerably more reliable than earlier versions. For example, Beck *et al.* (1962) found 54% agreement between four experienced clinicians when interviewing 153 patients. Söderberg *et al.* (2005) reported +.81 reliability with the most recent form of DSM (DSM-IV-TR).

DSM is claimed to have higher reliability than ICD because of the degree of specificity in the symptoms identified for each category. Nilsson *et al.* (2000) reported an inter-rater reliability of +.60 (or 60%) between clinicians using ICD.

Reliability of diagnoses of schizophrenia

There is evidence both for and against the reliability of a diagnosis of schizophrenia.

Pro – The diagnosis of schizophrenia has relatively high reliability (e.g. +.81 reported for schizophrenia whereas +.63 for anxiety disorders).

Anti – Read *et al.* (2004) reported that test-retest reliability was as low as +.37 and also described a 1970 study where 194 British and 134 American psychiatrists were asked to provide a diagnosis on the basis of a case description. 69% of the Americans diagnosed schizophrenia whilst only 2% of the British did so. They claim that there is no definitive evidence to suggest that the reliability of the diagnosis has improved since that date.

Evaluation

- Despite the rather low reliability of classification schemes, they are claimed to be useful because they are **better than nothing**. They enable research to be conducted linking syndromes to treatments and are better than just making a stab in the dark as to what treatment is likely to be most appropriate.
- Classification systems are **always being improved** and with increased understanding of mental disorders, the reliability should improve.

Validity

General issues

Validity concerns the extent to which a diagnosis represents something real. There are a number of approaches to establishing validity:

- **Reliability** – An unreliable diagnosis cannot, by definition, be valid.
- **Predictive validity** – If a diagnosis results in a successful treatment then the diagnosis must have been valid. Heather (1976) claimed that the same diagnosis had a 50 : 50 chance of leading to the same or a different treatment, which suggests that diagnoses lack validity.
- **Aetiological validity** – The cause of the disorder should be the same for all patients in that category.

Mental disorders are classified using **DSM** or **ICD**. The **DSM** (*Diagnostic and Statistical Manual of Mental Disorders*) is a list of typical symptoms for mental disorders, which is used to aid diagnosis of mental illness. DSM is used in America, whereas **ICD** (*International Classification of Diseases*) is used in Europe and the UK.

Studies often report a kappa statistic rather than a simple percent agreement; the kappa statistic (κ) is better because it takes into account the agreement occurring by chance.

It is important to remember that diagnosis of physical illness is not 100% reliable. However, physical illnesses have a (usually known) physical cause and, therefore, diagnoses of physical illnesses have the potential for greater reliability and validity.

- **Descriptive validity** – Patients in different diagnostic categories should differ from each other. Descriptive validity is reduced by **comorbidity**. Where comorbidity occurs it suggests that the 'illnesses' are not separate categories and thus not valid.
- **Cultural bias** – Western classification systems are culturally biased. The symptoms of a disorder are often culture-specific and, therefore, members of other cultural groups may be identified as ill when they exhibit behaviours that are normal within their own culture (e.g. hearing voices).

Comorbidity refers to the diagnosis of two or more conditions at the same time.

A classic study by David Rosenhan (1973) demonstrated the poor validity of psychiatric diagnosis. He arranged for 8 'normal' people to be examined by admitting doctors in psychiatric hospitals. The 'pseudopatients' were instructed to behave normally, except for reporting that they heard a voice. All except one was admitted as schizophrenic, and later released (between 2 and 52 days later) as schizophrenics in remission (this is a rare diagnosis which might suggest recognition of unusual circumstances). It would seem that the context mattered more than the symptoms, though it might be a case of a **Type II error** – the psychiatrists preferred to call a healthy person sick rather than a sick person healthy.

The lack of agreement between psychiatrists demonstrates low reliability.

What would happen if the hospital knew some patients were pseudopatients? Rosenhan described his study to the staff at one psychiatric hospital and told them to expect one or more pseudopatients over the next three months. In that time 193 patients were admitted and all staff were asked to rate the likelihood of whether they were 'real'. In fact, all patients were genuine but more than 20% were judged as pseudopatients by one member of staff and 10% were judged so by two members of staff.

Validity of diagnoses of schizophrenia

Culture bias – Cochrane (1977) found that more people of African-Caribbean origins were diagnosed as schizophrenic in the UK than whites (possibly 7 times as many). This may be because the disease has a genetic origin, but diagnosis rates for African-Caribbeans are not as high elsewhere in the world. It may be because members of minority ethnic groups in Britain have more stressful lives.

Evaluation

The **idiographic approach** is explained on page 185.

- The fact that diagnoses can be unreliable and inaccurate (invalid) suggests that they **should not be used**. However, the same is at least partly true of medical diagnosis generally, yet we wouldn't suggest abandoning that. There are alternatives, e.g. using a more **idiographic** approach that doesn't require classification (which is *nomothetic*), but emphasises listening and analysing each patient's problems.
- A major issue with psychiatric diagnoses is that they result in **labelling**, for example a person becomes a 'schizophrenic' rather than a person with schizophrenia, and this label tends to stick even when the disorder has disappeared. This problem with labelling is less true for physical diagnoses and, therefore, an invalid psychiatric diagnosis has more serious and lifelong implications. For this reason many critics would prefer to avoid the use of such labels. Another alternative is to use a system that focuses on the behaviours only.

Practice essays 9.1

(a) Outline the clinical characteristics of schizophrenia, with reference to examples.

(9 marks)

(b) To what extent are diagnoses of schizophrenia reliable and/or valid?

(16 marks)

9.2 Explanations of schizophrenia

After studying this section you should be able to describe and evaluate:

- *biological explanations of schizophrenia, for example, genetics and biochemistry*
- *psychological explanations of schizophrenia, for example, behavioural, cognitive, psychodynamic and socio-cultural.*

LEARNING SUMMARY

Biological explanations of schizophrenia

AQA A — U4
AQA B — U3

Genetic explanations

There is strong evidence that a predisposition for schizophrenia is inherited, and then life experiences trigger the condition (the **diathesis-stress model**, see page 54).

Individuals may inherit a gene or genes that cause their schizophrenia. Research suggests that it is not likely to be one gene (see gene mapping studies) and that such genes predispose individuals to develop the disorder, rather than being a certainty (identical MZ twins don't show 100% concordance).

Research evidence

Gene mapping involves comparing the genetic material from families who have schizophrenia with samples from families without schizophrenia to identify common factors.

Gene mapping – Sherrington *et al.* (1988) found evidence for a cluster of genes on chromosome 5, which might make an individual susceptible to schizophrenia. Subsequent studies have found a range of potential candidates on chromosomes 5, 6, 8, 9, 10, 11, 13, 18, 19 and 22 (Kendler *et al.*, 2000). Hahn *et al.* (2006) produced evidence that linked the gene associated with **neuregulin** with a predisposition for schizophrenia.

The abbreviation MZ stands for monozygotic (identical) and DZ for dizygotic (non-identical or fraternal).

Twin studies – Gottesman (1991) summarised about 40 studies, concluding that the concordance rate is about 48% for MZ twins but only 17% for DZ twins, indicating some environmental influence but a larger genetic component.

Adoption studies – Tienari (1991) reported on the Finnish adoption study, following 155 adopted children whose natural mothers were schizophrenic. In adulthood 10.3% of those with schizophrenic mothers had developed schizophrenia compared to only 1.1% of those without schizophrenic mothers.

Family studies – Kendler *et al.* (1985) found that first-degree relatives of schizophrenics are 18 times more likely to be similarly diagnosed. In the Copenhagen high-risk study, Parnas *et al.* (1993) followed 207 children (aged 10–18 at the start) who had schizophrenic mothers. At a 27-year follow-up 16% had been diagnosed as schizophrenic compared with 2% in a low-risk group.

Evaluation

- High concordance rates in MZ twins may be because they are **treated more similarly** than DZ twins (Loehlin and Nichols, 1976).
- Family similarities can also be explained by **shared environmental influences**.
- Genetic factors are involved but are **not solely responsible**. Less than 50% of children where one parent was schizophrenic develop the disorder (Fish *et al.*, 1992). The **diathesis-stress model** can be used to explain this. However, Rabkin (1980) found that schizophrenics do not report significantly more stressful episodes during the months preceding the initial onset of the disorder.

If schizophrenia is genetic then the genes may cause neuroanatomical and/or biochemical differences.

Neuroanatomical explanations

Known organic disorders, such as brain tumours, lead to psychotic states, which suggests an organic basis for schizophrenia.

Research has linked schizophrenia, particularly Type II, to abnormalities in brain structure. For example, Torrey (2002) found enlarged ventricles (the brain cavities that hold cerebrospinal fluid). This may be the result of having less developed parts of the brain. Kim *et al.* (2000) found evidence of smaller frontal lobes and abnormal blood flow to certain areas.

Post-mortem examinations of some schizophrenics show that their brains are 6% lighter and have fewer neurons in the cerebral cortex than 'normal' brains.

Biochemical explanations

The **dopamine hypothesis** (Snyder, 1976) proposes that schizophrenics have abnormally high levels of dopamine. This may be due to the fact that schizophrenics have abnormally high numbers of D2 receptors on receiving neurons, leading to more dopamine binding and more neurons firing. The original hypothesis was based on evidence that the drugs used to alleviate schizophrenic symptoms (**neuroleptics**) block dopamine synapses and the release of dopamine. In addition, the side-effects of neuroleptic drugs are similar to the symptoms of Parkinson's disease, a condition associated with low levels of dopamine, which is improved through the use of L-dopa (Grilly, 2002). Finally, evidence also comes from post-mortem examinations of schizophrenics, which show abnormally high levels of dopamine.

Revised dopamine hypothesis – The original dopamine hypothesis was revised by Davis *et al.* (1991) because it was recognised that dopamine (DA) was high in some patients, but not others. Also, a new drug, clozapine, is more effective in reducing schizophrenic symptoms, but blocks dopamine activity less. Therefore, the revised hypothesis suggests that:

* DA high in mesolimbic dopamine system (associated with positive symptoms) → <u>hyper</u>dopaminergia
* DA low in mesocortical dopamine system (and associated with negative symptoms) → <u>hypo</u>dopaminergia

The **glutamate hypothesis** (Olney and Farber, 1995) suggests that it is not dopamine that is the key, but it is implicated because of its role in glutamate production. DA receptors inhibit glutamate release and glutamate may be more closely related to root cause.

Evaluation

* Neurological differences may be a **cause or effect**.
* Neurological differences may be genetic or could arise from birth complications, i.e. **nurture rather than nature**. Harrison (1995) found that at least some schizophrenics may have experienced brain damage from anoxia (lack of oxygen) at birth. Torrey (1996) suggests a viral cause, which would explain why more schizophrenics were born in late winter.
* Neuroleptic drugs block dopamine fairly rapidly, yet they are **slow to reduce** the symptoms of schizophrenia.
* Healy (2000) suggests that **drug companies** have inappropriately promoted the dopamine hypothesis because it makes money for them.

Evolutionary explanations

Group splitting hypothesis – Stevens and Price (1996) suggest that some schizophrenic traits (e.g. bizarre beliefs, delusions) serve an adaptive function under certain conditions, such as when social groups become too big and they are more at risk from predation and have more difficulty with food; a 'crazy' individual may act as a leader and enable one subgroup to split off from a main group.

Origin of language theory – Crow (2000) proposes that schizophrenia is due to a disruption of language mechanisms. This is supported by the fact that schizophrenics often believe they are hearing voices and/or may use strange language (e.g. word salads). Language is normally highly adaptive but it might be that sometimes the brain malfunctions, giving rise to abnormal linguistic functions. Schizophrenia is the price that humans pay for language.

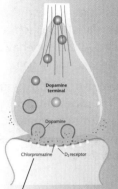

Diagram showing dopamine activity and D2 receptors on the receiving neuron.

Chlorpromazine, a drug that blocks symptoms of schizophrenia, occupies the dopamine site on the D₂ receptor, preventing receptor activation by dopamine.

Key points from AS

* You can read about neurotransmission in more detail in *Revise AS Unit 5.3, page 112.*

Key points from AS

* General criticisms of the biological approach to explaining abnormality can be found in *Revise AS Unit 7.1, page 151.*

It is important to remember that evolutionary explanations for mental disorders are based on the assumption that such disorders are inherited, or at least a predisposition for the disorder is inherited.

The evolutionary approach can be criticised for being determinist and not accounting for individual and cultural differences.

Psychological explanations of schizophrenia

Behavioural explanations

Labelling theory (Scheff, 1966) – Schizophrenia results from learning that escape to an inner world is rewarding. Individuals who have been labelled as schizophrenic then continue to act in ways that conform to the label. Bizarre behaviours are rewarded with attention and sympathy; this is known as secondary gain.

Operant conditioning – Some psychologists (e.g. Liberman, 1982) suggest that some children may receive abnormal reinforcements for social behaviours when they are young so they 'learn' to behave in bizarre ways to inappropriate stimuli. Subsequently, people avoid or respond strangely to the child's bizarre behaviour, which is further reinforcing and leads eventually to a psychotic state.

Evaluation

- The success of token economies (see page 103) with schizophrenia offers modest support for explanations based on operant conditioning.

Cognitive explanations

Many symptoms of schizophrenia relate to cognitive malfunction (e.g. hallucinations, disordered thinking), which suggests a cognitive basis for the abnormality. These malfunctions may be due to physiological abnormalities, for example, hallucinations may be produced by brain abnormalities and are, therefore, 'real'. However, other people are not likely to believe someone who reports hallucinations and, therefore, a sufferer may be labelled 'mad' and may also start to feel they are persecuted.

Evaluation

- Research has found evidence of **real hallucinations and other sensory problems** in schizophrenics (Elkins and Cromwell, 1994), which supports this explanation.

Psychodynamic explanations

Freud (1924) proposed that two psychological processes were involved in the development of schizophrenia:

1. **Regression to a pre-ego state** – A harsh emotional environment (such as a cold, unloving family) leads a person to regress to an infantile state (a pre-ego state) where they may talk (neologisms) and behave like a baby.
2. **Efforts to re-establish ego control** – The effect of regression is for the ego to try to re-take control, which results in other typical schizophrenic symptoms such as auditory hallucinations.

Evaluation

- There has been **little empirical support** for psychodynamic explanations.
- Family relations **may be an effect**. Oltmanns *et al.* (1999) found that parents of schizophrenics did behave differently from parents of other kinds of mental patient. Studies of schizophrenogenic families usually occur after the onset of the disease and, therefore, the dynamics have probably been altered by the stresses of having an ill son/daughter.

See page 72 for an explanation of operant conditioning.

Key points from AS

- General evaluations of the behaviourist approach to explaining abnormality can be found in *Revise AS Unit 7.1, page 153.*

Cognitive explanations are focused on maladaptive ways of thinking.

Key points from AS

- General evaluations of the cognitive approach to explaining abnormality can be found in *Revise AS Unit 7.1, page 154.*

Regression is a form of ego-defence where the ego deals with anxiety by regressing to an earlier state in life that was stress-free.

Key points from AS

- Bettelheim (1967) proposed that cold parenting could explain autism (the 'refrigerator mother'), see *Revise AS Unit 7.3, page 166.*

Key points from AS

- General evaluations of the psychodynamic approach to explaining abnormality can be found in *Revise AS Unit 7.1, page 153.*

Socio-cultural explanations

Socio-cultural explanations explain schizophrenia in terms of social and cultural factors, such as the sufferers' immediate family or their wider social circle.

Double-bind theory – Bateson *et al.* (1956) proposed that schizophrenia is a learned response to mutually-exclusive demands being made on a child and also conflicting messages. Prolonged exposure results in a child developing their own, internally consistent construction of reality. R.D. Laing (1959) regarded schizophrenia as a sane response to a disordered environment.

Expressed emotion (EE) – Another family factor that has been implicated in schizophrenia is expressed emotion – the extent to which a family communicates in a critical, hostile and over-emotional way. In fact, EE has been found to be particularly significant as a variable that prevents recovery; schizophrenics in high EE families have been found to be less likely to recover. For example, Vaughn and Leff (1976) found 51% relapse in schizophrenics returning to high EE homes, compared with 13% relapse for those returning to low EE homes.

Some of the other psychological explanations can also be seen as socio-cultural – such as *labelling theory* (labels provided by members of society) and *schizophrenogenic families* (the influence of others in your social group).

Social causation hypothesis – Members of lower social classes have more stressful lives, and this makes them more vulnerable to schizophrenia. However, it may be that developing schizophrenia leads to reduced social status (**social drift hypothesis**). Turner and Wagonfeld (1967) found that the fathers of schizophrenics tended to belong to the lower social classes.

Evaluation

- The genetic evidence shows that any account **must include biological factors**.
- Family abnormalities may be a **reasonable response** to a child with brain damage.
- If the family is at fault, **all children should develop the disorder**. This suggests that only vulnerable individuals are affected, or those who are made scapegoats.
- The importance of EE is supported by an adoption study, which showed that children whose natural mothers had schizophrenia were more likely to develop the disorder than their 'normal' adoptive siblings. However, this difference only emerged when the adopted family was rated as disturbed (Tienari *et al.*, 1994). This shows an **interaction between genetic vulnerability and environmental stressors** (the diathesis-stress model).
- Environmental factors may be more important in understanding the **course rather than the cause** of schizophrenia.

Practice essay 9.2

Discuss biological explanations of schizophrenia. *(25 marks)*

9.3 Treatments for schizophrenia

After studying this section you should be able to describe and evaluate:

- *biological therapies for schizophrenia, including their evaluation in terms of appropriateness and effectiveness*
- *psychological therapies for schizophrenia, for example, behavioural, psychodynamic and cognitive-behavioural, including their evaluation in terms of appropriateness and effectiveness.*

LEARNING SUMMARY

Biological therapies for schizophrenia

AQA A — U4
AQA B — U3

The term **psychotic** refers to a person who lacks contact with reality. Schizophrenia is a psychotic disorder.

Key points from AS

- For a diagram of a neuron synapse (the gap between two neurons) see *Revise AS Unit 5.3, page 112.*

Placebos are substances that have no pharmacological effects but the person taking them thinks they are the real thing. This means you can separate the psychological from the physical effects of being given a drug treatment.

Key points from AS

- General criticisms of drug therapies are given in *Revise AS Unit 7.2, page 156.*

Key points from AS

- ECT is described in *Revise AS Unit 7.2, page 157.*

Chemotherapy: drugs

Anti-psychotic drugs are used to treat psychotic illnesses, such as schizophrenia.

- **Typical anti-psychotics,** for example, *chlorpromazine*, are used to treat the positive symptoms of schizophrenia, such as hallucinations. They bind to dopamine receptors at the end of neurons and, thus, block dopamine action, reducing the positive symptoms.
- **Atypical anti-psychotics,** such as *clozapine*, treat negative symptoms of schizophrenia (such as reduced emotional expression) as well as positive symptoms. They act on the serotonin system as well as the dopamine system by temporarily occupying receptor sites and then allowing normal transmission. This may explain why side effects are less severe than when typical anti-psychotics are used.

Appropriateness and effectiveness

- Conventional anti-psychotics have a range of serious **side effects**, such as **extrapyramidal effects** – where patients develop movement disorders (e.g. muscle tremors) typical of patients with Parkinson's disease.
- There are serious side effects with the newer atypical anti-psychotics, for example, clozapine is linked with **agranulocytosis**, a potentially life-threatening drop in the number of white blood cells.
- Davis *et al.* (1989) looked at over 100 studies comparing anti-psychotic drugs with placebo treatment and found that the **drugs came out as more effective** in the vast majority of the studies. Overall, more than 70% of patients treated with conventional anti-psychotics were much improved after 6 weeks, compared with fewer than 25% of patients treated with a placebo only.
- Studies **comparing conventional anti-psychotics with the newer anti-psychotics** suggest that the former can be just as effective. For example, the CATIE study (2005), involving 1400 patients, found that the conventional anti-psychotic drug, *perphenazine*, was just as effective as the newer (and more expensive) atypical drugs, and no more likely to cause side-effects.

ECT

Appropriateness and effectiveness

- Tharyan and Adams (2005) report that ECT **remains a common treatment** option for people with schizophrenia. They reviewed 26 studies (about 800 patients) and concluded that courses of ECT resulted, in the short term, in better overall improvement in schizophrenics than the use of a placebo (sham treatment).
- However, drug therapies had greater success than ECT alone; anti-psychotic **drugs plus ECT produced the best outcomes.**

Psychological therapies for schizophrenia

AQA A | U4
AQA B | U3

A **secondary reinforcer** is one that has become reinforcing through association with things that are primary needs.

Key points from AS

- General criticisms of psychological therapies are given in *Revise AS Unit 7.1, pages 158–160.*

Your evaluation of treatments can include information about the reliability and validity of the diagnoses. If the original diagnosis lacks reliability/validity then the treatment may not be effective.

Key points from AS

- Psychoanalysis and CBT are described and evaluated in *Revise AS Unit 7.1, page 158 and 160 respectively.*

Psychotherapies such as psychoanalysis and CBT are only suitable for mental illnesses where some insight is retained, so they may not be especially suitable for schizophrenia.

The problem with a review of a number of studies (**meta-analysis**) is that they average a variety of results and are likely to produce rather inconclusive results.

There have been a number of well-publicised cases where a schizophrenic patient being cared for in the community has committed a murder. Usually, this is because the patient has stopped taken his/her medications.

Behavioural therapy: token economy (TE)

Institutionalised patients are given tokens when they engage in pre-defined correct/socially desirable behaviours. The tokens can be exchanged for food or privileges. They act as **secondary reinforcers**, whereas food and privileges are **primary reinforcers** (reinforcing in their own right). This system enables patients to cope better when living independently and may focus particularly on negative symptoms, such as poor motivation and social withdrawal.

Appropriateness and effectiveness

- Allyon and Azrin (1968) used TE to control the behaviour of 45 chronic schizophrenics who had been institutionalised for an average of 16 years. They were given tokens for making their beds or combing their hair. The number of **chores the patients performed each day increased** from about 5 to over 40.
- The drawback to this therapy is that it often fails to transfer to life outside the institution. McMonagle and Sultana (2000) reviewed several studies and found **low support for maintenance of behaviours beyond the treatment** programme. However, Woods *et al.* (1984) found fundamental long-term effects.
- The effectiveness of tokens **may be due to other factors**, such as being positively reinforcing for the nursing staff, who feel they are making positive gains and, therefore, are stimulated to persist. They also help to structure the situation and ensure consistent rewards.

Psychodynamic therapy: psychoanalysis

Spotnitz (1969) pioneered the use of psychoanalysis with schizophrenic patients. He believed that treatment needed to focus on redirecting aggression outwards rather than being inward-focused self-hate, which was at the root of serious mental disorders like schizophrenia. Spotnitz is credited with founding modern psychoanalysis.

Cognitive-behavioural therapy (CBT)

CBT is a recommended treatment for people with schizophrenia (Cochrane Review, 2006). This approach helps to link the person's feelings and patterns of thinking that underpin distress.

Appropriateness and effectiveness

- Sensky *et al.* (2000) compared CBT with a 'non-specific befriending control intervention'. **CBT was effective** in treating negative and positive symptoms that were resistant to standard anti-psychotic drugs, with a sustained effect over 9 months later.
- However, Jones *et al.* (2004) reviewed 30 studies of CBT and found fairly **minimal evidence of effectiveness** when treating schizophrenia.

The role of community care

The advent of drug therapies has meant many mental patients can be cared for in the community where they receive a mixture of care from mental health teams as well as structured psychotherapy (e.g. CBT).

Practice essays 9.3

(a) Outline the clinical characteristics of schizophrenia. *(5 marks)*

(b) Describe and evaluate **one** behavioural therapy for schizophrenia. *(10 marks)*

(c) Describe and evaluate **one** psychodynamic therapy for schizophrenia. *(10 marks)*

Chapter 10

Depression

10.1 Classification and diagnosis of depression

After studying this section you should be able to describe and evaluate:

Note that AQA A students only need to study **one** mental disorder, i.e. they only need to study chapter 9 or 10 or 11 or 12.

- clinical characteristics of depression
- issues surrounding the classification and diagnosis of depression, including reliability and validity.

LEARNING SUMMARY

Clinical characteristics of depression

| AQA A | U4 |
| AQA B | U3 |

Depression is a disorder of mood or affect. It may exist on its own or may be just one aspect of a more involved disorder. The clinical characteristics are listed below, organised into four main groups:

- **Emotional:** sadness, feelings of guilt, thoughts of suicide.
- **Motivational:** loss of interest and energy, shift in energy level (becoming lethargic or more agitated).
- **Cognitive:** difficulty concentrating and slowed thinking.
- **Somatic:** loss of, or increase in, appetite and weight; sleep disturbance (insomnia or oversleeping).

There are two forms of depression: unipolar (also called major depression), and bipolar or manic-depression. AQA A students do not need to study both but can read about bipolar disorder on page 164.

About 10% of men and 20% of women become clinically depressed at some time in their lives.

DSM-IV (see page 96) requires that the diagnosis of a major depressive episode requires that five of the above clinical characteristics occur nearly every day for a minimum of two weeks. In addition, a patient should either show a depressed mood or loss of interest and pleasure. The symptoms must also cause clinically significant distress or impairment in general functioning, nor be better accounted for by bereavement, i.e. the loss of a loved one. It may be useful to distinguish between **endogenous** depression (e.g. related to hormone changes or biochemical factors) and **reactive** depression (triggered by external events).

Issues surrounding the classification and diagnosis of depression

General issues related to reliability and validity of classification and diagnosis are discussed on pages 96–97.

Reliability

Inter-rater agreement – Brown *et al.* (2001) found reasonable inter-rater agreement in assessments made of about 350 patients, in terms of their anxiety and mood disorders, using DSM-IV.

Test-retest reliability – Moca *et al.* (2007) found high inter-rater reliability (.877) and test-retest reliability (.776) though these figures were lower than for schizophrenia.

There are times when we all feel depressed. The symptoms of clinical depression are similar to 'normal' depression, but more intense and long-lasting.

Validity

Descriptive validity – Zigler and Phillips (1961) found that the symptoms of depression were just as likely to be found in someone diagnosed with bipolar disorder as in someone labelled 'neurotic', and in 25% of those termed schizophrenic. This suggests that a diagnosis of depression conveys little information about a patient.

Practice essays 10.1

(a) Outline the clinical characteristics of depression, with reference to examples.
(9 marks)

(b) To what extent are diagnoses of depression reliable and/or valid? *(16 marks)*

10.2 Explanations of depression

After studying this section you should be able to describe and evaluate:

- *biological explanations of depression, for example, genetics, biochemistry*
- *psychological explanations of depression, for example, behavioural, cognitive, psychodynamic and socio-cultural.*

LEARNING SUMMARY

Biological explanations of depression

AQA A   U4
AQA B   U3

There is strong evidence that depression is related to biological factors, though not as strong as the evidence for schizophrenia (see pages 98–99).

Gene mapping involves comparing the genetic material from families who have depression with samples from families who don't have depression in order to identify common factors.

There is stronger evidence of genetic factors in bipolar disorder (see page 165).

If depression is genetic then the genes may cause neuroanatomical and/or biochemical differences.

Genetic explanations

Individuals may inherit a gene or genes that cause their depression. Research suggests that it is not likely to be one gene (see gene mapping studies) and that such genes predispose individuals to develop the disorder, rather than being a certainty (identical MZ twins don't show 100% concordance).

Research evidence

Gene mapping – Caspi *et al.* (2005) have found a link between abnormalities in the **5-HTT gene** and depression. 5-HTT is linked to the production of serotonin (see biochemical explanations below), so this research links genetic and biochemical explanations.

Twin studies – Kendler and Prescott (1999) studied nearly 4,000 pairs of US twins and found 39% heritability for depression. This study found no gender differences, whereas Bierut *et al.* (1999) found a stronger genetic component in female twins' depression.

Adoption studies – Wender *et al.* (1986) found that biological relatives of adopted depressives were about eight times more likely than adoptive relatives to have had major depression themselves. Wender *et al.* (1986) also found that adopted children were eight times more likely to develop depression if their biological parents had suffered from clinical depression.

Evaluation

- The research indicates **more environmental than genetic** influence.
- The 5-HTT gene has also been linked to a number of other disorders, such as autism, so it is **not a specific vulnerability factor** for depression – though of course depression does underlie a whole range of mental disorders.

Biochemical explanations: neurotransmitters

The **permissive amine theory** of mood disorder (Kety, 1975) suggests that depression is caused by a deficiency of **noradrenaline**. Noradrenaline is controlled by serotonin and dopamine. When levels of the latter are low, noradrenaline may fluctuate wildly, leading to depression. The theory refers to 'amine' because noradrenaline, serotonin and dopamine are all neurotransmitters of the monoamine group. In 'normal' circumstances these neurotransmitters are involved in arousal and mood, so it makes sense that they are involved in mood disorders.

The importance of **serotonin** is supported by the fact that one of the most successful anti-depressants (SSRIs) increases levels of serotonin (see page 109), and usually reduces the symptoms of depression. Other anti-depressants also increase levels of noradrenaline.

The **diathesis-stress model** suggests that people inherit a vulnerability (diathesis) to develop depression, but it only occurs when triggered by life experiences (stressors).

The effect of **dopamine** is also supported by the effectiveness of some anti-depressants – SSRIs also increase levels of dopamine. However, this effect may be slower than the effects for serotonin, which could explain why SSRIs do not have an immediate effect on depression (Zhou *et al.*, 2005).

Research evidence

Teuting *et al.* (1981) analysed the urine of depressed and normal people and found lower levels of products associated with noradrenaline in the depressed people.

Mann *et al.* (1996) found impaired serotonin production in people with depression.

Evaluation

- It is hard to know whether neurotransmitter changes are a **cause or effect** of depression.
- The effects of anti-depressants **are not the same** for everyone, which suggests that the causes are not likely to be the same.
- Anti-depressants raise neurotransmitter levels immediately, yet it may take weeks before there are psychological effects. In addition, the fact that there are also placebo effects (see page 102) suggests that biochemical explanations **do not provide a complete account of depression**.
- Anti-depressants are also used to treat other conditions (such as anorexia), which suggests that neurotransmitter dysfunction is not specific to major depression.

Hormonal causes of depression may explain why more women than men suffer from depression.

Biochemical explanations: hormones

Some forms of depression, are linked to hormonal changes, for example, endogenous disorders such as **post-partum depression** (PPD) and **pre-menstrual syndrome** (PMS), and reactive disorders such as **seasonal affective disorder** (triggered by changing day length, causing changes in melatonin levels, see page 16).

Research evidence

Abramowitz *et al.* (1982) found that 41% of women who were admitted to psychiatric hospital entered on or within a day of the start of their menstrual period.

About 20% of women report moderate depression in the first weeks after giving birth, however, Cooper (1988) found that a similar number of non-pregnant women reported feelings of depression.

Cortisol tends to be elevated in depressed patients. Carroll *et al.* (1980) showed that dexamethasone does not suppress cortisol in 50% of depressed individuals, whereas it does in normal individuals. This may be because levels of cortisol are so high in depressives they can't be suppressed.

PPD may be due to 'normal' hormonal cycles, or may be a reactive rather than an endogenous disorder – caused by lack of emotional support, low self-esteem and unrealistic ideas about motherhood.

Key points from AS

- General criticisms of the biological approach to explaining abnormality can be found in *Revise AS Unit 7.1, page 151*.

Key points from AS

- The hormone **cortisol** is produced when an individual is stressed or anxious – see *Revise AS Unit 5.1, page 98*.

Evaluation

- Hormonal changes could be an **effect rather than a cause**.
- Hormonal changes may act as a **predisposing factor**; depression occurs when there are other stressors, as in PPD (the **diathesis-stress model**, see page 54).

Evolutionary explanations

It's important to remember that evolutionary explanations for mental disorders are based on the assumption that such disorders are inherited, or at least a predisposition for the disorder is inherited.

Rank theory – Nesse and Williams (1995) suggest that depression is an adaptive response to losing rank, because it prevents further injury from re-engaging in combat. Conflicts are common in any social group and depression helps the individual to accept losing and settle for an inferior role. In time, depression became associated with other kinds of loss, such as loss of a loved one. 'Clinical depression' is a pathological outcome of an adaptive emotional mechanism.

The evolutionary approach can be criticised for being determinist and not accounting for individual and cultural differences.

Genome lag – Nesse and Williams (1995) suggest that depression may occur increasingly more because we are not adapted to live in urban situations. In addition, there are high commercial and achievement pressures in modern life, which are stressful. These can lead to depression because of our inability to cope with such aspects of modern life, things that we are not adapted for.

Psychological explanations of depression

AQA A ▶ U4
AQA B ▶ U3

Key points from AS

• General evaluations of the behaviourist approach to explaining abnormality can be found in *Revise AS Unit 7.1, page 153.*

Behavioural explanations

Learned helplessness – Seligman (1974) suggested that if an animal finds that its responses are ineffective, then it learns that there is no point in responding and, thereafter, behaves passively, which is a form of conditioning. This explanation was further developed by Abramson *et al.* (see below).

Reinforcement – Lewinsohn (1974) suggested that depressed people do very little and are socially withdrawn. This results in a lack of reinforcement and so they become trapped in a cycle of social withdrawal, perpetuating depression. Socially unskilled individuals are more likely to be socially withdrawn and this explains why they may be more prone to depression (see next page on socio-cultural explanations).

Research evidence

Hiroto and Seligman (1974) showed that college students who were exposed to uncontrollable aversive events (learned helplessness) were more likely to later fail on cognitive tasks.

Jacobson *et al.* (1996) found that reinforcement could be used to successfully treat depression (see page 110).

Cognitive explanations focus on the way a person *thinks* about their life; it is this style of thinking that creates depression.

Cognitive explanations

Attributional style – Abramson *et al.* (1978) applied the concept of learned helplessness to mental disorder, suggesting that depressed individuals have an attributional style where they tend to attribute failure to themselves (internal) rather than to external factors. Such individuals see these attributions as unchanging (stable) and as global, rather than specific. Abramson *et al.* (1989) extended their theory of attributional style into a broader **hopelessness theory**. Negative attributional style does not necessarily result in depression, for example, a person may just avoid traumatic experiences. But in cases where a person has a negative attributional style *and* believes that bad things are likely to happen (i.e. is hopeless), then depression is likely.

The cognitive triad – Beck (1967) suggested that depressed individuals hold negative thoughts about three things:

• **Themselves** – they regard themselves as helpless, worthless, and inadequate.
• **The world** – it is seen to contain obstacles that cannot be handled.
• **The future** – one's worthlessness prevents any improvements.

Such negative cognitions are self-defeating and lead to depression.

Research evidence

Seligman (1974) found that students who made stable, global attributions stayed depressed for longer after exams. However, Ford and Neale (1985) found that depressed students didn't underestimate their sense of control, contrary to the predictions of the theory.

Support for Beck comes from Bates *et al.* (1999), who found that depressed participants who were given negative automatic thought-like statements became more and more depressed.

Evaluation

• The success of **cognitive-behavioural therapies** in treating depression offers support for cognitive explanations (see page 110).
• The fact that there is a link between negative thoughts and depression does not mean that the former **caused** the latter.

Key points from AS

• Attribution theory is discussed in *Revise AS Unit 6.3, page 139.*

Attribution is the process of explaining causes of behaviour. We do not observe traits, we observe behaviours and infer personal attributes.

Beck's model has also been used to explain bipolar disorder, see page 166.

Key points from AS

• General evaluations of the cognitive approach to explaining abnormality can be found in *Revise AS Unit 7.1, page 154.*

Psychodynamic explanations

Freud suggested that loss in early life leads to depression later (he called it 'melancholia'). Repressed anger towards the lost person is directed inwards towards the self, reducing self-esteem. If loss is experienced later in adult life, this leads a person to re-experience early loss.

Bowlby (1973) suggested that separation from a primary caregiver in early childhood may increase susceptibility to depression later.

Research evidence

Bifulco *et al.* (1992) studied 249 women who, under the age of 17, had experienced maternal loss either through separation (for more than a year) or death. These women were twice as likely to suffer from depressive or anxiety disorders as adults, and this was particularly true where death occurred before the age of 6.

Barnes and Prosen (1985) found that men whose fathers had died during their childhood scored higher on a depression scale than 'normal' men.

Spitz (1945) used the term **anaclitic depression** to describe the severe and progressive depression found in institutionalised infants, resulting from a loss of attachments.

Evaluation

- The evidence is **inconsistent**, for example, Paykel (1981) reviewed studies and found that half weren't supportive of early loss as an explanation.

Socio-cultural explanations

Life events have been associated with depression, acting as stressors. Ohrenwend *et al.* (1986) found that depressed patients typically experienced higher levels of negative life events than normal in the year before a depressive episode.

Social networks – People with little social support are more likely to become depressed and also remain depressed. This is also related to having social skills; some people lack interpersonal skills and, therefore, find it difficult to maintain friendships, which makes it more likely that they will become depressed.

Research evidence

Kendler *et al.* (1995) found that the highest levels of depression were in women who were exposed to recent negative life events (such as an assault or serious marital problems) *and* were most genetically at risk for depression (i.e. the identical twin of a woman diagnosed with depression). This supports the **diathesis-stress model**.

Davila *et al.* (1995) found that adolescents with poor interpersonal problem-solving skills were more likely to become depressed, which supports the view that such characteristics are a cause of depression.

Brown and Harris (1978) studied depressed women in London and found that key factors were long-term relationship difficulties and being at home looking after children, i.e. life events and social factors.

Evaluation

- Poor social skills/reduced social circle could be a **cause or effect** of depression. Even if it is a cause, the resulting effect would be a downward spiral.

Key points from AS

- Bowlby's views on separation are discussed in *Revise AS Unit 3.1, page 53*.

Key points from AS

- General evaluations of the psychodynamic approach to explaining abnormality can be found in *Revise AS Unit 7.1, page 153*.

Socio-cultural explanations explain depression in terms of social and cultural factors, such as the sufferers' immediate family or their wider social circle.

The **life events** approach fits the **diathesis-stress model** where an individual has a vulnerability to depression, which is triggered by stressful life events.

Practice essay 10.2

Discuss biological explanations of depression. *(25 marks)*

10.3 Treatments for depression

After studying this section you should be able to describe and evaluate:

- *biological therapies for depression, including their evaluation in terms of appropriateness and effectiveness*
- *psychological therapies for depression, for example, behavioural, psychodynamic and cognitive-behavioural, including their evaluation in terms of appropriateness and effectiveness.*

LEARNING SUMMARY

Biological therapies for depression

AQA A ▶ U4
AQA B ▶ U3

Chemotherapy: drugs

Anti-depressant drugs (stimulants), such as Prozac, promote activity of noradrenaline and serotonin, which leads to increased arousal but can be affected by rebound (depression after initial euphoria).

- **Tricyclics** increase activity of noradrenaline and serotonin by blocking their re-uptake. When a neuron fires, the neurotransmitters are released into the synapse; they are then re-absorbed by the neuron, preventing further action. By blocking re-uptake the neurotransmitter levels are increased.
- **SSRIs (selective serotonin re-uptake inhibitors)** block mainly serotonin.
- **Selective noradrenaline re-uptake inhibitors** are also now available.

Appropriateness and effectiveness

- The fact that effectiveness **varies considerably between individuals** detracts from its power as a therapy. For example, Spiegel (1989) found that only 65% of depressed patients improved using tricyclics.
- Anti-depressants have been found to be **more effective than placebos**. For example, Furukawa *et al.* (2003) reviewed 35 studies comparing low dosage tricyclics with **placebos**, and found a significant beneficial effect for tricyclics.
- However, **placebo effects** are significant, which suggests that some of the effects of anti-depressants are psychological rather than biological.
- Anti-depressants have been linked to **suicidal and homicidal behaviour**, leading to several high-profile court cases against drug companies.

Electroconvulsive therapy (ECT)

Appropriateness and effectiveness

- ECT appears to be **successful for cases of severe depression**. Janicak *et al.* (1985) found that 80% of all severely depressed patients respond well to ECT, compared with 64% recovery when given drug therapy.
- However, Sackheim *et al.* (2001) found that 84% of patients **relapsed within 6 months**. Even when ECT is used in conjunction with anti-depressants, the relapse rate was relatively high (39%).

Light therapy

Light therapy is used for treating seasonal affective disorder (SAD). It uses very bright, full-spectrum lights, often at a particular time of day. It is often used in addition to drug therapy.

Appropriateness and effectiveness

- Tuunainen *et al.* (2004) reviewed a number of studies, which showed that high quality light therapy had a significant effect on SAD as compared to drugs.

Key points from AS

- For a diagram of a neuron synapse (the gap between two neurons) see *Revise AS Unit 5.3, page 112*.

Key points from AS

- General criticisms of drug therapies are given in *Revise AS Unit 7.2, page 156*.

Placebos are substances that have no pharmacological effects but the person taking them thinks they are the real thing. This means you can separate the psychological from the physical effects of being given a drug treatment.

Key points from AS

- ECT is described in *Revise AS Unit 7.2, page 157*.

On average, chronically depressed patients recover spontaneously after about three months. About 10% of patients remain depressed. Drug Therapies have proved useful.

Psychological therapies for depression

Behavioural therapy

Behavioural action (BA) – Jacobson *et al.* (1996) based a therapy on the behavioural view that reinforcement was the key; if you teach patients to elicit higher rates of reinforcement, their depression will lift (as Lewinsohn had suggested, see page 107). Jacobsen *et al.* claimed that cognitive methods are inefficient, whereas BA just focuses on the consequences of behaviour.

Social skills training – Patients are taught better social skills through reward and modelling.

Appropriateness and effectiveness

- Gortner *et al.* (1998) compared CBT and BA and found no significant differences even 24 months after treatment, i.e. the simpler method was just as efficient. However, in both treatment groups the level of success was 50% after treatment and 25% after two years.

Psychodynamic therapy

According to the psychodynamic view, depression has its origins in childhood. Therefore, unless these roots are explored and dealt with, the symptoms will reappear. Therefore, psychoanalysis is the only effective cure. **Short-term psychodynamic psychotherapies (STPP)** have been developed to make this process quicker.

Appropriateness and effectiveness

- The success of other therapies for treating depression suggests that it is **not always necessary to have insight** into the causes of the disorder.
- Henken *et al.* (2007) found that **family therapy** is an effective intervention in treating people of any age with depression.

Cognitive-behavioural therapy (CBT)

Beck (1976) used his concept of the cognitive triad to propose a treatment for depression; the therapist identifies the patient's self-defeating assumptions and substitutes more adaptive ones.

Rational-emotional behaviour therapy (REBT) – Ellis (1962) developed his own therapy, which also focused on changing irrational beliefs. Ellis suggested an ABC model: (A) Activating event leads to (B) Beliefs about the activating event, which leads to (C) Consequences. A therapist is directive and aggressive and challenges beliefs through **disputing**, e.g. asking the patient to justify the logic of the beliefs (logical disputing) or to consider the evidence for irrational beliefs (empirical disputing).

Appropriateness and effectiveness

- CBT can be **combined with drug therapy** to increase effectiveness. Keller *et al.* (2000) found a 73% response rate for combined therapy compared to 48% for one therapy alone.
- CBT is a **relatively short form** of psychotherapy, taking about 16 weeks, and the strategies can be applied to future situations.

Key points from AS

- General criticisms of psychological therapies are given in *Revise AS Unit 7.1, pages 158–160.*

Your evaluation of treatments can include information about the reliability and validity of the diagnoses. If the original diagnosis lacks reliability/validity then the treatment may not be effective.

Key points from AS

- Psychoanalysis and CBT are described and evaluated in *Revise AS Unit 7.1, pages 158 and 160 respectively.*

Cognitive explanations focus on thinking; cognitive-behavioural treatments are a combination of cognitive and behavioural approaches.

The American Psychiatric Association (2000) rated CBT as one of the best approaches to treating depression.

Practice essays 10.3

(a) Outline the clinical characteristics of depression. *(5 marks)*

(b) Describe **one** behavioural therapy for depression. *(10 marks)*

(c) Describe and evaluate **one** psychodynamic therapy for depression. *(10 marks)*

Chapter 11

Anxiety disorder – phobias

11.1 Classification and diagnosis of phobic disorders

After studying this section you should be able to describe and evaluate:

*Note that AQA A students only need to study **one** mental disorder, i.e. they only need to study chapter 9 or 10 or 11 or 12.*

- *clinical characteristics of phobic disorders*
- *issues surrounding the classification and diagnosis of phobic disorders, including reliability and validity.*

Clinical characteristics of phobic disorders

AQA A ▷ U4

About 50% of all clinically-diagnosed phobics are suffering from agoraphobia with panic disorder. However, many people do not seek treatment, which may disguise the frequency of specific and social phobias. The BBC website on phobias suggests a rate of about 1 in 10 people for simple phobias and about 2–3 in 100 for social phobias and agoraphobia.

All categories of phobias are twice as common in women as men.

Specific phobias generally have little impact on overall quality of life.

A phobic disorder involves extreme, persistent, and irrational fear, which is coupled with a lack of control and is strongly out of proportion with possible danger. DSM-IV (see page 96) includes various phobias within the category of anxiety disorders:

Agoraphobia (with or without panic disorders) is the fear of open spaces. When it is accompanied by panic disorder, the panic disorder usually starts first; fear of having another attack makes the individual feel insecure about being in public.

Social phobias are a fear of, for example, talking or eating in public; extreme concern about your own behaviour and the reactions of others.

Specific or simple phobias are fears of specific things, such as zoophobias (fear of animals), fear of natural environments (e.g. water, heights, the dark), fear of blood or injury, and fear of dangerous situations (e.g. being trapped).

The common diagnostic characteristics of phobias are as follows:

- Exposure to the feared stimulus nearly always produces a high level of anxiety.
- The anxiety experienced is out of proportion to the actual situation.
- The sufferer is aware of the extremity of their reaction.
- The feared situations are either avoided or responded to with great anxiety.
- Significant interference with life, or marked distress.

Issues surrounding the classification and diagnosis of phobic disorders

General issues related to reliability and validity of classification and diagnosis are discussed on pages 96–97.

Reliability

Inter-rater reliability – Skre *et al.* (1991) found high inter-rater reliability for social phobias – a kappa statistic of +.72 for three raters assessing 54 interviews.

Test–retest reliability – Kendler *et al.* (1999) assessed the patients on separate occasions, 8 years apart, concluding that single personal interviews lack reliability.

Fear and anxiety are adaptive responses. A fear becomes a phobia when it interferes with normal functioning.

Validity

Descriptive validity is poor, for example, Eysenck (1997) reported that up to two-thirds of patients with an anxiety disorder have also been diagnosed with one or more additional anxiety disorders.

Practice essays 11.1

(a) Outline the clinical characteristics of phobic disorders, with reference to examples.

(9 marks)

(b) To what extent are diagnoses of phobic disorders reliable and/or valid?

(16 marks)

11.2 Explanations of phobic disorders

After studying this section you should be able to describe and evaluate:

- *biological explanations of phobic disorders, for example, genetics and biochemistry*
- *psychological explanations of phobic disorders, for example, behavioural, cognitive, psychodynamic and socio-cultural.*

LEARNING SUMMARY

Biological explanations of phobic disorders

AQA A   U4

Gene mapping involves comparing the genetic material from families who have phobic disorders with samples from families without such disorders to identify common factors.

Genetic explanations

Individuals may inherit a gene or genes that cause their phobic disorder. Research suggests that it is not likely to be one gene (see gene mapping studies) and that such genes predispose individuals to develop the disorder, rather than being a certainty (identical MZ twins do not show 100% concordance).

Research evidence

Gene mapping – There is some evidence of a link between anxiety disorders and a gene related to serotonin (Lesch *et al.* (1996)).

Twin studies – Torgersen (1983) found 31% concordance for panic disorder with agoraphobia in MZ twins versus zero concordance in DZ twins, although none of them shared the same phobias. However, Kendler *et al.* (1992) found a lower concordance rate between MZ twins for agoraphobia than in DZ twins.

Family studies – Solyom *et al.* (1974) found that 45% of phobic patients studied had a family history of the disorder compared with 17% of 'normal' controls. Ost (1989), in a study on blood phobics, found that 64% had at least one close relative who also suffered from blood phobia.

If there is a genetic predisposition for phobic disorders, this does not mean they will inevitably develop. The **diathesis-stress model** suggests that such conditions only occur when triggered by life experiences (stressors).

Evaluation

- Individuals who are related may acquire phobias through **imitation** rather than genetic inheritance.
- Kendler *et al.* (1992) concluded that specific **phobias have a small genetic component** whereas agoraphobia appears to be more related to genetic vulnerability. They provided heritability estimates for different phobias of 67% for agoraphobia, 59% for blood/injury, 51% for social, and 47% for animal phobias.
- Phobias may involve genetic factors but require additional exposure to negative environmental influences (the **diathesis-stress model**).
- The evidence for a genetic basis for phobic disorders is **poor in relation to other disorders, such as schizophrenia** (see page 98).

If phobic disorders are genetic then the genes may cause neuroanatomical and/or biochemical differences.

Biochemical explanations

GABA – People who develop phobias tend to have higher levels of physiological arousal than normal, which means they are especially sensitive to their environment. This may be related to a dysfunction of GABA, which is normally produced to reduce anxiety levels. GABA reduces activity in the nervous system by slowing down transmission between nerve cells and, thus, makes a person feel calmer.

Key points from AS

- Both GABA and BZs are discussed in *Revise AS Unit 5.2, page 109.*

Biogenic amines – Another explanation is that neurotransmitters in the amine group (**noradrenalin, serotonin** and **dopamine**) may play a role in phobias. Van der Wee *et al.* (2008) found evidence that dopamine and serotonin levels may be abnormal in people with social phobias.

Evaluation

- The **success of chemotherapies** suggests that GABA and/or biogenic amines may be involved in phobic disorders (see page 116).
- However, it is likely that the success of chemotherapies is due to the fact that they reduce the anxiety component of the phobia and, therefore, enable a sufferer to cope. They **do not target the actual disorder**, which suggests that biochemical factors are not *causes* of phobic disorders.

Evolutionary explanations: biological preparedness

It is important to remember that evolutionary explanations for mental disorders are based on the assumption that such disorders are inherited, or at least a predisposition for the disorder is inherited.

Seligman (1971) described the concept of **biological preparedness**: that animals have an innate predisposition to develop certain 'ancient' fears because this would be an adaptive behaviour – enhancing their survival and thus reproductive success. In particular, animals would be biologically predisposed to acquire certain conditioned responses more easily than others, e.g. a fear of snakes or heights (see also page 74). It would be advantageous to have a predisposition to *learn* fears rather than inheriting a fixed fear of certain classes of object.

Note that this explanation suggests that phobias have to be learned; it is the predisposition for such learning that is inherited.

Research evidence

The evolutionary approach can be criticised for being **determinist** and not accounting for individual and cultural differences.

Garcia and Koelling (1966) demonstrated that rats had a predisposition to learn quickly to avoid substances that made them feel sick.

Bennett-Levy and Marteau (1984) found that fear was highly correlated with certain aspects of an animal's appearance – the more the animal's appearance was different to human form, the more the animal was feared. This suggests some innate preparedness.

Mineka *et al.* (1984) found that rhesus monkeys developed a fear of snakes if they saw another monkey showing fear to a snake – social learning. However, fears were not learned so rapidly if the monkey was seen behaving fearfully towards a flower. This supports the view that ancient fears are learned more readily.

DeSilva (1988) found that 88 phobic patients studied in Sri Lanka tended to exhibit fears that were biologically-based, demonstrating the universal (and, thus, innate) nature of such fears.

Evaluation

Genome lag could explain why innate fears tend not to relate to modern dangers – this is the concept that it takes time for our genes to evolve and better fit the current environment.

- This explains why people are **less likely to develop fears of modern day items** that are dangerous – such as electricity or cars. The reason is we are only biologically prepared to develop 'ancient' fears.
- This explanation can't account for **fears of harmless situations** or things, such as slugs. Though a further explanation may explain this – animals have evolved fears to things that are disgusting, which might also be adaptive.

Psychological explanations of phobic disorders

AQA A ▶ U4

Classical and operant conditioning are explained on page 72.

Behavioural explanations

Classical conditioning – Watson and Rayner (1920) conditioned 'Little Albert' to fear white furry objects by pairing a loud noise with a white furry object. It is likely that most phobias are learned through the association of trauma with some neutral stimulus. In addition, the fact that phobics avoid their feared situation means the response is never extinguished.

Operant conditioning – Mowrer (1947) proposed that the first stage involves classical conditioning followed by operant conditioning (**two-process theory**), because avoidance of the phobic stimulus reduces fear and is, therefore, reinforcing.

Social learning theory – Fears may be learned through imitation. Bandura and Rosenthal (1966) arranged for participants to watch someone else ostensibly receiving a painful electric shock every time a buzzer sounded. Later, the participants showed a fear response when they heard the buzzer. The experiment by Mineka *et al.* (see previous page) also demonstrated imitation.

Evaluation

- Learning explanations can be **combined with biological ones** – either in terms of genetic vulnerability (diathesis-stress model) or biological preparedness (we acquire ancient and adaptive fears more readily, see previous page).
- **Not everyone who is exposed to conditioning develops phobias.** For example, DiNardo *et al.* (1988) found that as many people without dog phobias as with reported negative experiences with dogs. However, many people do attribute their phobias to a specific incident (Sue *et al.*, 1994).
- **Stimulus generalisation** (see page 73) could be used to explain how a negative experience with one object has transferred to a fear of something else.
- The **success of behavioural therapies** in treating phobias supports their value as explanations (see page 116).

Key points from AS

- General evaluations of the behaviourist approach to explaining abnormality can be found in *Revise AS Unit 7.1, page 153.*

Cognitive explanations are focused on maladaptive ways of thinking.

Cognitive explanations

Phobias may be the result of irrational thoughts. For example, the sensation of crowding in a lift may develop into a cognition that lifts are associated with suffocation. This then turns into a fear of lifts, which may be generalised to other situations. So, it is the persons' irrational thoughts in response to an initial fearful situation that trigger off a phobia. Beck *et al.* (1985) suggested that people with phobias are most concerned with their fear of fear rather than fear of actual objects.

Research evidence

Eysenck (1997) reports research on biological challenges (e.g. breathing a mixture of carbon dioxide and oxygen). This often provokes a panic attack in patients suffering from panic disorder with agoraphobia, but rarely in normal controls. Panic-attack patients may differ in the way they *interpret* their bodily symptoms.

Williams *et al.* (1997) studied patients with agoraphobia and found that they were more concerned with their feelings of anxiety rather than their actual safety, which indicates that it is the patients' thoughts that are the problem.

Evaluation

- This approach can explain why **some people are more susceptible** than others to phobias – because of the tendency to think in irrational ways.
- The **success of cognitive-behavioural therapies** in treating phobias supports their value as explanations (see page 117).

Key points from AS

- General evaluations of the cognitive approach to explaining abnormality can be found in *Revise AS Unit 7.1, page 154.*

Psychodynamic explanations

Freud (1909) suggested that phobias arise as an ego defence for dealing with repressed anxieties. The anxiety is displaced onto the phobic object (another person or object), which symbolises the initial conflict. If the conflict is resolved the phobia will disappear.

Key points from AS

• Bowlby's views on separation are discussed in *Revise AS Unit 3.1, page 53.*

Bowlby (1973) suggested that agoraphobia might be linked to a fear of losing someone important. He suggested that the origins of phobias lie in early separation anxiety and overprotective parents.

Research evidence

Freud (1909) used the case study of 'Little Hans' to support his explanation of phobias. Hans developed a fear of horses and this was explained as a representation of the boy's unconscious fear of his father, because the horses' bridle represented his father's moustache. Hans' fear specifically was of being bitten by white horses, which was linked to an occasion when he heard a child being told not to touch a white horse because it might bite. Hans was actually scared that his mother would leave him because he asked his mother to touch his penis but she told him off for this. Therefore, not touching something was associated with the white horse. Finally, Hans was further fearful of horses pulling laden carts because the horse might fall over and die. This was linked to his fears related to pregnancy (like a laden cart) and his secret wish that his younger sister would die, a wish that made him feel guilty.

Gerslman *et al.* (1990) suggested, on the basis of a literature review, that phobics (especially social phobics and agoraphobics) had lower than normal parental affection and more parental control or over-protection. This might increase their levels of anxiety.

Key points from AS

• General evaluations of the psychodynamic approach to explaining abnormality can be found in *Revise AS Unit 7.1, page 153.*

Evaluation

- Hans might have developed his fear through **classical conditioning**.
- A case study of one child is **not reliable evidence**.
- In addition, the case study and interviews with Little Hans were recorded by his father so the data may have been affected by **leading questions and subjective interpretations**.
- Such data is **correlational** and doesn't demonstrate a causal link.

Socio-cultural explanations explain phobic disorders in terms of social and cultural factors such as the sufferers' immediate family or their wider social circle.

Socio-cultural explanations

Cultural attitudes might be linked to incidence of phobias. For example, Whiting (1966) considered the prevalence of phobias in other cultures and concluded that they were more common in societies that had stricter upbringings. This might also be related to psychodynamic explanations as stricter upbringings might lead to greater repression.

Research evidence

Cultural influences – Kirmayer (1991) reports a social phobia that is common in Japan but not elsewhere – *taijin kyofusho* is the fear of offending or harming others through one's own awkward social behaviour.

Social influences – Kleiner and Marshall (1987) report that 84% of agoraphobics had experienced family problems in the months before they had their first panic attack. This further supports the diathesis-stress model.

Practice essay 11.2

Discuss biological explanations of phobic disorders. *(25 marks)*

11.3 Treatments for phobic disorders

After studying this section you should be able to describe and evaluate:

- *biological therapies for phobic disorders, including their evaluation in terms of appropriateness and effectiveness*
- *psychological therapies for phobic disorders, for example, behavioural, psychodynamic and cognitive-behavioural therapies, including their evaluation in terms of appropriateness and effectiveness.*

LEARNING SUMMARY

Biological therapies for phobic disorders

AQA A ▸ U4

Key points from AS

- Anxiolytic drugs were reviewed in studies of stress for AS level, see *Revise AS Unit 5.2, page 109*.

Key points from AS

- General criticisms of drug therapies are given in *Revise AS Unit 7.2, page 156*.

Your evaluation of treatments can include information about the reliability and validity of the diagnoses. If the original diagnosis lacks reliability/ validity then the treatment may not be effective.

Chemotherapy: drugs

- **Anxiolytic drugs** are drugs that reduce anxiety, and may be used to treat phobias to reduce the accompanying anxiety. For example, **benzodiazepines** (BZs e.g. *Valium* and *Librium*) enhance the effect of the neurotransmitter **GABA**, and also reduce **serotonin** activity. The common side-effects of BZs are sleepiness and dependence.
- **Anti-depressants** are also used to treat phobias. For example, **SSRIs** (selective serotonin re-uptake indicators, see page 109) are used, which reduce levels of serotonin. **MAIOs** (monoamine oxidase inhibitor) are also used. These are an older class of anti-depressants, which increase serotonin and noradrenaline.

Evaluation in terms of appropriateness and effectiveness

- Drugs deal effectively with the symptoms of anxiety, for example, Kelly *et al.* found an **88% improvement after one year** of phobic patients being treated with anti-depressants.
- Phobias tend to be treated with psychological rather than biological techniques. However, drugs are **useful in reducing the anxiety** so a person is better able to benefit from psychotherapy. For example, Urukawa *et al.* (2007) reviewed 23 studies and found that combined therapies (anti-depressants and CBT) were more effective in the treatment of panic disorder with or without agoraphobia than either treatment alone.

Psychological therapies for phobic disorders

AQA A ▸ U4

Key points from AS

- General criticisms of psychological therapies are given in *Revise AS Unit 7.1, pages 158–160*.

Key points from AS

- SD was described and evaluated as part of your AS course, see *Revise AS Unit 7.2, pages 159*.

ERP (exposure with response prevention) was developed for obsessive compulsive disorder, but is also used with phobias. See page 124.

Behavioural therapy: Systematic de-sensitisation (SD)

SD is mainly used in the treatment of phobias (rather than other forms of mental disorder). It was devised by Wolpe (1958) and is a process in which a patient learns to pair the feared thing with relaxation rather than anxiety.

The basic steps are (1) teaching relaxation, (2) developing a de-sensitisation hierarchy, (3) visualising fearful scenes and (4) progressing through the hierarchy. The whole process typically takes 3–4 weeks but can be completed more quickly.

This is an example of classical conditioning because the patient is learning to associate the progressively more fearful stimulus with relaxation. It is characterised as **'counter-conditioning'** because the patient is replacing previously learned associations – between object and fear – with a new CS and CR (object and relaxation). **Reciprocal inhibition** also takes place because relaxation and fear are incompatible responses.

SD may involve simply imagining the feared stimulus (**covert desensitisation**) or may involve dealing with the feared object (**in vivo desensitisation**). An alternative is to skip the hierarchy and the relaxation and just experience being with the feared stimulus. This is called **flooding**.

Evaluation in terms of appropriateness and effectiveness

- McGrath *et al.* (1990) found that 75% of patients with phobias recover after a course of SD. However, **people may recover spontaneously** from phobias so the recovery rate would be almost as good with no treatment.
- **In vivo desensitisation tends to be more effective** than covert desensitisation.
- Marks (1973) suggests that SD works just because of exposure to the feared stimulus. Therefore, the success of SD **may have nothing to do with relaxation**.
- Klein *et al.* (1983) compared SD with supportive psychotherapy for patients with a social phobia (agoraphobia) or with a specific phobia. They found no difference in effectiveness (those receiving supportive psychotherapy had also done well), suggesting that the 'active ingredient' in SD or CBT may simply be the generation of **hopeful expectancies that their phobia can be overcome**.
- There are **ethical objections** to flooding and even some forms of SD, which may be quite traumatic.

Key points from AS

- Psychoanalysis and CBT are described and evaluated in *Revise AS Unit 7.1, pages 158 and 160 respectively.*

Psychodynamic therapy

The aim of psychoanalytic treatments is to uncover the repressed conflicts that are expressed as phobias, analyse what they mean to the patient, and substitute more realistic understandings of childhood events.

Evaluation in terms of appropriateness and effectiveness

- The case study of Little Hans (see page 115) suggests that **phobias can be 'cured' by dealing with the underlying issues**.
- Knijnik *et al.* (2004) found that a variation of psychoanalysis (**psychodynamic group treatment, or PGT**) was superior to a placebo control group in a 12–week randomised trial.

Cognitive-behavioural therapy (CBT)

REBT has been used with phobias, see page 110.

CBGT (cognitive-behavioural group therapy is CBT within a group setting) – Individuals with phobias follow a programme similar to systematic desensitisation (SD) but engage with group members who provide a safe and supportive environment. Each group member works through their hierarchy of fears, learning to relax through each stage. There is also a cognitive element to CBGT where patients are encouraged to replace the irrational beliefs they hold that lead to anxiety with more realistic and rational beliefs. During the simulation scenarios, group members challenge each other's irrational beliefs, giving the individual the opportunity for cognitive restructuring.

Evaluation in terms of appropriateness and effectiveness

- Beck *et al.* (1994) found CBT to be **more effective than supportive therapy, relaxation and drugs** in the treatment of panic disorder and agoraphobia.
- The **long-term effects** of CBT have also been shown to be superior to other techniques (Clark *et al.*, 1994).

Practice essays 11.3

(a) Outline the clinical characteristics of phobic disorders. *(5 marks)*
(b) Describe **one** behavioural therapy for phobic disorders. *(10 marks)*
(c) Describe and evaluate **one** psychodynamic therapy for phobic disorders.
(10 marks)

Chapter 12

Anxiety disorder – OCD

12.1 Classification and diagnosis of obsessive compulsive disorder

After studying this section you should be able to describe and evaluate:

Note that AQA A students only need to study **one** mental disorder, i.e. they only need to study chapter 9 or 10 or 11 or 12.

- clinical characteristics of obsessive compulsive disorder
- issues surrounding the classification and diagnosis of obsessive compulsive disorder, including reliability and validity.

LEARNING SUMMARY

Clinical characteristics of obsessive compulsive disorder (OCD)

AQA A   U4

In the general population, the prevalence of OCD is 1 to 2%, twice that of schizophrenia or panic disorder.

OCD is considered to be an anxiety disorder, and, therefore, shares some similarities with phobias. Namely, both are associated with high levels of anxiety.

The essential features of OCD are:

- Recurrent obsessions or compulsions present for at least two weeks:
  - **Obsessions** are persistent ideas, thoughts, impulses or images that are classed as inappropriate or forbidden, and which cause intense anxiety.
  - **Compulsions** develop as a means of controlling the obsessional thoughts. These compulsions are repetitive behaviours or thoughts, such as repeated hand-washing. Most OCD patients recognise that their compulsions are unreasonable but cannot control them. This creates further anxiety.
- The obsessions/compulsions are severe enough to be time consuming (i.e. they take more than one hour a day) or cause marked distress or significant impairment.
- The person recognises that the obsessions or compulsions are excessive.
- The obsessions/compulsions are not related to drug abuse or medication.

Issues surrounding the classification and diagnosis of OCD

General issues related to reliability and validity of classification and diagnosis are discussed on pages 96–97.

Tourette's syndrome is characterised by tics – sudden involuntary movements or vocalisations (such as swear words) that are repeated. These tics occur in spasms and may appear many times a day or only occasionally throughout a year. Individuals have some control over the tics but usually feel a compulsion to produce them. If the person tries to hold back the tics, this eventually leads to a strong outburst.

Reliability

Inter-rater reliability is reasonably high, for example, Williams *et al.* (1992) reported a kappa score of .59 (see page 96 for an explanation of a kappa score).

Test–retest reliability – Mannuza *et al.* (1989) reported a kappa score of .91 for a diagnosis of OCD using DSM-III-R (see page 96 for an explanation), based on two independent administrations of a structured interview.

Validity

Descriptive validity – Brown and Barlow (1992) reported high comorbidity (see page 97 for an explanation) with 50% of patients who were diagnosed with OCD also receiving a diagnosis of an additional mood or anxiety disorder. Baer *et al.* (1990) found that 50% of OCD patients also met the criteria for at least one personality disorder. There is also evidence of an overlap with **Tourette's syndrome**. Leckman and Chittenden (1990) found that between 36% and 52% of patients with Tourette's also meet the criteria for OCD. All of this suggests that OCD is not a separate category but perhaps better categorised as OCD spectrum disorders.

Practice essay 12.1

(a) Outline the clinical characteristics of obsessive compulsive disorder, with reference to examples. *(9 marks)*

(b) To what extent are diagnoses of obsessive compulsive disorder reliable and/or valid? *(16 marks)*

12.2 Explanations of obsessive compulsive disorder

After studying this section you should be able to describe and evaluate:

- *biological explanations of obsessive compulsive disorder, for example, genetics and biochemistry*
- *psychological explanations of obsessive compulsive disorder, for example, behavioural, cognitive, psychodynamic and socio-cultural.*

LEARNING SUMMARY

Biological explanations of obsessive compulsive disorder

 AQA A ▸ U4

Genetic explanations

Individuals may inherit a gene or genes that cause their phobic disorder. Research suggests that it is not likely to be one gene (see gene mapping studies) and that such genes predispose individuals to develop the disorder rather than being a certainty (identical MZ twins do not show 100% concordance).

Research evidence

Gene mapping – Karayiorgou *et al.* (1997) found evidence that a gene related to production of **COMT** was more common in OCD sufferers. This enzyme terminates the action of **dopamine** and **noradrenaline**. Dickel *et al.* (2006) found evidence that a **glutamate** transporter gene called **SLC1A1** might be related to OCD (glutamate production is linked to dopamine – see page 99). Both of these possibilities link to biochemical explanations (see below).

Twin studies – Billett *et al.* (1998) reviewed 14 twin studies which found that MZ twins were on average twice more likely to both develop OCD than DZ twins. Rasmussen and Tsuang (1986) reported concordance rates of 53–87% for OCD.

Family studies – Nestadt *et al.* (2000) found that people with a relative who had OCD were five times more likely to develop OCD at some time in their lives than members of the general population.

Evaluation

- The evidence for a genetic basis for OCD is **stronger than for other mental illnesses** such as depression. However, the same genes may be related to other disorders (e.g. Tourette's) and this would explain the comorbidity of such conditions.
- When relatives experience OCD the **actual symptoms may differ**, i.e. they are not obsessed by the same things. It is the predisposition to respond to situations in a certain way rather than the obsessions themselves that are inherited.

Biochemical explanations

OCD has been linked to low levels of the neurotransmitter **serotonin** and high levels of **dopamine**.

Research evidence

Jenicke (1992) reported that anti-depressants which reduced serotonin levels also reduced the symptoms of OCD, whereas anti-depressants which had a less dramatic effect on serotonin levels did not affect OCD. Some research suggests that 'classic' OCD is related to serotonin, whereas tic-related OCD is related to dopamine abnormalities (tic-related types include Tourette's syndrome and also nail-biting and trichotillamania – pulling out hair) (Van Ameringen *et al.*, 2001). Goodman *et al.*, (1992) found that drugs blocking dopamine were effective in treating OCD symptoms in patients who did not respond to SSRIs.

Gene mapping involves comparing the genetic material from families who have OCD with samples from families who don't have the disorder in order to identify common factors.

The **diathesis-stress model** suggests that people inherit a vulnerability (diathesis) to develop depression, but it only occurs when triggered by life experiences (stressors).

If OCD is genetic then the genes may cause neuroanatomical and/or biochemical differences.

Evaluation

- One problem with biochemical explanations is that it is not clear whether abnormalities are a **cause or effect**.
- The **success of drug therapies** supports the role of biochemical factors, for example SSRIs (which increase serotonin levels) have been shown to be effective (see page 123).
- The fact that a large number of OCD patients do not respond to anti-depressants that affect serotonin suggests that **other factors are involved**.
- The fact that anti-psychotics (which affect dopamine levels) can reduce the severity of OCD symptoms points to the involvement of **dopamine as well as serotonin**.

Neuroanatomical explanations

Brain scans indicate differences between OCD patients and normal individuals, in particular the pathway linking the **frontal lobe** (associated with thinking and decision making) to the **basal ganglia** (involved in planning and executing movements). There is also a link between the **orbitofrontal cortex** (OFC, in the frontal lobe) and the **caudate nucleus** (in the basal ganglia).

Research evidence

Baxter *et al.* (1987) used PET scans and found increased glucose metabolic rates in the left orbital gyrus of the frontal lobe in OCD patients, which became normal after patients received drug treatment or behaviour therapy.

Tailarach *et al.* (1973) found that electrical stimulation of parts of the frontal lobe induced stereotypic motions characteristic of OCD compulsions.

Murphy *et al.* (1997) investigated a link between the onset of OCD in childhood and Sydenham's chorea, a disorder associated with streptococcal infections. It may be that the immune response reacts with tissues in the basal ganglia, causing movement disorders and OCD symptoms. Infection-induced OCD has been successfully treated with drugs.

> There are also links between neuroanatomy, biochemistry and the outcome of gene mapping studies (see previous page).

Evaluation

- The role of key areas of the brain is further supported by the **effectiveness of psychosurgery** (see page 123).
- There are **links between this neuroanatomical explanation and the biochemical explanation** of OCD because low levels of serotonin cause the OFC and caudate nucleus to function poorly, and dopamine activity is associated with the basal ganglia. However, brain abnormalities may be a cause or an effect of the abnormal neurotransmitters.

Key points from AS

- General criticisms of the biological approach to explaining abnormality can be found in *Revise AS Unit 7.1, page 151*.

Evolutionary explanations

The adaptive nature of compulsions – It may be that some aspects of OCD behaviour are adaptive and, therefore, humans are predisposed to develop the disorder. For example, ritualistic behaviours often concern hygiene (e.g. repeated hand-washing) and may be adaptive insofar as extra vigilance over cleanliness might promote survival. Polimeni *et al.* (2003) further suggest that other compulsive behaviours – checking, counting, hoarding and requiring precision would all be beneficial to cultures focused on hunting and gathering (as in the **EEA**, see page 20) and would, therefore, be potentially adaptive.

Harm-avoidance strategies – Abed and de Pauw (1998) suggest that OCD is an extreme form of our evolved capacity to represent future scenarios and imagine the consequences of our own thoughts and actions in order to deal with risk situations before they happen.

> One should remember that evolutionary explanations for mental disorders are based on the assumption that such disorders are inherited, or at least a predisposition for the disorder is inherited.

> The evolutionary approach can be criticised for being determinist and not accounting for individual and cultural differences.

Psychological explanations of obsessive compulsive disorder

Behavioural explanations

Mowrer's two-process theory – This can be used to explain OCD (it is also used to explain phobias, see page 114):

- **Classical conditioning** – Some thoughts become associated with an event that creates anxiety and then they take on the associated properties of the event. For example, a mother looks at her baby and thinks 'I could smother this child'; such thoughts create intense anxiety and, in the future, just looking at the child creates intense anxiety.
- **Operant conditioning** – Distress and compulsive behaviours are maintained because the person learns to avoid the anxiety by escaping (e.g. going to wash their hands).

Superstition hypothesis – Skinner (1948) suggested that the chance association of a behaviour with a reinforcer can produce a link between body movements (routines) and superstitious behaviour. The pigeons he used in his experiments sometimes learned unique sequences of body movement because they just happened to be performing them when they were given food.

Research evidence

Carr (1974) demonstrated that compulsive behaviours can reduce anxiety; patients performed their compulsive rituals when activity in the autonomic nervous system (ANS) was high. Arousal of the ANS was reduced after performing the rituals.

Evaluation

- OCD patients are **not always able to identify a traumatic event** that may have triggered the disorder, and several obsessions can be present within one individual or obsessions can change without the occurrence of new traumas.
- The behavioural explanation has led to a successful therapy for OCD patients called **exposure and prevention therapy** (ERP), see page 124.
- The behaviourist approach cannot explain the development of **intrusive thoughts**, which are typical of OCD.

Cognitive explanations

OCD patients suffer from impaired information-processing (i.e. faulty thinking). People often have unwanted or intrusive thoughts (such as being infected by germs or harming someone), which are usually easily dismissed. However, for some people they cannot be ignored. Such people think in terms of rigidly defined categories or believe they should have total control, which are examples of maladaptive or faulty thinking. The thoughts create self-blame, depression and anxiety. Neutralising thoughts or acts reduce the obsessive thoughts and these become compulsive, because each time they are performed they reduce the unwanted thoughts. This makes them harder and harder to resist.

Evaluation

- There is some evidence that OCD patients do have **more intrusive thoughts than normal** people (Clark, 1992).
- There is no evidence to show that faulty thinking is the **cause rather than a consequence** of OCD symptoms.
- Some people have genetically-determined personality characteristics, which may predispose them to developing OCD, **linking cognitive explanations to genetic explanations** (Rachman and Hodges, 1987).

Classical and operant conditioning are explained on page 72.

You can read about Skinner and his pigeons on page 72.

Key points from AS

- General evaluations of the behaviourist approach to explaining abnormality can be found in *Revise AS Unit 7.1, page 153.*

Cognitive explanations are focused on maladaptive ways of thinking.

Key points from AS

- General evaluations of the cognitive approach to explaining abnormality can be found in *Revise AS Unit 7.1, page 154.*

Obsessive behaviours are common within 'normal' personalities and children often engage in behaviours that are obsessive-compulsive, such as avoiding the cracks in the pavement.

Psychodynamic explanations

Obsessive behaviour is linked to fixations in the anal stage of development. Freud suggested that children who experience conflicts during the anal phase of development (18 months to 3 years) may develop anal personality traits, i.e. characteristics related to 'control', such as orderliness, stubbornness, as well as an interest in collecting, possessing, and retaining objects. OCD may be an exaggeration of this personality type.

Unacceptable impulses dealt with by ego defences – Freud (1949) proposed that OCD develops when the id produces unacceptable impulses, which create anxiety for the ego and thus are dealt with by ego defences. The three most common ego defences for OCD are:

- **Isolation** – The ego isolates itself from the unacceptable impulses, but occasionally they intrude as obsessional thoughts.
- **Undoing** takes over when obsessional thoughts intrude. The ego deals with the anxiety by producing compulsive acts that symbolically undo the unacceptable impulses originating from the id. For example, compulsive hand-washing is a symbolical undoing.
- **Reaction formation** – Behaviours are performed that are opposite to the unacceptable impulses as a means of reducing anxiety, for example, being exceptionally kind when experiencing very aggressive impulses.

Feelings of inferiority – Adler (1931) produced a different psychodynamic explanation for OCD, which suggests that OCD develops because of feelings of inferiority or incompetence. Obsessions such as excessive cleansing allow the individual to develop mastery in some areas of life. Therefore, the treatment derived from this approach focuses on building confidence.

Evaluation

Key points from AS

- General evaluations of the psychodynamic approach to explaining abnormality can be found in *Revise AS Unit 7.1, page 153*.

- There is no evidence that people with **obsessive personality style** are any more likely to develop OCD (Peterson, 1992).
- Psychoanalysis (the therapy related to Freud's psychodynamic theory) may actually have a **negative effect** on OCD recovery, which does not support the Freudian explanation.

Socio-cultural explanations

Socio-cultural explanations explain schizophrenia in terms of social and cultural factors such as the sufferers' immediate family or their wider social circle.

Cultural factors play a significant role in OCD, but only in terms of the symptoms expressed rather than the core features of the disorder. Palanti (2008) compared prevalence rates across different national groups and found surprising consistency. Palanti also found that the symptoms take on the characteristics of the patient's culture, for example there was a correlation between compulsive washing and religious rituals among Egyptian Muslims. Fontenelle *et al.* (2004) found that aggressive and religious obsessions were typical of Brazilian and Middle Eastern samples.

Evaluation

Socio-cultural evidence emphasises the role of biological factors in the understanding of OCD because it seems to be **unaffected by different cultural practices**.

Practice essay 12.2

Discuss biological explanations of obsessive compulsive disorder.   *(25 marks)*

12.3 Treatments for obsessive compulsive disorder

After studying this section you should be able to describe and evaluate:

- *biological therapies for obsessive compulsive disorder, including their evaluation in terms of appropriateness and effectiveness*
- *psychological therapies for obsessive compulsive disorder, for example, behavioural, psychodynamic and cognitive-behavioural, including their evaluation in terms of appropriateness and effectiveness.*

LEARNING SUMMARY

Biological therapies for obsessive compulsive disorder

AQA A   U4

Key points from AS

- General criticisms of drug therapies are given in *Revise AS Unit 7.2, page 156.*

Placebos are substances that have no pharmacological effects but the person taking them thinks they are the real thing. This means you can separate the psychological from the physical effects of being given a drug treatment.

The reason for conducting a **cingulotomy** is that the one suspected cause of OCD is abnormalities in the brain, focused on the OFC and the caudate nucleus, which communicate via the cingulate gyrus.

Chemotherapy: drugs

Anti-depressant drugs that promote the activity of serotonin, such as **SSRIs** (selective serotonin re-uptake inhibitors) are used to treat OCD. (See more on anti-depressants on page 109.)

Anxiolytic drugs are drugs that reduce anxiety, and may be used to treat OCD. (See further details on page 116.)

Anti-psychotic drugs reduce levels of dopamine and have also been found to be effective with OCD patients. (See further details on page 102.)

Evaluation in terms of appropriateness and effectiveness

- SSRIs have been **shown to be effective.** For example, Soomro *et al.* (2008) reviewed 13 studies and found that people receiving SSRIs were twice as likely as those receiving a placebo to experience a reduction in clinical symptoms.
- Drug treatments **do not cure OCD** – Maina *et al.* (2001) report that patients relapse within a few weeks if their medication is stopped.

Psychosurgery

Psychosurgery involves either the removal of sections of the brain, or lesions (cuts) are made so that areas of the brain become 'functionally' removed. In extreme cases this method is used to treat OCD patients i.e. where the patient is incapacitated by the disorder. A **bilateral cingulotomy** is performed where the **cingulate gyrus** is functionally removed. Stereotactic devices and precise brain scanning techniques are used to locate the exact area of the brain to be altered.

Evaluation in terms of appropriateness and effectiveness

- It is an irreversible operation and even with refined modern techniques there may be **highly undesirable side effects.** In the 1950s and 60s some amygdalotomies resulted in patients who were confused, lacking in motivation, and unable to work (Eysenck and Eysenck, 1989).
- Cosgrove *et al.* (1996) report **successful treatment** of patients with depressive or anxiety disorders using cingulotomies. These patients had not benefited from all other available therapies. In contrast, Dougerty *et al.* (2002) studied 44 OCD patients who had been unresponsive to other treatments. Only 32% improved after a cingulomtomy and a further 14% were slightly improved. The reported side effects included memory deficits and incontinence as well as one case of seizures.
- It may be that psychosurgery simply **reduces motivation** and this explains the apparent reduction in symptoms (Sachdev and Hay, 1995).

Psychological therapies for obsessive compulsive disorder

Key points from AS

• General criticisms of psychological therapies are given in *Revise AS Unit 7.1, pages 158–160*.

Your evaluation of treatments can include information about the reliability and validity of the diagnoses. If the original diagnosis lacks reliability/validity then the treatment may not be effective.

Key points from AS

• Psychoanalysis and CBT are described and evaluated in *Revise AS Unit 7.2, pages 158 and 160*.

Behavioural therapy

Systematic desensitisation (SD) can be used to treat OCD (see page 116). A patient is exposed to an object that normally triggers their obsession and is trained to relax until the anxiety subsides.

Exposure and response prevention (ERP) was developed specifically for OCD. Patients are also exposed to situations that would normally trigger their obsessions but are prevented from producing their usual obsessive response. This is usually done as a form of homework where, for example, a patient with a cleanliness obsession is told that they must not clean the house for a week. This permits the patient to realise that obsessions which previously caused anxiety no longer produce this response, i.e. ERP permits re-learning to take place. OCD develops through reinforcements, but avoidance of anxiety-producing situations then prevents re-learning.

Evaluation in terms of appropriateness and effectiveness

• **Success rates are fairly high**, for example, Albucher *et al.* (1998) reported that 60–90% of OCD patients improve considerably using ERP.
• In addition, **relapse is much less of a problem** than for drug therapies; it is a lasting form of treatment.
• The therapy may produce quite **high levels of anxiety**, which may be traumatic and some patients may not persist. For that reason ERP is often combined with drug therapies.

Psychodynamic therapy

Psychoanalysis was the treatment of choice for OCD for many decades until the arrival of more modern psychotherapies. It is a suitable form of treatment for OCD because patients have some insight into their disorder.

Evaluation in terms of appropriateness and effectiveness

• Insight alone may **not be enough to 'cure' OCD**, given that the evidence suggests a strong biological component.

Cognitive-behavioural therapy (CBT)

Cognitive therapies focus more on changing obsessional *thoughts* whereas behavioural therapies focus on changing compulsive *behaviour*. One example of cognitive therapy is **habituation training** where patients are asked to revisit their obsessional thoughts over and over in order to reduce the fear they create. Some psychologists classify ERP as a form of cognitive therapy because it involves 'exposure', which may include exposure to frightening thoughts as well as to compulsive behaviours.

Evaluation in terms of appropriateness and effectiveness

• Gava *et al.* (2007) compared cognitive and/or behavioural treatments with control groups and found **symptom reduction from all psychotherapies** reviewed.

Practice essays 12.3

(a) Outline the clinical characteristics of obsessive compulsive disorder. *(5 marks)*
(b) Describe **one** behavioural therapy for obsessive compulsive disorder. *(10 marks)*
(c) Describe and evaluate **one** psychodynamic therapy for obsessive compulsive disorder. *(10 marks)*

Chapter 13

Media psychology

13.1 Media influence on social behaviour

After studying this section you should be able to describe and evaluate:

- explanations of media influences on pro- and anti-social behaviour
- the effects of video games and computers on young people.

LEARNING SUMMARY

Explanations of media influences on pro- and anti-social behaviour

AQA A   U4

The term '**media**' refers to any medium of communication – television, films and video most obviously but also books, magazines, plays, songs and so on.

It is easy to confuse **disinhibition** and **desensitisation** – one is concerned with changed social norms, the other is concerned with reduced emotional sensitivity.

Many programmes use **counter-stereotypes** (such as a black female doctor) to try to alter our stereotypical views. However, the deliberate manipulation of stereotypes, for good or bad, is ethically questionable because it presumes that certain stereotypes are preferable.

Imitation – We learn to behave in a pro- or anti-social manner from observational learning and vicarious reinforcement (**social learning theory**). This is especially likely if the observer identifies with the characters. Bandura *et al.*'s research (see page 40) shows that children imitate specific acts and also shows that general levels of aggression increase.

Disinhibition effect – Normally we are inhibited about behaving in certain ways. The media present social norms, which may change our view of what behaviours are common and acceptable.

Desensitisation – Exposure to violence may desensitise us so that we tolerate it more easily in real life. Drabman and Thomas (1975) showed young children a film which was either non-violent but exciting, or violent. The participants were then asked to monitor the behaviour of two younger children via a TV link. When the confederates started hitting each other, the children who had been exposed to the violent film were slower to call for help.

Cognitive priming – Cues in the media may later trigger pro- or anti-social thoughts and feelings. Josephson (1987) showed a violent TV programme involving a walkie-talkie to one group of boys, while another group watched a programme about motocross. Later, during a game of hockey, the most violent boys were those who were given instructions via a walkie-talkie *and* had watched the violent film.

Stereotypes – All media need to communicate a great deal of information in a relatively short time, so they use standard cultural stereotypes such as foreigners playing 'baddies', overweight people being depicted as 'jolly', and wolves as being big and bad. Such stereotypes may or may not reflect reality, and may be positive or negative. Gunter (1986) found that people who watch a lot of television hold more stereotyped beliefs, suggesting that the use of stereotypes on television does have an influence. Alternatively, people (e.g. children) who have a more simplistic cognitive style may prefer to watch more television.

Displacement effect – A media bias would be less harmful if it was sufficiently counterbalanced by experience of the real world. However, people who spend a lot of time watching television or reading books have less time for real interactions. Gerbner and Gross (1976) found that people who watch a lot of television rate the outside world as being more dangerous than it actually is (**deviance amplification**).

Stimulation hypothesis – Television is an ideal medium to present educational information, and is a resource much used by schools. *Sesame Street* provides preschool children with carefully considered material to promote emotional, social and intellectual development. The value of television and all media is related to what you actually watch, read or listen to.

Evaluation

- There are **individual differences**. For example, people who are more aggressive may watch anti-social programmes and/or are more influenced by them.

125

The effects of video games and computers on young people

AQA A   U4

Video games often include scenes of violent behaviour and have adult sexual content. For example, in *Grand Theft Auto* players have to murder police officers or plot against other racial groups (inciting racial hatred). One US court case involved a murderer's claims that he was inspired to shoot 3 police officers because of the game. We read about many criminals who blame violent behaviour on video games, but that doesn't mean it is the true cause.

The difference between video gaming and other media effects is that in the former the player is given a more active role and is often rewarded for committing crimes, thus, such behaviour might be expected to be repeated in everyday life.

The topic of 'computers' is a broad one and can encompass, for example, video gaming (above), educational programmes and content (strong pro-social value) and the use of email and the internet.

The effects of **deindividuation** (which can be pro-social as well as anti-social) are discussed on page 41.

Video games

Satcher (1999) reported on a survey of research by the US government. Research suggests that media violence is linked to aggressive behaviour but that the impact is relatively small compared to other factors, such as home background.

Freedman (2002) reviewed 200 relevant studies and concluded that there was little evidence of a causal link between gaming and violent behaviour.

Grossman (1995) argues that video games are 'murder simulators' and result in training children to use weapons. In addition, such games desensitise children to the act of murder. Grossman points to the fact that the US army uses similar techniques to train shooting responses in their soldiers.

Anderson (2000) testified to the US senate that research has shown consistent effects: increased aggressive behaviour, thoughts and feelings; increased physiological arousal; and decreased pro-social behaviour. Bushman and Anderson (2001) found that boys are more easily influenced than girls. However, there is evidence that individuals who are more prone to be aggressive are more likely to play video games.

Most studies focus on the effects of video games on violence, but it may also affect sexual behaviour and racial prejudice. Yao *et al.* (2006) found that sexually explicit video games prime thinking related to sex, encourage men to think of women as sex objects and increase the likelihood of inappropriate sexual behaviour. Dill and Thill (2007) found that video games portray both genders in a highly stereotyped fashion. Dill *et al.* (2008) found that men exposed to sex-typed video games were more tolerant of sexual harassment. Burgess *et al.* (2007) reported examples of racial stereotypes in video games and linked this to racist thinking.

Computers

A main concern with internet usage (**computer mediated communication** or **CMC**) is the formation of relationships over the internet. There are several issues:

- **Deception** – People can take on a false persona and this may allow them to target vulnerable individuals.
- **Deindividuation** leads to disinhibition – People can behave in ways that are atypical of them because their behaviour is usually governed more by social norms. This may increase anti-social behaviour. However, the **SIDE model** (social identity model of deindividuation) suggests that loss of personal identity is replaced by social identity, which means stronger social relationships are developed in such circumstances.
- **Lack of face-to-face (F2F) contact** means there are reduced cues leading to conversations in a social vacuum (Culnan and Markus, 1987). However, people have always formed relationships in non-F2F situations, such as penpals writing letters to each other.

On the other hand, internet relationships are good for people who are shy or who live in rural areas, who lack time and/or have physical handicaps. Young (1999) described the ACE model of CMC as Anonymity, Convenience and Escape.

Practice essays 13.1

(a) Describe **one** study related to the effects of video games on young people and evaluate the research methods used. *(10 marks)*

(b) Discuss explanations of media influences on pro- and anti-social behaviour. *(15 marks)*

13.2 Persuasion, attitude and change

After studying this section you should be able to describe and evaluate:

- *persuasion and attitude change, including Hovland-Yale and Elaboration Likelihood models*
- *the influence of attitudes on decision making, including roles of cognitive consistency/dissonance and self-perception*
- *explanations for the effectiveness of television in persuasion.*

LEARNING SUMMARY

Persuasion and attitude change

AQA A   U4

An **attitude** is a liking or disliking of an object based on cognitions about the object. It leads to a readiness to behave in a certain way.

The Hovland-Yale model is sometimes called the Yale Model of Communication after Yale University in the US, where the early research was conducted.

Key points from AS

- The topic of attitudes is considered in *Revise AS Unit 6.3, page 142.*

People resist attitude change because attitudes are a key element of one's personality. Attitudes can be changed through experience (learning), persuasion or brainwashing. Persuasive communications aim to induce a person to adopt a particular set of values and are commonly used, for example, in advertising and politics.

Hovland-Yale model

Hovland *et al.* (1953) identified key features to consider in relation to persuasive messages:

- The communicator or **source**, e.g. expertise, trustworthiness, likeability, status.
- The communication or **message**, e.g. order of arguments, form of conclusion.
- The **audience**, e.g. initial position, intelligence, self-esteem, personality.

They also identified four distinct steps in the persuasion process: attention, comprehension, acceptance and retention.

Zimbardo *et al.* (1977) used the model to generate suggestions for producing persuasive messages:

- The **source** of the message should be credible.
- The **argument** should be one-sided unless the audience is not sympathetic to the message, in which case a two-sided message is best.
- **Conclusions** should be stated rather than being left to the individual to work out.
- The **message** should be short, clear and direct. It should be vivid and not full of technical terms.
- The person should **actively** participate in receiving the message if possible.

The Hovland-Yale model has generated a vast amount of research, for example:

Source – Kiesler and Kiesler (1969) found that popular and attractive communicators were most effective. Miller *et al.* (1976) found that people who speak rapidly are more persuasive, possibly because it makes it sound as if they are more confident and knowledgeable.

Message – Hovland *et al.* (1949) found that when the audience is hostile, it is more effective to present both sides of an argument. Arkes *et al.* (1991) found that repeated messages were more persuasive.

Audience – Janis (1954) found that people who had low self-esteem were more easily persuaded. Allyn and Festinger (1961) found that people were more easily persuaded if they were distracted, rather than paying full attention.

Evaluation

- The model is **descriptive rather than explanatory**, in contrast with the Elaboration Likelihood model on the next page.

Elaboration Likelihood model (ELM)

Petty and Cacioppo (1986) presented a model to explain *how* people process persuasive messages (rather than describing the characteristics of persuasive messages, as in the Hovland-Yale model). Petty and Cacioppo suggested there are two alternatives:

1. The **central route** – Arguments are attended to carefully and elaborated by the message recipient. This route is likely to be followed for important messages only because it requires considerable cognitive effort. In such cases it is important for the message to be strong because persuasion will depend on the quality of the arguments.

2. The **peripheral route** – Only superficial cues are processed by the message recipient and, therefore, successful persuasion will be related to surface persuasion cues; the logic of the arguments is likely to be irrelevant. This is called 'peripheral' because people are affected by factors that are peripheral to the message itself.

The factors that affect the decision over which route to take are **motivation** and **ability to process the message** (e.g. lack of distraction). As these factors increase the central route then becomes more likely.

Motivation may be a function of personal relevance, accountability or a person's 'need for cognition' (i.e. enjoyment of thinking). Petty *et al.* (1981) assessed students' responses to arguments about whether an exam should be introduced for final year students. The message was either personally relevant (students were told their college was seriously considering this option) or not personally relevant, and the arguments given were persuasive or not. Petty *et al.* found that the strong (elaborated) arguments were most effective when the students were personally motivated but when the students were not personally motivated the status of the speaker (a peripheral cue) mattered more than the strength of the arguments.

Ability to process the message – Petty *et al.* (1976) varied the level of distraction and the quality of the argument. Participants in the high distraction condition agreed less with the message than those in the low distraction condition when the arguments were strong. But, when the arguments were weak, distraction had the opposite effect. This shows that distraction leads to the peripheral route.

Evaluation

- The model predicts that **attitude change will be greater if the central route is followed**, which is supported by a study by Chaiken (1980). Participants listened to arguments and were then contacted 10 days later; they were more likely to have maintained their new attitude if their attitude change had occurred via the central route (argument had had personal relevance and strong logic).

- The model **lacks predictive power** because it is difficult to predict the effect of certain variables in different contexts (Eagly and Chaiken, 1993).

- Petty *et al.* (2002) have **continued** to **adapt the model** to deal with such criticisms. They have attempted to specify the role of variables in different contexts, for example, source expertise is one such variable. This may in fact act as a biasing factor in conditions of high elaboration or may act as a peripheral cue in conditions of low elaboration.

- An alternative model by Chaiken (1980) (the **heuristic-systematic model**) uses two modes of processing. In this model messages which are listened to carefully are systematically processed (e.g. an analytic approach), otherwise heuristics (mental shortcuts) are used (e.g. judgments based on stereotypes). This model produces a wider range of predictions which are also more specific.

The ELM can be tested by varying (1) the strength/elaboration of message arguments and (2) the presence of peripheral cues (such as status or likeableness of source).

The influence of attitudes on decision making

AQA A ▶ U4

There is some debate about the extent to which attitudes are related to behaviour – if people change their attitudes, does their behaviour change as well? For example, you might convince someone that smoking is bad for their health but they continue smoking nevertheless.

Key points from AS

• The relationship between attitudes and behaviour is discussed in *Revise AS Unit 6.3, page 142*.

The role of cognitive consistency/dissonance

Festinger (1957) outlined the **theory of cognitive dissonance** – a general theory of what motivates human thought and behaviour, which is supported by a wealth of research. Cognitive dissonance occurs when a person holds two or more inconsistent views (or cognitions) and this creates a drive to create consistency.

Festinger and Carlsmith (1959) conducted an experiment where students were engaged to perform a very boring task (turning pegs on a board). Participants were paid $1 or $20. Afterwards they were asked to tell other participants what the job was like. Those paid least rated the task as more interesting – presumably because they experienced dissonance (boring task, no money so no reason to do it) and unconsciously had to rate the task as more interesting in order to reduce their dissonance.

Gibbons *et al.* (1997) found that smokers who gave up smoking after going to an anti-smoking clinic but who then restarted also had then lowered their perception of the danger of non-smoking – presumably in order to reduce their dissonance due to the decision to start smoking.

Brehm (1956) demonstrated **post-decisional dissonance**. Women were asked to rate various household items and then given their top two. They were asked to rate all the items again and Brehm found that ratings for their top two went up and other ratings went down – the women had altered their attitudes towards the items so they were more consistent with their choices, reducing any dissonant feelings that might have arisen from making the wrong choice.

Key points from AS

• **Self-perception theory** is related to attribution theory covered in *Revise AS Unit 6.3, page 139* which is a theory to explain how people construct explanations of their own behaviour. We do not observe traits, we observe behaviour and infer personal traits. We use this to infer the traits of other people and also for ourselves.

The link between self-perception theory and decision-making is that we discover our own attitudes through observing our behaviour, and these attitudes influence decisions.

The role of self-perception – self-perception theory

Bem (1972) suggested that when people are uncertain about their attitudes they infer what their attitudes are by observing their own behaviour. **Self-perception theory** may explain the results of dissonance experiments. Self-perception theory predicts that if a person is induced to perform a task for high rewards then task performance is attributed to factors outside the individual (i.e. 'I am doing it to get the reward') and the motivation to perform well is reduced. If the proposed reward is low then a person produces internal attributions (e.g. 'I am doing this because I like the task'), which results in higher motivation. In other words, if a person believes that their behaviour is caused by something external they assume it does not reflect their internal feelings. This is called the **overjustification effect**.

One outcome is that external rewards destroy internal motivations, as demonstrated by Lepper *et al.* (1973) in an experiment where nursery children were asked to draw some nice pictures. Some were told they would get a reward if their pictures were good. At the end all the children did actually receive a reward. When the children were observed a few days later, those children who had been promised a reward spent half as much time drawing as the other children, suggesting that their internal motivation had been destroyed by the expectation of external rewards.

Integrating dissonance and self-perception theories

Sherif and Sherif (1967) proposed **social judgment theory** – when making a decision, people have a **latitude of acceptance** and a **latitude of rejection**. A latitude of acceptance means that they will accept decisions that are around the same level, for example, if you decide that 30mph is a reasonable speed to drive in a built-up area then you would probably also accept 25mph and 35mph as reasonable speeds as well. A latitude of rejection means that you would be clear that driving at 15mph is too slow and 45mph is way too fast. Self-perception theory best accounts for decisions within the latitude of acceptance, whereas dissonance theory accounts for decisions within the latitude of rejection.

Explanations for the effectiveness of television in persuasion

AQA A ▶ U3
AQA B ▶ U3

The 'topic of television' includes advertisements that are both commercial and non-commercial (such as anti-smoking campaigns), programmes with political content that may change your views, and programmes related to health issues, etc.

The effectiveness of television in persuasion can also be related to social learning theory – figures on TV act as role models. In fact all of the explanations on page 125 for the pro- and anti-social effects of the media could be made relevant to the discussion on this page.

The models of attitude change examined on pages 127 and 128 can be used to explain the effectiveness of television in persuasion.

Hovland-Yale model

This model predicts that there are three factors that can account for the effectiveness (or not) of television:

- **Source** – TV often relies on expert sources who are attractive and have good verbal skills. Familiarity also increases their persuasiveness because we identify with them.
- **Message** – The medium is important so TV generally has greater influence than radio or magazines because it is more immediate and accessible. However, if the message is complex then written material may be better because people can go back over the arguments. Chaiken and Eagly (1983) found that when the message was easy to comprehend attitude change was greatest for video presentations, whereas difficult messages led to greatest attitude change when the message was written.
- **Audience** – Research shows that women are more persuadable than men, although this may only apply to male-oriented topics. When the topic is female-oriented men are more persuadable (Sistrunk and McDavid, 1971).

Elaboration Likelihood Model (ELM)

Persuasion is more likely to be effective if the listener is addressed via the central route. This can be achieved by making the message personally relevant, by presenting strong arguments, trying to make people scrutinise and think about your arguments, and by trying to avoid distractions.

Emotional influences

None of this may matter if you don't have people's attention. One way to do this is to start by emotionally involving the viewer, such as using fear or sentimentality. Emotion has an interesting effect on persuasion.

Good mood – When people are in a good mood they are less keen to have their mood spoiled and, therefore, more likely to take the peripheral route. Bless *et al.* (1990) demonstrated this, asking students to write about happy or sad events in their lives and then listening to speeches about college fees where the argument was either strong and well-reasoned or not. People in a sad mood (after writing about sad events) showed attitude change with the strong arguments only, people in a happy mood showed no attitude change in either condition.

Fear – Too much fear reduces persuasion; people become defensive and don't think rationally. However, Leventhal *et al.* (1967) found that showing people an anti-smoking film that scared them but then giving them a pamphlet to show them how to give up smoking (i.e. reduce their fear) was more effective than a film or pamphlet on its own.

Mediating factors

The effect of TV advertising/programmes can be moderated in children by active parental involvement. Huesmann and Bachrach (1988) reviewed research and concluded that TV has less influence on attitudes towards aggression than parental attitudes.

Practice essays 13.2

(a) Describe what research shows us about the Hovland-Yale model of attitude change. *(5 marks)*

(b) Describe and evaluate the influence of attitudes on decision-making. *(20 marks)*

13.3 The psychology of 'celebrity'

After studying this section you should be able to describe and evaluate:

- *the attraction of 'celebrity', including social psychological and evolutionary explanations*
- *research into intense fandom, for example, celebrity worship, stalking.*

LEARNING SUMMARY

The attraction of 'celebrity'

AQA A   U4

A **celebrity** is a famous, widely-recognised person who commands a high degree of public and media attention. It has been said that they are well known for being well known.

It is crucial that any discussions you have on this topic are firmly rooted in psychology rather than being idle banter!

The modern phenomenon of celebrity is linked to the media as they (magazines, TV, films) create fame. You couldn't have celebrity without the media. However the value of celebrity is linked to **gossip** – it is gossip on a global scale. Gossip is casual conversation about the personal affairs of other people.

The basis of evolutionary explanations is described on page 20. In a nutshell, we inherit certain mental modules because at some time in the past these enabled people to solve critical problems that were important for survival and reproduction. Thus, the behaviours are genetically based and adaptive – at least adaptive to that past environment (the EEA or environment of evolutionary adaptedness).

Social psychological explanations

Social learning theory (SLT) – Celebrities act as role models because we identify with them. They are also a source of vicarious reinforcement. SLT is explained on page 40.

Social construction theory – Celebrity is a social construction of the media, such as magazines and fan clubs on the internet. Social construction theory (or social constructionism) proposes that all of the phenomena around us (such as scientific knowledge, understanding gender roles, etc.) are constructed and maintained through social interactions; all knowledge is related to the social/cultural context. The media create the attractiveness of celebrity in order to serve their own ends (greater sales).

Social identity theory (SIT) (see page 63) – Membership of fan clubs and shared admiration for certain celebrities contributes to our social identity. The attraction of celebrity is that it is a means to define your social group and, therefore, yourself.

Group cohesion – Celebrities provide a common topic to talk about that helps build up social networks. It is safer to gossip about celebrities than about the people you know.

Leadership – Groups of people search for leaders, and celebrities may fulfill that function.

Evolutionary explanations

Gossip – One explanation of the evolution of language is that it allows a mechanism for gossip, so animals can pass on information about their social group. Dunbar *et al.* (1997) suggest people spend about 2/3 of their conversation time on social topics.

Successful reproduction – Gossiping is related to reproduction because the focus is on spreading information about who is successful in the mating game. This explains why so much celebrity gossip today is related to who is pregnant and who is getting together with whom or separating from whom. We gossip about relationships, especially those involving the alpha males or females (i.e. those individuals in a community to whom the others follow and defer). This approach also explains why celebrity interest is so concerned with beauty – because physical attractiveness is important for sexual selection and relationships.

Gender difference – The evolutionary approach can also explain why women are more interested in gossip and celebrity than men. Celebrity interest allows women to identify socially desirable men and compare notes on which men are better than others, to aid their own selection. When gossiping about other women they are considering the competition and learning how to copy alpha females.

Leadership – Humans are social animals and, therefore, any behaviour that enhances group dynamics is likely to be selected. One such adaptive behaviour is leadership; interest in celebrities is an offshoot of interest in and allegiance to a leader.

Research into intense fandom

> A **fan** is someone who has an intense liking for another person, a group of people or thing. A group of fans are a fanbase or fandom.

Celebrity worship

Maltby *et al.* (2003) developed a celebrity worship scale and gathered data from over 1,700 British people aged between 14 and 16. They categorised the responses into three dimensions, each typical of particular kinds of fans:

- **Entertainment-social** – attraction to celebrity because of entertainment value.
- **Intense-personal** – feelings of obsession towards celebrity.
- **Borderline-pathological** – uncontrolled behaviours and fantasies.

Low levels of fan worship (entertainment-social) are not related to any pathological behaviours (such as depression). Maltby *et al.* (2004) found that intense worship was related to higher levels of depression, anxiety, stress and illness.

> **Key points from AS**
>
> - **Cognitive therapy** is discussed in *Revise AS Unit 7.2, page 160.*

Celebrity worship has elements of obsessive love. Moore (2006) believes that rejection is the trigger for obsessive love. Treatment may involve cognitive therapy where the individual's irrational thoughts are challenged.

Hodgkinson (1991) suggests that there are several factors that contribute to obsessive love, such as having too much spare time (boredom), feeling vulnerable and lacking self-confidence, and perceiving oneself as a failure. All of this leads to needing an outlet for such anxieties and to seek an individual with the attributes one is seeking for oneself. In addition, a person's own feelings of unworthiness and insignificance are confirmed by the love that is sought, such as being 'in love' with someone famous.

Stalking

> **Stalking** refers to the obsessive following or observing of another person. Most cases of stalking do not escalate to the levels of reports that appear in the media.

Motivation – Mullen *et al.* (1999) studied reports of stalking and developed five categories that explain the reasons for stalking: intimacy seekers (those who wished to establish a close relationship with someone); rejected stalkers (those who had been rejected by the person they stalked); resentful (those who wished to punish someone who had wronged them); incompetent suitors (those who used this as a means to get a date) and sexually-motivated stalkers (which was solely male stalkers).

Gender – Purcell *et al.* (2002) studied 40 female stalkers and 150 male stalkers. The males reported more history of criminal offences and substance abuse. Females and males differed in terms of their motivation for stalking. The female stalkers generally were looking for intimacy and they usually stalked someone they knew, often someone who worked in a 'caring' profession (such as a nurse or teacher). Males showed a broader range of reasons for stalking.

> The term **'psychotic'** refers to individuals who are suffering from a mental disorder, which involves detachment from reality, such as schizophrenia.

Psychological profile – Kienlan *et al.* (1997) examined the case histories of 25 stalkers. One third had a diagnosed psychotic mental disorder (i.e. lack of contact with reality). The personality profile of the non-psychotic stalkers included traits such as anger, hostility, obsession, dependency and jealousy. The non-psychotic stalkers made more violent threats and carried out these threats. No single profile of the 'stalker personality' emerged.

Effect on victim – Pathe and Mullen (1997) asked 100 victims of stalking to complete a questionnaire. The effects reported were increased anxiety, intrusive recollections, plans to move house and/or leave job, and suicidal thoughts. These symptoms are similar to those related to post-traumatic stress disorder (PTSD).

Practice essays 13.3

(a) Outline social psychological explanations of the attraction of 'celebrity'.

(5 marks)

(b) Discuss research into intense fandom. Include research evidence in your answer.

(20 marks)

Chapter 14

The psychology of addictive behaviour

14.1 Models of addictive behaviour

After studying this section you should be able to describe and evaluate:

On pages 170–172 further research on substance use and abuse is covered, as required by AQA specification B

- *biological, cognitive and learning models of addiction, including explanations for initiation, maintenance and relapse*
- *explanations for specific addictions, including smoking and gambling.*

LEARNING SUMMARY

Biological models of addiction

AQA A ▶ U3
AQA B ▶ U3

Addiction occurs when the body relies on a substance for normal functioning. If the substance is removed, withdrawal symptoms may occur. There are physical (e.g. drugs) and psychological addictions (e.g. gambling), both of which draw on physical and psychological explanations.

When you are feeling depressed, dopamine levels are low. Increased dopamine (released when experiencing a reward) affects the reward centres of the brain and this is reinforcing (i.e. it encourages the behaviour to be repeated).

Any model of addiction should explain three aspects of addiction: initiation, maintenance and relapse. In the case of the biological model initiation can be explained by inheriting a genetic vulnerability (which would be triggered by life stressors), maintenance can be explained by activation of dopamine, which is reinforcing. Relapse may also be linked to dopamine, but is probably better explained by psychological factors.

Key points from AS

- General evaluations of the biological approach are relevant here. See, for example, *Revise AS Unit 7.1, page 151.*

Hereditary factors – Alcohol dependence is four times more likely in children whose parents are alcoholic (Sarafino, 1990). This is true even when the children have been adopted and it is their natural parents who are alcoholics.

Gene mapping studies (see page 98) have identified possible candidate genes. Blum *et al.* (1990) found an association between the **DRD2** (D2 dopamine receptor) gene and alcoholism; the gene leads to fewer dopamine receptors in the reward centre of the brain and, therefore, a person is more receptive to experiencing rewards. Subsequent research has found this gene to frequently be present in drug abusers, smokers, and other addictive, compulsive or impulsive disorders.

Physiological factors – The genetic explanation is linked to production of the neurotransmitter **dopamine**, which is a major component in the brain's reward pathways, i.e. it provides feelings of pleasure (a 'high') and is associated with reinforcement, encouraging an individual to repeat actions that led to its release. People with addictions may have higher than normal sensitivity to dopamine and/or low dopamine levels. Therefore, any increase is especially rewarding. Certain drugs have a direct effect on dopamine. For example, cocaine and amphetamines increase dopamine levels (cocaine prevents re-uptake, whereas amphetamine enhances dopamine release).

The addictive personality – Genetic explanations are also linked to the concept of the 'addictive personality'. Common factors have been identified, such as obsessiveness, impulsive behaviour, difficulty delaying gratification, disposition towards sensation-seeking and a general tolerance for deviance (Lang, 1983). Some of these traits have been linked to biological causes, for example, obsessive personality may be inherited and linked to low levels of serotonin (see obsessive-compulsive disorder on page 119).

Evaluation

- There is debate over the **role of the DRD2** gene. For example, Gelertner *et al.* (1993) concluded from a research review that no significant association between the DRD2 gene and alcoholism had been proven. A recent study (Riley, 2007) found that a neighbouring gene **ANKK1** might be a more likely candidate.
- Biological evidence is often based on **research with non-human animals** and may not be applicable to human behaviour.
- The biological model is linked to the **disease model** – which suggests that addiction is a disease state and, therefore, can be treated like a disease by giving appropriate drugs. Szasz (1974) suggests that the disease model is entirely inappropriate for addiction, which is linked to psychological factors.
- Addiction is such a personal experience that biological explanations are **unlikely to be very helpful**. In any case, genes cannot be the only explanation because not everyone with such genes becomes addicted. Therefore, psychological explanations are equally important.

Psychological models of addiction

AQA A ▶ U4
AQA B ▶ U3

Psychological explanations are more relevant to psychological addictions, although they also apply to physical addictions such as alcoholism and drug dependency.

Key points from AS

- Attribution theory, as an explanation of addiction, is explained in *Revise AS Unit 6.3, page 139*. It is an example of the cognitive approach to explaining addiction.

Biological explanations may be most relevant to the initiation of addiction. However, psychological factors may be more important in maintenance and relapse.

Classical and operant conditioning are explained on page 72.

Explanations based on the role of rewards link to biological explanations for addiction. The initial experience may be psychological (feeling a sense of reward or escape from negative feelings), which produces dopamine and activates the reward centre in the brain. This then leads to the maintenance of the addiction because of reinforcement.

See 'vulnerability for addiction' on page 136 – many of these factors can also be given as explanations of addiction.

Cognitive models of addiction

Cognitive explanations focus on the role of maladaptive cognitive processes. One example of this is the fact that addicts typically minimise the negative effects of their behaviour, focusing on the positive effects. This serves to maintain their addiction.

Another example is impaired decision-making abilities. Bechara and Damasio (2002) reported that a significant number of addicts selected options in an experiment that provided a higher immediate reward, even when they knew this strategy would be unprofitable in the long run. This behaviour resembles that of people who have experienced brain damage in their frontal cortex.

In addition, research using brain scanning techniques (e.g. Grant *et al.*, 1996) has shown heightened activity during craving in the areas of the frontal cortex that regulate decision-making, linking biology to cognitive explanations.

Psychodynamic model of addiction

The psychodynamic view is that addicts have dependency problems. In early childhood their needs for nurturance were not met and, therefore, in later life, they are not fully independent. This leaves them vulnerable to developing dependence relationships.

Learning models of addiction

Classical conditioning – Abusers come to associate drug use with certain situations and emotions. Those situations may then produce the euphoria of the drug-induced state. Meyer *et al.* (1995) found that just the sight of a hypodermic needle produced a sense of comfort for drug abusers.

Operant conditioning – This suggests that any behaviour that is rewarded will increase. Drug users experience a reduction of tension (negative reinforcement) and euphoria (positive reinforcement), which are both rewarding, increasing the likelihood that they will try the drug again. These rewards may also encourage them to use higher doses in order to increase the rewarding effects.

Once this stimulus–response link has been learned it may be resistant to unlearning because the user is afraid to experience life without the drug and, therefore, does not discover that they can cope without their addiction – a self-reinforcing cycle.

Evidence supports the negative reinforcement explanation. For example, Marlatt *et al.* (1975) found that participants drank more alcoholic drinks if they had taken part in a stressful taste task than an unstressful one.

Social learning theory – Addiction tends to run in families, which may be due to modelling and vicarious reinforcement rather than biological factors. In fact, research has shown that gambling often begins at home (Wynne *et al.*, 1996).

Evaluation

- Addiction patterns vary according to **social and cultural practices**. This supports the relevance of learning models.
- The **success and importance of psychological therapies** in treating addiction points to the role of cognitive factors at least in maintenance and relapse. Physical therapies rarely work on their own (see page 138).
- **Psychological models of addiction** are supported by the fact that not all addicts experience withdrawal symptoms, and also that biological factors cannot explain psychological addictions nor can they even explain physical addictions entirely.

Explanations for specific addictions

AQA A ▸ U4
AQA B ▸ U3

The statistics show that smoking is clearly very damaging to people's health. So why do people continue to smoke?

In 2004 25% of people in the UK aged 16 and over were smokers. Amongst the under-16s it is often girls who smoke more than boys.

The physiological effects of nicotine are discussed on page 171.

Smoking tobacco and nicotine

Social learning theory – The main reason why people start to smoke is probably imitation of desirable role models and peers. McKennell and Bynner (1969) found that smoking is associated with being attractive and tough. Therefore, pressure is put on the media to reduce examples of people smoking in films and on TV, and advertising of cigarettes is banned. The NHS 'stop smoking' website has stories of people who gave up to act as alternative role models.

Physical addiction – Addiction to smoking is explained in terms of nicotine, a substance that influences dopamine production and the reward centre in the brain. For that reason one of the ways to stop smoking is to replace the nicotine (i.e. with chewing gum, patches, nasal sprays). However, many people stop smoking without nicotine replacement or without experiencing any withdrawal symptoms. This supports the role of social and cognitive factors in smoking addiction.

Townsend *et al.* (1994) documented a negative correlation between the number of cigarettes smoked and the price of cigarettes, suggesting that people can stop if the immediate costs become too high. This further suggests that smoking addiction is not solely due to a physical addiction.

Social norms – Further support comes from the fact that the percentage of men who smoked used to be more than women, presumably because of social norms. However, today there is almost no gender difference, which is related to changing social norms about gender.

Gambling

About 1% of the adult population in Britain are problem gamblers. In 2005 the National Lottery collected £4.9 million. Gambling is claimed to be the fastest growing addiction in the US.

Cognitive distortions – In a study of fruit machine gambling Griffiths (1994) found that regular fruit machine gamblers (RGs), compared to non-regular users, were significantly more likely to use irrational verbalisations (e.g. 'I lost because I wasn't concentrating'). RGs also showed more evidence of flexible attributions (e.g. blaming failure on external factors and crediting success to their own skill). Anholt *et al.* (2003) found similar patterns of obsessive-compulsive thinking in OCD patients and compulsive gamblers, supporting the view that both groups have similar cognitive dysfunctions.

Personality – Loxton *et al.* (2008) found that problem gamblers were more impulsive, reward-driven and more sensitive to punishment than non-gamblers. Their reward-orientation and sensitivity to punishment would mean that success at gambling produced a stronger positive effect than in most people and that might be why they are more likely to continue gambling.

Key points from AS

- Making internal and external attributions is related to **locus of control** which is discussed on page 144 and also in *Revise AS Unit 6.2, page 135.*

Emotional factors – Gamblers Anonymous claims that the three key characteristics of a gambler are an inability to accept reality, emotional insecurity and immaturity. Gambling provides emotional comfort and permits the gambler to feel powerful. Wood and Griffiths (2007) interviewed 50 gamblers about the role gambling played in their lives. For most, the prime motive for gambling was as a means to escape and put them in a better mood. It enabled them to avoid their problems and 'fill the void'.

Biological factors may be significant as well. Zack and Poulos (2007) found that dopamine enhances the rewarding effects of gambling.

Practice essays 14.1

(a) Outline and evaluate the cognitive model as an explanation of initiation and maintenance of gambling behaviour.   *(10 marks)*

(b) Discuss the problem of relapse in relation to addiction. Include research evidence in your answer.   *(15 marks)*

14.2 Factors affecting addictive behaviour

After studying this section you should be able to describe and evaluate:

The role of the media in addictive behaviour can be explained in a similar way to explanations of pro- and anti-social behaviour (see page 125).

- *vulnerability to addiction including self-esteem, attributions for addiction and social context of addiction*
- *the role of the media in addictive behaviour.*

LEARNING SUMMARY

Vulnerability to addiction

AQA A   U4
AQA B   U3

Various factors have been linked to addiction and act as vulnerability factors, i.e. factors that make someone vulnerable to becoming addicted:

- **Low self-esteem** has been found in problem gamblers (Gupta and Derevensky, 1998), and in adolescents addicted to mobile phone use (Leung, 2007). Low self-esteem is likely to create dependency needs and lead to addiction in order to satisfy these needs.
- **Higher rates of depression** are related to low self-esteem. Addiction is a means of escaping reality (Gupta and Derevensky, 1998).
- **Greater risk takers** and sensation seekers (Zuckerman, 1996).

The explanations suggested for addictive behaviour on the previous pages can also be considered as factors that create a vulnerability to addictive behaviour – the initiation and maintenance of addictive behaviour as well as the problems with relapse.

Attributions for addiction

How do addicts explain their own addiction (i.e. provide an attribution)? **Attribution theory** is about how we explain the causes of our own and other people's behaviour. The **fundamental attribution error** suggests that people prefer to explain their own behaviour using situational attributions whereas they tend to explain other people's behaviour using dispositional explanations. This explanation may account for relapse behaviour in addicts. For example, Seneviratne and Saunders (2000) found that alcoholics were more likely to believe their relapse was due to situational factors whereas they believed that relapse in others was due to dispositional factors (such as low will power). This would hamper their ability to deal effectively with relapse because they view it as being outside their own control.

Key points from AS

- **Attribution theory** is discussed in *Revise AS Unit 6.3, page 139*.

Attribution is the process of explaining causes of behaviour. We do not observe traits, we observe behaviours and infer personal attributes.

Support for attribution theory as a factor in addiction comes from Robins *et al.* (1974) who found that US serviceman who were regular opium users when fighting in Vietnam found it easy to stop when returning to the US. The explanation is that they associated their addiction with external (environmental) cues, but once these were left behind they could give up. This explanation is supported by the fact that when people are successfully treated for addictions in a clinic they fail to transfer this to the outside world because they have attributed their behaviour (giving up) to the clinical setting.

Social context of addiction

Peer influences – Many addictions, such as smoking or alcohol, are a means of conforming to group norms and, therefore, being accepted by the group. Addiction may determine one's immediate circle of friends. For example, adolescent gamblers tend to make new friends through their gambling, so that old friendships are lost (Derevensky, 1999).

Explanations and vulnerabilities to addiction are important indicators of what treatments might be effective. The treatment of addiction is considered on page 138 onwards.

Poor environmental conditions – Tension and poverty are linked with drug addiction.

Practice essays 14.2

(a) Outline **two** explanations of vulnerability to addiction (for example, self-esteem, social context). *(10 marks)*

(b) Discuss the role of the media in addictive behaviour. *(15 marks)*

14.3 Reducing addictive behaviour

After studying this section you should be able to describe and evaluate:

- *models of prevention, including theory of reasoned action and theory of planned behaviour*
- *types of intervention, including biological, psychological, public health interventions and legislation, and their effectiveness.*

Models of prevention

Attitudes are discussed on page 127.

The TRA and TPB models are used generally with health behaviours (such as encouraging safe sex) and also used to understand attitudes generally (such as effective advertising strategies).

See also Prochaska's spiral model of behavioural change on page 172, another model of prevention.

Theory of reasoned action (TRA)

Ajzen and Fishbein (1980) developed a theory to explain how beliefs are linked to intentions about how to behave. They suggested that a behavioural intention is determined by (1) perceived facts and their personal consequences and (2) social norms. For example, smoking behaviour might be determined by (1) 'smoking causes cancer' (a fact) and (2) 'my parents smoke' (a social norm). This leads to (3) the intention 'I won't be so foolish' and finally (4) to a behaviour such as refusing a cigarette.

Evaluation

- This model enabled **clear predictions** about behaviour to be made, and generated useful research.
- However, there are various problems such as the model assumes there is a **direct link between thoughts and behaviour**, however, the evidence doesn't support this (e.g. DeFleur and Westie, 158).
- The model is also **limited to the effect of attitudes and social norms** on behaviour and assumes that **people behave rationally**, whereas this is not always true.

Theory of planned behaviour (TPB)

Ajzen (1988) modified the TRA model to produce the TPB model. This model includes the influence of perceived control, i.e. behavioural change depends on a third factor – your belief about whether you have control over a particular behaviour. Perceived control is affected by past experience and current obstacles. Perceived control may act on behavioural intention or may act directly on behaviour, and can, therefore, explain why intention is not always linked to behaviour.

A diagram of the theory of planned behaviour.

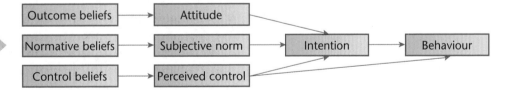

Evaluation

- This model still assumes that behaviours are **conscious, reasoned and planned**.
- TPB is **supported by** Oh and Hsu (2001) who sent questionnaires to about 400 gamblers living in the US state of Iowa, asking them about past gambling behaviour, attitudes, social norms, perceived behavioural control (i.e. budgetary affordability, self-controllability, perceived gambling skills, time availability), and behavioural intentions. Two months later they sent out a further questionnaire and found significant positive links between attitudes and behavioural intentions and behaviour, as the model predicts.

Types of intervention

Biological interventions

Detoxification programmes require medical supervision. One approach is to reduce the substance gradually. Alternatively, an addict may be required to quit in one go. Either way drugs may be used to reduce side effects, such as the use of anti-anxiety drugs to reduce anxiety.

Drug maintenance therapy – Substitute drugs are given, such as nicotine gum for smoking or giving **methadone** as a pharmacological substitute for heroin. Addicts become addicted to methadone but it can be taken by mouth and, therefore, the dangers of dirty needles are avoided. Methadone also doesn't have the same euphoric effects. The effectiveness may be due to several factors: the lack of euphoria may break the addiction cycle, and contextual dependency is lessened because methadone is oral and given by doctors.

Antagonist drugs are drugs that block or change the effects of the addictive drug. For example, the drug **antabuse** is given to alcoholics; if they drink anything alcoholic they almost immediately feel nauseous and develop a throbbing headache and other signs similar to a hangover.

Dopamine agonists such as L-dopa. One possible treatment for people who inherit a lack of D2 receptors is to be given drugs to stimulate these receptors. Such treatment may also benefit withdrawal symptoms because the effect of addiction can be to increase dopamine levels, which leads to a reduction in the number of dopamine receptors. The result is that when addictions are reduced there is less dopamine in the brain encouraging a person to renew their addiction in order to increase dopamine. Dopamine agonists do that for them.

There are two important criteria for assessing the effectiveness of any therapy for addiction:

(1) To what extent will addicts persist with the treatment? (If it is unpleasant they are likely to quit before completing treatment.)

(2) To what extent does the therapy prevent relapse?

Effectiveness

- Callahan (1980) found methadone therapy was successful as long as addicts were **prevented from continuing with other substance abuses**.
- Detoxification programmes tend to have a **high drop-out rate**, especially when not accompanied by some form of psychotherapy. This is likely to do with the fact that they are not pleasant and require considerable willpower.
- **Dopamine advice is contradictory**. For example, one study found that use of dopamine agonists for the treatment of Parkinson's disease actually led to pathological gambling rather than reduced it (Barclay and Vega, 2005) and Soares *et al.* (2003) found no benefit for cocaine addicts of using dopamine to reduce their symptoms during withdrawal.
- Biological treatments are not effective with psychological addictions, except where there is **comorbidity**, such as where a problem gambler is also suffering from severe depression. Use of anti-depressants may treat the depression and, therefore, remove one of the vulnerability factors for gambling.
- Biological interventions **assume that addiction is purely biological**. The fact that psychological factors are also important means that biologically-oriented treatment programmes must include psychological components in order to be successful. Amato *et al.* (2004) found that methadone treatment programmes had significantly improved success when used in combination with psychosocial interventions.

Comorbidity refers to the diagnosis of two or more conditions at the same time.

Psychological interventions

Aversion therapy – Negative affect is paired with the abused substance to recondition the patient. For example, the patient might be made to smoke a lot of cigarettes which makes them feel sick, then cigarette smoking is associated with nausea instead of being associated with pleasure. The success of **antabuse** (above) may be explained as a form of aversion therapy.

Key points from AS

- Aversion therapy is described in *Revise AS Unit 7.3, page 168*. It is based on the principles of classical conditioning.

Contingency management (CM) uses principles of **operant conditioning**; addicts are given rewards each time they produce drug-free urine samples. The rewards might be vouchers to be exchanged for clothing or food, or for patients being treated in a rehabilitation programme they might get extra time using the internet. Higgins *et al.* (1994) found that 75% of cocaine addicts using CM plus psychotherapy completed an outpatient treatment programme, compared to only 40% who received the psychotherapy only.

CM is similar to **token economy**, see page 103.

Cognitive-behavioural treatment (CBT) – Many programmes use CBT techniques, for example, self-help groups target the way a person thinks about their addiction. Specific CBT programmes include **behavioural self-control training** where patients are asked to keep a record of where and when they drink, smoke, gamble, etc. so they can become aware of when they are at risk. They are also taught coping strategies such as relaxation techniques to use when resisting temptation, assertiveness skills and also practical ideas such as sipping rather than gulping a drink.

Key points from AS

• CBT is described in *Revise AS Unit 7.2, page 160.*

Self-help groups, such as Alcoholics Anonymous (AA), provide social support and an opportunity to make a public statement of intention. This is important in attitude change (see theory of planned behaviour on page 137). They also provide successful role models, vicarious reinforcement and a social identity that empowers individuals.

Changing addictive behaviour requires a major shift in attitudes for the individual. In fact, they almost have to re-invent themselves – change friends, change habits and find new ways to gain pleasure.

Self-management strategies – This refers to methods without the benefit of formal treatment where individuals may employ a variety of the above techniques such as rewarding their behaviour or designing their own coping strategies. Such strategies may be carried out under professional guidance or with the use of self-help books.

Effectiveness

- Glasgow *et al.* (1985) found that people stop smoking by using **oral substitutes**, or rewards for quitting and punishments for backsliding.
- Ferri *et al.* (2006) reviewed research on the effectiveness of the **12-step AA programme** and did not find any greater success than other programmes. However, they acknowledged the problems in such research – the studies cover a variety of different programmes and individuals so it is difficult to draw firm conclusions. Self-help techniques are also difficult to assess because of the anonymity.
- According to the US Surgeon General, 95% of smokers **quit on their own** (self-management).

Public health interventions and legislation

Legislation and policing – Outlawing drugs may prevent some usage but it means that the sources are not regulated, thus, allowing poor quality substances, spread of diseases like Aids and association with crime. Anti-smoking bans may reduce cues to smoking in certain situations but actually may provide new cues, e.g. smoking areas outside pubs.

Health promotion campaigns

Key points from AS

• Social inoculation is similar to stress inoculation training (SIT), which was part of your AS studies. See *Revise AS Unit 5.2, page 107.*

Social inoculation – McGuire (1964) suggested that you can prepare people to resist temptation by giving them a set of strong counterarguments ('inoculation defence'), in the same way that inoculations provide us with antibodies. You can also provide them with 'supportive defence', which is strengthening the arguments they already hold.

Use of fear-arousing appeals – The use of fear may increase the persuasiveness of a message, for example, anti-smoking campaigns that show a picture of a diseased lung. See discussion of such appeals on page 130.

Identifying and targeting 'risk' groups – The New Zealand Government has recently launched a campaign to reduce problem gambling (Perese *et al.*, 2005). The primary target is raising general public awareness of the problem, but the secondary target is focus on high-risk groups such as young males (aged 18–24), who are unemployed or have low incomes. They are targeted because they have a high risk of gambling problems.

Effectiveness

- Health promotion campaigns **based on models of behaviour change** (such as the theory of planned behaviour) are more likely to be successful, though it is important that such models are related to cultural factors.
- The anti-smoking ban in the UK resulted in an 11% drop in cigarette sales during the first month of the ban in England (BBC, 2007). However, in the US stringent bans have **not resulted in continuing decreases in smoking**. 'Hardcore' smokers may become more defiant in the face of such bans; the same applies to all attempts to legislate against activities that are harmful.
- McAlister *et al.* (1980) found that a **local health promotion campaign** (anti-smoking) used in a high school reduced the likelihood of smoking by half.
- Jackson *et al.* (2002) evaluated an **anti-gambling campaign** in Australia and found a dramatic increase in helpline calls and 71% awareness of the campaign.
- Campaigns may be more effective if they **target 'risk' groups**.
- It is difficult to assess the effectiveness of any programme because **different measures can be used**, such as reduction among high-risk groups or changed attitudes in the general population.

Practice essays 14.3

(a) Assess the theory of reasoned action as a means of reducing addictive behaviour. *(5 marks)*

(b) Discuss types of intervention that can be used to reduce addictive behaviour. *(20 marks)*

Chapter 15
Anomalistic psychology

15.1 Theoretical and methodological issues in the study of anomalous experience

After studying this section you should be able to describe and evaluate:
- *issues of pseudoscience and scientific fraud*
- *controversies relating to Ganzfeld studies of ESP and studies of psychokinesis.*

LEARNING SUMMARY

Pseudoscience and scientific fraud

AQA A ▶ U4

The phrase **'anomalous experience'** refers to strange experiences that, as yet, have no proven explanation. It includes, but is not restricted to, paranormal phenomena.

Paranormal (or psi-phenomena) are those activities which cannot be explained using known laws and principles. 'Psi' is the hypothetical force underlying such phenomena.

The studies on the right show that scientific fraud occurs both in the pseudosciences and mainstream psychology.

Surveys indicate that about 60% of adults believe in paranormal phenomena, with more women than men being believers.

The term '**pseudoscience**' refers to practices that may look like they are evidence-based or claim to be scientific, but they are not. Scientific subjects use the scientific method, which is outlined on page 149. Pseudosciences (such as astrology or spiritualism) frequently rely on vague claims that cannot be tested (falsified). The importance of evidence-based research is that without it we can be easily fooled into believing fraudulent claims.

Some examples of scientific fraud:

- **Sir Cyril Burt and IQ testing** – Burt (1966) published data to support his original research on intelligence using data from twins. Both studies showed a high correlation in IQ scores for identical twins, supporting the role of genetic factors. However, Kamin (1974) accused Burt of inventing the data because the statistics in the two studies were too similar. Later, Gillie (1976) discovered that the research assistants Burt claimed to work with didn't exist. This claim was challenged but the conclusion appears to be that Burt was astonishingly dishonest (Mackintosh, 1995).
- **Soal and Bateman** used Zener cards to test ESP. These cards have 5 symbols repeated on 25 cards. The experimenter looks at each card and the participant reports what they think the experimenter is seeing. Soal and Bateman (1954) produced highly significant results with a man called Basil Shackleton. However, Marwick (1978) reanalysed Soal and Bateman's data and found some numbers had been added (fraud). When these were removed, the results were at chance level. Other researchers failed to replicate the original work by Rhine (1934), which had produced significant findings. Rhine suggested this was due to negative experimenter effects because other investigators were goats (non-believers).
- **Ganzfeld research** (see next page). Blackmore (1987) reported her observations of one Ganzfeld trial where the researcher (Sargent) had altered the procedures in such a way to reduce objectivity. For example, Sargent pushed one letter towards the subject when asking the subject to make his choice. Sargent rebutted the criticisms but stopped working in parapsychology after this.

The benefits of studying pseudoscience are to increase one's understanding of the importance of proof and disproof. This has been demonstrated in a study that looked at the effect of a course on pseudoscience on students' belief in the paranormal (Morier and Keeports, 2006). The course, called 'Science and pseudoscience', explored legitimate methods of scientific inquiry and compared them to the faulty, and often fraudulent, methods of the pseudosciences. Students doing an alternative course on 'psychology and law' were used as a control. At the beginning of term all the students completed the *Belief in the Paranormal Scale* and they again completed this at the end of term. The students in the 'Science and Pseudoscience' class demonstrated a substantially reduced belief in the paranormal relative to the control class.

Controversies relating to Ganzfeld studies of ESP

Ganzfeld is the German for 'total field'.

ESP (extrasensory perception) includes telepathy, clairvoyance and precognition – perceptions occurring outside any known sensory system.

The Ganzfeld technique was developed by Honorton (1974) as a method to test ESP. A receiver is placed in total isolation and to ensure full sensory isolation ping-pong ball halves are taped over their eyes and white noise is played through headphones. The sender is also isolated and concentrates on a picture randomly selected from four other pictures. The receiver tries to identify the image. Honorton (1985) analysed 28 studies using the Ganzfeld technique and found that 38% of the time participants were able to identify the correct picture. A chance level would be 25% correct guesses (1 in 4).

Demand characteristics occur in experimental research. Participants look for *cues* about what is expected of them. This means they are receptive to certain features of the experiment, such as leading questions. These features of the experiment almost *demand* a particular response from participants.

Hyman (1985) criticised the Ganzfeld work saying the experimental procedures were not rigorous enough and there were problems with the statistical analysis. When he reanalysed the same 28 studies he found that less than half of them had significant results, which might be because some experimenters are sheep (i.e. believers in paranormal phenomenon) and others are goats (i.e. non-believers). Believers might produce **demand characteristics** so that they found what they aimed to find. Honorton (1985) also did a meta-analysis and came up with different results to Hyman, supporting his original conclusions.

Honorton's automated trials were conducted under rigorous conditions where the receiver was in a sound-proof steel room. However, Wiseman claimed that this was not true for all trials.

Honorton *et al.* (1990) designed a fully automated project (auto Ganzfeld) to deal with the criticisms, producing a 34% hit rate, which was statistically significant. Hyman continued to doubt these findings, claiming that they could only be believed if replicated by an independent investigator. Milton and Wiseman (1999) conducted a meta-analysis of studies carried out by independent researchers and found no psi-effect. This was criticised for including all studies, including those with slightly different methods. When Bem *et al.* (2001) analysed just those studies using the strict Ganzfeld procedure a significant result was found.

Conclusions

- The findings **match up to the beliefs of the researcher**, i.e. those who do believe in ESP seem to find significant results, whereas those who are skeptical produce non-significant results.
- Hyman (1995) claims that a **theory needs to be put forward** explaining how such psi phenomena could occur. Until then, the results will be meaningless.

Controversies relating to studies of psychokinesis (PK)

Psychokinesis refers to situations where one person influences a physical event without direct intervention.

Macro-PK is cases of PK that have a large effect, such as being able to move objects or bend spoons. Weil (1974) was at first convinced by Uri Geller's ability to bend spoons until James Randi, a magician, demonstrated the same feats and showed Weil how they were done. Weil concluded that what we perceive is not the same as what is real; our beliefs alter what we perceive. Randi takes the view that psychic feats, such as spoon-bending, merely serve to increase our understanding of fraud.

Micro-PK involves small effects on probabilistic systems like dice throwing.

J.B. Rhine was one of the key figures in early research on the paranormal.

Rhine (1947) used a dice-throwing machine to try to demonstrate the power of the mind over random events. As the machine 'rolled' each die the participants had to try to influence the outcome. Rhine found significantly more 'hits' (the predicted outcome matched the actual outcome) than would be expected by chance. A review of nearly 150 dice-throwing studies by Radin and Ferrarui (1991) showed a weak but significant effect, overcoming criticisms that success was due to selective reporting or methodological flaws.

Check out your own belief in the paranormal – take an online test at www.queendom.com and search for 'Paranormal Beliefs Test'. You could correlate the results of this test with tests of other factors, such as personality.

Schmidt (1970) devised the equivalent of an electronic coin-tossing task. He asked participants to watch a circle of nine lamps. Whenever a lamp lit up, they had to try to make it move either clockwise or anti-clockwise by thinking about the direction they wished it to move in. The lamps used a strontium-90 radioactive source emitting particles at random intervals so that movement was caused by microscopic changes. Some participants appeared to be able to influence the subatomic processes.

Schmidt (1976) was also successful with another task, where a radioactive source generated random numbers that were converted into clicks on an audio-tape. Participants were able to influence the clicks, for example, making them mainly strong or weak, even when the tapes had been made some time in advance.

More recently, Stevens (1999) invited people accessing a web page to try to influence the path of laser beams. The path of the beam was altered significantly more often than in a control condition when there was no attempt to change its course.

Conclusions

- There is a large list of **successful PK studies**. However, attempts to replicate this research by skeptics have not been successful.
- **Magicians** who claim no special powers can often demonstrate psychic abilities, suggesting that other processes are at work.
- The results may be explained in terms of **participant and experimenter bias**. People who volunteer to be participants are likely to be believers and the same is true of experimenters. Schmeidler and McConnell (1958) found that believers in psi-phenomena (sheep) consistently scored higher than non-believers (goats) on tasks testing the paranormal. Non-believers often scored significantly below chance. Presumably, 'sheep' are more active than 'goats' in seeking cues from experimenters and acting on these cues. It is difficult to say which might come first, belief or experience, (i.e. do 'sheep' start off as non-believers and then experience leads them to believe, or does belief come first?). In either case the self-fulfilling prophecy would predict this cycle will be self-perpetuating.
- **Publication bias** – There is a tendency for positive paranormal research to be published, whereas studies that report no significance are rejected. This misrepresents the actual research that has taken place and produces a bias in favour of the existence of psi-phenomena. However, Honorton and Ferrari (1989) looked at over 300 forced-choice studies, finding a small but significant effect. They say this couldn't be due to selective reporting because, they calculated, one would have had to add a further 46 studies which reported no significance in order to reduce the significance effect.
- The James Randi Educational Foundation (JREF) has offered **$1 million** to anyone who can produce solid scientific evidence of psychic powers such as PK. To date no one has even passed the preliminary tests conducted in the claimant's own home.
- Randi (2003) has posed the question of why, if these special powers exist, have they **never been put to good use** and changed medicine or science?

Practice essays 15.1

(a) Outline and evaluate studies of psychokinesis.	*(15 marks)*
(b) Discuss issues related to scientific fraud.	*(10 marks)*

15.2 Factors underlying anomalous experience

After studying this topic you should be able to describe and evaluate:

- *cognitive, personality and biological factors underlying anomalous experience*
- *functions of paranormal and related beliefs, including their cultural significance*
- *the psychology of deception and self-deception, superstition, and coincidence.*

LEARNING SUMMARY

Factors underlying anomalous experience

AQA A   U4

If claims about anomalous experiences are unfounded, how can we explain why some people are fervent believers? If such beliefs are not unfounded, why do some people continue not to believe?

Cognitive factors

Cognitive biases – Thalbourne *et al.* (1995) suggest that low tolerance of ambiguity is associated with a fear of the paranormal.

Thinking style (intuitive vs. analytical) – Aarnio and Lindeman (2005) found an association between paranormal beliefs and tendency for intuitive thinking. They suggest that this might explain why more females believe in the paranormal – it is because they also prefer more intuitive approaches to thinking. However, other research has found a positive association between analytic thinking and belief in the paranormal (e.g. Wolfradt *et al.*, 1999) and some studies have found higher levels of paranormal belief in educated people (Farha and Stewart, 2006), although in the study by Aarnio and Lindeman psychology and medical students held fewest paranormal beliefs.

Cognitive illusions – Blackmore (1992) has explained psi-phenomena as a form of cognitive illusion. She argues that we are used to having explanations for everything and, if we haven't got one, we seek one. At least 'sheep' do; 'goats' accept that some things are simply random coincidences. 'Sheep' is a term used to refer to believers in anomalous experiences. 'Goats' are non-believers. Support of this was provided by Brugger *et al.* (1990) who found that goats were better at generating random numbers than sheep (they gave more consecutive repetitions of the same digit), i.e. they were able to cope with the nature of random occurrences better.

Personality factors

Locus of control – Malinowski (1948) suggested that belief in the paranormal gives people an illusion of control. People who have an external locus of control (externals) believe that events are often explained by factors outside their own control, such as luck. Tobayck and Milford (1983) demonstrated a positive correlation between being an 'external' and having a greater belief in paranormal phenomena. However, not all research has supported this. One suggestion is that some forms of psi-phenomena (such as superstition and spiritualism) correlate positively with an external locus of control, whereas others (such as pk) correlate negatively (Wolfradt, 1997). Davies and Kirkby (1985) found a positive correlation between internality and belief in psi.

Locus of control is also discussed on page 168.

Psychopathology – One element of some mental disorders is '**magical thinking**' (as seen in PK). This is a symptom of schizotypal personality disorder. Eckblad and Chapman (1983) found that people who scored highly on magical thinking also showed a predisposition to psychosis. Other research has found a link between holding paranormal beliefs and schizotypy (e.g. Thalbourne, 1994) and with manic-depressive experiences (Thalbourne and French, 1995).

Piaget, in his theory of cognitive development (see page 81), suggested that young children are prone to magical thinking, for example, believing in Father Christmas.

Neuroticism may be linked to paranormal beliefs. Williams *et al.* (2007) found a link in 280 adolescents, and Thalbourne *et al.* (1995) found a significant positive relationship between neuroticism and paranormal beliefs (specifically belief in psi, witchcraft, spiritualism, precognition and traditional religion).

Neuroticism is the tendency to experience negative emotional states such as anger, anxiety and depression.

From the evolutionary point of view it can be argued that, if ESP does exist, it would have high adaptive value – or would it?

The **EEA** (environment of evolutionary adaptedness) is the environment to which a species is adapted. The selective pressures at that time explain the behaviours that we observe today. In humans it is suggested that our EEA was the period from 1.8 million to 11,000 years ago when humans lived on the plains in Africa.

However, other researchers (e.g. Lester and Monaghan, 1995) have found no such relationship. Auton *et al.* (2003) found that high believers also scored highly on aggression (related to neuroticism) and defendence (i.e. not readily accepting criticism).

Biological factors

Evolutionary explanations – Paranormal beliefs are present in all cultures. This universality of paranormal beliefs suggests humans inherit a mental module which predisposes them to having such beliefs. If this is true then beliefs in the paranormal must be in some way adaptive, at least in the **EEA**. One suggestion is that such beliefs give comfort. In the face of uncertainty they stop people questing any further for answers and allow them to focus on more immediate concerns.

An alternative view is that it is a consequence of the adaptation of the human mind to seek explanations for events in the world. A desire to discover causes would be important in enabling humans to control their world. This desire leads to cognitive illusions, i.e. paranormal beliefs.

The significance of biological factors may be supported by universal similarities in paranormal beliefs. McClenon and Nooney (2003) analysed reports by anthropologists of anomalous experiences and found cross-culturally consistent features – belief in spirits, life after death and magical abilities.

The role of biological factors is further supported by genetic research on **religiosity**, which is related to anomalous experience. Koenig (2005) found that identical twins are more likely to have the same religious views than non-identical twins, which supports a genetic link.

Brain biochemistry – People with high levels of **dopamine** are more likely to regard coincidences as being meaningful and they pick out patterns where there are none. This was demonstrated in a study by Brugger *et al.* (2002) comparing people who either said they were believers ('sheep') or people who were skeptics ('goats'). The participants were shown both real faces and words, mixed together with jumbled up words; sheep were more likely to identify the jumbled words as more real than the goats. However, when the participants were given L-dopa, which increases levels of dopamine in the brain, both groups made the same errors. The drug did not increase the tendency of sheep to misinterpret the patterns.

Evaluation of factors underlying anomalous experience

- Other research (e.g. Sparks *et al.*, 1997) suggests that **social factors** are more important, such as having friends who believe in the paranormal.
- One of the problems with research on factors related to paranormal beliefs is that all research **relies on tests that assess belief in the paranormal**. Some tests include items that may not be considered to be 'paranormal experiences'.

Functions of paranormal and related beliefs

Dealing with uncertainty – The explanations outlined above lead us to suggest that paranormal and related beliefs provide answers in situations where there are no answers. They provide a means of dealing with uncertainty, though this is only true, as we have seen, for certain kinds of people (e.g. those who have intuitive ways of thinking or who tend towards neuroticism).

Sense of control – Watson *et al.* (2007) found an association between lack of a sense of control in childhood and tendency towards paranormal beliefs. This is linked to the explanation that paranormal beliefs provide an illusion of a sense of control.

Cultural significance – At a cultural level all beliefs perform an important function as part of shared cultural systems. A culture is defined as a shared set of values, norms and beliefs. Therefore, explanations of particular phenomena form a key part of what it is to belong to a community.

The psychology of deception and self-deception, superstition, and coincidence

Theory of mind (ToM) is the ability to understand what is going on in another person's mind, to 'guess' what they are thinking or feeling (see page 91).

Deception

The ability to deceive someone else depends on possessing a **theory of mind** and is seen as a sign of intelligence in animals. **Machiavellian intelligence** (see page 75) refers to the ability to intentionally deceive another individual. In order to intentionally deceive another individual one has to have an understanding of what they know, or don't know.

Pinker (2004) suggests that religious and paranormal beliefs evolved because of the benefits for the leaders – the magician, crystal-ball gazer, and shaman. The ability to deceive others gives the deceiver power.

Self-deception

Key points from AS

• Freudian explanations are explored in *Revise AS Unit 1.1, page 18*.

Self-deception can be related to the action of the unconscious and to Freudian explanations. According to Freud, thoughts that create anxiety are repressed into the unconscious to protect the ego (the action of **ego defences**). At a conscious level a person might believe that their reasons for action are, for example, honourable, but at an unconscious level the motivation may be quite different.

Key points from AS

• The accuracy of recall of paranormal events may be related to the study of eyewitness testimony, see *Revise AS Unit 2.2, page 35*. Memory is not always reliable. Some paranormal reports may be false memories.

In terms of belief in the paranormal, it may be that believers are deceiving themselves about the evidence. They may repress experience or repress evidence that runs counter to their beliefs. In addition, researchers who are believers may be deceiving themselves about the rigour of their investigations. Their wish to demonstrate psi-phenomenon means that some of their behaviours are repressed.

Superstition

Superstitions are beliefs that may be linked to ritual behaviours, performed with the belief that they will deal with something beyond our control, such as wearing a particular shirt to ensure your football team wins. Such beliefs or behaviours help a person deal with the unknown.

A **superstition** is a belief that is not based on knowledge or reasoned thinking, i.e. it is an irrational belief.

Skinner (1948) offered a behaviourist explanation for superstition. He suggested that the chance association of a behaviour with a reinforcer can produce a link between body movements (routines) and superstitious behaviour. The pigeons he used in his experiments sometimes learned unique sequences of body movement because they just happened to be performing them when they were given food.

People may acquire superstitions/superstitious behaviour through operant conditioning because in the past the behaviours have been associated with reducing the anxiety associated with uncertain events.

Coincidence

Coincidence is when two unrelated things happen together without any apparent causal connection.

When two unrelated things happen together it is a natural tendency to assume one has caused the other. For example, the presence of a spider and a person screaming leads to the assumption that the spider caused the scream. However, in some instances there is no cause yet some people prefer to impute a cause rather than be content with coincidence, a cognitive bias.

Practice essays 15.2

(a) Describe and evaluate personality factors that underlie anomalous experience. *(15 marks)*

(b) Discuss the function of deception and self-deception in relation to anomalous experience. *(10 marks)*

15.3 Belief in exceptional experience

After studying this topic you should be able to describe and evaluate:

- *research into psychic healing*
- *research into out-of-body and near-death experience*
- *research into psychic mediumship.*

Research into exceptional experience

AQA A   U4

Psychic healing aims to help people recover from illnesses by channelling energy into their bodies to re-energise them.

Research into psychic healing

Experiments – Krieger (1979) studied the effects of one psychic healer (Oskar Estebany) on a group of physically ill patients. She found that the haemoglobin levels of the patients he 'touched' were significantly higher after being treated than those of a control group of patients, and that the levels were still significantly higher a year later.

Distant healing studies are conducted to rule out any subtle communication/placebo effects; the psychic just focuses on a photo of the patient. Braud and Schlitz (1988) tested the effects on patients' galvanic skin response (see page 37), which is evidence of activity in the sympathetic nervous system. The healer is instructed to focus their influence for one-minute periods and at this time the patient's responses are recorded. They found significantly changed GSR patterns during periods of influence. In such cases the placebo effect cannot be operating because the patient doesn't know when the influence is occurring.

Skeptics suggest that psychic healing is no more than a placebo effect. **Placebos** are substances that have no pharmacological effects, but the person taking them thinks they are the real thing. This means you can separate the psychological from the physical effects of being given a drug treatment. A placebo effect occurs when someone thinks they are receiving treatment.

Studies with non-human animals – Grad (1976) studied the effects that Estebany had on a group of iodine-deficient mice (the lack of iodine creates a condition called *goiter*). The psychic placed his hands on their cages for 15 minutes, 10 times a week. In the control condition the mice's cages were warmed to simulate the effect of hands. Grad found that the rate of goiter development was slower in the experimental mice.

Evaluation

- Three explanations may account for **recovery from illness** (aside from psychic healing): it is spontaneous (people do recover spontaneously from many illnesses); it is temporary (a disabled person may walk again but relapses once out of the spotlight); it is due to a placebo effect (all physical disorders have a psychological element as demonstrated by the effectiveness of placebo therapies). Therefore, we cannot always be certain that recovery is due to psychic healing.

If psychic healing is a real phenomenon then why is it not widely used to treat people?

- The key question is the extent to which such studies were rigorously controlled – factors such as **experimenter effects and demand characteristics** may have acted as confounding factors, or the studies may have been fraudulent. However, the same criticisms are made of many psychological studies where, for example, the person who has designed the research also conducts it and may unwittingly communicate expectations. To deal with this we expect studies to be replicated; a practice not common in paranormal research.

Another classic case of experimenter effects with animals is shown in the case of Clever Hans, the horse who could apparently add up. It was discovered, through objective testing, that Hans was merely responding to his owner's cues.

- It is suggested that **non-human animals are not subject to unconscious suggestion** (placebo effects), but this is not true, as Rosenthal and Fode (1963) found in their classic study of experimenter effects on rats. Students were told they had to train rats to perform a task and were told that their rat was either dull or bright. The rats' performance was related to the students' expectations even though the rats had actually been randomly assigned.
- This research **has a serious side because some individuals make** considerable sums of money from claims of psychic healing.

Out of body experience (**OBE** or **OOBE**) involves a sensation of floating outside one's body and sometimes observing one's own body. It has been associated with near-death experiences (NDEs) which occur around the time of a person's death or potential death.

Research into out-of-body experience (OBE) and near-death experience (NDE)

Qualitative analysis – Green (1968) analysed 400 first-hand accounts of OBEs and provided a classification of them. In **parasomatic** cases the observer has another body distinct from their normal physical body; in **asomatic** cases the observer is unaware of having a body; in a small number of cases (4%) there was a connecting cord between the bodies.

Brain studies – Blanke *et al.* (2005) showed that experiences similar to OBEs could be elicited in 'normal' people if a particular area of the brain was activated electrically – this area is the **TPJ** (the right temporal-parietal junction where the temporal and parietal lobes come together).

About 1 in 10 people claim to have had an OBE.

Explanations – OBEs may be the result of dream states (i.e. on the edge of consciousness) or related to taking certain drugs. In both instances consciousness is separated from the physical self. Blackmore (1982) suggests that OBEs occur when a person loses contact with their sensory input while remaining conscious. The person's perceptions are fed from elsewhere.

Evaluation

- This research is **more credible** than other paranormal studies. The qualitative analyses have been verified by different researchers, supporting their validity. For example, Poynton (1975) analysed reports of OBEs in South Africa and found similar results to Green.
- The link to **possible explanations** is critical; phenomena do not make sense unless we can offer some account as to how they got there.

Research into psychic mediumship

Schwartz *et al.* (2001) conducted a controlled test of five mediums. A woman unknown to them recorded details of six significant losses she had experienced in the previous 10 years. Each medium interviewed the woman, who was only allowed to answer yes or no. The mediums' average accuracy was 83% compared to control interviewers who were 36% accurate. O'Keeffe and Wiseman (2005) asked five mediums to give readings for five volunteer sitters (totalling 25 readings). Each sitter read all 25 readings and was asked to rate how much each statement was appropriate to them. The ratings were actually lowest for the statements relevant to them.

A **psychic medium** is a person who can communicate with the spirits of dead people. Mediumship may involve telepathy (reading someone else's mind), clairvoyance (information from distant objects/people) and communication with the spirit world.

Remote viewing involves an experimenter going to a remote location, and then the medium reports any images that arise. Afterwards a judge tries to match images with a set of possible target locations. Targ and Puthoff (1977) reported higher than chance findings, but Marks and Kammann (1980) couldn't replicate this and suggested that the transcripts contained clues about previous targets.

Evaluation

- It is likely that psychic mediumship is impressive because **people only remember the things that were relevant to them**.
- The evidence above fits the common pattern – **believers obtain positive results**, non-believers don't. Gary Schwartz works with the research group VERITAS, investigating the continuity of life; Richard Wiseman is a skeptic.

Spiritualism has been brought into disrepute by the frequent cases of fraudulent activity.

Practice essays 15.3

(a) Outline **one or more** research studies that investigated psychic healing and consider what these studies tell us about exceptional experience. *(15 marks)*

(b) Critically evaluate research into psychic mediumship. *(10 marks)*

Chapter 16

Psychological research and scientific method

16.1 The application of scientific method

After studying this topic you should be able to describe and evaluate:

Science is knowledge gained through systematic and objective observation of, and experiments with, phenomena.

- *the major features of science, for example replicability, objectivity*
- *the scientific process, including theory construction, hypothesis testing, use of empirical methods, generation of laws/principles (e.g. Popper, Kuhn)*
- *validating new knowledge and the role of peer review.*

The major features of science

AQA A — U4
AQA B — U4

Popper (1969) argued that it was the possibility of **falsification** that separates science from pseudo-sciences.

There are several issues that can be debated:

- Is psychology a science?
- Is a scientific approach desirable in psychology?

You can read more about these issues on page 186.

Triangulation is achieved by comparing the findings from a number of different studies or using different methods within one study. Close agreement confirms the validity of the findings.

Kuhn's conception was that science develops through pre-science, to science, and then to revolution. On the other hand, Palermo (1971) argued that, far from being a pre-science, psychology has already undergone several paradigm shifts, such as structuralism (introspection), behaviourism, and information processing. It is now in the revolution phase.

Look at a list of references at the back of any Psychology textbook and you will see the names of many journals.

The key concepts of a science are: objectivity, control and manipulation of variables, replication (to confirm validity), and falsification (being able to reject a hypothesis).

The scientific process and the validation of new knowledge

The **hypothetico-deductive model** of science was proposed by Karl Popper (1935), suggesting that theories/laws about the world should come first and these should be used to generate expectations/hypotheses. These hypotheses can then be tested using experiments or other methods. This kind of science does not rely on chance observation but on deliberately organising opportunities to make observations.

1. Making observations, producing 'facts' (data about the world).
2. Constructing a theory to account for a set of related facts.
3. Generating expectations (hypotheses) from the theory.
4. Collecting data to test expectations.
5. Adjusting the theory in response to the data collected.

The **laboratory experiment** is the best, but not the only means of hypothesis testing, e.g. naturalistic observations use the scientific method. Qualitative methods sometimes aim to be subjective in their collection of data but objectivity is also possible, for example, through **triangulation** where results from a variety of studies can be compared to enhance validity.

Kuhn (1962) claimed that psychology could not be a science because, unlike other sciences, there is no single **paradigm** (i.e. shared set of assumptions about human behaviour and the methods appropriate to its study). It may be that psychology has yet to identify its paradigm, i.e. it is a **pre-science**. Others argue that psychology is a science with a number of paradigms, such as behaviourism.

The role of peer review

Scientists publish the results of their research in academic journals. These articles are subject to peer review (also called 'referring'), i.e. other academic psychologists read the article and judge whether the research is credible and valid. This ensures that a professional standard is maintained as well.

Some critics suggest that impartial review is an unachievable ideal, partly because research is conducted in a social world and social relationships affect objectivity. It is also not always possible to find a sufficiently knowledgeable person to conduct a review in a little-researched subject area.

16.2 Designing psychological investigations

After studying this topic you should be able to describe and evaluate:

AQA A ▸ U4

AS
- This unit is covered in *Revise AS Unit 4.1 and 4.2, pages 75–91.*

- selection and application of appropriate research methods
- implications of sampling strategies, for example, bias and generalising
- issues of reliability, including types of reliability, assessment of reliability, improving reliability, assessing and improving validity (internal and external)
- ethical considerations in design and conduct of psychological research.

16.3 Data analysis and reporting

After studying this topic you should be able to describe and evaluate:

AS
- Graphical representation is covered in *Revise AS Unit 4.3, pages 92–93.*

AS
- The analysis and interpretation of qualitative data is covered in *Revise AS Unit 7.3, page 94.*

- appropriate selection of graphical representations
- probability and significance, including the interpretation of significance and type 1/type 2 errors
- factors affecting choice of statistical test, including levels of measurement
- the use of inferential analysis, including Spearman's Rho, Mann-Whitney, Wilcoxon, Chi-squared
- analysis and interpretation of qualitative data
- conventions of reporting on psychological investigations.

Data analysis

AQA A ▸ U4
AQA B ▸ U4

Descriptive statistics (such as the mean or standard deviation or a graph) describe a set of data.

Inferential statistics give us a different kind of information – they tell us how likely it is that the pattern in a set of observed data occurred by chance and whether we can *infer* that the same pattern exists in the general population.

Two samples may differ but what we are really interested in is knowing how likely it is that the populations from which the samples were drawn are different.

Type 1 and Type 2 errors were used to describe the results of Rosenhan's study (see page 97).

Probability and significance

If we want to know whether men have better memories than women or vice versa, we might test the memories of a sample of men and a sample of women, and compare their scores. It is very unlikely that their scores will be identical, but what we want to know is whether the difference between the scores is **significant**, i.e. is the difference big enough to warrant a conclusion that men and women in the general population (as distinct from our sample) differ in their memory capacity? Or could the observed difference have occurred by chance and is, therefore, insignificant?

The idea of 'chance' is related to certainty. You can never be certain that an observed effect was due to chance or not, but you can state how certain you are. In general, psychologists use a **probability** of $p \leq 0.05$, this means that there is a 5% possibility that the results did occur by chance. In fact, what it really means is that there is a 5% probability of the results occurring if there is no real difference/association between the populations from which the samples were drawn. In some studies a more stringent level of significance is used, for example, if testing a new drug we want to be more certain. So researchers use $p \leq 0.01$ or even $p \leq 0.001$. This chosen value of 'p' is called the **significance level**.

Type 1 and type 2 errors

A type 1 error is a correct assumption that is mistakenly rejected, for example, rejecting a null hypothesis that is true. This may occur when using a level of significance that is too high (or lenient, e.g. 10%). A type 2 error occurs when an incorrect assumption is mistakenly accepted, for example, accepting a null hypothesis that is false. This might occur when selecting a level of significance that is too low (or stringent, e.g. 1%).

Critical values of T at 5% level (p 0.05)

N =	One tailed test	Two tailed test
5	T 0	
6	2	0
7	3	2
8	5 ≤	3
9	8	5
10	11	8
11	13	10
12	17	13
13	21	17
14	25	21
15	30	25
16	35	29
17	41	34
18	47	40
19	53	46
20	60	52
21	67	58
22	75	65
23	83	73
24	91	81
25	100	89

Factors affecting choice of statistical test

There are four statistical tests in the AQA A specification. The way to decide which one to use is to ask yourself the following questions:

1. Are your data in **frequencies** (i.e. nominal data)? If so, then you use Chi-squared.
2. **Are you looking to find out if your two samples are different or correlated?** If you are seeking to find out whether two samples are different you use a test of differences – either Mann-Whitney or Wilcoxon. If you are looking at a correlation then you use Spearman's rho.
3. **Experimental design** – Are your samples related (e.g. a repeated measures design is used) or are they independent (i.e. an independent groups design is used)? If they are related then you use Wilcoxon, if they are independent you use Mann-Whitney.
4. **Level of measurement?** There are four levels of measurement:
   Nominal – Data are in categories.
   Ordinal – Data are ordered in some way.
   Interval – Data are measured using units of equal intervals.
   Ratio – There is a true zero point.

Inferential tests

Spearman's Rho is used when a hypothesis predicts a *correlation* between two variables. The two sets of data are pairs of scores from one person or an associated event (such as scores from twins), i.e. they are related. The statistic that is produced is called **rho**.

Mann-Whitney test is used when a hypothesis predicts a *difference* between two sets of data. The two sets of data are pairs of scores from two separate groups, i.e. they are *independent*. The statistic that is produced is called **U**.

Wilcoxon test is used when a hypothesis predicts a *difference* between two sets of data. The two sets of data are pairs of scores from one person (or a matched pair), i.e. they are *related*. The statistic that is produced is called **T**.

Chi-squared test is used when a hypothesis predicts a *difference* between two conditions or an *association* between variables. The sets of data must be *independent* (no individual should have a score in more than one 'cell'). The data are in frequencies (nominal level of measurement). The statistic that is produced is called χ^2.

Observed and critical levels of significance

A statistical analysis is applied to a set of data and produces an **observed value**. In order to determine whether this observed value is significant it is compared to **critical values**, which are given in a table of critical values for that statistic. On the left is an example of a table of critical values for the Wilcoxon T test. In order to use the table, you need to know: (1) whether you had a directional hypothesis (which is a one-tailed test) or a non-directional hypothesis (two-tailed test) and (2) the number (N) of participants or participant pairs. This information means you can locate the appropriate critical value for your test. For example, if you had a one-tailed test and 19 participants, the critical value would be for T 53 at the 5% level of significance.

For the Wilcoxon test and the Mann-Whitney test the observed value must be equal to or less than the critical value for significance to be shown.

For the Chi-squared test and Spearman's rho the observed value must be equal to or greater than the critical value for significance to be shown.

Conventions of reporting on psychological investigations

Written reports of psychological investigations are published in academic journals, as described on page 149. The convention is to divide such reports into the following sections:

- A short summary or **abstract** at the beginning, which provides key details of the aims, participants, research methods and procedures, findings and conclusions.
- An **introduction** or **literature review** outlining previous research (theories and/or studies) which have led the researcher to the **aims/hypothesis** for this study.
- A description of the **method/procedures**. These should be sufficiently detailed so that someone else could replicate the study and, thus, be able to confirm the findings. Any questionnaires or tests used, or other materials, may be included in an appendix.
- The **results** are described and a summary of the raw data given (the actual scores or data for individual participants, called the 'raw data', is not given. Other descriptive statistics (graphs, tables, measures of central tendency) are included, and finally, inferential statistics indicating the significance of the results.
- A **discussion** of the results, including reference to other studies/theories and suggesting alterations to existing theories or proposing new theories.

Practice questions 16.3

A psychologist conducts a study into conformity to see whether gender differences vary with the kind of task undertaken. Two tasks are used in the experiment. Task one is a face-to-face conformity task, task two requires written answers.

Table 1 Results showing the number of people who conformed in each condition

	Task 1	Task 2	Total
Men	21	43	64
Women	31	33	64
	52	76	128

Critical values of Chi squared (x^2) at 5% level ($p \leq 0.05$)

df	One-tailed test	Two-tailed test
1	2.71	3.84

Observed value of x^2 must be EQUAL TO or GREATER THAN the critical value in this table for significance to be shown.

(a) Write a suitable directional hypothesis for this study. *(2 marks)*

(b) The Chi-squared value produced for this data is 3.36. Use the table of critical values to determine whether this would be significant at the 5% level (for a one-tailed test). *(1 mark)*

(c) Identify **one** factor that the psychologist had to take into account when deciding whether or not to use the Chi-squared (x^2) test. *(1 mark)*

(d) Sketch a suitable graph to display the results from this study. *(6 marks)*

(e) Describe **one** conclusion that you can draw based on the data in the table and the statistical significance. *(4 marks)*

(f) Outline the key features of the scientific method. *(6 marks)*

(g) Identify **one** strength and **one** limitation of the scientific method. *(4 marks)*

(h) The psychologist wanted to find out more about why men and women conformed in different situations and decided to conduct some follow-up interviews. Describe the design decisions that would be necessary, including some questions that would be used. Make sure you cover all the procedural details that he would need to plan. *(10 marks)*

See pages 9–11 for a breakdown of the marking criteria used to mark this question.

This student has wisely managed to avoid starting the essay with a description of the clinical characteristics of schizophrenia. You should only provide these if specifically required in the question, otherwise start immediately with a description of the explanations.

The answer shows a detailed and thorough knowledge of biological explanations for schizophrenia. The AO2/evaluation/commentary points are scattered throughout the answer – paragraph 2 ends with an AO2 point and paragraph 3 starts with one.

The use of research throughout the essay could be credited as AO1 or AO2 – the studies have been presented as part of the descriptive content of the essay, but could have been turned into effective AO2 if key phrases had been used (e.g. 'this explanation is demonstrated by…') and/or if the conclusions from the studies were emphasised (e.g. 'This study indicates that…').

In the end the decision about whether to credit material as AO1 or AO2 is not of major significance here because there is sufficient of both. In some essays an examiner might choose to credit some material as AO2 because there is plenty of AO1 and not enough AO2.

This essay certainly has plenty of accurate and detailed AO1 (**9 out of 9 AO1 marks**). The AO2 contains reference to approaches since the topic of the essay is on the biological approach, therefore, **13 out of 16 AO2 marks**.

The total mark is 22 out of 25 marks.

1

"Research into schizophrenia shows there is a major genetic component but the fact that concordance rates between identical twins is never 100% means that there must be environmental contributions."

Discuss biological explanations of schizophrenia.   *(25 marks)*

Schizophrenia is a psychiatric disorder involving loss of control with reality and a range of symptoms. There is considerable evidence that genetic factors are involved. This view considers that certain individuals possess certain genes that predispose an individual to schizophrenia. This means that it is inherited and we would expect to find that relatives have similar chances of developing the disorder. Indeed, research has found that first degree relatives of people with schizophrenia are 18 times more likely to be affected than the general population.

Identical (monozygotic, MZ) twins would be expected to have a similar chance of having schizophrenia since they carry the same genes. Research by Gottesman and Shields has found higher concordance rates (where both twins have the disorder) in MZ twins than DZ (dizygotic) twins who only share 50% of their genes. However, if schizophrenia was solely caused by genes then we would expect 100% concordance in MZ twins. Since this is not found then other factors must also be involved.

MZ twin studies have the advantage of controlling for genetics but the disadvantage of not controlling for environment. One way to get round this is to study MZ twins reared apart. Twin studies show similar concordance rates even when they have been reared apart, but the samples used in these studies tend to be rather small and family problems may have been the reason for the separation.

A genetic predetermination could lead to abnormalities in the brain. There is strong support for the idea that high dopamine levels are involved in schizophrenia. Dopamine is a neurotransmitter in the brain and post mortems have found higher levels than normal in the brains of schizophrenics. It has also been found that those drugs that are known to reduce dopamine (antipsychotic drugs) also reduce schizophrenic symptoms. However, this evidence tends to be correlational and we can't know whether the dopamine levels cause schizophrenia or schizophrenia causes high dopamine levels.

MRI scans have found that schizophrenics have enlarged ventricles in their brain and post-mortems have found that the brains of schizophrenics are lighter. This could reflect loss of cells in the brain and could explain the cognitive symptoms, such as poor attention, distractability and poor memory. This again could be a cause or effect of schizophrenia.

Viruses might also be involved as they could invade and disrupt brain development in the foetus. Research by Mednick has found a higher rate of schizophrenia in people exposed to flu in the second trimester of pregnancy, a time when there is greatest cortical development. Crow suggested that a retrovirus was incorporated into DNA and this was transmitted between generations. This would explain the fact that there is gradual brain damage and why schizophrenia spontaneously appears in families.

Adoption studies support the genetic explanation for schizophrenia. Tienari found that children who had been adopted away from a schizophrenic biological mother were still more likely to get it than a children adopted from non-schizophrenic parents, despite being raised in a different environment. Marcus also found that 22/50 children from 1 or 2 affected parents got it, and only 4/50 from healthy parents did. This supports the view that genetics has a strong role. However, not all high risk participants got it, indicating that other factors are involved.

2

(a) Outline and evaluate Ganzfeld studies of ESP. *(10 marks)*

(b) Discuss the functions of paranormal and related beliefs, including their cultural significance. *(15 marks)*

(a) Honorton first devised the Ganzfeld technique as a way to investigate ESP (extra sensory perception). This is the ability to perceive what is in another person's mind without direct contact. Honorton devised a way to cut out any signals – the participant who was receiving signals from someone else would be in a separate room and have no contact with anyone else. They also have ping pong balls taped to their eyes and cotton wool in their ears to cut out any extra sensory information. The sender concentrates on one of four pictures selected randomly by the experimenter and the receiver says which picture he thinks it is.

Honorton and other people used this technique to study ESP and concluded that people did demonstrate ESP because they did slightly better than chance with their identification of the image 'sent'. If it was chance then you would expect 25% 'hits' but people on average did better than this.

Some people don't believe these results and think that the experimenter influenced the choices in some way. However, Honorton repeated his studies using an automated technique and still found more hits than would be expected by chance. When Wiseman reviewed the evidence he found the opposite was true. The average result was poorer than chance. Both sides have argued back and forth and there really isn't a conclusion. It is possible that the results are related to the beliefs of the researcher – people who believe in ESP seem to find support, whereas people who don't believe don't find support.

(b) There are many reasons suggested about why people believe in ESP and other paranormal phenomena, and the function this serves for them. One such function could be related to a person's cultural background. Different cultures have different beliefs about ghosts and spirits, water diving, ESP and so on. Paranormal beliefs such as belief in spirits are embodied in your culture. Children learn about the stories and explanations related to paranormal phenomena when they are young. They are part of things like fairy tales. The important thing is that such stories bind a group of people together and are an integral part of the culture. Culture is defined as the rules and customs shared by a group of people so it is just these stories that are a key part of what is meant by a culture.

Of course, on the negative side, this cultural importance may mean it is quite hard to stop people believing in such things as witchcraft or folk methods used to treat mental illness. And the knowledge people have today may not be accepted by the cultural group, which is not good for them.

Probably the most important function of beliefs in paranormal and related beliefs is it helps people deal with the unknown, with things that don't have an explanation. It makes some people feel very unsafe because they don't know why some things happen, such as seeing things in the sky, and no one can explain why those things are there. So people want an explanation and if there isn't one they will invent something or accept whatever explanation is offered.

There are individual differences in this because some people are more happy to accept uncertainty whereas others seek answers and, therefore, are more accepting of paranormal explanations. In fact the quest for explanations is a natural part of the way human minds work and this is adaptive. Humans seek explanations and their desire for such explanations means that they do find real explanations and this kind of scientific question enables them to find ways to control things in their world. This wish for explanations is an example of determinism.

See pages 9–11 for a breakdown of the marking criteria used to mark this question.

(a) In this part of the question there is a mixture of AO1 and AO2 marks. The student has given an accurate and detailed description of the Ganzfeld technique plus a reasonably accurate report of the findings of such studies, though key details are lacking (such as the actual percentages). However, there are only a few marks available for AO1 so this is sufficient for **4 out of 4 AO1 marks**. The evaluation is rather superficial and basic, tending towards 'rudimentary' rather than 'reasonable'. Therefore, **2 out of 6 AO2 marks**.

(b) The second part of this question contains a higher amount of marks and, therefore, more time should have been spent on this part of the answer, especially the evaluative component. There is some evaluation in paragraphs 2 and 4 but this is rudimentary. However, this is not a topic that lends itself to evaluation; research studies might have been used to comment on, for example, the individual differences.

There is also the question of synopticity – issues, debates and approaches. Determinism was thrown in right at the end, but not in a very meaningful way. It could be argued that humans tend to be determinist in their approach to understanding the world and, therefore, such an approach by scientists is a natural form of thinking. **5 out of 5 AO1 marks, 2 out of 10 AO2 marks.**

The total mark is 13 out of 25 marks.

See pages 9–11 for a breakdown of the marking criteria used to mark this question.

3

A psychologist wishes to investigate whether people in a group will decide on a riskier course of action than individuals making a decision on their own. In order to investigate this the psychologist gave participants a scenario to consider: A young man has decided to take a gap year before going to university and can't decide whether to (a) travel with a group of friends (the safer decision) or (b) travel on his own (the riskier decision). The psychologist sought participants for this study by advertising on the noticeboard at the university where he worked. He selected the first 40 students who volunteered and asked each participant to select one of the options after considering the scenario. Half of the participants were allowed to discuss their views with a small group of other participants before registering their opinion. The other half read the scenario on their own.

The results from the study are shown in the table below.

Table 1 Decision made by participants in groups or on their own

	Safer decision (choice a)	Riskier decision (choice b)
Participants who discussed the scenario in a group	8	12
Participants who made their decision on their own	15	5

The psychologist decided to use a Chi-squared test to analyse the results. The Chi-squared analysis produced a value of 5.01.

Table 2 Critical values of Chi-squared for a one-tailed test where $df = 1$

Significance level	0.10	0.05	0.01
Observed value of Chi-squared	2.71	3.84	6.64

All of the answers given are fully correct, except for part (h).

(a) State an appropriate directional hypothesis for the above study. *(2 marks)*

People who discuss a scenario produce a riskier decision than people who do not discuss the scenario.

In part (a) the answer would not receive full marks if it did not include mention of both levels of the IV.

(b) Identify the target population in the above study. *(1 mark)*

The target population is the group of people from which the sample was taken, which in this case would have been the students at that university who read the advertisement.

(c) Identify the type of experimental design used in the above study. *(1 mark)*

It is an independent groups design.

(d) Identify **one** possible uncontrolled variable in the study and describe the effect it may have had. *(3 marks)*

One possible uncontrolled variable would be the fact that students had taken gap years themselves and this would affect their judgement. This would affect the results if it happened that there was an uneven distribution of people who had taken gap years in one of the experimental conditions.

In part (e) the candidate has given two answers, both of which are correct and well explained. However, if the first answer had been wrong the candidate would have received 0 marks because, in the research methods section, only the first answer is marked. This is because you could give a range of answers, knowing that one of them is going to be correct.

(e) Describe how you would have dealt with this uncontrolled variable. *(3 marks)*

To control this I would have allocated participants randomly to the two experimental conditions, which should mean that there should be no bias. Alternatively I could have asked people beforehand about their own travel experience and excluded anyone who had travelled.

The answer for (f) is fully correct; another possible reason is that a test of association was required.

(f) Give **two** reasons why a Chi-squared test was used to analyse the results of the above study.   *(2 marks)*

The data was nominal data, in other words it was in frequencies. And also the samples were independent – no person was represented in more than one category.

The answer for (g) is fully correct; if the candidate had written 'the level of probability' this would be given only 1 mark.

(g) What is meant in Table 2 by the phrase 'significance level'?   *(2 marks)*

The phrase means that the probability that the results can be attributed to chance factors rather than the IV.

(h) Explain what conclusion could be drawn from the statistical results.   *(4 marks)*

Chi-square is significant at the 5% level but not at the 1% level. The 5% level is adequate so there is a significant difference in whether people discuss things as a group or not, in that groups seem to produce a riskier result than a person just working on his/her own.

The answer for (h) is only worth 2 marks because the full evidence has not been given – the answer should mention that it is significant at the 5% level because the observed value is 5.01, which is greater than the critical value at 5% (which is 2.71).

(i) Briefly describe the major features of science, with reference to the study described above.   *(5 marks)*

Two of the key principles of science are replicability and objectivity. In this study it would be important for the psychologist to record his procedures in detail so that someone else could repeat the study. He would also aim to be objective, which is why he would get participants to note down their decision instead of discussing it with the psychologist, which might be subjective. The control of extraneous variables is also part of objectivity. Another feature of science is hypothesis testing. The aim is to see if you can falsify your hypothesis, in which case it is wrong.

In part (i) there is sufficient detail for the full 5 marks.

(j) The psychologist was further interested in why people made the decisions they made and, therefore, decided to conduct a further study following the same procedures but interviewing the participants afterwards. This time the psychologist thought he would involve a wider target population. Describe in detail the procedures that would be involved in this follow-up study, including sampling methods, ethical issues, instructions to participants, and questions that might be asked.   *(12 marks)*

In order to get a wider sample the psychologist might place the advertisement in a newspaper, which would mean you would get people of all ages and different occupations.

Once the main study is over the psychologist would ask each participant if they would be happy to discuss the scenario further. The psychologist should deal with ethical issues by explaining the aims of this part of the study (i.e. to find out the reasons behind their decisions) and remind the participants that all of their answers would be confidential and that they had the right to withdraw at any time from the interviews.

The candidate has provided a detailed description of key design decisions that would need to be taken in extending the original project, so **12 out of 12 marks**.

The psychologist should then take each participant one at a time to discuss the situation further. The psychologist might have a few questions fixed to start off the interview but would think of questions as the interview went along in order to respond to the answers that the participant was giving. This would allow the maximum amount of information to be collected.

The questions might start with 'What were the reasons behind the choice you made?' and 'What factors do you think were most important in that choice?'. It would be particularly important to interview the people who had been in a group discussion to see what effect the group discussion had on their final decision. If the participant had been in a group discussion it would be important to consider the effect of the other group members, so questions might be asked about the arguments presented by other group members. The psychologist might also ask people what their initial view might have been to see whether it had changed. It would also be important to ask people about what factors might have influenced their decision, such as personal experiences.

The total mark is 33 out of 35 marks.

Child development

17.1 Social Development

After studying this topic you should be able to describe and evaluate:

AS

- The first part of this unit (early relationships, attachment, privation and deprivation) is covered in *Revise AS Unit 3.1, pages 52–63.*

- early relationships: attachment and the role of caregiver-infant interactions in the development of attachment, including reference to human and animal studies; function of attachment; secure and insecure attachments; measuring attachment; possible short-term and long-term consequences of privation and deprivation; Romanian orphan studies: effects of institutionalisation, age-related benefits of adoption (Rutter et al); the work of Bowlby, Schaffer, Ainsworth and van IJzendoorn
- later relationships: the development of friendship in childhood and adolescence; age-related change in friendship; sex differences in children's friendship; research into the causes and consequences of popularity and rejection.

Later relationships: the development of friendship in childhood and adolescence

AQA B ▶ U3

Age-related change in friendship

A friend is more than a 'peer'; friendship implies an emotional aspect and includes elements of mutual trust, assistance, understanding, respect and intimacy.

Howes (1988) notes that toddlers have begun to form friendships – they direct more attention to one playmate and their friendships are characterised by sharing things like toys or food. After the age of 2 they develop more friendships and are able to distinguish between different types of friends.

Damon (1977) suggested three stages in the development of friendship based on interviews with children where he asked them about their friendships:

- Under 8 years: Children are egocentric in their thinking (see Piaget's theory, page 81), so friendships tend to be focused on the child's own needs. Friendships are rather short-lived and quickly formed and reformed.
- Between 8 and 11 years: Friendships based on mutual interests and kindness are valued.
- Over 11 years: More sharing of personal information, longer-lasting relationships.

Bigelow and LaGaipa (1975) confirmed the view that early friendships are based more on mutual activities, whereas later friendships are related to loyalty, similarity and acceptance. Selman (1980) used social dilemmas to investigate the development of friendships and empathy. He identified 5 stages, which are outlined on page 91.

Sex differences in children's friendship

Friendships are important in gender development where same-sex friends reinforce gender stereotypes (see page 65).

Waldrop and Halverson (1975) found a reversal in playmate choices in boys and girls around the age of 7. Up to this age boys have relatively 'intensive' relationships with same-sex peers whereas girls have 'extensive' relationships, i.e. relationships with a wider and mixed sex group. After the age of 7 girls foster a few best friends (intensive and same-sex), whereas boys become more interested in larger groups or gangs. Omark *et al.* (1973) report that this is found in other cultures, which suggests an innate basis for such behaviour, perhaps related to the roles boys and girls take on in adulthood. Girls focus more on friendship as a source of intimacy and confidantes, whereas boys' friendships tend to be more based on joint activities. This may be related to females' general orientation towards interpersonal matters (Eagly, 1978).

Research into the causes and consequences of popularity and rejection

The importance of social skills has led to social skills training programmes as a way to help rejected children improve their social relationships.

Role-taking skills refer to the ability to take the perspective of someone else, i.e. to 'stand in their shoes'. Such skills are related to social skills generally. Empathy and role-taking skills are discussed on pages 88 and 91.

The **continuity hypothesis** is based on Bowlby's theory of attachment, suggesting a 'continuity' between infant relationships and later adult relationships.

Causes of popularity and rejection

Social skills – Dodge *et al.* (1983) observed 5-year-olds at play and noticed that popular children displayed more sensitive social skills than rejected children. If the children were watching others at play the popular children gradually joined in by making group-oriented statements, whereas the rejected children tended to barge in and behave aggressively. The rejected children were also uncooperative, self-serving and critical, all characteristics that led to their rejection. Other children were classified as neglected (they just watched) or average. Coie *et al.* (1982) describe another group, called 'controversial', who are aggressive but good at social skills.

Cognitive skills – Popular children have better **role-taking skills** and also tend to have higher IQs than rejected children (Shaffer, 2002). Inadequate social skills are associated with low IQ (Cartledge and Milburn, 1986).

Parenting styles – A number of studies have linked authoritative parenting style to popularity, where a parent is firm but fair (for example, Dekovic and Janssens, 2002). Highly authoritarian parenting, which relies on power assertion, tends to be associated with rejected children.

Sroufe *et al.* (2005) showed that securely attached children are more likely to be popular in school (the **continuity hypothesis**). Such children also go on to be good parents and form trusting adult relationships – as a consequence of secure attachment, not popularity.

Physical attractiveness – Vaughn and Langlois (1983) found a correlation between physical attractiveness and popularity in pre-school children.

Consequences of popularity and rejection

Mental illness – Cowen *et al.* (1973) used longitudinal data from a study of 800 children in New York state. Those children who received negative ratings at age 8 were three times more likely to have sought psychiatric help in the following 11 years.

Delinquency – Dishion *et al.* (1991) suggested that 'rejected' children band together and form deviant cliques in adolescence. Kupersmidt and Coie (1990) used data from a longitudinal study to show that children identified as 'rejected' at age 11 were more likely to have been suspended from school later and three times more likely than normal children to have been in trouble with the police.

Evaluation

- A lot of the data are correlational, though some studies have shown a causal link, for example, Ladd and Golter (1988) found that argumentative behaviour at age 3 predicted later unpopularity. Dodge (1983) found that rejected children continue to be rejected even when with unfamiliar peers, supporting a causal link.
- On the other hand the link between rejection and later consequences **may be due to common factors** such as poor social skills. In other words, mental illness may not be due to peer rejection but both are due to poor social skills.

Practice essays 17.1

(a) Suggest **one** way that researchers could investigate attachment in infants. *(3 marks)*

(b) Describe and briefly evaluate **one** cause of popularity. *(5 marks)*

(c) Describe and evaluate the development of friendship in childhood and adolescence. *(12 marks)*

17.2 Cognitive Development

After studying this topic you should be able to describe and evaluate:

Piaget's theory of cognitive development is covered on pages 81–82.

- *Piaget's theory of cognitive development: schemas: adaptation, assimilation and accommodation; Piaget's stages of intellectual development; characteristics of these stages, including object permanence, conservation, egocentrism, class inclusion; Piaget's research, including the three mountains experiment and conservation experiments*
- *alternative approaches to children's cognition*

Vygotsky's theory of cognitive development is covered on pages 82–83.

- *Vygotsky and cognitive development within a social and cultural context; Vygotsky's zone of proximal development; scaffolding; guided participation in sociocultural activity; nativist explanations and early infant abilities, including knowledge of the physical world (Baillargeon); the information processing approach: Siegler's research into problem-solving strategies.*

LEARNING SUMMARY

Alternative approaches to children's cognition

AQA B ▶ U3

Nativism is the view that abilities are innate. The nativist view of cognitive development suggests that infants are born with substantial knowledge about the physical world.

Key points from AS

- There are two views of perception – one view says that we interpret what we see on the basis of expectations (Gregory's view) see *Revise AS Unit 2.4, page 46*.
  These expectations resolve ambiguities in perceptual data and incomplete data. The other view is that sensory input is sufficiently rich to explain our perceptions. This latter view was developed by James Gibson, see *Revise AS Unit 2.4, page 45*.

Object permanence is the realisation that objects continue to exist even when they cannot be seen. Piaget claimed that this developed after the age of 8 months.

Criticisms of research using infants can be found on page 26.

Nativist explanations of cognitive development

Piaget's view was that the earliest stage of cognitive development was a perceptual stage (the sensorimotor stage). Therefore, theories of perceptual development are relevant to cognitive development. In Piaget's view sensory input is not sufficient on its own for perception of the world because such data is often ambiguous and incomplete and so infants have to learn to interpret their world through interactions with the world. In contrast, nativists believe that infants possess many innate perceptual and cognitive abilities. Gibson and Gibson (1955) developed this view in their **differentiation theory**, the view that perceptual (and cognitive) development is a process of learning to see the differences between objects, i.e. through a process called *differentiation*. As babies develop they can learn to make distinctions between objects and events that they were not able to make initially. Their early inabilities are not due to lack of cognitive skills; they simply lack the ability to differentiate.

Renee Baillargeon was another researcher who argued that infants know more about perception than Piaget claimed and she conducted research to demonstrate this. For example, Baillargeon and DeVos (1991) showed that infants aged 3–4 months demonstrated **object permanence** when tested on various tasks. In the rolling car task there was a large or small carrot sliding along a track and hidden at one point by a screen with a large window. The track is arranged so that the large carrot should be visible as it passes behind the window (but in fact doesn't appear), whereas the small carrot (not as broad) should remain hidden. The infants looked longer at the large carrot presumably expecting the top half to be visible behind the window.

Infants have also been shown to have other innate cognitive abilities. For example, Wynn (1992) assessed their arithmetic ability. 5-month-old infants were shown a series of pictures where, in one case, picture 1 shows a mouse placed behind a screen, picture 2 shows a second mouse placed behind the screen and then in picture 3 the screen slides down and either two mice or one mouse are shown. The infant should only show surprise at one mouse if he/she can add. Surprise was measured in terms of time spent looking at the picture. 5-month-olds showed rudimentary addition and subtraction abilities.

Gopnik and Meltzoff (1997) take an intermediate position with a **'theory' theory**, proposing that infants do have substantial innate knowledge, but cognitive development does require the construction of theories (hypotheses about how the world works), which are tested against reality.

The **information-processing approach** is based on computer analogies – input, output, storage, programmes, routines and so on. Information-processing theories assume that one person is more intelligent than another because they can process information more efficiently.

Key points from AS

- For information on 'working memory' see *Revise AS Unit 2.1, page 29.*

The information-processing approach suggests that cognitive development is related to age-related changes in (1) what the brain can do (use of M space), and (2) the use of strategies. Piaget's theory has been viewed as an information-processing approach because it too focused on age-related changes to brain maturity and the development of more sophisticated strategies.

Piaget's theory suggested that children of different ages were typified by particular strategies.

The information-processing approach to explaining intelligence is presented on page 69.

The information-processing approach

Case's theory – Case (1992) suggested that information-processing ability is related to **mental space** (M space), a concept rather similar to 'working memory'. There is a limit to the amount of information that can be held in M space at any one time, but processing efficiency increases with age:

- **The brain matures** – changes in the myelin sheath (a fatty protective layer around the nerves which increases), leads to faster neural transmission rates. Cowan *et al.* (1999) compared the abilities of children and adults to be able to recall digits presented in a way that prevented any rehearsal. Average span of apprehension (i.e. ability to hold information in mind without doing any operation on it) was 3.5 digits for adults, 3 for older children and 2.5 for 6 year olds.
- **Cognitive strategies** develop. As children get older the amount of M space needed for well-practised mental tasks is reduced, thus increasing the amount of available space. Chi (1978) tested M space by comparing the ability of child chess experts and adults who had no chess experience. The task was their ability to remember chess board positions. The children could recall more, presumably because they had developed relevant strategies through experience.
- **Metacognitive skills** (thinking about thinking) are important for efficient use of M space, for example, being aware of what words you don't understand when reading something, monitoring your own progress on a mental task, etc.

Siegler's model – There are also age-related changes to the quantity and quality of information-processing strategies. Siegler *et al.* (1996) formulated the **adaptive strategy choice model**, which suggests that at any one time a child has a variety of different strategies that can be used. With increasing age more sophisticated and powerful strategies develop, but a child will fall back on simpler strategies when faced with new tasks.

Siegler (1976) tested children on a Piagetian task where a child is shown a balance with a number of weights (different sizes) on either side. The child is asked to predict whether the scale will tip one way or the other. Siegler worked out four possible strategies that could be used to solve the problem, for example, number (the side with most weights will tip down) or distance (the side with weights further from the fulcrum will tip down). Siegler gave children a variety of problems and found that 5-year-olds used number strategy and were 89% correct when given the conflict-weight problem (one side has more weights and the other side has weights at a further distance), whereas 17-year-olds who tended to use the more sophisticated distance strategy were only correct 51% of the time on such problems, though they obviously did better on other types of problems. This shows that there is not a simple relationship between strategies and success on solving problems.

Siegler *et al.* (1996) looked at children's arithmetic strategies. Very young children use a *sum strategy* (when adding 5 + 3 counting every number singly, i.e. 1 and 2 and 3 and 4 and 5 and 6 and 7 and 8), older children use a *min strategy* (start from 5 and add one at a time, i.e. 6 and 7 and 8). The most sophisticated strategy is 'knowing' the answer, called *fact retrieval* (i.e. they just know that 5 + 3 is 8).

Practice essays 17.2

(a) Describe what Vygotsky meant by the zone of proximal development.

(3 marks)

(b) Outline and evaluate **one** method used by Piaget to investigate cognitive development. *(5 marks)*

(c) Describe and evaluate nativist explanations of cognitive development.

(12 marks)

17.3 Moral development

After studying this topic you should be able to describe and evaluate:

Kohlberg's theory of moral development is covered on pages 87–88.

Eisenberg's model of pro-social reasoning is covered on pages 88–89.

- Piaget's stages of moral development: pre-moral judgement, moral realism and moral relativism
- Kohlberg's pre-conventional, conventional and post-conventional levels; the stages of moral reasoning within these levels; ways of investigating moral development, including the use of moral comparisons and moral dilemmas
- alternatives to Piaget and Kohlberg
- Eisenberg's model of pro-social reasoning, including hedonistic, needs, approval, self-reflective and internalised orientations
- Gilligan's ethic of care: differences between boys and girls; Gilligan's three levels of moral development
- Damon's research into distributive justice
- psychodynamic explanations of moral development; the role of the superego.

LEARNING SUMMARY

Piaget's theory of moral development

AQA B   U3

Both Piaget and Kohlberg's theories are cognitive-developmental theories, characterised by identifying innately-determined stages of development.

Children in the stage of moral relativity recognise that morals are not absolute, for example, there are some situations where it is acceptable to lie.

Piaget (1932) proposed a stage theory based on investigations with children and moral stories (see research evidence).

age (approx)	stage	rules
0–5 years	Pre–moral judgement	Rules not understood
5–9 years	Moral realism	Rules exist as real things (**realism**). Actions evaluated in terms of **consequences**. Punishment in terms of **atonement**: make up for damage done (expiatory).
9+ years	Moral relativity	Rules mutually agreed and changeable (**relativism**). Actions evaluated in terms of **intentions**. Punishment in terms of **principle of reciprocity**, where punishment fits the crime.

Research evidence

Piaget believed that moral development was in part due to maturation, but also due to exposure to the views of others that cause the child to question his/her own values.

Realism vs. relativism – Piaget (1932) played a game of marbles with a group of children and asked questions about the rules. Children under 3 used no rules at all. By the age of 5 rules were seen as 'untouchable' and from some semi-mystical authority. By the age of 10 children understood that people had invented the rules and they could be changed but only if all players agreed. Linaza (1984) found the same sequence of development in Spanish children, supporting the universal nature of such stages.

An example of Piaget's paired moral stories was one boy who accidentally broke lots of plates whereas another boy deliberately threw one plate down and broke it. Which one should be punished most severely?

Intentions vs. consequences – Piaget presented pairs of moral stories to children where one story had greater consequences but the intentions were good. He asked who was naughtiest and why. The **heteronomous** younger child could distinguish between intentional and unintentional actions but based their judgment on the severity of outcome. The **autonomous** older child used the motive/intention as the means for judgment. However, Nelson (1973) found that even 3-year-olds can make judgments about intentions if the information is made explicit.

Hartshorne and May (1928) found little consistency in moral behaviour. A child who cheated in one situation didn't in another. They also found that immoral behaviour was more governed by the probability of being caught than any principles of morality.

Evaluation

- The game of marbles is a **rather insignificant** example of morals.
- The moral stories **confound intentions and consequences**, making it difficult for younger children. Armsby (1971) manipulated the stories so there was a small amount of deliberate damage or a large amount of accidental damage. He found that younger children did take intention into account.
- Piaget **introduced the idea of stages**, which are related to cognitive maturity.
- This account does not explain moral inconsistency (see Hartshorne and May on the left and Gerson and Damon on the next page), and ignores emotional influences.

Alternatives to Piaget and Kohlberg

AQA B   U3

Eisenberg's model of pro-social reasoning is an alternative approach to that of Piaget and Kohlberg. It is described and evaluated on pages 88–89.

Gilligan entitled her book '*In a different voice*' because she argued that women were not inferior – just different – to men.

Gilligan's ethic of care

Carol Gilligan (1982) suggested that Kohlberg made the error of assuming there was only one moral perspective, one of justice and fairness, whereas women tend to operate an ethic of care. Gilligan based her stage theory (below) on interviews with women facing real-life dilemmas (about abortions).

Gilligan explained why women were more 'caring' – she suggested that their **'interconnectness'** stems from identifying with their mother. In contrast, men have to separate early from their mother in order to form a separate masculine identity. This separation heightens boys' awareness of the power differences between themselves and adults, and so makes them more concerned with inequality (justice).

stage	justice perspective	care perspective
1	Uphold moral standards and withstand pressure to deviate	Concern with what others say and how choices might affect relationships.
2	Justice plus mercy. Principles are most important but one should consider others' feelings.	Sacrificing one's own concerns to the welfare of others. Relationships are more important than conventional rules.
3	Everyone is best served by universal laws, though there are some exceptions to the rule.	Aiming for a balance between valuing the individual and trying not to hurt anyone.

Research evidence

Gilligan and Attanucci (1988) asked a group of men and women to produce accounts of their own moral dilemmas. Overall, men favoured a justice orientation and women favoured a care orientation.

Garmon *et al*. (1996) tested over 500 people and found that women were more likely to refer to care issues.

Eisenberg *et al*. (1987) found that girls aged 10–12 gave more caring responses than boys, although this may be because girls mature earlier.

Evaluation

- The findings may be due to **demand characteristics**. Eisenberg and Lennon (1983) found that, if participants knew researchers were looking at empathetic behaviour, they portrayed themselves more like that.
- Walker (1984) reviewed 79 studies and found **variable support**; some studies found no gender difference and some found that males were more caring.
- If a man's moral perspective was assessed using Gilligan's stage theory, he might appear to be morally inferior to women – so Gilligan's approach might also be seen as **gender-biased**.

Key points from AS

- Freud's view of moral development is part of his psychodynamic theory see *Revise AS Unit 1.1, page 19*.

The phallic stage and the process of identification that occurs in that stage are also important for gender identity.

Erikson's theory of social development (see page 39) is also a psychodynamic theory. He de-emphasised the unconscious and emphasised the social world. Each stage of life is marked by a crisis, which must be confronted and resolved. Both parents influence the development of moral behaviour, which is a product of the superego (determining what is acceptable or not) and the ego (inhibiting undesirable impulses of the id). Since the ego is the rational component of the personality, morality must be related to cognitive development generally.

Key points from AS

- General criticisms of Freud's theory of personality development can be used to evaluate this account, see *Revise AS Unit 1.1, page 19* and also *AS Unit 7.1, page 153*.

Damon's research on distributive justice shows that children are capable of more sophisticated moral judgments than Kohlberg had predicted in his theory.

Psychodynamic explanations of moral development

Freud suggested that moral development is related to the **phallic stage** and emergence of the **superego**. Around the age of 3 years a child's sexual interest focuses on their genitalia and they feel desire for their opposite-sex parent (the **Oedipus complex**). This makes them see their same-sex parent as a rival. The child feels unconscious hostility, resulting in guilt. The child also feels anxiety and fear of punishment should his true desires be discovered. Resolution occurs through identification with the same-sex parent. **Identification** is the process of 'taking on' the attitudes and ideas of another person.

Freud explained the strong bonds between dominant parents and their children as the result of a threatening parent producing a greater fear of punishment, which leads to a stronger sense of identification.

The Oedipus complex only explains moral development in boys. Freud proposed that girls go through a similar conflict – they recognise they haven't got a penis and blame their mother, thus, their father becomes their love-object and the girl substitutes her '**penis envy**' with a desire to have a child. This ultimately leads to identification with her mother. However, the resolution of penis envy is less satisfactory than resolution of the Oedipus conflict and therefore, according to Freud, girls have inferior moral development compared to boys.

The internalised parent – The ego-ideal rewards you when you behave in accordance with parental moral values. It is the source of feelings of pride and self-satisfaction, acting as the 'rewarding' parent. Your conscience punishes you when you do something wrong. It is an internal representation of the 'punishing' parent and is composed of prohibitions imposed on you by your parents. The conscience appears at age 5 or 6 and is a source of 'guilt feelings'.

Unsatisfactory resolution of the phallic stage results in problems such as amorality, homosexuality or rebelliousness.

Research evidence

Freud predicted an inverse relationship between guilt and wrongdoing: the more guilt a person experiences the less likely they are to do wrong. MacKinnon (1938) gave nearly 100 participants a test and left them alone with the answer book. Of those who cheated (about 50%) most said they did not feel guilty, which confirms the inverse relationship between guilt and wrongdoing.

Inconsistency of moral behaviour – Freudian theory suggests that moral behaviour should be consistent because of the conscience, though there is the possibility of some inconsistency because of irrational behaviour by the id. Hartshorne and May's study (see previous page) found little consistency in moral behaviour.

Another example of inconsistency can be seen in Damon's research into distributive justice. Gersen and Damon (1978) showed that children don't distribute rewards as fairly as they said they would. In a pretend situation children gave an average of 18% of candy bars to themselves. In a real test a few months later, this rose to 29%.

Practice essays 17.3

(a) Explain what Piaget meant by the terms 'moral realism' and 'moral relativism'. *(4 marks)*

(b) Outline and evaluate **one** method that was used by Kohlberg to investigate moral development. *(4 marks)*

(c) Describe and evaluate Gilligan's approach to explaining moral development. *(12 marks)*

Applied Psychology

18.1 Cognition and law

Face recognition is covered on pages 29–30.

AS

• Research on eyewitness testimony is covered in *Revise AS Unit 2.2, pages 35–37*.

• recognising and remembering faces: processes involved in recognition of faces; explanations for face recognition, including feature analysis and holistic forms; the construction of likenesses using composite systems; identification procedures: simultaneous and sequential line-ups

• recalling events: factors affecting the reliability of eyewitness accounts and eyewitness identification, including post-event contamination; improving eyewitness recall, including features of the cognitive interview; children as eyewitnesses; flashbulb memory: memory for shocking events

• the false memory debate: controversy surrounding the recovery of repressed memories; the existence of false memories; evidence relating to repression and false memory; ethical and theoretical implications of the false memory debate.

LEARNING SUMMARY

The false memory debate

AQA B ▶ U3

A **false memory** is a memory for something that did not happen, but which feels as if it is a true memory. **False memory syndrome (FMS)** refers to a memory of a traumatic experience, such as sexual abuse, which rules a person's entire life, disrupting normal functioning.

Key points from AS

• Repressed memories and motivated forgetting are discussed in *Revise AS Unit 2.3, pages 41–42*.

The ethical implications relate to the extent to which psychiatrists should encourage recovered memories, and, thus, might be instrumental in creating them.

The theoretical implications relate to the extent to which this evidence can be seen as supporting or challenging the concept of motivated forgetting.

Controversy surrounding the recovery of repressed memories

FMS advocates, such as Elizabeth Loftus, believe memories are confabulations, i.e. reconstructed memories put together from fragments of real and imaginary events that might include stories seen on TV or suggestions made by therapists. The danger of FMS is that it has resulted in wrongful accusations and lawsuits – both by those who have been accused, and also by those who thought they had recovered memories during therapy but later realised these were false memories.

Others, such as Dallam (2002), argue that repression is an unconscious strategy for dealing with traumatic experiences, well documented by research. This supports the view that false memories are real.

The existence of false memories

Evidence for FMS

Loftus and Pickrell (1995) conducted a study referred to as 'lost in the mall'. They interviewed participants about childhood events, implanting a memory about having been lost in a shopping mall when younger (they were told a close relative had reported the incident). About 20% of the participants came to believe in their false memories to such an extent that they still clung to them even after being debriefed.

Evidence against FMS

Pezdek (1995) suggested that people may accept relatively innocuous memories (such as the ones above) but they may not accept suggested traumatic memories. In a similar study she found that no participants remembered an innocuous memory (of receiving a painful enema as a child from their parent).

Practice essay 18.1

Discuss evidence relating to repression and false memories.   *(20 marks)*

18.2 Schizophrenia and mood disorders

After studying this topic you should be able to describe and evaluate:

Schizophrenia is discussed on pages 95–104.

Unipolar depression is discussed on pages 105–110, including seasonal affective disorder.

- classification of schizophrenia, including sub-types; symptoms and diagnosis; explanations, including biological and cognitive; sociocultural explanations: labelling and family dysfunction; treatments of schizophrenia, including anti-psychotic drugs, behavioural treatments and psychotherapy; the role of community care; evaluation of these treatments
- mood disorders: unipolar and bipolar depression; seasonal affective disorder (SAD); symptoms and diagnosis of mood disorders; explanations, including biological, cognitive, behavioural and psychodynamic; treatments of mood disorders, including biological and cognitive; evaluation of these treatments.

LEARNING SUMMARY

Biological explanations of bipolar disorder (BD)

AQA B   U3

Bipolar disorder is also referred to as manic-depression because many sufferers oscillate between mania (being hyperactive, elated, making grandiose plans) and depression. There are often long periods of normal behaviour in between the manic or depressive phase, though in some sufferers the episodes alternate even within one day. Bipolar I disorder refers to full manic and depressive episodes; bipolar II disorder refers to milder manic episodes that alternate with depression over time.

About 1% of the population experience bipolar disorder.

The manic phase of bipolar disorder has been related to creativity and charismatic leadership, and, therefore, would be an adaptive trait. Many artists and famous leaders have been manic-depressives (e.g. Winston Churchill, Abraham Lincoln, Vincent Van Gogh, Robbie Williams, Stephen Fry). However, for most it is a crippling disorder that ruins their lives.

Genetic explanations

Individuals may inherit a gene or genes that cause BD. Such genes predispose individuals to develop the disorder – this is the **diathesis-stress model** described on page 54.

Research evidence

Gene mapping – Egeland *et al.* (1987) studied the Amish, an American religious sect who have a high incidence of BD, and a cluster of genes on chromosome 11, which were present in 63% of those with the disorder. However, subsequent research (e.g. Hodgkinson *et al.*, 1987) failed to find any common marker on chromosome 11. Continuing research has identified other possibilities. Recently, Gurling *et al.* (2006) found evidence that the '**Slynar**' **gene**, on chromosome 12, may be implicated. It is present in about 10% of cases. Some studies also show links between BD and schizophrenia, pointing to a shared genetic cause.

Twin studies – Durand and Barlow (2000) report a concordance rate of 80% for identical (MZ) twins, as compared to only 16% for non-identical (DZ) twins, showing a high genetic component for BD.

Adoption studies – Gershon (1983) looked at adopted individuals with manic depression. 2% of their adoptive parents had the disorder whereas 30% of their biological parents had it.

Family studies – In families of individuals with BD, first-degree relatives (i.e. parents, children, siblings) are more likely to have a mood disorder than the relatives of those who do not have BD (Davis and Palladino, 2000). This suggests a genetic basis for mood disorders generally.

Neuroanatomical explanation

Zubieta *et al.* (2000) studied the brains of 16 people with BD using PET scans and found 30% more brain cells in certain areas of the brain – areas containing signaling cells that release the brain chemicals dopamine, serotonin and noradrenaline.

Biochemical explanation

The **permissive amine theory** of mood disorder (see page 105) has also been used to explain BD. When serotonin is low noradrenalin fluctuates wildly causing highs and lows (serotonin and noradrenalin are biogenic amines).

Psychological explanations of bipolar depression

AQA B ▸ U3

Key points from AS

- General evaluations for biological and psychological explanations of abnormality can be found in *Revise AS Unit 7.1, pages 151–155.*

Behavioural explanations

The fact that BD runs in families can be explained in terms of environmental rather than biological factors. It may be that such families reward particular behaviours, for example, praise or attention is given for grandiose plans so that such behaviours are encouraged. It may also be that family members with the disorder act as role models; having a parent with a tendency towards manic behaviour could influence a child.

Psychodynamic explanations

One psychodynamic suggestion is that bipolar depression results from alternating dominance of the personality by the superego (depression) and the ego (elation).

Freud in fact placed BD under the heading of 'psychosis', along with schizophrenia, i.e. a disorder where the patient does not have insight into their condition.

Cognitive explanations

Linear schematic processing model

Beck (1976) extended his concept of the negative triad, which is an explanation of depression (see page 107). He suggested that mania was the opposite of depression. In the case of mania, sufferers had a positive cognitive triad of self, world and future, and positive cognitive distortions. For example, they saw themselves as extremely attractive and powerful, saw the world filled with wonderful possibilities, and the future with unlimited opportunities. Typical cognitive distortions include underestimating risks, minimising problems, and seeking immediate gratification.

Integrative model

Beck (1996) recognised the failure of his earlier model of BD to take biological factors into account; given the research evidence it is clearly important to include such factors. Therefore, his new model includes two key additions: the concepts of 'modes' and 'charges'. **Modes** are methods of responding to specific demands or problems, for example, 'primal modes' have evolved from prehistory as survival reactions (and are therefore biological). When a mode is activated this leads to increased physiological activity and the person becomes 'charged'. **Charges** are energy levels.

Socio-cultural explanations: life events

Psychological factors are important as a trigger for the onset of the disorder. It is likely that people inherit susceptibility for BD but the disorder only appears as a consequence of stressful life events, such as the death of a close family member or friend, or the loss of one's job. Once the disorder has developed it then seems to have a life of its own, which may suggest that certain neurotransmitter dysfunctions have been triggered.

Evaluation

- The importance of psychological explanations is supported by the fact that **drug therapy on its own is not effective**.
- Not all individuals who inherit a genetic susceptibility develop BD, therefore, **psychological factors must be important in triggering** the disorder, as described by the diathesis-stress model (see page 54).

Therapies for bipolar depression

ECT may be used in the treatment of bipolar disorder, especially for the depression component (see page 102).

Biological therapies: drugs

The most commonly prescribed drug for BD is **anti-manic drugs**, especially *lithium*. It is often referred to as a 'maintenance treatment' because patients must continue to take the drug even when apparently recovered in order to prevent further episodes. Lithium relieves the depressive episodes as well as the mania, though to a lesser degree. **Anti-depressants** are prescribed for depressive episodes, as well as **anti-psychotic drugs** for acute mania episodes to slow the individual down.

Evaluation

Key points from AS

- General criticisms of drug therapies and psychological treatments are included in *Revise AS Unit 7.2, page 156*.

- The effectiveness of lithium depends on getting **the correct dosage** – too low a dose will have little effect, whereas too high a dose results in lithium intoxication (or poisoning).
- As long as patients continue taking **lithium the results are impressive**. For example, Viguera *et al.* (2000) report that more than 60% of patients with mania improve with lithium. Stuppes *et al.* (1991) found that relapse was 28 times greater when patients stopped taking lithium so it is important to continue taking the medication even when the symptoms have stopped.
- On the other hand, drug therapies are **not totally effective**. Kulhara *et al.* (1999) report that 30% of patients do not improve when taking lithium (which may in part be due to receiving the wrong dosage or not taking their medication).

Psychological therapies

Cognitive therapy – Basco and Rush (1995) list some of the aims of cognitive therapy: to facilitate acceptance of the disorder and the need for treatment; to help the individual recognise and manage psychosocial stressors and interpersonal problems; to improve medication adherence; to teach strategies to cope with depression and hypomania; to teach early recognition of relapse symptoms and coping techniques; to improve self-management through homework assignments; and to identify and modify negative automatic thoughts.

Family focused therapy (Miklowitz and Goldstein, 1997) recognises the role of the family in the care of people with BD. The treatment lasts over 9 months and involves education (family members are taught about treatments for BD, how to recognise the onset of episodes and to develop a relapse prevention plan); patient and family are taught communication skills and are given help with how to deal with specific family problems.

Evaluation

- **STEP-BD** (Systematic Treatment Enhancement Program for BD) is a large-scale US longitudinal study. In 2007 they reported that 64% of the cohort followed had recovered after psychotherapy, compared to 52% of a control group getting just case management, and they did it an average of 110 days faster. Family focused therapy (FFT) made for the best outcomes.
- **Psychotherapy alone is rarely effective** in treating BD (Klerman *et al.*, 1994), but the same is true for using lithium therapy alone.

Practice essays 18.2

(a) Explain the differences between unipolar and bipolar disorder. *(4 marks)*

(b) Briefly describe **one** treatment for bipolar disorder. *(4 marks)*

(c) Describe and evaluate **at least one** biological explanation of bipolar disorder. Refer to empirical evidence in your answer. *(12 marks)*

18.3 Stress and stress management

After studying this topic you should be able to describe and evaluate:

- *stress and illness: the role of the autonomic nervous system (ANS) and endocrine system functions in mediating and responding to stress*
- *ways of measuring stress, including physiological, behavioural and self-report techniques; the role of personal variables, including behaviour types A, B and C, locus of control and hardiness in mediating responses to stress*
- *stress management: problem-focused and emotion-focused strategies, the role of defence mechanisms in coping with stress, including repression, regression, rationalisation and denial*
- *techniques of stress management: behavioural approaches, including biofeedback and systematic desensitisation; cognitive therapy; the role of social factors in coping with stress: social support, including types of social support.*

**L E A R N I N G
S U M M A R Y**

AS

- Most of the topics on stress and stress management are covered in *Revise AS Unit 5.1 and 5.2, pages 98–110.*

Extra stress topics for AQA B

AQA B ▷ U3

The **ANS** (autonomic nervous system) controls our response to stress; the sympathetic branch of the ANS is aroused by a stressful situation.

Key points from AS

- The Daily Hassles and Uplifts Scale, and other scales, are discussed in *Revise AS Unit 5.1 pages 101 and 102.*

Ways of measuring stress

Physiological – The **galvanic skin response (GSR)** indicates stress arousal by measuring activity of the ANS. When the ANS is aroused the electrical conductivity of the skin is altered and this is measured by attaching electrodes to the skin.

Behavioural – Signs of ANS activity include sweating, rapid pulse, raised heart rate, flushed face – so stress can be measured by assessing these behavioural signs.

Self-report techniques – There are a vast array of questionnaires that can be used to assess stress, including SRRS (Holmes and Rahe, 1967) and also the Daily Hassles and Uplifts Scale (DeLongis *et al.*,1982).

Locus of control in mediating stress responses

Locus of control (Rotter, 1996) refers to where you place the responsibility (or blame) for things that happen to you.

Locus of control can be measured using Rotter's Locus of Control Scale.

- **Internals** have an internal locus of control, i.e. they believe they are responsible for the things that happen to them.
- **Externals** have an external locus of control. This can make one feel comfortable because when things go wrong, you blame someone or something else ('a bad workman blames his tools'). On the other hand this makes an individual feel that things 'happen to them'. Life is simply a matter of luck or fate.

Taking control is a way to reduce levels of stress.

Individuals who have a high internal locus of control feel less stress and are less disrupted by it. For example, Kim *et al.* (1997) found that children who were 'internals' showed fewer signs of stress when their parents divorced. Cohen *et al.* (1993) found that participants were more likely to develop a cold if they felt their lives were unpredictable and uncontrollable; the likelihood to become ill is linked to a weaker immune system, which is a sign of stress. Rodin and Langer (1977) found that residents in a nursing home were likely to live longer if they were given a greater sense of control (e.g. how they arranged the furniture in their rooms, when they could receive visitors).

The role of defence mechanisms in coping with stress

Freud (1910) suggested that we unconsciously deal with anxiety by means of ego defence mechanisms, such as:

- **Repression** – placing uncomfortable thoughts in the unconscious, e.g. you might forget that a favourite pet had died because you failed to feed it.
- **Regression** – a person behaves in a way that in the past may have brought about relief from the anxiety-provoking situation.
- **Rationalisation** – things that create anxiety are dealt with in a rational or logical manner in order to avoid the emotional content.
- **Denial** – simply denying the existence of something that is threatening. However, denying the existence of the thing does not make it go away.

Such ego defences can be effective in protecting the individual from overwhelming anxiety in the short-term, but in the long-term may be counterproductive. One study found that the use of denial following an HIV diagnosis was associated with more rapid disease progression in HIV-seropositive gay men (Ironson *et al.* 1994).

The role of social factors in coping with stress

Social support – Research has shown that social support has a significant effect on stress. For example, Kamarck *et al.* (1990) recruited 39 female psychology student volunteers to perform a difficult mental task (stressful) while their physiological reactions were monitored. Each participant attended the lab session alone or they were asked to bring a close same-sex friend who was told to touch the participant on the wrist throughout the mental task. In general the participants who were with a friend showed lower physiological reactions than those who were alone.

Kiecolt-Glaser *et al.* (1984) looked at **T-cell activity** (an indicator of immune system activity) in the blood of students before and after taking exams. They also gave students a questionnaire at the beginning of the study, which looked at psychiatric symptoms, loneliness and life events. Levels of T-cells were higher during the month before the students took exams, and dropped during the examination period itself. What is notable is that the effect was strongest in those students who said they were lonely/lacked friends. This indicates the importance of social support in enhancing the functioning of the immune system and, thus, resisting stress.

Nuckolls *et al.* (1972) studied 170 pregnant women. The women with high life stress and low social support had more early pregnancy complications than those with high life stress and high social support (91% vs. 33%).

Brown and Harris (1978) interviewed 400 women living in Camberwell, London. Some of them had experienced a stressful event in the preceding year, yet not all developed any serious psychological problems, such as depression. Those who did develop such problems shared one important factor, the absence of a close, supportive relationship.

Types of social support – Family and friends provide social support. Social support may also be provided in self-help groups.

Practice essays 18.4

(a) Explain **one** method that could be used to measure stress. *(3 marks)*

(b) Distinguish between *problem-focused* and *emotion-focused* strategies for coping with stress. *(5 marks)*

(c) Describe and evaluate **one** stress management technique. Refer to evidence in your answer. *(12 marks)*

18.4 Substance abuse

After studying this topic you should be able to describe and evaluate:

Explanations of substance abuse (addiction) are discussed on pages 133–136.

Treatments of substance abuse (addiction) are discussed on pages 137–140.

- *use and abuse: distinctions between addiction and physical dependence; psychological dependence, tolerance and withdrawal; solvent abuse, tobacco and nicotine, alcohol, stimulants and depressants; explanations for substance abuse: hereditary factors; personality characteristics and social factors, including peer influences*
- *treatment and prevention: psychological treatments and their effectiveness, including aversion therapy and self-management; prevention techniques; identifying and targeting 'risk' groups; use of fear-arousing appeals; social inoculation; health promotion/education in treatment and prevention; the stages of behaviour change proposed in the Prochaska model.*

LEARNING SUMMARY

Use and abuse

AQA B　　U3

Many substances are *used* for genuine medical purposes. The term *abuse* refers to the harmful use of such substances.

Distinctions between addiction and physical dependence

Addiction refers to *psychological* dependence on a drug, which is separate from the *physical* dependence.

Physical dependence refers to the effects of abrupt discontinuation of a drug. This can be the result of long-term use of a legal or an illegal drug. Characteristics of physical dependence include:

- **Tolerance or habituation** – The body increasingly adapts to the substance and needs larger doses to achieve the same effect. These increases eventually level off.
- **Withdrawal** – When the substance is discontinued the person may experience symptoms such as anxiety, cravings, hallucinations, nausea and 'the shakes'.

Psychological dependence

Addiction and psychological dependence relate to feelings of well-being, whereas physical dependence relates to a physical craving.

Psychological dependence is related to the reinforcing properties of substance abuse – using such substances creates a sense of pleasure and this is positively reinforcing; not taking the drug is a negative experience, which acts as a punisher. Thus, addiction is maintained. In addition, as we saw on page 134, addiction can be explained in terms of faulty cognitions and also in terms of psychological vulnerabilities such as low self-esteem or dependency needs.

It has recently been recognised that addictions to physical substances (such as drugs) and psychological activities (such as gambling) share many of the same symptoms. Substance abuse may appear to be solely physical, whereas the psychological elements may be equally or even more critical in dealing with the problems. Conversely, something like gambling may appear to be solely psychological, whereas the activation of reward circuits in the brain may create a dopamine addiction.

The physical effects experienced by gamblers may be explained in terms of the role of dopamine in addictive behaviours, see page 133.

Griffiths (1995) has listed six components of addiction:

- **Salience** – The addiction is highly important to the individual.
- **Euphoria** – The addictive behaviour makes the individual feel 'high'.
- **Tolerance** – Over time, a drug user increases the dosage; a gambler increases the stakes to gain the same 'high'.
- **Withdrawal** symptoms are experienced by gamblers as well as drug addicts.
- **Conflict** with others and with themselves.
- **Relapse** is always likely even after giving up for a long period, the individual is always vulnerable and must resist key triggers.

Examples of substance abuse

A solvent is a substance that dissolves other substances. Water is a solvent, however, solvent abuse refers specifically to volatile solvents (i.e. solvents that evaporate rapidly) such as dry cleaning fluids, nail polish remover, butane gas, glue or turpentine (paint solvent).

Research on alcoholism is included on pages 133–134.

DSM is explained on page 96.

Stimulants are drugs that increase alertness either by increasing activity in the autonomic nervous system (ANS) or central nervous system (CNS), or both.

Research on cocaine abuse is described on pages 133, 138 and 139.

Depressants have a calming effect on the CNS. They increase the activity of the neurotransmitter GABA, which is the body's natural means of reducing anxiety.

Alcohol is also a depressant.

Solvent abuse

Solvent abuse involves sniffing or breathing in solvents. The effect is similar to drinking – initial euphoria followed by a lowering of inhibitions. The after-effects may be like a hangover, however, long-term use can include kidney and liver damage and even death; over 1,000 people have died in the UK in the last 20 years (Ives, 1999). Unlike most drugs, solvents are not addictive in themselves; it is a purely psychological addiction.

Research has identified certain vulnerability factors such as children in the care of local authorities ('looked after' children). Melrose (2000) also identifies two other groups: young offenders and school excludees. He also notes that children are likely to come from unstable or abusive family backgrounds.

Alcohol

Alcohol abuse (alcoholism) is classed as a chronic disease (American Medical Association). The distinction between alcohol use and abuse is that the latter involves physical and social harm, including problems with tolerance, withdrawal and an uncontrollable urge to drink. It is included in the DSM classification of mental disorder.

Current evidence suggests that there is a considerable genetic component (Dick and Bierut, 2005). Addiction to alcohol is a mixture of physical and psychological dependence.

Stimulants

Amphetamines increase alertness and concentration, as well as heart rate and blood pressure. They stimulate the CNS and the sympathetic branch of the ANS and also increase levels of dopamine. They are prescribed for narcolepsy (see page 24) and major depression.

Cocaine is primarily prescribed for its anaesthetic properties, but it is also a stimulant. It too increases levels of dopamine in the brain.

Nicotine is the chemical associated with smoking addiction (see page 135). It is a stimulant and leads to physical dependence because of its capacity to release dopamine, which then may also lead to sensations of reward and relaxation. Research suggests that some people are predisposed to smoking because they have a mutation in a gene (**CYP2A6**) that helps to rid the body more rapidly of nicotine (Pianezza *et al.*, 1998).

Caffeine is found in coffee, tea, many soft drinks and, to a lesser extent, in chocolate. Drinking coffee is a common way to keep awake and many people avoid it because of its stimulant properties. It reduces levels of the neurotransmitter adenosine in the brain, which leads to increased dopamine activity. It is regarded as highly addictive and leads to a physical dependence. People quickly develop a tolerance and also experience symptoms of withdrawal.

Depressants

Barbiturates are prescribed as anti-depressants and also for sleep. Common names include 'purple hearts' or 'blue heavens'. They are abused as a form of anxiety relief and because they reduce inhibitions. Their use has declined dramatically because even a slight overdose can be fatal and also because they are highly addictive and withdrawal symptoms can be life-threatening.

Benzodiazepines (BZs), such as Valium, are also used as anti-depressants. BZs reduce anxiety levels and are, therefore, relaxing. They can be dangerous when taken with alcohol but on their own they are relatively harmless. They have replaced barbiturates because they are less addictive but they are not without psychological and physical dependence. They also produce unpleasant side effects such as slurred speech and difficulty breathing. Long-term use has been linked to anorexia.

Treatment and prevention

Some aspects of treatment and prevention are discussed on pages 137–140.

Prochaska's spiral model of behavioural change

Prochaska *et al.* (1992) proposed a model that explained both professionally-motivated and personally-motivated changes in health behaviour:

- **Precontemplation** – The person is unaware of a problem and, therefore, has no intention to change their behaviour.
- **Contemplation** – The person is thinking about doing something in relation to the problem. People may stay in this stage for a long period of time (even several years).
- **Preparation** – The person has decided to take action and may have begun to make some minimal changes. They may, for example, have started to reduce the number of cigarettes they smoke.
- **Action** – The person has made changes to their behaviour or environment for a significant period of time (ranging between 1 day and 6 months). Many people focus on this stage as being critical, whereas the early stages are equally important in bringing about change.
- **Maintenance** – Continued action in maintaining change, most importantly focused on preventing relapse. A person can be said to be in the maintenance stage if they have been able to remain free of their addiction for more than 6 months.

The model is a spiral because people are usually not successful at the first attempt so they have to repeat these steps several times, each time getting further towards action and maintenance. Prochaska *et al.* suggested that smokers usually have to make three or four attempts before they reach the maintenance stage. People also may not go through the stages in a linear fashion.

Effectiveness

- This model incorporates **behaviour as well as attitudes**, and is realistic about the need to repeat the steps several times before behaviour change can be accomplished.
- DiClemente *et al.* (1982) provided **evidence to support the model** in a study of about 1500 smokers (white American females who started smoking at about 16 years of age). Those who were in the preparation stage at the beginning of the study were more likely to have tried to quit smoking or actually succeeded when assessed 6 months later as compared to those in earlier stages.

Practice essays 18.4

(a) Explain the difference between *addiction* and *physical dependence*.

(4 marks)

(b) Describe **one** method used to treat alcohol addiction. *(4 marks)*

(c) Describe and evaluate explanations of substance abuse that are related to inherited factors. Refer to evidence in your answer. *(12 marks)*

18.5 Forensic psychology

After studying this topic you should be able to describe and evaluate:

- *offending behaviour: problems in defining crime; measuring crime, including official statistics and alternatives (victim surveys and self-report measures); offender profiling, including typology and geographical approaches; theories of offending; physiological approaches: atavistic form and somatotype theories; biological explanations, including genetic transmission; psychodynamic and learning theory explanations, including social learning; Eysenck's theory of the criminal personality*
- *treatment of offenders: the role of custodial sentencing; effectiveness of custodial sentencing, including recidivism; alternatives to custodial sentencing; treatment programmes: behaviour modification; social skills training and anger management; evaluation of these treatment programmes.*

LEARNING SUMMARY

Offending behaviour

AQA B   U3

Crime is the breach of a rule or law that has been created by a governing authority.

In order for any society to function effectively, it is necessary to prohibit certain behaviours, especially those that harm other people or their property.

Key points from AS

- Self-report techniques are discussed in *Revise AS Unit 4.1 page 78.*

Offender profiling is a method of identifying the perpetrator of a crime based on an analysis of the nature of the offence and the manner in which it was committed.

Typology means the study of types.

Problems in defining crime

Crime is defined with reference to a particular society's rules, therefore, there is no single definition of crime that isn't circular – crime is what is designated as criminal by the relevant authorities. Certain offences are universally regarded as criminal, such as murder. However, murder may be classified according to intention (the French have *crime passionnel* – crime of passion – which results in a lesser sentence). Another issue is the consideration of 'how much' (for example, stealing one sweet may not be regarded as a criminal act) and also what counts as a mitigating factor (for example, murdering someone who has injured your child).

Measuring crime

Official statistics – The Home Office publish *Criminal Statistics* containing a record of the number and types of crimes recorded by the police in England and Wales. One drawback with this is that many crimes go unreported so it is not an accurate picture, yet it is important in forming public perceptions, changes in law and policing policy.

Victim surveys and self-report measures – The *British Crime Survey* is conducted every two years in the UK of people over the age of 16, asking about their experiences of victimisation in the previous year. This permits access to unreported crimes. However, questionnaires have problems in obtaining reliable data.

Offender profiling

Typology – The FBI was the first to use offender profiling and the typology approach. The process involves:
(1) assimilation (information including the crime scene, victim and witnesses).
(2) classification (integrating the information and classifying the type of criminal e.g. as organised or disorganised – an organised criminal is skilled and leaves few clues, a disorganised criminal is impulsive and lacks social skills).
(3) construction of a behavioural sequence (reconstruction of the crime).

Geographical approaches are relevant to serial crimes and focus on making geographical links between various crimes to help catch the criminal. Ideally, a minimum of five crimes is required to build up a geographic profile that will help track the criminal. Geographic profiling complements the typological approach.

Theories of offending

AQA B   U3

Atavism is the tendency to revert to ancestral type.

'Soma' means 'body', so somatotype means 'body type'.

Eysenck's theory (on page 175) is a biological explanation of offender behaviour.

Key points from AS
• Freudian concepts are explained in *Revise AS Unit 1.1, page 19.*

The superego is important in moral development, see page 163.

Key points from AS
• Bowlby's research is discussed in *Revise AS Unit 3.1, page 53.*

Physiological approaches

Atavistic form – Lombroso (1876) proposed that some people are born with a strong, innate predisposition to behave anti-socially. This is essentially a 'throwback' to an earlier human type (which he called *homo delinquens*). Individuals actually look different: a narrow sloping brow (low in intellect), prominent jaw (strong in passion), and extra nipples, toes and fingers. They were adapted to survival in the wild but could not cope with social living and could not distinguish right from wrong.

Evaluation

• Goring (1913) reported a study comparing the physical features of 3000 convicts with 3000 non-criminals and found **no significant differences** in any features.

Somatotype theories – Sheldon *et al.* (1949) proposed that there were three basic body types: **endomorphs** (fat and soft), **ectomorphs** (thin and fragile) and **mesomorphs** (muscular and hard). Mesomorphs are also aggressive and insensitive to other people's feelings and, thus, potentially criminals. Sheldon rated people on a scale of 1 to 7 according to the amount of each of the three components they showed and used this to rate criminals and normal people, demonstrating that criminals tended to be mesomorphs.

Evaluation

• This explanation has **received some support**, for example, Cortes and Gatti (1972) conducted a study of 100 delinquents and found that 57% were mesomorphic, whereas only 16% were ectomorphic compared with 19% and 33% respectively for controls. Most research, however, has not been supportive.

• Even if there is a correlation between physique and criminality this **doesn't demonstrate a cause**; there may be some common factor, which causes both physique and criminality, such as home environment.

Biological explanations

Various studies have looked at the link between genes and criminality as evidence of the genetic basis of aggression (see page 44).

Psychodynamic explanations

Criminality can be explained in terms of the superego, which develops during the phallic stage when a child identifies with their same-sex parent. Some children develop a weak superego because their same-sex parent is absent or unloving, which results in selfishness and uncontrolled aggression. Alternatively, criminality may be explained by identification with a deviant parent, resulting in a deviant superego. Freud called this phenomenon **pseudoheredity**, i.e. non-genetic inheritance.

Bowlby (1946) proposed that certain delinquents (**affectionless psychopaths**) were unable to feel empathy for other people and that is why they commit crimes. Bowlby suggested that affectionless psychopathy was caused by attachment bonds being disturbed in early life. This was supported by Bowlby's study of delinquents (Bowlby, 1944); 86% of the affectionless psychopaths had experienced frequent early separations.

Evaluation

• Psychoanalysts do not claim to account for all types of crime in terms of unconscious conflicts. For example, Kline (1987) suggests that white collar crimes and even **some aggressive crimes are rational** rather than irrational.

• This approach **does address the importance of emotional factors** in criminal behaviour.

Learning theory explanations

Classical and operant conditioning are explained on page 72.

- **Classical conditioning** involves learning to associate one thing with another, so a child may learn to associate stealing sweets with excitement.
- **Operant conditioning** involves learning by the consequences of your actions; criminal behaviour is learned and maintained by the rewards it brings.
- **Social learning theory** – we learn from observing others and model the behaviours that are rewarded (due to **vicarious reinforcement**).

The theory of differential association – Sutherland (1947) argued that criminal behaviour, like all behaviour, is learned through social interactions. Social groups are defined in terms of the norms they share and for some social groups there are norms that are favourable towards criminal activities as well as norms that are unfavourable. The term **differential association** reflects the ratio of favourable to non-favourable definitions of crime.

Evaluation

- This theory **explains why crime rates are higher in some neighbourhoods** than in others, and not just poor neighbourhoods. 'White collar crimes' are committed by professional middle classes who view such behaviours as acceptable.
- The theory does **not explain more impulsive, emotional crimes**.

Eysenck's theory of the criminal personality

Sensation seeking has also been associated with addictive behaviour. (See page 136.)

Eysenck (1977) proposed that criminality is produced by an interaction between personality (which is genetically based) and the environment. Eysenck's theory of personality identified three dimensions: extraversion-introversion (E); neuroticism-stability (N); psychoticism-normality (P). Criminality is associated with **extraversion** – extraverts are impulsive, have a high need for excitement and danger, and lose their temper easily. Extraverts are also harder to condition and, therefore, less affected by reinforcement and punishment. Eysenck proposed that the dimension of extraversion-introversion is based on activity of the **reticular activating system (RAS)**, a part of the brain responsible for arousal levels. In extraverts, the RAS inhibits incoming sensations and, therefore, the person seeks arousal.

Neuroticism is the tendency to experience negative emotional states such as anger, anxiety and depression.

According to Eysenck **neuroticism** may also be linked to criminality, a trait which is also biologically based. People who score highly on neuroticism have a more reactive ANS, they tend to be high on emotionality, are jumpy and anxious, and find it very difficult to cope with stress. Finally, **psychoticism** involves a hostile and uncaring attitude to others, cold cruelty and a lack of empathy.

Evaluation

- There is **poor evidence that extraversion is consistently linked** to the traits suggested by Eysenck. For example, Zuckerman *et al.* (1988) didn't find sensation seeking was related to extraversion.
- Some **studies have found support** – criminals score more highly than non-criminals on the scales of extraversion, neuroticism and psychoticism, as measured by the Eysenck Personality Questionnaire (EPQ). However, important variables (such as socioeconomic class, cultural background and intelligence) were not controlled (Dwyer, 2001).
- Many other **studies have not been supportive**. For example, Bartol *et al.* (1979) compared EPQ scores of 400 male prisoners with controls and did find that robbers were high on extraversion, but overall the criminals were less extravert than the control group.
- The theory **does recognise that both biology and the environment** may be important determinants of criminality.

Treatment of offenders

AQA B   U3

A **custodial sentence** is a punishment where a person is kept in custody, i.e. some form of prison.

The role of custodial sentencing

There are four main functions that prisons serve:

- **Incapacitation** to protect other members of society.
- **Rehabilitation** through education and/or treatment.
- **Punishment** to decrease the probability that a behaviour will be repeated.
- **Deterrence** to discourage people from committing crimes in the first place.

Effectiveness of custodial sentencing

Recidivism refers to repeating criminal behaviour.

Recidivism rates suggest that prison does not act as an effective punishment or deterrent. In the US rates stand at about 60% compared to 50% in the UK (BBC, 2005). One possible explanation for the difference is the greater emphasis on education and rehabilitation in UK prisons.

Type of criminal – Glaser (1983) concluded, from a review of evidence, that supervision in the community is better for new offenders since prison often encourages and reinforces criminal behaviour. This is particularly true for 'low risk' offenders.

Two judges, Davies and Raymond (2000), argue that a longer jail sentence does not deter others, nor does it discourage the criminal himself; sentences are often imposed as a result of public demand. Many crimes are committed under the influence of alcohol or during an emotional rage, therefore, the perpetrator is not making rational choices based on the likelihood of punishment.

Length of sentence – Walker and Farrington (1981) found that the length of sentence made little difference to rates of reoffending among habitual offenders. Some argue that a short sentence has the greatest effect, especially for first offenders.

Alternatives to custodial sentencing

Alternatives include being given a caution, a fine, a community order, or a community order with an unpaid work requirement.

Treatment programmes

Behaviour modification is a form of operant conditioning where a person is rewarded for desirable behaviours in order to increase such behaviour.

One example of behaviour management is token economy, which is discussed on page 103.

Social skills training (SST) – Since criminals often lack appropriate social skills, programmes may focus on the acquisition of such skills, which involves modelling the behaviour of someone else and/or role play.

Anger management – Impulsive people may need to learn to become desensitised to disconnect anger and fear arising in frustrating situations. Therapeutic approaches usually include frustration tolerance training as well as meditation and relaxation techniques.

Evaluation of these treatment programmes

One issue for any treatment programme is the longevity of the effects – often changes are just short-term or do not transfer to the real world.

- Goldstein (1986) reviewed 30 studies of SST with delinquent teenagers and found **participants had acquired certain skills**, such as how to negotiate with a probation officer. However, not many could transfer these skills to everyday life.
- Blackburn (1993) suggests SST may be useful with criminals who have serious social difficulties, but it **does not have much value for the majority of offenders**.
- Anger management courses have had **mixed success**. For example, Ireland (2000) assessed the effect of an anger management course on 50 prisoners and found considerable improvement in most of the prisoners as measured by questionnaires, although 8% showed a deterioration after completing the course.

Practice essays 18.5

(a) Describe and evaluate **two** methods used to measure crime. *(8 marks)*

(b) Discuss biological explanations of crime. *(12 marks)*

1

(a) A group of psychology students are going to replicate Piaget's study of conservation in young children.

(i) Describe a suitable sample of children that should be used in order to demonstrate age differences in conservation. *(2 marks)*

(ii) Identify suitable materials that might be used to test the children's ability to conserve. *(2 marks)*

1. (a) (i) A reasonable answer but should mention why the age of 7 has been selected e.g. explain the age divide for pre-operational/ concrete op. stages. **1 out of 2 marks.**

(i) They could use some children under the age of 7 and some over the age of 7 because around the age of 7 is the age when children become able to conserve. They wouldn't use very young children because they couldn't cope.

1. (a) (ii) The answer would be better if the student had referred to the actual task, but there is sufficient for **1 out of 2 marks.**

(ii) You could use counters to show conservation of number, clay for conservation of mass, and beakers of water for conservation of volume.

(b) Outline the nativist approach to explaining cognitive development. *(4 marks)*

Nativists are people who believe in nature rather than nurture. So the nativist approach is one where psychologists have suggested that infants are more capable than Piaget suggested. Piaget suggested that children acquire schemas through the processes of assimilation and accommodation. At first infants have very few innate schemas but these develop through interactions with the world. Nativists like Baillargeon suggest that children are more capable than Piaget suggested.

1. (b) This is a competent answer; the candidate makes three clear points and, therefore, gains **3 out of 4 marks.**

(c) Describe and evaluate Vygotsky's theory of cognitive development. *(12 marks)*

Vygotsky's view of cognitive development was that the main driving force was social interactions. A child is led through the ZPD (zone of proximal development) because experts lead them through it. Experts are people with greater knowledge. Experts are one kind of social interaction. The other kind is culture more generally. We are surrounded by cultural things such as language and the internet, and these things provide us with the stimulus to develop cognitively.

Vygotsky suggested that there are two kinds of mental functions: elementary ones and more complex ones (higher functions). All children are born with elementary mental functions, and animals have these too – things like attention and perception. Through social interactions these functions are transformed into higher level cognitive abilities.

Vygotsky's theory has been used to develop the idea of scaffolding in education where a child is guided in the learning process but not told what to do except when the child is floundering. The expert essentially provides a scaffold for the learning and this helps them through the ZPD.

There is some research evidence to support Vygotsky's theory, but not as much as Piaget's because Vygotsky's theory is less easy to test. Research on scaffolding has shown that it is an effective way to learn, for example, a study by McNaughton and Leyland. There is also evidence from other cultures which shows how cognitive development is different and this is related to the culture surrounding the child.

Vygotsky's theory can be contrasted with Piaget's theory, which is more representative of European capitalist society and which focuses on the importance of the individual. Piaget felt each child should invent knowledge through his/her own self-discovery whereas Vygotsky felt knowledge should be socially constructed. In fact, both of their theories recommend active learning so in some ways the theories have similarities. They may be appropriate to different cultures.

1. (c) This answer provides a reasonable amount of description and evaluation, however key details are missing, for example there is no explanation of the ZPD (what it means). There is also no mention of the different speech shown by children as they develop cognitively and this is important to Vygotsky.

The evaluation (final two paragraphs) also contains some useful points but these could have been further explained in order to score top marks, for example, providing more understanding of the active learning strategies recommended by both approaches.

The evaluation carries more weight than the description so only **6 out of 12 marks.**

2

(a) Distinguish between the concepts of privation and deprivation. *(4 marks)*

Privation refers to the lack of any attachments whereas deprivation refers to the loss of attachments. It is suggested that privation has more serious consequences whereas children may recover from early deprivation.

(b) A psychologist intends to study the attachment behaviours of young children when playing with their father. Describe **two** behaviours that might be studied and how they could be measured. *(4 marks)*

The psychologist might look at reunion behaviour. When the father comes into a room the way the child greets his/her father is related to how securely attached the child is. Another behaviour that might be studied is the distance between the child and his/her father while the child is playing. Secure children are not so clingy.

(c) Describe and evaluate Bowlby's work on early relationships. *(12 marks)*

Bowlby's first research looked at the effects of deprivation on a child's emotional development. He proposed the maternal deprivation hypothesis, which stated that children who experience frequent early separations from their mother figure will later become maladjusted. Bowlby said that there was a critical period for this development – children under the age of 2 would be affected. He supported this with his study of juvenile delinquents. He showed that the children who became affectionless psychopaths had experienced frequent early separations. However, Rutter said Bowlby was wrong in claiming that this is true of all children and also Bowlby overlooked the fact that there is a difference between privation and deprivation.

Bowlby further developed his original hypothesis and it became a theory of attachment. This theory focuses more on the benefits of attachment rather than on the consequences of deprivation. It is an evolutionary theory because it is concerned with the way that attachment is something that is adaptive – attachment increases the likelihood that an animal or baby will survive. This is similar to the process of imprinting that Lorenz documented in his study of goslings that imprinted on a goose or on Lorenz depending who they saw first.

Bowlby suggested that this early attachment relationship forms the basis for later relationships in a person's life. The kind of attachment relationship the infant has with its mother figure leads them to expect the same, for better or worse, from relationships later in life, like with their romantic partners or with their own children.

It's always difficult to get evidence to support evolutionary explanations but one piece of evidence is from Hazan and Shaver who did find a link between the kind of attachment a child experiences early in life and their later relationships. They found that children who are securely attached go on to form more trusting relationships. However, this study was a questionnaire where people had to recall their early childhood so the data may not be entirely reliable. Bowlby's theory of attachment also included the concepts of primary and secondary attachments. Children are attached most to one person in terms of emotional development. This is most likely to be a child's mother but could be their father or someone else. This attachment is probably related to the quality of the contact with the other person. Children also develop secondary attachments that are also important.

2. (a) The answer to this question is brief regarding privation and deprivation, but enough for **2 out of 4 marks**. In the second sentence an example of the serious consequences should have been given for an extra mark and the difference between them is not explained enough.

2. (b) The first sentence is sufficient for 1 mark but does not go on and say how this can be measured. The other behaviour mentioned is not explained sufficiently for 1 mark and again this does not say how it can be measured. **1 out of 4 marks.**

2. (c) This is a competent and thorough answer. It provides a clear description of Bowlby's theories showing sound and accurate knowledge and understanding.

There are good references to other studies that back up Bowlby's theory. There are also evaluative comments throughout the essay, however, the evaluation is perhaps not as full as the description – and it is critical to focus on evaluation as more weight is placed on AO2 marks. **10 out of 12 marks.**

Chapter 19
Approaches, debates and methods in psychology

19.1 Approaches in psychology

After studying this topic you should be able to describe and evaluate:

AS

- A discussion of all six approaches is presented in *Revise AS Unit 1.1, pages 13–21.*

Classical and operant conditioning are explained on page 72.

- the biological approach: assumptions and application of the biological approach; the role of the central and autonomic nervous system in behaviour; the genetic basis of behaviour; strengths and limitations of the biological approach
- the behaviourist approach: assumptions and application of the behaviourist approach; key concepts including stimulus, response and reinforcement; types of reinforcement; classical and operant conditioning as applied to human behaviour; strengths and limitations of the behaviourist approach
- the social learning theory approach: social learning theory as a bridge between traditional behaviourism and the cognitive approach; assumptions and application of social learning theory; the role of mediational processes in learning, motivation and performance of behaviour; observational learning and the role of vicarious reinforcement; strengths and limitations of social learning theory
- the cognitive approach: assumptions and application of the cognitive approach, including the idea that thoughts influence behaviour; information processing and how this applies to human behaviour and thought; use of computer analogies in understanding behaviour; strengths and limitations of the cognitive approach
- the psychodynamic approach: assumptions and application of the psychodynamic approach; Freud's approach to personality structure and dynamics; unconscious mental processes; psychosexual stages of development; Freud's use of case studies to highlight concepts; post-Freudian theories including Erikson and at least one other; strengths and limitations of the psychodynamic approach
- the humanistic approach: assumptions and application of the humanistic approach; the person-centred approach of Rogers and Maslow; rejection of the traditional scientific approach and experimentation; the importance within humanistic psychology of valuing individual experience, promoting personal growth, the concepts of freewill and holism; strengths and limitations of the humanistic approach
- the extent to which different approaches overlap and complement each other. The value of individual approaches and the merits of taking an eclectic approach to explaining human behaviour and in the application of psychology.

LEARNING SUMMARY

On the next page there is a table comparing the approaches in terms of the various debates listed on page 181. The discussion of each of the debates (pages 180–186) provides useful information related to the value of each approach and the merits of an eclectic approach.

Comparison of the approaches

AQA B U3

	The biological approach	The behaviourist approach	The social learning approach	The psychodynamic approach	The cognitive approach	The humanistic approach
Causes of behaviour	Internal, physical	External, psychological	External (observational learning) and internal (cognitive representations)	Internal, biological/ psychological	Internal, cognitive	Internal, psychological
Determinism / free will	We are determined by internal factors and/or inherited factors, both of which are outside our control.	Environmental determinism: we are controlled by external factors.	Reciprocal determinism: a person's behaviour both influences and is influenced by personal factors.	Psychic determinism: causes of behaviour are unconscious and hidden from us.	Thoughts determine behaviour, therefore, the individual has control (free will).	Each individual is responsible for making their own choices.
Nature and nurture	Biological systems are innate (nature) but experience may modify them (e.g. changed hormone levels when stressed).	All behaviour is learned (nurture), though the capacity to be conditioned is innate.	Behaviour is learned through direct and indirect reinforcement, but biological factors are not ignored.	Behaviour is driven by innate systems, but outcome is the result of an interaction with experience (nurture).	Faulty thoughts may be innate or due to experience. They may be a cause or effect of mental disorder.	Behaviour is affected by life experiences, which shape self-esteem, and also by an individual's self-determination.
Reductionism and holism	Reduces behaviour to basic biological components.	Reduces behaviour to stimulus-response units.	Reduces behaviour to effects of learning.	Reduces behaviour to a set of hypothetical mental structures and processes.	Reduces behaviour to thoughts, beliefs and attitudes.	Emphasises the importance of the whole person.
Idiographic / nomothetic	Nomothetic.	Nomothetic.	Idiographic and nomothetic (reciprocal determinism).	Idiographic, though also produced generalisations.	Nomothetic.	Idiographic.
Scientific status	Lends itself to experimental study. Often uses non-human animals because of ethical objections.	Highly objective and experiment-based approach.	An experimental approach.	Relied on case studies and subjective interpretation; may better reflect the complexity of human behaviour.	Highly experimental approach. Propositions can be easily tested.	Qualitative research (e.g. unstructured interviews), but this can be a scientific approach.

19.2 Debates in psychology

After studying this topic you should be able to describe and evaluate:

- free will and determinism, hard determinism and soft determinism; biological, environmental and psychic determinism; the scientific emphasis on causal explanations
- the nature–nurture debate, the relative importance of heredity and environment in determining behaviour; an interactionist approach
- holism and reductionism, the strengths and limitations of reductionist and holistic explanations; an interactionist approach
- idiographic and nomothetic approaches, the strengths and limitations of idiographic versus nomothetic research
- psychology and science, the features and principles of the scientific approach: a paradigm; the role of theory; hypothesis testing; empirical methods and replication; generalisation; the subject matter of psychology: overt behaviour versus subjective, private experience; the role of peer review in validating research; strengths and limitations of the scientific approach in psychology.

LEARNING SUMMARY

A **debate** is an argument between two alternative positions. None of the debates studied in this section are simply 'one or the other', it is a question of weighing up the relative strengths and limitations of each side of the debate.

Free will and determinism

AQA B ▷ U4

Behaviour can be determined by internal or external forces.

Key points from AS

- Psychological explanations of stress are given in *Revise AS Unit 5.1 page 98.*

This view of behaviour may be more applicable to non-human animals where learning has less influence on behaviour.

Key points from AS

- Prejudice is discussed in *Revise AS Unit 6.3 page 143.*

Kinds of determinism

Biological determinism – Behaviour is determined by internal (biological) factors, e.g. physiological explanations of stress and genetic explanations of gender development (see page 59).

Environmental determinism – The behaviourist view is that we are controlled by external forces. Skinner said that freedom was an illusion, maintained because we are unaware of the environmental causes of behaviour. The social learning approach suggests that our behaviour is controlled by vicarious/indirect reinforcement (environmental), but also by direct reinforcement.

Psychic determinism – Freud also thought that freedom was an illusion, because the actual causes of our behaviour are unconscious and, therefore, hidden from us.

The scientific emphasis on causal explanations – Science is based on the assumption that one thing causes (determines) another. Scientific research can be used to predict behaviour and manipulate it, e.g. reducing prejudice. Free will denies such relationships.

Issues related to determinism

Where do you think a cognitive psychologist would stand on the free will–determinism debate?

Moral responsibility – When a person commits an anti-social act, the cause of their behaviour may be due to biological (inherited) or social (e.g. the media) causes. We cannot hold individuals legally responsible for their actions if the causes were outside their control. Criminals have used this argument to 'excuse' their behaviour – their actions were not their fault and, therefore, they shouldn't be punished. Free will, on the other hand, suggests that we are each morally responsible for our actions.

At any time, would your behaviour have been different if you had willed it? Believers in free will say 'Yes'.

Lack of determinism – Both Heisenberg's **uncertainty principle** (1927) and Hilborn's **chaos theory** (1994) suggest that even in a hard science such as physics there are no purely deterministic relationships. The uncertainty principle states that the act of making an observation changes the observation, thus no objective research is ever possible. Chaos theory proposes that very small changes in initial conditions can result in major and unpredictable changes later.

181

Free will

Individuals have an active role in determining their behaviour, i.e. they are free to choose.

Humanistic psychologists (such as Maslow and Rogers) believe we exercise choice in our behaviour. Rogers believed that it is only by taking responsibility for all aspects of your own behaviour that an individual can be well-adjusted and capable of self-actualisation. Maslow also used the concept of self-actualisation and regarded it as the highest form of motivation.

Sartre, an existentialist philosopher, said that we are 'condemned to be free'; freedom is a burden because we must each be totally responsible for our behaviour and we must each respect each other's views. The law embodies this view.

Reconciling determinism and free will

Hard versus soft determinism

Soft determinism offers a way to make determinism compatible with moral responsibility.

William James (1890) proposed a way that the determinism–free will debate can be resolved, which he called 'soft determinism'. He suggested that we can separate behaviour into a physical and mental realm. It is the physical that is determined, whereas the mental realm is subject to free will.

Elizabeth Valentine (1992) proposed a different form of 'soft determinism'. She described it as the view that behaviour is always determined, it just sometimes appears to be less determined. Behaviour that is highly constrained by a situation appears involuntary; behaviour that is less constrained by a situation appears voluntary.

Westcott (1982) conducted a study to demonstrate the validity of this view. University students were asked to indicate the extent to which they 'felt free' in 28 different situations. They reported that they felt most free in situations requiring self-direction, absence of responsibility, performing a skilled behaviour, or when behaviour would result in escape from an unpleasant situation (i.e. where there was little constraint). They felt least free in situations characterised as 'prevention from without', 'diffuse unpleasant affect', 'conflict and indecision' and when they recognised that there were limits on their behaviour, for example having to take their abilities into account when selecting course options (i.e. where there was most constraint).

Freedom within constraints

Absolute free will means that behaviour is not determined in any lawful way. However, even humanistic psychologists believe that behaviour is governed by conscious decisions, which have some regularity. Heather (1976) resolved this by suggesting that much of behaviour is predictable, but not inevitable. Individuals are free to choose their behaviour, but this is usually from within a fairly limited repertoire.

The nature–nurture debate

AQA B U4

Nature refers to behaviour that is determined by inherited factors, whereas nurture is the influence of environmental factors such as learning and experience.

This debate is sometimes called the 'heredity versus environment debate'.

Key points from AS

• Bowlby's theory is discussed in *Revise AS Unit 2.1, page 53*.

'Empirical' means to discover something directly through one's own senses. Empiricists argue that all behaviour is acquired directly through experience.

Key points from AS

• Gregory's theory of perception is discussed in *Revise AS Unit 2.4, page 46*.

Nature versus nurture was once a heated philosophical debate, but now it is accepted that our genetic blueprint provides certain limitations through which the environment can express itself.

The diathesis-stress model (page 54) is a similar concept where potential is modified to produce phenotype.

Both Piaget and Freud suggested that development is 'driven' by biological changes. Adult characteristics are the consequence of the interaction between these biological factors and experience (nature and nurture).

Key points from AS

• Theories of perception cover both nature and nurture, see *Revise AS Unit 2.4, pages 43–48*.

IQ is a classic example of the nature–nurture debate (see page 78–79).

Nature

The 'nature' position is sometimes called 'nativism' or 'heredity'. It is the belief that human characteristics are largely inherited or native to an individual, a view espoused by the Greek philosopher Plato and later notably by the French philosopher Rousseau who believed that children were noble savages, and they should be allowed to follow their natural inclinations and inherent sense of goodness. This European view led to, e.g. Piaget's concept of the child actively engaged in his cognitive development.

Some examples of explanations where inherited factors are seen to be uppermost: evolutionary explanations of behaviour (e.g. Bowlby's theory), and biological accounts of aggression (page 43), mental illness (e.g. page 98) and gender development (page 53).

Nurture

The 'nurture' position is sometimes referred to as 'empiricism' or 'the environment'. Locke, a 17th Century philosopher, suggested that all babies are born alike; their minds can be described as a blank slate (*tabula Rasa*). Their development is passively moulded by empirical, sensory experiences. This view developed into the behaviourist view of environmental control.

Some examples of explanations in terms of environmental factors include Gregory's theory of perception, learning theories of aggression (page 40), gender development (page 61) and mental disorder (e.g. page 100).

Nature or nurture? An interactionist approach

Hebb (1949) pointed out that the question of 'nature or nurture' is like asking whether a field's area is determined more by its length or by its width. However, we can still consider the contributory factors.

Gottesman (1963) described a **reaction range**, e.g. our potential height is inherited but actual height is determined by factors such as diet. Potential is your **genotype** (the actual genes that an individual has) and realised potential is your **phenotype** (an individual's observable characteristics).

Phenylketonuria (PKU) is given as the classic example of gene-environment interaction. It is an inherited metabolic disorder where phenylketones build up and cause brain damage unless the child is given a diet (nurture) low in phenylalanine. Nature interacts with diet to produce the final phenotype, which may or may not be brain damage, depending on the child's diet.

Practical implications

If behaviour is entirely due to heredity then intervention would have little effect on the development of children. Herrnstein and Murray (1994), the authors of *The Bell Curve*, argue that we can't significantly change IQ and, therefore, intervention programmes are a waste of money. If intelligence can be boosted by experience then intervention programmes make sense. The evidence suggests that such programmes have a positive effect, supporting the 'nurture' position (page 79).

If behaviour is learned it can be manipulated by others. Skinner (1948) wrote a novel, *Walden Two*, describing how an ideal environment could be created to engineer human behaviour. If behaviour is learned it can be unlearned. Behaviourist principles are used to shape the behaviour of prisoners and mental patients, assuming that their behaviour is learned rather than innate. However, if such behaviours are biological then we should treat them with drugs.

Holism and reductionism

Holism is the view that systems as a whole should be studied rather than focusing on the constituent parts, and suggests that we cannot predict how the whole system will behave from a knowledge of the individual components.

Reductionism is any attempt to reduce a complex set of phenomena to some more basic components.

Most determinist explanations are reductionist, and vice versa.

Key points from AS

- Perception is discussed in *Revise AS Unit 2.4, page 44*.

You can work out the strengths and limitations of holistic explanations by reversing the reductionist arguments.

Examples of reductionism

Environmental reductionism – Reducing behaviour to the effect of environmental stimuli, as in behaviourist explanations of gender development (page 61) and mental illness (e.g. page 100). This approach overlooks innate influences and has potential for abuse through social manipulation.

Biological reductionism – Explaining behaviour in terms of physiological and genetic mechanisms, for example, biological explanations of gender development (page 59) and mental illness (e.g. page 98). However, this diverts attention from other, more social explanations and can result in over-use of biochemical methods of control (e.g. for mental illness or treatment of jet lag).

Machine reductionism – Explaining behaviour in information-processing terms. However, interconnectionist networks have been described by Penrose (1990), which are holist insofar as the network behaves differently than the individual parts.

Experimental reductionism – Use of controlled laboratory studies to understand similar behaviours in everyday life, may lack ecological validity.

Examples of holism

Gestalt psychologists argued that the whole does not equal the sum of the parts. They applied these principles to perception.

Humanistic psychologists (e.g. Rogers, 1951) believe that the individual reacts as an organised whole, rather than a set of stimulus–response (S–R) links.

Cognitive systems like memory and intelligence are examples of the value of a holistic approach. They are complex systems whose behaviour is related to the activity of neurons, genes and so on; yet the whole system cannot be simply predicted from these lower level units.

An eclectic approach

Relevant data is gathered together from various sources and disciplines, e.g. understanding the causes of schizophrenia involves both reductionist and holist explanations, or using data from brain scans to understand cognitive processes (see page 114).

Strengths and limitations

Strengths of the reductionist approach

- Reductionism may be a **necessary part** of understanding how things work.
- Reductionist arguments are **easier to test empirically**.
- Reductionist explanations may be correct or appropriate; they are incomplete because **psychological research has yet to identify all the facts**.

Limitations of the reductionist approach

- Reductionist explanations may **oversimplify complex problems** that have no single answer, taking attention away from other levels of explanation so that we fail to usefully understand behaviour.
- Reductionist explanations **may not answer the question**. Valentine (1992) suggests that physiological explanations focus on structures, whereas more holist explanations are concerned with process (see 'levels of explanation' on the next page).

An interactionist approach

Rose (1976) suggested that the controversy over reductionism is due to a semantic confusion.

If psychologists attempt to 'explain away' psychological phenomena using reductionist concepts, the result is unsatisfactory. However, if one accepts that there is a hierarchy of **levels of explanation**, then it is possible to see that reductionist explanations are one form of discourse and contribute to explaining behaviour. Rose proposed that physical explanations are at the bottom, moving through chemical, anatomical-biochemical, physiological, psychological (mentalistic), social psychological and, finally, sociological explanations.

Idiographic and nomothetic approaches

AQA B ▶ U4

The **idiographic approach** is an approach to research that focuses more on the individual case as a means of understanding behaviour, rather than aiming to formulate general laws of behaviour (the nomothetic approach).

'Nomos' means 'law'.

The **idiographic approach** involves the study of individuals and the unique insights each individual gives us about human behaviour. It is the approach favoured by humanistic psychology and also the approach taken by Freud in his case histories. Case studies focus on individuals, such as the study of Jenny undertaken by Allport as a means to study personality. He analysed 300 letters written by 'Jenny', arguing that this idiographic perspective could tell us more about human behaviour and personality than could the use of personality tests, which provide statistical information.

The idiographic approach typically uses qualitative methods such as unstructured interviews, case studies, introspection, etc. Such techniques allow new insights to be presented. The approach is typical of humanistic and psychoanalytic psychologists.

The **nomothetic approach** involves the study of a large number of people and then seeks to make generalisations or develop laws/theories about their behaviour. This is the goal of the scientific approach. The biological, behaviourist and cognitive approaches are concerned with general laws of behaviour. In fact, most psychological research focused on generalisations, for example, research on gender focuses on the way that men on the whole and women on the whole differ from one another.

Strengths and limitations

Strengths of the idiographic approach

You can work out the strengths and limitations of nomothetic approach by reversing the idiographic arguments.

- Recognises the **uniqueness** of each person.
- Sees the world from the **perspective of the individual**.
- A **more holist approach** to understanding behaviour, rather than reducing it to particular elements.

Limitations of the idiographic approach

- Tends to be **less scientific** insofar as the approach does not aim to make generalisations. However, qualitative methods are not unscientific in that they seek verification through empirical evidence.
- Makes it **more difficult to produce predictions** about how people will behave. Such predictions can be useful, for example, in producing drugs to treat mental illness.

An interactionist approach

A number of approaches actually combine the two approaches. Freud used idiographic methods to study people, but also used those insights to make generalisations about human development in his theory of personality.

Bandura's concept of reciprocal determinism embraces the uniqueness of each person and the laws of behaviour and the environment. He proposed that our behaviour is determined by the environment (conditioning) but our behaviour also shapes the environments we are in.

185

Psychology and science

AQA A ▸ U4
AQA B ▸ U4

The features and principles of the scientific approach and the role of peer review are presented on page 149.

The subject matter of psychology

Psychology has been defined as the science of behaviour and experience, which points out the two strands of interest:

(1) psychologists seek to study overt behaviour and use objective, nomothetic methods to do this

(2) they also seek to understand subjective, private experience and tend to use more idiographic and qualitative methods.

Strengths and limitations of the scientific approach

The word 'science' refers both to the body of knowledge and the methods used to obtain that knowledge.

Strengths

- The scientific method enables **theories to be constructed and tested** through the collection of objective, verifiable data. Without a scientific approach we are easily beguiled by pseudoscientific explanations.
- The scientific approach enables us to **make generalisations** about people and **apply this knowledge constructively** in, for example, reducing prejudice and treating mental disorders. The applications themselves can then be evaluated using the scientific method.

Limitations

- The problems of bias in science are especially problematic in psychology where the object of study is active and intelligent. Experimental artifacts, such as **experimenter bias**, **demand characteristics**, and **sample bias** mean that it may be impossible to conduct objective and repeatable research.
- Science may be an **impossible ideal** even in the 'hard sciences' such as physics. No investigator is ever truly objective and no observations are unaffected by the process of being observed, as indicated by Heisenberg's uncertainty principle (page 181).
- **Social representation theory** suggests that scientific knowledge is not a timeless concept, but a feature of a particular group of people at a particular time in history. Scientific beliefs are subject to the same group pressures of other groups, i.e. not objective.
- Even if one accepted that psychology was scientific, we must ask what **relevance** this approach has to the understanding of human behaviour.
- The scientific approach is both determinist and reductionist. This means that scientific experiments may not have **ecological validity** because what is studied is very divorced from everyday life (i.e. it lacks **mundane realism**).
- All scientific research is based on **restricted samples**. In psychology these are culturally and socially biased, producing theories that are not universally valid.
- Humanistic psychologists feel that objective data can tell us little about subjective experience. It has statistical, but **not human, meaning**. New research methods are needed to properly investigate human behaviour, such as qualitative methods.

Key points from AS

- These concepts are explained in *Revise AS Unit 4.2, pages 82 and 84*.

Social representation theory emphasises the way that we represent *social* knowledge and how this knowledge is unconsciously shaped by *social* groups, i.e. such representations are social in two ways.

Mundane realism refers to things that are similar to everyday activities.

Key points from AS

- Qualitative data is discussed in *Revise AS Unit 4.3, page 94*.

Practice essays 19.3

(a) Outline what is meant by the terms 'hard determinism' and 'soft determinism' in psychology. *(4 marks)*

(b) Explain the idiographic approach to the study of human behaviour, using examples in your answer. *(4 marks)*

(c) Discuss the nature–nurture debate in psychology, with reference to **at least one** topic area in psychology. *(12 marks)*

19.3 Methods in psychology

After studying this topic you should be able to describe and evaluate:

Inferential statistics:
- *statistical inference: the concepts of probability and levels of significance; hypothesis testing: null and alternative (experimental or research) hypothesis*
- *one and two tailed tests, Type I and Type II errors; positive, negative and zero correlation; limitations of sampling techniques and generalisation of results*
- *statistical tests: use of non-parametric and parametric tests; statistical tests of difference: the sign test, Wilcoxon signed ranks test, Mann-Whitney, related (repeated measures) and independent tests; statistical tests of association: Spearman's rank order correlation, Pearson's product moment correlation, the Chi-squared test; factors affecting the choice of statistical test, including levels of measurement, type of experimental design; criteria for parametric testing: interval data; normal distribution; homogeneity of variance.*

Students should have experience of designing and conducting informal classroom research using a variety of methods. They will be expected to analyse data collected in investigations and draw conclusions based on research findings. They will be required to draw on these experiences to answer questions in the examination for this unit.

Issues in research:
- *strengths and limitations of different methods of research; strengths and limitations of qualitative and quantitative data*
- *reliability and validity applied generally across all methods of investigation; types of reliability and validity; ways of assessing reliability and validity*
- *critical understanding of the importance of ethical considerations within the social and cultural environment; ethical considerations in the design and conduct of psychological research.*

In addition to the topics listed on the right, candidates are expected to draw on topics studied in the AS course, such as research methods and design.

AS

- These are covered on pages 151–152 and also in *Revise AS Units 4.1, 4.2 and 4.3, pages 75–94.*

AS

- These topics were covered in *Revise AS Units 4.1 and 4.2, page 75–91.*

LEARNING SUMMARY

Inferential tests: Non-parametric and parametric tests

AQA B   U4

The inferential statistical tests described on page 151 are all non-parametric tests. Another group of inferential tests are called **parametric tests**. These are distinguished by the fact that they have been developed based on certain assumptions about the data they test. The assumptions are that:

1. The level of measurement is **interval** or **ratio** (levels of measurement are described on page 151). '**Plastic interval scales**' are also acceptable – these are scales where the intervals have been arbitrarily determined, such as on a rating scale. We can assume, for the purpose of analysis, that the intervals are equal.

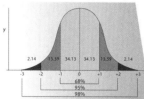

In a **normal distribution** 34.13% of the data scores are 1 standard deviation below the mean and an equal number are 1 standard deviation above the mean, i.e. 68.26% are within 1 standard deviation of the mean. 95% of the scores are within 2 standard deviations of the mean.

The **standard deviation** is calculated by working out the difference between each score and the mean and calculating the mean of these differences.

2. The data are drawn from a population that has a **normal distribution**. Note that it is not the sample that must be normally distributed but the **population**. A normal distribution is a bell-shaped distribution, where most scores cluster around the mean with an equal number of scores above and below the mean, as illustrated on the left. We expect many physical and psychological characteristics to be normally distributed, such as IQ and shoe sizes.

3. The **variances** of the two samples are not significantly different (i.e. they are homogenous or the same). The variance is related to the **standard deviation** of a set of data – it is the standard deviation squared. When looking at related samples, differences in variances should not distort the result (Coolican, 1996). Therefore, we do not need to be too concerned about variance when dealing with related measures. When looking at independent samples, the best way to ensure similar variances is to collect samples that are similar in size.

However, parametric tests are quite robust – they are reliable unless the parametric assumptions are met quite poorly. The reason for preferring to use a parametric test is that they are more powerful, i.e. they can detect a significant difference when the actual difference/relationship between the data is smaller.

Which test should be used?

Design/Data	Non-parametric		Parametric
	Nominal data	Ordinal data	Interval data
Association/ Correlation	Association: Chi-squared test	Correlation: Spearman's rank order correlation correlation	Correlation: Pearson's product moment
Independent samples	Chi-squared	Mann-Whitney	Independent t-test
Repeated measures (and matched pairs)	Sign test	Wilcoxon signed ranks	Related t-test

Looking up the critical value for each test

For some tests a statistical result is significant if the observed value is greater than the critical value. Sometimes it is significant if the observed value is less than the critical value. The letter 'r' can sort this out for you!

The observed value should be greater than the critical value for:
Spearman, Pearson, Chi-Squared, Related t-test, Unrelated t-test (each test name, like the word 'greater' has a letter 'r' in it).

The observed value should be less than the critical value for:
Wilcoxon, Mann-Whitney, Sign test (there is no letter 'r' to be found!)

Practice questions 19.3

See practice questions on page 152.

1

(a) Describe **two** methods used by biological psychologists to investigate human behaviour, and give examples for each. *(4 marks)*

One method used by biological psychologists is twin studies. This is used to see whether a particular trait, such as schizophrenia is genetically inherited or not. Another method is brain scans which are used, for example, to see what part of the brain is active when a person is engaged on a particular task or to see if the brain of a schizophrenic is different to a normal person's brain.

(b) Outline **two** strengths of the behaviourist approach. *(4 marks)*

One strength is that it is easy to conduct experiments to show whether certain behaviours are acquired through reinforcement. A second strength is that this approach has led to many applications, such as therapies for treating mental disorders.

(c) Discuss the psychodynamic approach in psychology. Refer to **at least one** other approach in your answer. *(12 marks)*

The psychodynamic approach is associated with Freud's theory of psychoanalysis. This theory proposes that our personalities develop as a result of interactions between biological forces and life events. The personality is divided into three elements. The id is the primitive self, driven by the pleasure principle. The second element, the ego, develops towards the end of a baby's first year and is driven by the reality principle. The id and ego are inevitably in conflict because the id wants what it wants, whereas the ego takes reality into account. Around the age of four the superego develops. The superego is your ideal self and your moral self. The id and ego are in conflict and this creates anxiety. In order to protect itself from anxiety the ego has certain ego defences such as repression, where any thought or event that creates anxiety is repressed into the unconscious mind. Another ego defence is projection where a person projects their anxious feelings onto something else.

Freud also suggested that there are stages of psychosexual development. These stages are biologically determined (all children go through the same stages) but the outcome of each stage depends on individual experiences and these experiences shape adult personality. The first stage is the oral stage, in the first year of life when pleasure is derived from the mouth. A baby who experiences too much or too little pleasure in this stage will be fixated on it later in life and is described as having an oral personality. This may mean that they like to do things such as chew on a pencil or smoke, or it may mean they are pessimistic (frustrated in the oral stage) or optimistic (overindulged in the oral stage). The next stage is the anal stage followed by the phallic stage where focus is on the child's genitals. In this stage a boy goes through the Oedipus conflict where he desires his mother and, therefore, sees his father as a rival. Eventually, the conflict is resolved, which leads the boy to identify with his father and, thus, develop important moral values. Lack of identification will affect moral development. Girls go through a different conflict and their resolution isn't as strong so Freud said this explains why girls have a less well-developed sense of moral values.

Freud has received lots of criticisms because his theory is based on a small group of neurotic Viennese Victorian women and may not really apply to other people. He has also been criticised because his theory was too focused on sex and Erikson proposed a similar psychodynamic theory which had social instead of sexual conflicts.

2

(a) Explain what is meant by the terms 'nomothetic' and 'idiographic'. *(4 marks)*

Nomothetic refers to making generalisations about people, whereas idiographic is when you just study one individual.

2. (a) The question asks for an explanation but the answer only gives a brief description of each term. **2 out of 4 marks.**

(b) Outline why some psychologists favour reductionist explanations of human behaviour. *(4 marks)*

Reductionist approaches are desirable because they are simpler and mean that you identify individual factors and can then conduct experiments to look at causes and effects.

2. (b) Even though the question only asks for an 'outline' there is insufficient detail in the answer. The student should have expanded on the fact that such approaches are simpler (in what way) and gone on to say what factors can be experimented on. **2 out of 4 marks.**

(c) Discuss the nature and nurture debate in psychology. In your answer, refer to **at least two** topics that you have studied in psychology. *(12 marks)*

It is agreed by psychologists that behaviour is not simply all nature or all nurture. There is some interaction or relationship between these two. Hebb made the point that trying to separate them was like trying to decide whether the length or width of a rectangle contributed more to its area. This shows that it cannot be an either/or question. They interact.

The nature–nurture issue has been studied in many areas of psychology: perception, mental illness and probably most notably in the area of intelligence. Aspects of perception are hard-wired, such as our ability to see colour and perceive form. But a considerable amount of perception is affected by expectations because much sensory input is incomplete. We fill in the gaps using expectations. This means that there are cultural differences in perception because of different experiences. For example, Segall et al. (1963) suggested that people who live in carpentered environments are more likely to be fooled by visual illusions based on depth cues.

Mental illnesses such as schizophrenia have been explained in terms of the diathesis–stress model which again expresses this interaction between nature and nurture. The principle is that some individuals are born with genes for a mental disorder, but the disorder only surfaces when there are triggers (stressors). This explains why the concordance rates in twins is not 100%, but does not explain why few schizophrenics report stressful episodes in the months leading up to the initial onset of the disorder (Rabkin, 1980).

In the case of intelligence much research has looked at twins. If an individual's intelligence is entirely due to nature then we would expect identical twins, even those reared apart, to have identical intelligence. They don't (e.g. Pederson et al., 1992). However, they do have greater similarity in IQ (and many other personality variables) than non-identical twins. It is better to compare identical and non-identical twins because one presumes that each pair has more similar nurture experiences than brother and sister who are genetically as similar as non-identical twins but there are age differences. However, recently the idea of micro-environment has been raised. Each individual creates their immediate environment and this effect of the environment is related to aspects of their genetic self. For example, if they are an innately attractive baby then people treat them better and this attractiveness creates a halo effect – people who are attractive are seen as possessing many other desirable qualities. Such effects can be self-fulfilling. In the case of identical twins they will create more similar micro-environments than non-identical twins who look and behave more differently. Thus, we can see that genes interact with environment such that environmental influences are at least in part genetic.

2. (c) The answer contains a very good descriptive element, as is common in student answers. At least two topics are referred to, as required in the question, but there is no clear explanation of what is meant by nature or nurture.

The evaluation is weak because there is not much reference to the debate in the essay, nor are nature and nurture compared. The part of the essay that referred to twin studies and intelligence is muddled.

7 out of 12 marks.

See page 155 for a student answer to a research methods question.